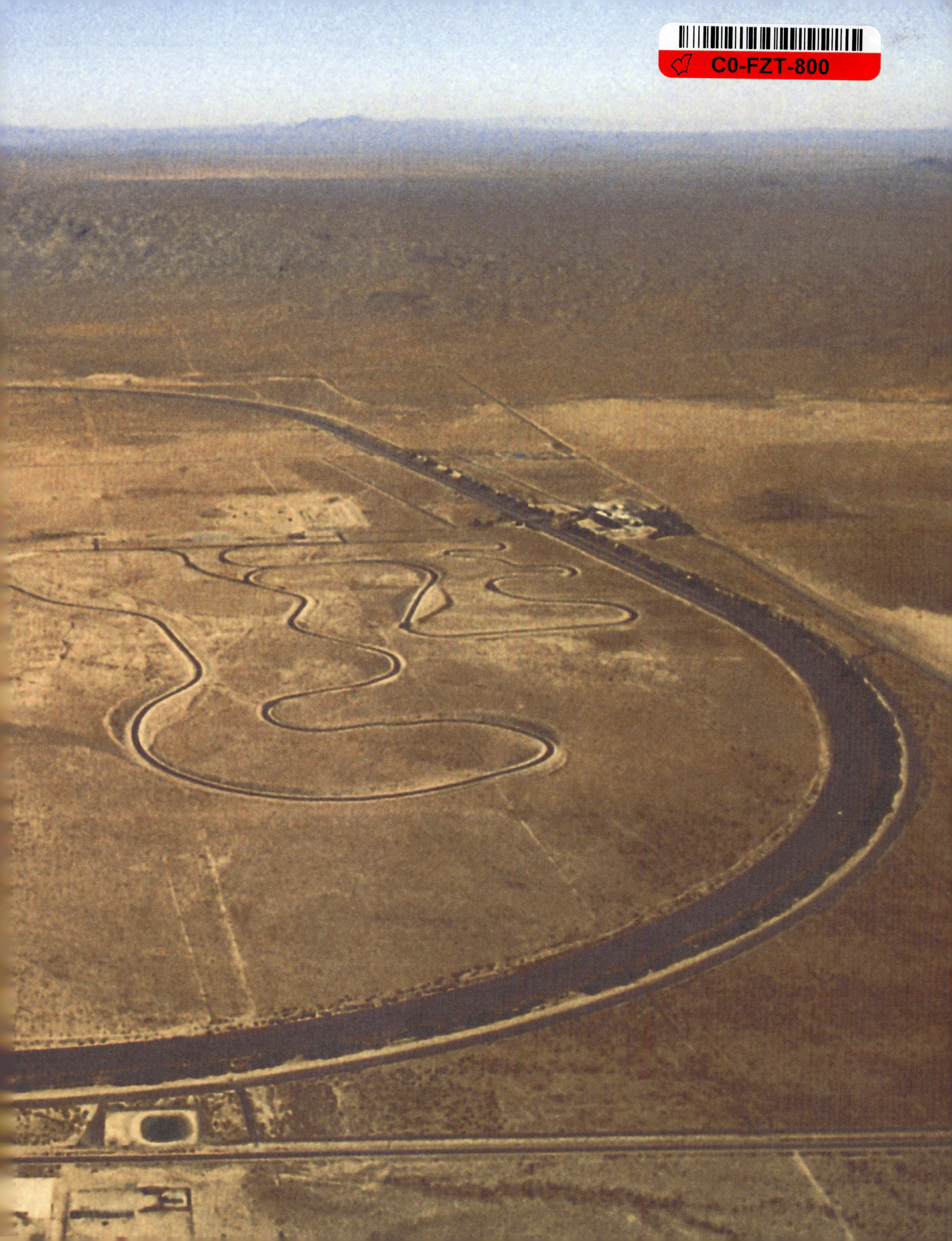

ROSA BARBA

WHITE IS AN IMAGE

10. April 2016

ROSA BARBA

WHITE IS AN IMAGE

WITH ESSAYS BY

LYNNE COOKE

ELISABETH LEBOVICI

RAIMUNDAS MALASAUSKAS

FRANCESCO MANACORDA

NATAŠA PETREŠIN-BACHELEZ

IAN WHITE

HATJE
CANTZ

CONTENTS

AN IDEA IN THREE DIMENSIONS

IAN WHITE

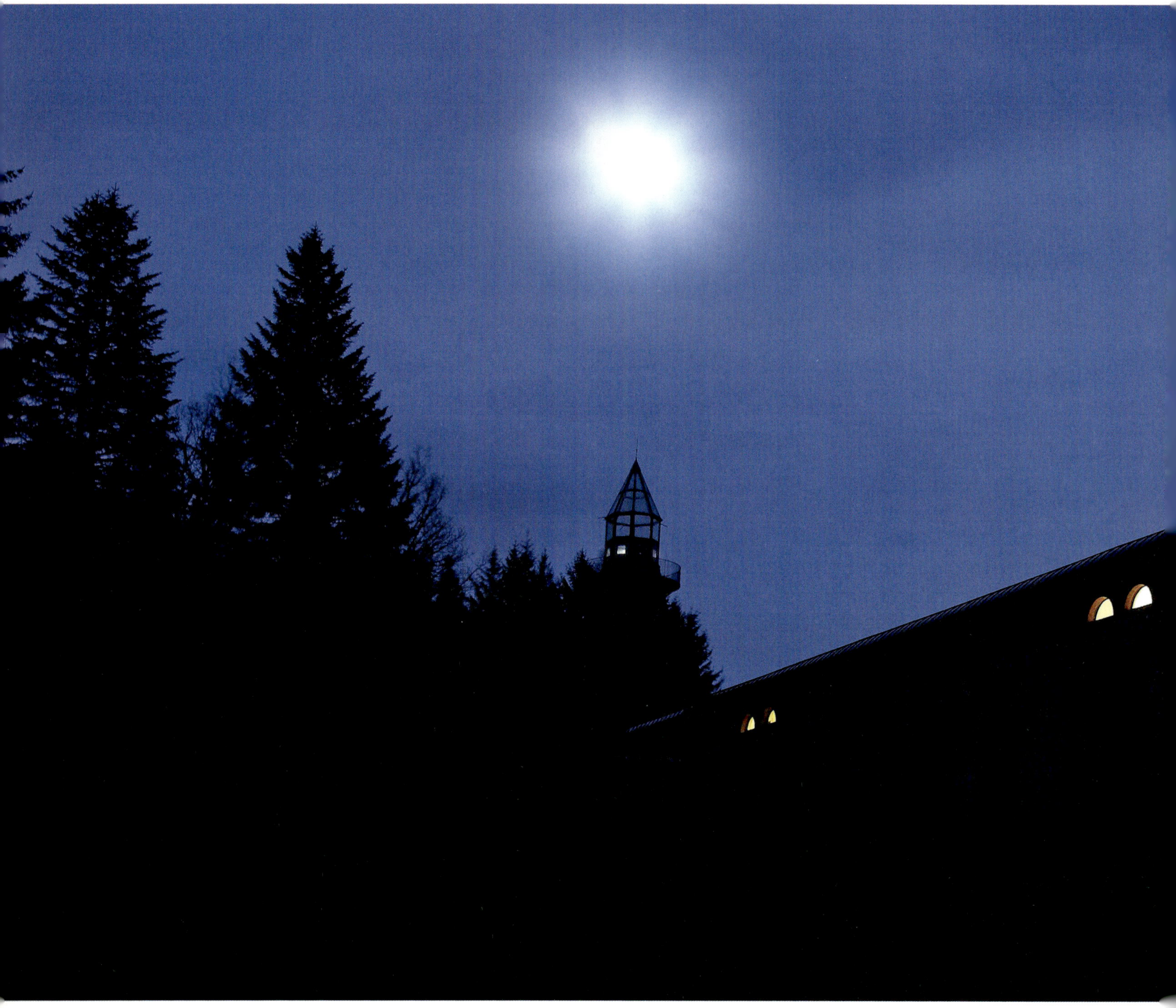

White Museum (2010), installation view, Centre international d'art et du paysage de l'île de Vassivière, 2010

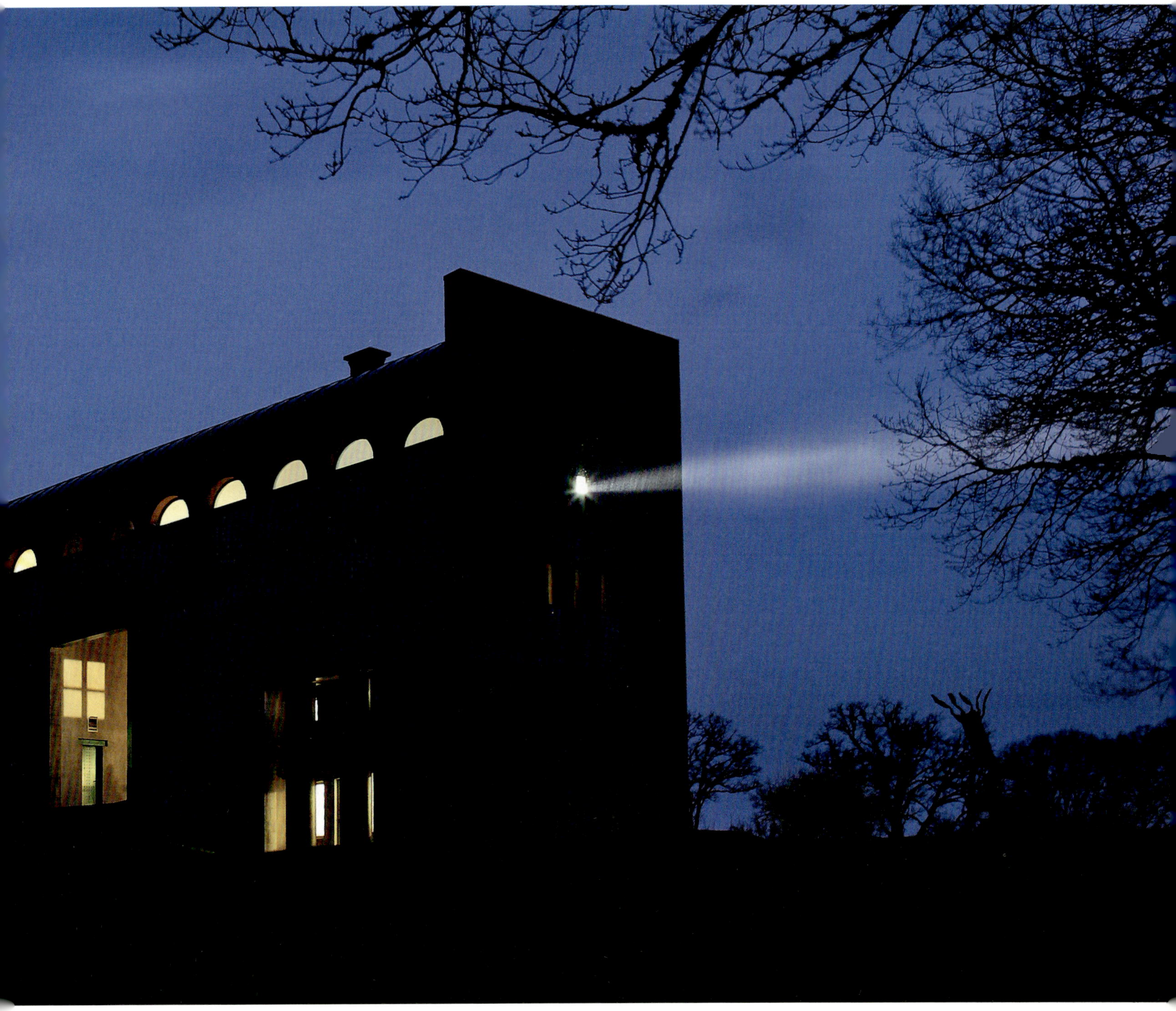

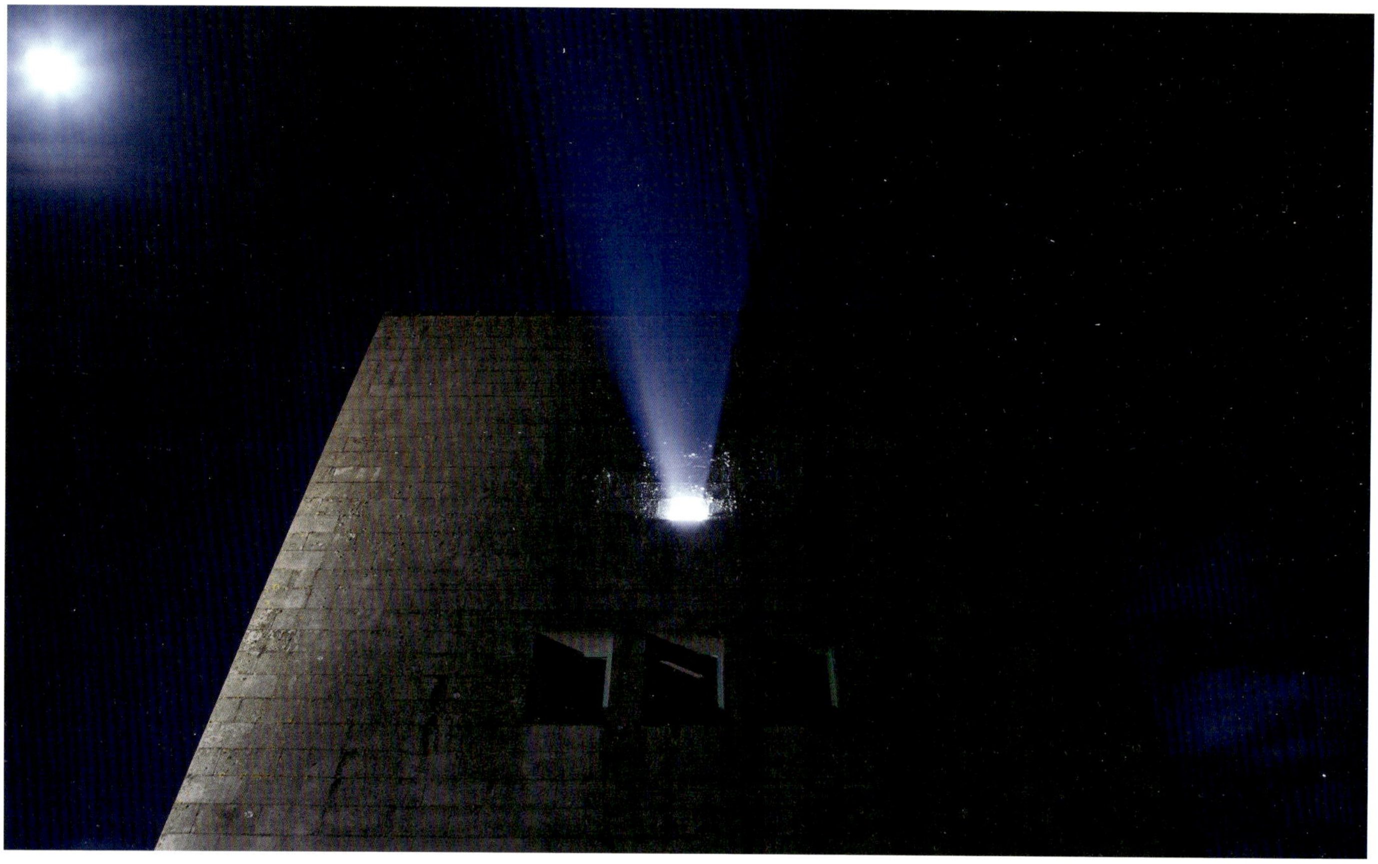

Above and pages 14–15: *White Museum* (2010), installation view, Centre international d'art et du paysage de l'île de Vassivière, 2010
Pages 12–13: *White Museum Soundtrack* (2010)
Pages 16–17: *Enigmatic Whistler* (2009) and *They Come and Go* (2009), installation view, Centre international d'art et du paysage de l'île de Vassivière, 2010
Pages 18–19: *The Indifferent Back of a View Rather Than Its Face* (2009)
Pages 20–21: *The Personal Experience behind Its Description* (2009) and *The Indifferent Back of a View Rather Than Its Face* (2009), installation view, Centre international d'art et du paysage de l'île de Vassivière, 2010

> "The ashes now began to fall upon us, though in no great quantity. I looked back; a dense dark mist seemed to be following us, spreading itself over the country like a cloud. 'Let us turn out of the high-road,' I said, 'while we can still see, for fear that, should we fall in the road, we should be pressed to death in the dark, by the crowds that are following us.' We had scarcely sat down when night came upon us, not such as we have when the sky is cloudy, or when there is no moon, but that of a room when it is shut up, and all the lights put out."

Pliny's letter to Tacitus (LXVI) on the dangers at Misenum[1]

Catastrophes are terrible. But so is a catastrophe waiting to happen. A catastrophe waiting to happen might be more dangerous. It might not exist. It might not be ignored. Maybe it is entirely conceptual, an imagined territory with ambiguous borders and irrational (special) laws, a great, consuming space carved out of life to serve as a waiting room (one from which there is no escape) where fear or threat, inevitability, truth, rumor, evidence, analysis, invisibility, and fiction become the levers by which power is wielded. A state of absolute unknowing, like absolute darkness, the catastrophe-in-waiting is useful to those in power and to those who want to seize it by means of the peculiar, amplified importance it grants to the control of information (how it is illuminated) and the time and space in which they have to do this. It also represents a set of possibilities—terrible perhaps, but also potentially utopian—a soft, easy ground appealing to the absolutes of idealisms and idealists irrespective of rank.

Thus one could paraphrase the British political documentary filmmaker Adam Curtis's 2004 BBC television series *The Power of Nightmares*. In it he proposed that modern-day politicians have found a way to recoup power by remodeling themselves no longer as ideologues or civic managers, but as protectors—protecting the public, their subjects, in particular from the threat (figured as immense) of international terrorism. In other words he describes the terrible use-value for those in power of the public's conviction that there is a catastrophe-in-waiting. It's a mind game. The opening sequence of each episode over which Curtis speaks this one-line outline features a series of images (all of Curtis's films combine archival material with interviews as the vehicle for his arguments) that partly evoke a period of recent history, establishing a fiction of impending doom and preparing the viewer for the story that is about to be told: stadium lights dim, an empty television (news?) studio is dismantled, car headlights illuminate a tiny part of the road being traveled, stately chandeliers are turned off, shadows expand . . . In short, darkness descends as a metaphor for the exploitable state of unknowing we could also ascribe to the catastrophe-in-waiting, and darkness descends as it does in the auditorium as the very condition of that ultimate narrative experience, industrial cinema. The disaster movie might be one of its definitive genres, but the catastrophe-in-waiting is both the situation and a condition of industrial cinema.

It is within this frame that I want to position a discussion of the work of Rosa Barba, not because it proposes an argument about the political use of a fear of international terrorism, but because of its subtle interrogation and co-option of industrial cinema-as-subject via various kinds of what might be understood as "stagings"—of "the local," the nonactor, gesture, genre, information, expertise and authority, the mundane—or removals from a social realism within which they were observed and which qualifies them as components of the work, to be framed, redesigned, represented. The effect of this contests and recasts truth and fiction, myth and reality, metaphor and material, to a disorienting degree that ultimately extends into a conceptual practice that also recasts the viewer's own staging as an act of radical and exhilarating reversal—from being the receiver of an image (a subject of control) to being in and among its engine room(s), looking out.

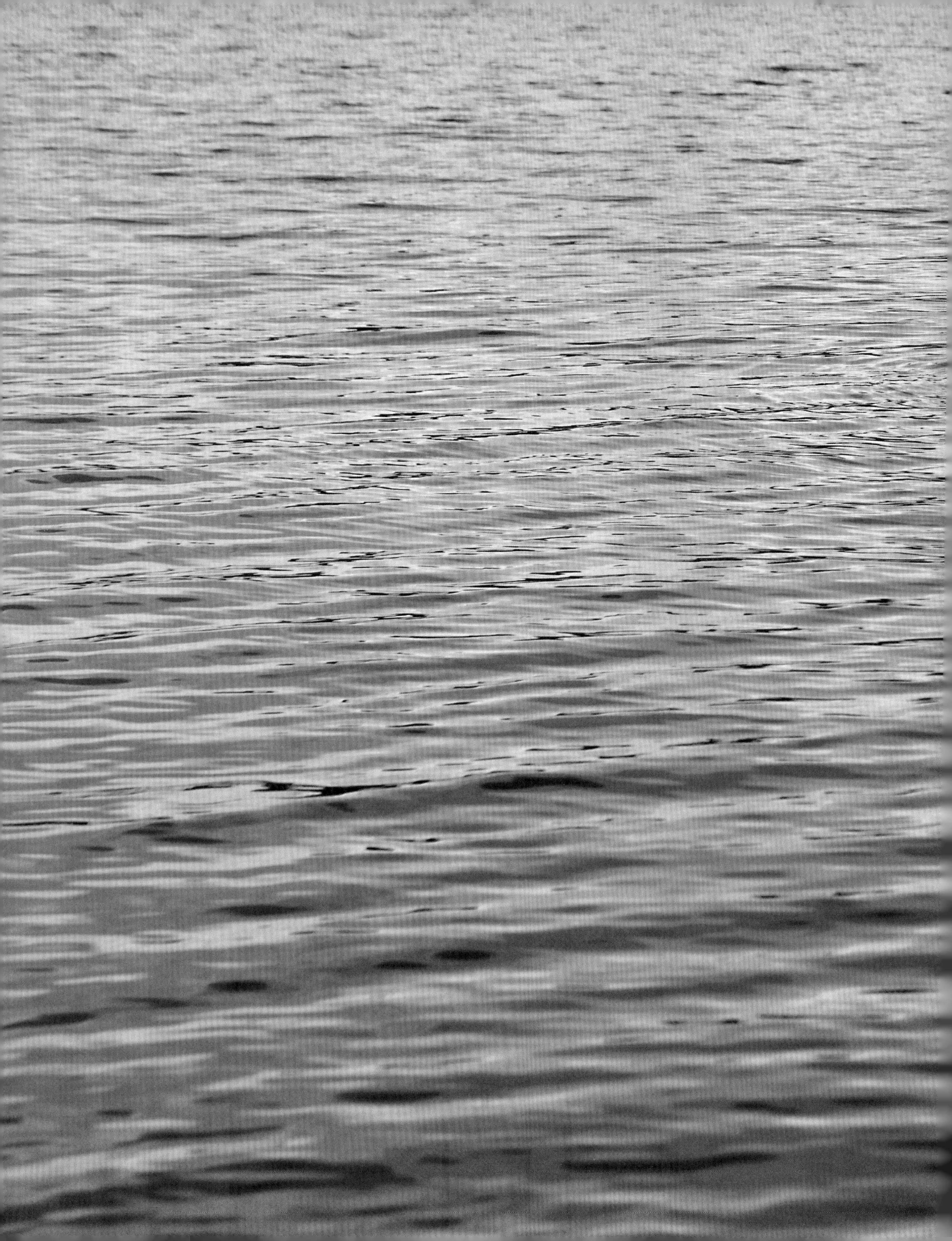

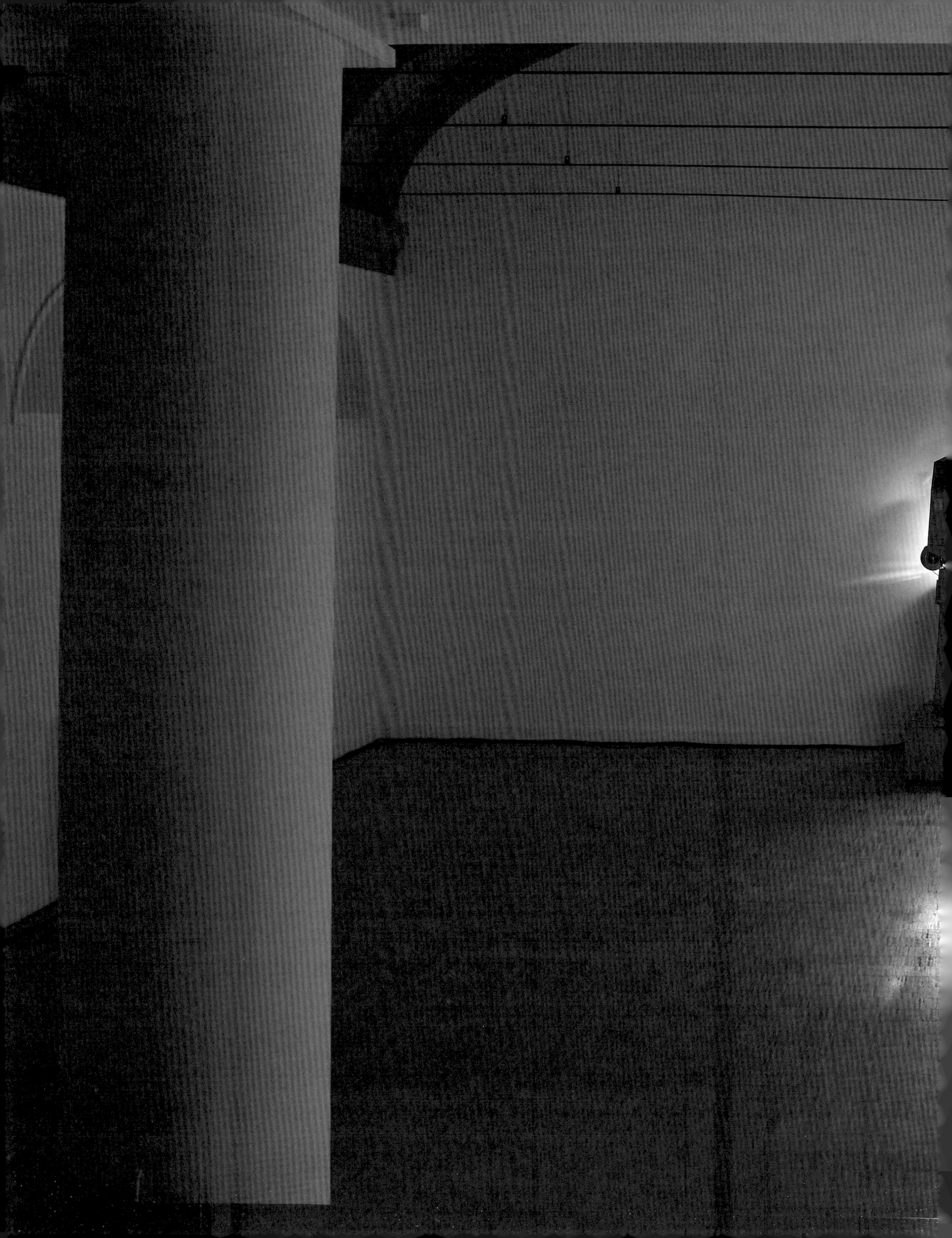

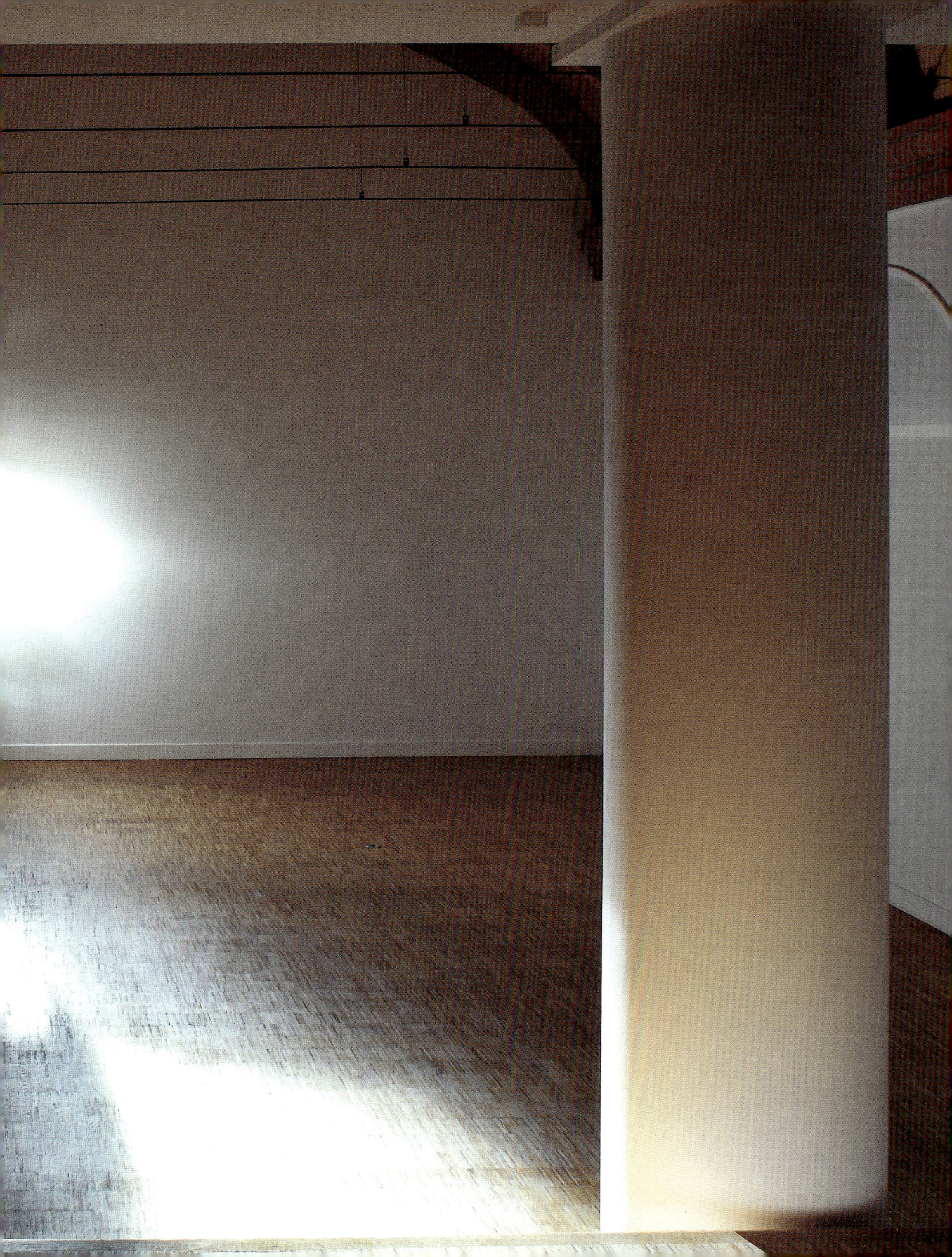

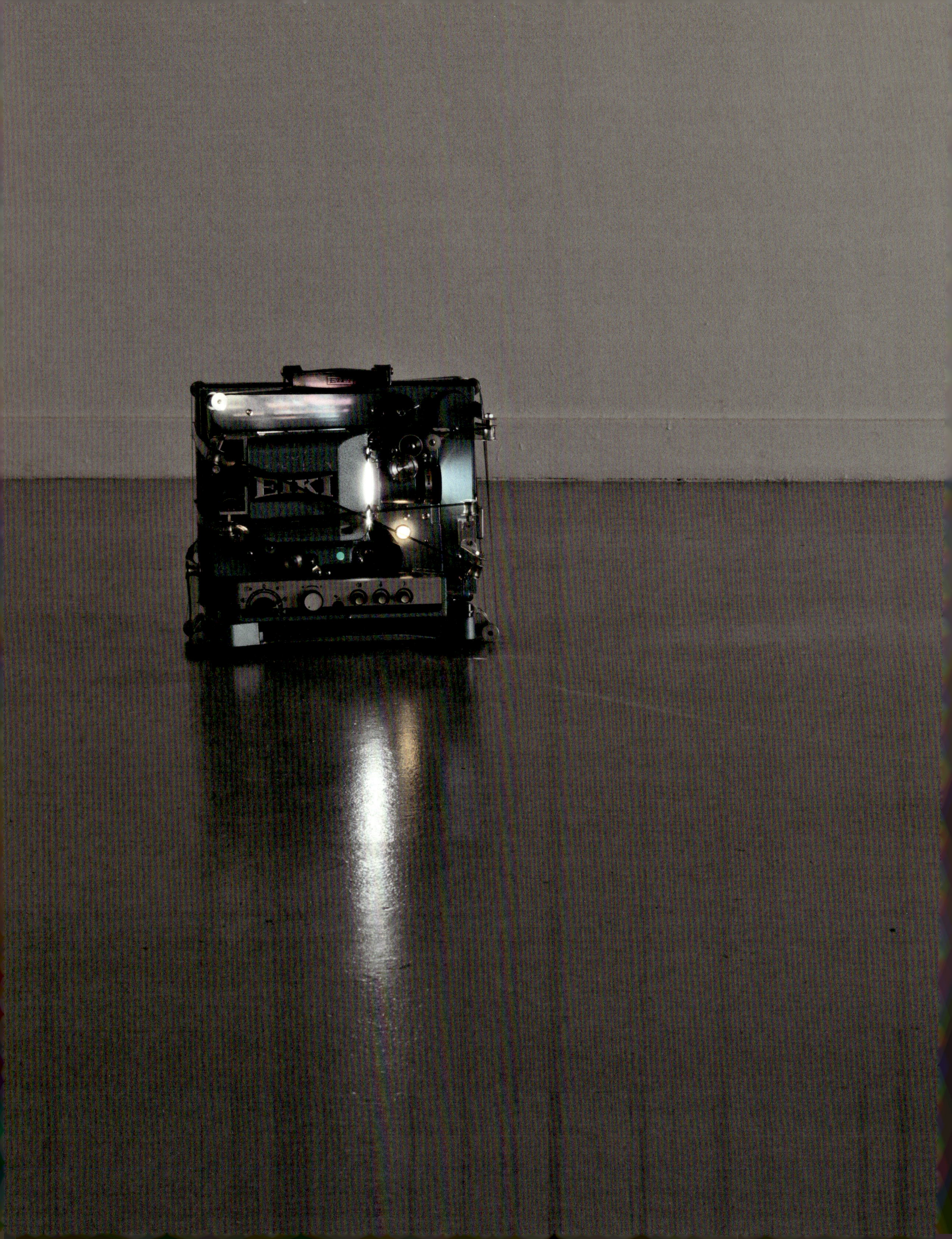
EIKI

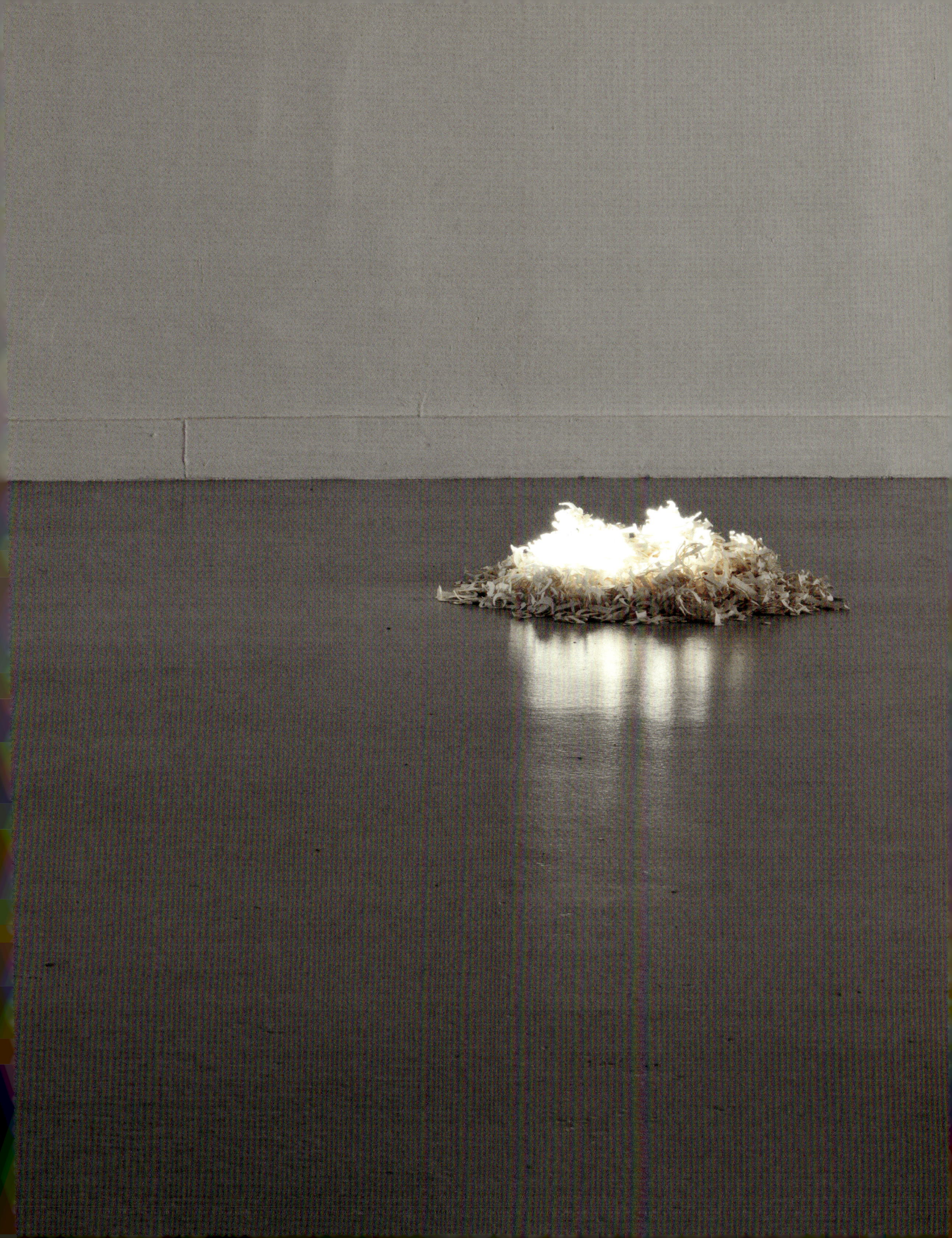

dream I kept filling so
smaller shapes, and my n
too impatient and excite
And every time I ha
somebody would start sc
awoke screaming too, t
anonymous shriek, with
exultation, but with no
more - if there had bee
particular sunset. The w

e kind of spectacle with
se was bleeding but I was
to do anything about it.
that dream, suddenly
eaming behind me, and I
as prolonging the initial
its initial note of rising
eaning attached to it any
a meaning. I recall one
ole thing was like some

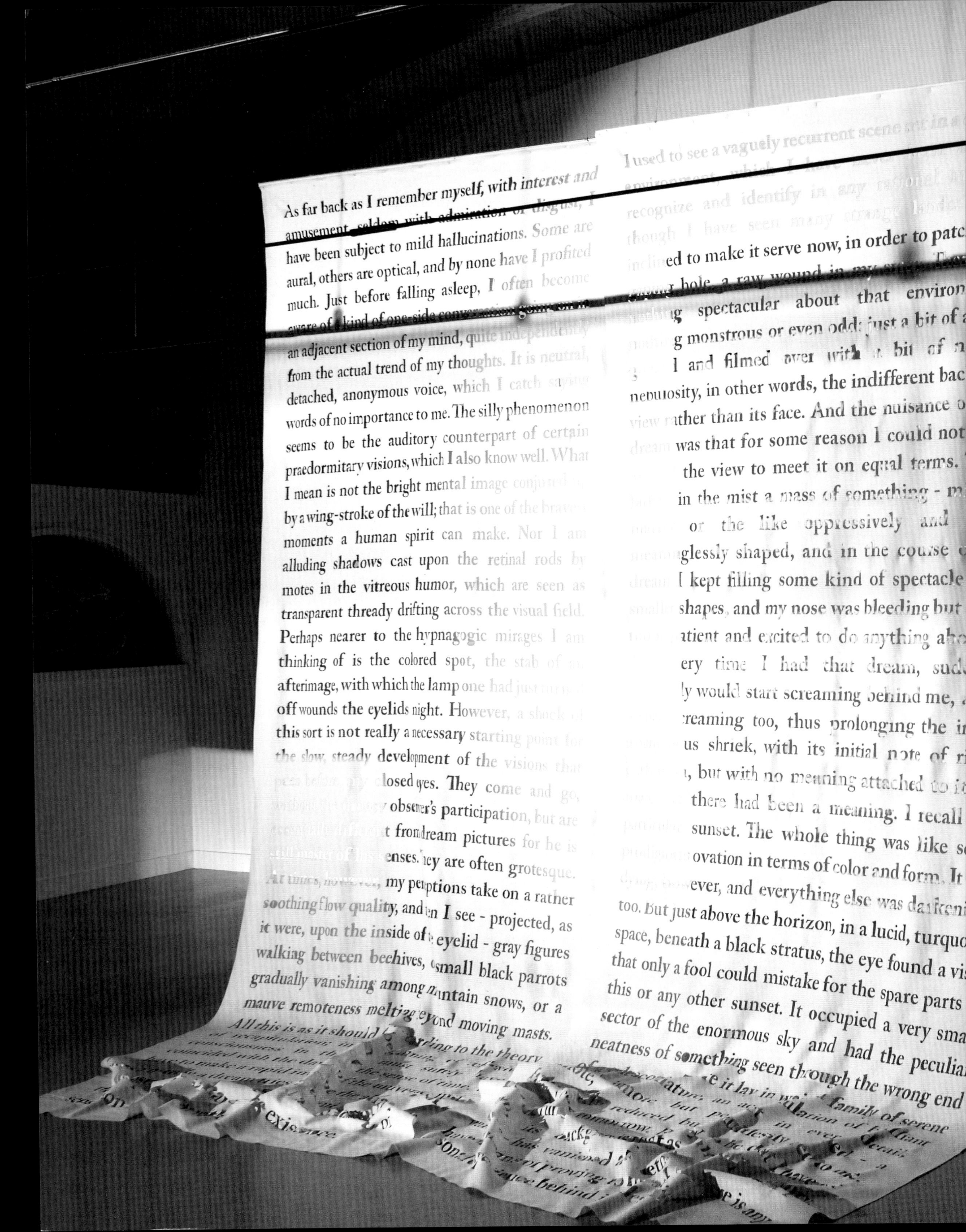
As far back as I remember myself, with interest and
have been subject to mild hallucinations. Some are
aural, others are optical, and by none have I profited
much. Just before falling asleep, I often become
an adjacent section of my mind, quite independently
from the actual trend of my thoughts. It is neutral,
detached, anonymous voice, which I catch saying
words of no importance to me. The silly phenomenon
seems to be the auditory counterpart of certain
praedormitary visions, which I also know well. What
I mean is not the bright mental image conjured
by a wing-stroke of the will; that is one of the bravest
moments a human spirit can make. Nor I am
alluding shadows cast upon the retinal rods by
motes in the vitreous humor, which are seen as
transparent thready drifting across the visual field.
Perhaps nearer to the hypnagogic mirages I am
thinking of is the colored spot, the stab of an
afterimage, with which the lamp one had just turned
off wounds the eyelids night. However, a shock of
this sort is not really a necessary starting point for
the slow, steady development of the visions that
losed eyes. They come and go,
observer's participation, but are
t from dream pictures for he is
enses. hey are often grotesque.
my perptions take on a rather
soothing flow quality, and en I see - projected, as
it were, upon the inside of eyelid - gray figures
walking between beehives, small black parrots
gradually vanishing among ntain snows, or a
mauve remoteness melting eyond moving masts.
I used to see a vaguely recurrent scene set in a
recognize and identify in any rational
ed to make it serve now, in order to patc
g spectacular about that environ
g monstrous or even odd: just a bit of
l and filmed over with a bit of
nebulosity, in other words, the indifferent bac
view rather than its face. And the nuisance o
was that for some reason I could not
the view to meet it on equal terms.
in the mist a mass of something - m
or the like oppressively and
glessly shaped, and in the course
I kept filling some kind of spectacle
shapes, and my nose was bleeding but
atient and excited to do anything abo
ery time I had that dream, sud
ly would start screaming behind me,
reaming too, thus prolonging the i
us shriek, with its initial note of
, but with no meaning attached to i
there had been a meaning. I recall
sunset. The whole thing was like s
ovation in terms of color and form. It
ever, and everything else was darkeni
too. But just above the horizon, in a lucid, turquo
space, beneath a black stratus, the eye found a vi
that only a fool could mistake for the spare parts
this or any other sunset. It occupied a very sma
sector of the enormous sky and had the peculia
neatness of something seen through the wrong end
All this is as it should

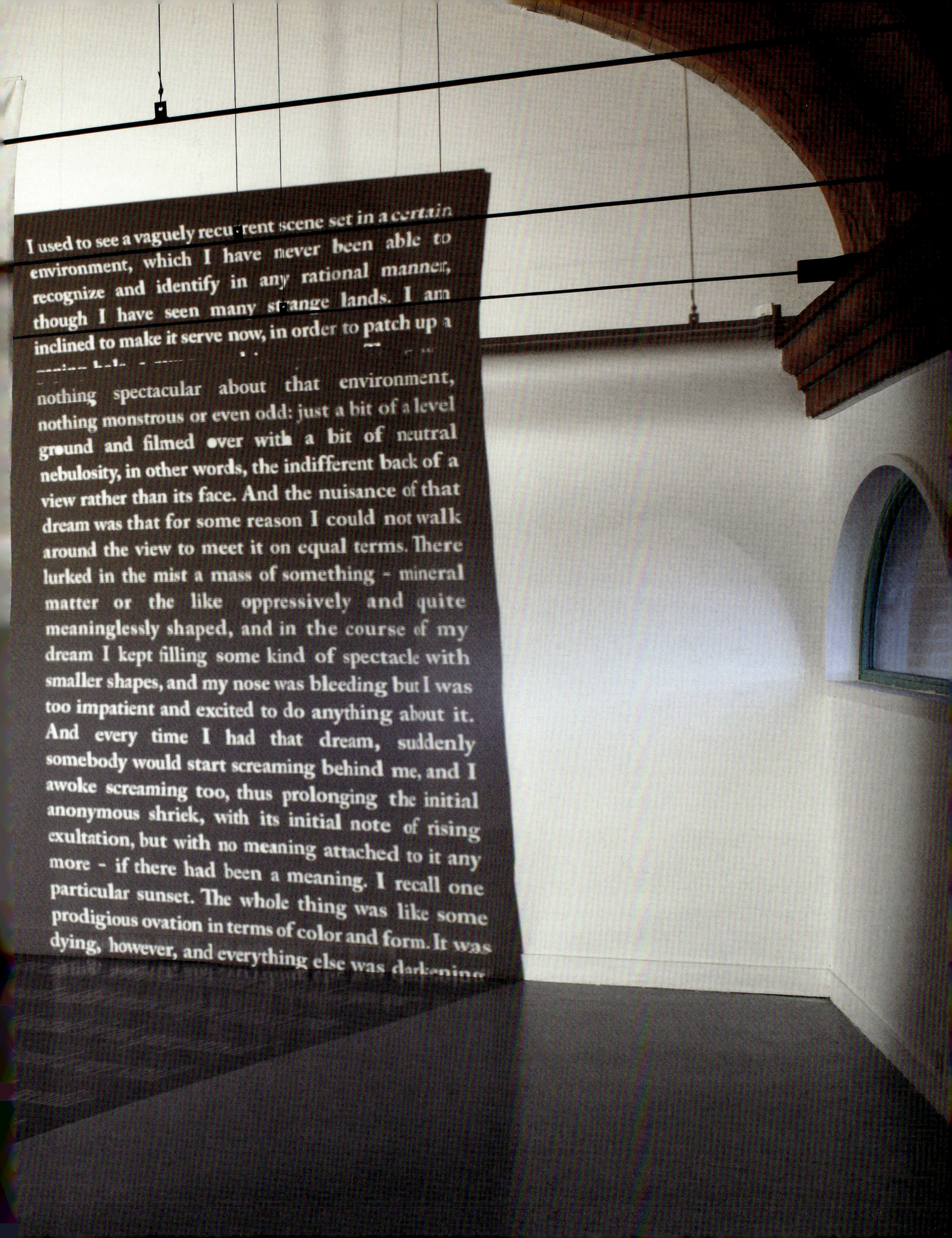
I used to see a vaguely recurrent scene set in a certain
environment, which I have never been able to
recognize and identify in any rational manner,
though I have seen many strange lands. I am
inclined to make it serve now, in order to patch up a
nothing spectacular about that environment,
nothing monstrous or even odd: just a bit of a level
ground and filmed over with a bit of neutral
nebulosity, in other words, the indifferent back of a
view rather than its face. And the nuisance of that
dream was that for some reason I could not walk
around the view to meet it on equal terms. There
lurked in the mist a mass of something - mineral
matter or the like oppressively and quite
meaninglessly shaped, and in the course of my
dream I kept filling some kind of spectacle with
smaller shapes, and my nose was bleeding but I was
too impatient and excited to do anything about it.
And every time I had that dream, suddenly
somebody would start screaming behind me, and I
awoke screaming too, thus prolonging the initial
anonymous shriek, with its initial note of rising
exultation, but with no meaning attached to it any
more - if there had been a meaning. I recall one
particular sunset. The whole thing was like some
prodigious ovation in terms of color and form. It was
dying, however, and everything else was darkening

Often Barba's work represents pre- or post-apocalyptic, seemingly abandoned communities occupied by the proposition of a central threat of disaster wherein both those depicted and the disasters that threaten them might equally be read as actual and fictional—to the extent that whether they are one or the other becomes not irrelevant, but an ambiguity that is the very means by which the works themselves function conceptually. It is a variation on the "leap of faith" requested of an audience in the theater auditorium, but one that instead of an immersion into believable storytelling leans toward establishing a meta-narrative. In their different ways, the films *Panzano* (2000), made with Ulrike Molsen, and *Outwardly from Earth's Center* (2007) function explicitly around such a framework (as does the online work *Vertiginous Mapping* [2008]). *The Empirical Effect* (2010) does so as well, and it is this work that I want to focus on as a sort of structural crystallization that can be traced backwards and further understood in Barba's earlier works, and extended to brief meditations on the artist's sculptures of 16-millimeter film projectors, the viewer's position in relation to them, and their gathering together into exhibitions where individual works become the component parts of an overarching constellation.

The Empirical Effect is shot on the slopes surrounding the still-active volcano Mount Vesuvius located outside of Naples in central Italy, the eruption of which in AD 79 bequeathed us the impeccably preserved Pompeii, the definitive archaeological subject, as well as the earliest description of a volcanic eruption, which was written by Pliny the Younger and from which the quotation that opens this text is drawn. The volcano's last major eruption occurred in 1944 and the next is allegedly imminent, the length of the volcano's silence and inactivity being in inverse proportion to the increasing volume of analysis and speculation, its manipulation and contestation, and the expected size of the eruption to come. Silence and inactivity are both the emblems and the function of threat. You would imagine that nobody lives there, and yet the slopes are more populous now than ever before. All of this is nonetheless a situation of which the film provides, significantly, only an elliptical account, as if to render fact an anecdote.

The film opens with a voice-over of a nature we could describe as cinematic—the booming voice of a man is heard, partly informing about and partly mythologizing (via the expectation of an ominous narrative) the activity of Vesuvius, and ending with a warning to flee spoken over an image of what looks like dark, boiling lava, smoke, and smoldering coals. Expectation is staged. There is a sense of ominousness. But that is not how the work progresses. A genre is staged only for it to be then abandoned: Cut to a grid of scientific monitoring equipment, electronics, maybe seismographs. An empty building, designed for a purpose that is neither residential nor civic, but for the kind of research that requires a special kind of architecture. No people. Archival footage of a street scene, probably early-twentieth-century. Promenaders looking at a mountain, Vesuvius. Archaic measuring equipment, still in glass vitrines, unused. Suddenly, an aerial shot of the slopes around Vesuvius from a helicopter—a chopper—that we hear, and that reveals villas and villages, like the opening shots of a Mediterranean *Dynasty*. Now the film cuts back to the building, which we'll call a research center. A map of the region covers the floor, and magically a group of mainly older people appear, not touching each other, standing there like objects (strangely desocialized, but also calm, at home, and on stage), and among them are a number of bleating sheep. They begin to examine the maps, enacting investigation, their considered movements and their pace intimating choreography; they are at once present and engaged, but also half-removed, as if they are also agents. One woman is wearing dark glasses with a wide, white plastic frame that recalls the world of science fiction, or that famous photograph of a uniform cinema audience wearing 3-D glasses to watch a film in Guy Debord's *The Society of the Spectacle*. They are gesturing to each other and speaking, but we do not hear what they say. Technical equipment is wheeled in, as alien to them as they are to it, physically and functionally—their examinations of it and how this technology seems to appear to them are equally strange. Still, they get to work. An archivist is heard describing the population's communion with their environment as both a malediction and a benediction: they are at risk of disaster and devastation, but they are there by choice, for the special kind of rebirth that is its result . . .

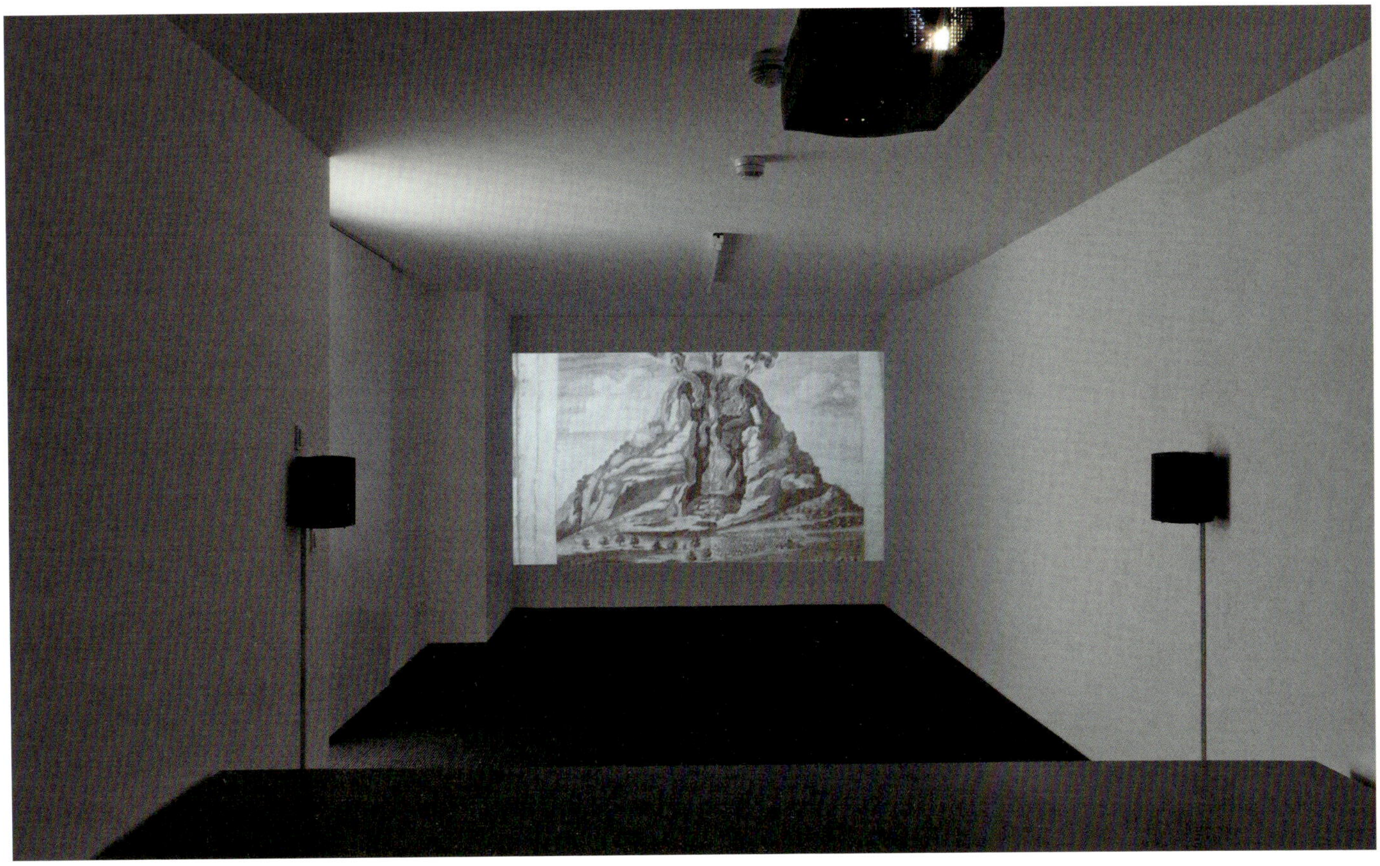

The Empirical Effect (2010), installation view, Sprüth Magers, Berlin, 2010

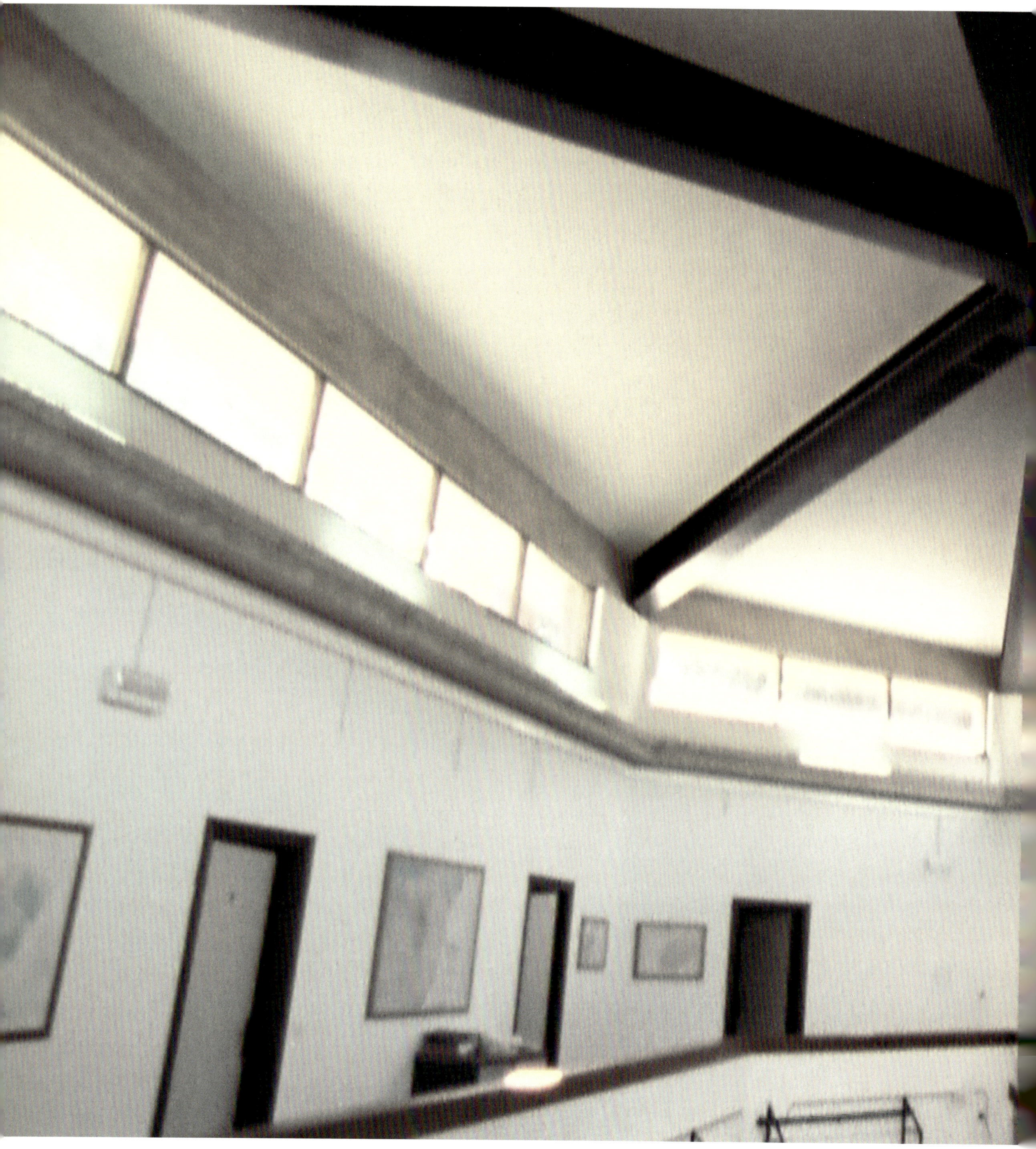

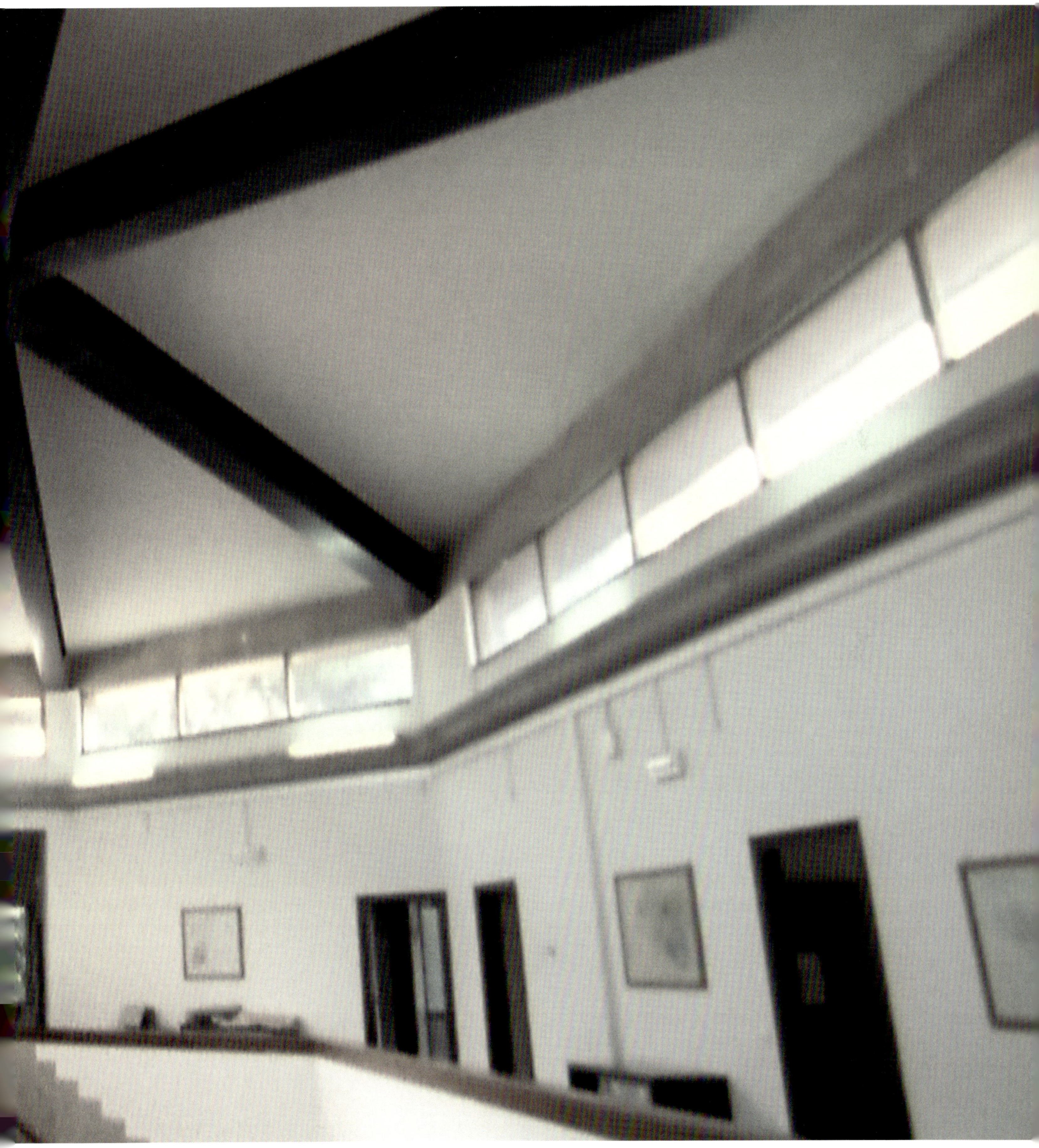

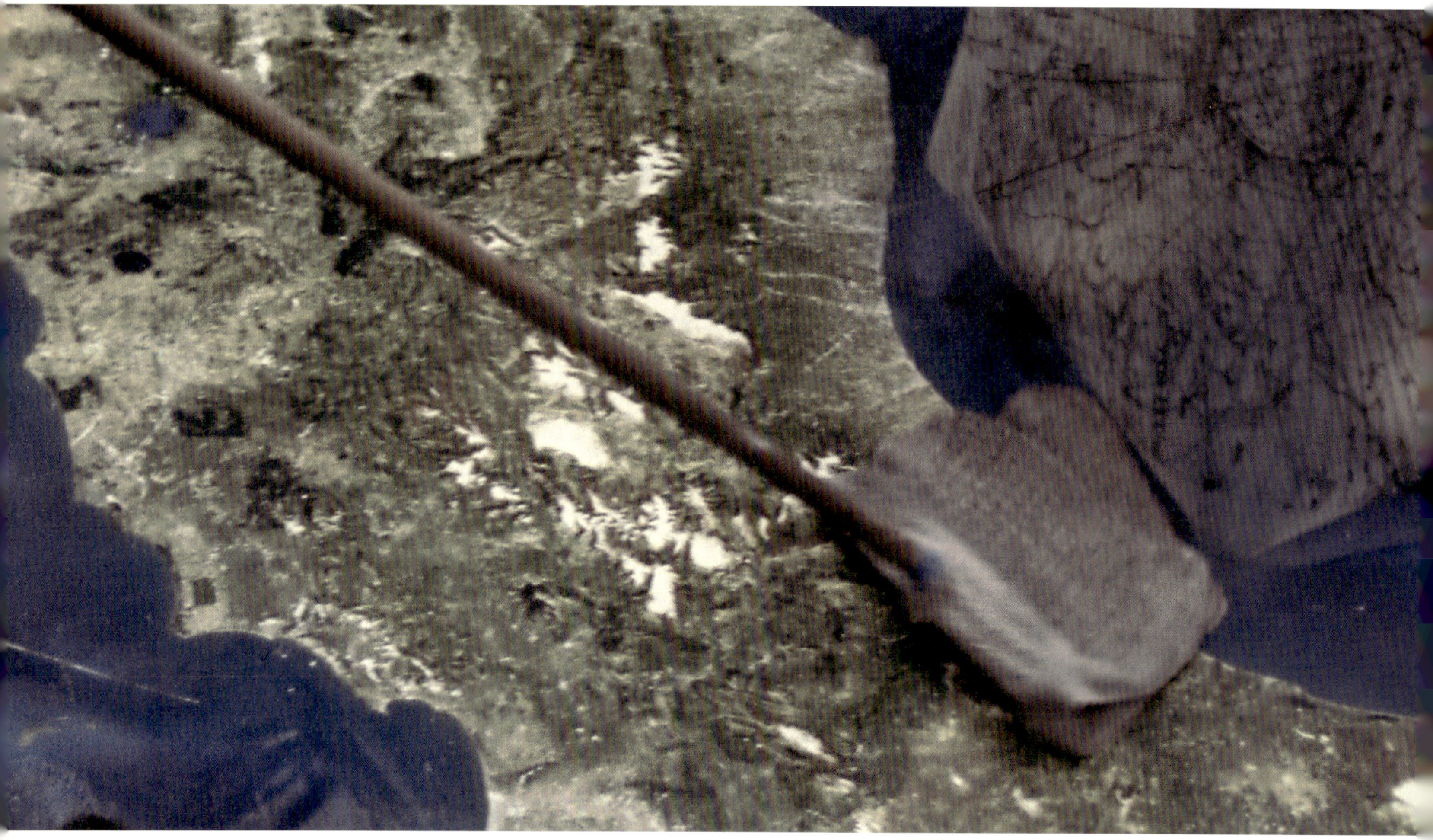

Above, right, and pages 24–25: *The Empirical Effect* (2010)

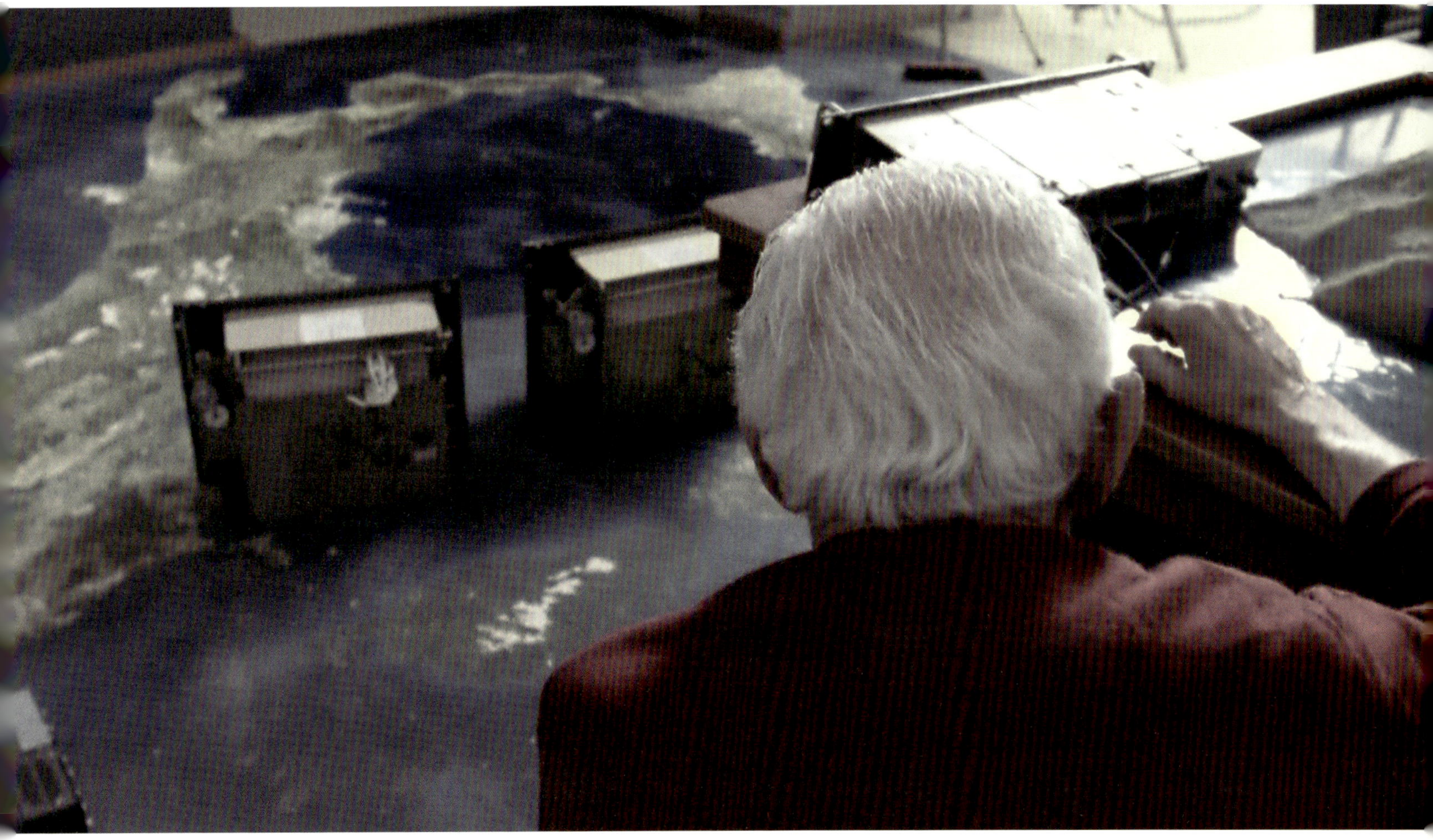

And so the work goes on, a paced irregular patterning of anachronisms, different registers, intimating genres and scenes, to the extent that we do not notice the material's incoherence because we are in and among it—or rather, what we see and hear is coherent *because* we are in and among it. Nothing appears that is not staged somehow: scientific inquiry is scenery and enactment; mystery, like physical movement, is choreographed, with heads upturned to the sky, as if to point; the camera explores architecture with smooth symmetry, not the shakiness of a hand or the instability of an eye; the group of older people reappear like a Greek chorus but without commentating, and ultimately singing and dancing. The absurd is equal to argument. Different systems of inquiry (cinematic, documentary, scientific, amateur, mystical, theatrical) coexist; there is no truth in *that* sense. We are not being told anything, no fact, no story, no opinion. This series of scenes is not the portrait of common experience, but rather its interpretation and transformation into emblematic representations of ideas, translations into a field of performance and representation—and by being so, it is closer to something material as opposed to further away from it. The security of a grand narrative promised by the film's opening is destabilized into a variety of modes through which this situation might be thought or experienced rather than told, as being in and of a medium.

Towards the end of the film a row of four old men, sitting in a line on a sofa, wave their arms above their heads in time with each other. A simulated siren engulfs the soundtrack. For the first time, instead of isolated individuals or the chorus of older people, larger groups of people of various ages are seen "running" through the streets (that is, they are running *as if* there were an emergency, performing the instruction "run as if there is an emergency"). Some are carrying an object—a plaster figurine of the Madonna, a photograph, a plastic bag. They are enacting evacuation. It might be an actual evacuation drill. Here, in the film, it *is* evacuation, not a documentation of it. The register of what we see is the equivalent of any of the staged situations that have come before. What a local community might have been asked to do by a local government to test the official plans for dealing with an eruption now—to prove how long it would take to entirely evacuate the region and to demonstrate how much and what kind of transportation would be the most efficient, what kind of a warning time would be necessary for everyone to reach safety, or other such things that online reports of these drills give accounts of—is a proof that is equivalent to anything else presented in this work. A radical inversion occurs in this moment. The film itself becomes a proof of its own fictions, investigations, and representations. An external "reality" is subsumed into the work's own: when filmed, something acted in actuality becomes a kind of actual. Community is not depicted but constructed, a communism of representations and a manifestation of an altogether different kind of empiricism than that which involves observing the outside world. A community (of viewers) is established through our act of looking and the collective agreement now, according to these terms, that it suggests about what we can and cannot say, not about the record of an actual, perilous situation, but about the work itself—its truths and its lies, its records and their nature, its layers of staging. A hyper-realism, divulged from and by the situation and condition of industrial cinema, which could also now be understood as a catastrophe-in-waiting, has become the work's subject.

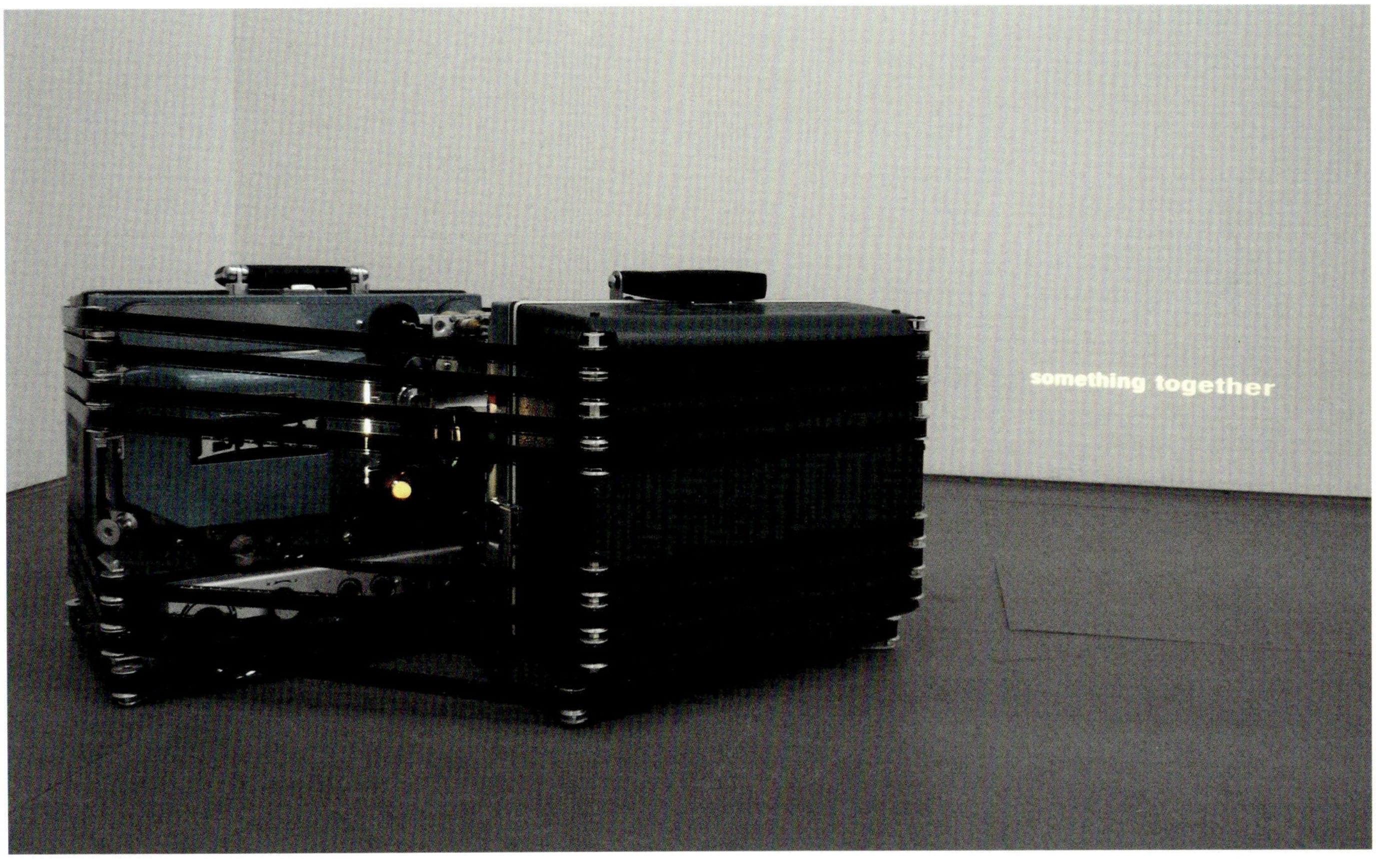

Double-Whistler (2011), installation view, carlier | gebauer, Berlin, 2011

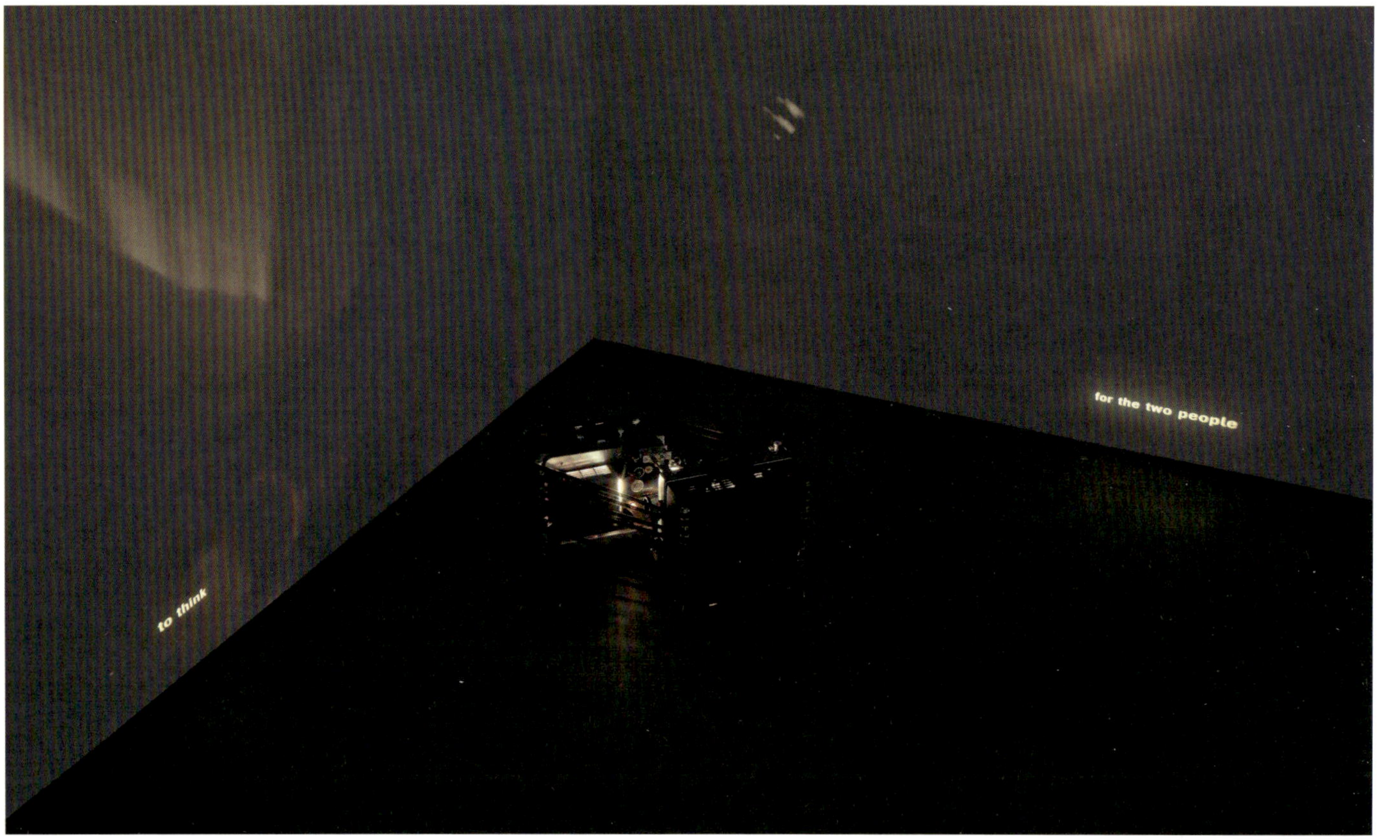

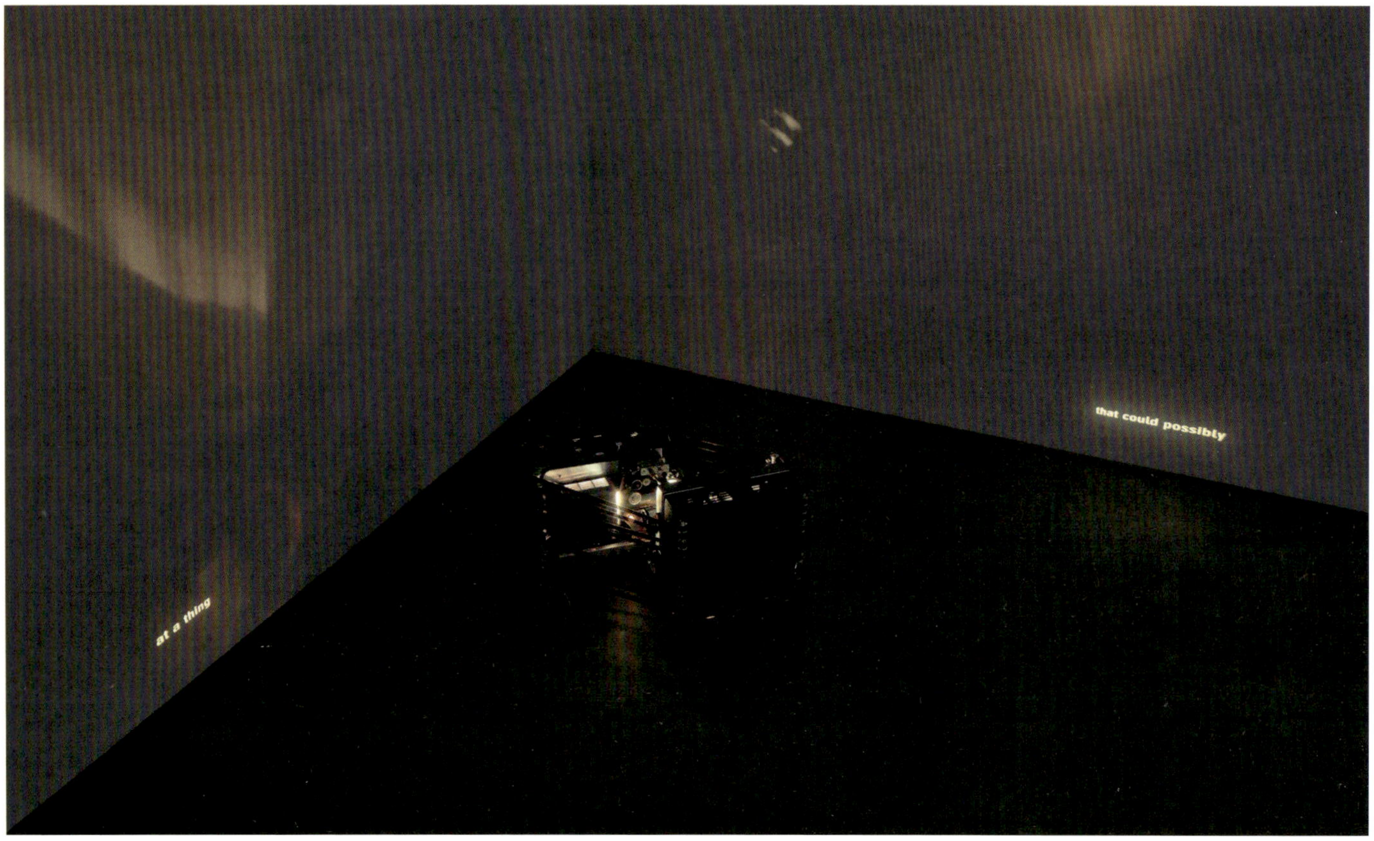

Double-Whistler (2011), installation view, carlier | gebauer, Berlin, 2011

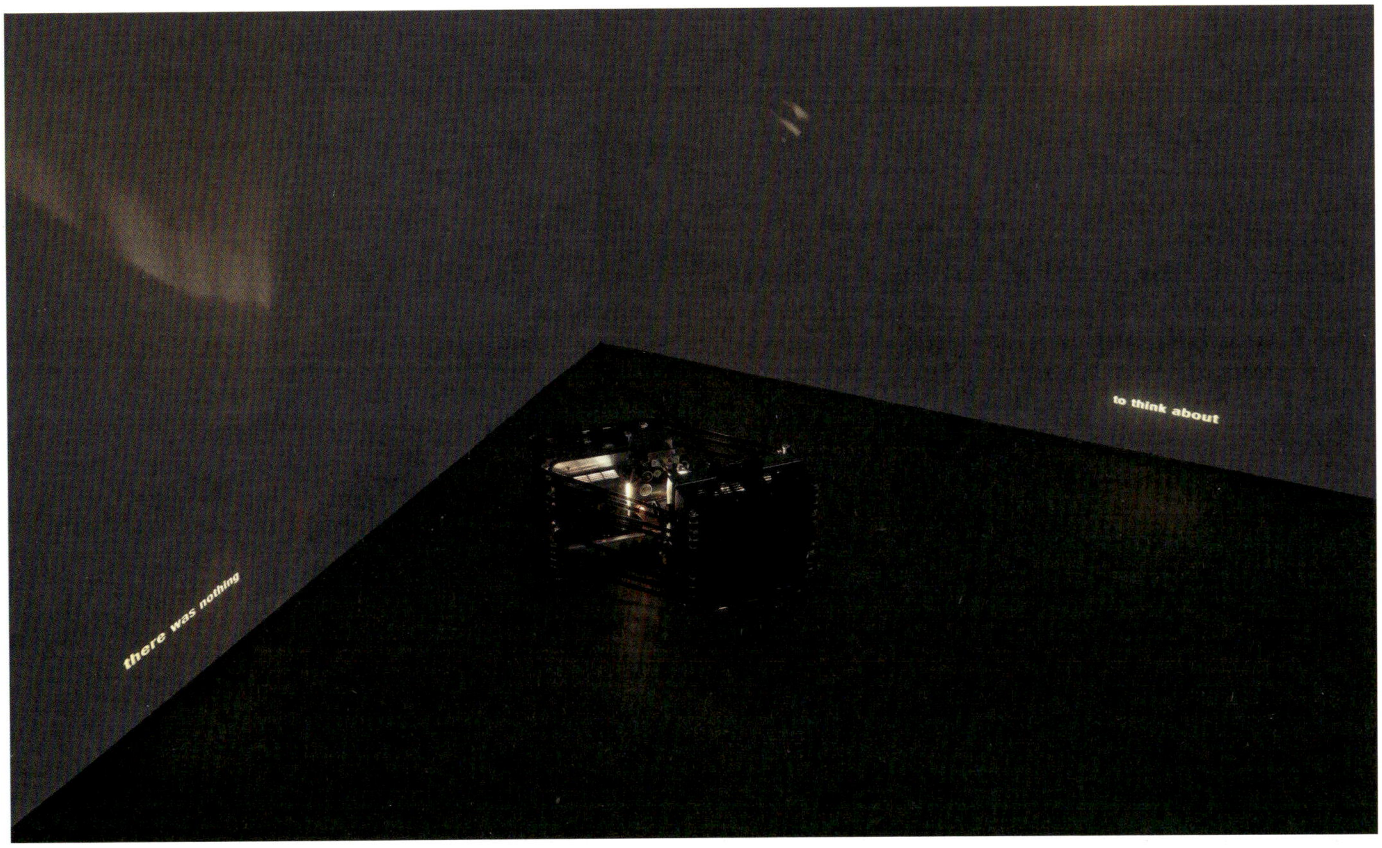
there was nothing
to think about

because
and second

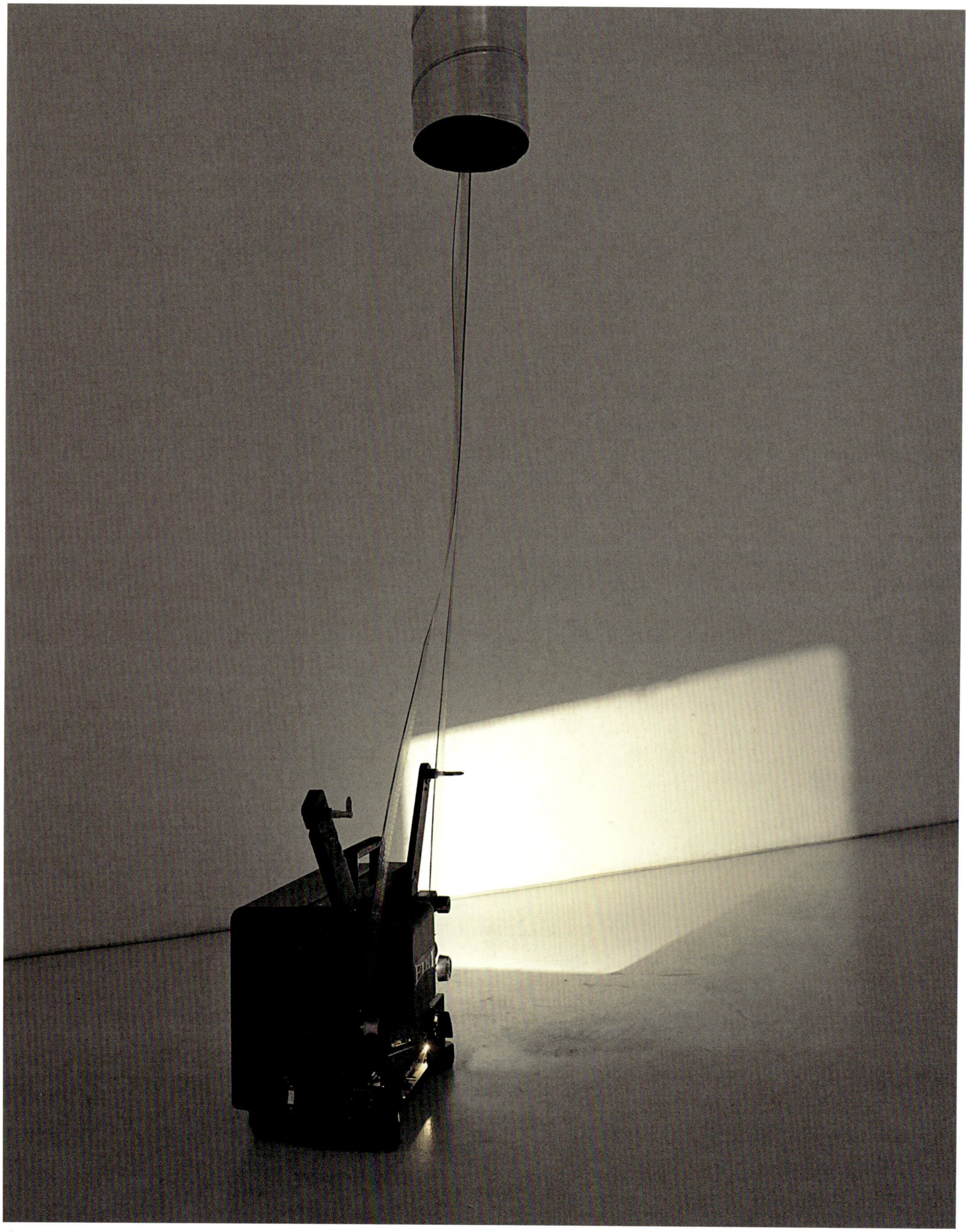

Above: *One Way Out* (2009), installation view, Galleria Giò Marconi, Milan, 2009
Pages 34–35: *Invisible Act* (2010)
Pages 36–37: *Free Post Mersey Tunnel* (2010), installation view, Liverpool Biennial, 2010

Many of *The Empirical Effect's* devices can be traced back through Barba's previous work, especially *Outwardly from Earth's Center,* with which the film shares much, and the more associative, filmically self-referential dramas of *Panzano.*
The development of a particular model across these three works can be mapped and is significant. It is first established in *Panzano.* Like the other two, this film is also both a portrait (of a three-way relationship between two men and a woman) and a constructed reality, the enactment of a set of personal relations developed into a representation after observation, collaboration, and translation—a making strange of an actual situation through various cinematic-theatrical effects (nonsync sound, lighting, framing, script, etc.). Not only do each of the three people it depicts occupy a role that is scripted, but they are also shown in what we assume is their own habitat, an isolated, rural, impoverished, ramshackle home. Yet they appear there by the magic of superimposition, through an empty armchair suddenly flickering into an occupied one, etc., and the subtext (the imminent catastrophe) is their fear (or the threat) of each other's disappearance. They are both actually and cinematically existing (like all actors, in a way, only here the paradox is pronounced), the two things depending on each other just as the three people do, one always being contingent upon the other. Dramas that emulate melodramas absurdly play out between them. At one point the older man tells the younger, over a game of table soccer, that the woman did not sleep in her bed last night: incomprehension, powerlessness, jealousy (?), and fear ensue. But what I want to draw attention to is the climax of the film: Brilliant and blinding, otherworldly lights flood the house. Is the older man abducted by aliens? He walks towards the light, sees a young man there and then, suddenly, it is cried that he is gone and never coming back. Which means, of course, that he is neither in the house nor in the film. However, he does return, conjured from the darkness, as the mourning younger man rests his head on the woman's shoulder and she says: "Close your eyes and he will come back." Conjured from the darkness, he returns, at least in the film, if not actually in the room, as a—or *the*—cinematic presence. It is an image that we know and doubt and are glad for, one witnessed by them both and by us as the ghost and the material of the medium.
Outwardly from Earth's Center is closer to *The Empirical Effect* than to *Panzano,* as it, too, is an examination of a location (relations, but not a relationship) in peril: a seemingly barely populated island that is continuously drifting towards the North Pole at the rate of several meters per year. The film presents a range of "inhabitants" and "experts" whom we know by their occupation rather than their names, much as we would in a storybook: the Lighthouse-Keeper, the Archaeologists, the Architect, the Archivist, etc. Their different kinds of theories (or mythologies) and solutions to the island's problem are both subject to and the product of Barba's staging—they are situated within the sublime, and information is presented in a theatrical space, projected onto screens as on a set for the drama and mystery of only half-explained charts and diagrams, or reported as folklore yet figured in official papers. These stories are intercut with Bergmanesque shots of a solitary person on a beach staring out to sea, monochrome, quintessentially romantic, and a series of shots of rock formations over which a man's voice is heard as if responding to a Rorschach test, naming what he sees in each of them as if to ask whether we see them too, as if to exemplify a directional act of framing and its problems. Clearly, like *The Empirical Effect,* this film is concerned with a set of proofs that overlap with, contradict, supplant, and fantasize around this other catastrophe-in-process. And as in this other work, they come to assume parity because of the work's enveloping function, its own consuming act of creation. That is, this work too is not a document, or a record of an actual situation, but a projection of one through a vocabulary that is visual, fantastical, its own proof (equivalent among relatives), and cinematic.
Towards the end of the film large wooden stakes are piled into the sand like vertical hieroglyphs. Huge, thick ice-encrusted ropes are dragged around them. In an aerial shot of the island, rays of sun strike the land through the clouds, a formation mirrored by the ropes, which are now many and are seen as taut, dark lines radiating (like sunbeams) from the island's shoreline to an off-camera tethering place. The island is "saved," which is to say that the impossible solution to a fantastical problem that is itself an emblem or an exploration of the possibilities of social cohesion is made possible: in film, and with our agreement to its fictions that it also precipitates.
It is this model that *The Empirical Effect* develops further, as if the film could be read as a breakthrough. After we imagine the population to have "fled" to safety, the choruslike group of older people remains. There's no sense of triumph, but there is a sense of relaxation. They dance on a terrace overlooking the sea with a gentle abandon that suggests that all the testing, proving, evidence-gathering, comparing, re-presenting, competing, and experiencing was not in vain but was as fictional and as actual as the eruption they were trying to anticipate, which both has and has not occurred, for it has (only) occurred within and through a complex web of fiction that we might not even need to notice, which is the film alone, as a special kind of actuality.

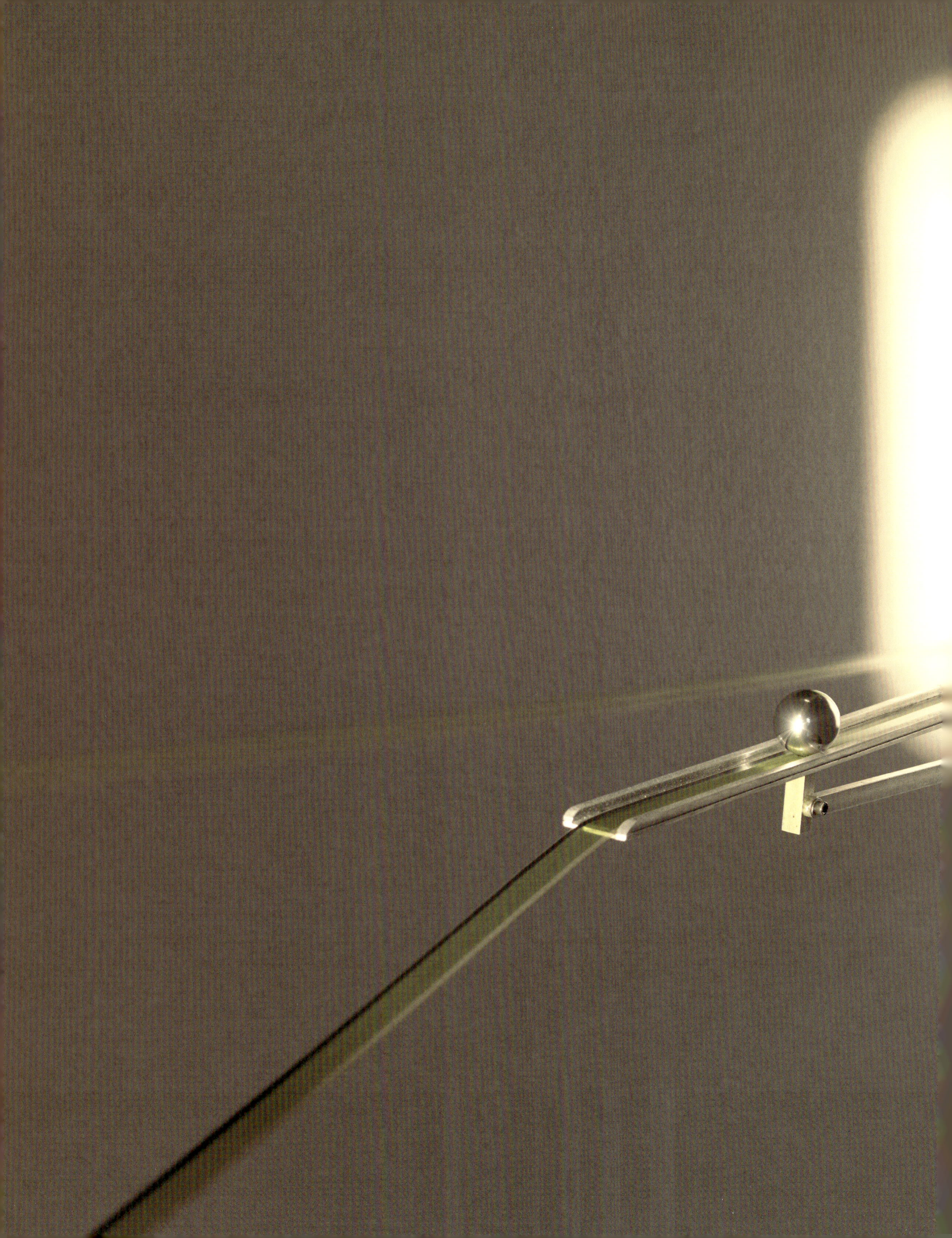

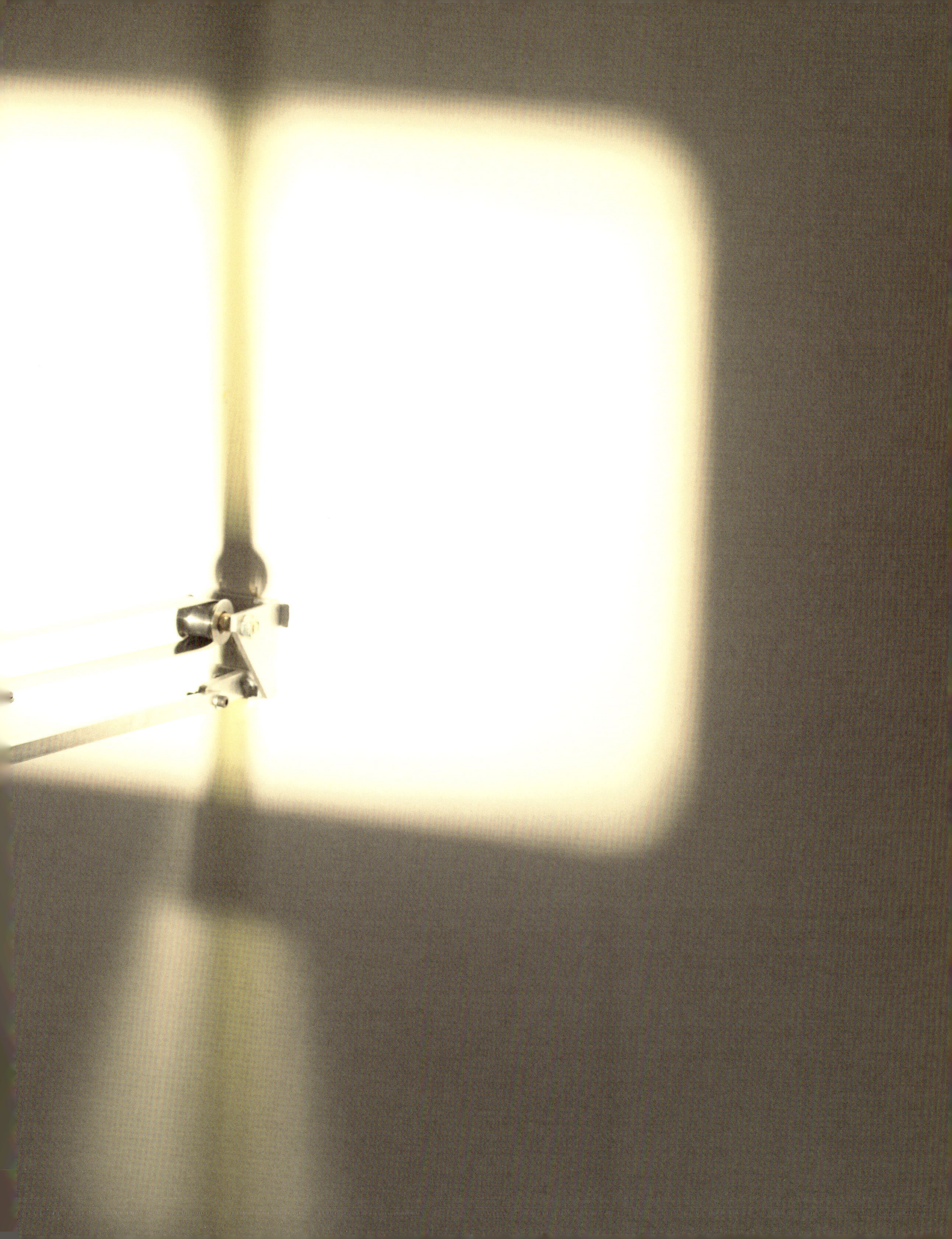

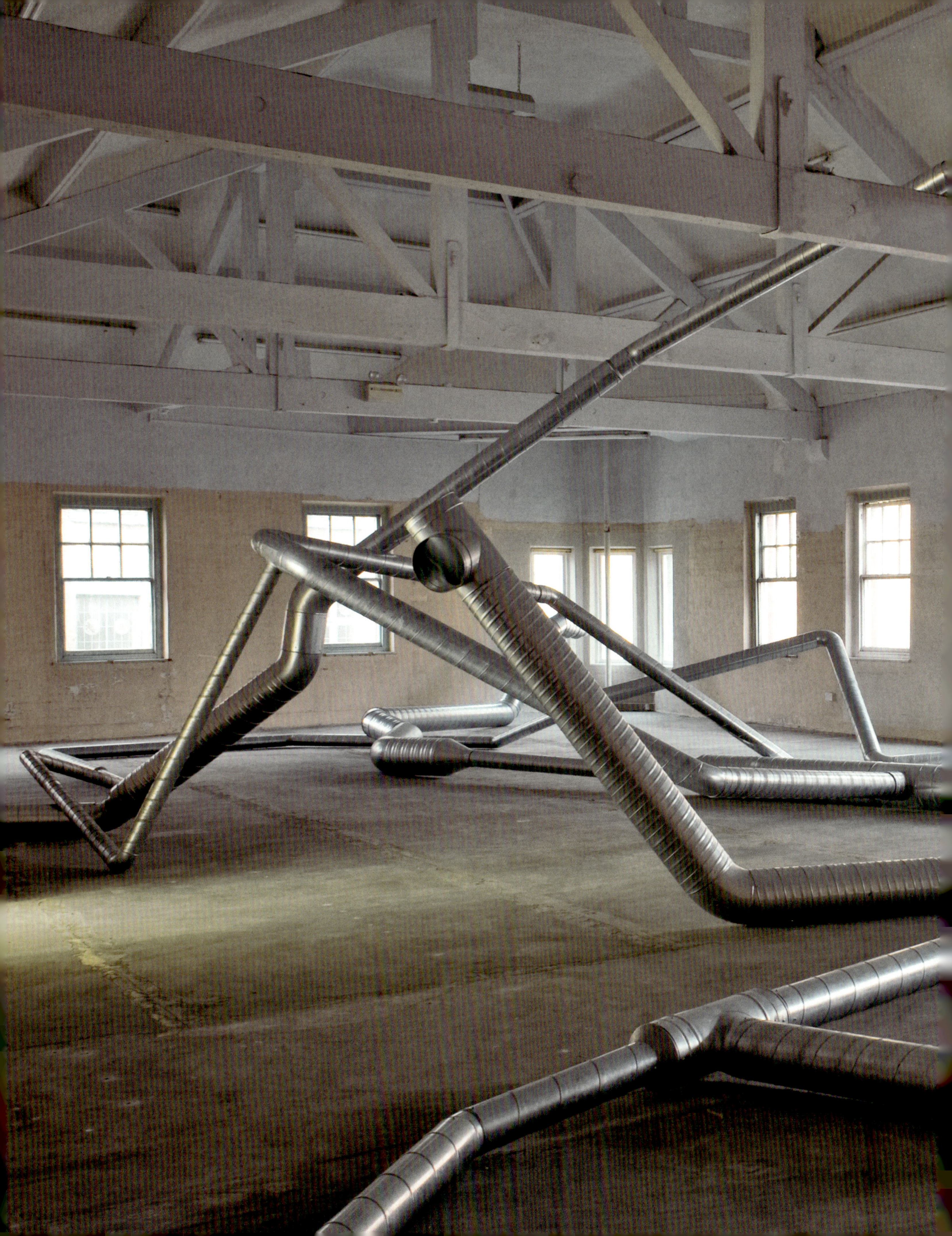

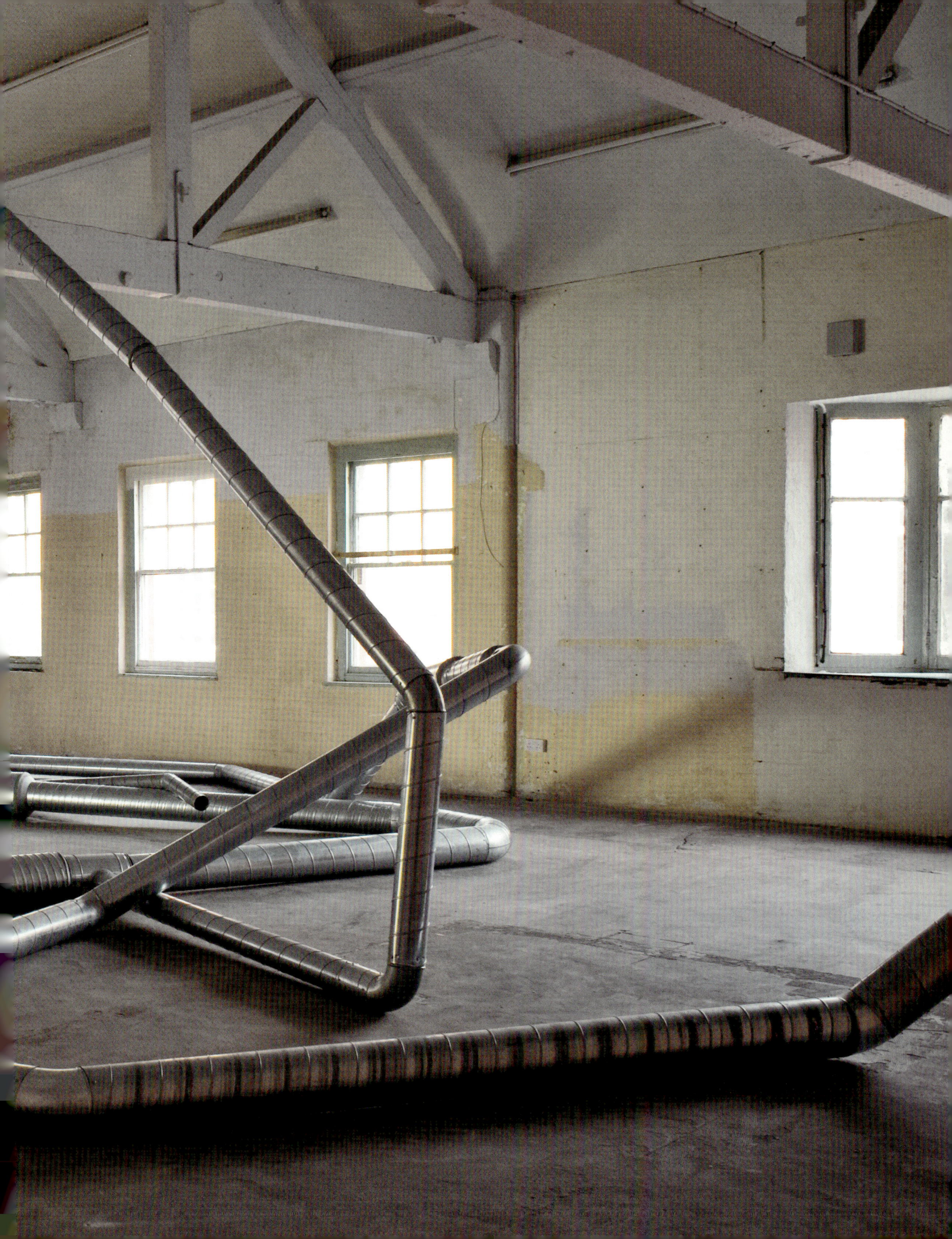

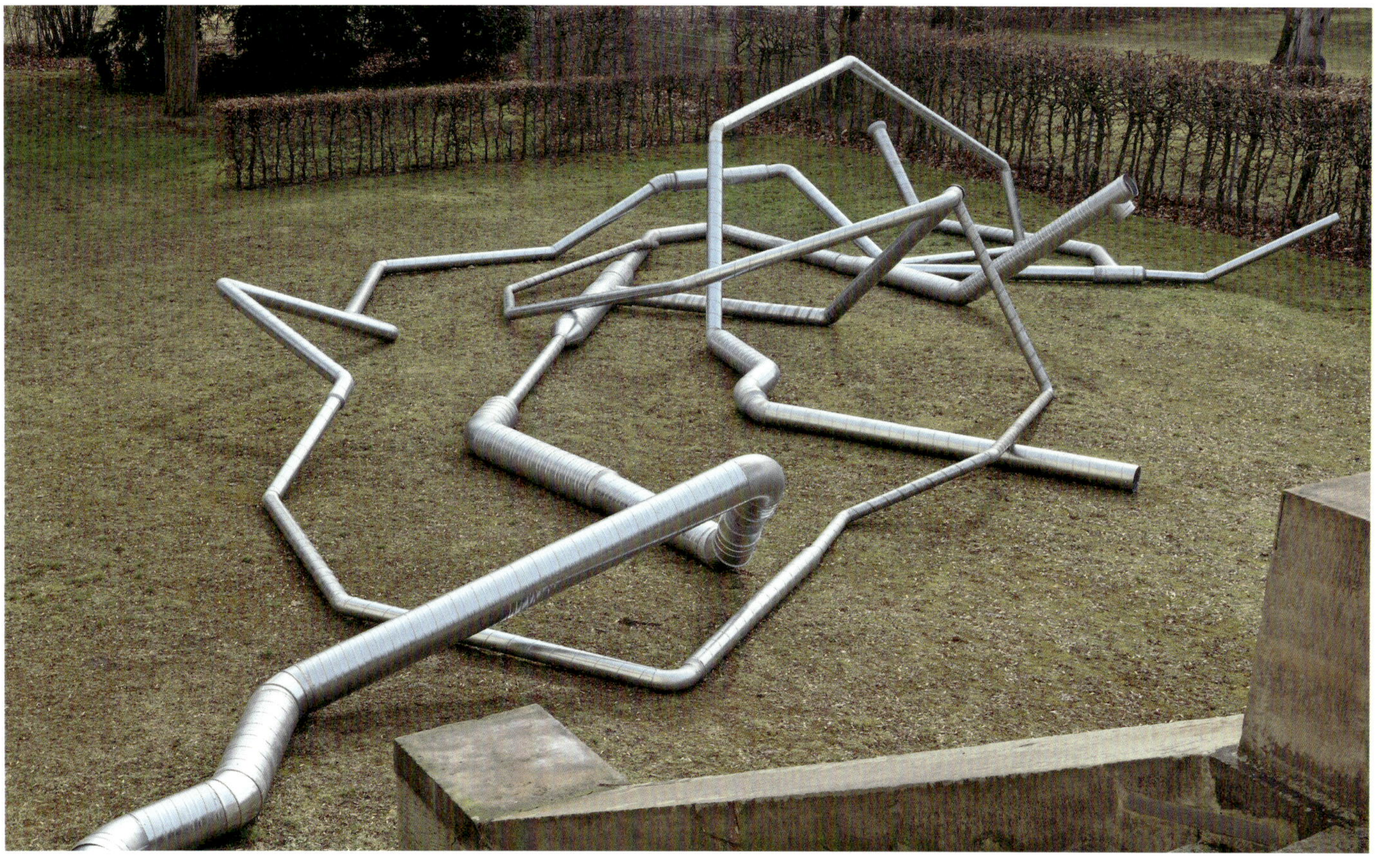

Above: *Free Post Mersey Tunnel* (2010), installation view, Kunstverein Braunschweig, 2011
Pages 40–41: *Stating the Real Sublime* (2009), installation view, Tate Modern, London, 2010
Pages 42–43: *One Way Out* (2010), installation view, Centre international d'art et du paysage de l'île de Vassivière, 2010

My point is that both of the endings of the two earlier films lead to that of *The Empirical Effect*. They similarly offer the suggestion of something joyous, not disastrous, having occurred, something akin to liberation, and I'd suggest that this is both an operation of filmmaking itself and our escape from the trappings of control that are the other pleasures of industrial cinema to which we might agree to be subjected (like happily choosing to live next to an active volcano). If the situation and condition of industrial cinema ultimately is read as Barba's (meta)subject, what is effected is a kind of turning inside-out of that situation and condition such that it becomes surface content and might be occupied and dismantled at the same time and by its own means.

There are two connected thoughts that extend from this. The first concerns Barba's sculptures of 16-millimeter film projectors, in which the projector itself, in various arrangements, projects nothing or just its own beam and is proposed as an object. *Stating the Real Sublime* (2009) is a good example of this. Here a projector hangs from the ceiling by the very same clear celluloid that it is projecting, the empty film spooling through a series of pulleys and around the body of the machine that is suspended by it. At first glance it might be read as a novelty. What is this machine? The celluloid/support holds no images; it is functioning, but not in the standard way, which makes it almost fetishistic. It is almost as if it is wearing its inside on the outside, or the material that it usually ingests and transforms into the ultimate immaterial artwork, which is the projected image, is its cradle. But there is no image, just a machine that is caught, held, running on its own mechanisms. Self-contained and strangely inside-out without quite being so mechanically. In my mind, it comes to stand for something. Its subject is not formalism. It is an image of itself that positions me alongside it (I am alongside it) while affiliating me to a similar unpronounceable inside-outness. It becomes like a living thing. I am occupying and dismantling both it and myself. I am subject to the situation and condition of an idea of cinema—one that is now over there, let's say an industrial cinema—in which I am not participating physically, architecturally, or perceptually but of which I am a function to the extent that, conceptually, this is both its metaphor and its content. Its weightlessness is also a bodilessness and infinity.

Furthermore, a similar enveloping (of the body, of the machine, of concept and metaphor) begins to occur when a number of these works are shown together, combinations of projector-sculptures and projected films. Structurally, they provide images of each other and come to incorporate the viewer into this conceptual engine room as the means of a reimagining and the revealing of a set of relations that elsewhere constitute subjection. No better is this exemplified than in Barba's 2010 exhibition *Is It a Two-Dimensional Analogy or a Metaphor?*, which occupied almost every space of the unique postmodernist buildings of the Centre international d'art et du paysage on the île de Vassivière. In fact, it claimed the building and the viewer's movement through it and beyond as the work itself. One was propelled from the tower of a mock lighthouse along the beam of a 70-millimeter projector into the galleries proper and confronted with the diagram of a projector (and of our own movement) discovered in an aerial shot of a car-testing track in the Californian desert, and then pushed further through the building into a room with projector-sculptures and films-as-text cut out from sheets of felt hung from the ceiling like scenery. One passed through a door—all of this transpiring in the same linear direction—into an unfurnished lecture-theater-type space that had become a projection box in which another huge projector was positioned at a small window. After dark, this threw a static rectangle of light onto the grass, trees, and bushes below, which moved like the frames of a film that were viewable from a pure white room, a museum no less, beneath the lecture theater. Here, nature has become image, and the viewer is still, while the earth is turning. You are inside the mechanisms of control that you were (otherwise) subjected to outside. This is industrial cinema with the lights on, an idea in three dimensions.

Note

1. Translated by William Melmoth and revised by F. C. T. Bosanquet. Consulted online at: http://ancienthistory.about.com/od/pompeii/a/PlinyPompeii.htm (last accessed February 2, 2011).

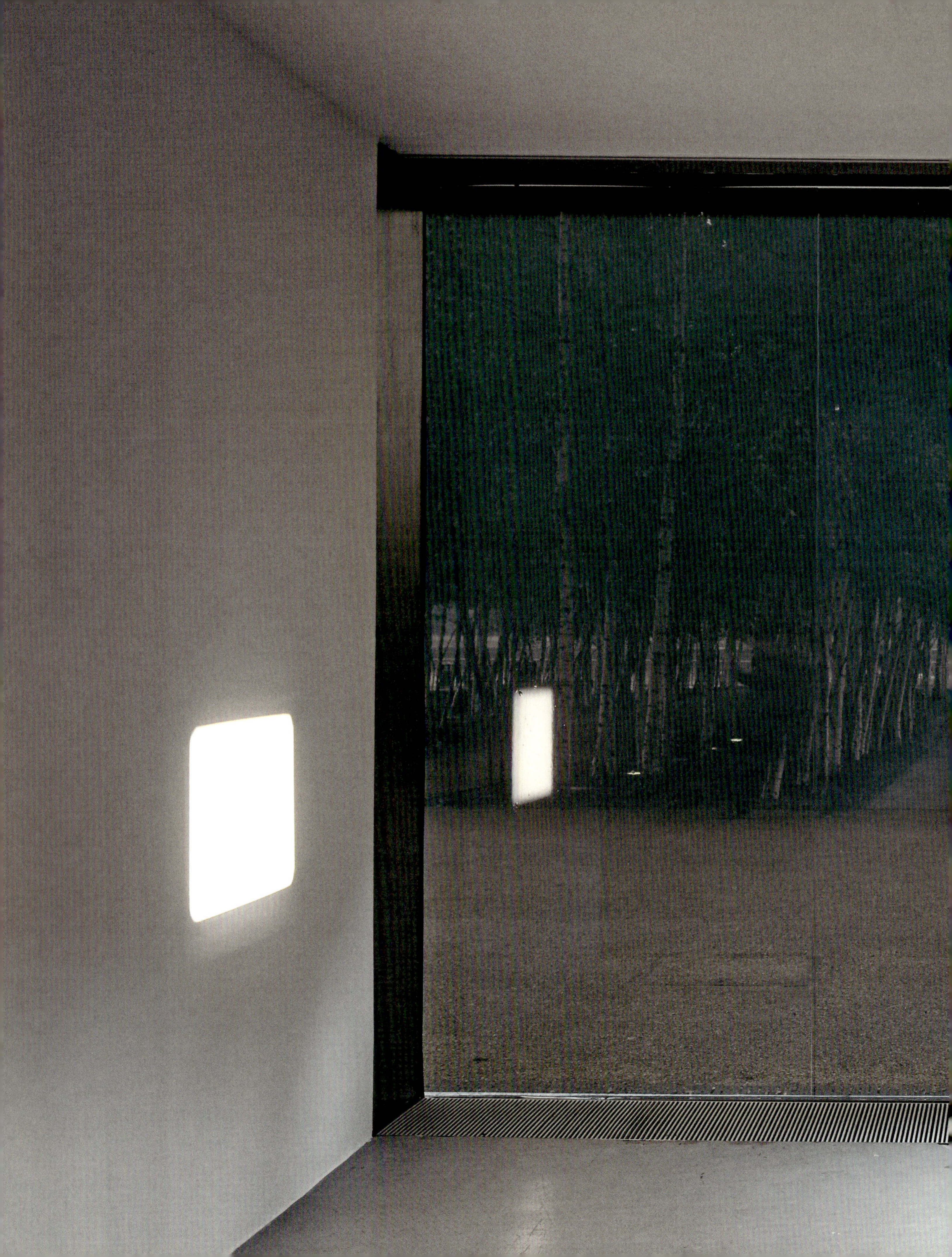

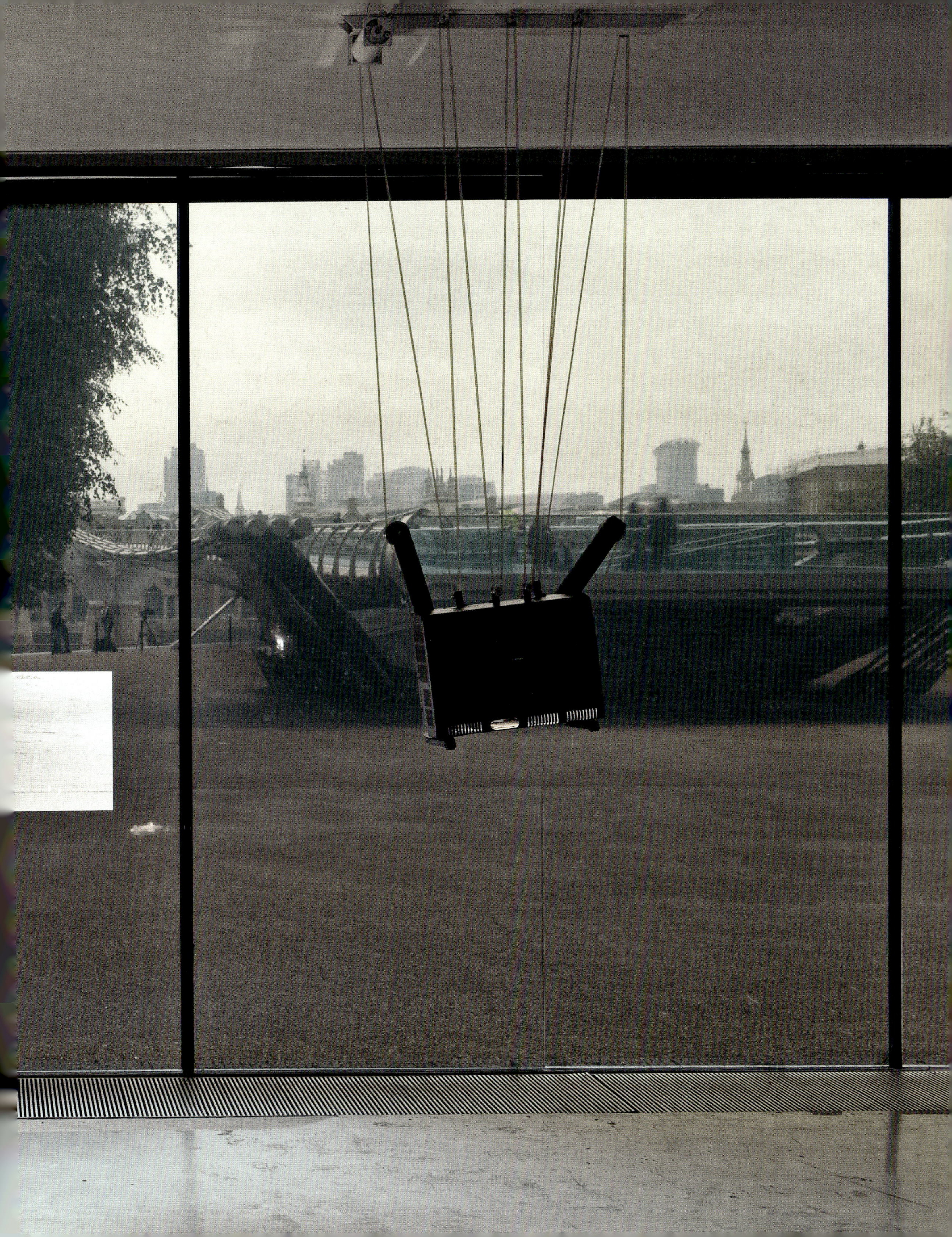

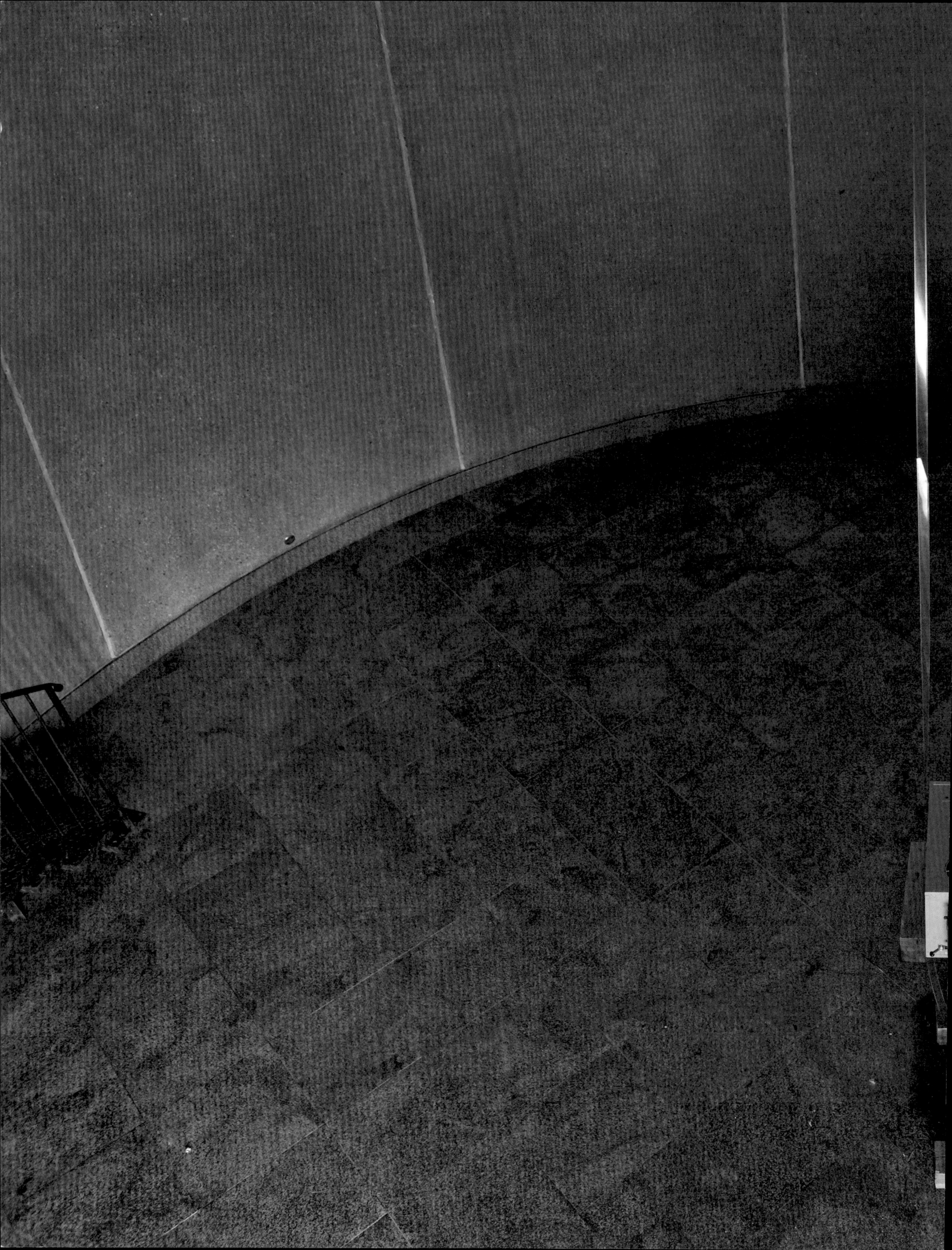

LOOKING FOR ROSA BARBA

ELISABETH LEBOVICI

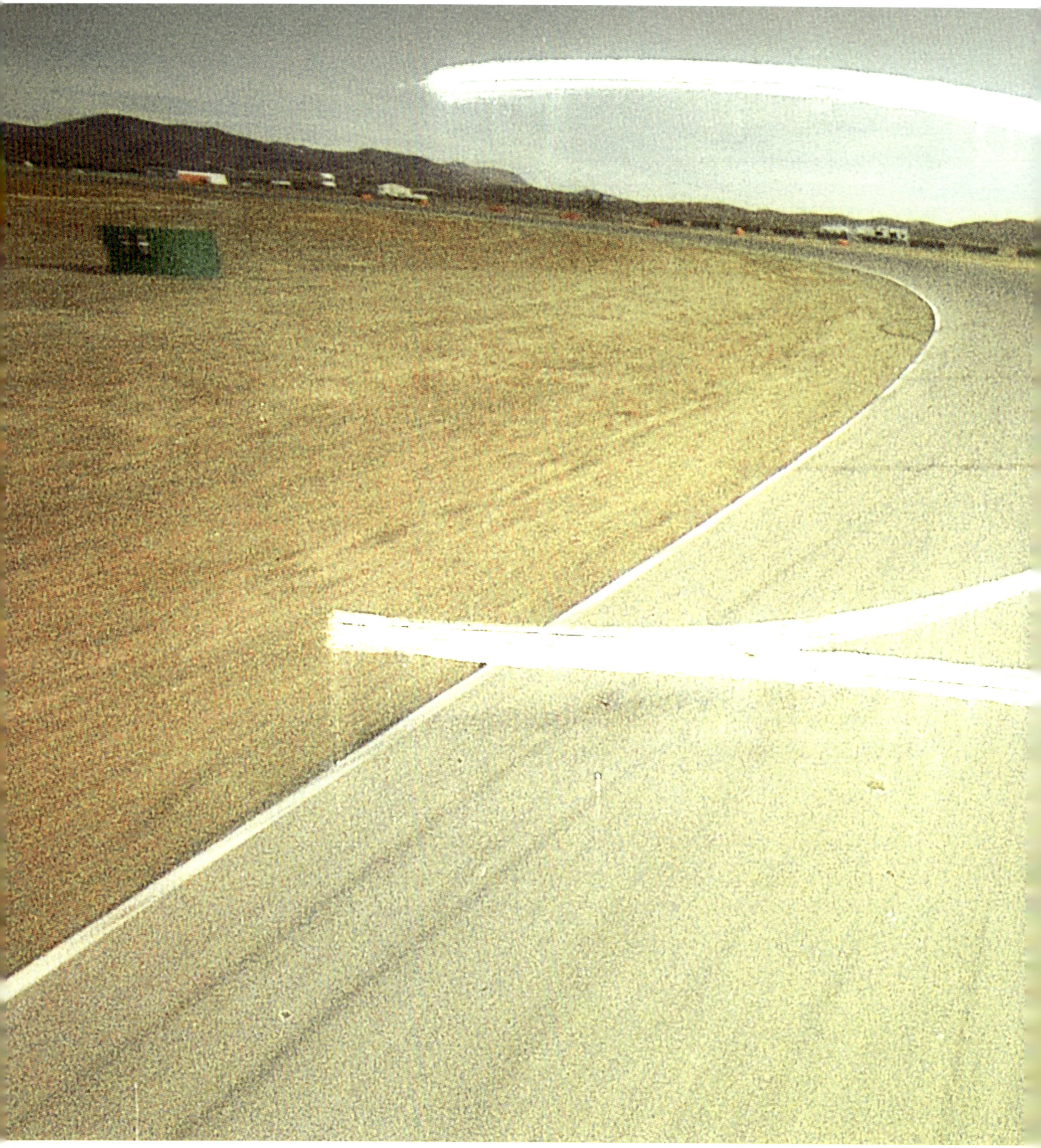

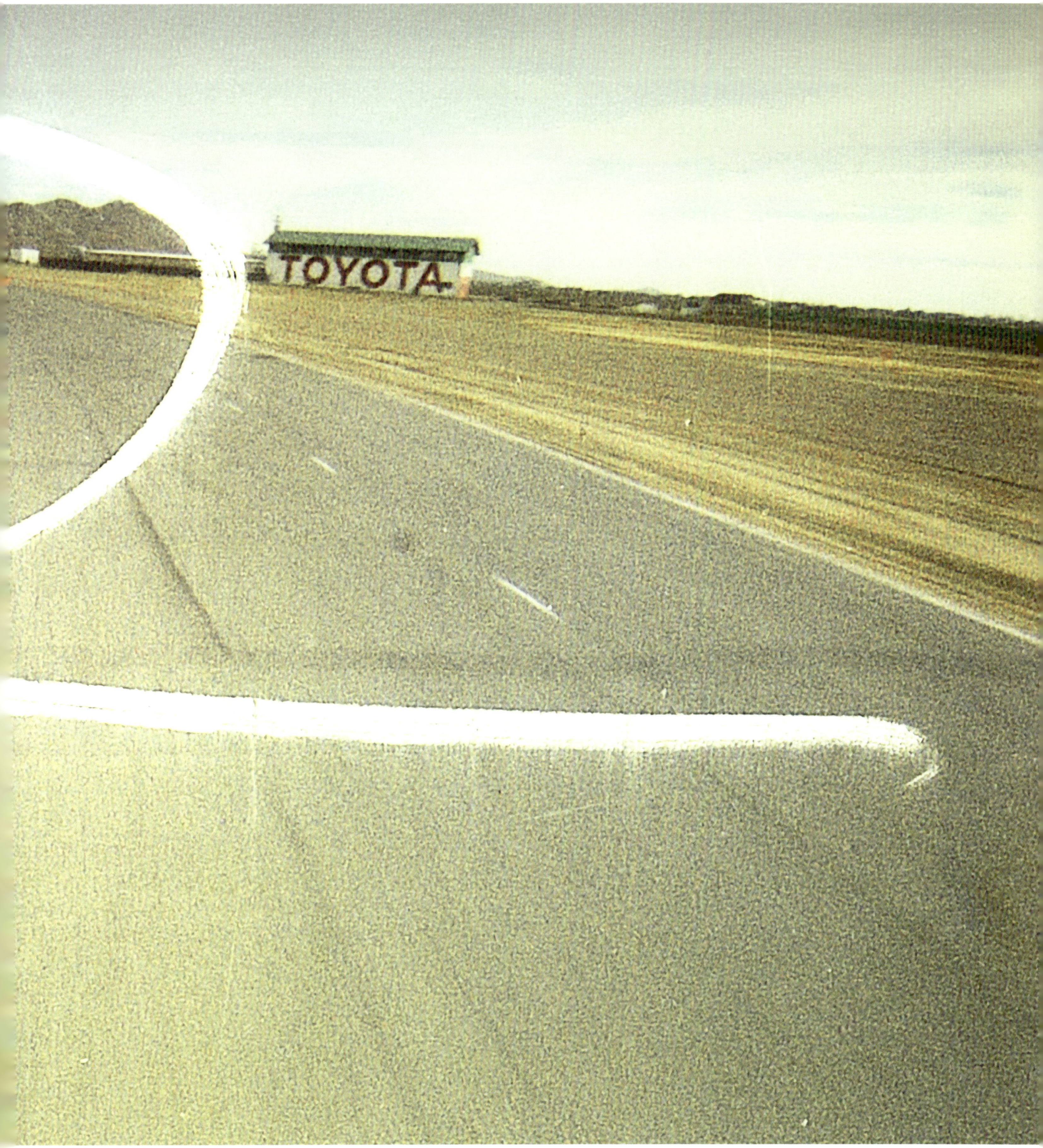
TOYOTA

I. Full Circle

It's not because Rosa Barba's recent exhibition took place on the island in Lake Vassivière—a landscape transformed into a screen by the artist's use of the Art Center building as a gigantic light / movie projector—that her work appeared to me as an archipelago. The motif of an island and its surroundings features frequently in her oeuvre, in the form of sites, maps, arbitrarily marked-out desert territories, cirques, circuits, circular roads, exhibition rooms, films rolled up in their cans, and film loops projected as eternal returns yet at the same time made visible as tangible paths. Such is the case of the baroque trajectory of one of these loops, which exits a projector hanging several meters above the floor of Aldo Rossi's cavernous tower at Vassivière and is then drawn endlessly upward to the space's highest point, where it coils and then cascades back down. These islets come with sound, too, electronic ritornelli or the noise of projectors and ventilation systems, or conversations whose meaning eludes you. At the Venice Biennale in 2009 a chorus of texts was choreographed via five projectors, which, like sound-emitting ids, accompanied words written on a screen—an evocation of the inserts that used to provide the dialogue for silent movies. What grips us in Rosa Barba's production is not only the areas her works demarcate, but the dramas taking shape within those areas, inceptive narratives mixing science and technoscience, fiction and science fiction, and "collapsing into the sun of their radiant (ir)reality-war."[1] Often, in this way, a threat wells up without our being able to work out whether it comes from some still-secret past or from a future the narratives anticipate, or whether it has its origins in the images to which it refers or in the machines that are part of the performative present of the installation: the island threatening to drift away in the sea and separate itself from the world linking the narratives to us, and the lost continent where the ruins of a forgotten event—*Forgotten* being one of Barba's fictional countries—intermingle in a nonlinear, nonchronological, noncanonical, and, let us dare to imagine, "nonmale" temporality.[2] The following text is also an archipelago, a network of islands, slowly drifting. Triggered by the works and referencing them, it is intended to be not a substitute for the actual experience of viewing them, but rather a movement that, as we seek out Rosa Barba, seems to have forgotten itself within or been distracted by the momentum of the search.

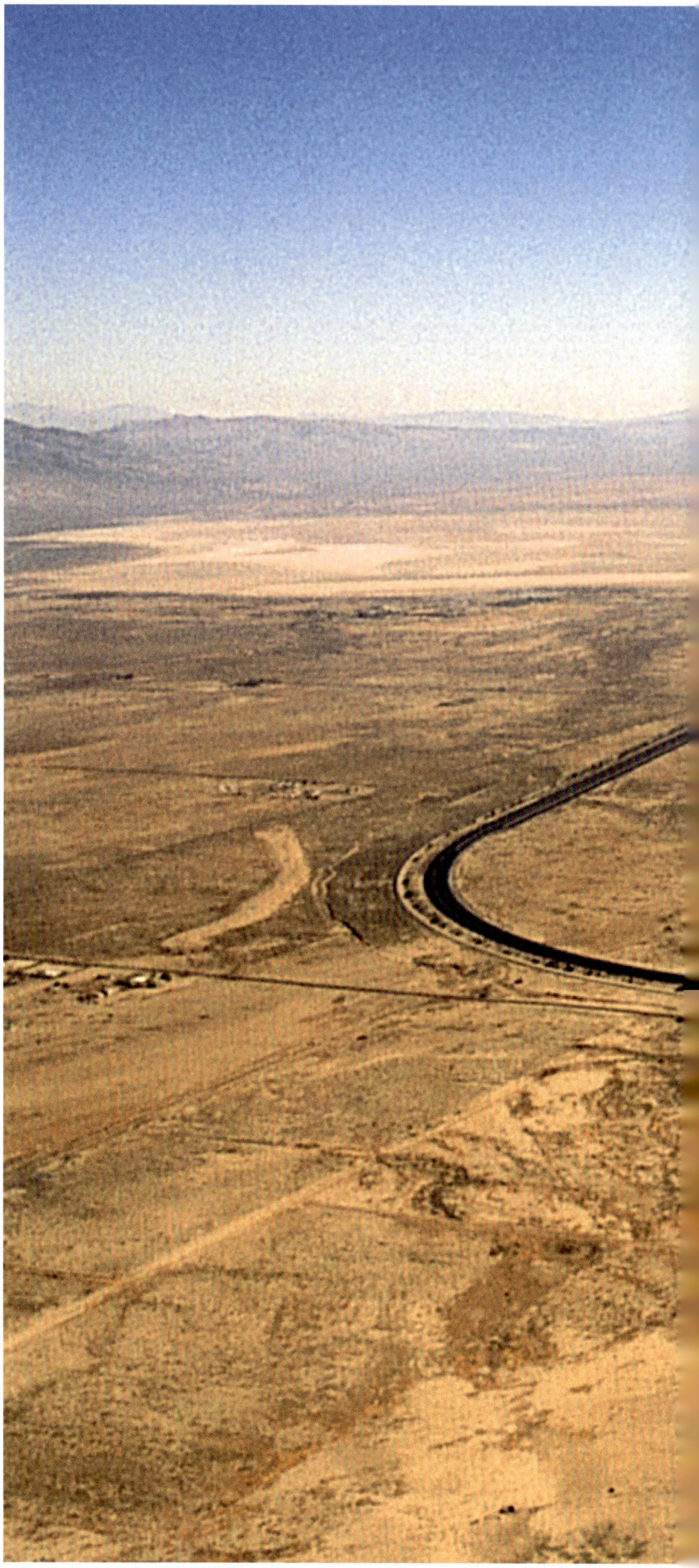

Right: *The Long Road* (2010). Collection of the Louisiana Museum of Modern Art, Humlebæk, Denmark
Preceding pages: *The Long Road* (2007), untitled still

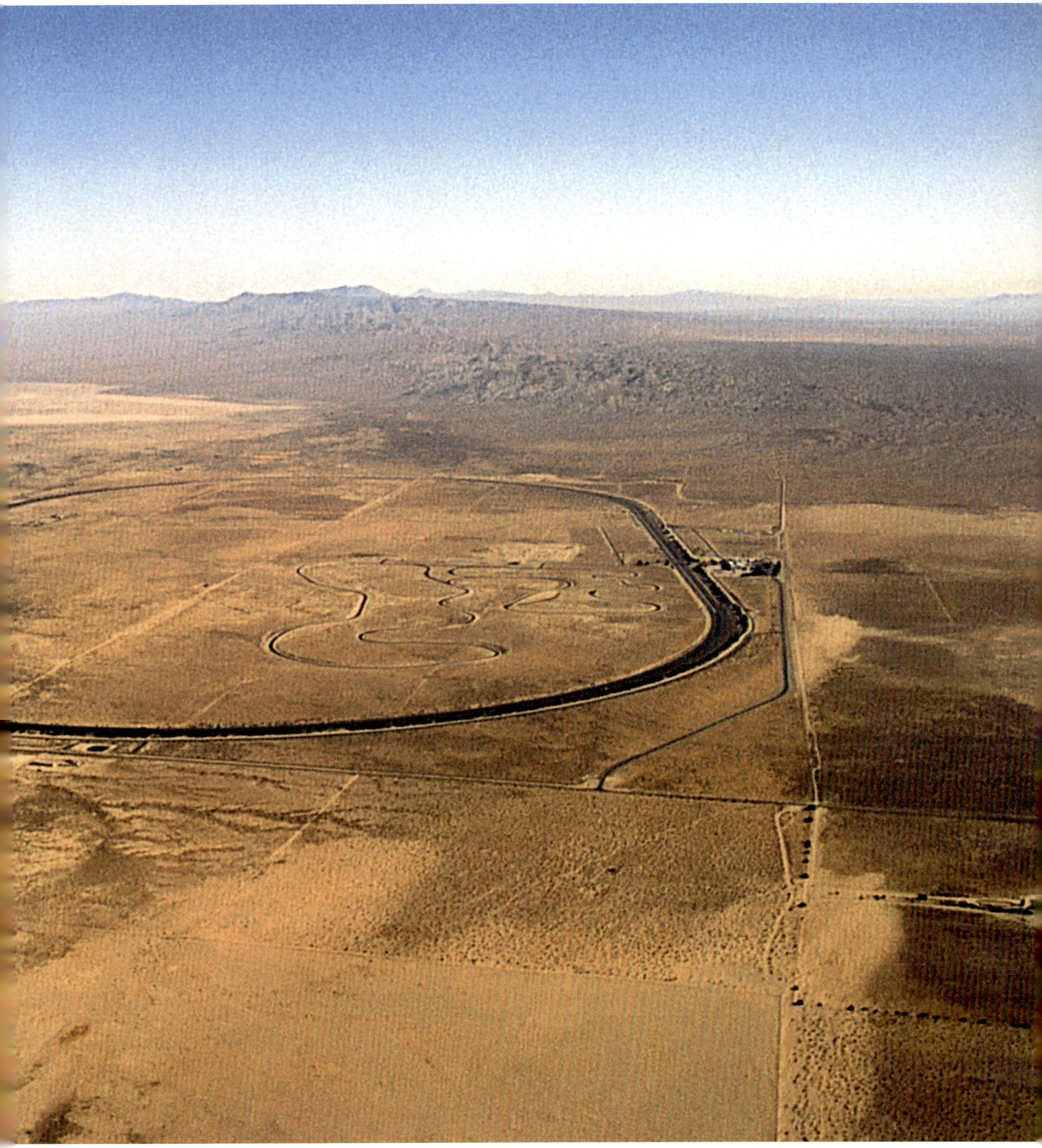

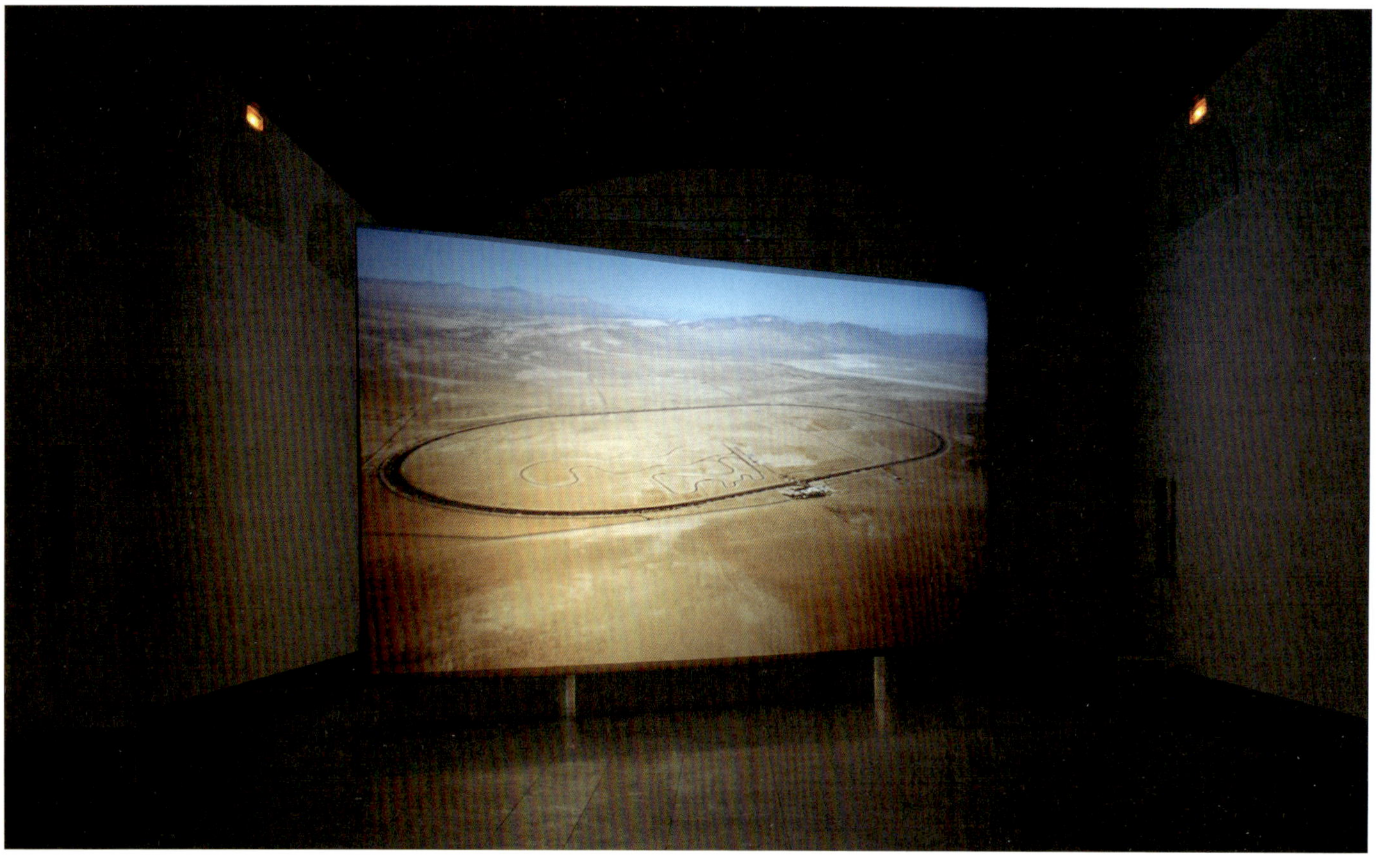

Above and right: *The Long Road* (2010), installation view, Centre international d'art et du paysage de l'île de Vassivière, 2010

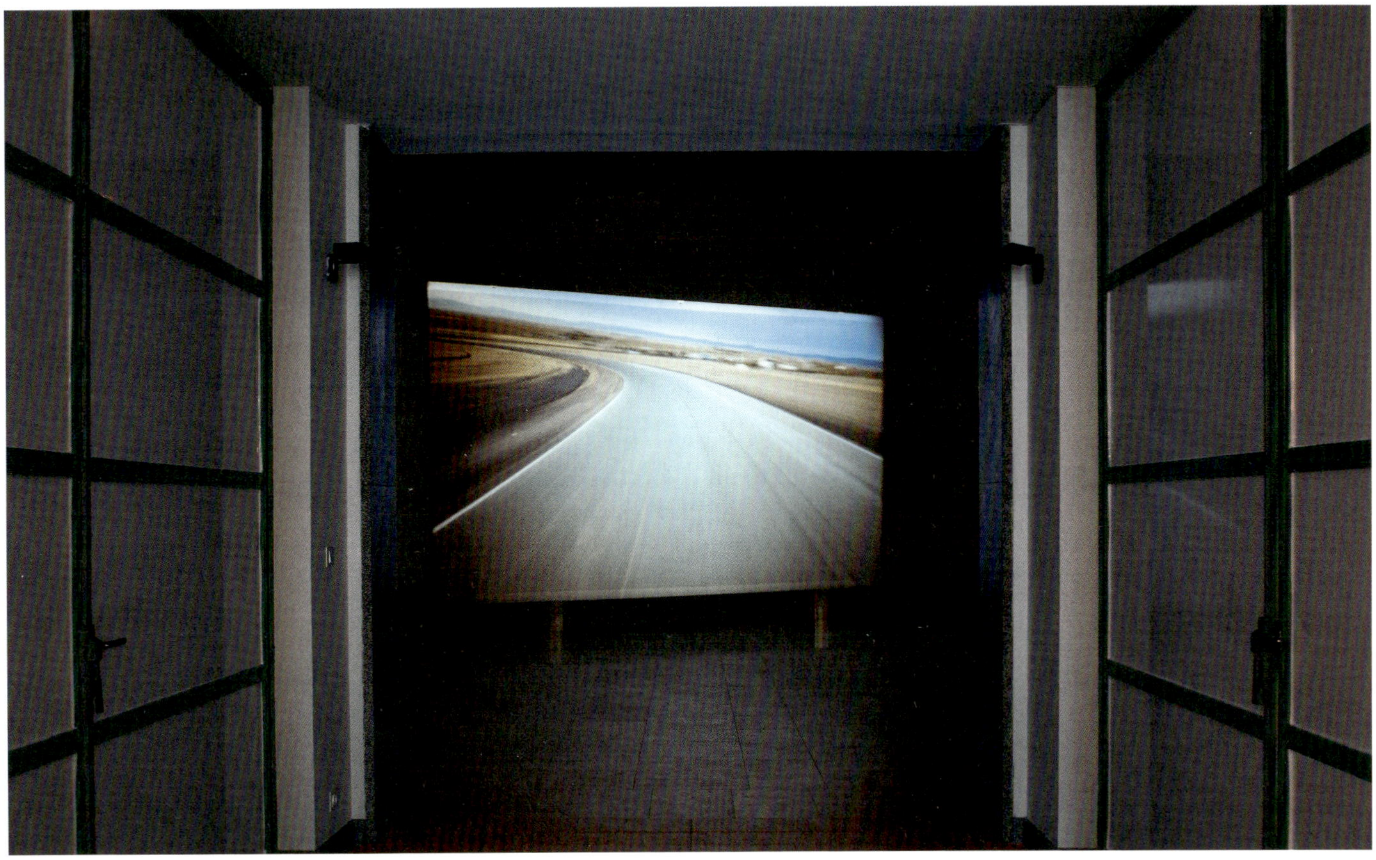

II. "The Crack-Up"

In Nicolas Poussin's *The Shepherds of Arcadia* of 1638 (Musée du Louvre, Paris), four figures are gathered around a bulky tomb set in a wild, not particularly rustic-looking landscape of trees which are either storm-damaged or whose dried-out leaves mimic the forms of a host of gray-white clouds—traditionally speaking, Arcadia is an island "far from all coastlines." Standing on the right, a woman in profile has her hand on the shoulder of a young shepherd; leaning on his staff, the shepherd is looking at her and pointing with thumb and index finger at something the two other shepherds on the left are trying to decipher. One of them, standing in a nonchalantly off-balance pose with his legs crossed one over the other, is leaning on the tomb, while the third, bearded and on one knee, is tracing with his fingertip the inscription visible on the stone: "Et In Arcadia Ego." Or rather, "Et In Arcadia E/go," for a flaw or crack in the stone has cut through the last word. Thus the Ego is cut in two, as one of the shepherds sees his cast shadow take the shape of the Grim Reaper's scythe.
Poussin's painting has turned an inscription on a stone in a garden into a focal point for conversation, beginning with the one transpiring between the members of the group inspecting the inscriptions, and continuing with those between art historians—such as Panofsky, Blunt, Klein, Gombrich, Marin, and others—who have dialogued via their writings. Each of these eminent men has sought, either laboriously or inspiredly, to read the signs' true meaning and, by extension, to commit himself to an interpretation of the work. In the same way, during a series of encounters after World War II, artists, art historians, and art critics racked their collective brains over where aesthetics was going.
And because Rosa Barba quoted the event as a reference, the "Western Round Table on Modern Art" has made a comeback on today's art scene. The encounters that bore this title took place in San Francisco in 1949 with the purpose of bringing "a representation of the best informed opinion of the time to bear on questions about art today."[3] But was it not also, for the participants, a matter of justifying their own authority with a riposte to those who were calling it into question? Now accessible on the marvelous online Ubu network, this Western in the form of a conversation brilliantly makes its point as Duchamp, Bateson, Wright, "Schoenburg" [*sic*], and others underscore the male unanimity of those taking part: "A bunch of guys trying to think. Still more difficult, we were trying to think aloud and trying to communicate with each other—trying to get things clear that have never been gotten clear."[4] They were new shepherds, then. Arcadia had made way for the West, for the word that designates both the Occident and the Wild West, which also includes the West as depicted in film. So here a broad overview was entrusted to a gang of white cowboys trying to make headway into the already outdated future of their civilization and their cultures, and forgetting that every vision is personified in a body: "All Western cultural narratives about objectivity are allegories of the ideologies governing the relations of what we call mind and body, distance and responsibility."[5] It was also in 1949 that Simone de Beauvoir published *The Second Sex*.
What did these men fail to say about this inscription with no verb—this "Et In Arcadia Ego"? Was it incomplete? Was it complete? Its translation, which varies between "I too was in Arcadia" and "Even in Arcadia, I am," attributes the words alternately to the dead man and to death. And from here on in things diverge, starting with the inscription: the four words that link the dead and death, and subvert the landscape we are shown. The tomb speaks, but what is it saying? Whether the warning is being issued by death or by a man who is dead and already in his grave, something dramatic has been introduced into the realm of the pastoral that, as the land of bliss, should be invulnerable to decay and decrepitude. Meanwhile the female figure remains upright, neither leaning forward nor attempting to decipher anything. She is a pensive image, parallel to the picture plane and ultimately alone: is it not through her that a second gaze is at work, signaling a process of visualization which it is not painting's task to represent? In this case, the split is its signal.
The split is the key given to us by Louise Bourgeois. This is where the issue of seduction breaks into the art text. Bourgeois explains the narrative of her oeuvre via what she specifically calls "the crack-up in the family, caused by my father bringing his mistresses into the house."[6] To see stealthily or from below is also to actively personify a gaze, and Bourgeois in turn suggested the activation of that gaze to and by her viewers. Aesthetics slips into this family fissure through a number of images that, rather than conjuring up the psyche of the person who made them, trigger a kind of subjective fault line in the viewer.[7] And this is what Rosa Barba does with her *Split Fields,* a work whose black-and-white graininess turns the collective fantasy—at once social, economic, and political—of the potential collapse of the villages close to Mount Vesuvius into a ghostly apparition.
In the Turbine Hall at Tate Modern, *Shibboleth,* a work by the Colombian artist Doris Salcedo, consisted of a zigzag crevasse dug into the concrete floor—"a negative space," says the artist: "It suggests the hole of History, which marks the fathomless difference separating whites from non-whites"—a line of demarcation that has left an indelible scar on the floor of the London institution.

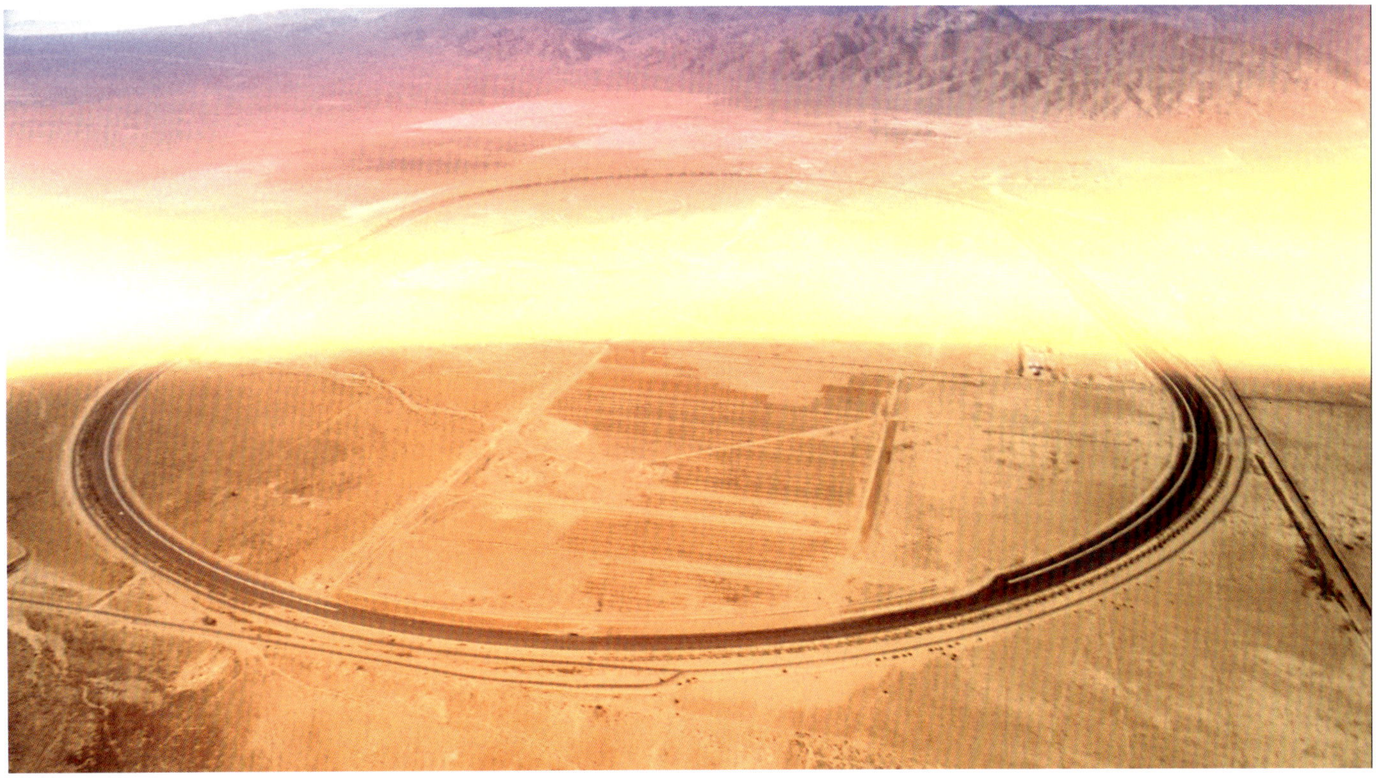

Above: *The Long Road* (2010), untitled still
Following pages: *Rosa Barba* (2010), installation view, Tate Modern, London, 2010

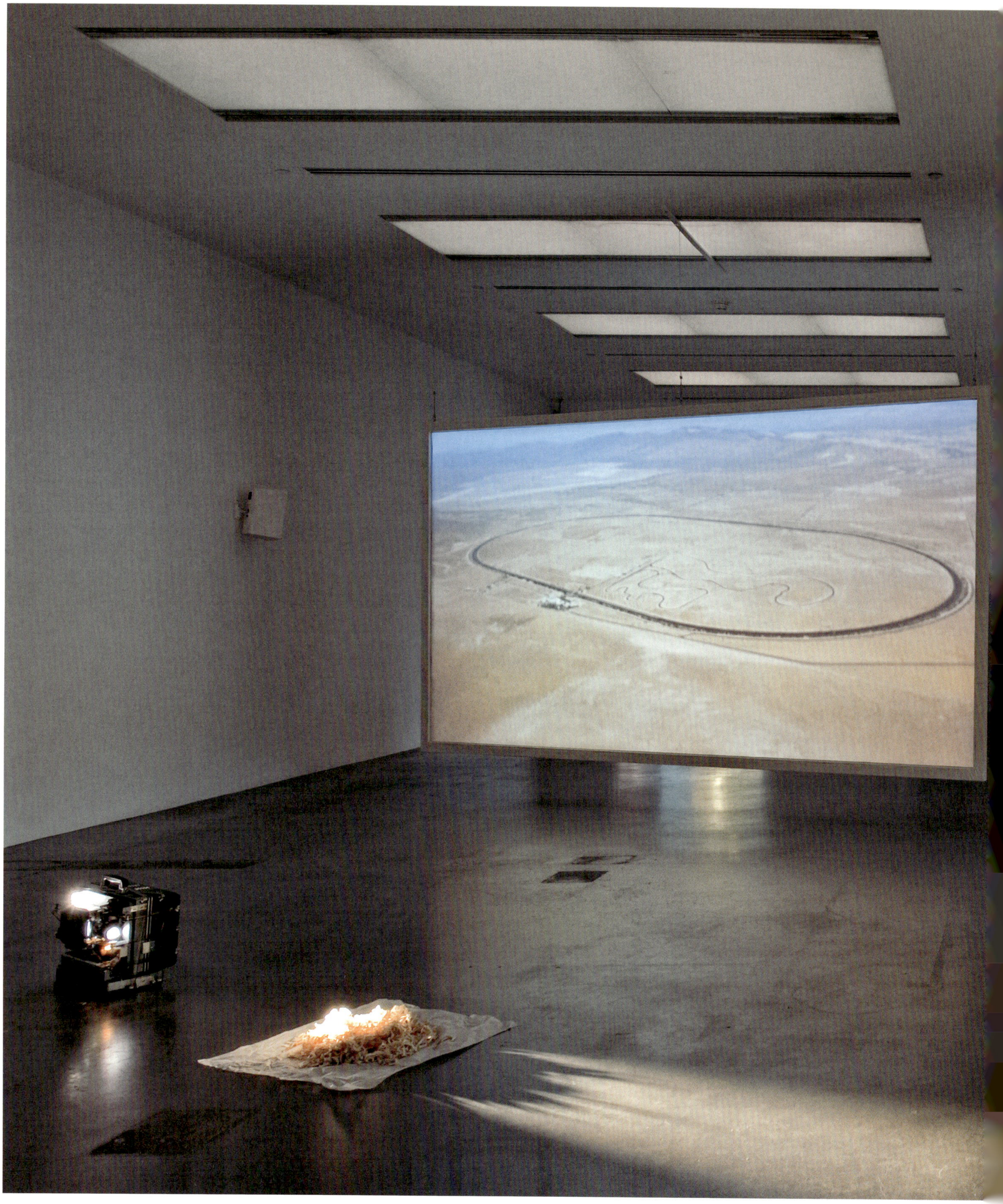

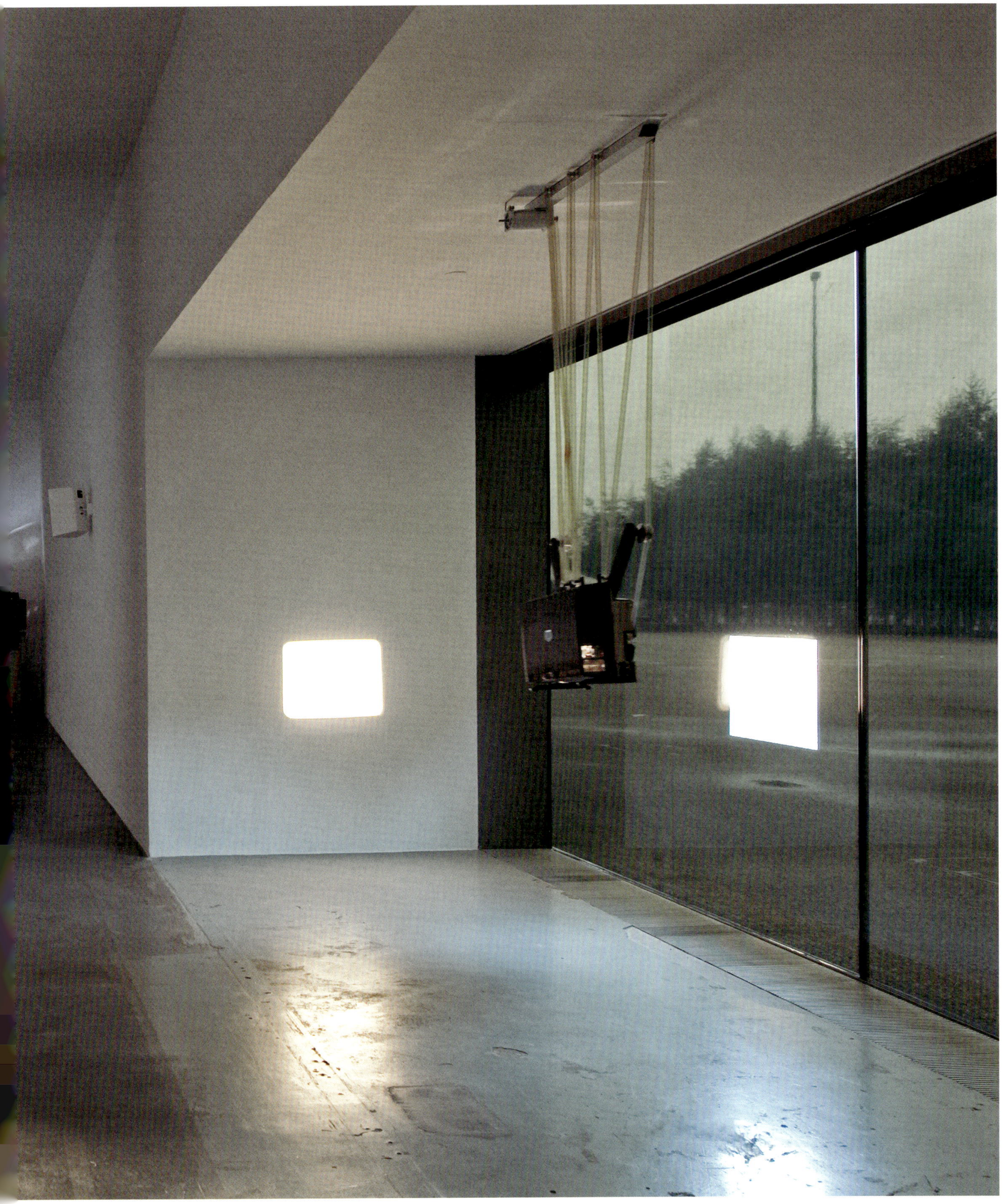

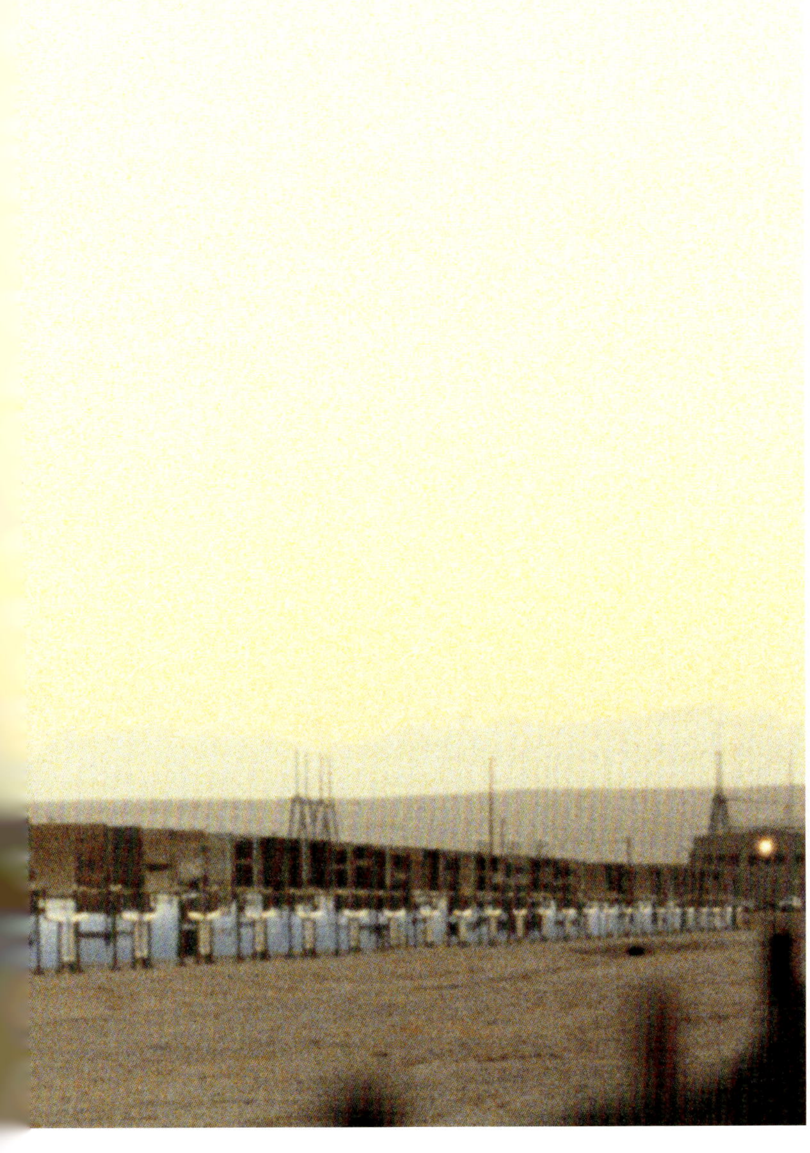

III. Stories from the Landscape

In her novel *The Song of the Lark,* American writer Willa Cather speaks of Panther Canyon as an abrupt fissure in the Arizona desert:

> The canyon walls, for the first two hundred feet below the surface, were perpendicular cliffs striped with even-running strata of rock. From there on to the bottom the sides were less abrupt, were shelving, and lightly fringed with piñons and dwarf cedars. The effect was that of a gentler canyon within a wilder one. The dead city lay at the point where the perpendicular outer wall ceased and the V-shaped inner gorge began. There a stratum of rock, softer than those above, had been hollowed out by the action of time until it was like a deep groove running along the sides of the canyon. In this hollow (like a great fold in the rock) the Ancient People had built their houses of yellowish stone and mortar.[8]

They Shine (2007), untitled still

Aggressive and gentle, inhabited and uninhabited: the canyon is a place imbued with a whole range of emotions. This passage, with its description of the canyon as one of the fault lines shaping the enigmatic history of this country, is "the most thoroughly elaborated female landscape in literature."[9]

Inside the fissure, then, one finds an entire native people, ecological builders revealed by the song of the earth. Willa Cather—or, rather, Thea Kronborg, the singer who is the novel's protagonist—speaks of remnants of the pottery made by the Indian women: for both her and them these archaeological remains are a potential focal point for aesthetic explorations. This kind of transformation is a theme one comes upon often when examining the impact of women on the canonical history of the arts, if one remains receptive to such nonclassical activities as the crafts and working with clay and ceramics. Between the process of creation effected by what we call nature and that effected by fiction, a passageway is hollowed out, one that is also a landscape: "It is when the first semblance of organic form is achieved that a work of art exhibits its general symbolic possibilities, like a statement imperfectly made or even merely indicated, but understandable in its general intent."[10] Thus states Susanne Langer, a somewhat forgotten philosopher who puts the emphasis on a "feeling" that is not solely one of pleasure, but is also identified with the experienced space of the world, i.e., what takes place in the life of the mind.

The evolution of the term "landscape" goes hand in hand with this view of things: initially signifying a form of aesthetic depiction—drawn, painted, or textual—it later came to mean a view (and thus a point of view), and then, an aesthetic intervention within a place; and the word ultimately drifted through time and space until it came to designate, as J. M. Coetzee has put it, "both a specific terrain and the general character of that terrain."[11] Landscape is an arrangement—an aesthetic composition and an emphasis. To quote Rosa Barba, "So then, it was a story that emerged from a landscape."[12]

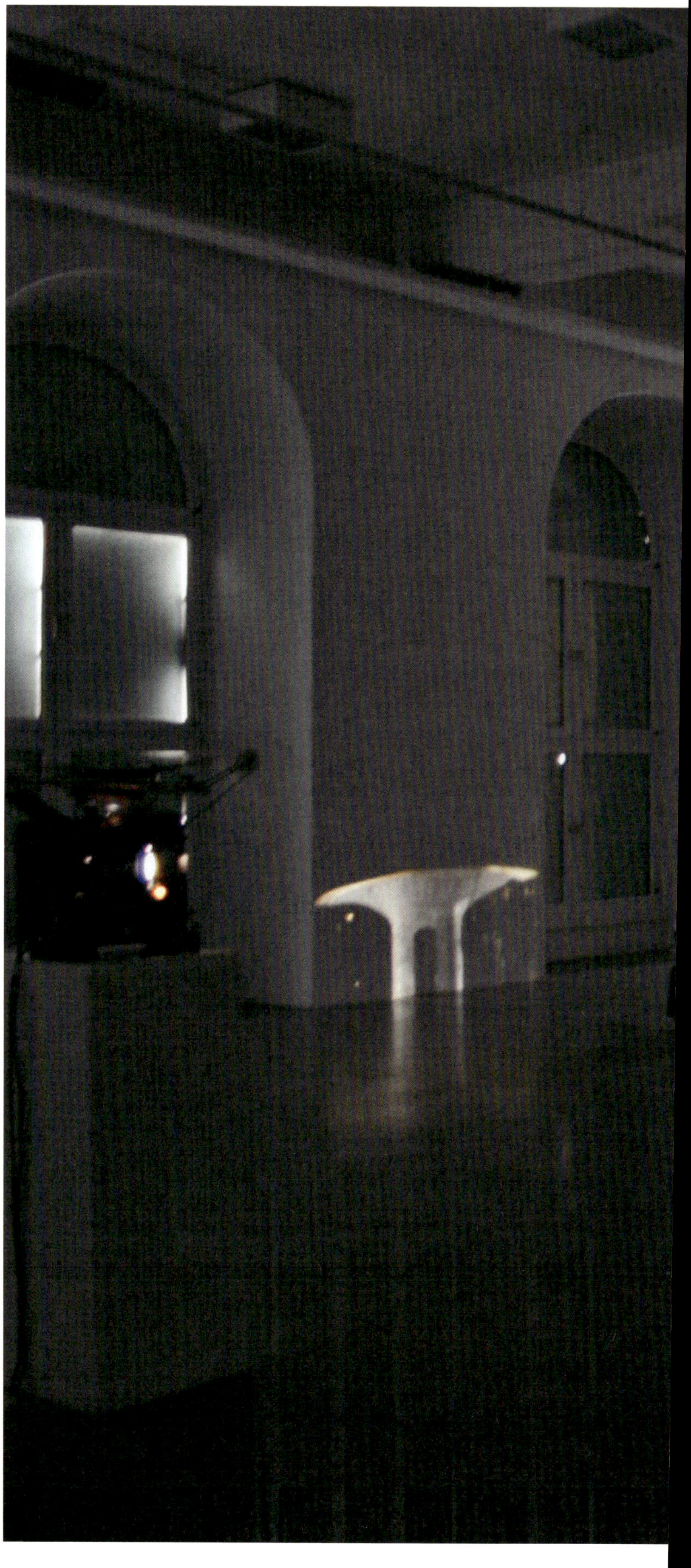

Right: *Parachutable* (2005), installation view, Kasseler Kunstverein, Fridericianum e.V. Kassel, 2005
Following pages: *They Shine* (2007)

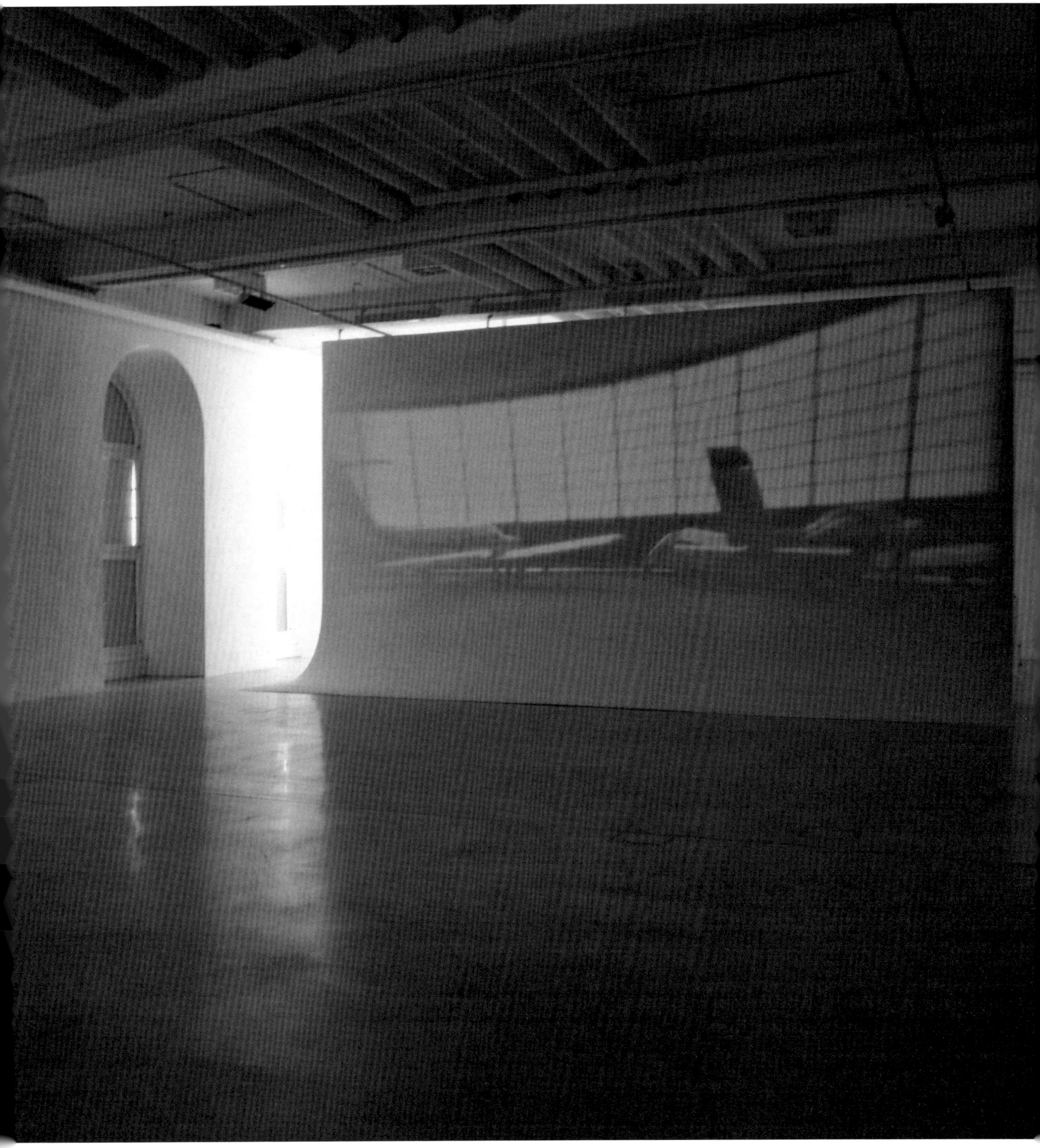

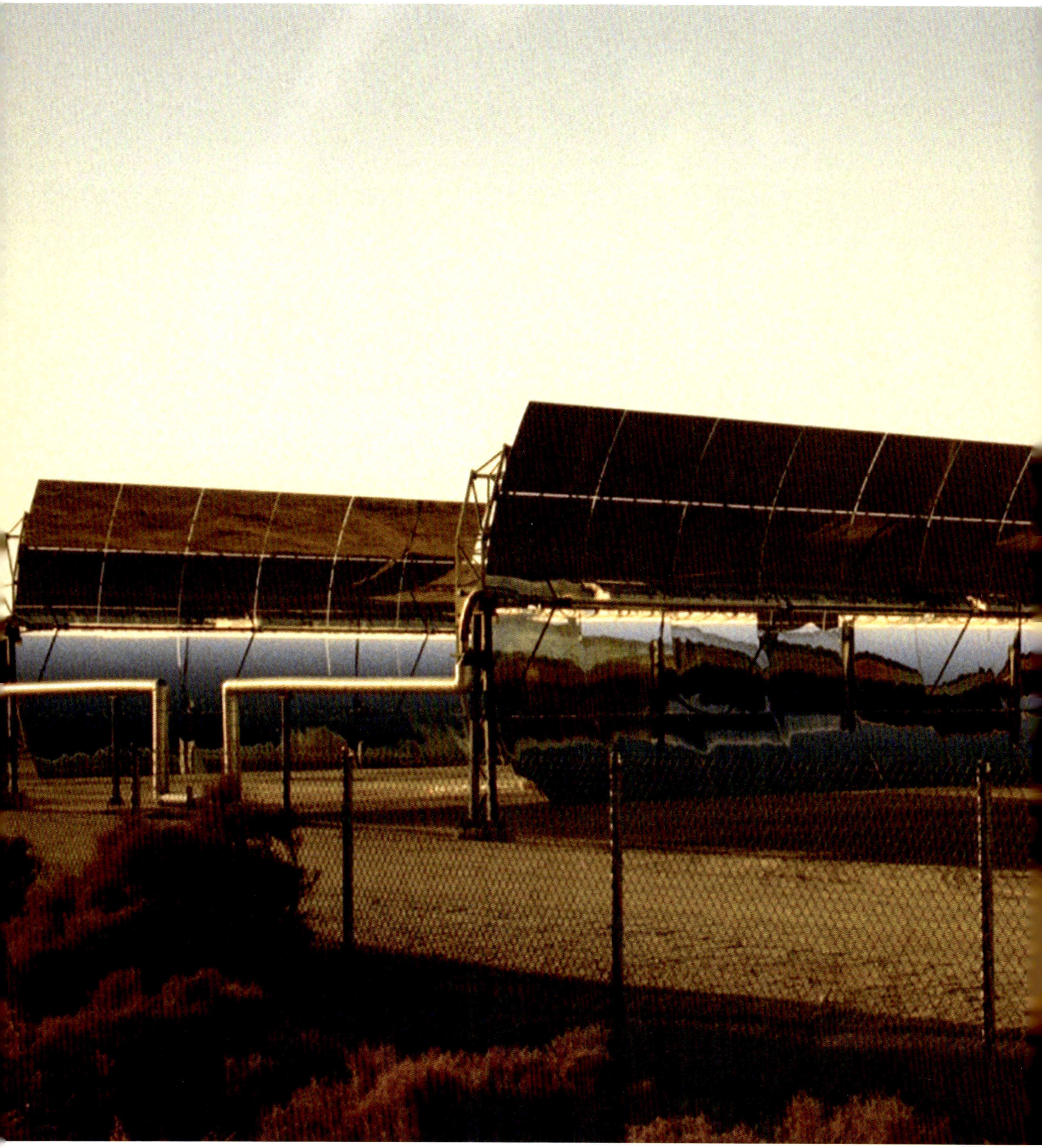

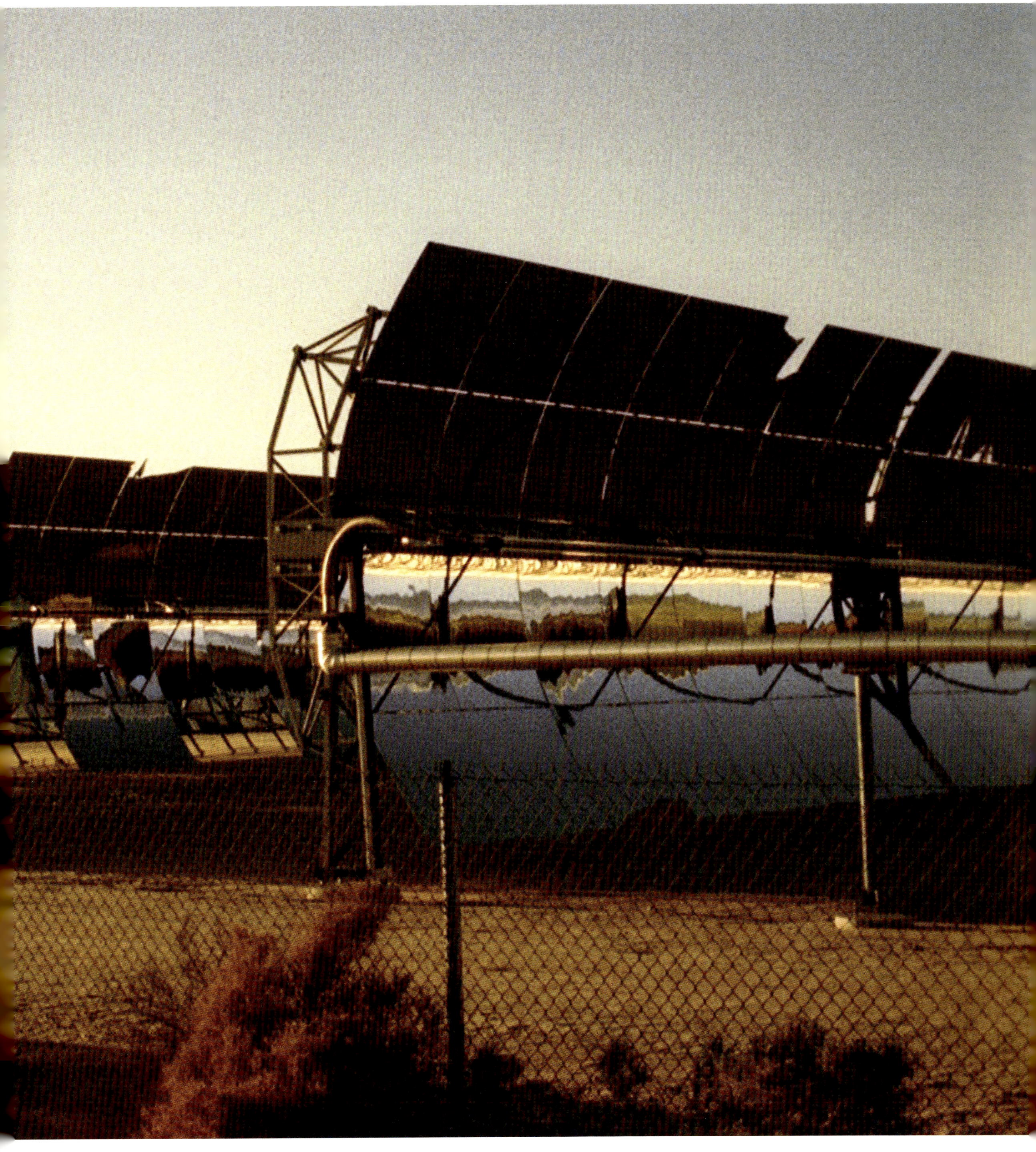

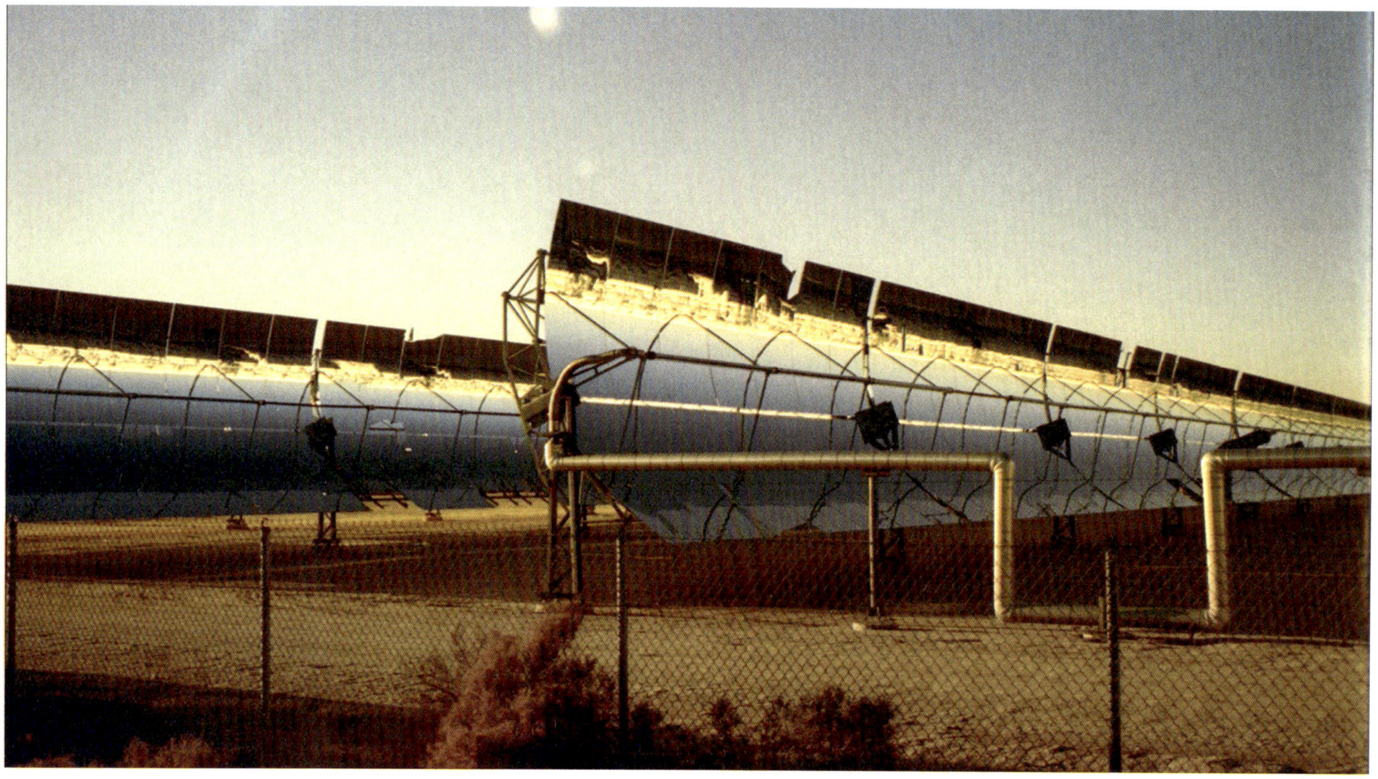

They Shine (2007)

"They shine."
"They shine, he says! All right, but how?
How do they shine? Tell me how!"
"Uh, they twinkle – they blink – they wink
and move."
"How clever it is! They wink! Yes, they wink!
But when do they move?
Do you know when?"

They move, just before they vanish.

"There is a huge town being built behind them, with streets, squares, dormitories, storehouses; hollowing out a dwelling-place for themselves and their families. At a place where rain cannot penetrate, they cultivate the surface and pierce it with galleries, which lengthen into long communicating streets, subdivided into short ones, crossing one another here and there, sometimes ascending, sometimes descending, and opening into large spaces."

They Shine (2007), soundtrack script excerpt

IV. The Ecosystem of Collaborations

Panzano (2000) is a collaboration involving Rosa Barba, Ulrike Molsen, and Valeria, Claudio, and Dino, survivors of one of the great utopias of the 1970s, antipsychiatry. It is also a model, of a far-too-neglected kind, or of an ecology-of-life alert to the relationships between human beings or other things—which here is the camera, television, or talent-show hero—and their environment; it is a model that includes from the outset processes of creation and cultural products. The film's ecosystem is not the village in Tuscany where it was shot, but the screen space, where shifts from the optical to the haptic involve overexposure and compositions using the physicality of everybody and everything concerned, including technology. The "camera eye" combines with the virtuality of potential stories and the chemistry of overlay techniques, as well as with the splits taking place between outside and inside. *Panzano* could be described as the landscape of the fissure, a gaping maw.

And what if this experimental microclimate spread to untillable desert lands? Calling up another part of the world and another time—the American West in the early twentieth century—Jonathan Goldberg narrates a collaboration, which remains fictional because it failed to take place, between two women who traveled within the same vast territory: the writer Willa Cather—now better known for having applied the word "queer" to sexual deviance in letters written in 1890—and Laura Gilpin, one of the preeminent photographers of the Navajo and Pueblo peoples from 1920 until her death in 1979.[13] Here the Western falls outside the epic canon of the building of white, male America and the urge to move and control borders that also structures a vision of the desert as monument and monolith: "Et In Arcadia Ego." In her desert, Laura Gilpin photographs American "antiquity" as the realm of a unity between canyons—nature's sculptures—the Indians' houses, and the pottery the Indians produce, which for her symbolizes *The Enduring Navajo,* the title of one of her most famous books. In Cather's writings the landscape and its flora and fauna—including the Sinagua pottery to be found there—form a symphonic texture in which metamorphosing corpuscles mingle and transpose their influences and styles; at the same time, however, their materiality also suggests the sensitive membrane of the human diaphragm, the muscle that structures breathing for song. The music of the canyon also becomes part of a harmony involving birdsong, the sounds of cicadas and other insects, and the rhythms of certain ceremonies. In writing, then, the site becomes a resonator for the vitality of the body. The important thing for Gilpin as a photographer was to render oblivion visible—to show what once was and is now no more—even if this involved recreating the site of a tranquil existence by having living Indians (mostly women) pose in exchange for money. This is a way of working that has bothered more than one devotee, but what Gilpin inscribes in her images, writes Goldberg, is a projection that is part of her reserved, noninvasive way of uniting these women, their environment, and their artifacts. The pottery items in the photographs are intermediaries, "monuments of great beauty . . . They have given us in their art a virility and beauty of design beside which much of our own becomes weak and somewhat insignificant. Above all they have endured."[14] The link between Cather's writing and Gilpin's photographs—which might be briefly summed up in sexual terms, namely, their homosexuality—emerges as something more subtle when the focus is to present the desert as a place of intuitive, vital knowledge that seeks no explanation. As in Poussin's *Shepherds of Arcadia,* the task of the female character is not to decipher the power of signs, but, on the contrary, to turn away from it, not out of indifference, but because she is already a sign in the language used by males.

"Et in Arcadia E/go": Arcadia is no longer a utopia. The E/go is sliced through by a line that expresses antithesis—a dystopia—in the same way as when Monique Wittig relates an experience in a language that does not establish m/e as a subject in her book *The Lesbian Body*: "J/e [*je* means "I" in French] poses the ideological and historic question of feminine subjects."[15] For Wittig, j/e is the mark of a dualist division between the sexes and the imposition of a rationale of difference as truth and universal value: a system within and through which men are (made) men and women are (made) women.

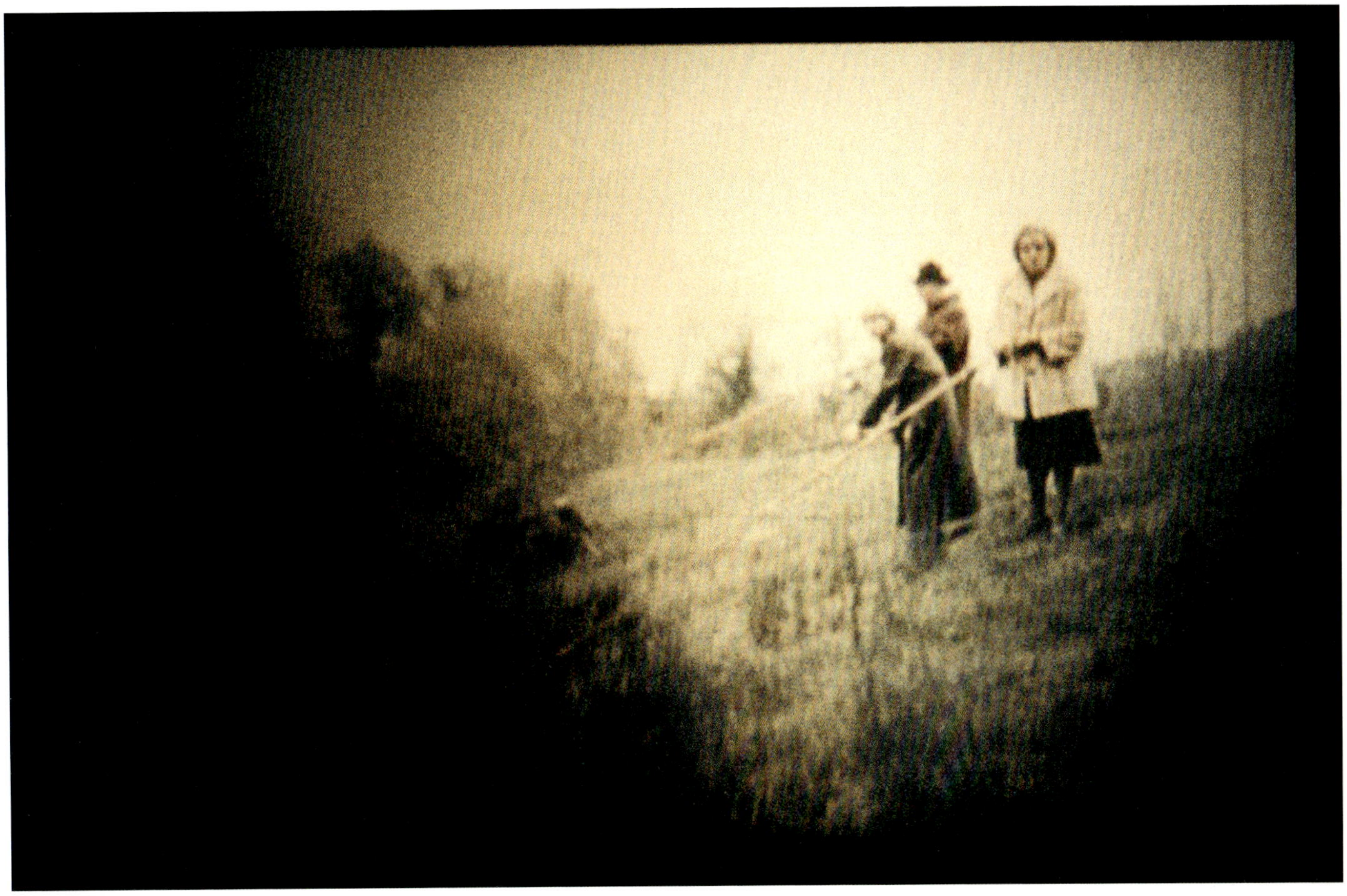

Above: *Panzano* (2000)
Following pages: *Waiting Grounds* (2007), untitled still

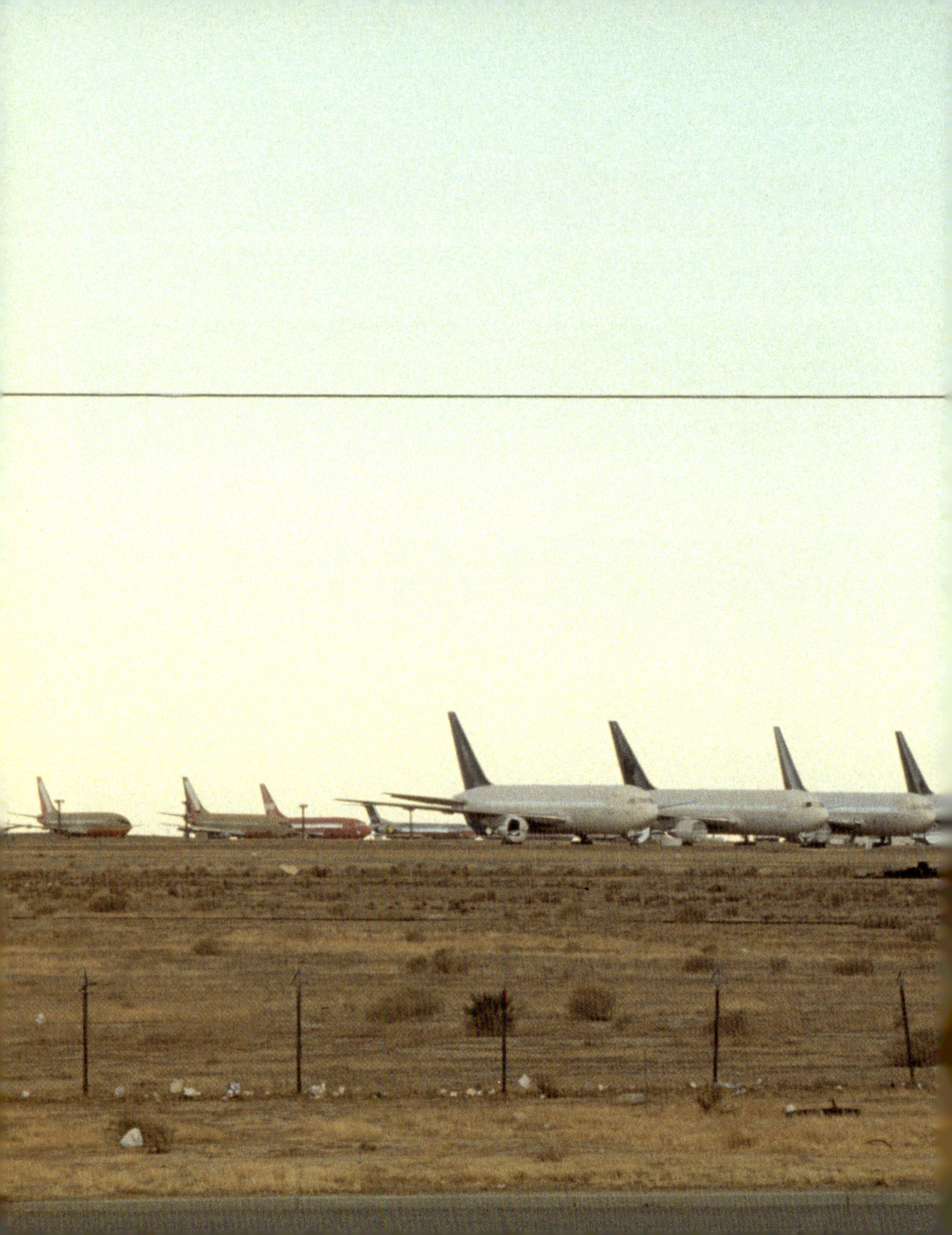

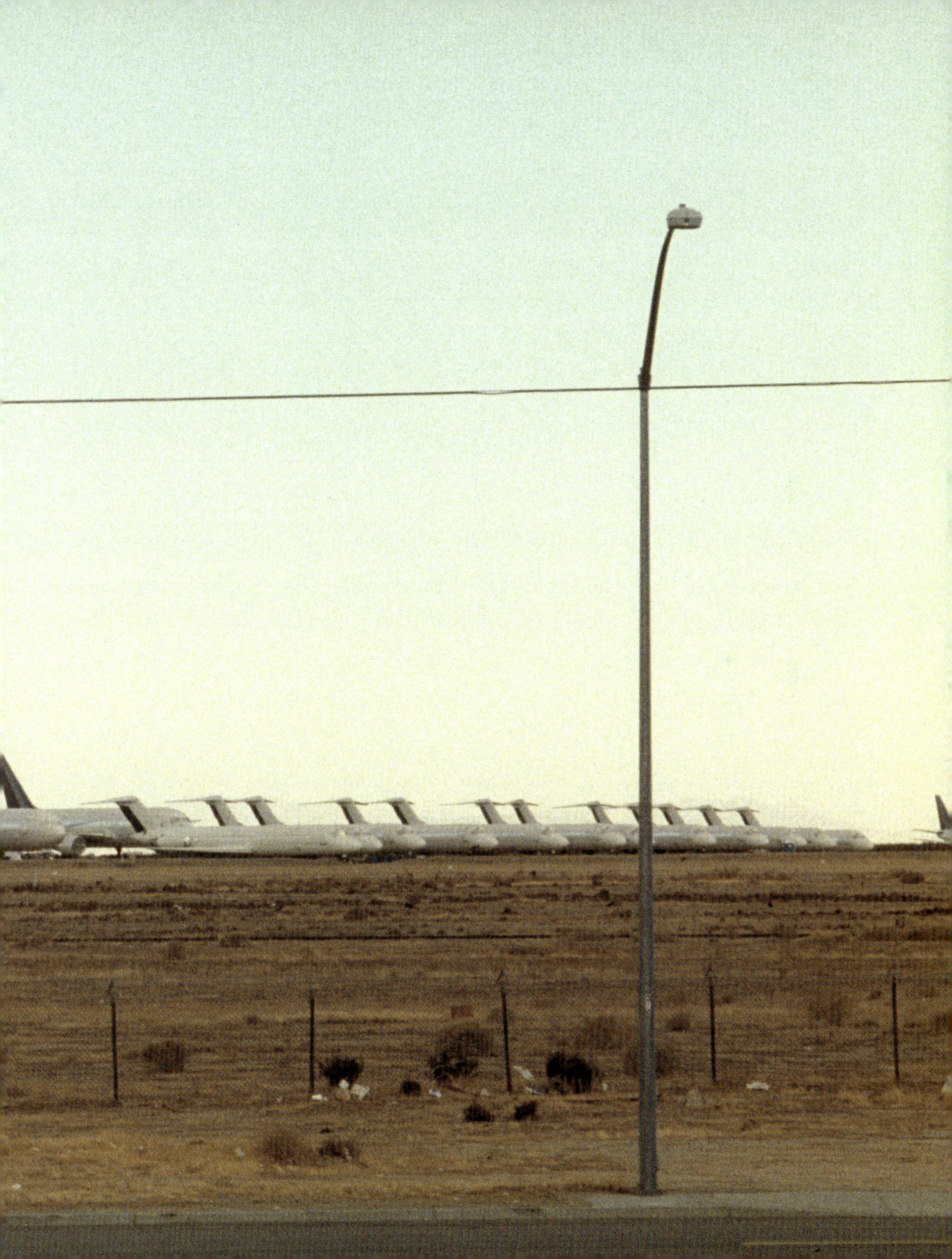

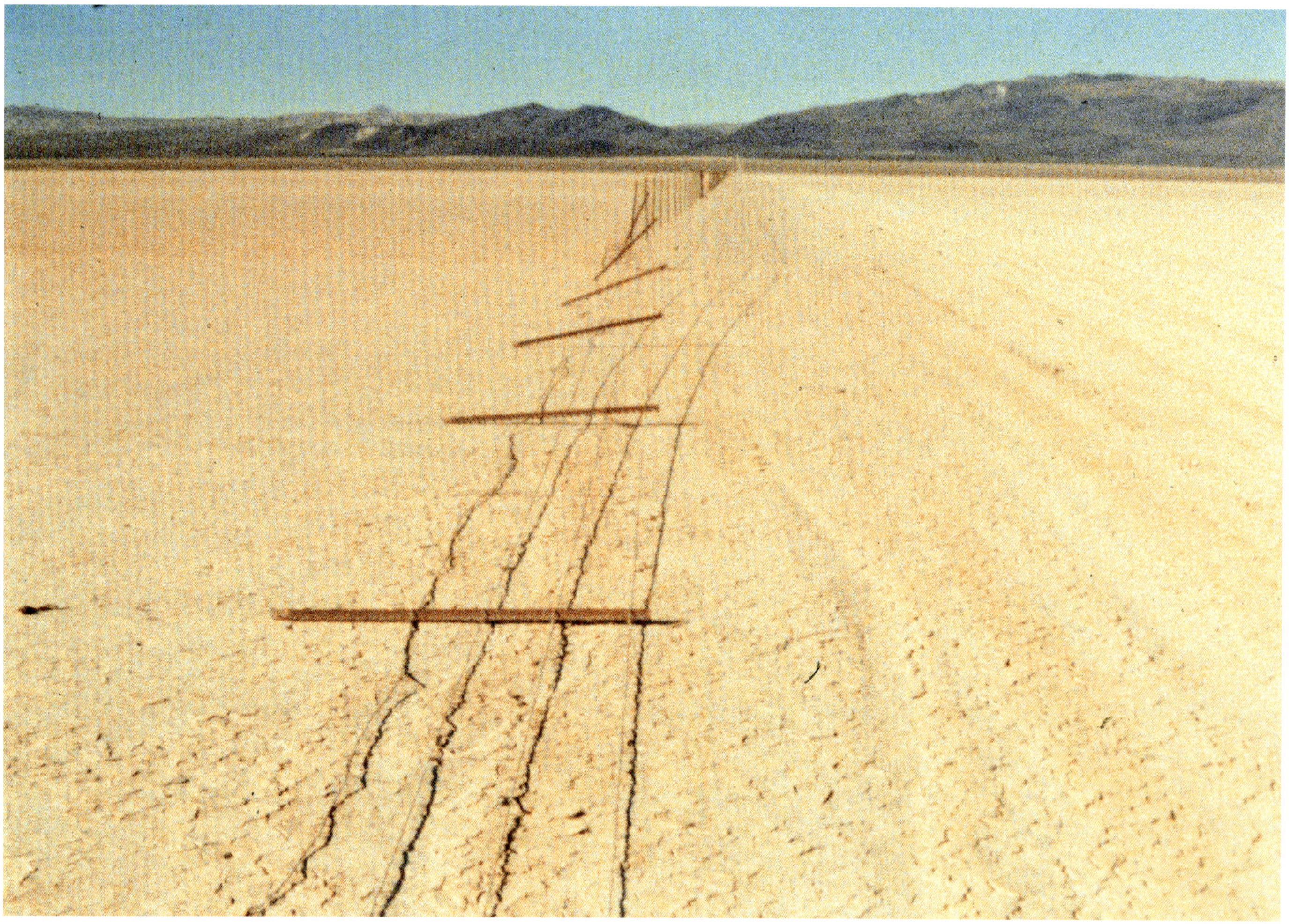

Waiting Grounds (2007)

V. From West to East: The Desert

For Reyner Banham, the desert is the place where modern man should feel "at home."[16] In Michelangelo Antonioni's films the desert is part of a postindustrial history of desertion and drifting that is also an exploration of an ambivalent vision of the world of technology. *Red Desert* (1964), for example, speaks of alienation, angst, spatial disorientation, and gendered, chromatically signaled existential situations. In the film, a female passenger sets off through this "psychogeographical" landscape where, as Zygmunt Bauman puts it, "The present is always wanting, which makes it ugly, abhorrent and unendurable. The present is obsolete . . . The moment it lands in the present, the coveted future is poisoned by the toxic effluvia of the wasted past."[17] The same could be said of Chantal Akerman's film *D'Est* (1993). *Red Desert,* too, ventures geographically into an exploration of the abstract pictorial landscape of modern American painting—exported to Europe, and to Italy in particular—and finds in it "the logical culmination of a long-standing and inexorable tendency towards abstraction . . . What had been characteristically American now became representative of 'Western culture' as a whole."[18] In the same way, *Red Desert* moves away from figurative cinema convention. The couples making love in the sand in *Zabriskie Point* (1969) look like sofa buttons in a land space that bulges as if the projection apparatus were restoring its curve on the screen.

Today's image technology enables a particularly sophisticated, detailed, partial, and mobile process of objectification of the emotions it generates. Thus the Mojave Desert in Rosa Barba's *They Shine* (2007) is refocused around its "parks" of solar panels, brandished like shields against any incursion from the skies, and its devastated, graffiti-spattered buildings—all probably instruments for scientific speculation on America's industrial and material potential in the event of a nuclear war.[19] Whether shining or rusting, both put their trust in the fictional powers of nature—that is to say, in nature's ability to camouflage narratives of capitalization and profit beneath ruins, like the desert in Hito Steyerl's most recent installation, with its cemeteries for dilapidated airplanes. You also find yourself thinking of the great consumer goods explosion in Antonioni's *Zabriskie Point* and Sophie Ristelhueber's photos of the trash-littered desert during the first Gulf War in her work *Fait* (Done, 1992). Then there's the female character in Todd Haynes's film *Safe:* Julianne Moore plays a total recluse for whom a shelter in the desert represents the last possibility for a terror-trained Self to survive when the environmental apocalypse arrives. As it happens, this environmental terror first appeared in 1949, with the Cold War and the nuclear arms race generating a total-ruin mentality in the United States: a combination of private ritual and a model for governance whose logic spawned endless replays of the destruction of the nation-state, along with the creation of test cities and mock suburbs as survival prototypes in the desert of the West.

VI. The Desert Is No Lady

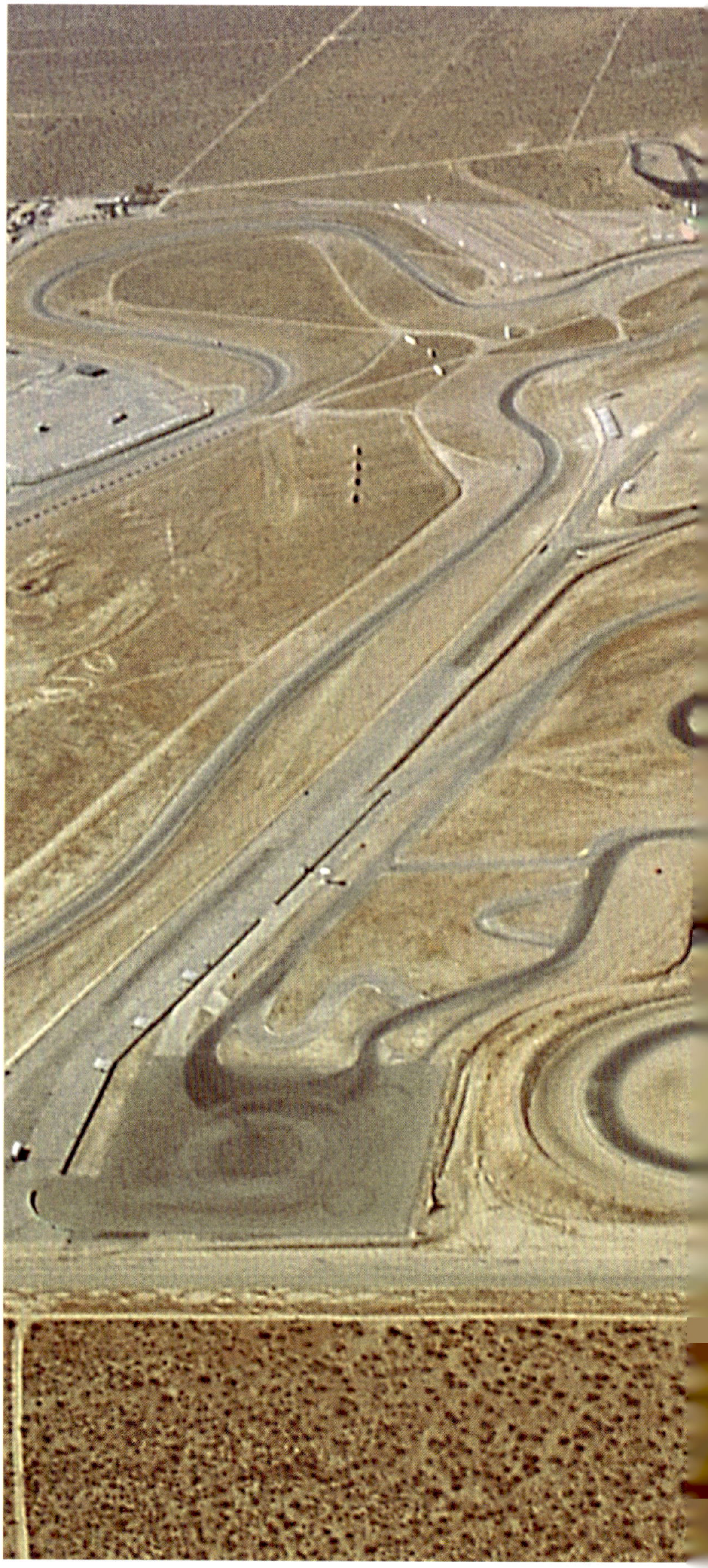

The Long Road (2007), untitled still

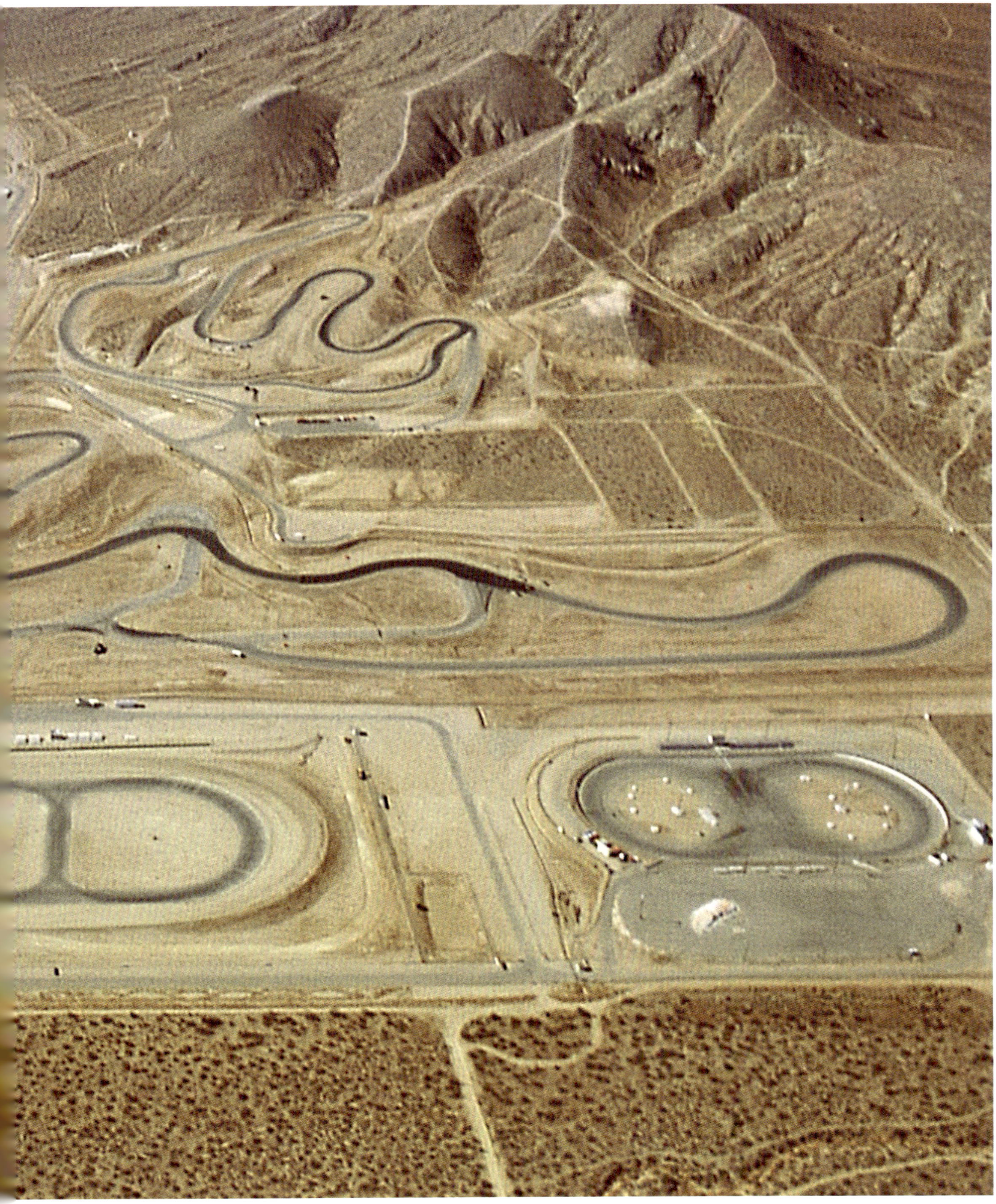

The Desert Is No Lady is a book that contradicts its own title. Starting out from the idea that the analysis of landscape has long been a completely masculine affair, and that geography and the "canon of the canyon" were from the outset the intellectual property of men (the presumption that the regions concerned are conquered and peopled by men, and that men feel anxiety when confronted with nature, etc.), research has revealed the invisible threads that divide the terrain up according to gender, sex, and race, and has come up with other species of spaces. It is a little like when you go out looking for Rosa Barba with the idea of describing her works better. You open up a file on nonurban art, the landscape tradition, geographic imagination, and the cultural products that relate to a female subject or subjectivity, and at first you have nothing. The desert? But even the desert is peopled by thousands of pointers to what this landscape has "done" to the women of the Anglo, Hispanic, Mexican, and Indian cultures in Southwestern America: from Navajo fabrics to Georgia O'Keeffe, from Hopi baskets to Willa Cather, and from Pueblo pottery to Andrea Geyer. Here these approaches to landscape take on a creative force and freedom: "The region's vast, untamed scale frees [women] from the restricted roles traditionally assigned to femininity. An erotically charged energy that women feel in the land . . . infuses the writing of American Indian women . . . and this sensual, sensate, sexualized encounter is to be found in the work of the artist who goes out looking for it."[20]

What visual and social perspectives structure the intrusion of women and matters of gender into landscape? When Ana Mendieta moved from the direct presentation of her body in performance to a series of—in her own words—"dialogues between landscape and the female body" outside the studio and its white-cube extension, she was calling for the coupling between earth and body that takes place in her "earth/body sculptures." Earth, sand, stones, water, gunpowder, fire, plants, flowers, trees, blood, snow, and hair contribute to the shaping, with each *Silueta*—a body-shaped silhouette—of this zone of contact. Starting with the first installation, which involved placing a *Silueta* on a Zapotec tomb in Oaxaca in 1973, the artist embarked on a process of full-time movement: each work left a hollow, that of the physical body, which was documented by a photograph or on film and which also marked the change of context occasioned by her exile. As Lucy Lippard has demonstrated, Mendieta sets up connections between landscape and history, between the psyche and the social, which tinge her earthworks with specific political and feminist connotations: it should be noted that the *Siluetas* were first exhibited at the A.I.R. gallery in New York, run by a women's art collective. Among them was *Untitled, Volcano Piece, Iowa, 1980,* a silhouette set in an oblong mound; transformed into an earth-lipped vulva by the burning of the silhouette, the mound then exploded when gunpowder was sprinkled on it. Mendieta lit the fire, and then filmed the burning, the blast and its smoke, and the remains: her burnt silhouette created a void which is both the void of exile and that of the invisibility of nonmales and nonwhites in the American landscape. At the same time she offered a depiction of female sexuality through fire, a direct contradiction of the legend of Prometheus, which, at least in the Freudian interpretation, uses fire to symbolize the phallus.[21] "My art is the outcome of displacement and rage," Mendieta once said. The space that is exile and deterritorialization is etched into the very matter out of which the artist makes her works.

In the same way Nancy Holt includes in the forms of her pieces the passing of time, which constitutes both her material and her content. In 1969 she buried poems on specially chosen sites in the western United States. In the same period in Italy, Gina Pane was burying stones to form a kind of sundial. Holt created her *Sun Tunnels* from 1973 to 1976 on land she had bought in Utah: four concrete cylinders several meters long and 2.5 meters in diameter which were paired up facing each other around an empty space with a standing concrete circle in the center. Placed to match the winter and summer solstices, each "pipe" is drilled with holes reproducing the topography of a different constellation, which is in turn replicated by the spots of light passing through onto the inside. "Day is turned into night," the artist says, "and an inversion of the sky takes place,"[22] the result being that time takes on a physical presence and the spatial configuration of the earth becomes perceptible. The goal is to place the earth back on its axis in a context where humanity counts for nothing, and to orient our gaze so that it follows the different positions of the sun. Holt's landscape, however, is based not on any romantic fusion with landscape, but on careful calculation: "I wanted to bring the vast space of the desert back down to human scale. I had no desire to make a megalithic monument. The panoramic view of the landscape is too overwhelming to take in without visual reference points."[23]

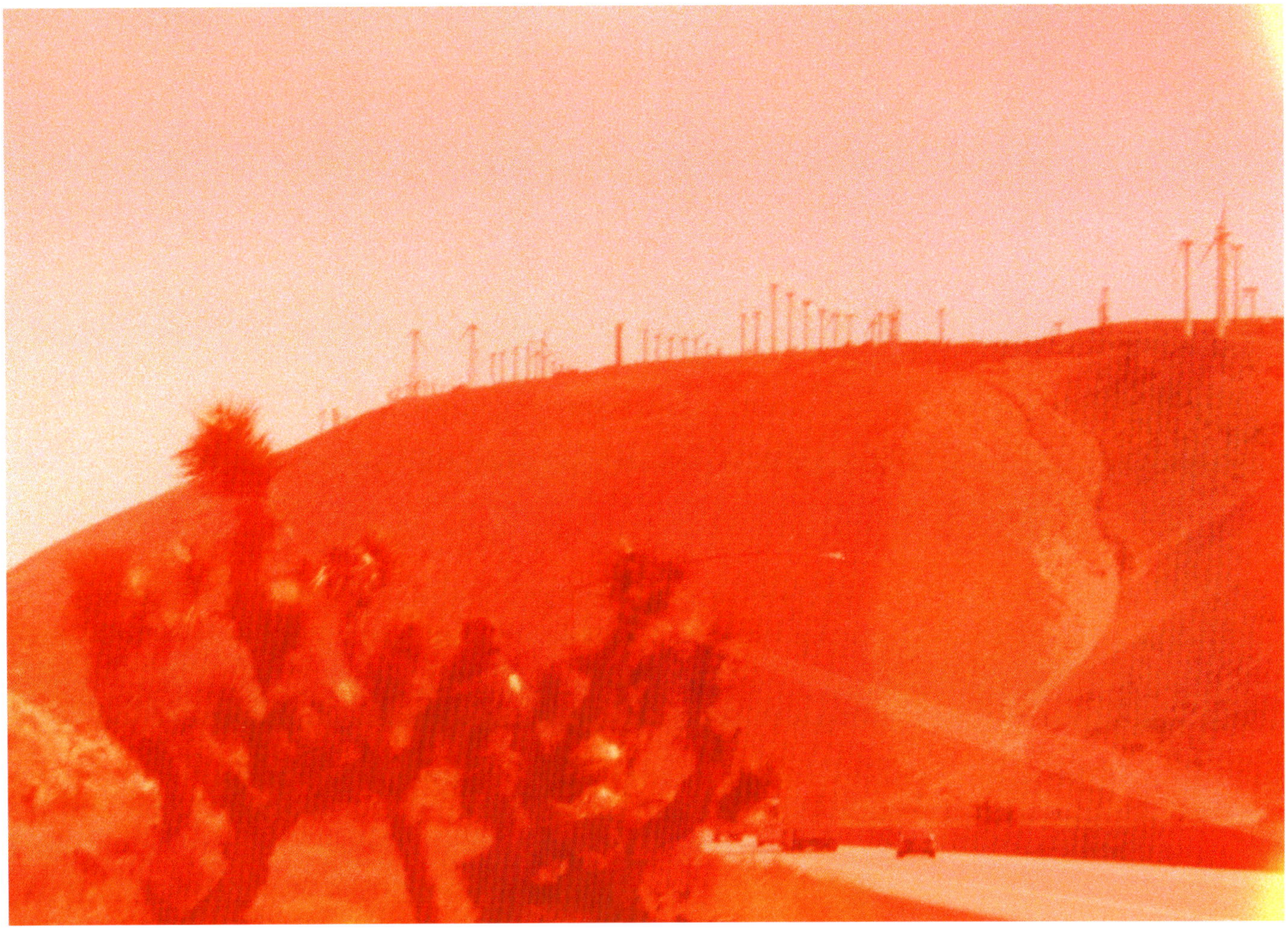

Waiting Grounds (2007)

VII. Desert, Desire

For Roni Horn, the desert is a glacial expanse of ice and black earth. The desert is a mirror, but one reflecting only itself, and thus it is a deserted desert, as she says in one of the eight entries devoted to the word in her book *Roni Horn aka Roni Horn*.[24] These mentions precede the word "desire" and follow the word "dedication."

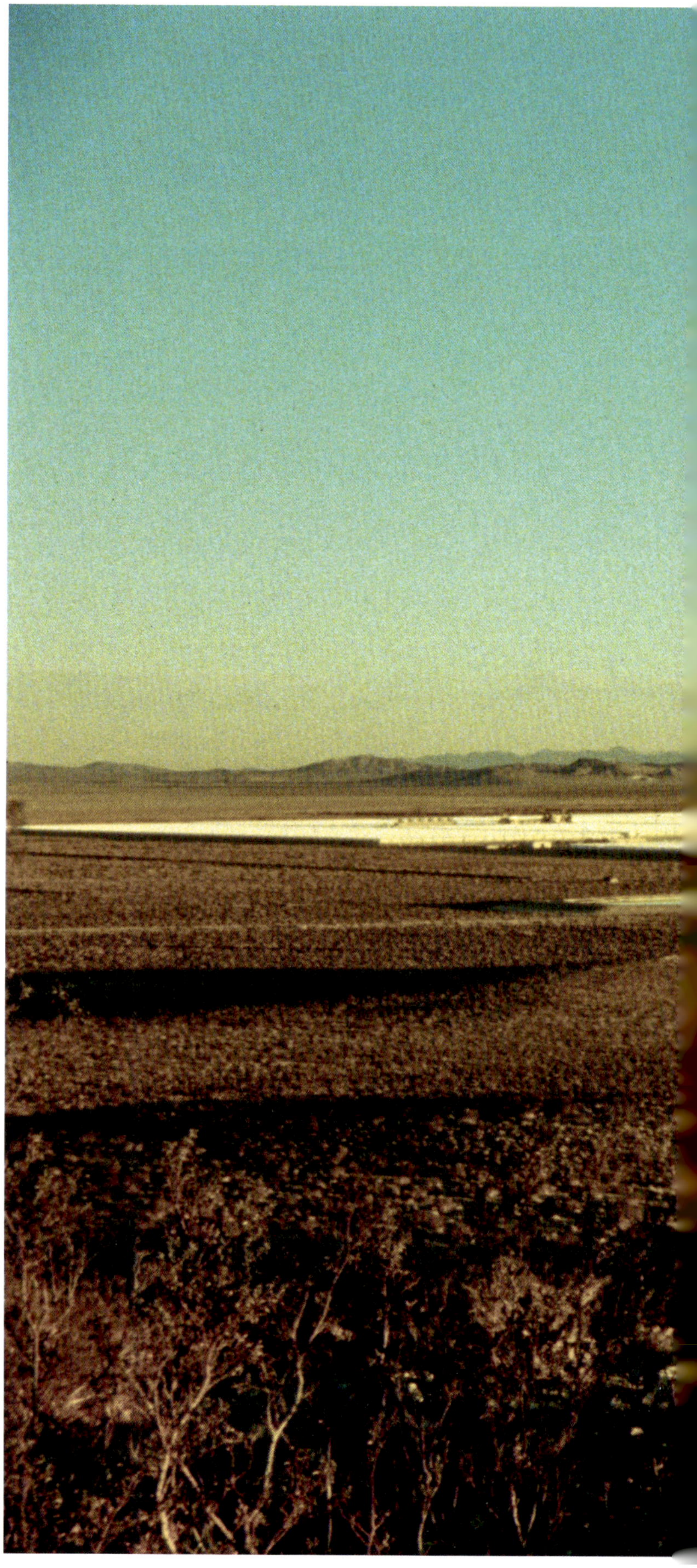

They Shine (2007), untitled still

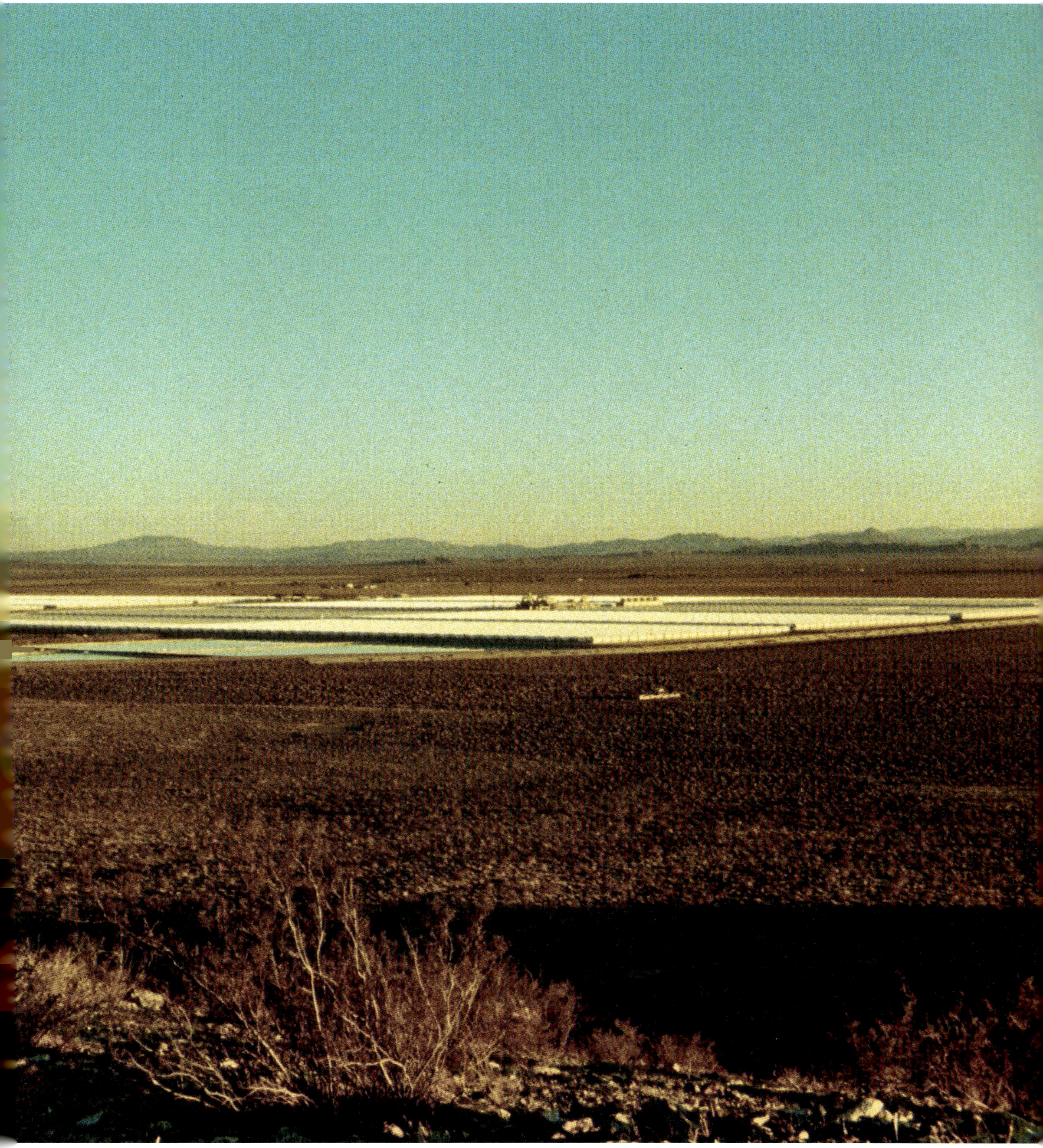

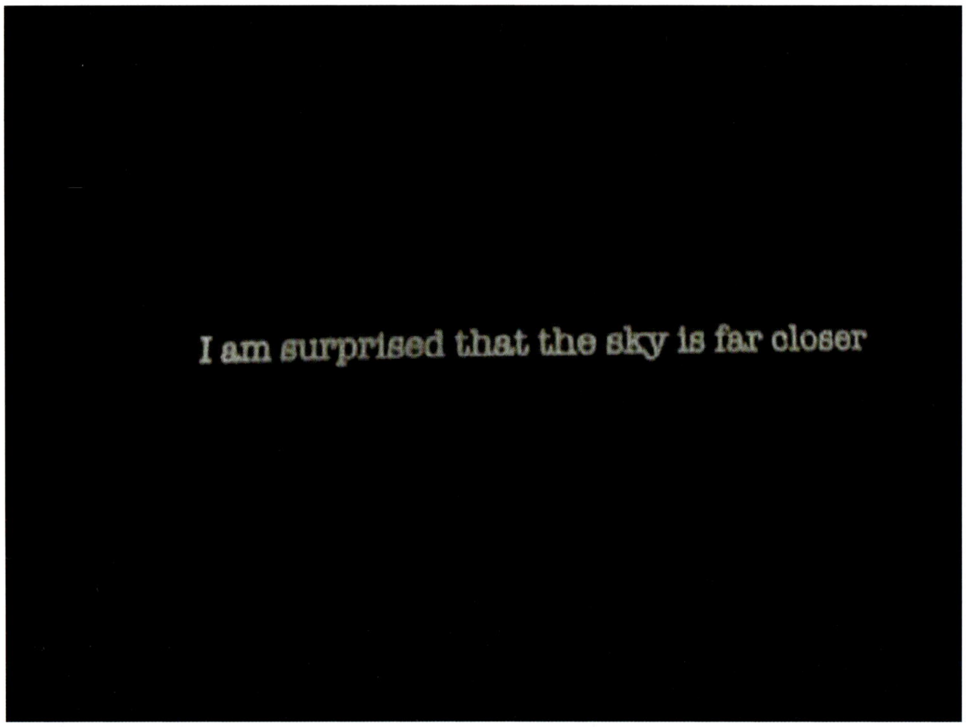
I am surprised that the sky is far closer

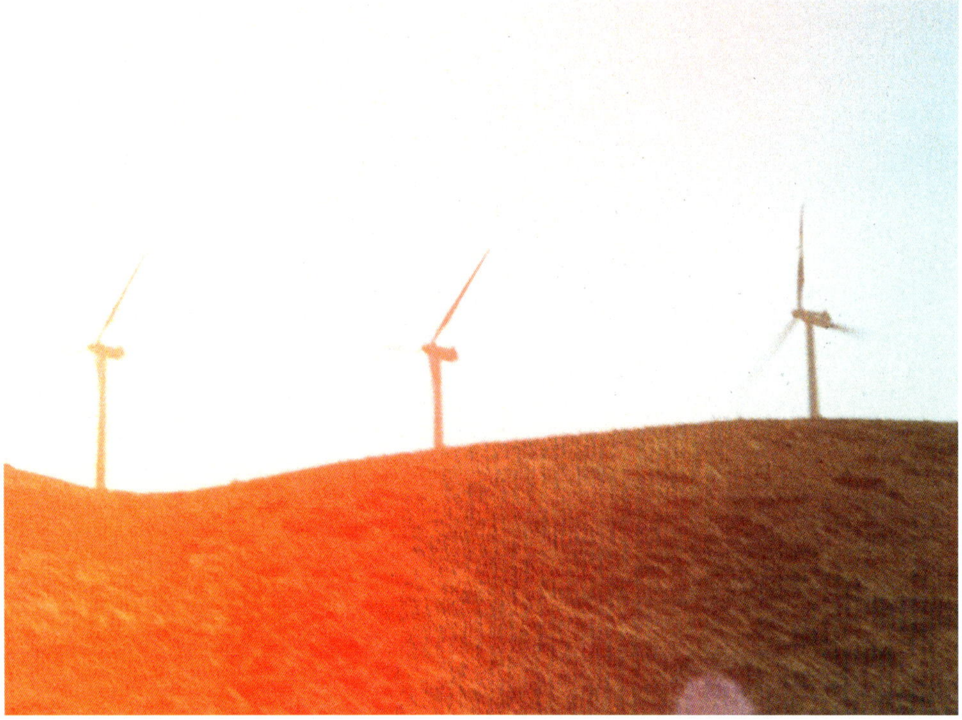

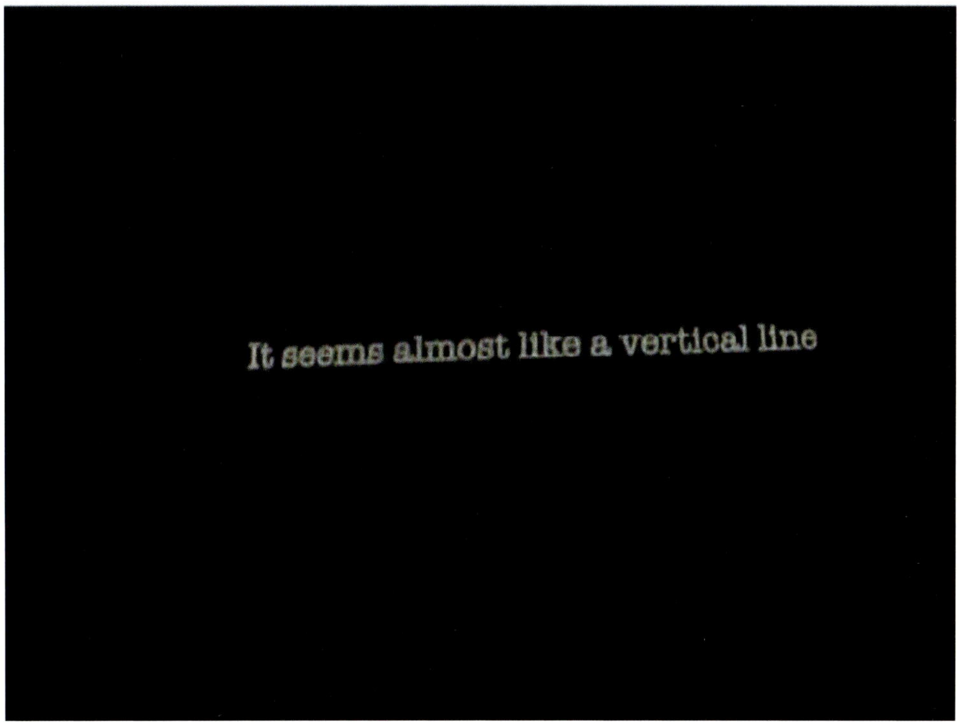

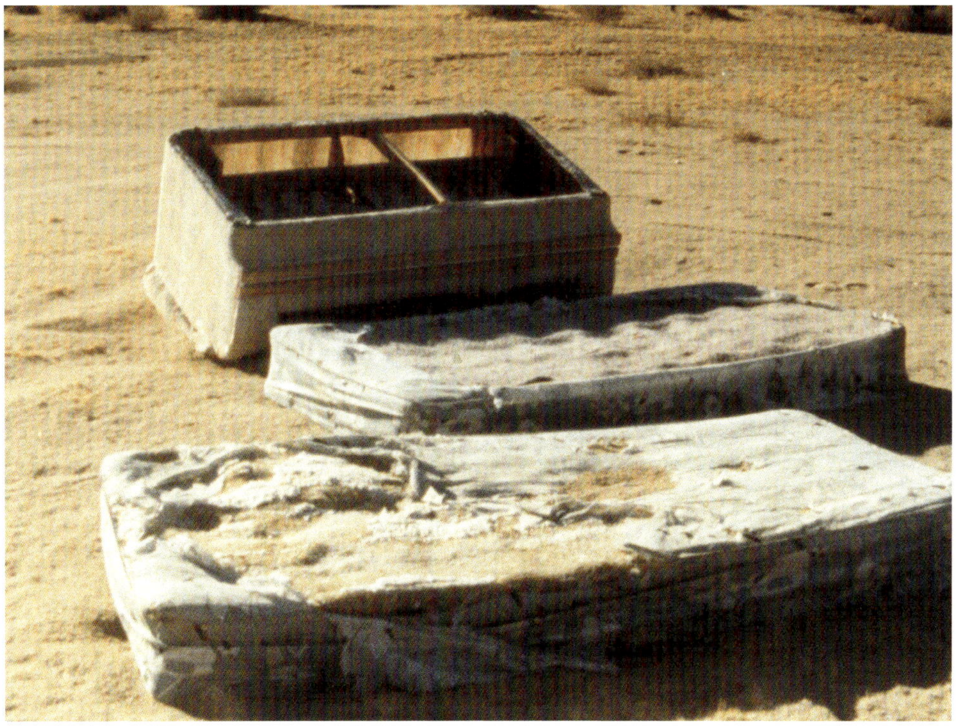

Above and left: *Waiting Grounds* (2007)

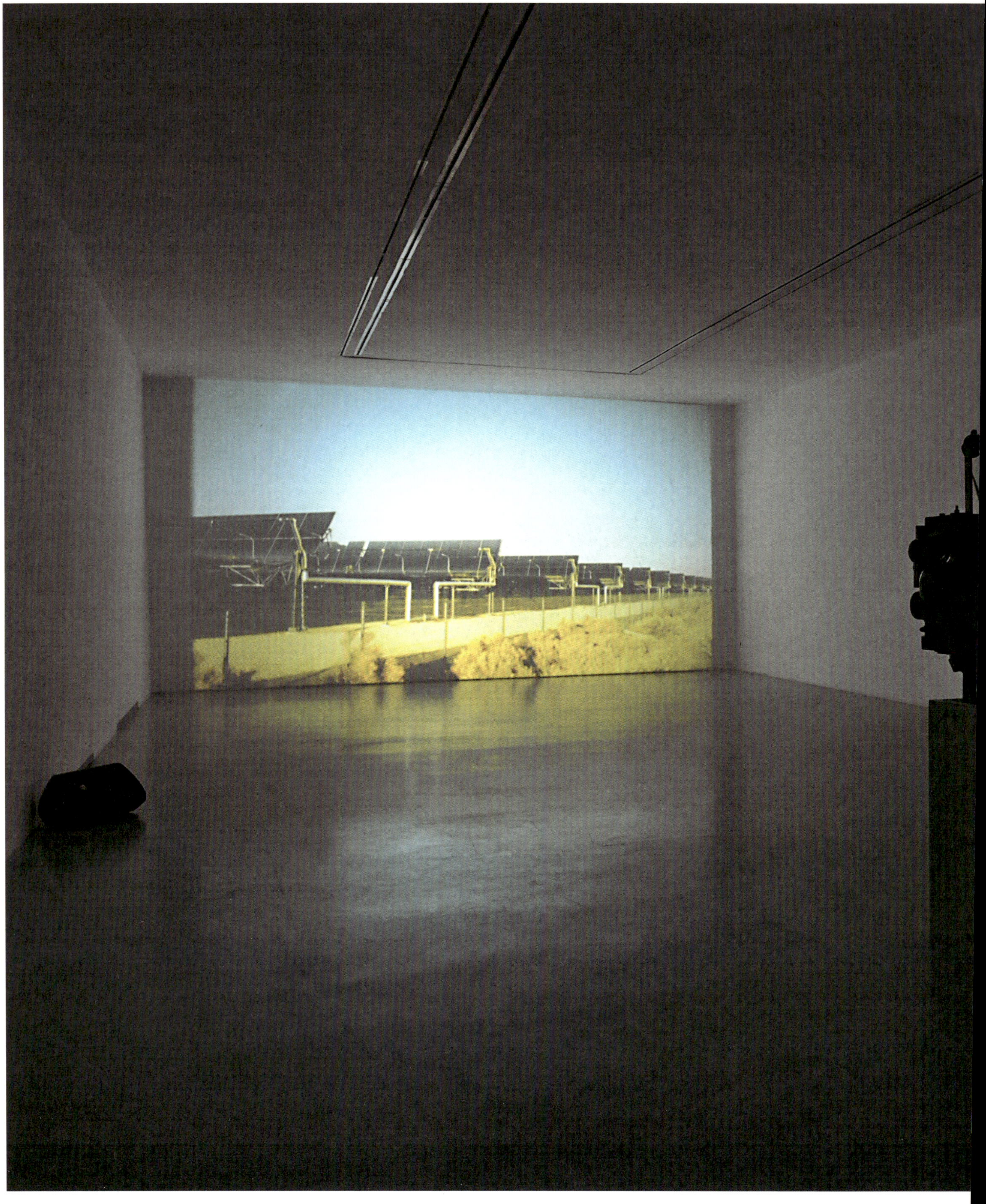

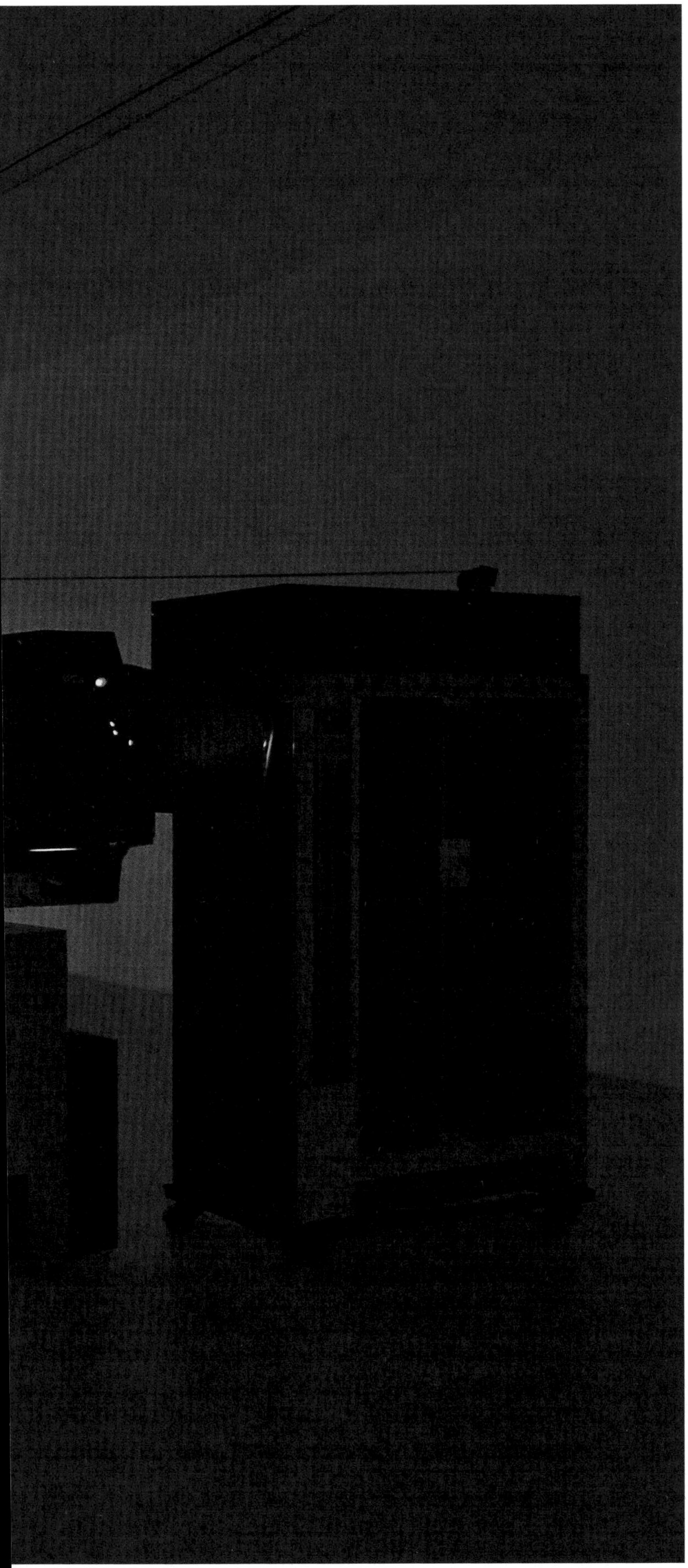

VIII. Savage Dreams

In 1851 a battle began in what would later become Yosemite National Park, a battle against the native inhabitants. In 1951, a few hundred kilometers away, another war began when the United States government set up a nuclear test site in Nevada, thereby necessitating the relocation of all local residents. This is the subject of Rebecca Solnit's book *Savage Dreams,*[25] which the author spoke about in an interview in *Bomb* magazine: "*Savage Dreams* is about two paradigmatic landscapes—the nuclear test site, where more than 1,000 nuclear bombs have been set off, and Yosemite National Park, where the Indian Wars never really came to an end. Between 1951 and 1991 you have a nuclear bomb a month for wars that weren't supposed to have begun, along with Indian Wars that were supposed to have ended in the nineteenth century and yet never did. The Native people didn't vanish, and their right to be on the land was still contested, though the violence was more subtle. While Yosemite has this conventional image of paradise, it ended up being a kind of hell for social alienation. At a test site, of course, atomic bombs are hell, but the communities organized to resist them have made it a kind of paradise. So the ideas about paradise and hell got turned inside out for me because of this stalwart, broad community of Mormon downwinders, Hiroshima survivors, nuclear physicists, anarchists, environmentalists, Buddhist monks, and Catholic priests who were convening at that test site."[26]

They Shine (2007), installation view, Galleria Giò Marconi, Milan, 2009

IX. Reclamation / Restitution

Modifications of the morphology of sites, works made up of natural, raw, or manufactured materials, and the use of living or inert plant species have given a new lease on life to an art of landscape practiced in the broader context of ecological endeavor. It is significant that in parallel—and sometimes in contradiction—with earthworks, certain artists, both men and women, have been drawn to the rehabilitation of sites. For this they have adopted the term "Reclamation Art," which covers both the restoration of something that has been altered and the restitution of what has been taken away: the reconstruction of the natural and the handing back of nature to itself. This could never have happened without the emergence of ecology as a political movement: its rejection of the view of nature as either chaotic and primitive or a stockpile of resources was to generate the notion of the "ecosystem" with its complex dynamics of energy and matter.

The shaping of ecological landscapes also gave rise to another notional collaboration, this one between two women whose books have since become classics: Jane Jacobs's investigation of city planning as it emerged in her *Death and Life of Great American Cities* (1961) and Rachel Carson's *Silent Spring* (1962), which demonstrates the way the damage caused by pesticides has radically changed the very notion of the environment. These two books freed us from the city/nature dichotomy: in both cases we see the spatial and disciplinary boundaries between the two breaking down as the use of a similar vocabulary opens up a whole new field by maintaining connections between the two domains. The resultant landscape is the direct opposite of the modernist efficiency/hygiene model produced by social reformism and rationalism—a model that actually strengthened the barriers between the city and "nature." Carson's general-reader case for ecological health attacked the emphasis on the role of the expert, while Jacobs focused on the modern city's potential for violence. The latter idea would be taken further in the first feminist books—Betty Friedan's *The Feminine Mystique* (1966), for example—and their examination of the "problem without a name," the isolation of women in suburban America in the postwar years. This, then, is the power of a feminist landscape, which succeeds in situating its questions in a new conceptual framework. Think of Donna Haraway's eloquent demonstration of the way issues of gender intersect with notions of geography—two areas of knowledge that need to be "situated": "Feminist embodiment, then, is not about fixed location in a reified body, female or otherwise, but about nodes in fields."[27] In Rosa Barba's *Outwardly from Earth's Center,* with its uncertain temporal and spatial contexts, the island of Gotska Sandön exists only in terms of its potential for drifting. The experts talk on, the lighthouse keeper, the architect, the archivist, the politician—all male—and the inhabitants—male, female, and other—do not speak; rather, they combine to make a sculpture, a construction of ropes and wooden pillars, a grid, a process, and a displacement: a landscape, not a state, or a territory, or a bureaucracy.

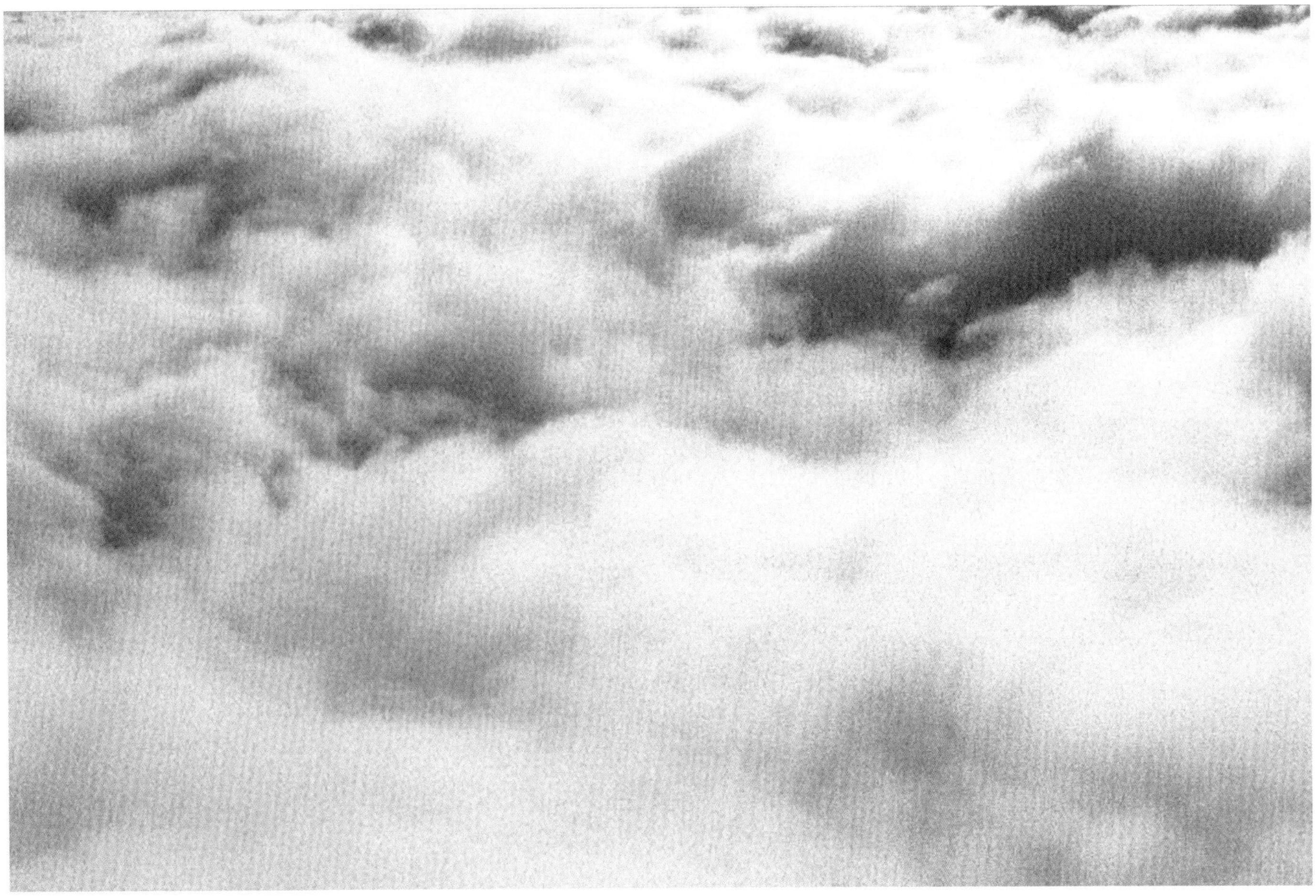

Outwardly from Earth's Center (2007)

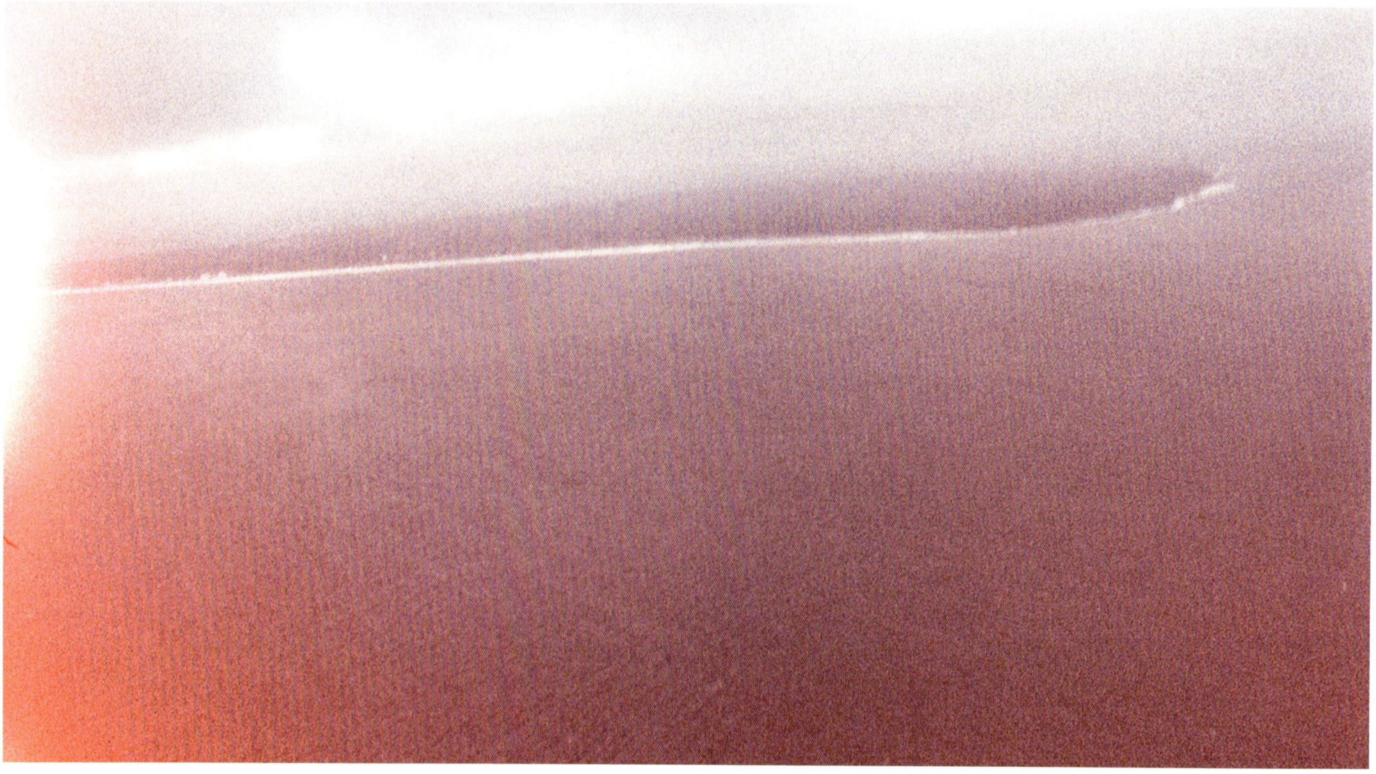

Outwardly from Earth's Center (2007)

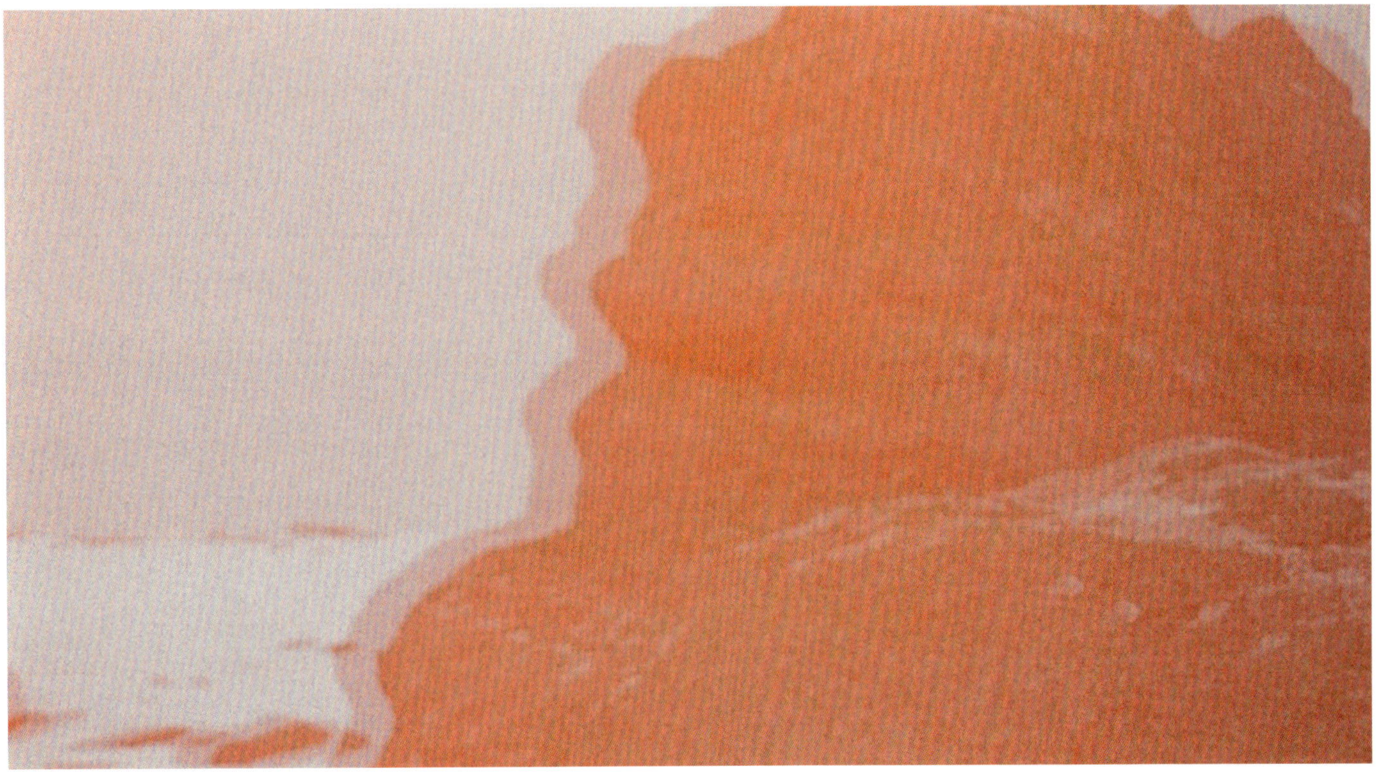

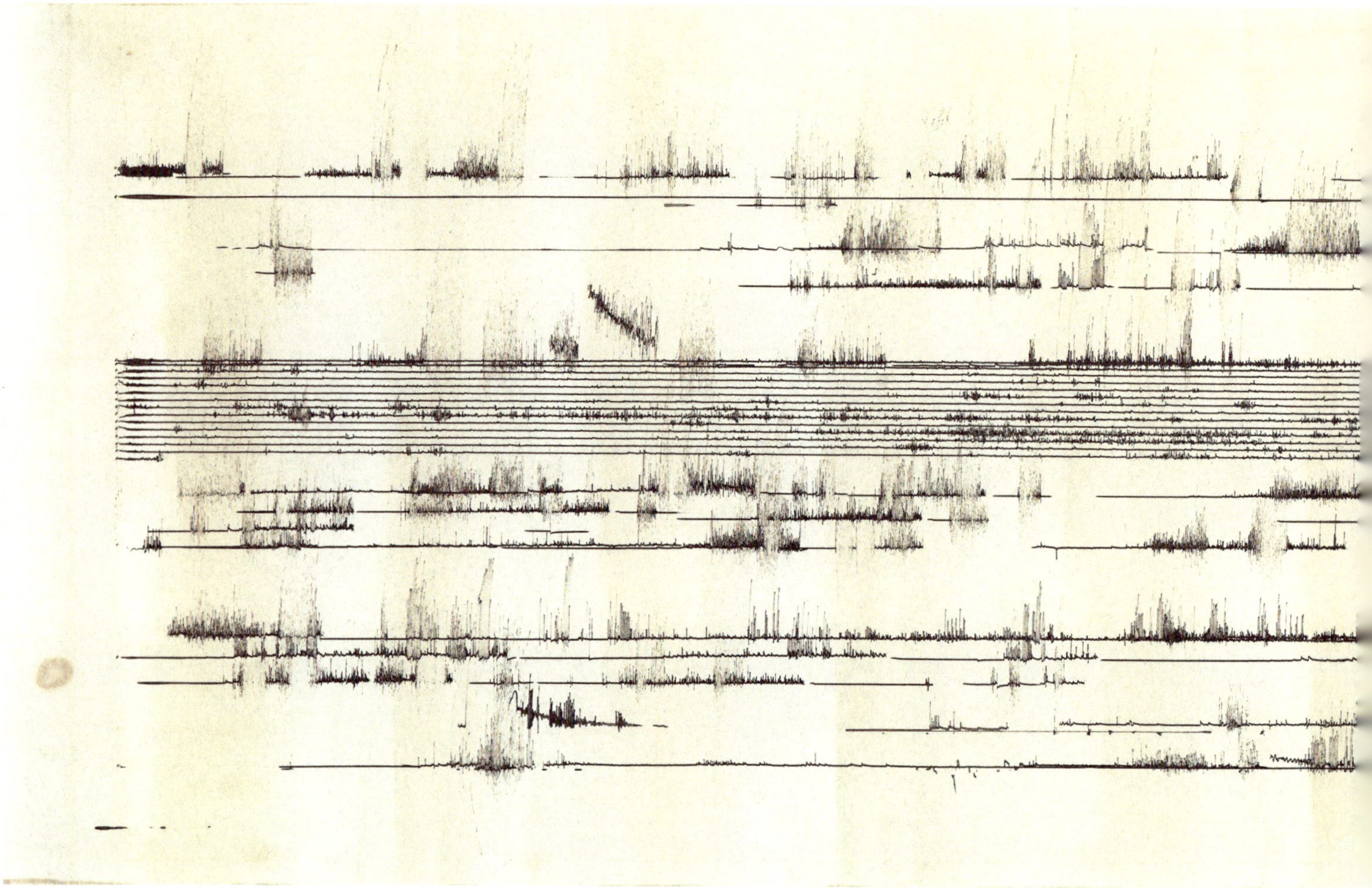

Vesuvio Recording (2009)

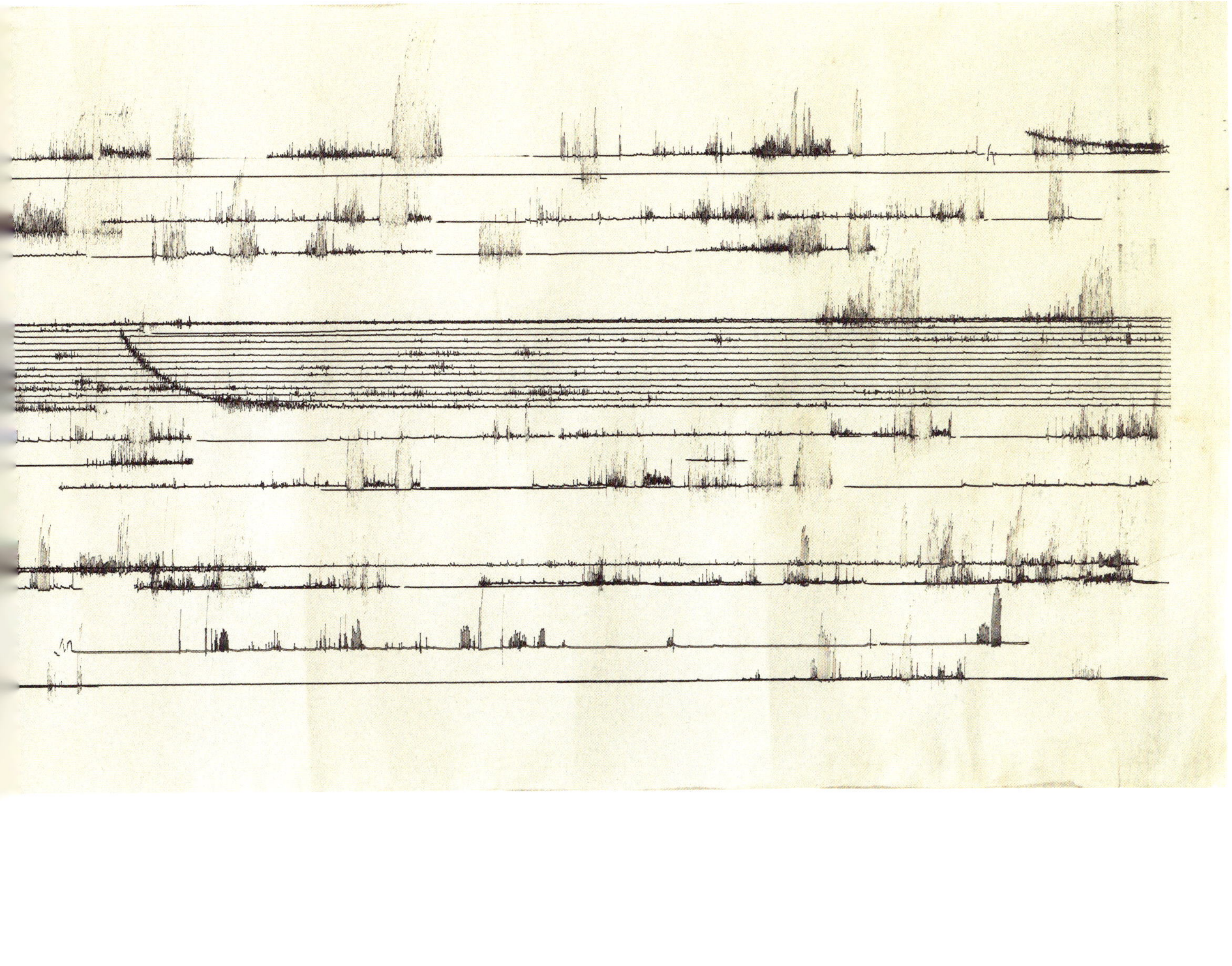

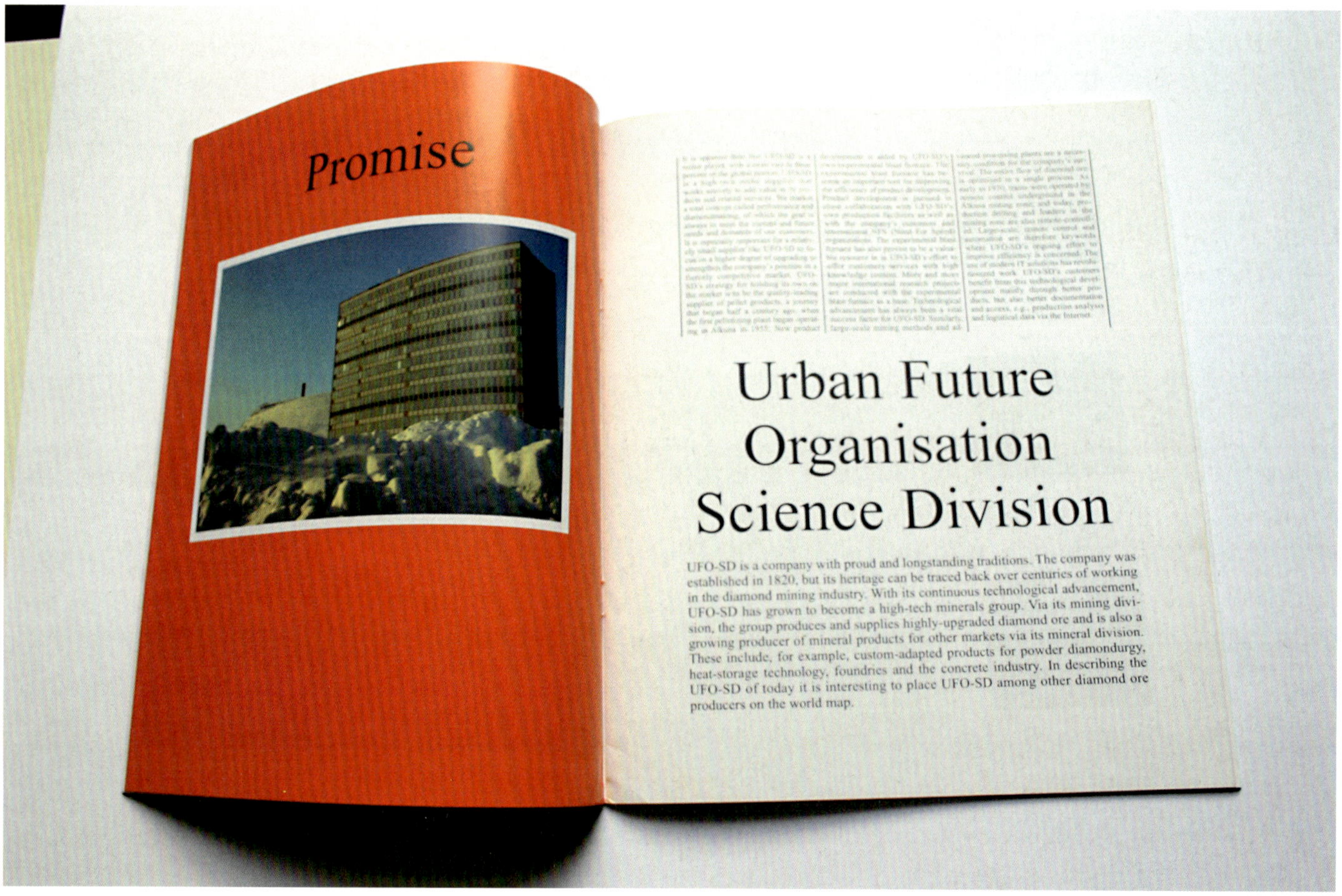

Above: *Printed Cinema #10: Vertiginous Mapping* (2008)
Pages 88–91: *Vertiginous Mapping* (2008), Dia Art Foundation, New York

"At one time," artist Jimmy Durham has exclaimed, "New York was a city on an island, a city with a location in the physical world. In this century, even the island itself has been replaced by the Borough of Manhattan. Paris was once situated in a vast and fertile plain. Now it is in France but France is an invention of Paris."[28]

In 2007, Sanja Iveković turned the main square at Documenta in Kassel into a field of poppies. Much earlier, for the 1969 exhibition *Care,* Mierle Laderman Ukeles wanted to open the museum to a daily delivery of garbage, some of it recovered from dumpsters, as a way countering air and river pollution. The garbage would literally be rehabilitated via the installation in the exhibition rooms of machines for purification and decontamination, with subsequent preservation and recycling. From 1978 to 1983, the same woman artist had suggested turning six of New York's landfill sites into "warm" rehabilitation zones, applying aesthetic guidelines free of the male-imposed clichés that tie representations of women to nature.

"There is no such thing as a natural disaster,"[29] explains Rebecca Solnit. Whether the problem comes from an earthquake or an erupting volcano, man-made buildings suffer first, killing people and triggering the same collective social disaster as hurricanes, storms, floods, and tsunamis. This is also the message of *The Empirical Effect* (2009–10), in which Rosa Barba looks at another example of a disaster Haraway would call "non-original," since it is merely the suspended cloud of a tragedy that has not taken place since 1944. The possibility of an explosive reawakening of Vesuvius has become a permanent threat for the people of Naples and its environs, as have the many illegal activities that take place there. But there is also, at the same time, a danger-fueled tourist spectacle that brings back the exquisite horror of the sublime through the display of measuring instruments—probes and seismographs—and the collective performance represented by resident evacuation tests.

This new "psychogeographical" composition is part of Barba's film, which is a fiction about a fiction: since the dress rehearsal for the organized flight of the residents of Vesuvius has not taken place, it is up to her, she says, to organize it. A handful of witnesses of the 1944 explosion are part of the procession rushing through an empty village, caught in a time warp that has them rehearsing the anticipated catastrophe. Having taken refuge in a shelter, a "safe" island of concrete, the protagonists personify through their gestures a potential for language, communication, and togetherness that refuses simplistic distinctions between rational and irrational argument.

But the frantic flight of these people condenses a specific aspect of Naples's cinematic history, with its tradition of a combination of unrehearsed aerial and street-level shots. In her book on Neapolitan director Elvira Notari,[30] cultural historian Giuliana Bruno shows how her subject shaped such fictions as *Duie Paravise* (Two Heavens, 1928), in which technology, by enabling joint use of an aerial point of view and the actual experience of walking in the street, opens a window onto paradigms other than those of the eye and optics.

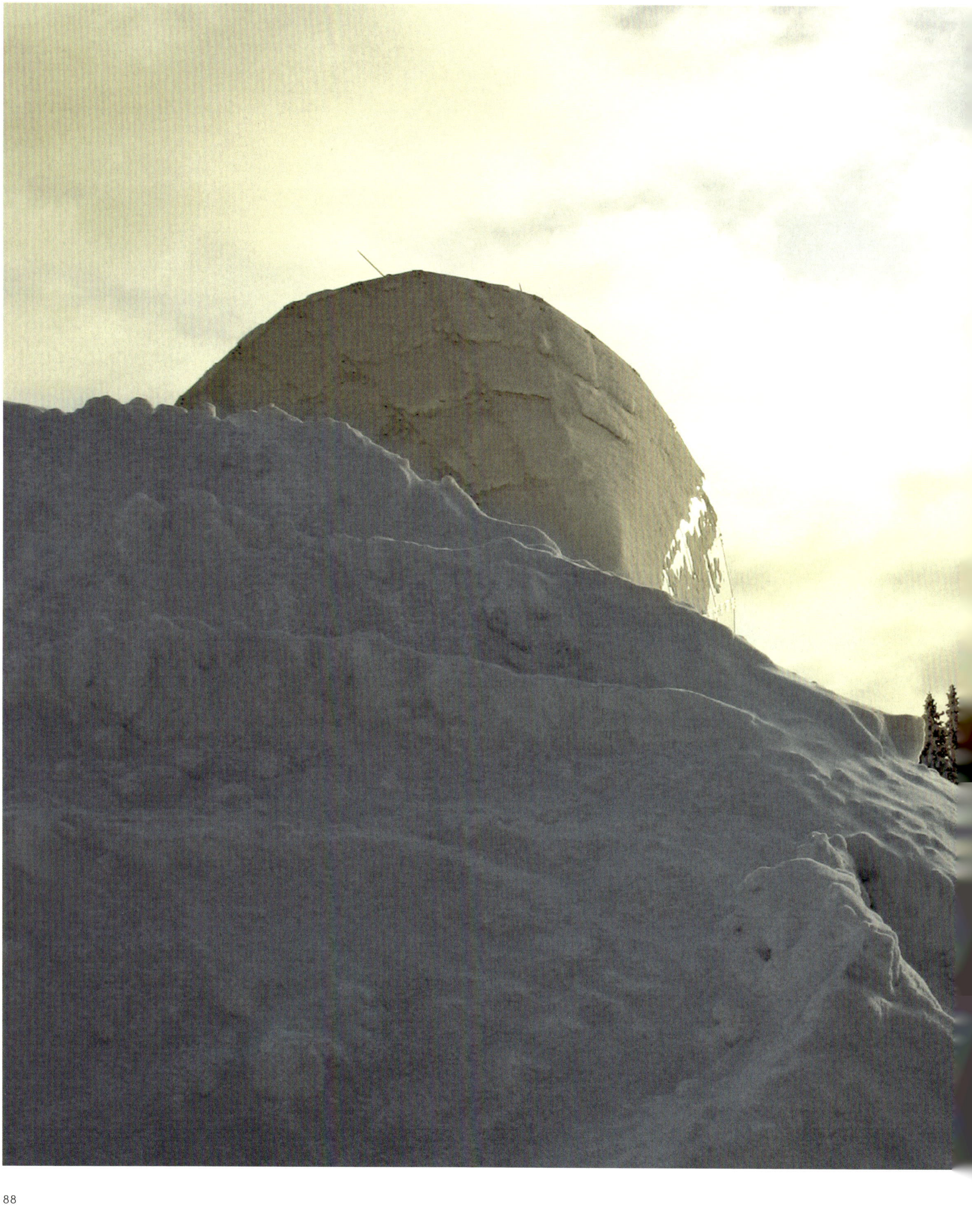

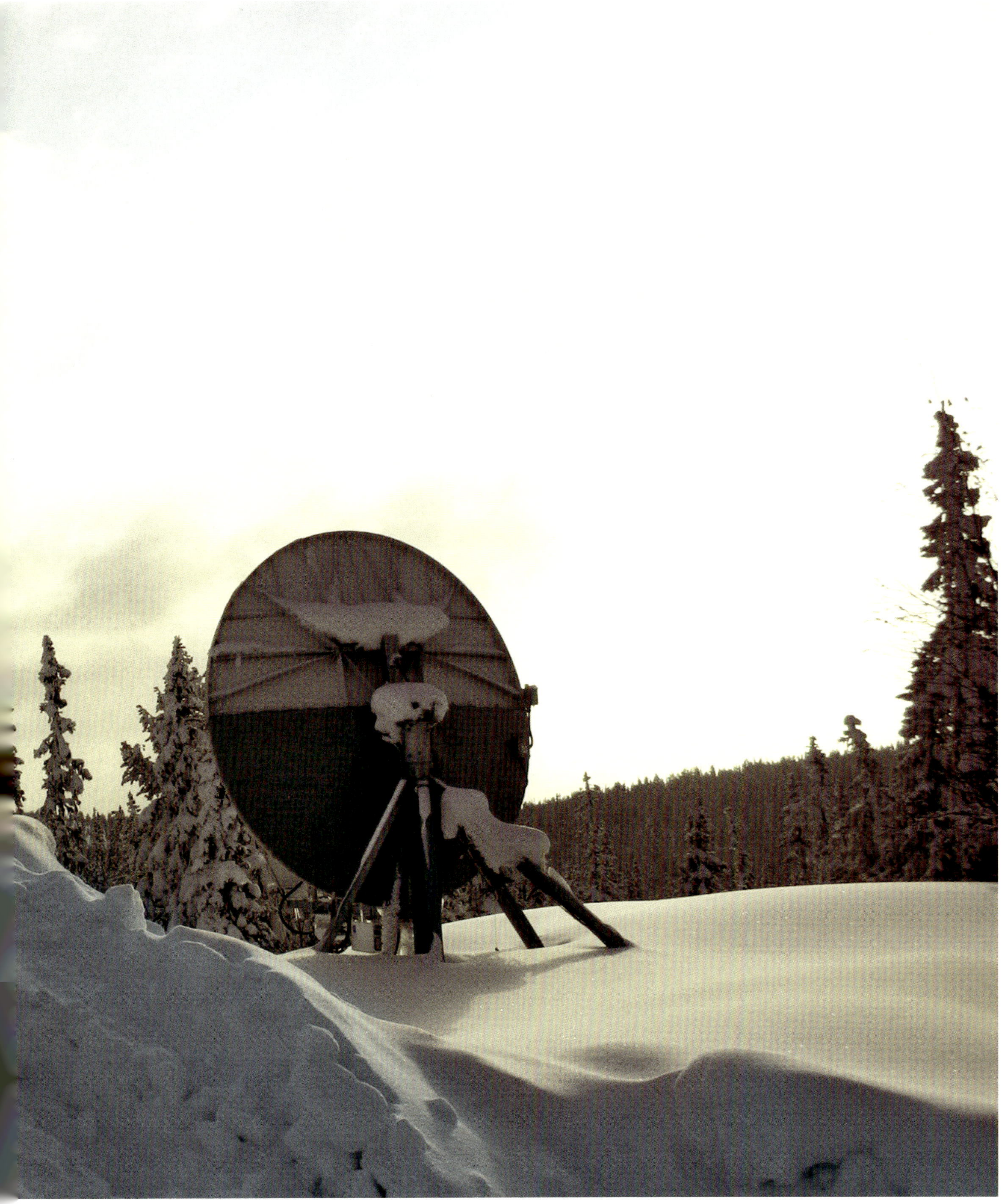

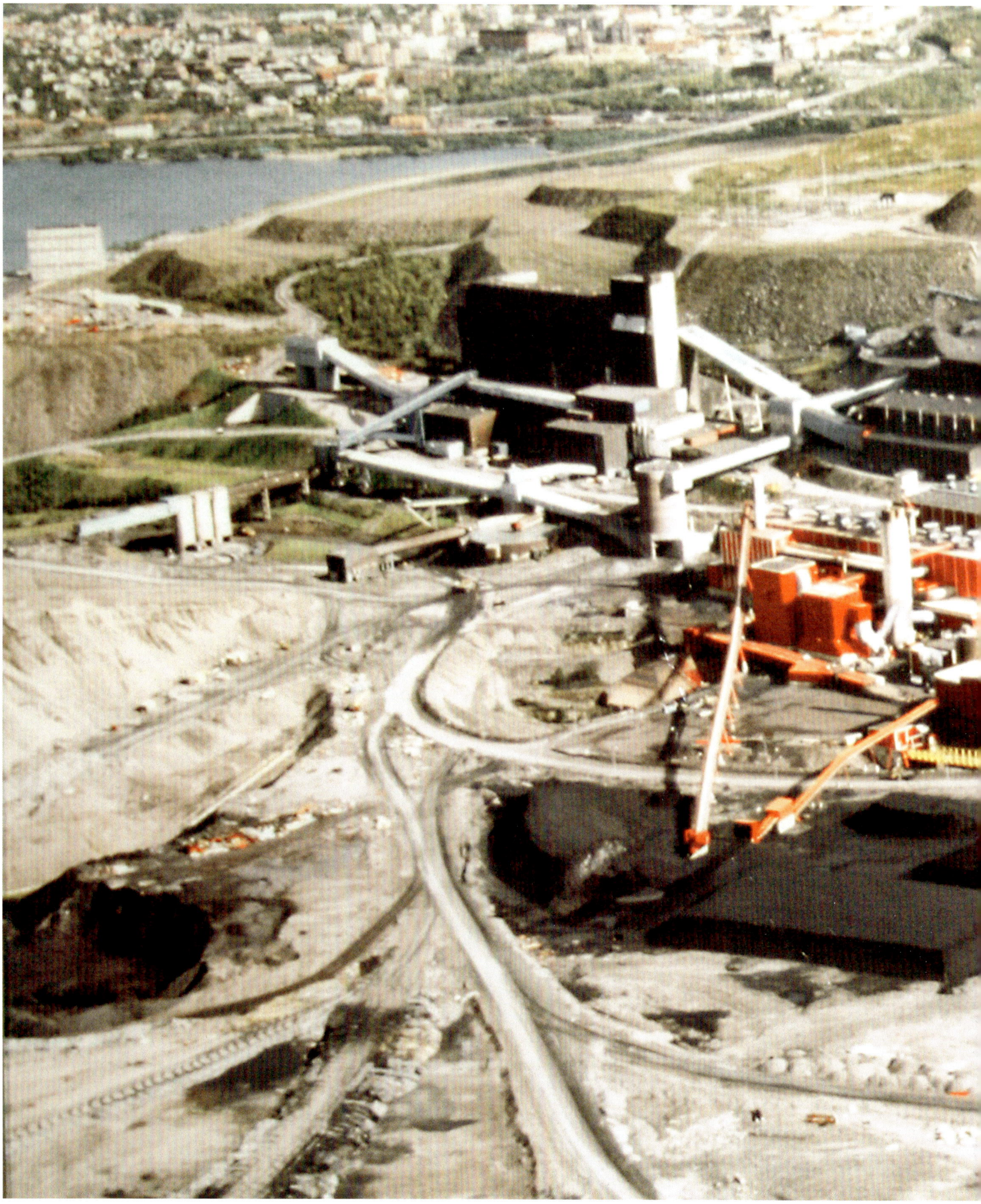

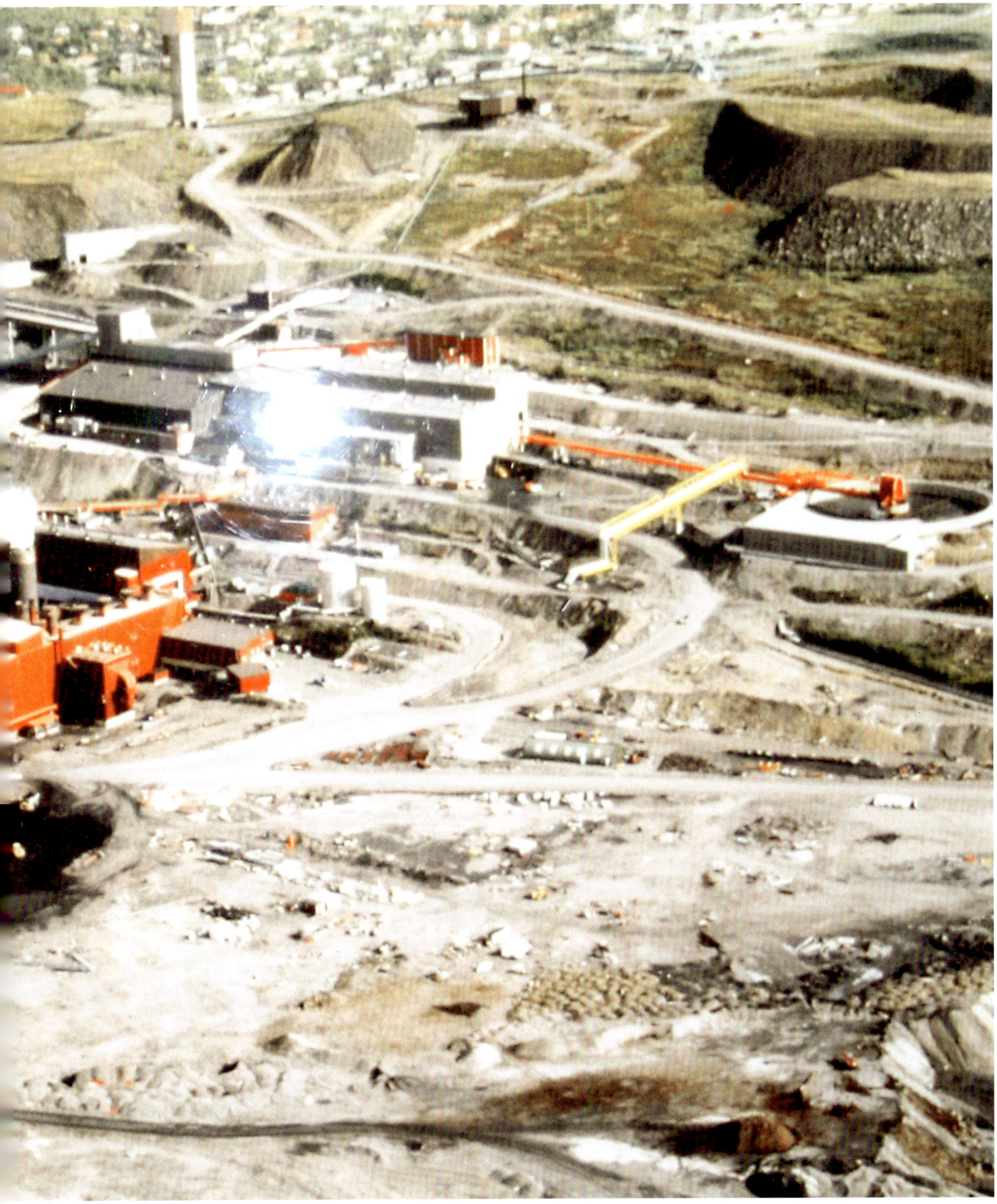

XI. Vertiginous Mapping

Working from Mademoiselle de Scudéry's *Carte du Pays de Tendre* and its carefully drawn topography—published in 1654 as a portrayal of an itinerary of the emotions, a lovers' journey, an interior landscape providing "a geographical map of the relational space," and "an open cartographic text whose many potential touring options produce a cumulative effect"[31]—Giuliana Bruno reinvents cinema space and the movement of what she calls the "spatiovisual" arts. The invention of cinema as a kinetic cultural locus brought with it an era of circulation that becomes more and more complex as one attempts, as Rosa Barba does, to integrate into the map the drift inherent in the process and the very tools of cartography: the outcome is vertiginous mapping—"vertiginous" because it includes in its texture both images and technology, screens and projectors, architecture and machines. Barba turns cinema itself into a ruin of the future, a form of science fiction left behind by twenty-first-century cyberspace. As Web networks continue to expand, Bruno asks, is not our spatial culture endlessly reinventing the impulse to make contact and to be connected, to propose virtual space as habitable and inhabited?

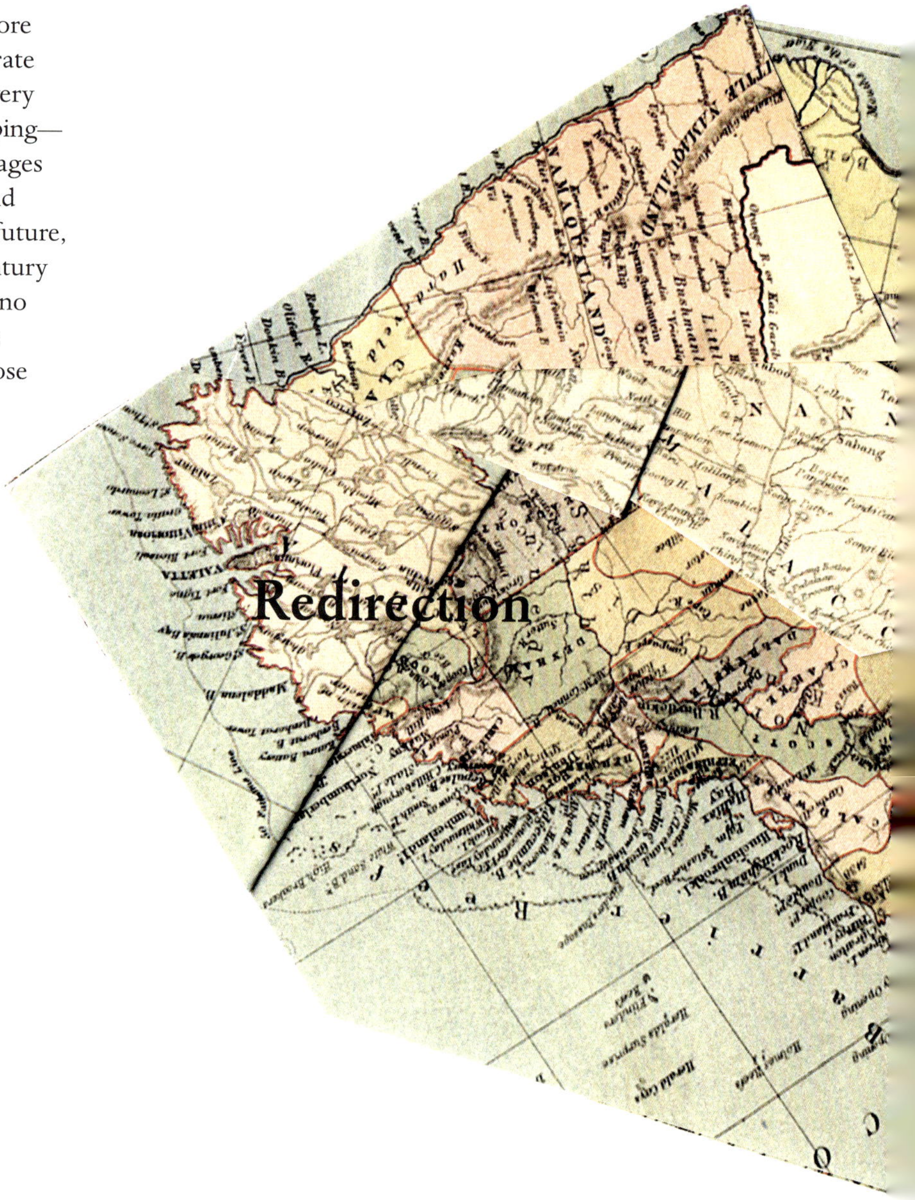

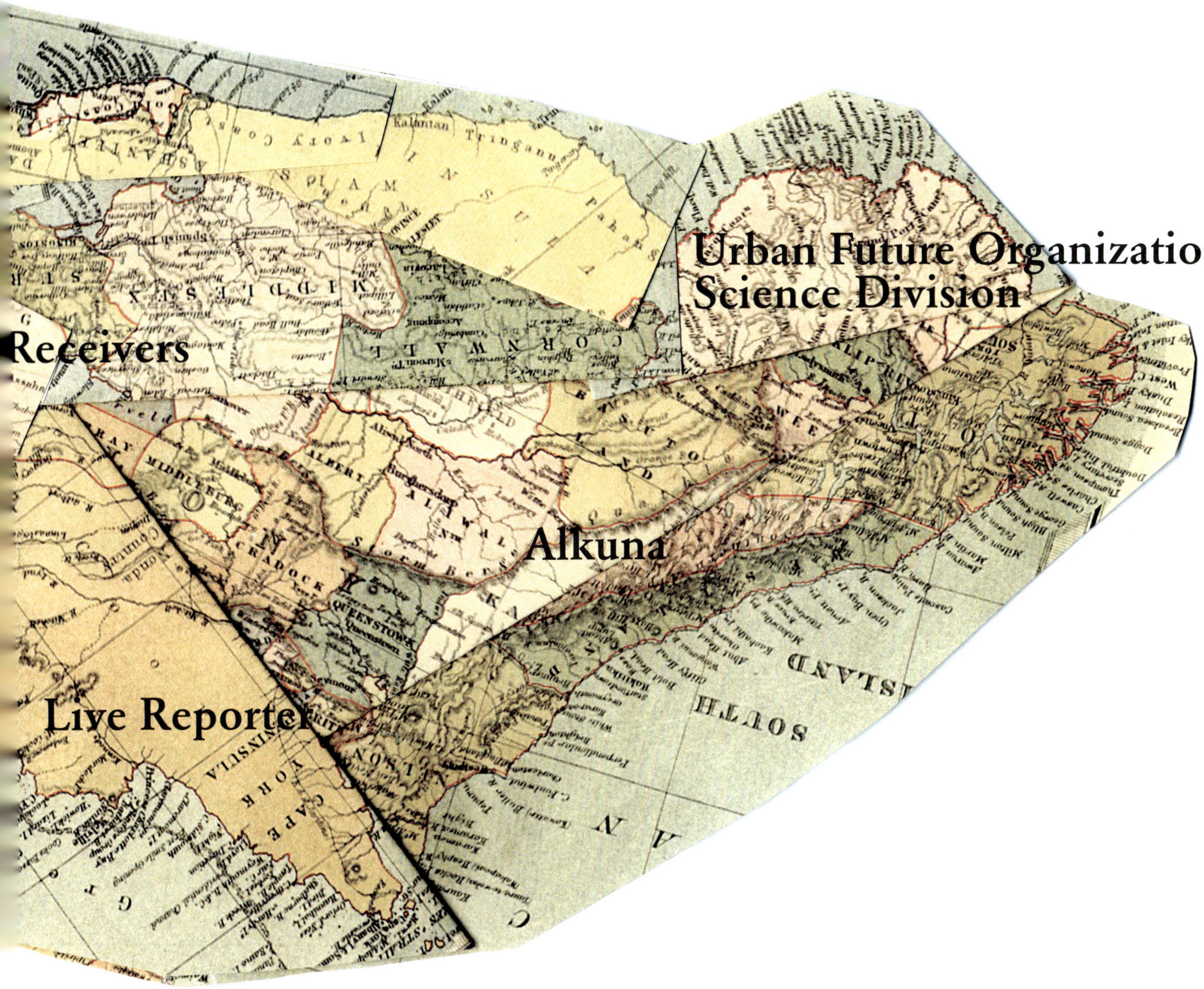

Vertiginous Mapping (2008), Dia Art Foundation, New York

XII. “Facts Run on Light Beams These Days.”[32]

Notes

1. Donna Haraway, "Situated Knowledges: The Science Question in Feminism and the Privilege of Partial Perspective," *Feminist Studies* 14, no. 3 (Autumn 1988), p. 577.
2. Regarding the refutation of the canonical model of an "anteriority narrative," see Mieke Bal, *Louise Bourgeois' Spider: The Architecture of Art-Writing* (Chicago and London: University of Chicago Press, 2001).
3. "The Western Round Table on Modern Art (1949)," ed. Douglas MacAgy. Consulted online at: http://www.ubu.com/historical/wrtma/index.html (last accessed on March 8, 2011).
4. Ibid.
5. Haraway 1988 (see note 1), p. 583.
6. Louise Bourgeois, in an interview by Bernard Marcadé in Camille Guichard's film *Louise Bourgeois* (New York, February 1993).
7. Bal 2001 (see note 2).
8. Willa Cather, *The Song of the Lark* (Boston: Houghton, 1915), p. 297.
9. Ellen Moers, quoted in Ann Moseley, "The Creative Ecology of Walnut Canyon," in *Cather Studies,* vol. 5. Consulted online at: http://cather.unl.edu/cs005_moseley.html (last accessed on March 8, 2011).
10. Susanne K. Langer, *Feeling and Form: A Theory of Art* (New York: Scribner's, 1953), p. 122.
11. J. M. Coetzee, quoted in Katie Brewer Ball and Julia Steinmetz, "Call for Papers: Feminist Landscapes," in *Women & Performance: A Journal of Feminist Theory.* This call for papers appeared on different Web sites with the deadline for submission as January 1, 2010.
12. Rosa Barba, *Printed Cinema #3: Accidental Suspension* (2005) .
13. Jonathan Goldberg, "Photographic Relations: Laura Gilpin, Willa Cather," *American Literature* 70, no. 1 (March 1998), pp. 63–95. Consulted online at: http://www.jstor.org/stable/2902456 (last accessed on March 8, 2011).
14. Jonathan Goldberg, *Willa Cather and Others* (Durham, NC: Duke University Press, 2001), pp. 158–59.
15. Monique Wittig, "Author's Note," in idem, *The Lesbian Body,* trans. David Le Vay (Boston: Beacon, 1986), pp. 10–11.
16. Reyner Banham, *Scenes in America Deserta* (Cambridge, MA: MIT Press, 1989).
17. Zygmunt Bauman, *Modernity and Ambivalence* (Cambridge, UK: Polity, 1991), p. 11.
18. Serge Guilbaut, *How New York Stole the Idea of Modern Art: Abstract Expressionism, Freedom and the Cold War,* trans. Arthur Goldhammer (Chicago: University of Chicago Press, 1983), p. 177.
19. See Joseph Masco, "Fantastic City: Engineering Ruins in Cold War America," *Cabinet* 20 (Winter 2005–2006), pp. 85–88.
20. Vera Norwood and Janice Monk, eds., *The Desert Is No Lady: Southwestern Landscapes in Women's Writing and Art* (New Haven: Yale University Press, 1987), p. 87 (this quotation has been partly retranslated from the French version of the present essay).
21. Sigmund Freud, "The Acquisition and Control of Fire," in *The Standard Edition of the Complete Psychological Works of Sigmund Freud, Vol. XXII (1932–36): New Introductory Lectures on Psycho-Analysis and Other Works,* pp. 183–94.
22. Nancy Holt, "Sun Tunnels," *Artforum* (April 1977), pp. 34–35.
23. Ibid.
24. Briony Fer and Roni Horn, *Roni Horn aka Roni Horn* (London: Steidl, 2009).
25. Rebecca Solnit, *Savage Dreams* (Berkeley: University of California Press, 2000).
26. Astra Taylor, "Rebecca Solnit," *Bomb* 109 (Fall 2009), http://bombsite.com/issues/109/articles/3327.
27. Donna Haraway, *Simians, Cyborgs and Women: The Reinvention of Nature* (New York: Routledge, 1990), p. 195.
28. Jimmy Durham, "Artists' Pages," *Art Journal* 51, no. 2: "Art and Ecology" (Summer 1992), p. 14.
29. Rebecca Solnit interview, consulted online at: http://believermag.com/issues/200909/?read=interview_solnit (last accessed on March 8, 2011).
30. Giuliana Bruno, *Streetwalking on a Ruined Map: Cultural Theory and the City Films of Elvira Notari* (Princeton: Princeton University Press, 1993).
31. Giuliana Bruno, *Atlas of Emotion: Journeys in Art, Architecture and Films* (New York: Verso, 2002). This is a book to be read in its entirety.
32. Donna Haraway, "Situated Knowledges: The Science Question in Feminism and the Privilege of Partial Perspective," in Haraway 1990 (see note 27), p. 248, n. 2.

ROSA BARBA'S UNFILMED FILMS

FRANCESCO MANACORDA
&
RAIMUNDAS MALASAUSKAS

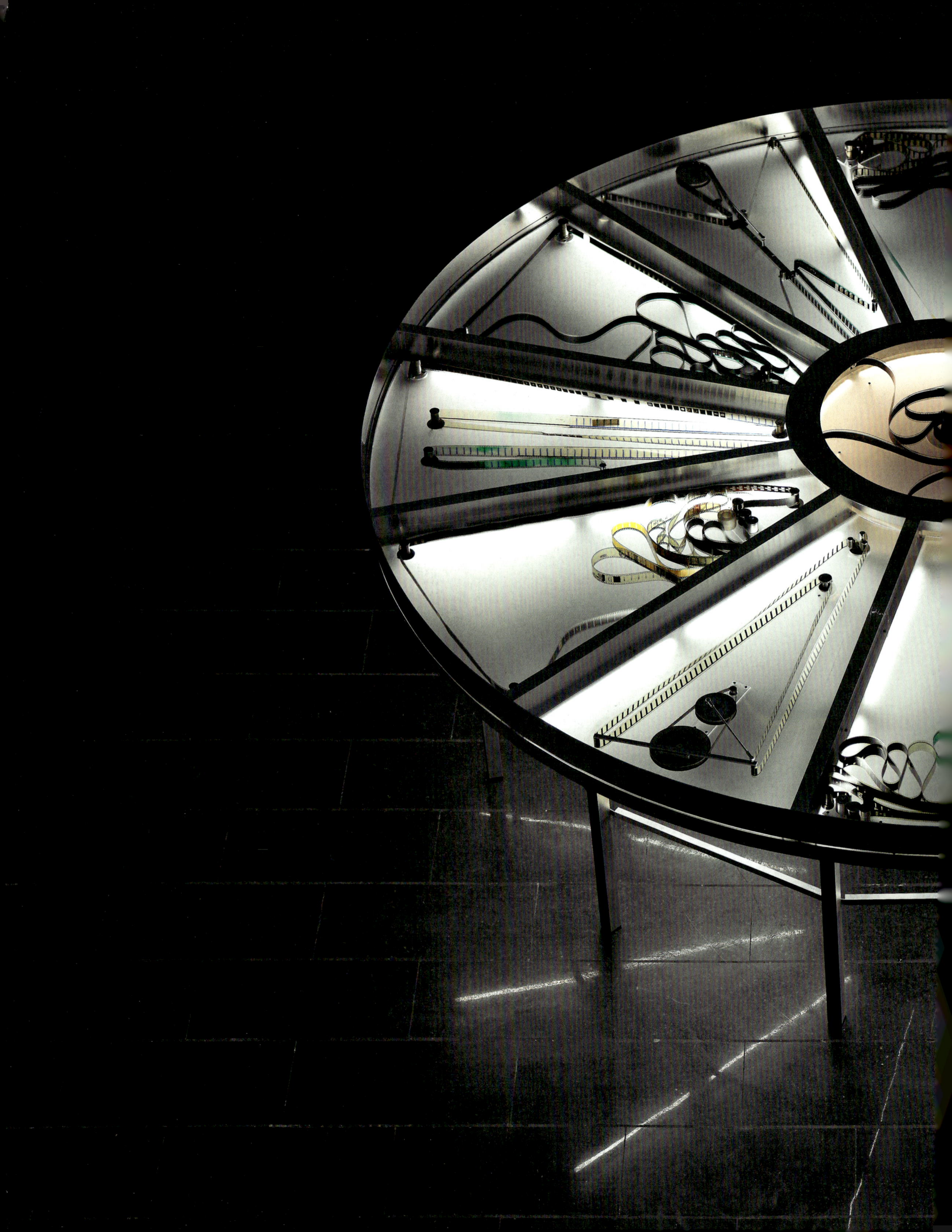

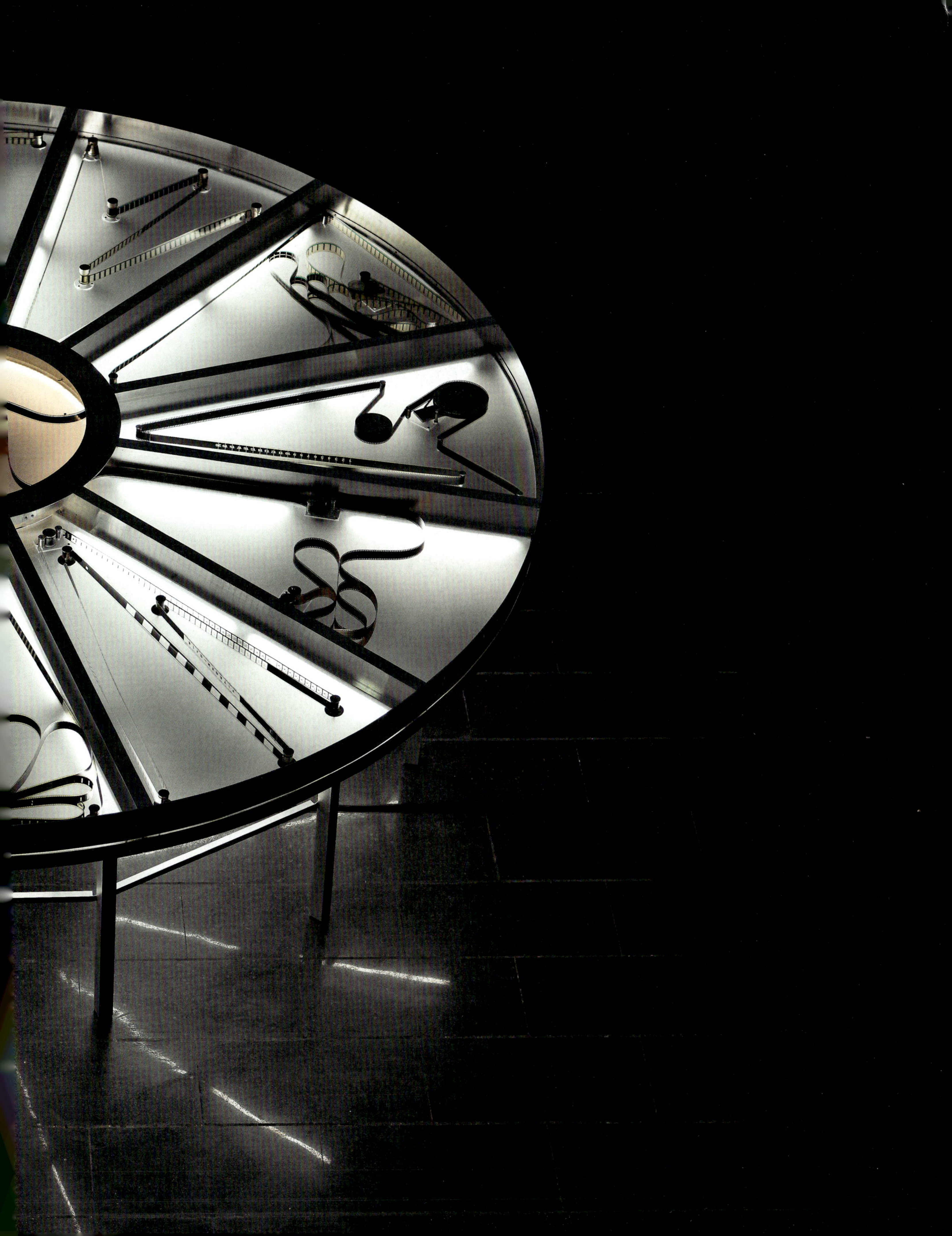

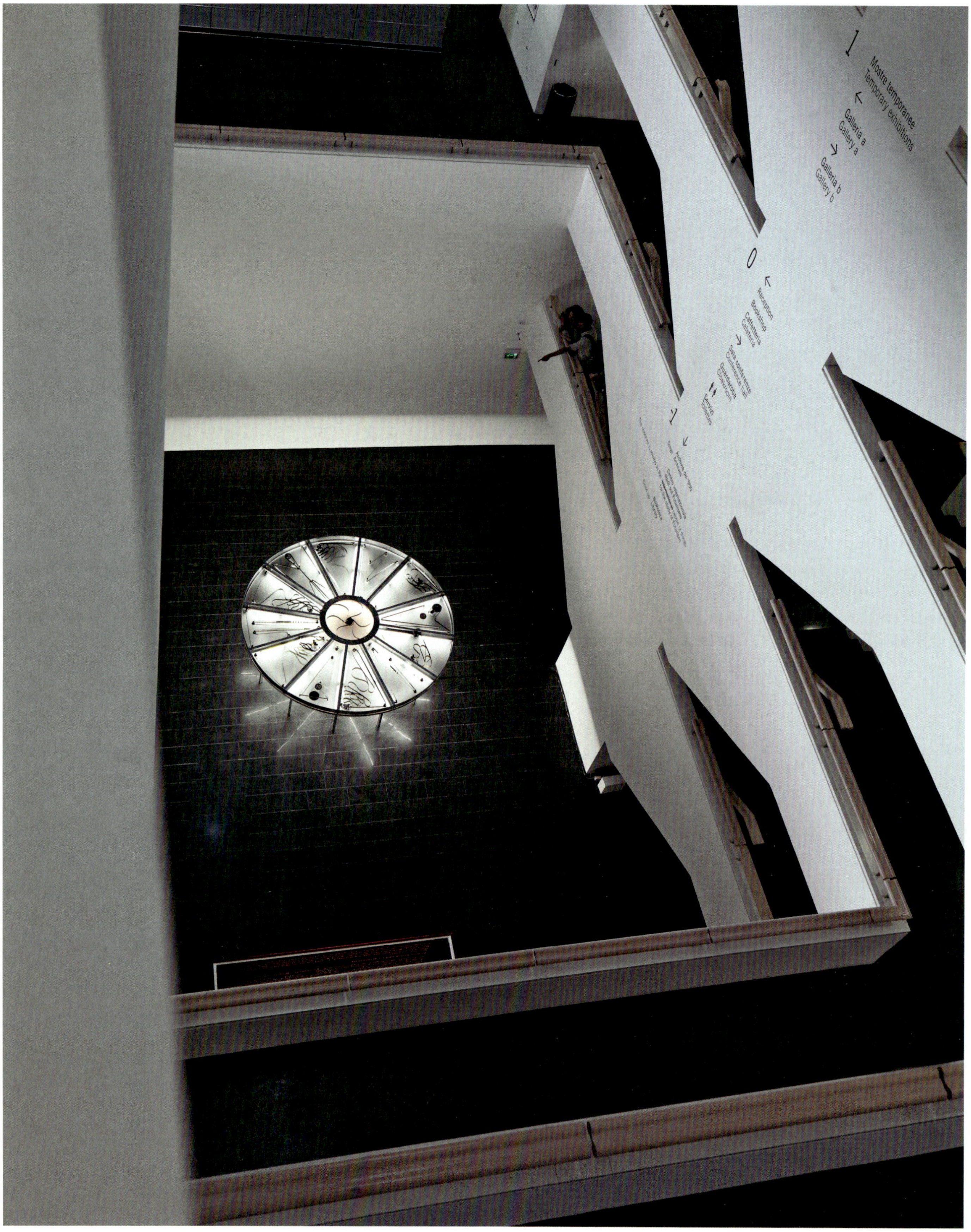

Above and preceding pages: *Stage Archive* (2011), installation view, Mart – Museo di Arte Moderna e Contemporanea di Trento e Rovereto, Rovereto, 2011
Following pages: *Stage Archive* (2011)

In his famous 1874 piano suite "Pictures at an Exhibition," Modest Mussorgsky transposed into music his account of a visit to an exhibition of the work of his friend, the artist and architect Viktor Hartmann. The ten movements are each linked to individual works, the majority of which cannot be identified now. Titles of the works are used for each movement, but the majority of them are lost or their identity uncertain. Due to this disconnection, the music functions as a spectacular archival ghost of a past experience whose source material is not available to the listener any- more in its original medium. Its evocative power allows us to conjure up potential images from the darkness of a memory that was never recorded visually, or a film whose images have been erased by decay, leaving behind the "second-degree" aural trace that once accompanied them. From the point of view of textual analysis, this piece puts listeners into a state of forced amnesia for which the music tries to compensate.

Rosa Barba's series *The Hidden Conference* (2010–11)—like, in general, her later works on the notion of the archive—functions in a mirrored, reverse relationship to "Pictures at an Exhibition." The artist uses different collections of stored cultural data (paintings, sculptures, works on paper) as a reservoir of characters that can be activated in a possible film whose script is generated through their fortuitous contiguity in the storeroom. The potential of museum storage areas and archives resides in the artist's eye, in the dormant roles that collected items can play in a plot. Connections between artworks or documents are used to form a story, and the archive itself is turned into a theater stage on which works are given roles that take into account their identities within a complex choreography.

Elements in unexhibited collections thus become the protagonists of the multiple untold, nonlinear stories that have brought them together. Like letters in the alphabet, documents can be used to utter single words, complete sentences, or multiple scripts. This combinatory game is not dissimilar from museum work: it results in something akin to the archaeologist's effort to reconstruct a buried past from which he only has received some fragments. From these fragments, a whole story—or, rather, in the case of the archaeologist, history—has to be reconstructed, pieced together, and evoked. The difference between archaeological work and Barba's narratives lies in the unity of materials that the archaeologist can guarantee through the geographical location of his findings and the carbon dating that confirms their simultaneity. Conversely, the multiple possibilities inside an archive are by definition in search of a story, not necessarily *his*tory, and Barba seems to be inclined to allow them to coalesce on her celluloid storyboard and form discontinuous permutations. Are these possible futures that never took place? Are they multiple universes explored by mathematical probability games? Or are they, once more, theatrical plays resulting from a séance that tried to reanimate the potential fiction latent in the works confined in the rooms we have built to store collective memory?

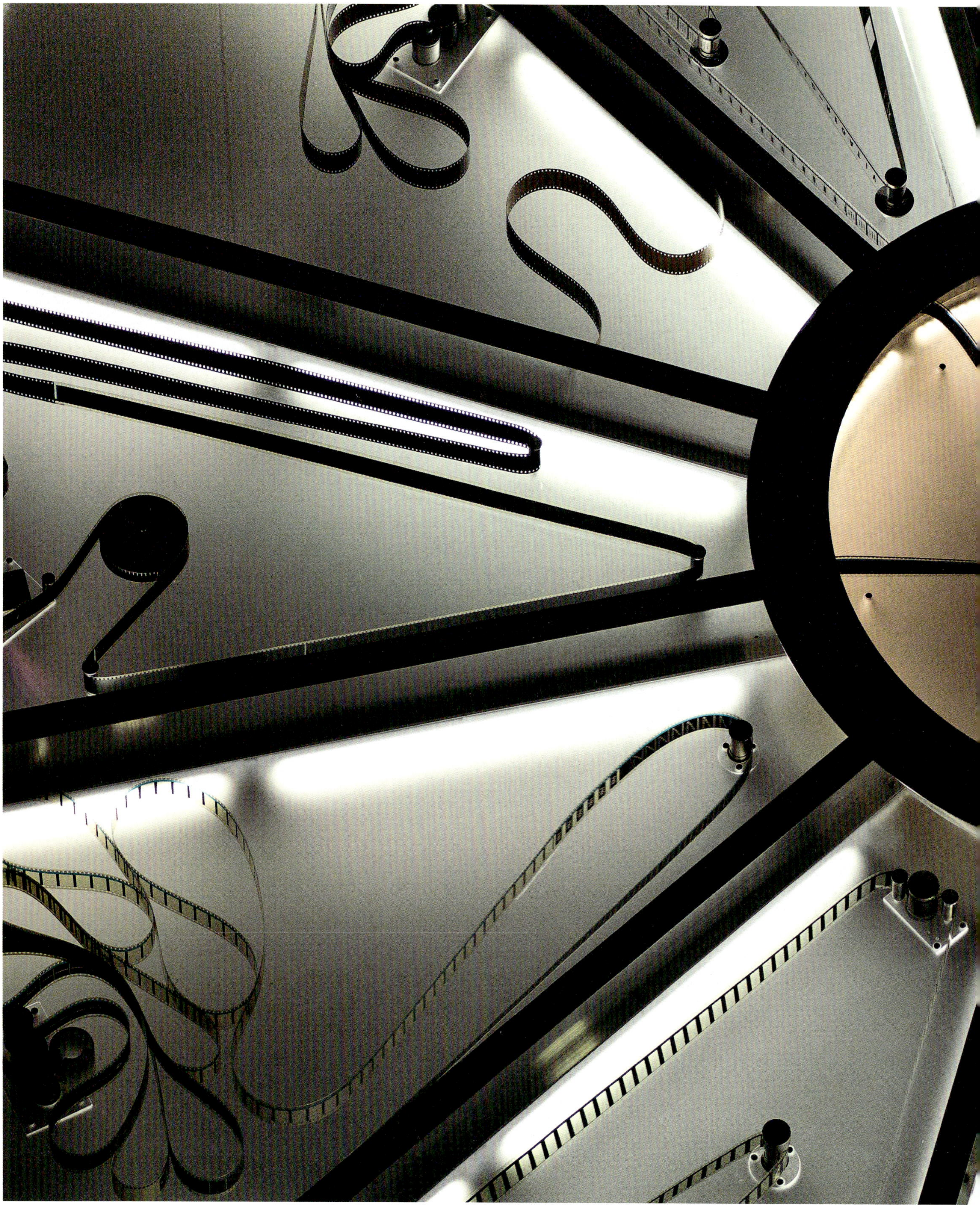

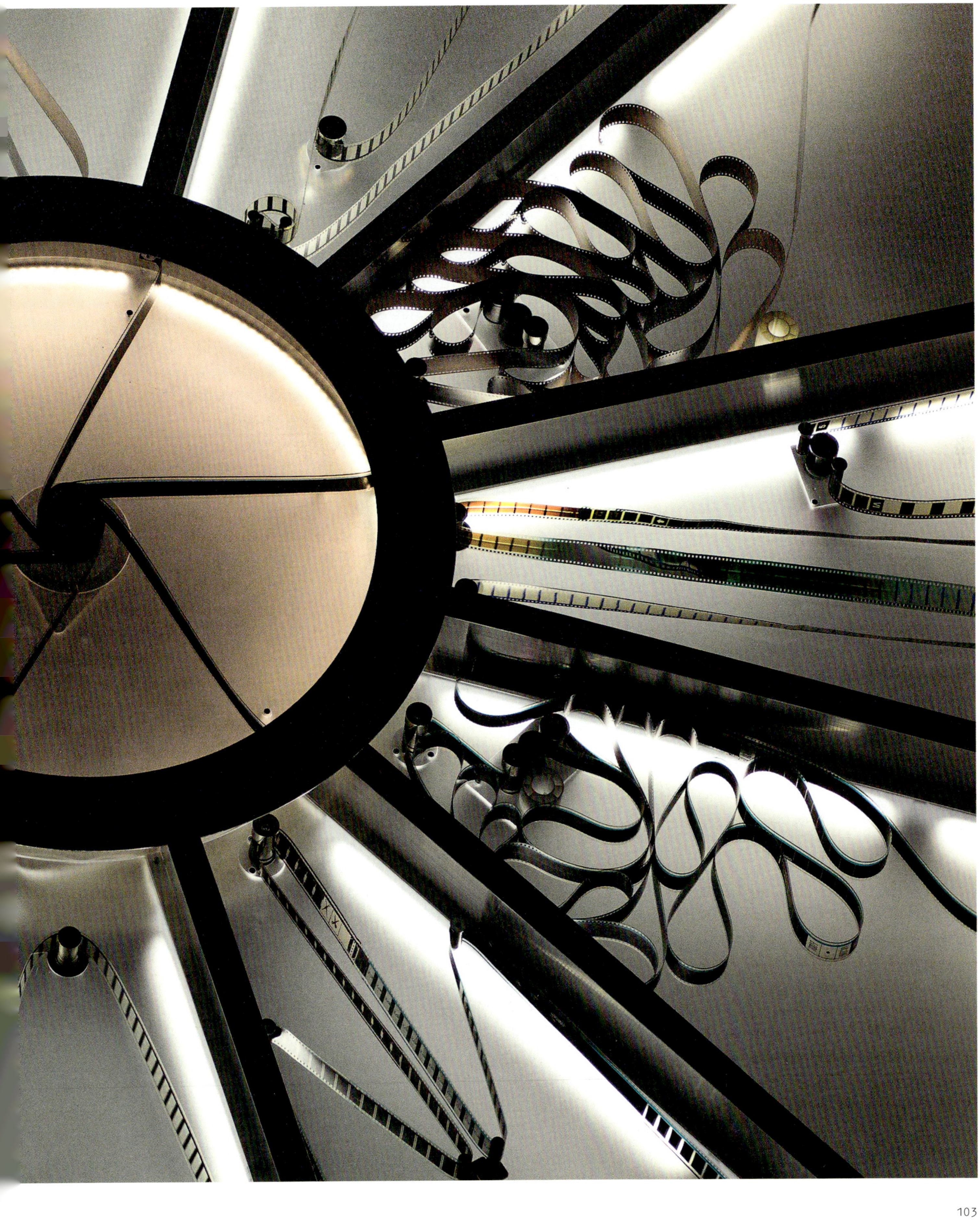

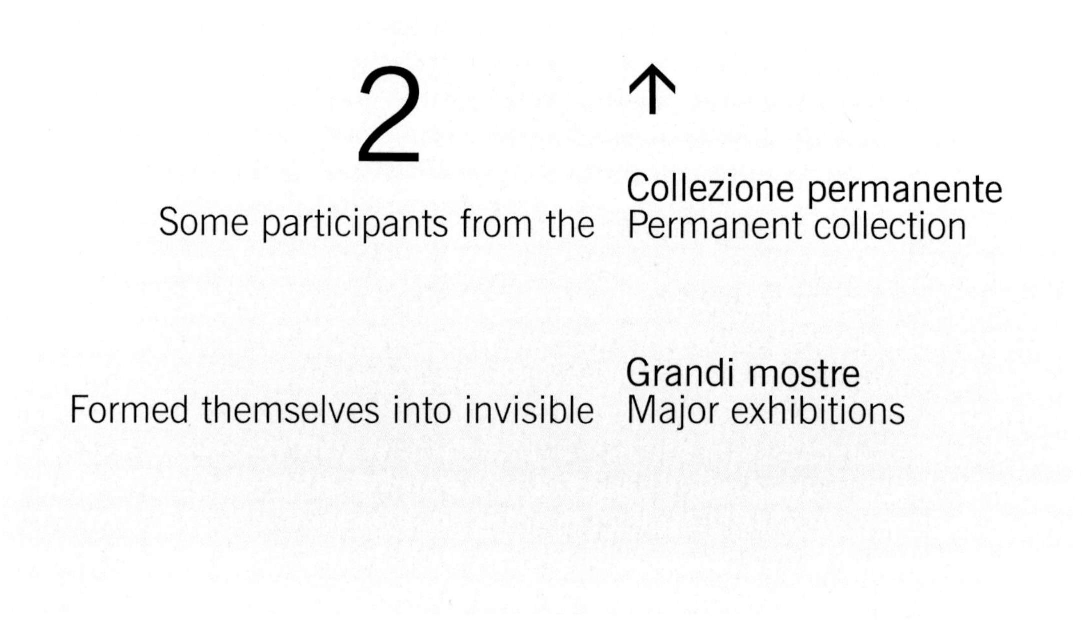

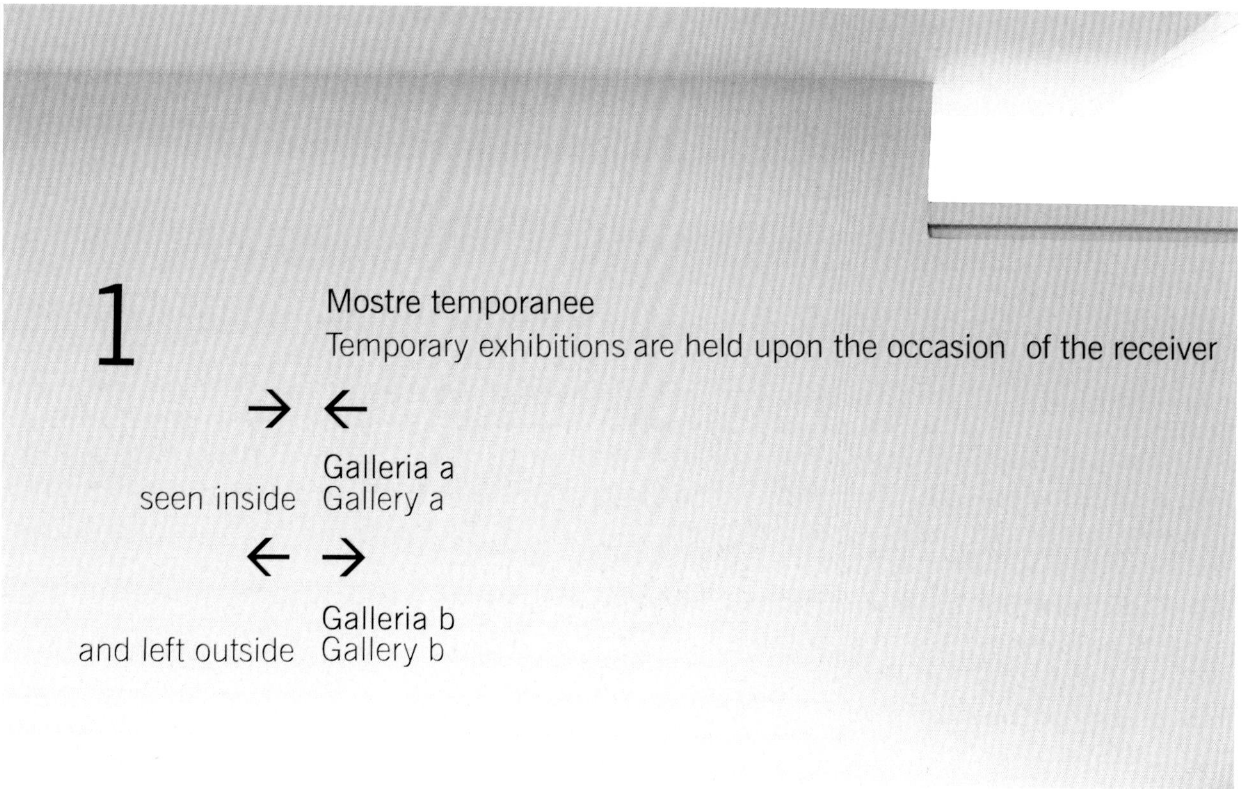

No Titles (2011), installation view, Mart – Museo di Arte Moderna e Contemporanea di Trento e Rovereto, Rovereto, 2011

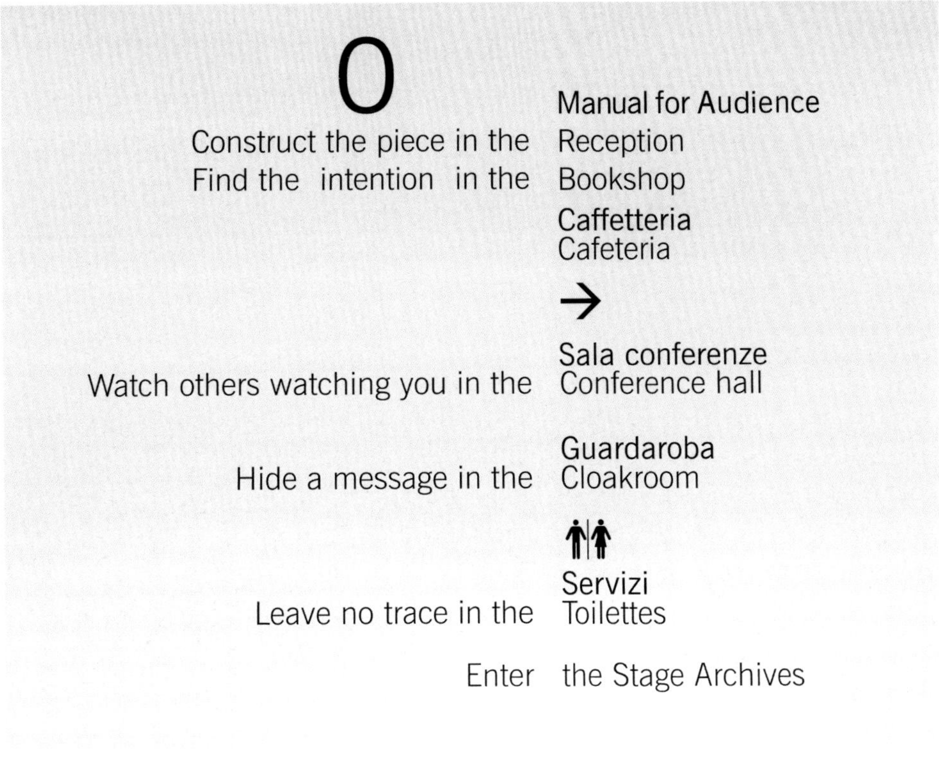
0
Manual for Audience
Construct the piece in the Reception
Find the intention in the Bookshop
Caffetteria
Cafeteria
→
Sala conferenze
Watch others watching you in the Conference hall
Guardaroba
Hide a message in the Cloakroom
Servizi
Leave no trace in the Toilettes
Enter the Stage Archives

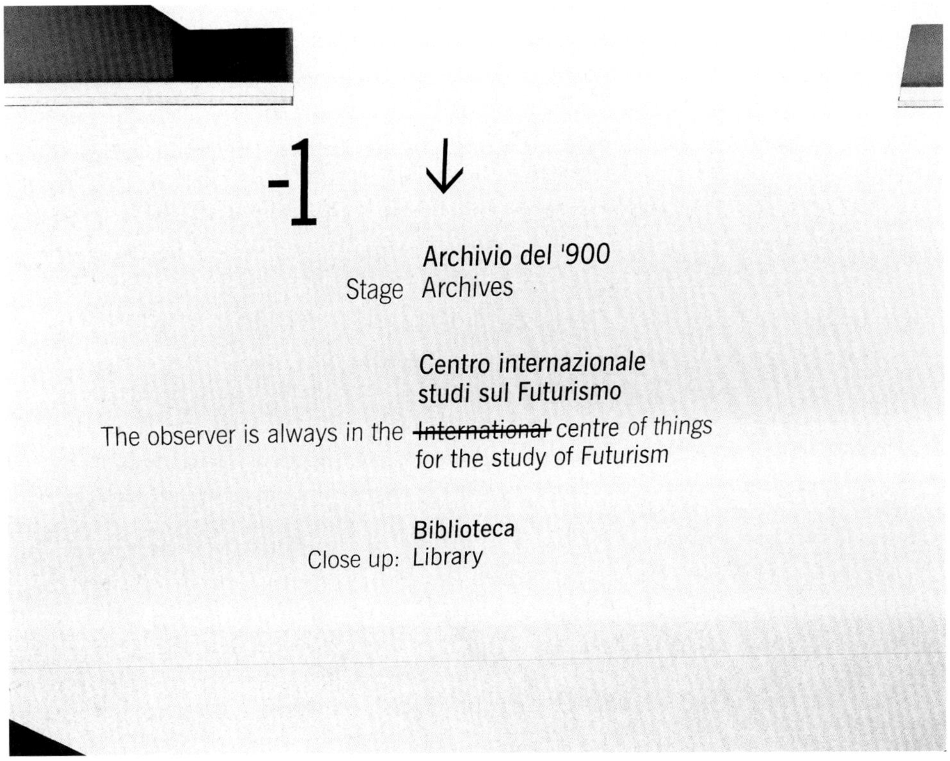
-1 ↓
Archivio del '900
Stage Archives
Centro internazionale
studi sul Futurismo
The observer is always in the ~~International~~ centre of things
for the study of Futurism
Biblioteca
Close up: Library

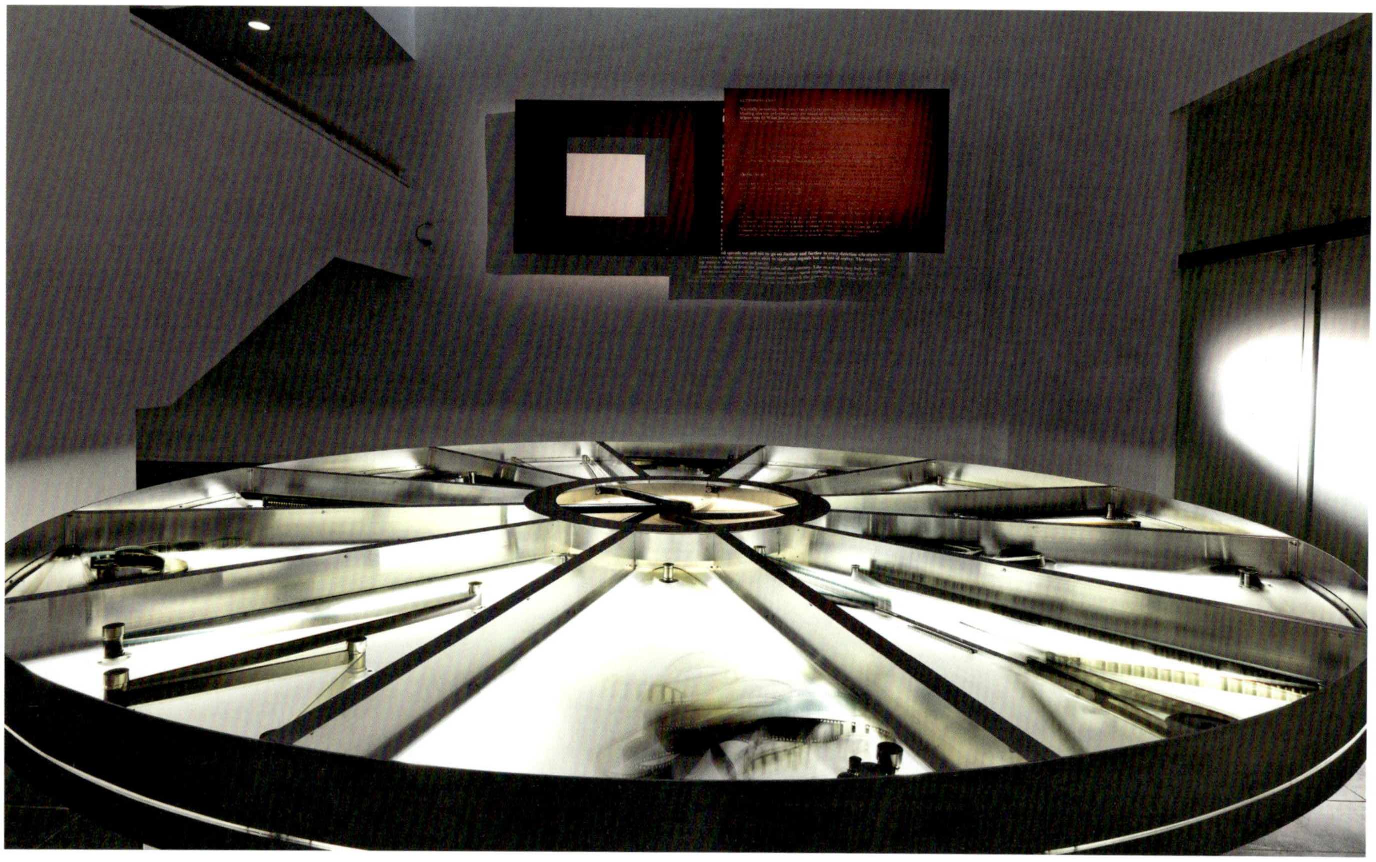

Above: *Stage Archive* (2011), installation view, Mart – Museo di Arte Moderna e Contemporanea di Trento e Rovereto, Rovereto, 2011
Following pages: *Theory in Order to Shed Light* (2011), installation view, Mart – Museo di Arte Moderna e Contemporanea di Trento e Rovereto, Rovereto, 2011

For the show in Rovereto, Barba has planned an installation in front of the door that gives access to the archive. The mise-en-scène involves a lamp and a theater curtain hanging on the threshold that separates the exhibition from the storeroom. The monumental round light fixture is installed on the floor and displays a long celluloid films, which move slowly on top of the lit surface like a snake. The lamp functions as a science-fiction film apparatus that filters the past and converts it into a potential future. If in a traditional film projector the light passes through the celluloid to allow ghostly, immaterial images to dance on a white screen, then in this modified version, the celluloid allows the light to leak through towards the archive door, as if to magnetically attract onto its surface the potential film characters confined in the "changing rooms" behind the theater curtain. In this sense, the lamp is a camera rather than a projector—a séance tool capable of reanimating inanimate objects. The film inside the lamp aims at conjuring up the manifold possible untold stories emerging from the archive, and for this reason it is still unexposed. Documents, artworks, photographs, and scripts are drawn towards the film as if the celluloid had been chemically treated to attract cultural content onto its surface.

Within the documents left behind by Depero, there are some unrealized scripts for a Futurist film. In these, an artist reaches success through the invention of a fully automated theater. In his notes, Depero describes "mechanical animals, automated savages dancing, multicolored butterflies flying, moustached masks dancing, constructed shadows dancing, a rain of cigarettes . . . " Elements such as these are like worlds submerged in the memory of someone else, recalling the stories emerging from Raimundas Malasauskas's interview with Mr. Pechalat,[1] the narrative fragments of a village now kept underwater. Like the sounds of Lake Vassivière's frozen surface cracking at night that Pechalat describes, the archive shouts out to those who are willing to listen. What is underwater can easily be resuscitated like a mechanical ballet.

The two distant worlds of Pechalat and Futurism come together in *Underwater Forward Amnesia,* the new film that Barba has realized after three years of research conducted in collaboration with Malasauskas and myself in Vassivière and Trento. Lasting an entire day, the projection recalls the sounds and scenery of an underwater world as if it were the reverse of an archive: it is a stage set without a related story, because its story has been totally erased from memory. Fragments of other histories "stolen" from several unconnected archives can inhabit the set just as fashion models are able to wear different dresses, one after the other. As in a Futuristic mechanical play, stories unfold in what looks like a future reversal of Atlantis—a once-abandoned submerged civilization that is later reinhabited after an environmental disaster made it impossible for humans to live on the ground. The film manages to sustain a sense of timelessness despite its twenty-four-hour duration; everything that is immersed in water acquires the appearance of a world seen through the crystal ball of a long-dead fortune-teller. Will the future still need fiction to give order to the world?

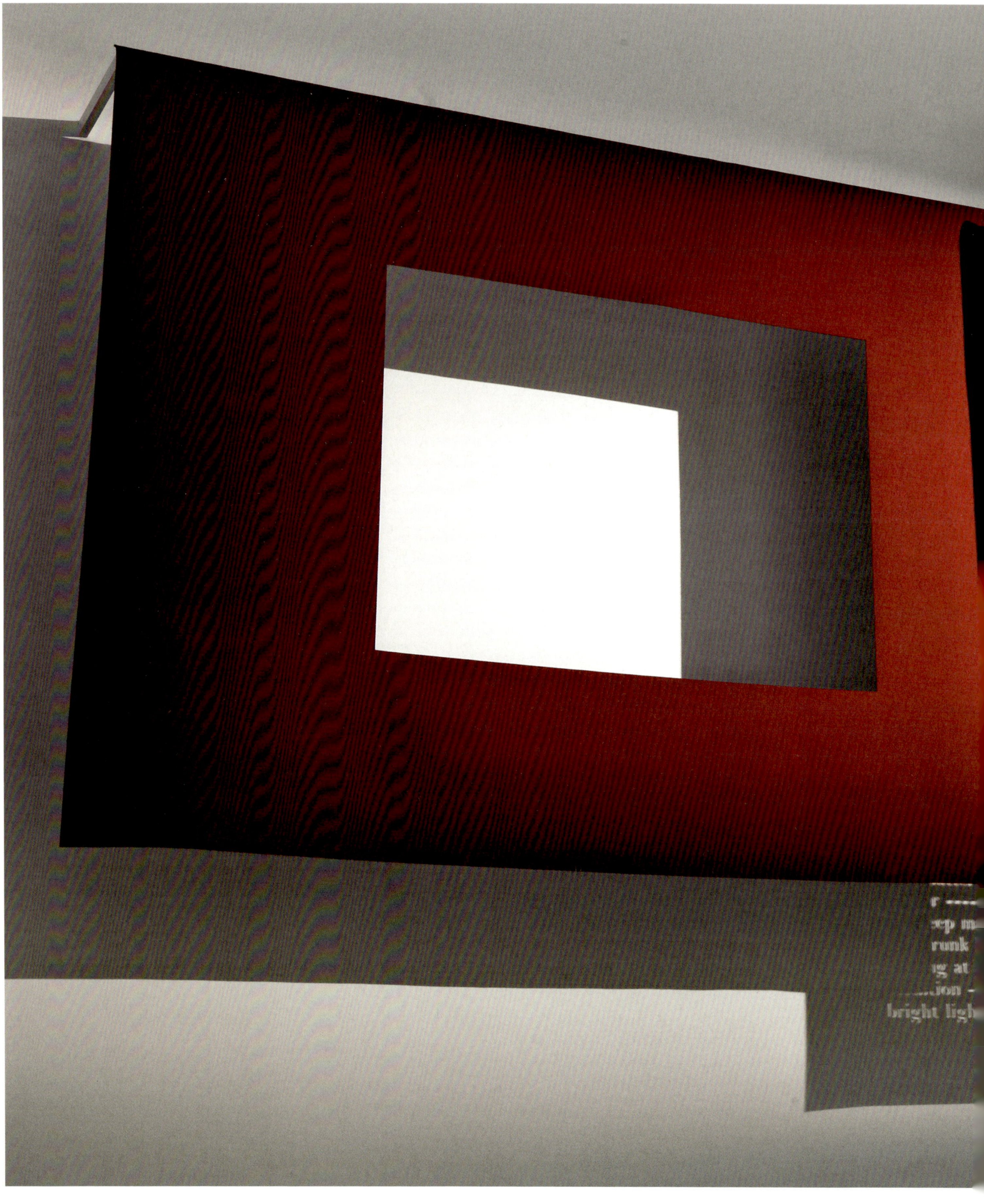

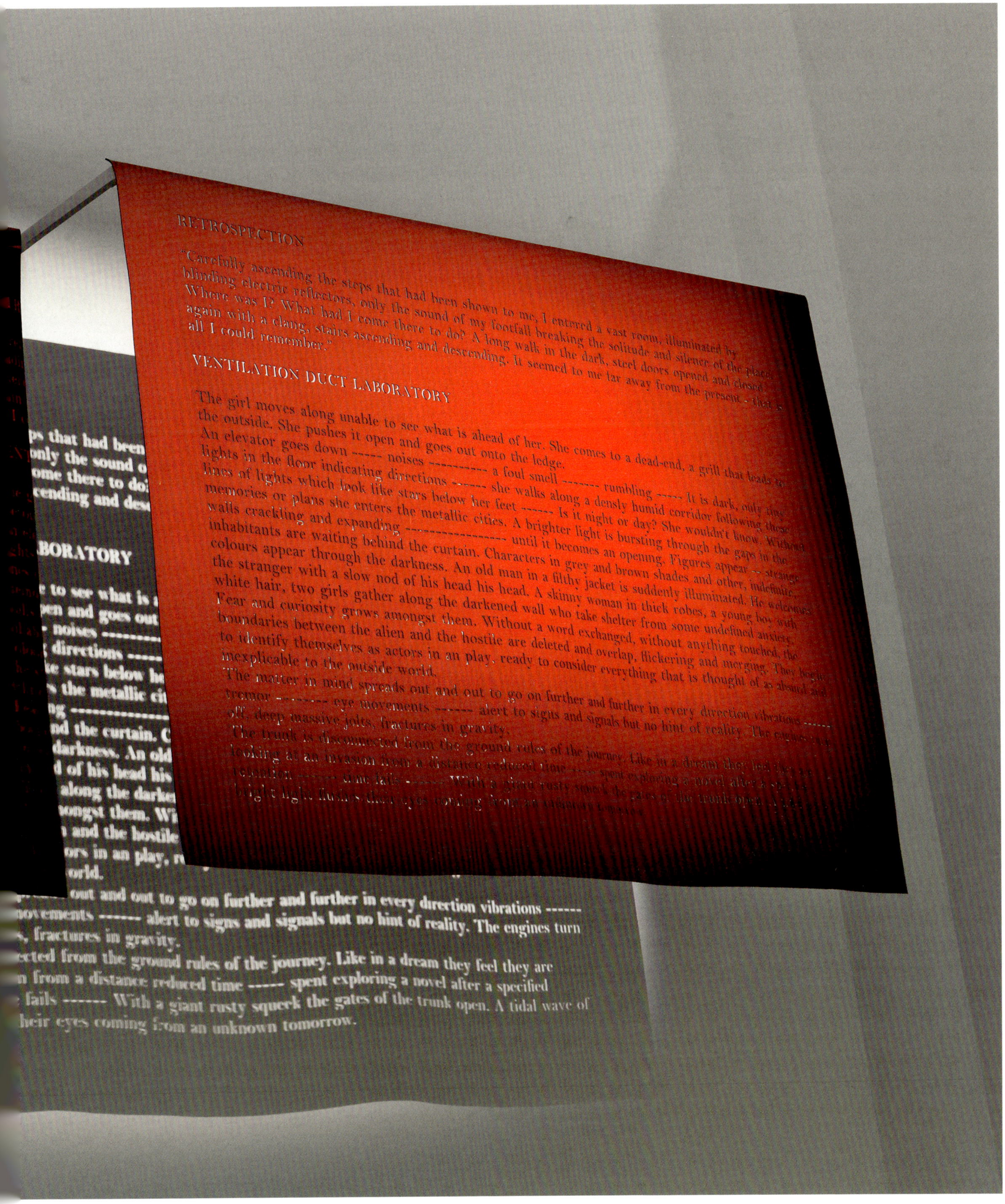
RETROSPECTION
"Carefully ascending the steps that had been shown to me, I entered a vast room, illuminated by
blinding electric reflectors, only the sound of my footfall breaking the solitude and silence of the place.
Where was I? What had I come there to do? A long walk in the dark, steel doors opened and closed
again with a clang, stairs ascending and descending. It seemed to me far away from the present - that
all I could remember."
VENTILATION DUCT LABORATORY
The girl moves along unable to see what is ahead of her. She comes to a dead-end, a grill that leads to
the outside. She pushes it open and goes out onto the ledge.
An elevator goes down ----- noises ---------- a foul smell ------- rumbling ----- It is dark, only the
lights in the floor indicating directions ------ she walks along a densly humid corridor following these
lines of lights which look like stars below her feet ------ Is it night or day? She wouldn't know. Without
memories or plans she enters the metallic cities. A brighter light is bursting through the gaps in the
walls crackling and expanding ----------------- until it becomes an opening. Figures appear -- strange
inhabitants are waiting behind the curtain. Characters in grey and brown shades and other, indefinite
colours appear through the darkness. An old man in a filthy jacket is suddenly illuminated. He welcomes
the stranger with a slow nod of his head his head. A skinny woman in thick robes, a young boy with
white hair, two girls gather along the darkened wall who take shelter from some undefined anxiety.
Fear and curiosity grows amongst them. Without a word exchanged, without anything touched, the
boundaries between the alien and the hostile are deleted and overlap, flickering and merging. They begin
to identify themselves as actors in an play, ready to consider everything that is thought of as absurd and
inexplicable to the outside world.
The matter in mind spreads out and out to go on further and further in every direction vibrations ------
tremor -------- eye movements ------ alert to signs and signals but no hint of reality. The engines turn
off, deep massive jolts, fractures in gravity.
The trunk is disconnected from the ground rules of the journey. Like in a dream they feel they are
looking at an invasion from a distance reduced time ----- spent exploring a novel after a specified
time fails ------ With a giant rusty squeek the gates of the trunk open. A tidal wave of
bright light flushes their eyes coming from an unknown tomorrow.

By definition, every archive tends to the construction of a fictional completeness; each tries to impose a different kind of homogeneity on a heterogeneous series of individualities. This scientific drive overlooks the fortuity with which collections and archives are often gathered, and the nonlinear potential for collective fictions is precisely the element that scientific thought overlooks. However, although perhaps being a misuse of the intellectual tool, the archive as a reservoir of stories can tie together visions of alternative worlds from the past with others from the future. Some time ago I met with Arlette Farge, a French historian who specializes in archival work, to interview her about the notion of "the document," and the most interesting aspect of her practice that emerged from the conversation was her method for fully understanding an archival document:

> At a certain moment I realized that if I really wanted to work on the eighteenth century, I couldn't just take notes and sum things up. I said to myself that if I made a series of index cards the way historians do, I would never succeed. The material that I was not acquainted with, and which I was trying to decode, seemed to me to be so rich that I forced myself—but I didn't mind that—to copy things, to venture into syntax and vocabulary, and I was quite convinced—which you will find thoroughly naïve—that even the movement of my body as I was in the process of writing could give me ideas! My immersion was a lengthy process, but I enjoyed it; I copied things out for hours and hours, and I felt that that particular movement gave me some kind of inspiration, rather than summing up sentences and following arguments, punctuation, and hesitations, step by step. I imagined the voices and I heard sounds. My immersion was not anything imaginary; rather, it was a feeling of "being with."

In this account, documents are like scripts, and the act of copying them becomes an actor's performance designed to fully fit in the role of the character to be evoked. If in scientific work the evocation needs to be considered as emerging from the past, then within fiction the space–time continuum can be reversed and the character evoked can be thought of as traveling from the future. Barba takes this intuition further by imagining anthropomorphized archival holdings as being in search of a shared script. Like in the famous Pirandello drama *Sei personaggi in cerca d'autore* (Six Characters in Search of an Author), the storage room conceived as a stage provides individualities lacking a plot with the opportunity to have their say about the reasons they are found there or about the absurdity of such a condition. Archives and storage rooms are full of these potential actors, all of them capable of playing roles in different tragedies and of inventing a utopian world from which they stem. They are kept as dead bodies ready to be reanimated, unseen in the dark. Robert Smithson's definition of museums as graveyards could be further qualified to postulate that storerooms, being invisible to museum visitors, are the spaces in which to house the undead. The potential of a storeroom's contents does not reside in the possibility of being wheeled out into the exhibition space, but rather in the séancelike process that makes them protagonists of an untold story taking place in an unspecified future.

Note

1. See the text by Raimundas Malasauskas in this volume, pp. 124–29.

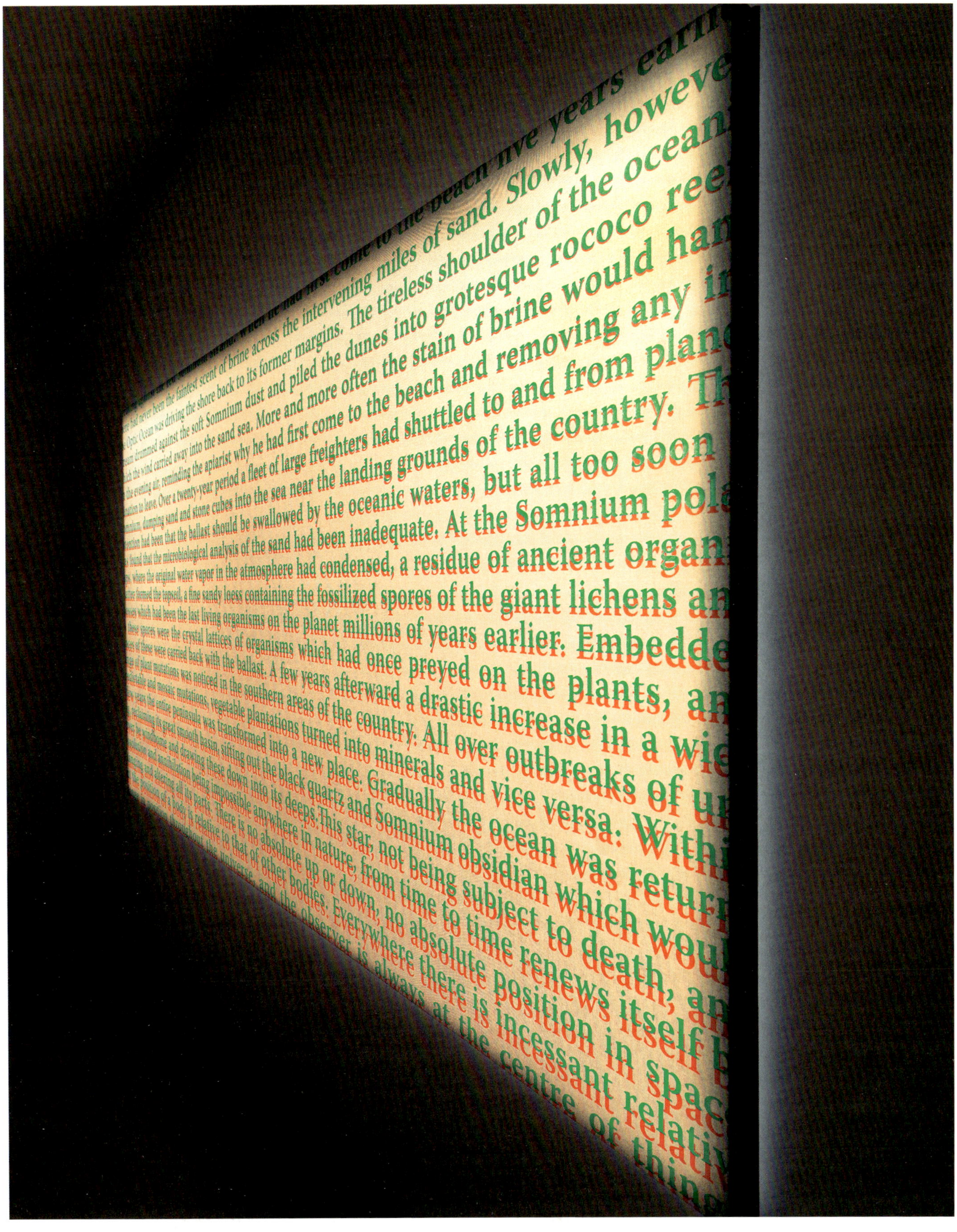

Optic Ocean (2011), installation view, Fondazione Galleria Civica–Centro di Ricerca sulla Contemporaneità di Trento, Trent, 2011

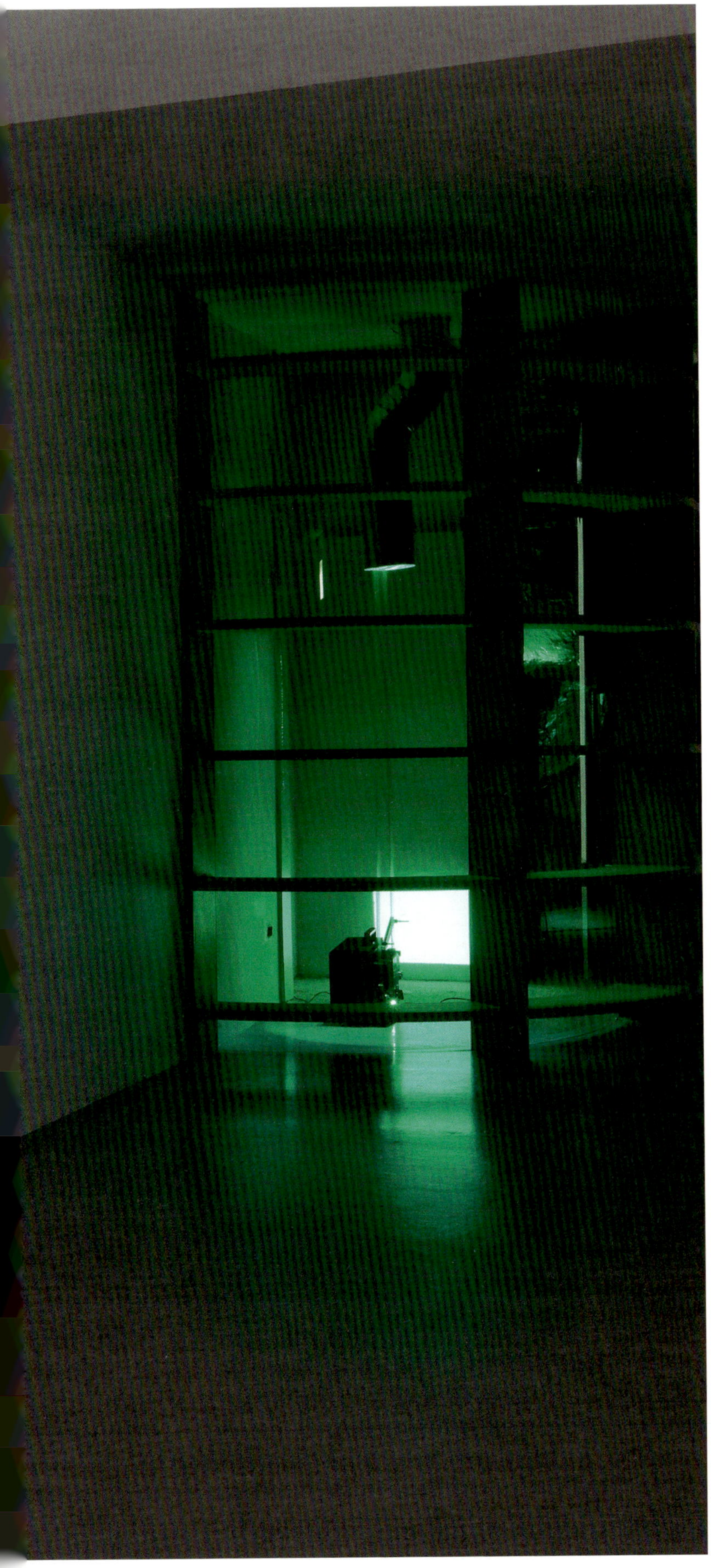

Left: *Time Machine* (2007) and *One Way Out* (2009), installation view, Fondazione Galleria Civica–Centro di Ricerca sulla Contemporaneità di Trento, Trent, 2011
Pages 114–17: *Time Machine* (2007), installation view, Stedelijk Museum Bureau Amsterdam, 2007
Pages 118–23 and 130–31: *White Museum* (2010), installation view, Centre international d'art et du paysage de l'île de Vassivière, 2010

T H E T I M E M A C H I N E FADE IN: Leo the Lion ROARS over the FANFARE, then FADE OUT: GLIDING OBJECTS IN A WIDE DARK VOID - (ANIMATION) Out of the SILENT darkness a short white fluted column surmounted by a SUNDIAL appears. It floats in,
CLOCK accompanied by the sound of DRIPPING WATER. A MEDIEVAL CLOCK with weights arises as its horizontal escapement TICKS LOUDLY. Mean-while the sundial, hourglass and water clock return, drifting at diverse angles across the screen. THE SOUND of
in to mingle with all the drifting objects. The BIG BEN is TOLLING Then a GREAT BELL. DEAFENING SOUNDS NOW COME FROM ALL DIRECTIONS, as the time K devices weave across the screen and, reaching CRESCENDO STOP abruptly. A mellow VOICE begins
ched countryside. Only the laboratory, a converted greenhouse, is dark, shaded from the moonlight by a majestic, leafless oak. A two-horse carriage, in the style of the turn of the century, lingers in the driveway. Beyond all this, the River Thames takes a sharp cu
who hastily hands her his rumpled cloak and hat, then rushes toward: INT. LIBRARY A pleasant Edwardian room, the shelves are stacked tightly with volumes of books, many of ancient Vintage. Three men are seated in a rough circle, motionless, obviously await
SHOTS DR. PHILIP HILLYER is an imposing businessman, wearing full sideburns. He stares stonily at the last empty chair, then at Filby with annoyance. ANTHONY BRIDEWELL, a man of the world, impeccably attired in the latest fashion, welcomes Filby the only
it shut and glares at EMPTY CHAIR - MED. SHOT Conspicuously unoccupied. GRANDFATHER CLOCK - CLOSE SHOT Reaching the hour of eight, it begins to STRIKE ITS YELLOW CHIMES. Other timepieces JOIN IN the announcement. GROUPSHOT The men look
KEMP (unscrews the cigar from his tight lips) This is such a confounded waste of time! If he's not coming, I've any number of more important things to do. All heads turn as Mrs. Watchett enters, closing the door quietly behind her. With an envelope in her hand s
we are. (to Mrs. Watchett) How long has he been gone? MRS. WATCHETT (nervously) I can't rightly say, sir. - Several days. I hardly catch a glimpse of him lately. He never leaves the laboratory and comes out only to nibble at his meals...but he did tell me days a
George merely says that if he is not here by eight we're to begin without him. Kemp tears the note out of Filby's hand and reads it hurriedly. Meanwhile, Mrs. Watchett swings the door open and turns around. MRS. WATCHETT Dinner is served, gentlemen! BRIDE
LYER He's making fools of us by inviting us here and then not showing up It's not the behavior of a gentleman. KEMP To say nothing of the waste of time. DR. HILLYER (agreeing) To say nothing of the waste of time. Bridewell, already seated at the heavily laden c
cook in the world. - I think I'll drink to that!The glass barely touches his lips as he freezes at the SOUND OF DROPPING TRAYS and a PIERCING SCREAM. All look in the direction of another door across the room. THE DOOR - FULL SHOT It bursts inward and Mrs. W
All stare o.s., Hillyer with the carving knife clasped in his hand. CORRIDOR THROUGH DOORWAY - FULL SHOT We see the figure of a man approaching, a black silhouette against the pale glow at the end of the passage. He is bent with exhaustion and sways as he
to speak of him). At this instant he is in a sorry state. His clothing is tattered and dirty, his face pale, bruised and scratched and his eyes glazed with fatigue. For a moment he hesitates as if dazzled by the light and then takes another swaying step into the room.
a frantic glance at Dr. Hillyer back at the table. The Time Traveller, however, moves forward under his own power. TIME TRAVELLER I'm all right...just some food. and a drink. He reaches the table and sinks into his chair. With trembling hands Bridewell tries to p
Meanwhile, Mrs. Watchett hovers over the Time Traveller like a mother hen. MRS. WATCHETT (half apology, half concern) I didn't recognize you!...it was so dark. The CAMERA MOVES IN as she dishes up a bowl of soup for him, but he pushes it away. TIME TRA
Well, can't you speak, man? What happened to you? Aren't you going to tell us BRIDEWELL Leave him alone, can't you? TIME TRAVELLER (swallowing It's all right. - I want to tell. FILBY It will keep, George. Eat, rest a little. TIME TRAVELLER No! I must tel
together five days ago, the last day of Eighteen Hundred Ninety Nine. Slowly the CAMERA MOVES IN CLOSER while everyone listens so intensely that, aside from the Time Traveller's VOICE, only the TICKING of a pendulum CLOCK is heard SLOWLY DISSOLVE: I
BACK to reveal the LIBRARY. The Time Traveller, wearing casual tweeds and smoking a pipe, sits in his favorite chair behind the Ebony Box. Across from him in another chair sits Dr. Hillyer puffing his cigar. Bridewell and Filby have glasses in their hands -- B
always maintained what this nation needs is a reliable timepiece The Navy needs one. The Army needs one. - For the artillery you know. KEMP (leaning forward) Couldn't do better, George. So that's why you've been in hiding. Clever of you, indeed! FILBY (study
avid interest. FILBY Go on, George.TIME TRAVELLER Now, as you know, the difficulty in explaining the fourth dimension is that it cannot be seen or felt it must be thought of. FILBY If you don't mind, George, would you refresh me on the first three dimensions.
left or right, two dimensions. When I move up and down, three dimensions. (a bright idea lights up his face. At last he can get ahold of the box, but Filby interferes before Dr. Hillyer can get his fingers on it and he has to be satisfied with merely pointing) For instan
forward in his chair. TIME TRAVELLER On the contrary, Doctor! The fourth dimension is as true and as real a dimension as any of the other three. In fact, they couldn't exist without it. DR. HILLYER (enters the SHOT) How do you mean? TIME TRAVELLER Well
LYER (impatiently) All right! But what's in that box? TIME TRAVELLER I'm coming to that. But first, consider! Why is it that we usually ignore the fourth dimension? Because we have no freedom to move in it. We can move in the other three -- up, down, forwa
understand. TIME TRAVELLER Look! There are a lot of things in the world you don't understand, aren't there? KEMP Of course! Quite a number. TIME TRAVELLER But you don't refuse to believe in them because of that? KEMP Not if I can see the proof with my
se at its lightness, and takes it to the Time Traveller. George opens it with great care and brings forth a mechanical device TIME TRAVELLER I've told you. The larger model can carry a passenger on a journey through Time. - Not through Space, mind you, but th
LER That's the most important question to which I hope to find an answer. Can Man control his destiny? Can he change the shape of things to come? TIME TRAVELLER'S VOICE Imagine that this cigar is the Time Traveller. Now, this lever in front of him controls
lose my model forever. That is why I need witnesses.They look at each other, uncertain whether he is joking or not. Bridewell stoops with difficulty to examine the table. KEMP go ahead. TIME TRAVELLER You're ready then? Despite disbelief, there is a tense siler
HUM is heard. CLOSE ON THE MEN - LOW ANGLE The men stare in fascination as the CAMERA PANS and the HUMMING INCREASES. INSERT: GLASSES - CHANDELIER - VASE The glasses on the silver tray rattle and clink against each other. The gas lights of
SHRIEK and STOPS abruptly. BACK TO CLOSE ON MEN - LOW ANGLE The sudden silence is almost unbearable. They stare at the empty table. The CAMERA PANS. DR. HILLYER (touches his cigar pocket) I'll be damned! TIME TRAVELLER (almost to himself)
slowly turns to the Time Traveller. DR. HILLYER Where did it go? TIME TRAVELLER (recovering) Go? Nowhere in the usual sense. It's still here.(indicating space where the Machine stood) But it's no longer in the present. It's traveling through time - to the futur
31st, 1899, while the model you saw is perhaps a hundred years away. This room, or even this house, may no longer exist a hundred years from now. But the Time Machine is occupying the same space it did a moment before it went off on its journey. Dr. Hillyer r
ER (getting angry) Space is space! It doesn't change!The same space that is here now should be here a hundred or even a thousand years from now. TIME TRAVELLER No! Time changes space. This flat ground we're standing on now could have been at the botto
For my part, I intend to take a journey into the future. - Unless someone else prefers to volunteer. There is no response.BRIDEWELL (chuckling)I say, George. Suppose you go off and get lost in the fiftieth century! How will you find your way back? TIME TRAVELL
a number of ways of doing a disappearing trick! But a man of your ability should not bother with such nonsense. CLOSE ON DR. HILLIER - MOVING SHOT He gets up from his chair. DR. HILLYER (unable to resist the temptation for sarcasm) There's a war on, yo
in the b.g.TIME TRAVELLER (looks up at Filby) What do you think? FILBY (hesitating slightly, and then) I think Dr. Hillyer has a point, George. Lazily the Time Traveller toys with the lid of the Ebony Box, then closes it with a SNAP. He looks up and nods. DR. HII
Machine disappeared. BRIDEWELL (concerned) Are you all right, George? TIME TRAVELLER Of course, I am. DR. HILLYER'S VOICE Coming, Bridewell? Reluctantly Bridewell leaves the library followed by the Time Traveller. INT. ENTRANCE HALL - FULL SHOT
Year. - Goodbye, George -Happy Twentieth Century. - Etc. Bridewell clasps the Time Traveller's shoulder, reassuringly. EXT. COTTAGE - LONG SHOT - (DUSK) - (MATTE) In contrast to the previous SHOT this is a snow- less wintery day. The visitors are boarding t
THE CARRIAGE As it pulls away, Bridewell leans out, waving. From the opposite direction another carriage full of NOISY YOUNG PEOPLE THUNDERS by. In early New Year's Eve REVELRY they TOOT their toy HORNS at the Time Traveller. BACK TO THE TIME TR
picks it up. INSERT: NEWSPAPER A ROLL OF DRUMS in military fashion ACCENTS the headline that the Boer Army has won another victory. CLOSE ON TIME TRAVELLER He closes his eyes and, added to the DRUMS, we HEAR the call to battle by a DISTANT B
even in the darkness WE CAN OBSERVE that he is an angry man. He strikes a match and lights the overhead gas fixture. The light comes up and the MUSIC STOPS as he stares across the room to see: FILBY - MED. SHOT sitting in a chair near the fireplace. FILB
goes to the fireplace and stirs the coals. The CAMERA FOLLOWS TIME TRAVELLER I appreciate your gesture, David, but if you don't mind I'd ratheryou left me alone. FILBY You have changed, George. Enormously. TIME TRAVELLER I'm sorry. FILBY (looks up to
for the time I was born into. - It seems people aren't dying fast enough these days. They call upon science to invent new, more efficient weapons to depopulate the earth. FILBY I quite agree with you. But herewe are and we have to make the best of it. TIME TRA
TRAVELLER You saw the experiment this afternoon, didn't you? FILBYI saw a toy machine vanish. But I'm certain there are a number of ways of doing that trick. Any magician at the Hippodrome could probably do it. TIME TRAVELLER (angrily) It was no trick!
life. (and then) George, I speak to you as a friend. More, as a brother. If that machine can do what you say it can...destroy it. Destroy it, George, before it destroys you. Distant SOUNDS of NEW YEAR'S CELEBRATIONS are HEARD: TIME TRAVELLER You must ha
the old century out by myself.FILBY (rising) Have it your own way. He goes to the door. AT THE DOOR Filby stops, then turns around.FILBY Will you promise me that you won't leave the house tonight? TIME TRAVELLER I promise you, I won't walk out of the door
others with you? FILBY (with a warm smile) Whatever you say, George. - Happy New Year. TIME TRAVELLER (shaking hands) And a very happy New Year to you, David.Filby pats his arm before he leaves. The Time Traveller stands there until he hears the FRO
dinner engagement. At this point Mrs. Watchett, with his velvet smoking jacket over her arm, appears in the doorway and walks up to him. MRS. WATCHETT Will you be having supper in this evening, sir? TIME TRAVELLER (while ex-changing jackets with Mrs. W
turns to go as the Time Traveller calls after her. TIME TRAVELLER Oh, Mrs. Watchett! (as she responds) I've invited Mr. Filby and the others to dinner next Friday.(and then) Happy New Year, Mrs. Watchett. MRS. WATCHETT Happy New Year, sir. Mrs. Watchett
the old calendar with the new one. Then, he hastily scribbles a note which he puts into an envelope and places it prominently on the table. He rises and mounts the steps that lead to: INT. CORRIDOR - MOVING SHOT The Time Traveller walks slowly toward a close
a greenhouse. Only a few potted plants remain. The glass walls are obscured from view from the garden by rows of tall growing plants. Only the glass skylight is clear. Thick, dark, low-hanging clouds are passing beneath the moon, dimming its light and leaving
Machine. It is a duplicate of the miniature model already seen.However, its size gives it a majestic quality. Nickel, ivory and crystalline quartz gleam and sparkle. While the miniature possessed a delicate, appealing note, the full size Machine has an ominous loo
Here a crystalline lever is attached to a polishing buffer.The Time Traveller sets it in motion, polishing the crystal lever until its rough edges disappear and it sparkles like a fine cut diamond. As he works, his lips purse and he softly STARTS TO WHISTLE the mela
that his settling himself into the saddle is any more than aroutine position he has taken before to work on the Machine.Then he leans back in the saddle and gazes up at: INSERT: SKYLIGHT - (STOP MOTION OR ANIMATION) Passing clouds. BACK TO TIME TRAV
THE CONTROL PANEL The luminous dials show: "31 December 1899." The meters and indicators start to BUZZ and whirl. The glow increases.BACK TO TIME TRAVELLER His expression is taut as he looks around, then down to the control panel. TIME TRAVELLE
As he starts to look up and around, slowly. TIME TRAVELLER'S VOICE- I stopped.WHAT HE SEES - MOVING SHOT Starting at the WINDOW with frost around the edges and icicles outside, we move around the room PASSING THE WORKBENCH over to the DOOR. D
said 9:31 when I started and now it was 11:09...and the candle, shorter by inches.BACK TO TIME TRAVELLER He looks amazed, then pulls his old fashioned watch from his pocket by its gold chain. It flips open showing almost "9:32." TIME TRAVELLER'S VOICE A
of the candle flickers with the speed of a bee's wing, melting the candle down. The CAMERA MOVES to the window where the frost has spread and the icicles continue to grow.Light comes up behind so that the crystals glitter like gems and the sun starts to rise. TIM
SKYLIGHT - MED. SHOT - (STOP MOTION OR ANIMATION) As the sun arches majestically. TIME TRAVELLER'S VOICE arc in less than a minute... INSERT: POT OF FLOWERS - (STOCK AND/OR STOP MOTION) As they close. TIME TRAVELLER'S VOICE to see flow
Watchett leaps into the garden, pauses the briefest instant to sprinkle the flowers, then with the speed of wind streaks away. BACK TO TIME TRAVELLER A trace of a smile, then apprehension. TIME TRAVELLER'S VOICE And as yet I was travelling very slowly!
TIME TRAVELLER As he looks up. INSERT OF SKYLIGHT - (STOP MOTION OR ANIMATION) The sun soars across the sky, night falls. Pin points of stars streak by and dawn comes. The sun is chased by the stars again and again. Faster and faster. VERY CLOSE
or icicles. The snow has disappeared, replaced by the lush green of Spring.While the vines of a morning Glory grow up and around the window like a snake and the flowers open and close, we see the following through repeated fast flashes. The sun hops swiftly ac
TIME TRAVELLER Quick flashes of lightning on the Time Traveller's face followed by a series of SHORT THUNDERCLAPS. TIME TRAVELLER'S VOICE It became intoxicating. To see an entire storm in a few seconds. So I pushed the lever on toward even greater spe
-- the moon passing through its phases and the sun shifting its position with the seasons. BRANCHES - CLOSE SHOT - (ANIMATION) Leaves grow quickly. Flowers appear and turn into small green apples. Growing larger, they turn red and fall. The leaves gradual
now green; they spread, shiver and pass away. Snow flashes across the country, vanishes and is followed by the brief bright green of Spring.TIME TRAVELLER'S VOICE Thirteen years had passed...fourteen fifteen...sixteen...and then...Gradually soot, dirt and gri
VOICE In the year nineteen hundred seventeen...I stopped. The flickering of passing days and nights slows and the HUMMING SOUND GRADUALLY DIMINISHES. The dial stops on "13 September 1917". TIME TRAVELLER - MED. SHOT The CAMERA PULLS BACK
door. Dust falls as he opens it and enters the corridor. INT. LIBRARY The dim light and the protective sheets covering the furnishings previously seen, lend the room a ghostly appearance. Tilted paintings reveal faded spots on the walls and the dust is inches thic
his once prized possessions. There is NO TICKING now. The hands of the clocks, each pair indicating a different time, seem to guard the past. CLOSE ON TIME TRAVELLER - MOVING SHOT Curiosity takes the Time Traveller from the library, through the ENTRANC
of daylight illuminates the dusty interior. The Time Traveller moves into the open driveway that is now taken over by weeds. EXT. COTTAGE - LONG SHOT - DAY The Time Traveller takes a deep breath and looks curiously around. Everything is overgrown with vi
ve geographical movement. For instance, the sharp curve of the River Thames in the distance will remain even after the house itself has disappeared.) CLOSE ON TIME TRAVELLER Suddenly the SOUND OF AN APPROACHING ENGINE catches his attention. He loo
dressed for the period, is in the window. The driver, in the uniform of a Second Lieutenant of the First World War, steps out of the car. The Time Traveller walks over to see his old friend, sans moustache. TWO SHOT TIME TRAVELLER (glibly) Going to a masquer
was a remarkable resemblance. - I'm James Filby. TIME TRAVELLER Was? JAMES FILBY Were you a friend of father's? TIME TRAVELLER Yes...yes...I've been away. JAMES FILBY He was killed in the war...a year ago. TIME TRAVELLER (aghast) No!...It can't be
even go inside. TIME TRAVELLER Why is that? JAMES FILBY My father was executor of the inventor's estate and he refused to liquidate it. (adds with a smile) I often chided him on that account, but he felt positive that the owner would return some day. - Some
front, sir? TIME TRAVELLER Front? What front? JAMES FILBY Why the war, of course. TIME TRAVELLER What war? JAMES FILBY Great heavens, man, don't you know we've been at war with Germany since nineteen fourteen? I thought perhaps you had see
(hesitantly) Then...goodbye, sir. The Time Traveller nods and James Filby slowly turns and, glancing back repeatedly, enters the Department Store. CLOSE ON TIME TRAVELLER 97 He speaks almost to himself. TIME TRAVELLER Goodbye, Jaime. With the bitte
(STOCK AND ANIMATION) ACCENT on MUSIC, then as the HUMMING OF THE TIME MACHINE takes over, suddenly panes of GLASS BREAK one after another, giving a clear view of a sky full of SWIRLIING TURBULENT CLOUDS. DISSOLVE TO: CLOSE ON TIME T
hour, or even for a second to observe, then go ahead for a year or two. - Thus I was able to see the changing world in a series of glimpses. Something catches his interest. He pulls back the lever to SLOW DOWN. EXT. STREET - FULL SHOT - (NIGHT) - (STOP MOTI
A distant CLOCK STRIKES ELEVEN. BACK TO TIME TRAVELLER Speaks surprised.TIME TRAVELLER Good heavens, that's a dress? MANNEQUIN - MED. SHOT From her pretty face with the funny hat, the CAMERA PANS DOWN to the hem line of her skirt, twelv
SHOT - (DAYS & NIGHTS) (ANIMATION) As the years speed by INTERRUPTED BY SHORT BLURS, the dresses of the mannequin change. The skirts get shorter and shorter, then drop inch by inch while the hair styles vary. The bosom appears to swell with the s
LERATED manner. He looks down at the instruments. INSERT OF DIALS Showing the passage of time. October, November December of 1939 and January, February, March, April, May of the year 1940 are peeling off. The instruments vibrate erratically. CLOSE C
The Time Traveller HEARS the SCREAMS of DIVING PLANES. He stops the Machine and looks up at: SKYLIGHT - MED. SHOT - (NIGHT) - (STOCK) Through the panes of broken glass we see a clear but limited glimpse of the night sky that is swept by beams of sea
met earthward, balls of streaking flame and fire. CLOSE ON TIME TRAVELLER Gazing up at the grim spectacle.TIME TRAVELLER'S VOICE The last time I had stopped was in nineteen seventeen, twenty three years ago. And the war with Germany was still wagin
but to prepare even more effective means of destroying one another. I decided to push on into time and see the outcome. He looks down at:INSERT OF DIALS Denoting the movement of the Machine through time. The dials spin from 1940 to 1959 where the HUMI
- FULL SHOT - (DAY) In bikini bathing suit. A car, a 1959 model, passes by. CLOSE ON TIME TRAVELLER Smiling. TIME TRAVELLER'S VOICE It vas reassuring to find that she hadn't changed. Only her costume. Provocative to say the least. I wondered what she
SIREN HOWLS, menacingly. BACK ON TIME TRAVELLER His smile becomes a puzzled stare at what he sees. EXT. STREET IN 1966 - LONG SHOT - (DAY) People are racing along the sidewalk. The SOUND OF MORE DEEP-THROATED SIRENS from all directions co
the doll she has dropped as her FATHER returns from the shelter. He gathers her up in his arms and rushes back to safety. In a few seconds the streets are deserted. TIME MACHINE AT EDGE OF PARK - FULL SHOT The Time Traveller gets out and looks arour
below. Meanwhile, through a loudspeaker o.s., a melodious SYMPHONY ORCHESTRA is heard softly, until a BURST OF CHORDS attracts the Time Traveller's attention. EXT. STORE WINDOW - FULL SHOT A TELEVISION CABINET on display. The set isoperating
and the doors fly wide open. He stops startled, looking about to see who opened them. Seeing no one, he starts slowly forward. INT. DEPARTMENT STORE - LONG SHOT From the TV set BLARES MUSIC that gradually becomes the UNDERSCORE for the SCENE. T
FOOTSTEPS. He looks off. REVERSE SHOT Coming from the office is THE WARDEN, dressed in a plastic suit. He also wears an armband and a white crash helmet, both bearing the insignia of "Civilian Defense." MUMBLES are heard from beneath his mask as th
thing. Makes more noise than it does sense TIME TRAVELLER (recognizing him) Filby!WARDEN My name is Mister Filby. - Didn't you hear the air raid siren? TIME TRAVELLER You mean that horrible screeching? WARDEN It wasn't constructed for its aestheti
on, young man. We'd better be going before the mushrooms start sprouting. (looks at Time Traveller with renewed interest) You do look familiar. Haven't we met somewhere before? TIME TRAVELLER Indeed we have. Right here. Many years ago. WARDEN I w
ble. You haven't changed. You're not a day older. And your clothes... TIME TRAVELLER I'm afraid it's going to take me a little time to explain... You see... There is an insistent, EAR PIECING SIREN. It lasts for three seconds. WARDEN The last alert... hurry! He g
Hurry! Hide 'til the All Clear! He descends into the air raid shelter. CLOSE ON TIME TRAVELLER - MOVING SHOT He looks puzzled.TIME TRAVELLER All clear? (yells) I've got to talk to you.The Time Traveller looks up as he hears the APPROACHING SIRENS OF
FLASH. He stops and looks startled. VIEW THROUGH THE STREETS - LONG SHOT - (STOCK, MINIATURE, SPLIT) A SATELLITE travels over the city in the distance. The flash is followed by an EXPLOSION and a giant cobalt mushroom begins to rise over the hor
ruins. Only a single, large structure in the f.g. remains standing for a moment, then it also collapses in an instant. TIME TRAVELLER'S VOICE The labor of centuries gone in an instant. The ground shudders with an OMINOUS sound and sudden a great rent appea
IN THE GROUND - (STOCK) The smoke and steam give way to a spluttering of red hot lava which swells slowly at first in a rising tide and then spilling over begins to EXPLODE into the air. BACK ON TIME TRAVELLER The Time Machine is shaken violently, but
ures in the f.g. dissolve into smoke and flame and the upper parts come tumbling down into the rising red flood. Then the incoming rush of the river meets the flowing tide of lava. The two opposite elements, molten rock and cold green water, dwar the ruined c
directly toward the Time Machine. TIME TRAVELLER'S VOICE Then I saw my own danger. I too was to be engulfed! CLOSE ON TIME TRAVELLER As he sees his great peril. TIME TRAVELLER'S VOICE But to go back was unthinkable. He jams the lever forward to
the Machine is permeated with a dull red glow which seems to flow like mist all about the Time Traveller. TIME TRAVELLER'S VOICE Only my speed through time saved me from being roasted alive and encased in stone forever. INSERT OF DIALS They are spir
prayed...wondering how many centuries, how many eons must pass before the wind and rain could wear away the mountain that enclosed me. In the pitch darkness there are only the sounds of the HUMMING TIME MACHINE and the SLOW LABORED BREATH
DIALS They roll very fast. We can distinguish only the passing of years -- 70,000...80,000...90,000.100,000. Then the matchlight flickers and goes out leaving only the dial's own faint glow. BACK ON TIME TRAVELLER Once again there is darkness and the MON
HIGH PITCHED HUMMING INCREASES TIME TRAVELLER'S VOICE The centuries rolled by. - I put my trust in time and waited for the rock to wear down around me. A white light from above begins to permeate the dark- ness. The Time Traveller looks up, his fa
sunlight returns. The Machine is now finally entirely above ground, the only distinct object in the whirling transparent landscape. EXT. TIME TRAVELLER - CLOSE SHOT As he smiles gratefully up at the sky. TIME TRAVELLER'S VOICE I was free again! There
wars! - Had man finally learned to control both the elements and themselves? - I had to stop and find out. TIME TRAVELLER - MED. SHOT As he eagerly pulls hard on the lever, the HUMMING DECREASES and the dial freezes on: "23 November 802,701". THERE
Thick mist eddies about his face, undulating dreamily, revealing enough to see that he is unconscious. Blood seeps from a gash across his forehead. He dazedly opens his eyes to find that he is gazing across the dewey, green turf. Then he looks up. EXT. THE SP
weeping birch tree barely touches its outspread wings.THE TIME TRAVELLER - MED. SHOT He shakes the cobwebs out of his head and, FOLLOWED BY THE CAMERA, rises with difficulty. Still half- dazed he presses a handkerchief to his temple, as he loosens h
have been a temple. Vines mat the ancient walls, seemingly holding them together. BACK TO TIME TRAVELLER He smiles. TIME TRAVELLER (to himself) At last I've found a Paradise. He starts off toward the building WHISTLING his favorite tune. "The Land
completely and more bountiful than ever before.VARIETY OF FLOWERS - MOVING SHOT The CAMERA PANS under boughs laden with orchids and a multitude of other gorgeous blossoms. TIME TRAVELLER'S VOICE Flowers everywhere... the whole landscape one
red and broken with age. TIME TRAVELLER'S VOICE (surprised) Unrepaired for centuries! Maybe unlived in for as long.(then) It would be no Paradise if it belonged to me alone. INT. ENTRANCE - MED. SHOT Shooting through the ARCHWAY we see the Time T
streams through windows where half the panes of stained glass are broken. Faded curtains droop in dusty folds along the walls, and at random about the floor are low tables, some heavily fractured, loaded with bowls of fruit. His FOOTSTEPS ECHO through the
leaves. At considerable distance upstream, the PEOPLE OF THE FUTURE are swimming in a natural pool and sunning themselves on a beach of white sand. They are small, but delicately formed. Their grace and beauty fits perfectly into this splendid new world.
sens her robe which drifts to the sand and she dives deep into the crystal water. CLOSE ON TIME TRAVELLER He smiles philosophically and leans back against a tree trunk, watching the distant swimmers, reassured. TIME TRAVELLER (musingly, to himself) S
LY. The other people turn their heads toward her, but make no move to help. CLOSE ON GIRL She has caught a ledge of rock and clings. Two little men, their bare feet dangling in the water, sit nearby but ignore the Girl's plight. TIME TRAVELLER - MOVING SH
ting go.TIME TRAVELLER - MOVING SHOT Reaching the ledge, he pushes past the people nearby and grasps the Girl's wrist just as her fingers slip. Quickly, he pulls her out of the river's turbulent current and lifts her up in his arms. GIRL - EXTREME CLOSE U
YOUNG MAN and the MAN IN WHITE. They return the Time Traveller's look of scorn with pleasant smiles as if they do not know the meaning of a mean look. TIME TRAVELLER & GIRL - EXTREME CLOSE, MOVING SHOT The CAMERA FOLLOWS him as he str
without a word, walks away. The Time Traveller stares after her in astonishment. The disconcerned people, now all dressed in multi- colored robes, are leaving the pool. They walk past the Time Traveller as though he was a part of the scenery, merely adding t
the steps to see if any will turn back to either welcome him or resent his intrusion, but they move on with lack of interest, completely. He sits down on the steps, thoroughly perplexed at this utter indifference TIME TRAVELLER - MED. SHOT THE GIRL Why did
you drown. Not one of them so much as lifted a finger. (shakes his head) A curious attitude - in a curious world.(a pause, then a smile) Aren't you the least bit interested in what I am...where I come from? THE GIRL (innocently) Should I be? TIME TRAVELLE
The Girl makes no reply. Instead she gazes off at the sun which is low in the heavens. Shadows have already fallen over the distant hills. TIME TRAVELLER What's your name? THE GIRL Weena. TIME TRAVELLER How do you spell that? WEENA Spell? TIME
INSERT OF DUST The stick now writes in the dust: " E L O I " BACK TO SCENE A shadow crosses her face. Suddenly she springs to her feet, concerned. WEENA Come. We must go in. TIME TRAVELLER (rising) Why? What's wrong? WEENA (anxiously) It is ge
branches with his free hand. After he passes one of the bushes, a white indistinct creature dashes out of it and disappears in the darkness. TIME TRAVELLER - MOVING SHOT He straightens slowly, his eyes narrowed. Nervously he looks around, then steps o
SHOT - THE TIME TRAVELLER He pauses momentarily against Rock Wall. He sees Eloi, apparently too confused to move. TIME TRAVELLER Weena! Go on! Go on the steps! CLOSE SHOT - AT ROCK - WEENA AND YOUNG MAN Weena spots the still flickering t
Time Traveller with his Machine FADING, leaving the present. Then the CAMERA MOVES ACROSS the workbench to the corner where we last saw the Time Machine. It is not there! The CAMERA WHIPS to the other corner. Nor is it there! A few sheets of paper

it becomes clearly visible, then drifts off as though moving in some huge orbit. Next an HOURGLASS floats in from the left of the screen. The faint HISSING OF RUNNING SAND breaks the stillness of space. As the hourglass glides across the screen, it is met by a GREEK WATER
es continues to MOUNT. A FIGURE wheels past, with the face of a clock and the body carved like a drummer of the 14th century, BEATING the hour. A SMALL CLOCK bears a golden angel with hammer in hands as it STRIKES A BELL. ANOTHER TIMEPIECE, with CHIMES, floats
EME of the picture, "The Land Of The Leal". Simultaneously, the screen reveals the MAIN TITLE: THE TIME MACHINE "THE LAND OF THE LEAL" FADE IN: EXT. COTTAGE - LONG SHOT - (NIGHT) - (MATTE) Warm lights pour through the windows, spreading over the snow-pat-
re hurries up to the front door and KNOCKS on it impatiently. AT THE DOOR The knock is answered by MRS. WATCHETT, the housekeeper, a thin, tense woman with iron gray hair. The CAMERA ENTERS the HALL with DAVID FILBY, anamiable red-haired young man of sc ence,
occupants for the two empty chairs. The silence is accentuated by the merry CRACKLING of logs in the fireplace and the capricious TICKING of innumerable timepieces about the room. Filby enters, pauses to glance down, then embarrassedly takes his chair. SERIES OF CLOSE
lifting his glass of whiskey. WALTER KEMP, a middle aged man with keen black piercing eyes, angrily chews onhis Havana.Filby fidgets uncomfortably in his chair as Hillyer glances impatiently at his watch, comparing time with a GRANDFATHER CLOCK behind him, then snap
til the CHIMES, BELLS ETC. FADE away. Dr. Hillyer angrily slaps on the arm of his leather chair. DR. HILLYE I say, this is outright rude of the man! FILBEY He's undoubtedly been detained. That's all. Bridewell, filling his glass, is trying to say some-thing but is interrupted by
esitating. DR. HILLYER Speak up -- what is it, woman? She is taken aback for a moment, then walks over to Filby and hands him the open envelope. He takes his time in extracting the note. BRIDEWELL Well...are we or are we not invited to dinner? FILBY (reading) Apparently
night and left these instructions. (pointing to note) FILBY Thank you, Mrs. Watchett. A faint, nervous smile is her acknowledgement and with that she retreats toward the door. DR. HILLYER (indicating the note) What does it say, Filby? What's wrong? FILBY Nothing really. -
lass down) First sensible thing I've heard all evening. He rises and starts for the dining room. The others follow. FILBY, HILLYER & KEMP - MOVING SHOT As they walk toward the DINING ROOM. FILBY This is peculiar. He is usually very prompt, precise and punctual. DR. HIL-
a glass of wine for himself while the others settle down. This time the chair at the head of the table is conspicuously unoccupied. BRIDWELL (arises, lifting his glass) One thing I will say for George, he keeps the best cellar in the south of England...and Mrs. Watchett is the finest
lying, dashes down the steps panic-stricken into the room. The CAMERA RUSHES with her to the table where the men have come to their feet. Clutching Filby's arm, she points toward the long corridor now revealed by the open door. MRS. WATCHETT (frightened) There!...there.
mping. The man comes closer, his features still blacked out by shadows, but as he nears the doorway, the light from the room strikes first his legs, then his body and finally his face. Here he stops. This is our first meeting with the TIME TRAVELLER (for so it will be convenient
EWELL - MOVING SHOT They come to life. Bridewell, noticing the glass of wine still in his hand, quickly gulps it down before rushing with Filby toward the Time Traveller FILBY Good lord! - What's happened? Reaching him, each seizes an elbow to support him. Bridewell throws
f wine, spilling most of it over the tablecloth. The Time Traveller looks up at him with a wry smile. TIME TRAVELLER Are you all right? A stunned Bridewell is unable to speak while the Time Traveller empties his glass. BRIDEWELL (a delayed answer) Of course. I'm...all right.
m hungry for meat! Mrs. Watchett grasps the carving knife from Dr. Hillyer and, with a single slash, cuts off a huge portion of beef and loads it onto his plate. GROUPSHOT The Time Traveller eats, the men watching him curiously. Finally Dr. Hillyer leans forward. DR. HILLYER
ill remember. FILBY Relax, try to relax a bit. You've all the time in the world. CLOSE ON THE TIME TRAVELLER As he looks up, amused. TIME TRAVELLER You're right, David. (almost to himself) That's exactly what I have. All the time in the world!. ever since we were all
ON TABLE - CLOSE SHOT (AFTERNOON) (NOTE: The Slow Dissolve from the previous shot should give the effect of the Ebony Box emerging from the Time Traveller's brain.) TIME TRAVELLER'S VOICE There in that box rests the result of two years' labor. The CAMERA DRAWS
are looking at the box TIME TRAVELLER (continues) I wanted to finish the job before the new century began. - I barely made it. BRIDEWELL Marvelous. DR. HILLYER (stands up) What is it? TIME TRAVELLER Well, it has to do with time. DR. HILLYER (steps to box) I've
veller's reaction) I don't believe George is referring to a new kind of timepiece TIME TRAVELLER When I speak of time, I'm referring to the fourth dimension. A perplexed look comes over Bridewell's face.Dr. Hillyer registers concern. Kemp looks troubled. Only Filby expresses
lly, Filby, they must have taught you something at school! BRIDEWELL (baiting Dr. Hillyer) Suppose you explain it, Doctor. DR. HILLYER Certainly! (he demonstrates pompously) When I move in a straight line, forward or backward, that's one dimension. - When I move to the
ree dimensions: length, breadth, and height. BRIDEWELL (amazed) Well, then, what's the fourth dimension? DR. HILLYER Well, that's...that's mere theory! No one can really say what the fourth dimension is or even that it exists. THE TIME TRAVELLER - MED. SHOT Leaning
has the first three dimensions, as you said. But what if it didn't exist in Time? It wouldn't exist at all, would it? DR. HILLYER No. TIME TRAVELLER So - for an object to exist at all, it must exist in the fourth dimension....and that fourth dimension is duration....Time! DR. HIL-
ways. But when it comes to Time, we are prisoners. Do you follow me, Anthony? GROUP SHOT In the f.g., Bridewell who has been sitting with a glazed, dreamy look, suddenly jumps. KEMP George! You've given a most lucid explanation and all that! But I don't think I entirely
TRAVELLER Good! All I'm asking you to do now is to witness a demonstration of the possibility of movement in the fourth dimension. (to Dr. Hillyer) Philip, will you please hand me that box? All eyes turn to Dr. Hillyer as he eagerly rushes to the table, lifts the box with surpri-
EWELL Oh, I say George! If you start floating around in the future, aren't you likely to mess things up for the rest of us? DR. HILLYER The future is already there. It's irrevocable and cannot be changed. CLOSE ON TIME TRAVELLER He answers thoughtfully. TIME TRAVEL-
rd pressure sends the Machine into the future, backward pressure into the past. And the harder the pressure the faster the Machine travels. GROUPSHOT - LOW ANGLE All eyebrows are raised. TIME TRAVELLER This experiment can be performed only once. If it succeeds, I
finger on the lever. Then he pauses. TIME TRAVELLER Doctor Hillyer, would you care to lend me your hand? Dr. Hillyer extends his hand hesitantly, smiling weakly. INSERT OF MODEL Using Dr. Hillyer's forefinger, the Time Traveller presses the lever forward. A LOW-PITCHED
cker rapidly. A vase shudders and moves slightly o the mantel INSERT OF MODEL As the vibration increases, the outline of the model is blurred and gradually becomes transparent, until the Machine with the cigar has vanished utterly. The HUMMING HAS REACHED A HIGH
wallows. Bridewell, with his mouth open, stares at the table. Now he looks at the glass of champagne in his hand and places it on the mantelpiece as far out of reach as he can. Then, suddenly reversing his decision, he retrieves the glass and gulps it down. TWO SHOT Dr. Hillyer
R. HILLYER Do you seriously expect us to believe that? TIME TRAVELLER Certainly. DR. HILLYER But you just said it hasn't really moved. TIME TRAVELLER That's correct. DR. HILLYER Then why can't we see it? TIME TRAVELLER Because we're in this room on December
the top of the table. DR. HILLYER (exasperated) If it occupies the same space, I should be able to feel it. TIME TRAVELLER You must remember that the space you've just put your hand through is today's space. You can't put your hand into the space of tomorrow. DR. HILLY-
lion years ago. And a million years from now it could be the interior of a huge mountain. Dr. Hillyer turns away, speechless. GROUP SHOT Kemp steps forward. KEMP Suppose what you say is true. Exactly what do you suggest we do with such a contraption? TIME TRAVELLER
) That's a calculated risk I'm prepared to take. Dr. Hillyer, having controlled his fury, now exchanges significant glances with Kemp and turns back with an air of reasonableness. DR. HILLYER Now listen, George! I don't know what you take us for, but we're not fools. There are
are putting up a pretty stiff fight in South Africa and our country needs inventors like you. I can put you in touch with the War Office if you wish. He walks over to the Time Traveller who is sitting near the table on which stands the empty Ebony Box with its lid open. Filby is
being sensible. I'll take care of it first thing in the New Year. BACK TO GROUP SHOT Everyone rises. DR. HILLYER Well, time to go. KEMP Yes, we all have our plans fo tonight. Dr. Hillyer and Kemp head toward the door. Bridewell lingers at the table where the model of the Time
ut on their capes, overcoats, scarfs, gloves and hats, preparing for the cold weather outside, the Time Traveller steps to the door and grasps the handle. TIME TRAVELLER Thanks for coming. He opens the door and they file past him, Bridewell at the rear. AD LIBS Happy New
waits them in the drive. DR. HILLYER Come on, Bridewell. Bridewell glances back to the Time Traveller, then submits and, with a CRACK OF A WHIP, the carriage moves off. EXT. ENTRANCE - FULL SHOT The Time Traveller, a silhouette framed in the door way, waves to them.
dful of their salutations he turns and enters the cottage. INT. ENTRANCE HALL - MED SHOT The Time Traveller slowly closes the door and leans his back against it, staring into space. Thinking. - He spots a newspaper on a nearby table, apparently left by one of his guests, and
BRASS, FIFES and HORNS join the BUGLE and DRUMS to take up a MILITANT OVERTURE. He loosens his collar, then with sudden resolution strides toward OMITTED INT. LIBRARY - LONG SHOT The Time Traveller crosses to his writing table in the f.g. He stands there and
ter stay. TIME TRAVELLER'S VOICE You needn't have troubled yourself I'm all right. FILBY No you're not. - You've been behaving oddly for over a month now. (and then) I'm not leaving until you tell me what's on your mind.TIME TRAVELLER - MED. SHOT Deep in thought, he
you answer me one question honestly? TIME TRAVELLER I'll try. FILBY Why this preoccupation with Time? TIME TRAVELLER (sharply) Why not? FILBY Don't go simple on me, George! TIME TRAVELLER (a beat, then calmly) If you want to know the truth, I don't much care
have to. I don't. FILBY (making a half- hearted attempt at levity) All right. Take a journey on your contraption. What would you become? A Greek? A Roman? One of the Pharaohs? TIME TRAVELLER I prefer the future. FILBY You're not seriously saying you can do it? TIME
o see the full-scale model? FILBY No, I would not! I have no desire to tempt the laws of Providence and I don't think you should. It's notfor man to trifle with. TIME TRAVELLER Now you sound like Hillyer and Kemp.FILBY There is something in their common sense attitude to
ear's Eve. Don't let me keep you. FILBY Mary isn't well. We decided to stay home with the baby. But why don't you come home with me. You haven't seen little Jaime for a long time.TIME TRAVELLER I can't. FILBY What's stopping you? TIME TRAVELLER I just want to see
led by this strange promise, turns to go as the Time Traveller puts down the poker and steps up to him.TIME TRAVELLER David! Please don't think me unfriendly! - Come over to dinner next Friday. Won't you? FILBY Very well. TIME TRAVELLER Fine...and will you bring the
hen, FOLLOWED BY THE CAMERA, he goes to the writing table and sits down. AT THE WRITING TABLE The Time Traveller opens a drawer and takes out the new calendar that reads: "1900, Welcome New Century. "He flips a few pages to find the next Friday and jots down the
on't think so, Mrs. Watchett. Why don't you take the evening off and celebrate. MRS. WATCHETT Thank you, sir, but if you won't be needing me I think I'll turn in early and get some sleep (indicating revelers outside) If I can. - Goodnight, sir. TIME TRAVELLER Goodnight. She
oor after her. Once again the Time Traveller is alone. He looks at the old calendar that reads: "December 31. 1899," rips the final sheet from the pad, crumples it into a tight little ball and tosses it into the hearth where it burns. With slow and deliberate movements he replaces
of the passageway. Here he pauses momentarily, removes the key from his pocket, unlocks the door, then slowly swings it open as the MUSIC STARTS the THEME of the picture. INT. LABORATORY - FULL SHOT - (NIGHT) The laboratory has the appearance of having once been
e of dark shadows. As the slow moving clouds pass overhead, a shaft of moonlight seeps through and we SEE workbenches, numerous tools, sheets of drawings and scientific instruments situated around the perimeter. But the most conspicuous object in the room is the Time
noonlight seems to render it alive and give it the power of movement. CLOSE ON TIME TRAVELLER - MOVING SHOT Staring at the Machine, hypnotized by his own crafts- manship, he locks the door with accustomed movement, then crosses to a workbench and lights a candle.
"The Land Of The Leal." A clock near him on the workbench reads: "9:30." Satisfied with the buffing, he removes the gleaming handle and crosses to the Machine. He settles into the saddle and affixes the crystalline lever. There is no sign of urgency in his movements to betray
wards for several moments. Then his hand slowly reaches forth and his fingers encircle the lever. - Gently he urges it forward. A HUMMING SOUND, similar to the one made by the model, but MORE RESONANT starts and a soft glow wells up from within the Machine. INSERT:
d...and the laboratory grew faint around me... INSERT OF PANEL The figures spin, the needles vibrate. Then almost at once the Time Traveller's hand reaches for the lever and jerks it over to halt the Machine. The HUMMING LESSENS and FADES. BACK TO TIME TRAVELLER
R the: TIME TRAVELLER'S VOICE No change; everything exactly as it bad been before. - But no! THE CAMERA SWINGS BACK TO THE WORKBENCH, CLOSE, where the clock now shows "11:09" and the candle has burned shorter. TIME TRAVELLER'S VOICE (excited) The clock
h which was in the machine with me, only a few seconds had passed. Pleased, he puts his watch away and reaches for the lever, looking off toward the: WORKBENCH - (ANIMATION) The HUMMING SOUND STARTS again and, while the hands of the clock circle the dial, the flame
THE MACHINE - MED. SHOT The rays of the early Morning sun slide down the lab-oratory wall and sweep across the Time Traveller and his Machine. A trace of a smile -- and then, he looks up and squints. TIME TRAVELLER'S VOICE It was disconcerting to see the sun INSERT:
yes for the night, changes that normally took hours, occuring in seconds, was beautiful. During this it has turned into night and a little SNAIL rushes across the ground beneath the plant, and thenthe flowers start to open again. Light begins to flood the scene. In the b.g. Mrs.
t if I went faster?! His hand shoves the lever farther over toward the future position. THE HUMMING SOUND RISES TO HIGHER PITCH. The Time Traveller lurches in his seat, clings to the controls and looks at the dials. INSERT: CLOSE ON DIALS They are spinning. BACK TO
LER His eyes gleam with a mad light, half pleasure, half pain. His face is illuminated by the alternatingflashes of light, each one indicating the passage of another day. He turns toward the: WINDOW - FULL SHOT - (ANIMATION, STOP MOTION & STOCK) Without a trace of frost
night falls and the stars circle the North Star The sun appears and disappears be-)hind the whirling clouds. At night the moon races through tumultuous clouds. On the following day the sky darkens with thunderheads. There is a cataract of lightning and THUNDER. BACK ON
ater pressure on the lever. The HUMMING INCREASES. The alternate flashes of light become a flicker almost too fast for the eye to follow. EXT. TREE IN GARDEN - FULL SHOT - (ANIMATION) Its shadows, cast by the sun and the moon, dance around the trunk, faster and faster
nd disappear. Suddenly the bare branches are covered with snow for a few seconds, then again burst into green leaves and blossoms. EXT. DISTANT HILLSIDE - FULL SHOT - (ANIMATION) through the window we see the trees grow and change like puffs of vapor -- now brown,
the windows from the outside and darkness prevails. CLOSE ON TIME TRAVELLER His brow is beaded with perspiration. Alarmed,he grabs the handle of the Time Machine. INSERT: THE DIALS The hand of the Time Traveller quickly pulls back the lever. TIME TRAVELLER'S
his Machine and glances with astonishment around the interior of the laboratory. The once clear windows are now dirty and boarded up. The world outside is completely obscured from view. Only faint light penetrating cracks indicates that it is day outdoors. He crosses to the
n the dining room seen in the b.g. Cobwebs are everywhere. The floor SQUEAKS on every footfall as the Time Traveller, coming down the steps from the corridor, enters the room and looks about. THE SHELVES - TIME TRAVELLER'S P.O.V. Among his books still rest the clocks,
t door. It refuses to respond to his attempt to open it. Even when he uses his shoulder it does not budge. He steps back and flings his full weight against it and with a WRENCHING SOUND it gives slightly. Under continued pressure the nailed boards outside give way and a flood
he house is boarded up. He starts to wander around, thinking, investigating. (NOTE: The house is situated upon a site with distinctive landmarks that will stay recognizable during his journey into the future, thereby giving a clear conception that time-travelling does not invol-
EXT. ROAD - LONG SHOT - (DAY) Coming up the hill on a narrow dusty road is a car of 1916 vintage, with the HORN HONKING. The CAMERA PANS with it, up to a SMALL STORE across the street. The sign above the entrance reads: "Filby's Department Store". A MANNEQUIN,
ok rather silly without your moustache, old man! FILBY (puzzled) Were you addressing me, sir? TIME TRAVELLER (positively) Filby! I expected more of an enthusiastic greeting from FILBY (smiles as he interrupts) I'm afraid you have me confusedwith my father, sir. There
izes its truth) I'm sorry to hear that. (pause, then hesitantly points) And the gentleman who used to live across the street? JAMES FILBY Oh, him. Some inventor who disappeared around the turn of the century. - If you're interested in that house, forget it. You can't buy it or
s think it's haunted. (stares at Time Traveller curiously, studying the strange cut of his clothes) Who are you, sir? TIME TRAVELLER Just a stranger who once knew your father. JAMES FILBY I see. (still curious at the Time Traveller's abstract attitude) Have you been at the
...or maybe... (noticing confusion, adds with a note of compassion) Perhaps a cup of tea would make you feel better. Won't you come in? TIME TRAVELLER No...no, thank you. JAMES FILBY ou're sure you're alright, sir? TIME TRAVELLER Yes, I'm quite alright. JAMES FILBY
his old friend, David Filby, he slowly walks across the street and returns to the cottage. INT. LABORATORY - FULL SHOT The Time Traveller approaches the Machine, steps up into the seat, throws his head back and grimly shoves the lever forward. SKYLIGHT - FULL SHOT -
ICKERS of days and nights, as well as the HUMMING, INCREASES and DECREASES, in accordance with his manipulation of the controls. Over this: TIME TRAVELLER'S VOICE As I went along, I gained experience in handling the Machine. I found that I could stop for a day, an
of wind, pedestrians streak across the pavement. The bright lights of the night pop out one after another leaving a sparingly illuminated street. The HUMMING SUBSIDES. The mannequin previously seen in the show window now wears the clothing of the "Roaring Twenties".
floor. BACK TO TIME TRAVELLER A smile appears on his face. TIME TRAVELLER'S VOICE This was intriguing. I wondered just how far women would permit this to go. He pushes the lever ahead. Flashes and HUMMING INCREASE and we: BLUR TO: THE MANNEQUIN - FULL
flattens a the neckline rises. During this: TIME TRAVELLER'S VOICE I began to grow fond of that mannequin. Maybe because, like me, she didn't age. THE TIME TRAVELLER - MED. SHOT Suddenly he hears the SOUNDS OF AIRPLANES and EXPLOSIONS in a strangely ACCE-
ER. He stares at the dials with much concern as he is PITCHED back and forth in his Machine. TIME TRAVELLER'S VOICE Suddenly, in nineteen forty I began to be buffeted from side to side. My first thought was that the Machine had a mechanical defect or a part had worn out.
-AIRCRAFT batteries are FIRING as a squadron of Nazi fighter planes are caught in the criss- cross beams of light. The sky is pierced with ack ack. Then, following the sound OF APPROACHING RAF. FIGHTER PLANES, a dog fight ensues. Several of the planes are hit and plum-
th flying machines. It didn't seem possible they could go on fighting all these years and still have the means of fighting. Then I realized the truth of the matter. This was a new war. There must have been an interval of peace in between these wars. Yet they had learned nothing
DES and the dials again come to a stop. TIME TRAVELLER'S VOICE The fighting in the sky lasted only a few moments. By nineteen forty five it was over, but I continued on a few more years before pausing for another glimpse of my silent, never aging friend. THE MANNEQUIN
years hence. With a grin he throws the lever forward. INSERT OF DIALS HUMMING INCREASES and the years spin, 1960, 1961 and so on until it finally STOPS on 1966. BACK AT THE MANNEQUIN Dressed in the sleek dress of the future. First a distant, then a close AIR RAID
leave their cars of the period in disorder. The running is purposive, however. All are entering particular buildings or, like those closest to the Time Traveller, are descending a stairway from the sidewalk down below street level. Some glance sky-ward. A LITTLE GIRL picks up
TRAVELLER'S VOICE At first I wondered if my Machine and I were the cause of the panic. I was to soon find out we weren't. He starts off toward the sidewalk, the CAMERA MOVING with him. At the descending subway stairway he stops and peers downward, but sees no one
mphony orchestra led by one of the popular conductors of tomorrow. The CAMERA SWINGS to the modern ENTRANCE of FILBY'S DEPARTMENT STORE just as the Time Traveller reaches the two broad glass doors. As he steps forward he intercepts the rays of electronic eyes
nters and turns his attention to other products of tomorrow -- refrigerators, vacuum cleaners, reducing belts, etc. As his keen mind grasps the significance of each, he smiles with approval, proud of his fellow man. His delight increases until he is interrupted by APPROACHING
him to the Time Traveller. TIME TRAVELLER (shakes his head) I can't understand you. The warden takes off his helmet. He is David Filby's son, James, whom we saw in 1917 as a young man. He is now in his mid-sixties. WARDEN (looking at helmet) Confounded radio in this
but to warn silly young fools like yourself to get down into the shelter. Now go on. TIME TRAVELLER But I'm perfectly comfortable and I find your store magnificent. What splendid achievements, what gigantic strides mankind has taken, what...WARDEN (interrupting) Come
the exact time escapes me TIME TRAVELLER It was two wars ago, I believe. Nineteen seventeen. WARDEN (awed) Why now I recall. He inquired about my father -- and the house that used to be across the way. (stops and stares at the Time Traveller) But no...that's impossi-
ller by the arm and drags him out. ON THE STREET - FULL SHOT pulls himself free. TIME TRAVELLER Listen to me! It's important. WARDEN (points to sky) Look! An atomic satellite zeroing in! That's important!! The Warden runs, looks back over shoulder, calling. WARDEN
Alarmed, he runs across the street directly in the path of the ambulance that threads its way between the cars left in disorder on the road. The driver spins the steering wheel and the ambulance tilts crazily in trying to avoid the Time Traveller. Suddenly there is a BLINDING
NE As the Time Traveller tries again to rush toward his Machine, the shockwaves reach him and throw him to the ground. He looks back, desperately. THE CITY - LONG SHOT - (MINIATURE) Through the thick cloud of smoke and dust we see the once proud city of the future in
t ahead, as though the earth were being torn apart. It zig zags down the street and from the widening fissure clouds of smoke and steam rise. TIME TRAVELLER'S VOICE But then Mother Earth, aroused by man's violence, responded with volcanic violence or her own! CHASM
manages to crawl into it. THE THAMES - LONG SHOT - (STOCK) As the river spills over it bed and turns into another direction. THE STREETS - (STOCK, MINIATURE, SPLIT) With red hot lava swirling around the bases of the remaining buildings. The lower parts of the struct-
ward each other and meet with explosive fury. The air is rent with the SINGING HISS of water and the CRACKLING of cooling rock. Steam whitens the sky. THE TIME MACHINE - LONG SHOT - (STOCK) - (PROCESS) Out of the tumult a flow of red hot lava turns aside and leaps
n. The HUMMING SOARS TO A VERY HIGH PITCH. THE ENCROACHING LAVA - (STOCK) It has been approaching with the speed of a torrent, but now it literally leaps forward in a blinding red haze that engulfs the entire scene. THE TIME MACHINE - MED. SHOT The interior of
tinguish anything in the gradually fading red glow. EXTREME CLOSE ON TIME TRAVELLER His face is bathed in sweat. His eyes search the growing darkness. TIME TRAVELLER'S VOICE The molten rock cooled. (he closes his burning eyes as the last of the light vanishes) I
veller. Then a match flickers. The CAMERA SCARES BACK. The Time Traveller holds up a burning matchstick, his face glistening with perspiration as he leans forward to look at the dials.TIME TRAVELLER'S VOICE (whispering) Darkness...darkness for centuries. INSERT OF
e Time Machine. He breathes heavily and tries to calm himself. TIME TRAVELLER'S VOICE I wondered if there was still war being waged on the ground above me if man would still exist on earth, when I saw the sun again. As he speaks, the Time Machine goes faster and faster.
e relief. WHAT HE SEES: Rocks deteriorate and a bright blue sky bursts into view EXT. TIME MACHINE AND GROUND NEARBY - LONG SHOT Everything is a blur except the Time Machine with its passenger. The black rock on the surface slowly melts away and the flickering
several great buildings set wide apart by green landscape -- a landscape which no longer changes color even though trees spring up like plumes of green smoke. TIME TRAVELLER'S VOICE Thousands of centuries passed, but the earth stayed green! There was no winter! No
THUNDER and the Time Machine suddenly goes into a spin. The CAMERA ZOOMS BACK TO A FULL HIGH SHOT as the machine keels over. The friction caused by the intrusion creates a pitiless HAIL, and we SLOWLY DISSOLVE TO: EXT. TIME TRAVELLER - CLOSE SHOT - (DAY)
LOW ANGLE - (MATTE) The vapor rises like a curtain to disclose a great bronze pedestal, green with verdigris, whereon clawed feet support the white marble figure of an immense Sphinx. The figure has the face of a woman, the body of a huge cat and the tail of a serpent. A
es into the Machine, pockets the lever and surveys his surroundings. LANDSCAPE - LONG SHOT - (MATTE) It looks like a garden untended for centuries. The trees and shrubs are laden with strange blossoms or exotic fruits. In the distance there is a building that might once
AMERA ACCOMPANIES him as he looks about with interest. WHAT HE SEES - MOVING SHOT Strange, exotic fruits bend the branches of the TREES, some purplish and gourd-shaped, others suggesting giant raspberries, mangoes, etc. TIME TRAVELLER'S VOICE Nature tamed
sign of weeds or briars. EXT. ENTRANCE TO GREAT BUILDING - LONG SHOT - (DAY) The Time Traveller pauses and looks up at the building. ACROSS FACADE - PAN DOWN - (MINIATURE?) Vines creep up the crevices. The ornamental stone work, while rich in detail, is weathe-
teps and enter the building. INT. THE GREAT HALL - FULL SHOT - (MATTE) - (DAY) In the background across the hall, the Time Traveller halts. He is dwarfed by the height of the vaulted ceiling. Although ancient in appearance, everything is ultra modern in design. Sunlight
me Traveller crosses to A TABLE - MED. SHOT TIME TRAVELLER (shouting) Anyone here? But an ECHO is his only answer. Curiously he retraces his steps and leaves the great hall. EXT. THE POOL - LONG SHOT - (DAY) The Time Traveller's VIEW is partially obscured by the
remely lovely, surrounded by fern trees, and with the water plunging into it from a high waterfall. Below the pool the stream emerges in a swift torrent. ANOTHER, CLOSER SHOT A beautiful GIRL, dressed in a silken robe of white and gold, starts running. As she runs, she loo-
e. He pauses, thinking back on what he has just said. TIME TRAVELLER Well, and why not? Suddenly a SHRILL SCREAM COMES OVER from the pool. He turns. THE POOL - LONG SHOT The Girl has swum out too far and is caught by the swift torrent. She CRIES OUT PITEOUS-
m the foliage, rushes to the bank, points toward the Girl and tries to attract the attention of those near her on the bank. TIME TRAVELLER Help her!. No one moves. He runs toward the ledge. BACK TO THE GIRL Her grasp on the ledge grows weaker. She is at the point of let-
Time Traveller bewildered, she shows neither fear nor gratitude. TIME TRAVELLER - EXTREME CLOSE UP Gazing back at the Girl thoroughly puzzled. He turns and glances down at the two little people on the ledge. CLOSE TWO SHOT These two men will later be known as the
y takes off his jacket and throws it around her. He looks at her for the first time sees the almost ultimate in feminine beauty. TIME TRAVELLER Are you all right? TIME TRAVELLER & GIRL - FULL SHOT Wearing his velvet jacket very appealingly, she calmly rises, turns and,
SE ON TIME TRAVELLER Perplexed DISSOLVE TO: EXT. ENTRANCE TO THE GREAT BUILDING - (SUNSET) Shooting toward the ARCHWAY. The sun is sinking as the last stragglers of the little people enter the great hall. The Time Traveller slowly follows them. He pauses on
LER Why did I what? THE GIRL Come after me. TIME TRAVELLER (ironic) I did it to save your life, young lady, which I'm afraid doesn't hold much meaning for you or anyone else. THE GIRL (simply) It doesn't. TIME TRAVELLER Must have been fifty of your friends watching
ou'd better take me to someone a bit older I can talk to. THE GIRL There is no one older. The Time Traveller is suddenly struck by the truth of her words. All of the little people seem to be of the Girl's age or younger. TIME TRAVELLER Doesn't anyone age in this land of yours?
Can't you write? Look! He bends over, picks up a stick and starts to draw on the ground INSERT: DUST As the stick writes out: " W E E N A " BACK TO SCENE She shows little interest. TIME TRAVELLER And what are your people called? WEENA (as if he ought to know) Eloi.
s his hand and pulls him toward. INT. THE GREAT HALL - LONG SHOT - (MATTE) - (DAY) EXT. TIME TRAVELLER ON THE PATH - (NIGHT) Holding his torch high, the Time Traveller hurries toward the bushes around the edge of the lawn looking for his Machine, beating the
ves. BACK TO THE FOOTPRINTS THE CAMERA CONTINUES TO FOLLOW the grooves straight across the lawn to the flagstones around the white sphinx. There are dark scratches on the stones leading to the wide panel in the base of the pedestal. Here the marks end. CLOSE
ard it. INT. LABORATORY - LONG SHOT - (NIGHT) The Time Machine has returned, but it is resting in the far corner of the room instead of in the spot where we originally saw it. In the gloom, the Time Traveller clambers pain-fully from the Machine. SLOW DISSOLVE TO: The
center of the floor. EXT. COTTAGE - LONG SHOT - Drifting like a curtain, the snow falls quietly as Filby, a solitary figure in the night, pauses a moment to look up at the sky, then selects a path and starts walking the long way home. Without looking back .FADE OUT. THE END

ilt up on the windows from the outside
os out of his Machine and glances with a
well as in the dining room seen in the b
o the front door. It refuses to respond to
owers. The house is boarded up. He sta
d toward: EXT. ROAD - LONG SHOT - (DA
? You look rather silly without your m
as he realizes its truth) I'm sorry to hea
ereabouts think it's haunted. (stares at
n France...or maybe... (noticing confusi
death for his old friend, David Filby, he
R The FLICKERS of days and nights, as
the speed of wind, pedestrians streak a
rom the floor. BACK TO TIME TRAVELL
kline and flattens a the neckline rises.
RAVELLER He stares at the dials with
nts. ANTI-AIRCRAFT batteries are FIRI
he air with flying machines. It didn't se
E SUBSIDES and the dials again come
like ten years hence. With a grin he thr
Drivers leave their cars of the period i

d darkness prevails. CLOSE ON TIME T
tonishment around the interior of the la
. Cobwebs are everywhere. The floor SC
is attempt to open it. Even when he use
s to wander around, thinking, investigat
) Coming up the hill on a narrow dusty
stache, old man! FILBY (puzzled) Were
hat. (pause, then hesitantly points) An
me Traveller curiously, studying the st
, adds with a note of compassion) Perha
owly walks across the street and return
ell as the HUMMING, INCREASES and D
oss the pavement. The bright lights of t
R A smile appears on his face. TIME TF
ring this: TIME TRAVELLER'S VOICE I
ch concern as he is PITCHED back and
as a squadron of Nazi fighter planes ar
n possible they could go on fighting all t
a stop. TIME TRAVELLER'S VOICE The
s the lever forward. INSERT OF DIALS
disorder. The running is purposive, how

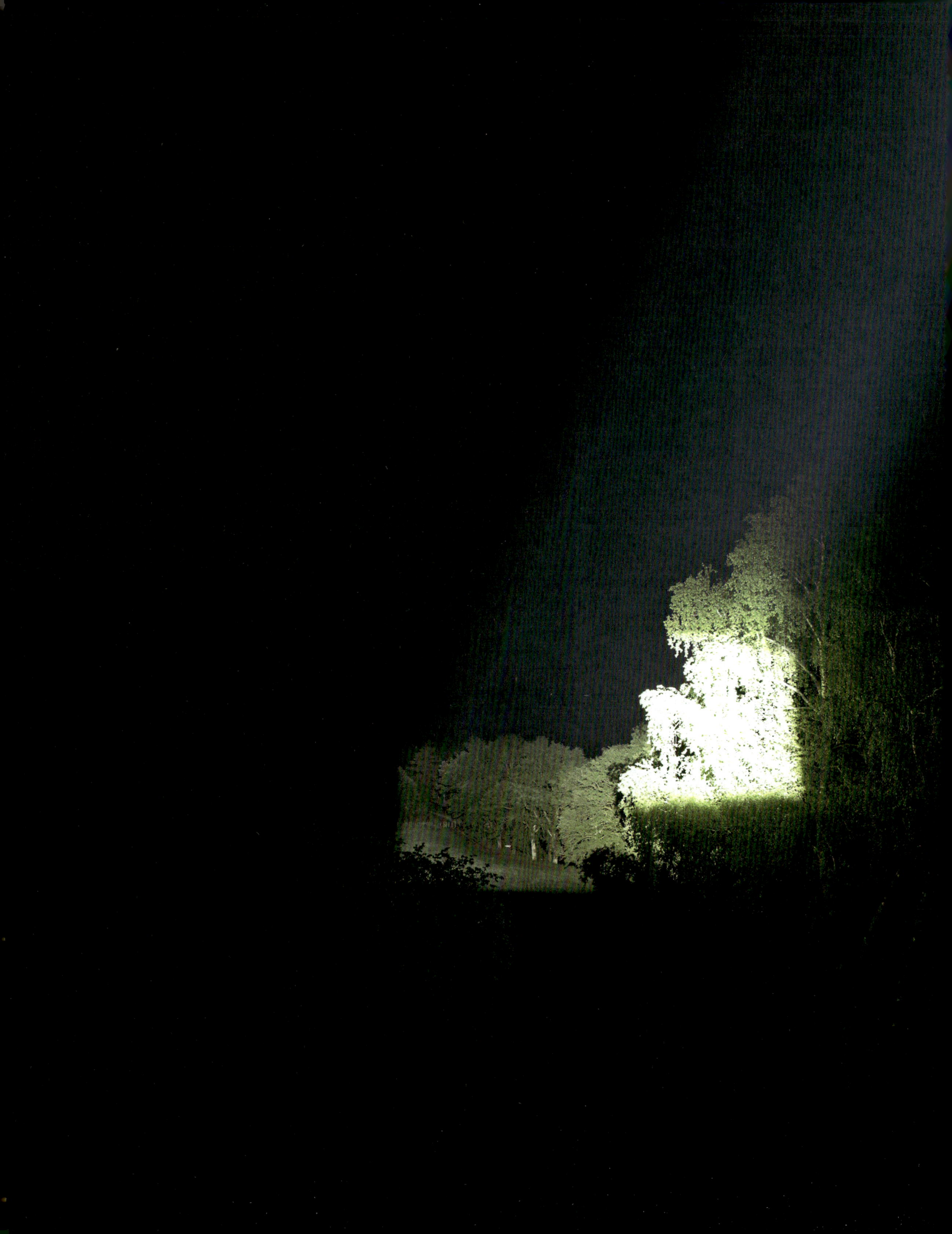

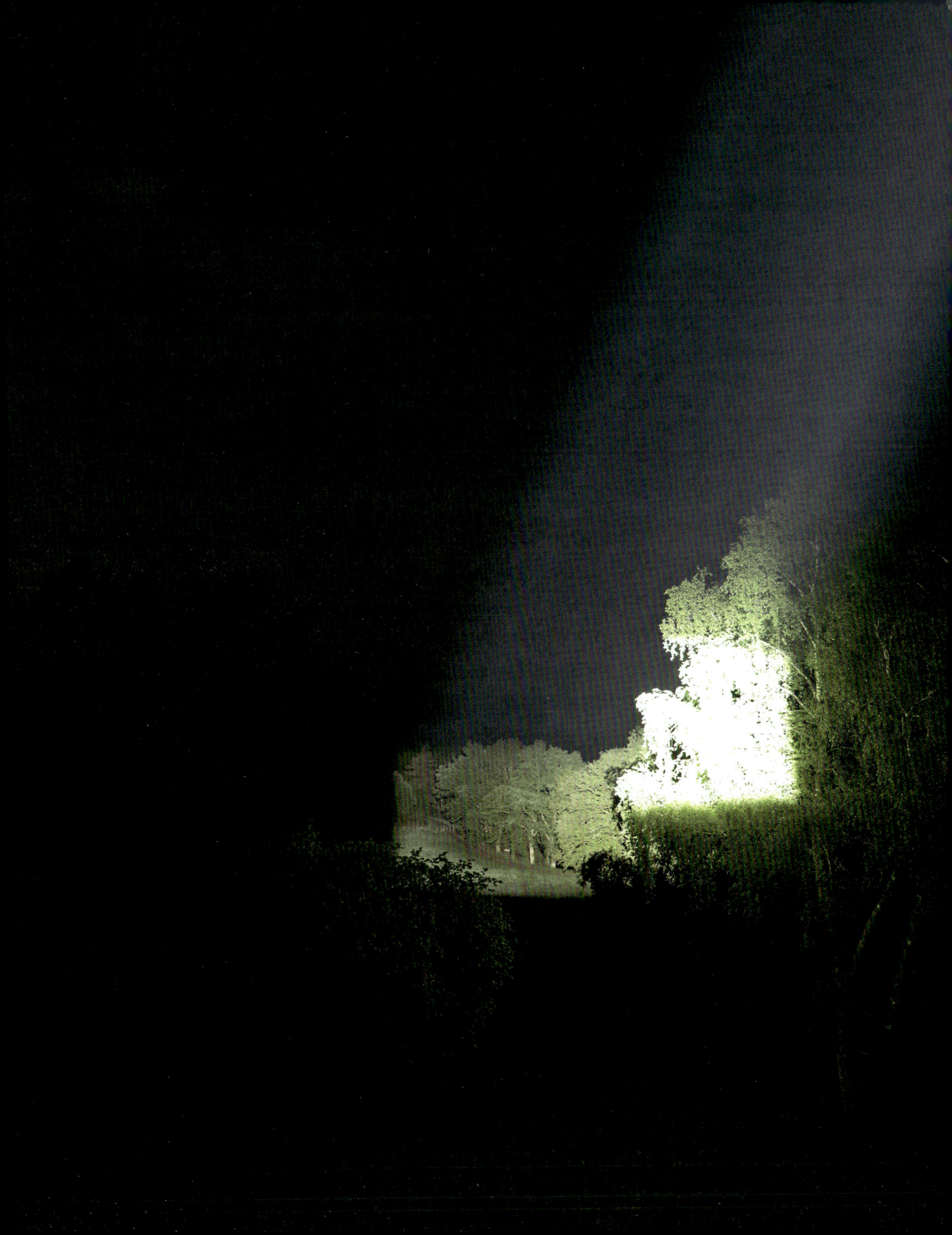

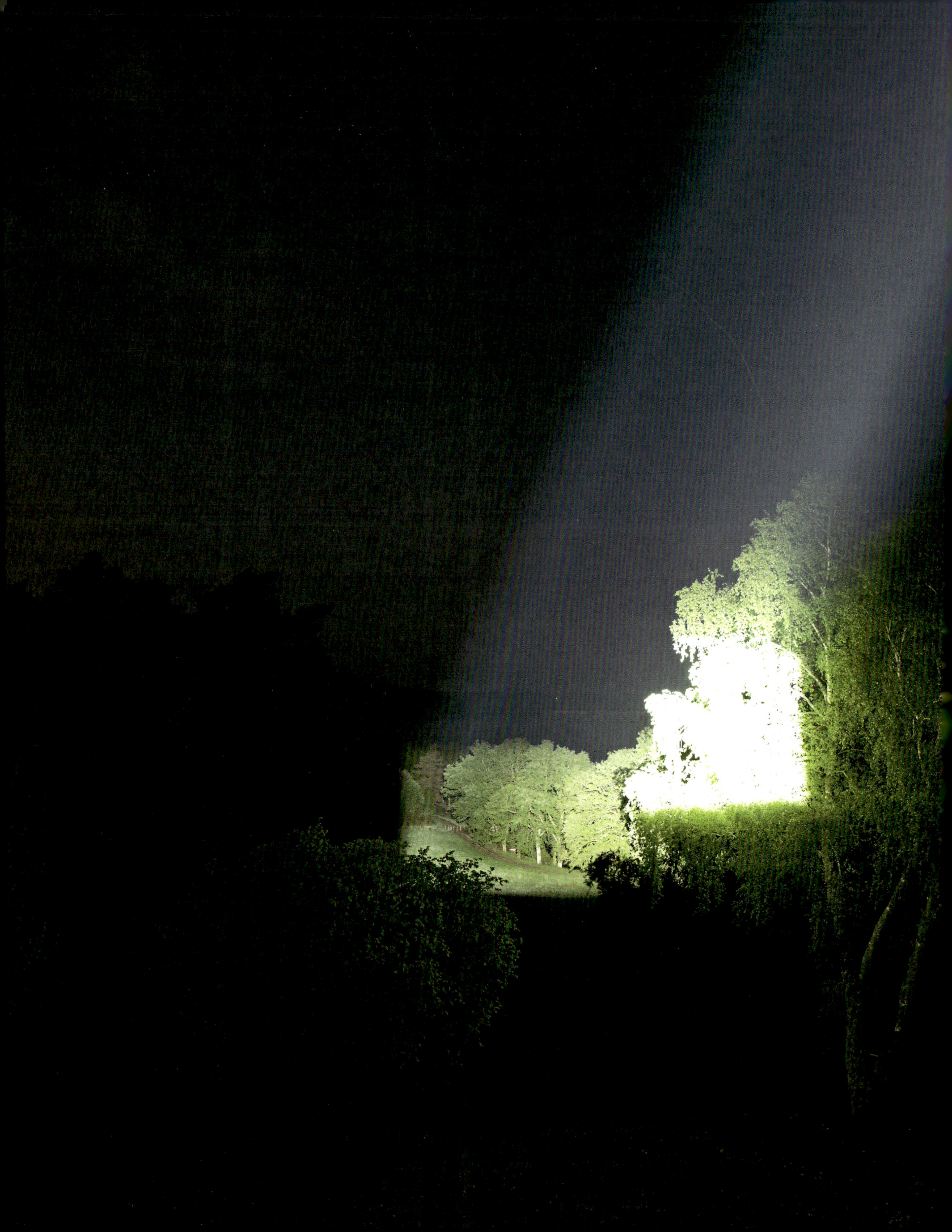

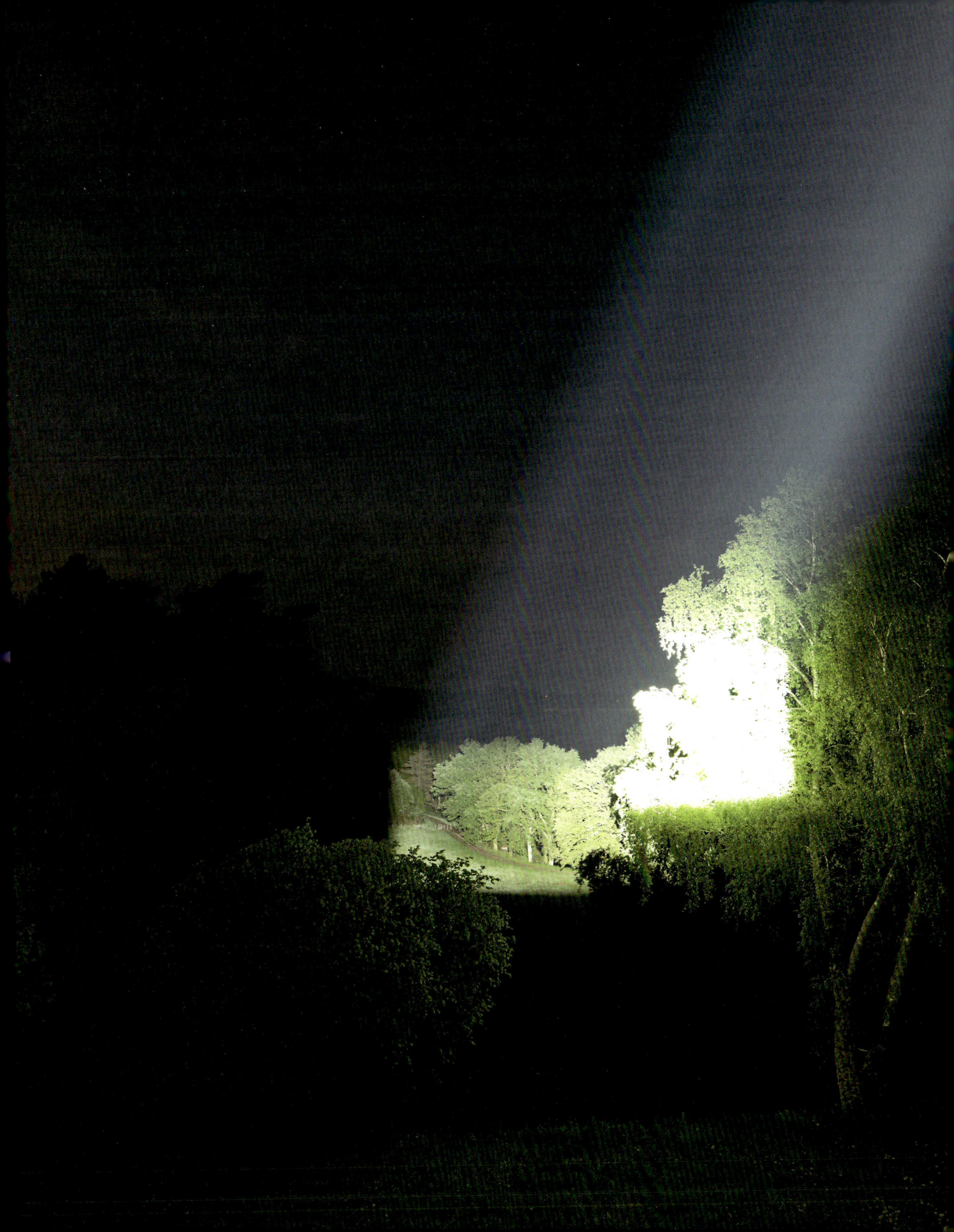

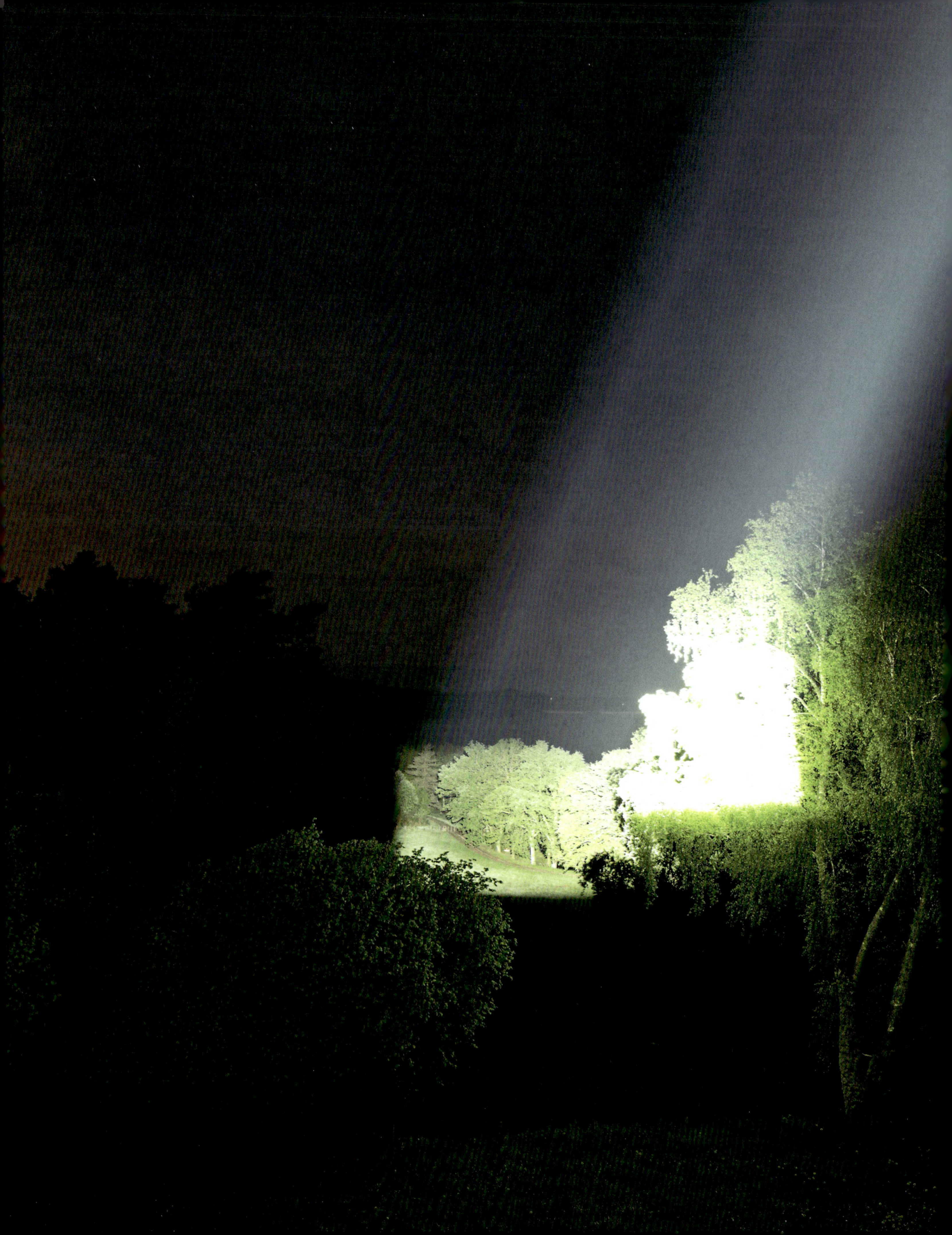

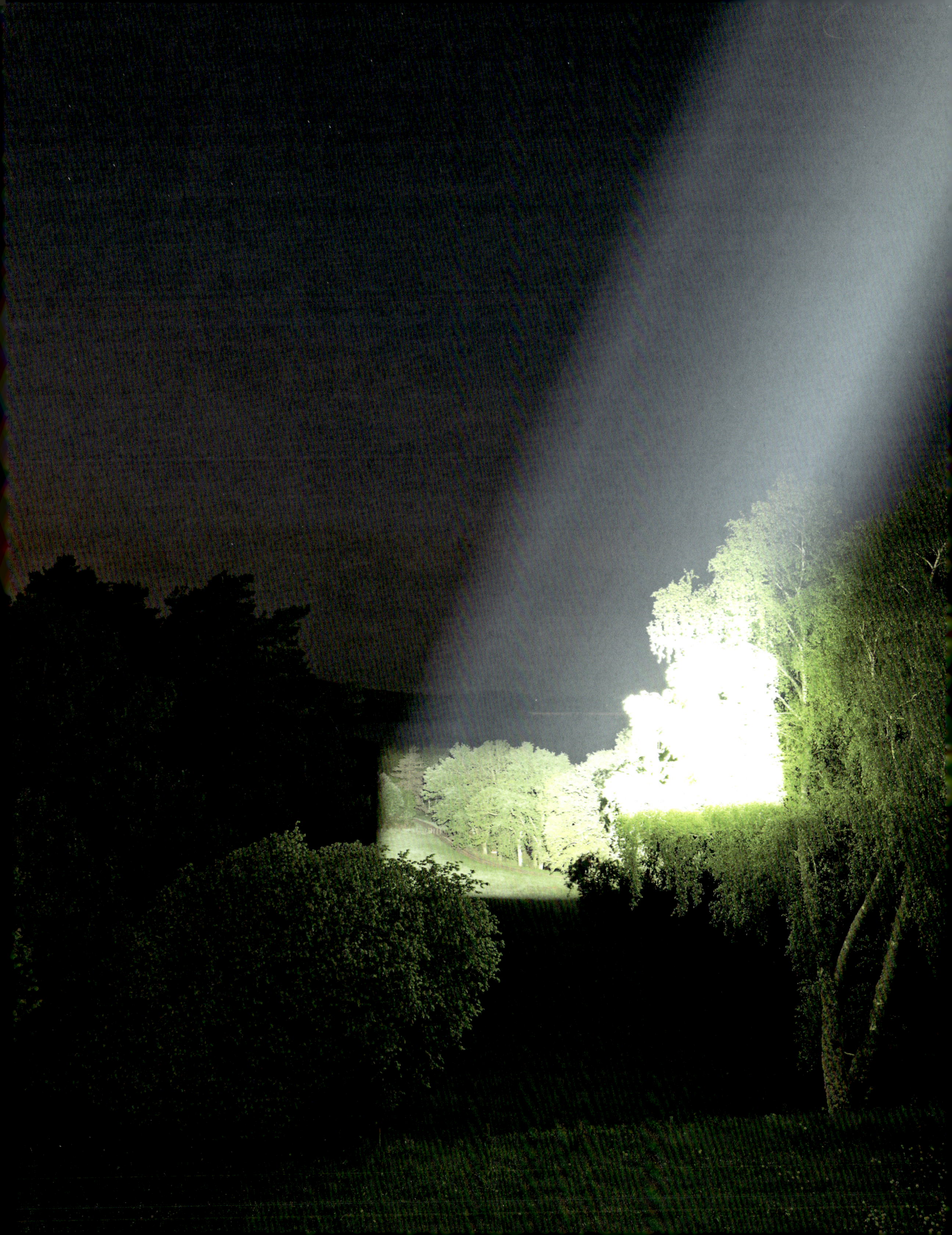

Dear Rosa,

Thanks for asking again for an update about the mission. Not much has happened lately, I have to admit, but there are several things that may be worthy of your attention.
Yesterday we walked the bridge leading from the shore to the island in the middle of the lake. Almost at the same time your e-mail arrived, we'd reached the island. After going up and down the tower, seeing hundreds of meters of celluloid, and listening to the low frequencies emanating from the water, we took a walk around the island with Alexandra. I don't remember if we'd finished the walk, but one thing that I got stuck on most was the fact that the island was a recent creation of human hands. It felt as if we were walking around something that had existed there for ages. I was stunned. My whole perception of where we were shifted: I understood that we were standing on top of a little hill that got surrounded by water and became an island only some years ago.
This is when Alexandra told me that there has been a man living on this island since the time the island was not an island at all. This man, she said, knows the history of the island best, because he is older than the island itself. Can you believe it? I don't think there is another person on earth who is older than the island he inhabits.
Without hesitating we went to meet him. I felt he must know something that has the potential to accomplish my mission in seeking out new possibilities for your film. This man must know something that could obliquely translate into the forms and trajectories of your work, through the poetry of suspended signifying chains and repeated promises.
Monsieur Pechalat, the man living on the island, welcomed us warmly into his house. Several cats, red in color, if I remember correctly, were snuggled around the place. He was genuine and kind, and eager to answer my questions. I kept asking about simple things in no particular order: his life on the island, the life of the island itself, and the shared memory of the man and the island—everything that could help extract some facts that we could adapt in the script later. I was curious about the time when the island became an island, about the dreams he had when sleeping on the island, and about any scenes or images that he could remember in close detail.
They say that water has a memory too, and I was wondering whether he had a chance to witness it. I was curious about those moments that sometimes emerge from our memory in full detail—for example, that brief moment from many years ago that hasn't crossed your mind for half a century but suddenly unfolds in your mind as if it happened just two minutes ago. Or perhaps in two minutes to come: the future must be enfolded in the past like water is in water, mustn't it?
It is not only because of this enfolding of the future in the past that you should not blame me for missing deadlines. First of all, I am chrono-dyslexic; second, my daughter has been undergoing something for the first time in her life. She will not tell me what it is, but it keeps me more distracted than usual. Yesterday she hung up after I tried to console her with a story of the first image I remember—I thought the subject of the first image fit the whole conversation. It was a color photo of a crocodile in the pages of *Soviet Encyclopedia* that I happened to open one day when I was a kid. "It can still bite," I laughed to my daughter, expecting to cheer her up. And that's when she hung up.
Chrono-dyslexia is easier to understand though: it is a chronic condition sort of like involuntary time traveling. You asked me last time "when" I was in time, and I could not tell you exactly, remember? This is what I am going through—a state

of being somewhere that has no beginning and no end, yet each time it is over you feel like it will never happen again. This makes me prematurely melancholic. Time traveling relies on multiple paradoxes. One of them is a belief that the past (like the future) stays static and does not change (like a kind of frozen monadic bubble or a fossil). According to this belief, if someone from the year 2012 goes back to the summer of 1989 in Berlin, they find the Berlin Wall still standing intact. Yet disgruntled Germans are already gathering to tear it down. So the sequence of events is an entirely familiar playback of public record. But imagine what happens when you go back in time and discover that all of the things in the past have changed as much as your life did, but not in the direction you've expected or in the sequence of events that led to the present you think you know. Following this idea, one no longer jumps from one time to another like skipping from one track to another track on one's MP3 player. Instead you are left with your own devices and perhaps more time for time.

"So, since when have you been here, Monsieur?" I asked Mr. Pechalat. "Your story may be recorded not only in the wind passing through the trees on the island, but also on the surface of Rosa Barba's film."

"I've been here since 1936—it's been ages!—staying at the same place."

"Were you born here?"

"No, I was born in Eymoutiers."

"Why did you come to live here?"

"It was work. I came with my parents, who had taken a farm on the island, which wasn't an island then, as there was no water all around it. We continued working for Mrs. Pascal. I stayed with her, and when the dam was built she kept me on. A lot of people from the flooded villages left. I was on a mountain and so I didn't leave; I stayed in Vassivière. I kept working for her until she died, and even afterwards. And then the joint local commission in charge of the area came and took over the island. It changed life; things weren't the same at all. It's very difficult . . . I don't know how to explain it to you. Life was turned upside-down; it was not the same work anymore. We kept the property, we had the cattle—we had many things. On the other hand, of course, it was saddening to see the water rise. When the dam was completed, we were seeing the water rise slowly and we had a lot of invaders, because it made the vermin come up—rats, snakes . . . That was bringing them closer. The snakes were passing through the courtyard. You just had to see that; it was amazing. We say vermin, but everything—the hares, the rabbits, every sort of game—came here along with the snakes and the rats; they came here, and we were invaded."

"When did they fill the lake?"

"They started work in 1946, and the lake started to fill in 1949. On Christmas Eve that year, dam wasn't complete yet; it was only half finished. But the water was not troublesome to work with. The materials needed were coming via air. It was like the cable cars you see in the mountains: they were bringing the little carts that were unloading cement on the dam."

"It took them three years to prepare the place before water arrived? What went on between 1946 and 1949?"

"They were working by hand. There were very few mechanical tools, just some; a lot was done manually. There were 3,500 workers at the time."

(Rosa, don't be surprised that it may take us three years to produce the script. I wish we were 3,500 workers capable of turning the lingering potentiality into the bonds of the present. But meanwhile it is only Francesco, submerged in the archive, and myself, dumped in this forest. Our efforts may overlap, but not necessarily in the same history. Do you think a belief in the latent potential of the world around us binds us? I doubt it. I am rather sceptical about all those artists claiming that they produce potentialities. I think they are lazy and cerebral. It is as if I were to claim that I produce laziness. Of course, I will never say that. But if it takes us three years to produce a script—well, take it as a sign of my fidelity to the pursuit rather than as a failure, God bless us.)

"Was the dam conceived before the Second World War?"

"No, they started it right afterward. There was trouble in Indochina. The war was just finished when they started because there wasn't enough light or enough central heating. Now there is forest everywhere, but before it was all heather moor, cattle that we farmed, and very little wood; the cattle was farmed in little herds, not large ones like today. There were a lot of crops: rye, oats, potatoes . . . It was a lot at the time."

"Between 1946 and 1949 when the government proposed that people go somewhere else, why did you decide to stay?"

"I was on a mountain; the ones down below, they had to go. I was the one in the water."

"Weren't you worried about staying in a kind of isolated situation—being stranded on a island?"

"I didn't even think about it. It changed life; pages were turned, so to speak. In a way, we jumped forward. The harder part was when the lake was drained in 1995. To see all the land barren . . . Then it was a hard blow to see the land where I lived again. I had the chance to see that from a helicopter, to explain to people where there had once been a bridge, a mill, a church . . . "

(I would suggest we add the Centre international d'art et du paysage to this list of places submerged under water. Our script should escalate a disaster and introduce a parallel history through parallel montage. We don't have to be too literal, but we have to exercise our right to be parallel. The building by Aldo Rossi and Xavier Fabre becomes a part of the landscape in a way that is no different from a submerged church or a mill.)

"Before the arrival of the water, did they destroy everything?"

"They demolished everything—the trees were all cut down, the houses, dynamited. You see the little pile of stones? They dynamited everything because of the boats. At Vaugelade the mill was still intact and, somewhere else, so was the church, but I don't remember where. But now the water has probably destroyed everything."

"Did you go inside that church before the war?"

"No, never. I don't know the place. Some said that there was a cemetery at the bottom of the lake, but that's not true. Vassivière was just a village. The true Vassivière is here."

(I think we have to retrieve more than just associations from the water. We have to work on the parallax intensities. Perhaps moments of change, transition, and solitude could be of particular interest. A memory of something distant, like the man diving into water in 1949 converging with a memory of something closer, like the memory of last Christmas or of a George Michael song, or even closer—like a song that you heard just this morning, remember? Are these possible futures that never took place? Are they multiple universes explored by mathematical probability games? Or are they once more theatrical plays resulting from a séance that tried to reanimate the potential fiction present in the water confined in the lake?)

"In three days, the water reached everywhere. How was it for you? The landscape changed immediately, didn't it?"
"Of course. We saw it disappear. The stumps of the cut trees, the water was overflowing them; we couldn't see them anymore. We were happy without being really happy; we didn't know what it was. We had never see a dam. The people weren't against the dam, because they had just emerged from the war: they had suffered so much that it was OK. But afterwards, the police were needed to protect the other dam projects, because people didn't want to give away the land. I remember a project in Creuse, long after the war, that the people managed to stop. Today there's only a ruined housed there, and there are people coming back, but the land still belongs to the EDF."
"Were there many friends you never saw again?"
"There are some that I completely lost track of; they've gone somewhere like Creuse, in cities. Being mostly women, they left after the war; they didn't stay in the countryside. They were fed up with farming as they were growing old, and even if they weren't old and moved to the cities—Paris, Lyon—I lost track of them. Some come back to visit, people who know me, but I don't know them anymore because they're old. It's mostly women that left for the cities, because the work here is tiring. It's very hard to be a farmer, and that's why they left."

(Imagine you are the last creature on earth: your love for the void is bound to its destiny, your stories will never be told again (even by someone else), and your voice counts for nothing. "You are the last creature on earth," reminds a disclaimer. But suddenly your eye catches a mosquito bursting with blood on the white wall of the room, the room you've just entered. Whose blood is it? Where is it from? What kind of information does it contain? Is there some message in it from the generations that lived before the end of humanity? Or a retro-virus to be reactivated? Would it prolong the end of the world or would it invert it? Would it inadvertently make you immortal—you, who just a minute ago was the last creature on Earth?)

"So, in the beginning there was no bridge? How did you deal with that?"
"The bridge was rising with the water. All the EDF's work had begun at the same time—everything was done at the same time, for there were 3,500 workers. The bridge, the dam, the road, everything at the same time . . . "
"When did you get a television?"
"A lot later, long after the dam. I couldn't afford it, it was too expensive."
"Were you going to the movies?"
"To go to the movies you needed to go to Eymoutiers, which was too far—fifteen kilometers on foot. Afterward, one opened in Beaumont, but it wasn't large. Now it's easy. You take the car and you go far; you can go to the movies in Limoges even if, in fact, you don't go. At Eymoutiers there are some who go because there is a movie every week, I believe. Before there weren't any cars like there are now; cars were extremely rare."
"What was your favorite movie?"
"The movies? I don't remember them all."

(The unremembered movies remind me of a party that once took place at the end of an unfinished highway in Germany. Thrown by the Techno-enthusiasts of the early Rave era, it attracted a wide array of Cyberglam creatures of the mid-nineteen-nineties that looked so eerie that the whole scene could have been a film set. In fact, when the cops arrived to shut the party down, the ravers said, "We are shooting a movie." The cops didn't question whether it was a film set about the future or a film set about something else. Cinematographic credibility saved the party. The ravers' film has never been shot, of course, but that party still burns in my memory due to the fact that it was never filmed. Right at the edge of the unfinished autobahn, there was a Ballardian frontier. "We are all movies"—remember Terence McKenna?)

"Earlier, you said something about the moment when the animals and the vermin arrived on the island. What happened exactly?"

"It's the water that brought the beasts, the snakes, and the rats closer. The rats were the most annoying: they were eating potatoes in the fields, and grain. We had to poison them because they were too numerous. The rats weren't that nasty, but the snakes were. A rat can bite but it can't kill; snakes, on the other hand, were killing the animals and biting people."

"But aren't snakes good at killing the rats?"

"Yes, they were eating them, but not all of them—there were too many. And then I was afraid of the snakes. There were asps, adders, grass snakes . . . It's said that grass snakes are harmless, but there is still venom in them anyhow. I saw a woman drop dead; many were bitten . . . I saw this woman fall: she was holding handfuls of wheat, which you had to tie manually, and when she reached out the snake struck and she died. When the doctor came, she was already dead. Once you've been bitten, you never forget. In the past there were healers, but that was a long time ago. When you where bitten by a snake, I don't know what he would do, for I was never told, but he would perform some kind of secret thing that I don't know about and in the end you were cured. It's a time that is older than I am, one I never knew. But if you didn't go to see this person, you'd die."

(I think we should ask Francesco to develop the figures of the snakes through serpentines of film on the floor. He should tell everybody how it spins and collects the dust of metaphors. We could also use it as an opportunity to imply the ghost of *Ophisthostoma Verniculum*. That is the name of a special creature that scientists discovered recently. However, when the creature was exposed to discovery, it died. This is not such an unusual example of a relationship between science and unknown phenomena: the apparatus of identification kills its object of focus. It is therefore not surprising that even the name of the creature has disappeared from Google.)

"Why did people choose the healer and not the doctor?"

"Because doctors couldn't do anything; there were no injections at that time."

"Is there a small island called 'the snakes' island'?"

"The name was given to make the island seem more significant. There were actually snakes on all seven islands; the larger the island, the larger the number of snakes."

"Does the lake freeze sometimes?"

"Yes, I walked across ice that was forty centimeters thick in 1954 and it was minus 27°C; it made a nice floor. When the lake was filling it didn't make noise, but when it was coming down, when the ice was breaking, it made a noise at night like thunder. We could hear the cracks . . . It was formidable. This year, the frost was as thin as a sheet of paper."

(The description of this sound should be translated into something emanating from the water, maybe another type of sound or a frequency that shatters our indifference, expectations, and dreams. Did I tell you that I've dreamed of broken iPhone screens a few times lately? Again and again, I've dreamed of those crushed screens of immersion—crushed surfaces of infinite, depthless perspective, the crushed ice of touch, crushed metaphors. The ringtones were intact though; they woke me up each time.)

"Do you remember when the art center was built?"
"Yes, there were discussions about it, but I can't remember which year it all started, even though I worked on the construction site with the sculptures and bringing equipment."
"When the art center came, did you think that more exiting things were going to happen on the island?"
"I can't say. Those things are beyond my ken; they're beyond me. It's kind of peculiar, the art center. They do unbelievable things there. It's another world that's beyond me."
"Do you see the exhibitions there?"
"Usually, each of them."
"Have you ever gotten bored, living here on the island?"
"For the moment, I'm feeling down, but you've got to live with it. I don't have a car to go out with anymore; I rolled it. I had the accident in Pierrefitte, outside the village. In broad daylight, I fell asleep and bumped the embankment, and the car tipped over. I didn't have a scratch on me, but the car was totaled. Me, I could have cured myself, but the car is no more. They revoked my licence because of the accident and because I'm too old, but I'm going to try getting another one. Nobody was hurt, but they don't want to insure me anymore."
"You should be taking a helicopter again! . . . When you were in the helicopter that time, what was it like?"
"Nothing. I was happy; it was good to see the land I once knew, because the lake, its 1,000 hectares . . . It was quite a trip; it lasted over an hour. I was happy. It was a nice ride for me. Every place, every bridge, road, everything . . . It was like being on the moon: the soil had dried, and there were cracks, like in the desert, big enough to put your hand inside, and it was barren, with no more greenery—nothing was left but stumps and crushed houses. Of course, it's kind of sad, but for someone who knew the place, who used to live there, to see all the recesses . . . I know I'll never see it like that again."
"Do many people come to see you, as we have today, to talk to you about the history of the island?"
"Yes, there were a lot, but they are fewer now. Perhaps it's less interesting, or not at all so. In the past, many came. Sometimes the visits lasted all day long."

(Rosa, I am telling you, your film on the island should last all day long . . . A day-long projection full of things that already happened and things that have not yet happened—in the same beam of light, remember . . . ?)

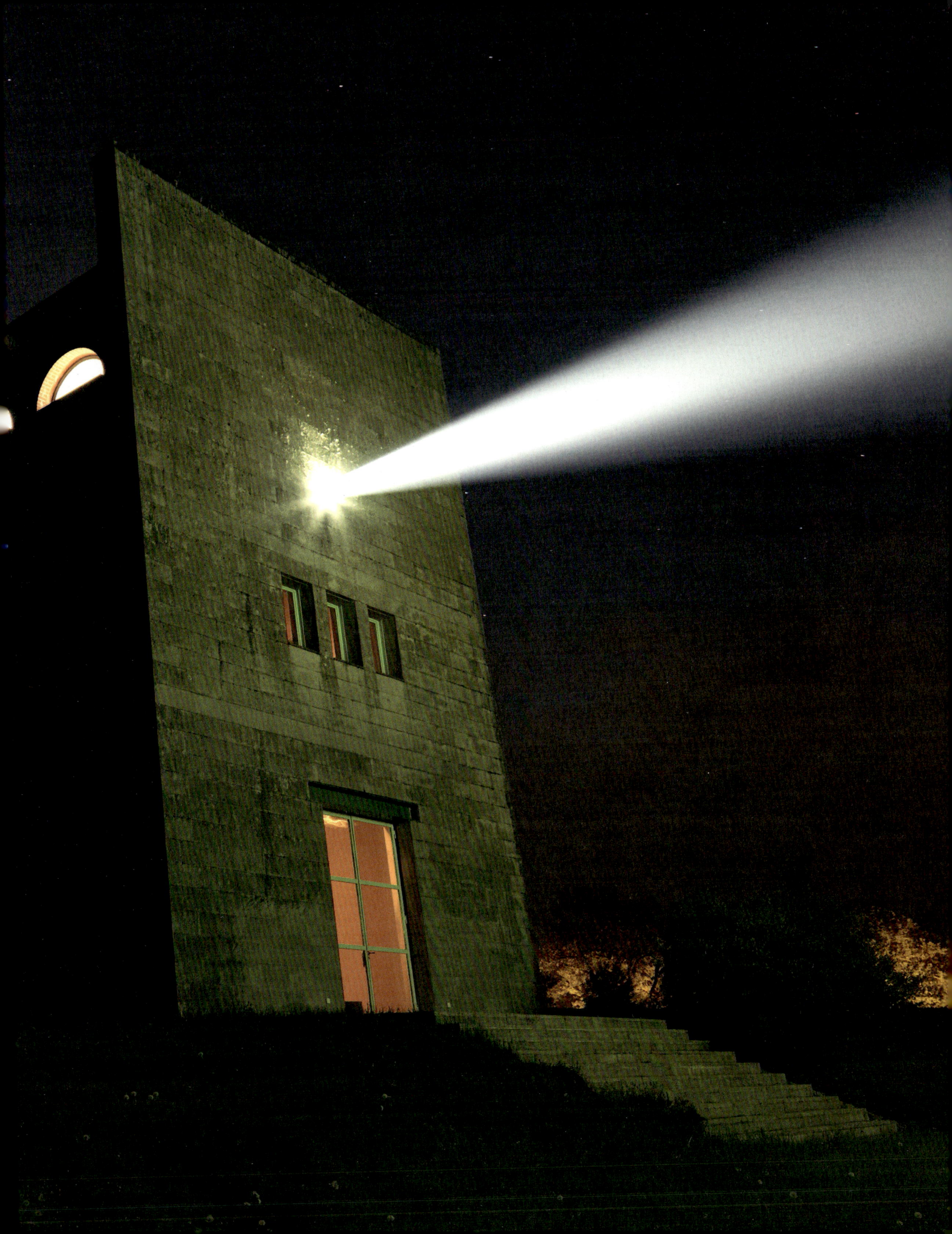

ON PERFORMING THE TRACES THAT PEOPLE LEAVE BEHIND IN HISTORY

NATAŠA PETREŠIN-BACHELEZ

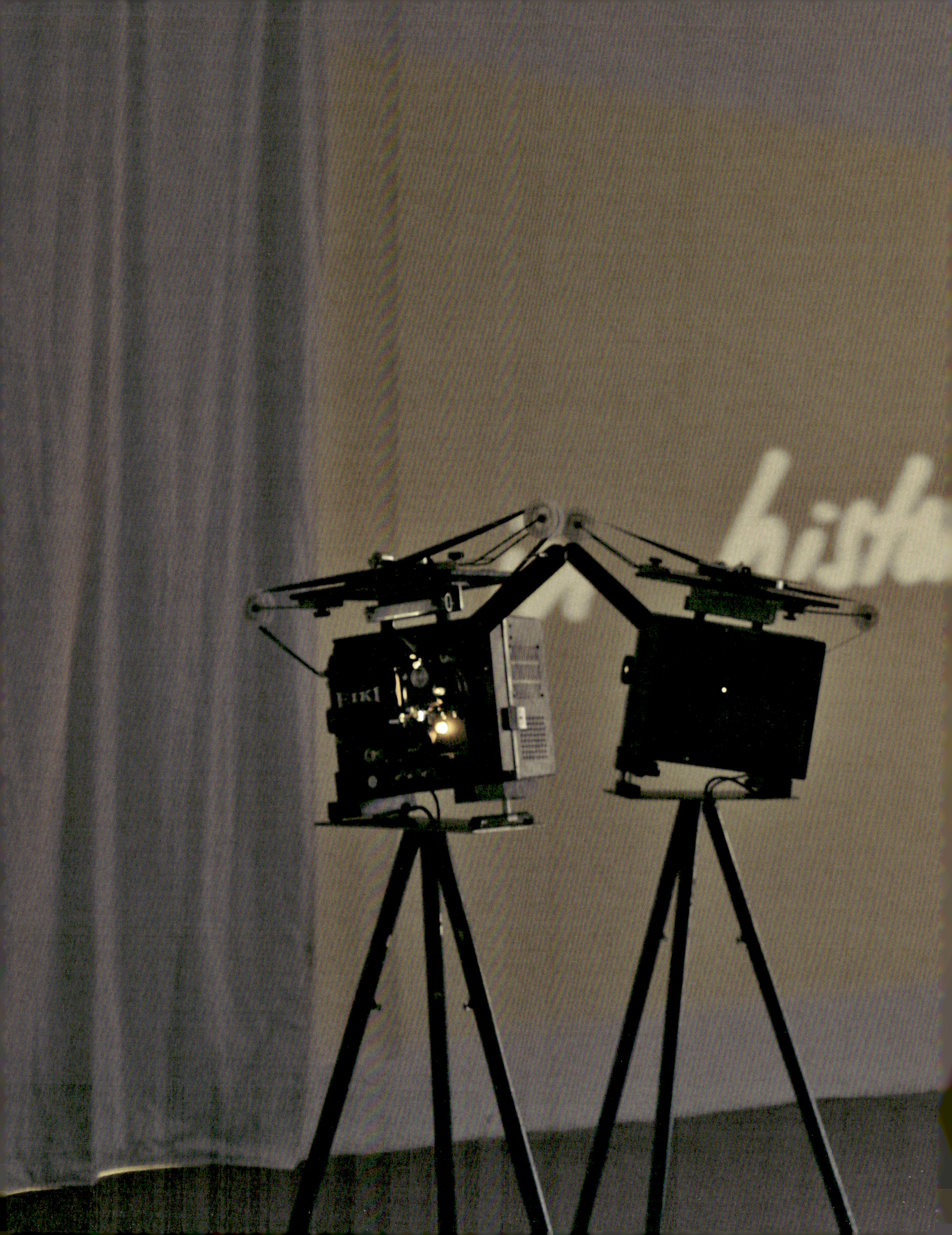
EIKI

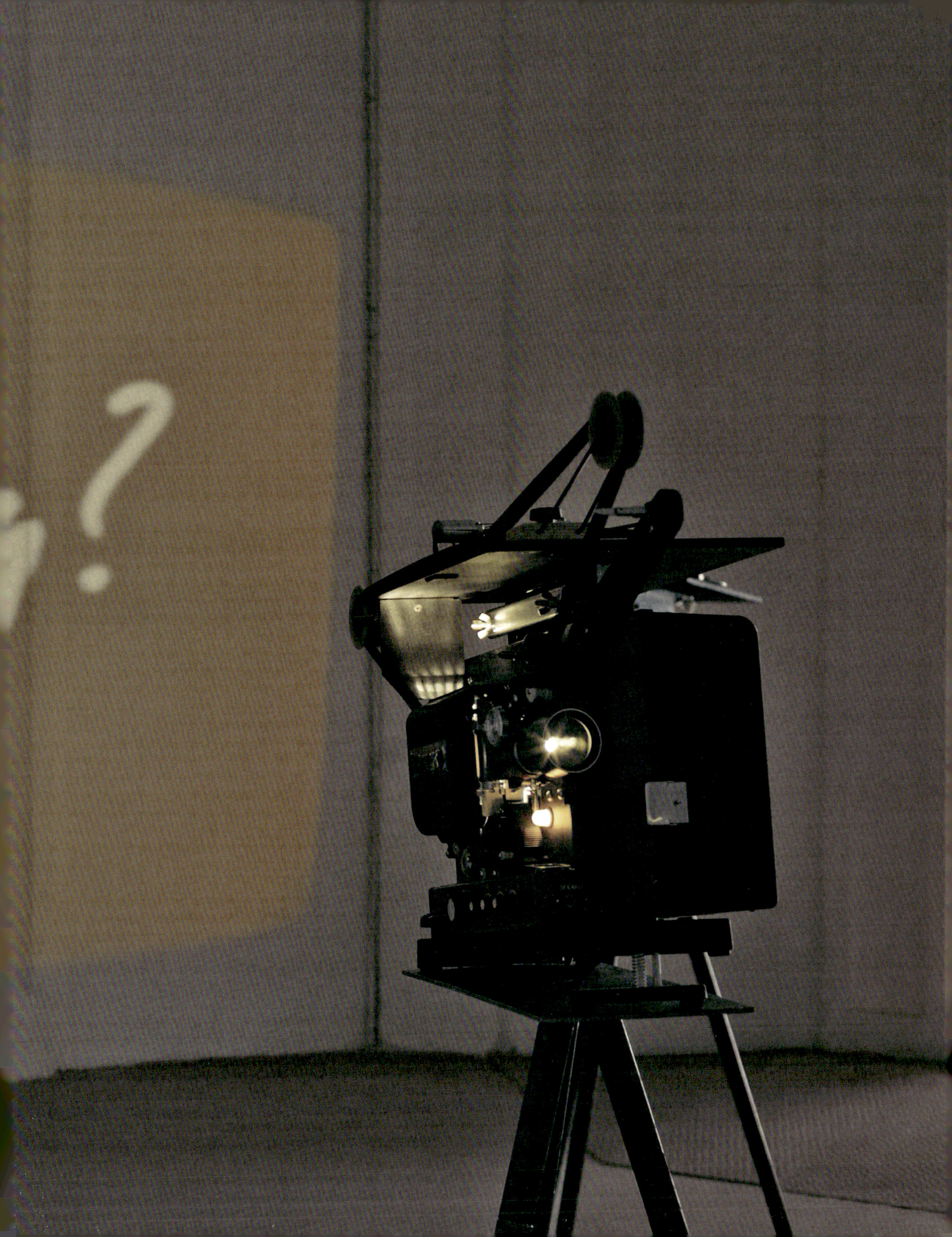

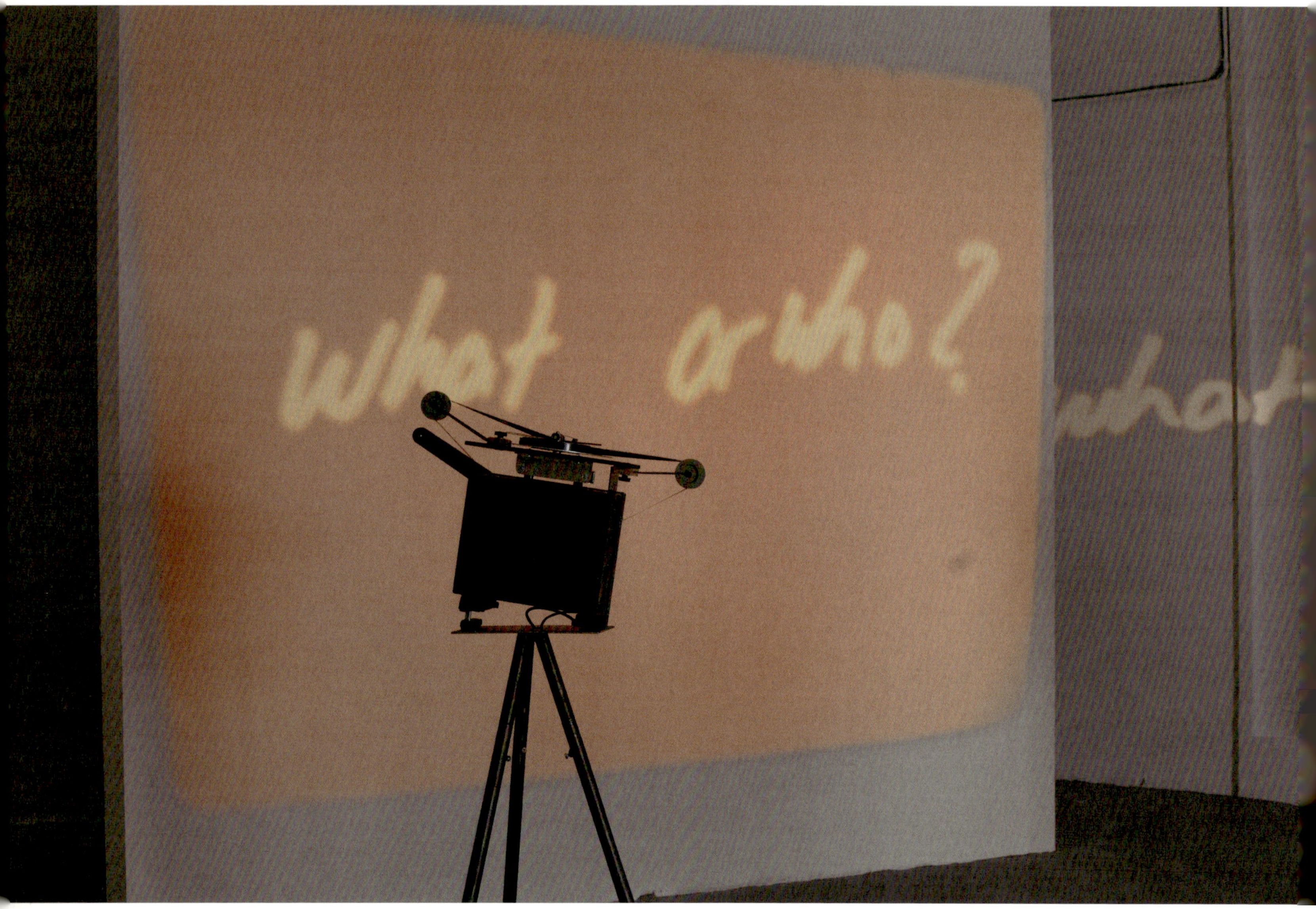

Above, right, preceding pages, and following pages: *Coro Spezzato: The Future Lasts One Day* (2009), installation view, Palazzo delle Esposizioni, 52nd Venice Biennale, 2009
Collection of the FRAC Franche-Comté, Besançon

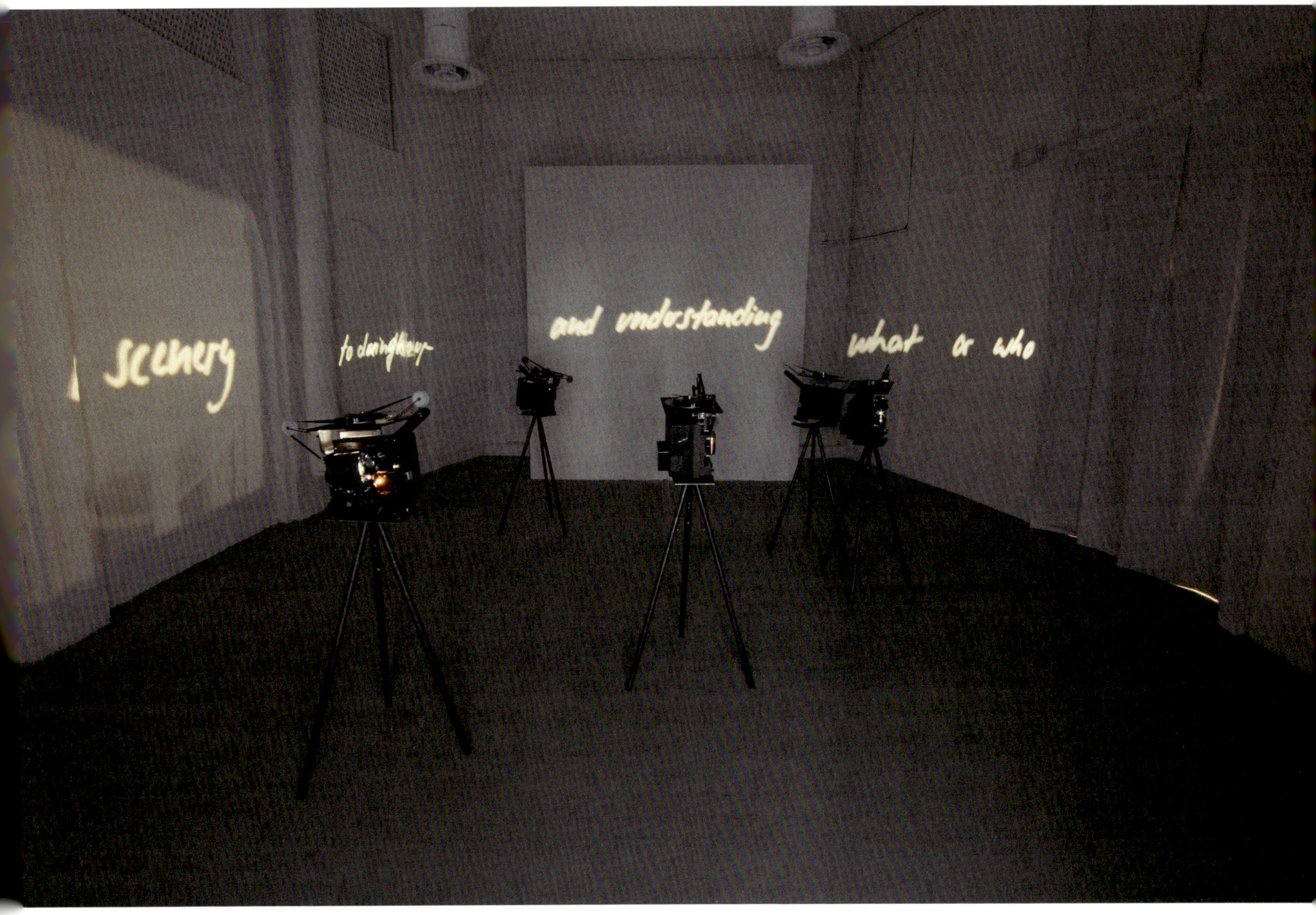
scenery
and understanding
what or who

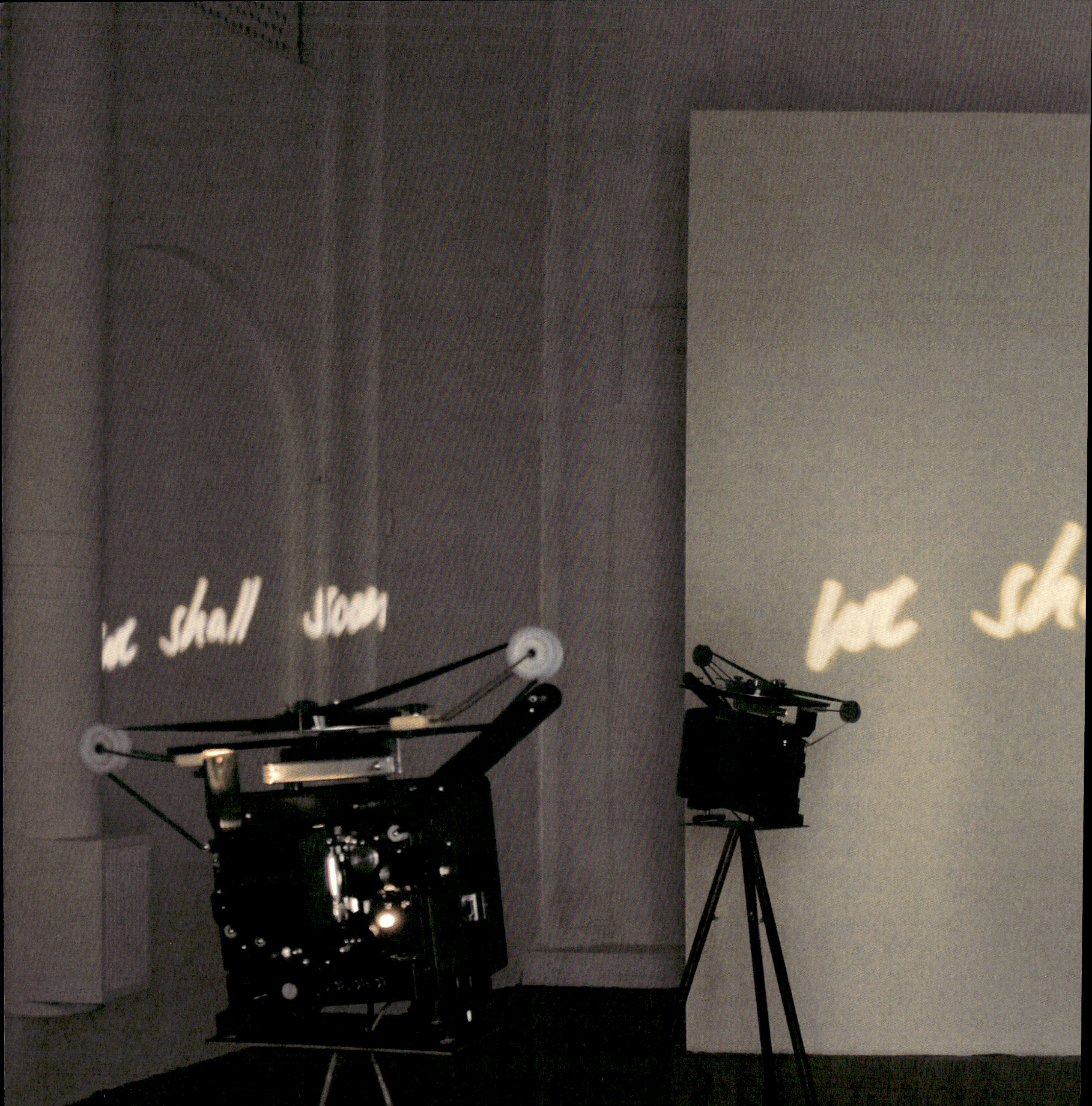
we shall

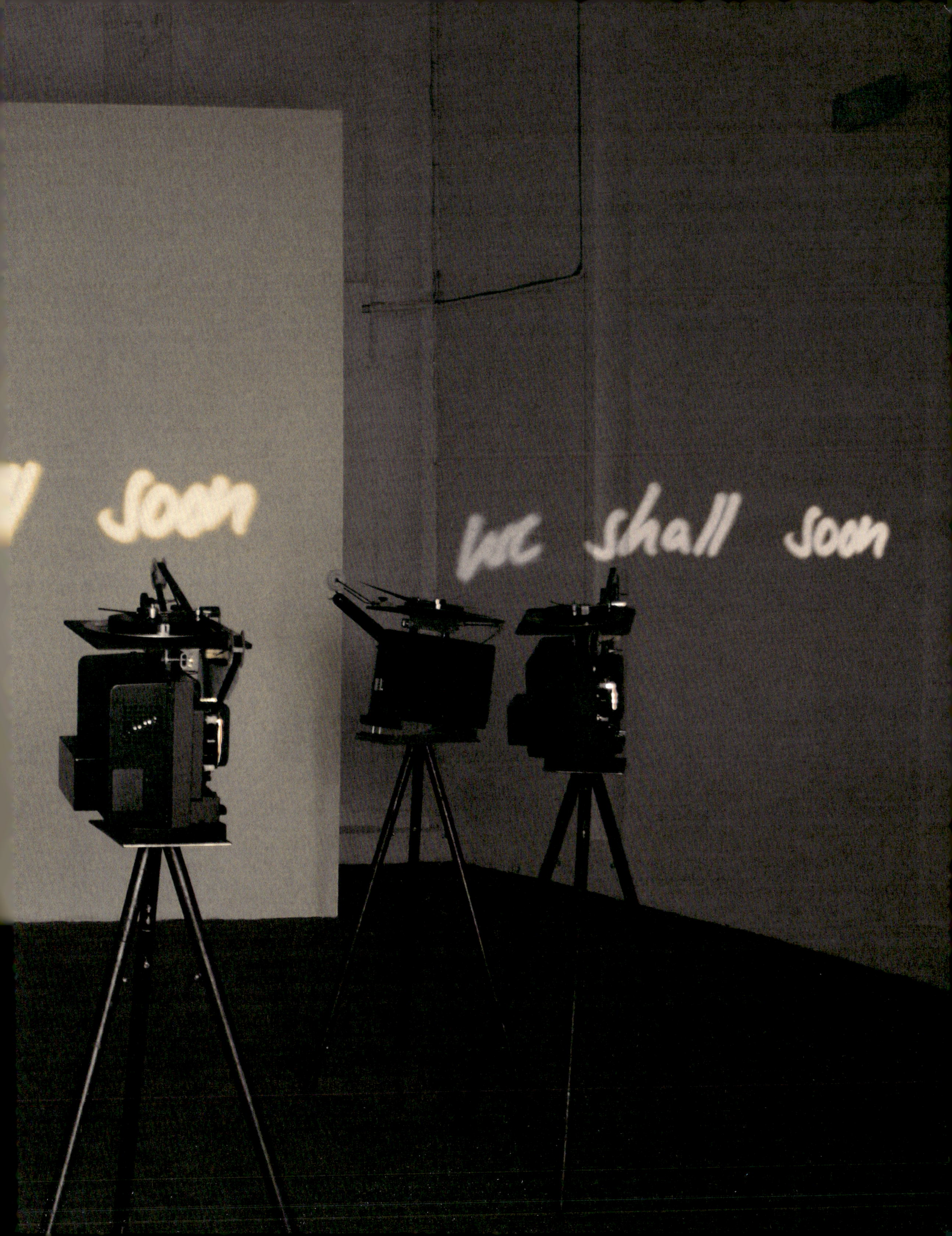
soon
we shall soon

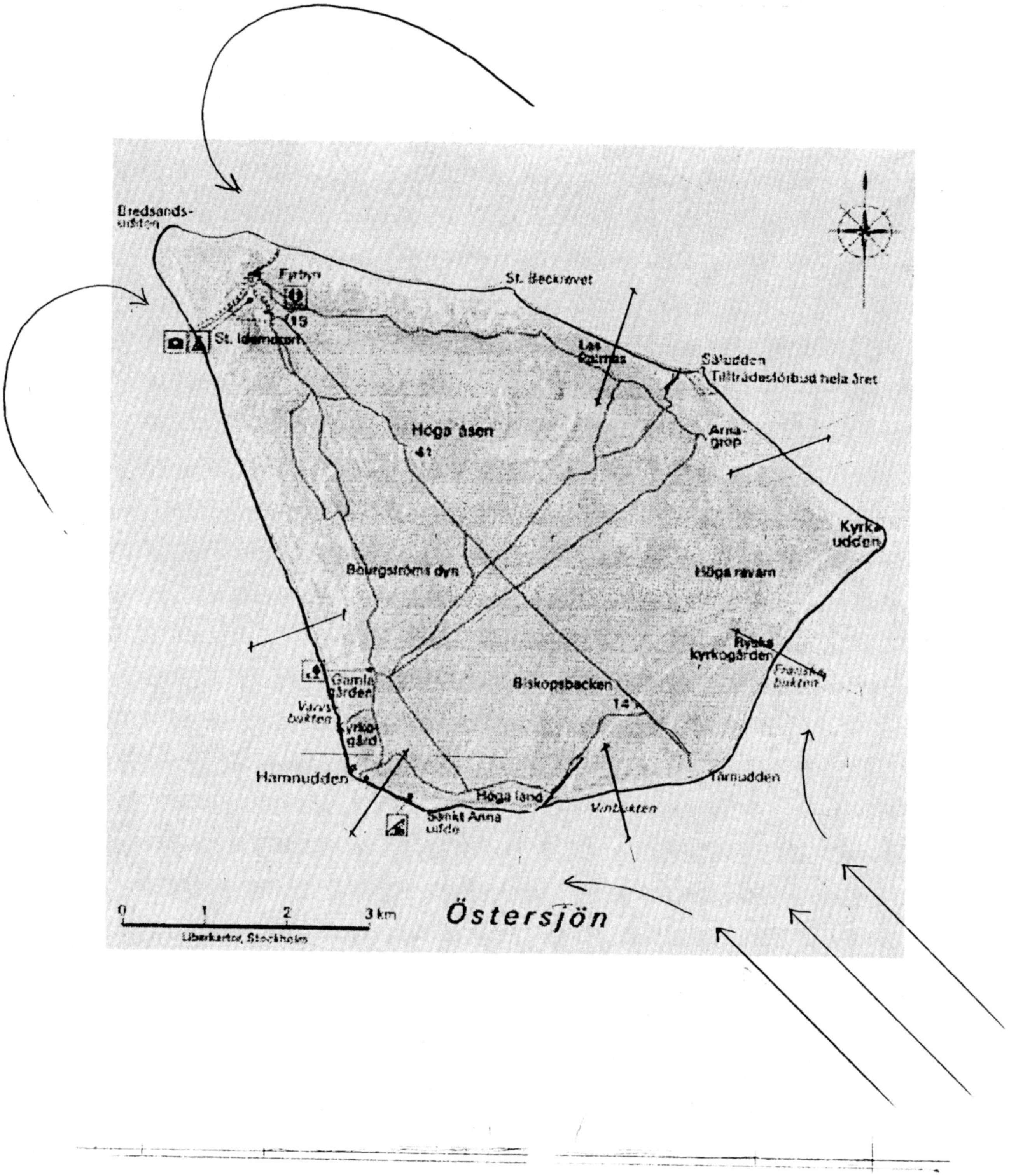

Outwardly from Earth's Center (2007)

In some recent writings, Rosa Barba's exhibitions have been referred to as "choreographed installations."[1] If we can claim that Barba transposes the notions of kinetic installation and of the performer onto the film projectors and her camera (especially in the films *They Shine* [2007], in which we follow the rotating movement of solar panels in the Mojave Desert, and *The Long Road* [2010], in which the provisional racetrack is "drawn" in circles with the camera filming from a bird's-eye perspective), then choreography should be employed here in its broadest sense, leaving behind its Greek roots as "dance-writing" to be perceived as a directorial act, one that designs and organizes movement in space. This starting point provides an exciting parallel to Barba's working relationship with the individuals or groups of people in at least three of her films—*Panzano* (2000), *Outwardly from Earth's Center* (2007), and *The Empirical Effect* (2010)—in which this specific relationship becomes concrete when there are moments of group appearances including dialogues, speeches, and movement.

In *Panzano,* which was Barba's first film and was made with Ulrike Molsen, the two artists worked on a regular basis for some months with two men and a woman who had been living in an experimental psychotherapeutic community in a village in Tuscany. We observe the three people—who, in Ian White's words, have been "orchestrated"[2]—in vaguely defined and interchangeable roles (sometimes representing a couple and their child, and at other times merely evoking the possibility that what we see might be an atypical family with its daily habits and conversations) as they actually act out their everyday experience of living in the village. By watching how their relationships form and unravel among them, however, another imaginative activity for the viewer begins to unfold, that of wondering about the filming process itself, through which the two filmmakers allowed the narration of the film to emerge delicately as the people involved behaved and expressed themselves as they chose.

The curious Swedish island Gotska Sandön is the subject of the film *Outwardly from Earth's Center,* in which a real situation—the island's slow drift towards the North Pole—is "inhabited by" a fictional one recounting how the residents of the island attempt to anchor the island in order to prevent its geological destiny from unfolding. The topic is presented at first through several interview-like monologues that introduce us to the Lighthouse-Keeper, the Architect, the Archaeologists, the Politician, and the Archivist, each one filmed in his or her own context and presenting the material on which they work. The scene with the Architect offers another discerned analogy with the format of a lecture performance, whereby the Architect himself appears in a theatrical setup in front of white screens on which images are projected, and what he says and shows is out of sync with his narration, which we are made to hear. Then another performative part of the film begins, the one in which the electronic music and soundscape composed by Jan St. Werner and Folke Rabe offer an eerie backdrop to the very slow, painstaking physical movement of the inhabitants, who put wooden branches around the beach and drag the ropes from the woods to the boats and further into the sea, which is the scene, shot from above, with which the film ends. The focus on the ropes, and on the way the people dragging them totter and wobble while struggling with their heavy weight, almost floating with the ropes as they get them tied to the boats, is spectacular in its aesthetic composition and performative quality. In the above-mentioned text by Ian White, this particular scene reminds him of the "friends and performers in Joan Jonas' *Wind,*"[3] a filmed performance from 1968 in which a group of performers moves through a windswept landscape.

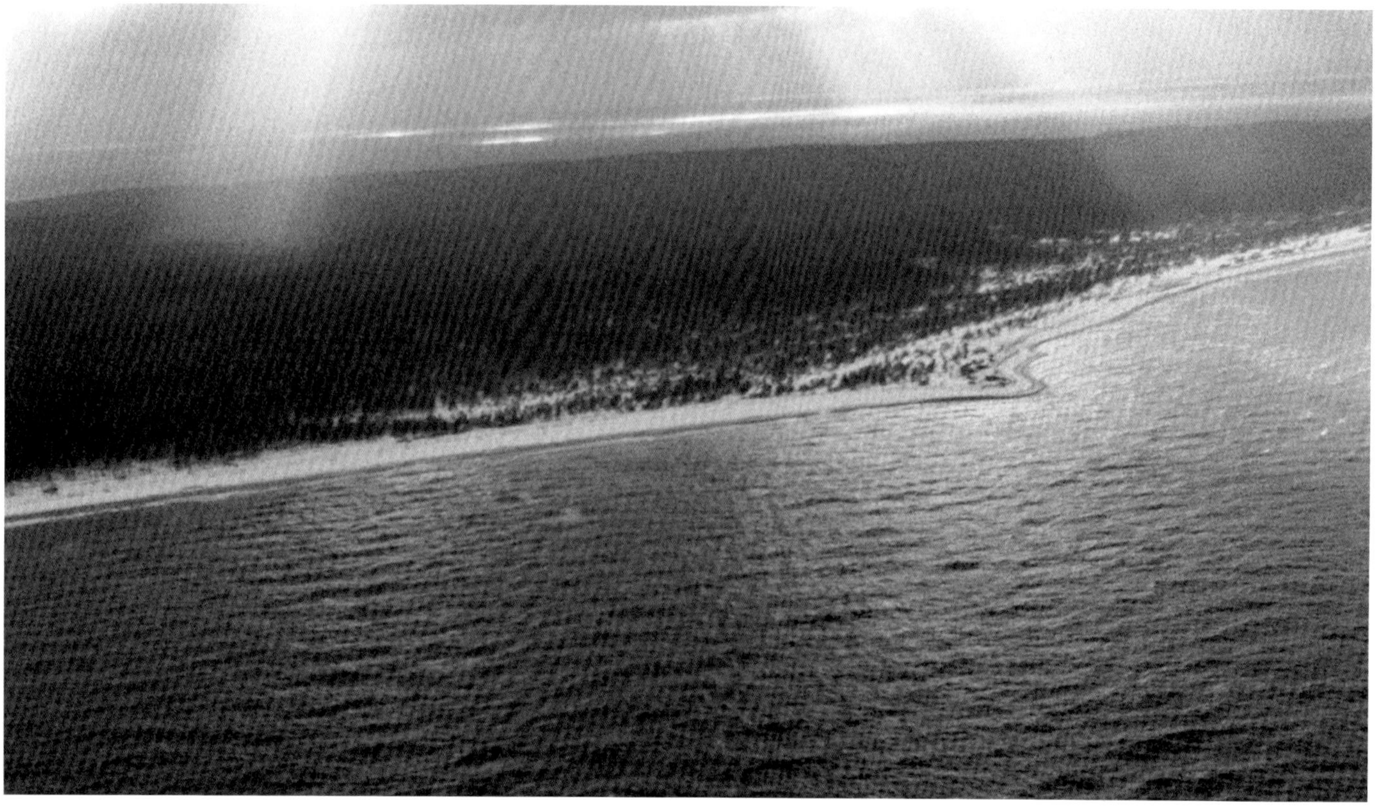

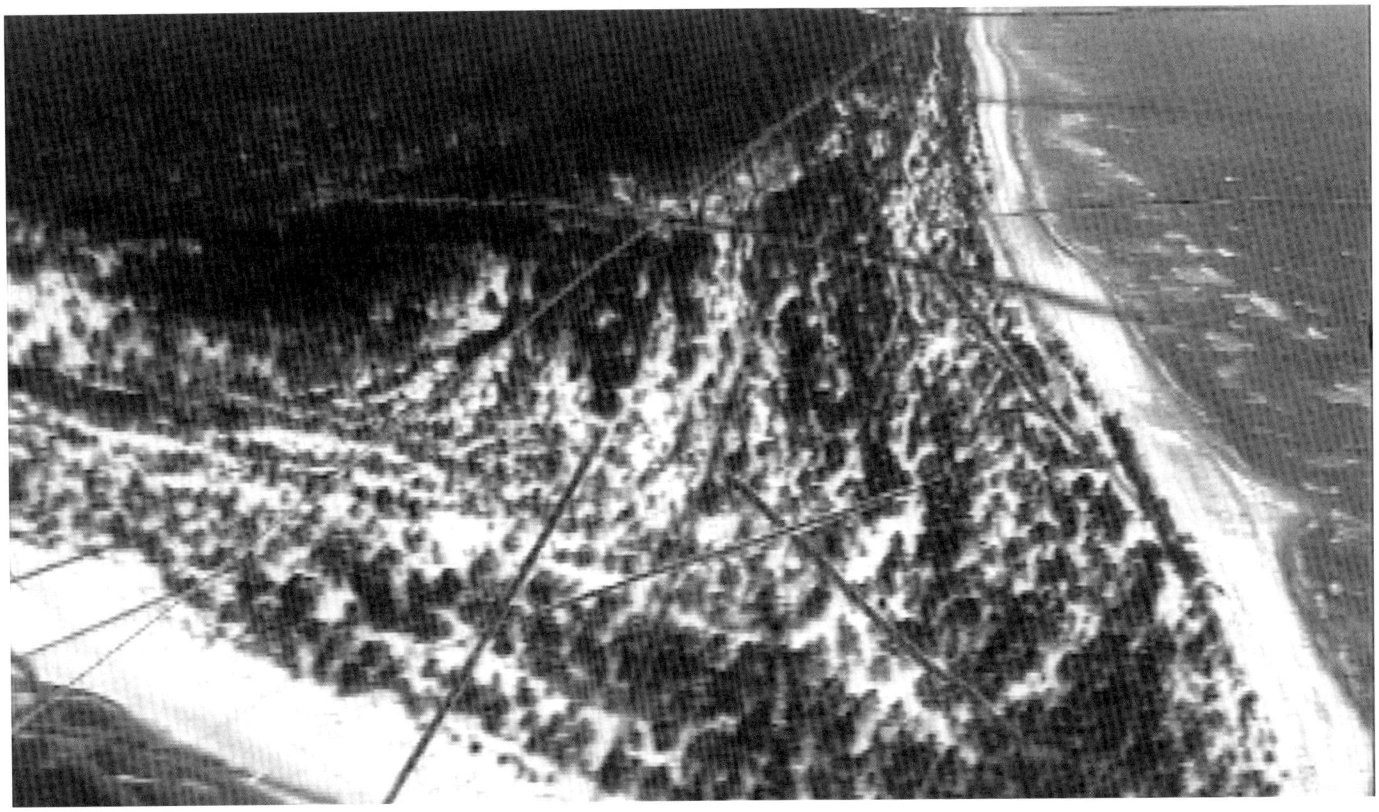

Left, above, and following pages: *Outwardly from Earth's Center* (2007)

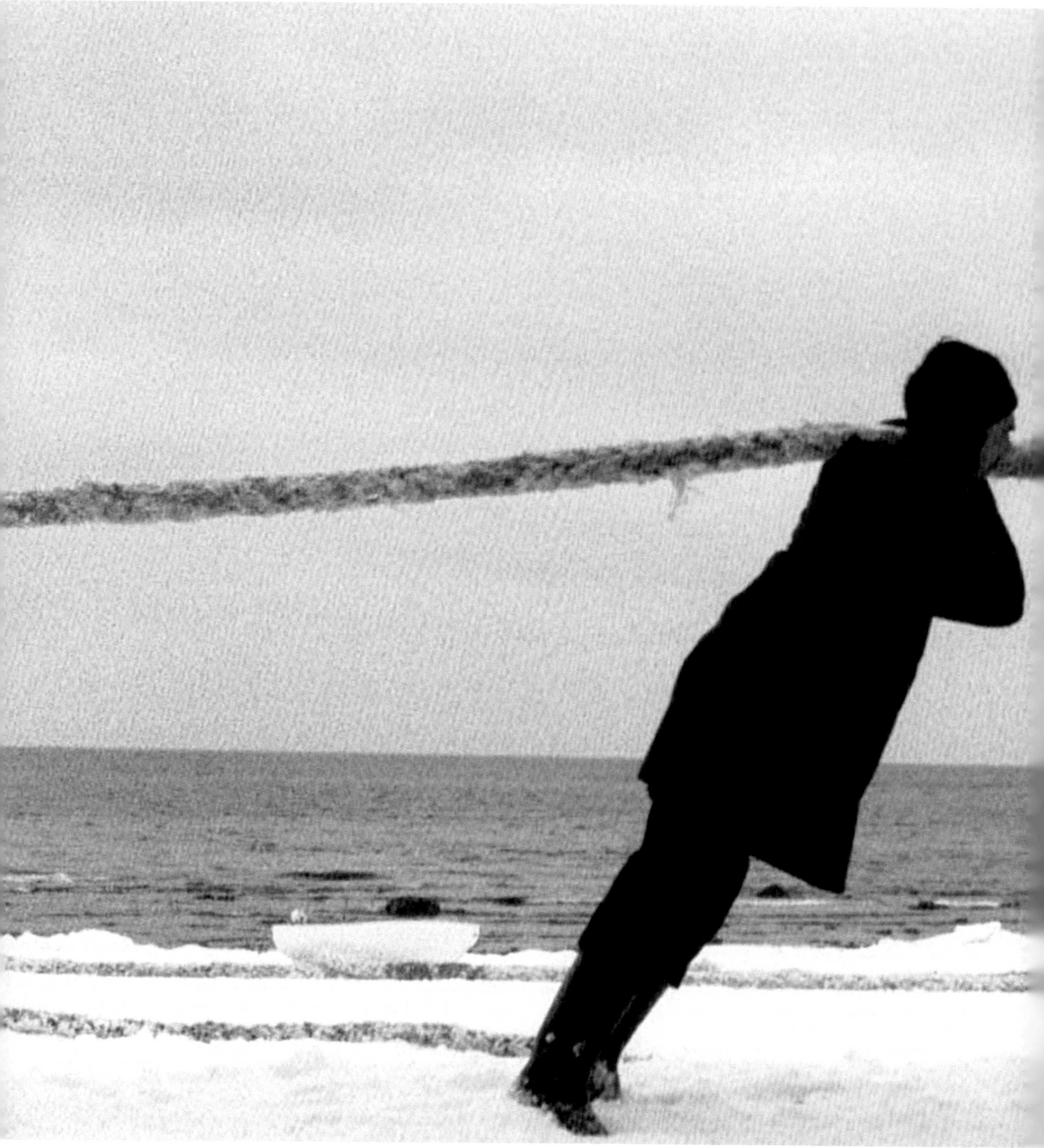

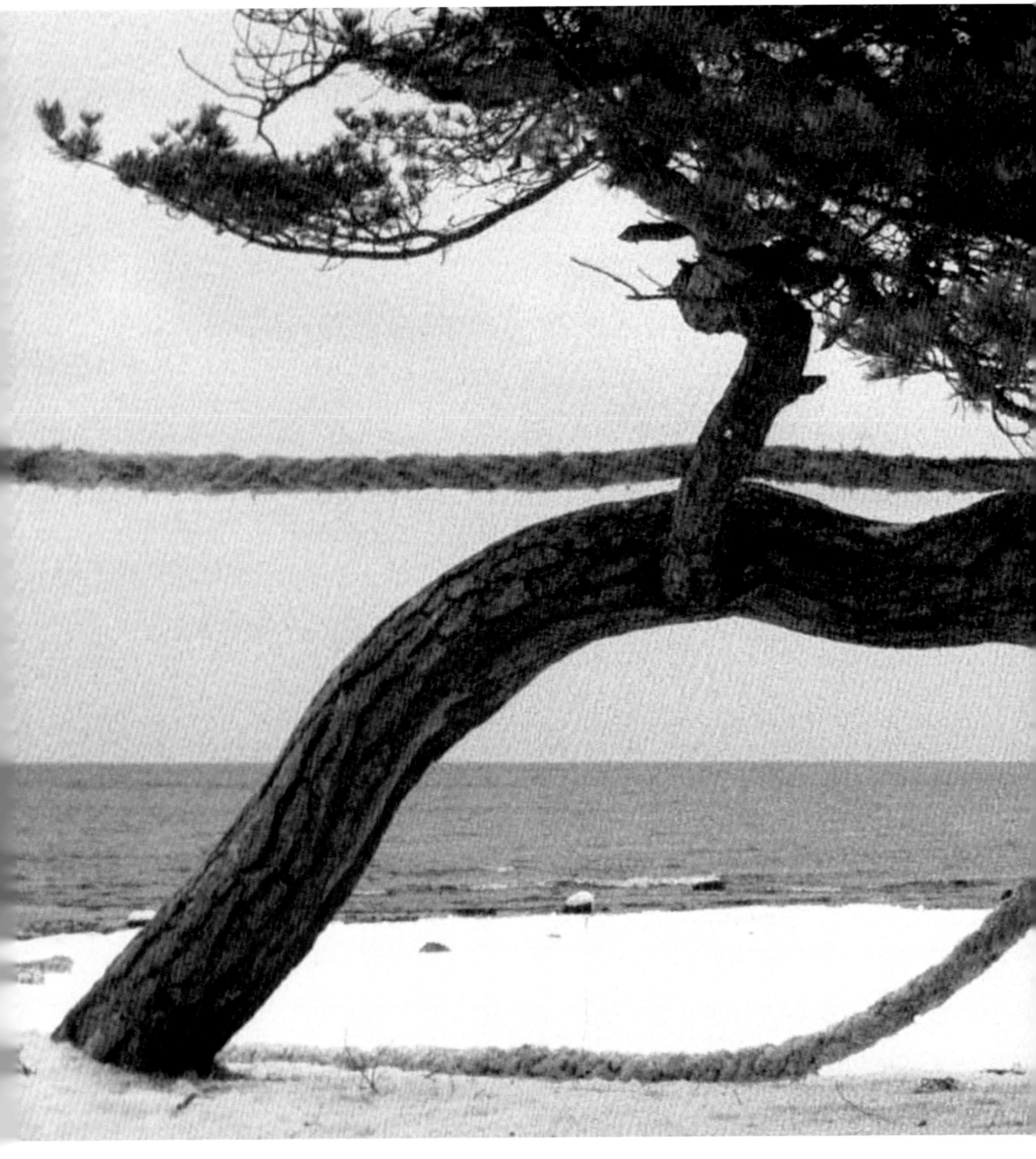

Enigmatically, *The Empirical Effect,* another of Barba's films, addresses human attempts to tame nature and is comprised of similar collective performances in which the memories of the characters involved interact with the scenario of a violent reawakening of Mount Vesuvius. For this film, Barba assembled and worked with two different groups that included many inhabitants of the constantly endangered "red zone" found at the foot of the volcano, as well as some of those who survived Vesuvius's last catastrophic eruption in 1944. The old observatory (Osservatorio Vesuviano) in Naples, which is situated near the volcano's crater, serves as the scenographic platform for the first part of the film and thus offers an important allusion to a performance that enrolls within a theater of memory. A smaller group of older people moves around the seismographic machines in the observatory, interacting with each other around the model of Vesuvius without speaking, and the sheep walk around and stare, and they occupy with the actors their place on the large map of Italy—and with the presence of the latter, a metaphor that the artist associates with the volcano is deployed in the film: we are observing an aspect of the unstable relationship between society and politics in contemporary Italy. One of the men in the group brings in old machines that the others unpack and disassemble, and they browse through books and black-and-white photos that hint at some unknown archival material that appears again later in the film in the form of the Lumière brothers' movies of Naples. The importance of showing the archival material as a means of consolidating the plausibility of the film's narration and in order to stimulate our curiosity about authenticity in Barba's fictional proposals is already brought into question in *Outwardly from the Earth's Center* through the role of the Archivist. What follows is another strongly performative sequence in which the group is seated in a classroomlike space watching a slide show or a film, but we only see them and their bodies as projection screens, for on their faces, glasses, and seated bodies we can see the reflections of what appears to be undecipherable archival material. We are witness to a silent performance in which their own memories are projected back onto their bodies. The artist herself has described the atmosphere of the community portrayed in this film as a "society [that] lives at a high level of tension, yet [is] paralyzed and somnambulistic." The focus on this particular group is shifted to a mass of people running out from their homes and down the streets, looking at the sky as if the volcano has already erupted.[4] While there is some expectation that we will see the lava eruption and chaos in the scenes that follow, Barba decides to slow the tempo of this potent atmosphere with the introduction of a final sequence with the first group of actors. In this sequence, they are on a large terrace of the observatory, dancing and singing traditional songs. Eventually, however, they stand still with their backs to the camera. The film's last image could again be seen as a performance, as it is shot from far away and presents a montage that repeats the same scene from the same point of view, but with only one person slightly moving around in the (otherwise immobile) group of people.

These specific "collective performances"[5] have been conducted and recorded for the film and follow a precise set of negotiations between the actors and the filmmaker as well as improvisation. In contemporary dance and performance terminology, choreography and improvisation are no longer antonyms, for improvisation can be included in choreographed pieces and can itself also be choreographed. Similarly, organizing her group of "actors," as Barba prefers to call them, into coherent performative entities is a result of a process whereby the artist tells them about her way of envisioning the narrative and the film and they are invited to enact—or react to—this based on who they are, what they represent to the artist, and how they feel the narrative should be presented in the film: "I invite people to come together and perform their memories (through facts, documents) in a kind of collective performance; it is the peak of the fictional part of the films. I tell them about my ideas for the films, but even more I tell them why I am interested in working with them on them. We talk much more about it during the shooting itself, although in the beginning, when I have just met them, we don't speak about it a lot. It is a bit of a chemical reaction between them and me. As soon as the camera rolls, the space turns into a stage, and they start to perform with me."[6] The characters that appear in the above-mentioned films are never played by professionally trained actors, but rather by individuals who are deeply connected with the location or subject that is represented in each film. In Barba's words, the people who are selected to participate "are carrying the story of this chosen location with them, and I invite them to tell this story in a performative frame, which I set. This frame is then only a drawing from which to start, and is then extended or broken by them during shooting. I give them instructions, but they are free to do with them what they want."[7]

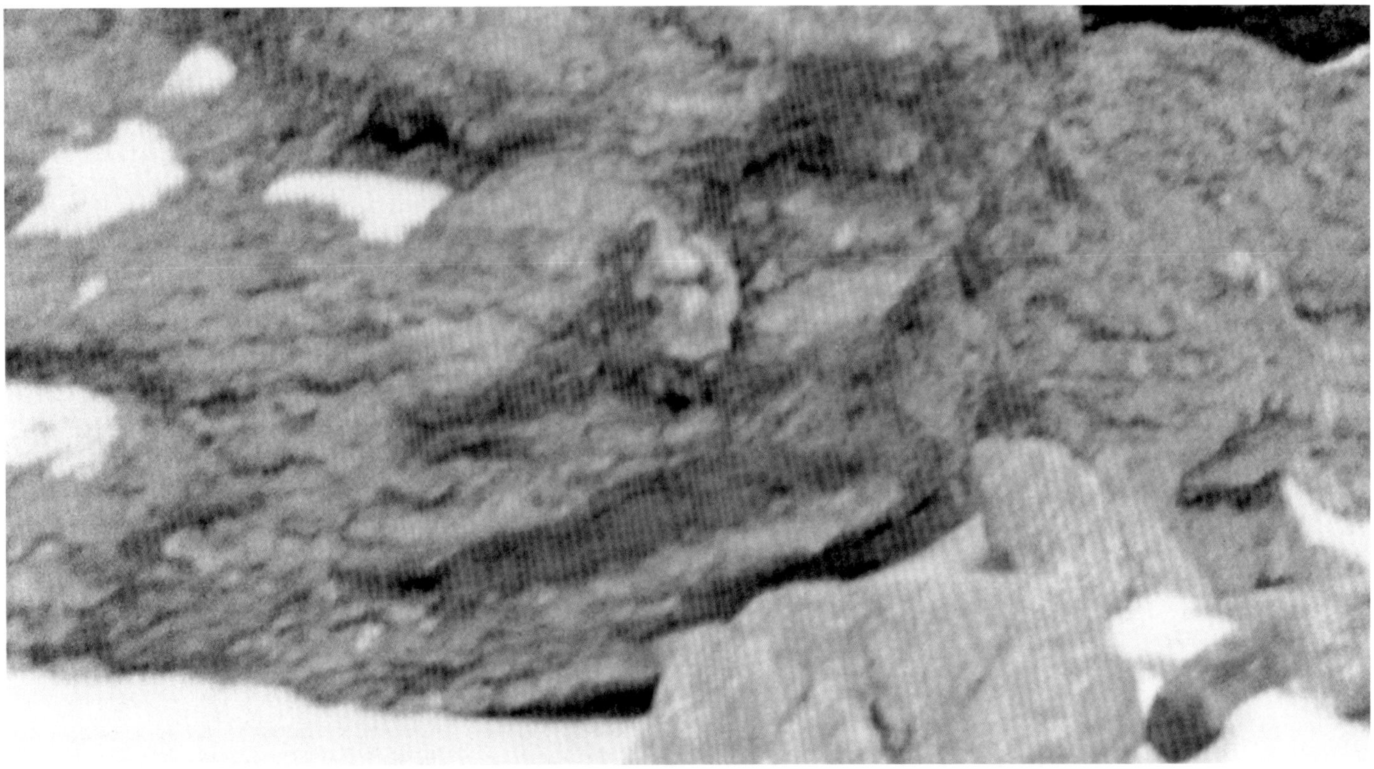

Outwardly from Earth's Center (2007)

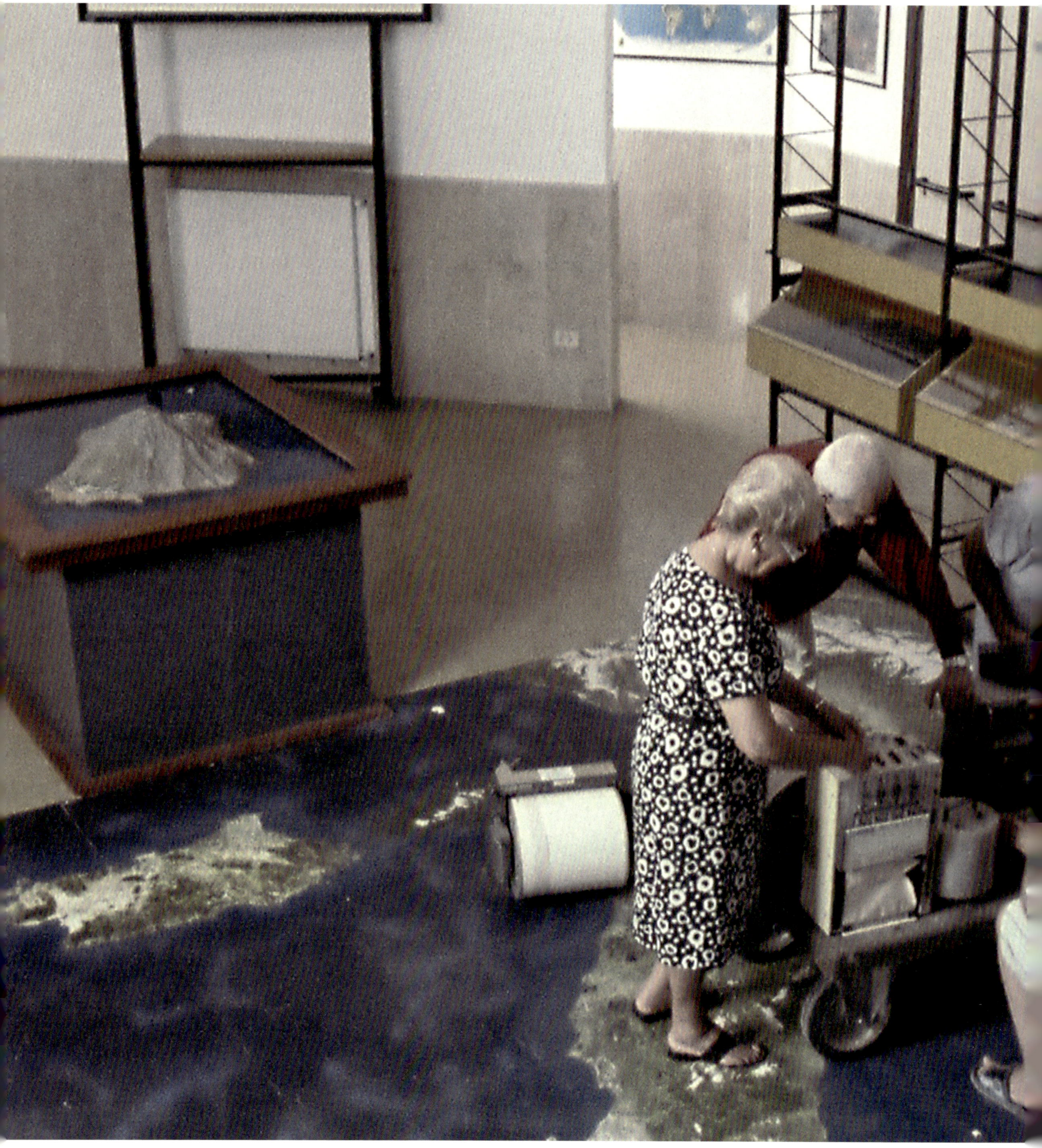

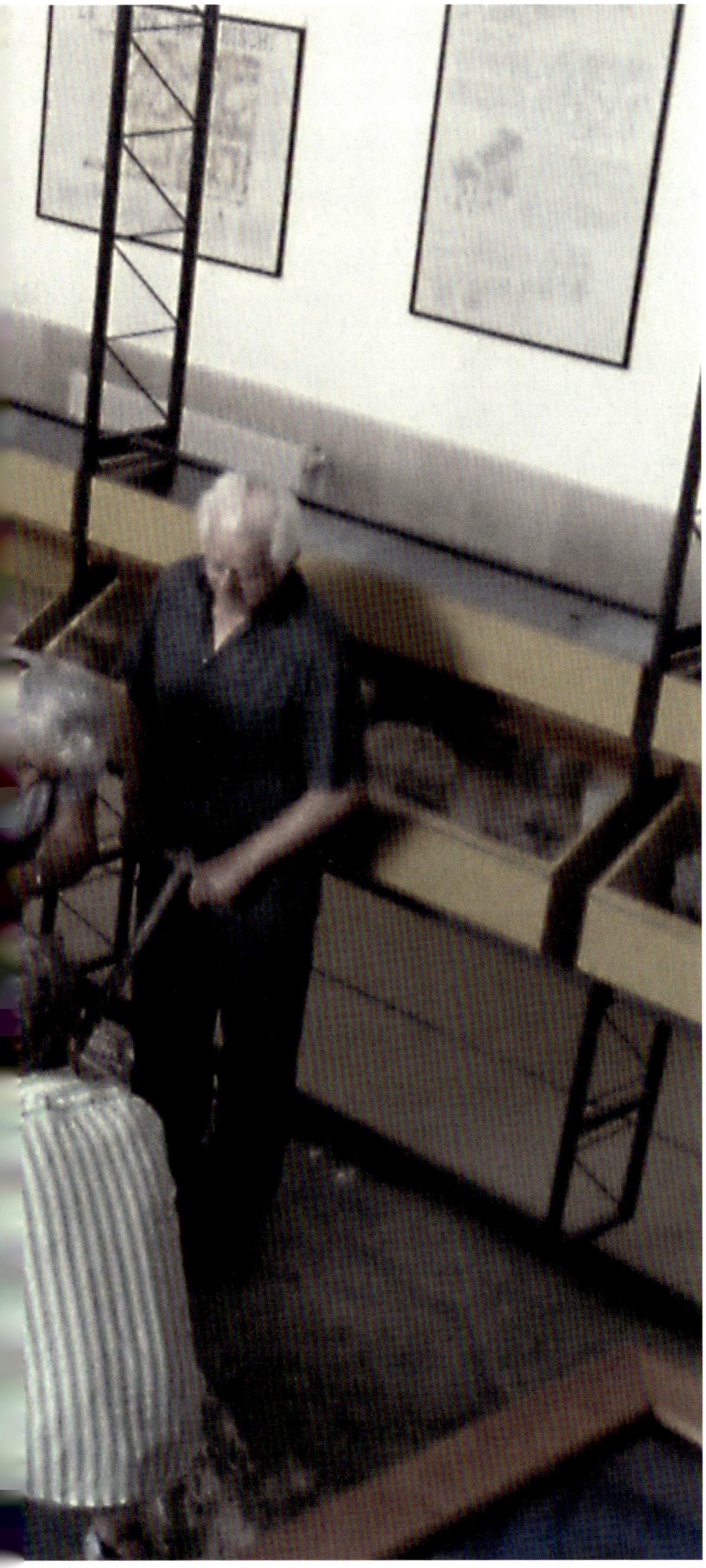

Especially in the film *The Empirical Effect,* the method employed of inviting people to perform their own memories in conjunction with imagining a fictional narrative comes close to the most recent developments in choreography, which are concerned with the production of kinesthetic sensations and with the affective relationship with the viewer through the use of imagination and language in the choreographic process. Mette Ingvartsen, Alice Chauchat, and Eszter Salamon are three of the younger generation of choreographers who are putting emphasis on the use of language to stimulate the imagination and to inspire sensations about a given movement in the performer himself.

Let me point to two examples in which some correspondence can be found in the "choreographic process" evident in Barba's films. In the working process that informed Salamon's show *NVSBL* (2006), in which four female dancers advance across the stage so slowly that their movement is rendered imperceptible,

> action and sensation merge in one process for performers, as well as for the spectators, yet in another distribution: for the performers, actions are initiated by sensation, and for the spectators, perception demands such effort that it is experienced as action. . . . [T]he problem that the performers were to confront was imagining and feigning movement, the place in the body where it is initiated, the corresponding quality that it has, the image it could take in another context. The system that could provide a quasi-physiological insight into the body and that would, therefore, require animating sensations with images and fictions about the movement was Body-Mind Centering (BMC). . . . Apart from BMC, the performers implemented another technique of expression. In order to compose their faces and enrich the quality in the movements of the overall body, they were conjuring images of expressions, the memory they had of the dynamic of certain moods and emotions, or placing the movements they were doing then and there into another environment, with a quality that it could not have actually, but only virtually on stage; for example, how it would feel to do this movement while running, remembering the sensation of running, while not running.[8]

Left and following pages: *The Empirical Effect* (2010)

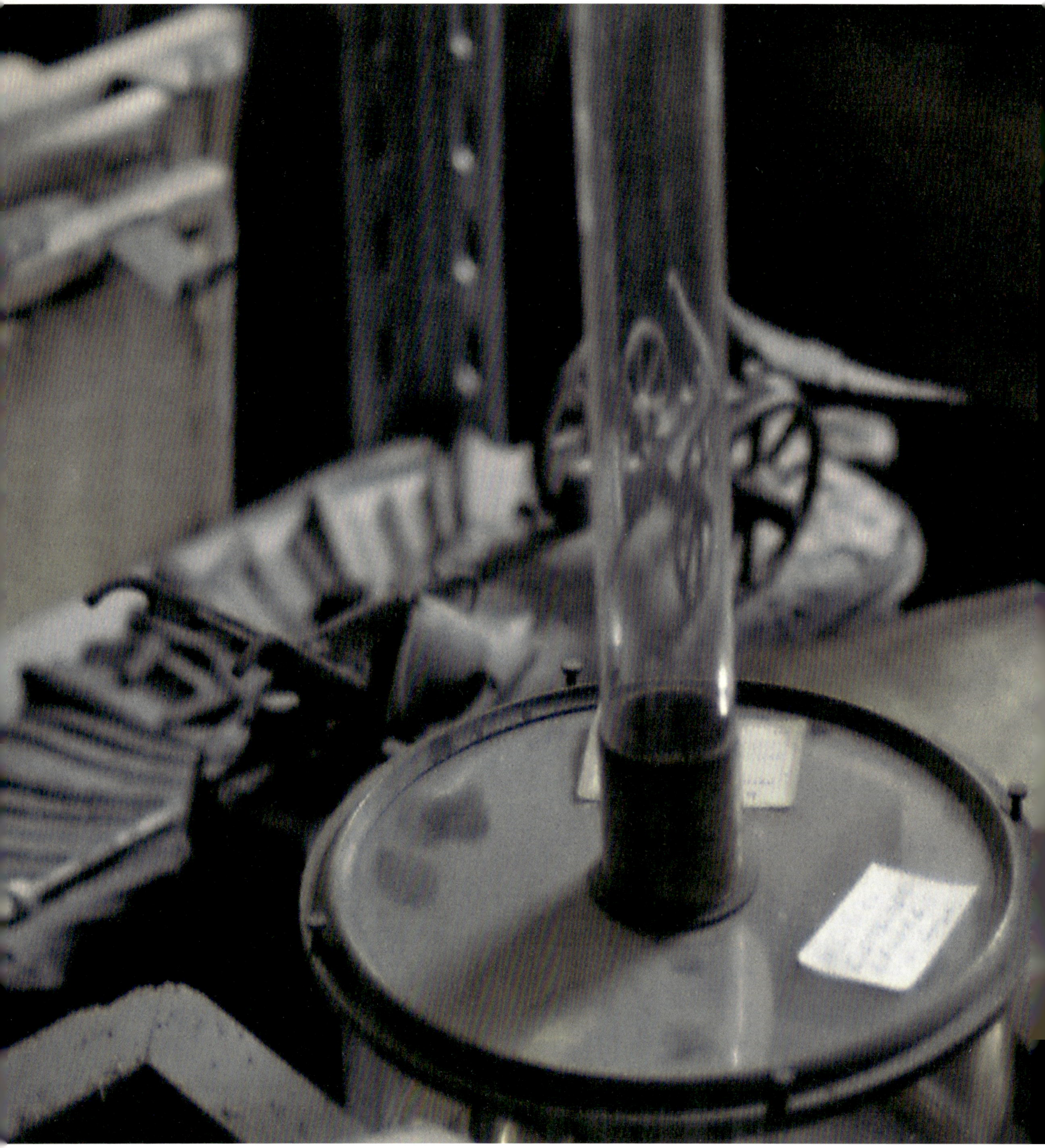

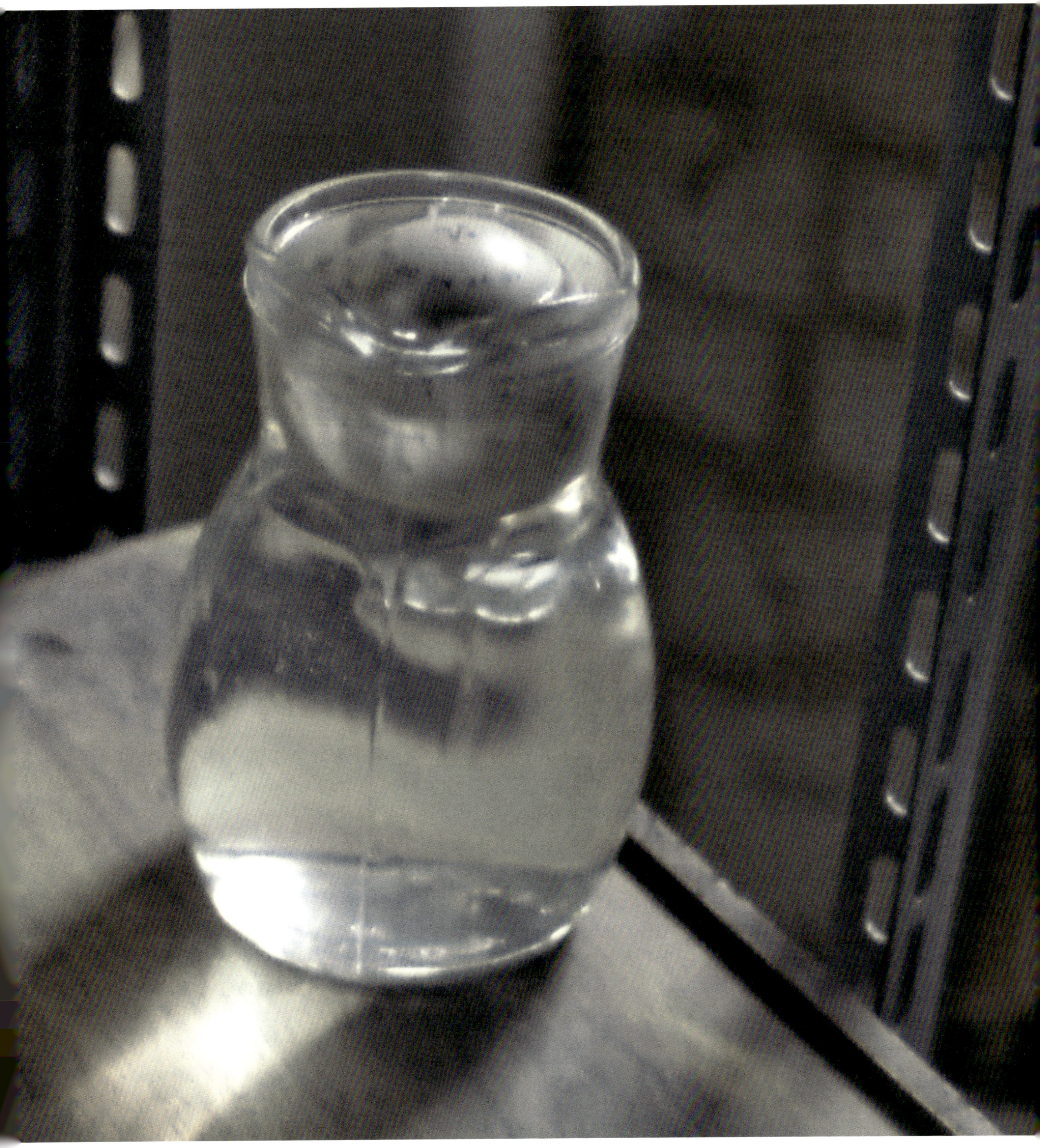

Danish choreographer Mette Ingvartsen wrote a short manifesto entitled "On Site-Specific Performance" that also echoes the atmosphere of space and its memory that Barba employs in her films:

> 1. Site-specific performance insists on using preexisting environments as the starting point for its creation, thus using the environment as a backdrop, [as a] stage-set or even as a performer.
> 2. Site-specific performance lets the artistic idea emerge out of an actual, social and/or political situation[,] however not reducing the expression to the reproduction of this situation.
> 3. Site-specific performance reactivates its location and offers a new "sight" on the specific.
> 4. Site-specific performance is conditioned and influenced by a particular space and should condition and influence this space in return.
> 5. Site-specific performance lets go of the autonomy of art and the neutrality of the theater space.
> 6. Site-specific performance creates a fiction within the reality of the place, suggesting the spectator . . . rethink her/his "natural" perceptions.
> 7. Site-specific performance melts into the environment where it is performed, becoming indistinguishable from the reality of the place.
> 8. Site-specific performance produces doubt about what belongs to the situation that is performed, versus what belonged to the situation already beforehand.
> 9. Site-specific performance cannot be toured, as it is integral to the place it has been made in. However the strategies used can be reinstated or readapted to other contexts and produce new site-specificities.
> 10. Site-specific performance addresses and treats formats, conventions and expectations of performed expressions, [and also] questions logics of [the] reproduction, circulation and commodification of performance works.[9]

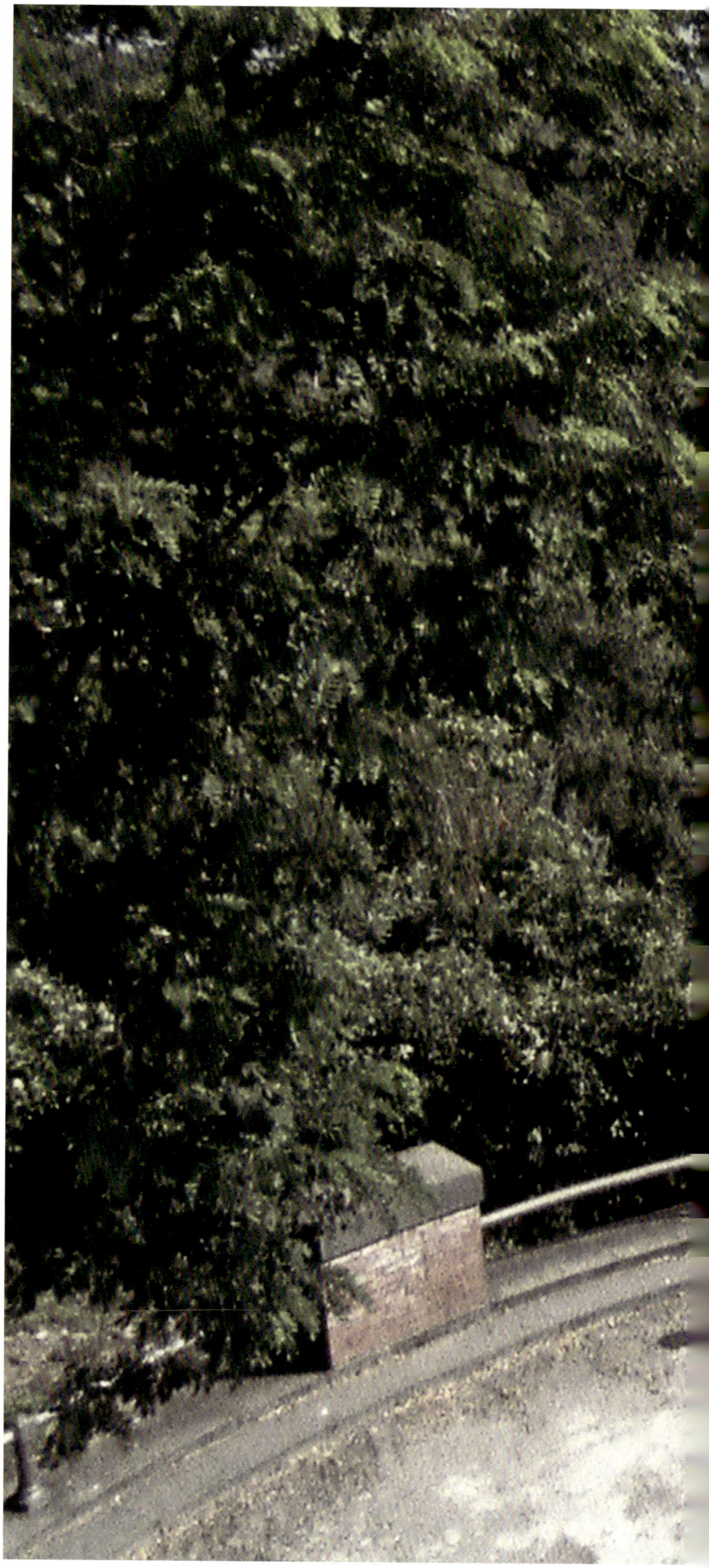

The Empirical Effect (2010)

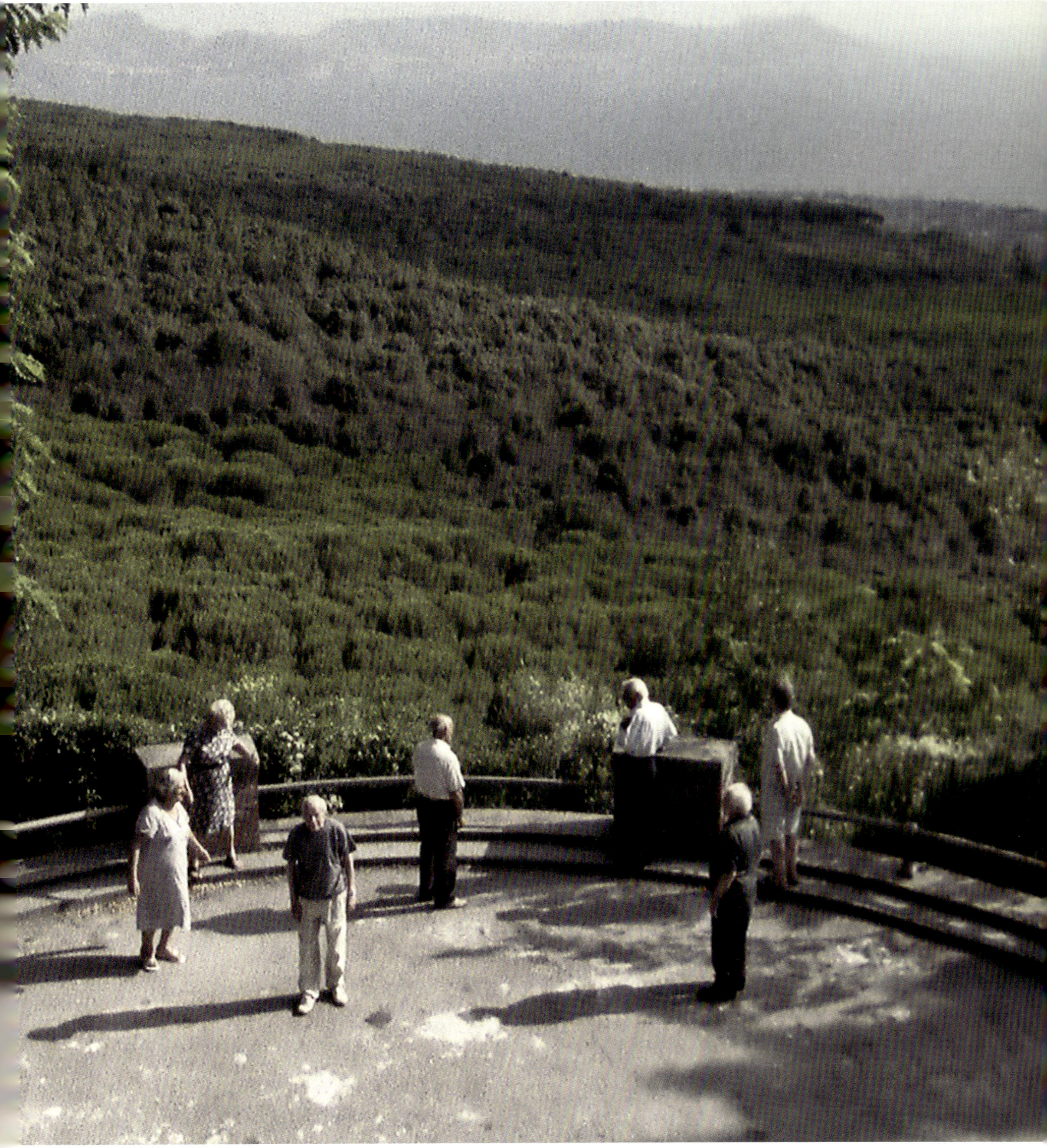

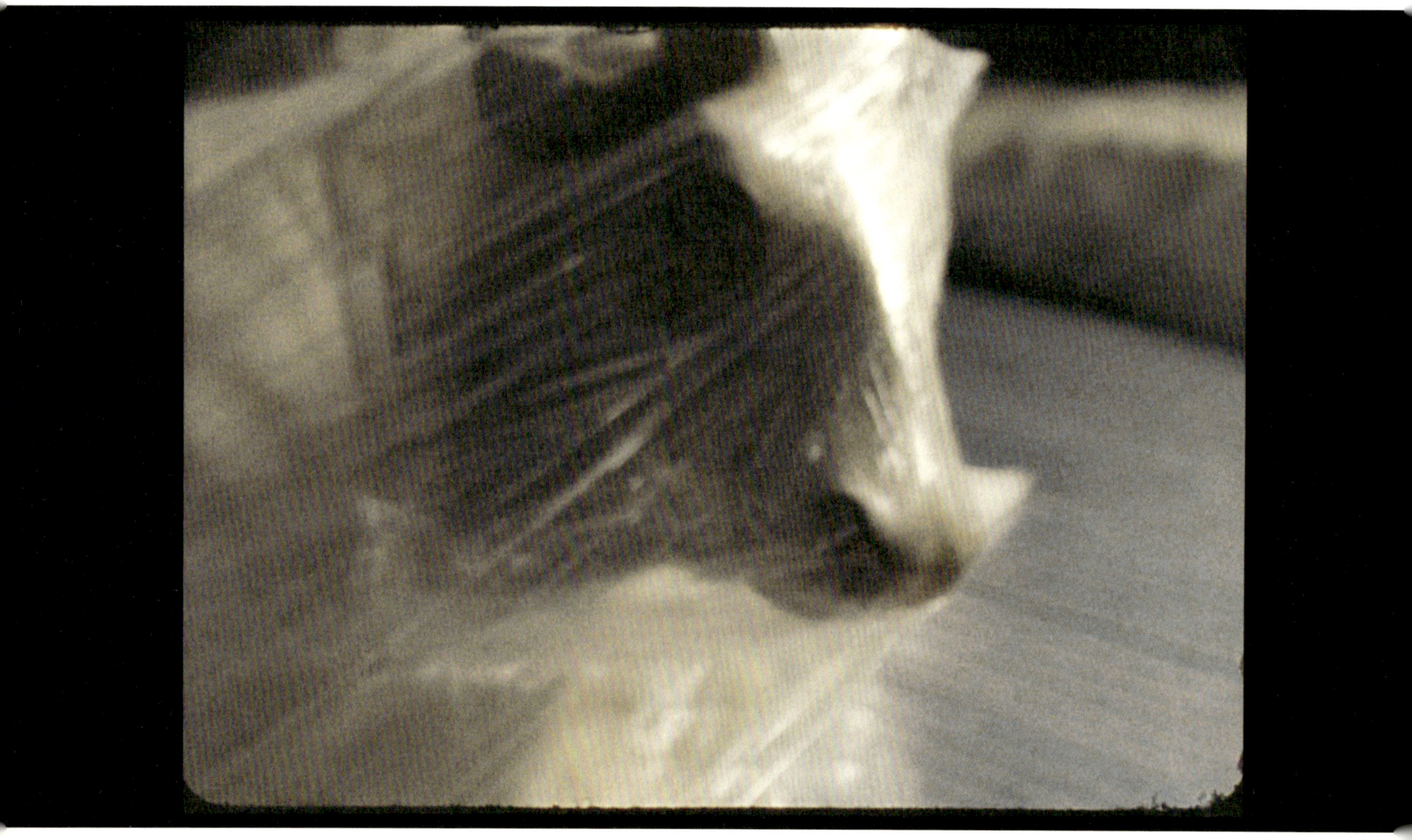

Above and following pages: *The Hidden Conference: A Fractured Play* (2011)

In her two most recent films, this very special filmed "site-specific performance" extends beyond the human protagonists onto the camera itself (as in *A Private Tableaux,* 2010) and onto the art objects kept in museum storage (as in *The Hidden Conference: About the Discontinuous History of Things We See and Don't See,* 2011). In *A Private Tableaux,* the movement of the camera is "scripted" by the lines, marks, drawings, and scratches that engineers and scientists have left behind over the years while conducting research on the stability of subterranean architecture. The camera draws out details of wall drawings and the accompanying electronic sounds of the researchers and, later on, sounds that seem to come from building construction, and responds kinesthetically to the swinging light that enables it to capture some elusive forms in the dark.

The Hidden Conference is a dialogue-free yet nonetheless performative film evoking the discussions one can imagine artworks in museum storage spaces might have with one another. It is a work in progress that confirms Barba's continuing investigation of cultural storage areas and archives. In the first part of the film, the camera slowly weaves a narrative around small sculptures sitting on shelves, providing close-ups of them and creating a chiaroscuro atmosphere as if it were presenting the spectators with the story's main protagonists. In the second part of the film, the storage area transforms itself into a stage upon which theatrical entries and exits are performed by the iron walls on which the paintings are stored. The soundscape, as is always the case in Barba's films and installations, is an equal partner in supporting the fictionalization process.

It is in these examples that we can see Rosa Barba's interest in bringing into visibility, as the artist herself puts it, the ways in which human inner landscapes interact with the natural landscapes she presents in her films and, furthermore, the ways in which emotions, memories, and other experiential or lived realities materialize human traces in history.

Notes

1. "In this exhibition, Barba's carefully choreographed installation divides viewers' attention between the projected image and [the] projector itself, posing questions as to which is the narrative and which the narrator." Excerpt from the press release of Barba's exhibition at the Tate Modern, London, September 15, 2010–January 8, 2011; consulted online at: http://www.tate.org.uk/modern/exhibitions/rosabarba/default.shtm (last accessed on March 23, 2011).

2. Ian White, "Ian White on Rosa Barba," *Camera Austria,* no. 101 (2008), pp. 21–26.

3. See note 2.

4. These scenes were shot during the annual drill that all of the inhabitants of the red zone must perform in preparation for the eventuality of an emergency mass evacuation.

5. Barba used this term in her talk at the "Something You Should Know" seminar at the École des hautes études en sciences sociales (EHESS) in Paris in May 2010. Barba's precise formulation was, in fact, what sparked the present essay, and I would like to thank her warmly for all of our exchanges about this notion.

6. Rosa Barba in conversation with the author, November 2010.

7. Ibid.

8. Eszter Salamon, quoted in Bojana Cveji, "Researching: A Public Interview with Eszter Salamon," in *6M1L* (n.p.: Everybodys Publications, 2009), pp. 84–85. Body-Mind Centering is an integrated approach to transformative experience through movement re-education that has recently been used widely in contemporary choreography. Developed by Bonnie Bainbridge Cohen, it is an experiential study based on the embodiment and application of anatomical, physiological, psychophysical, and developmental principles through the utilization of movement, touch, voice, and mind.

9. See http://www.everybodystoolbox.net/?q=node/160 (last accessed March 23, 2011).

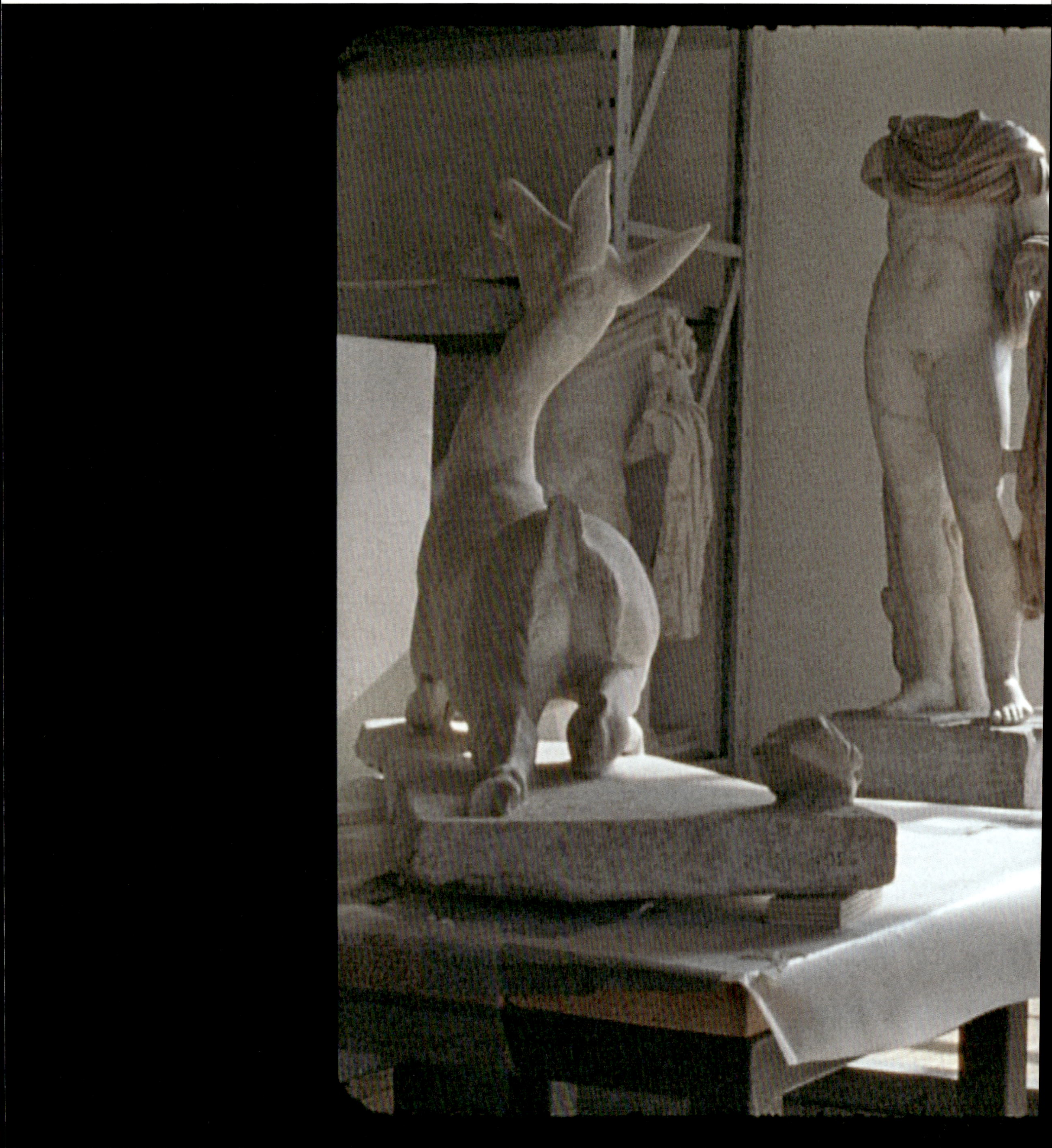

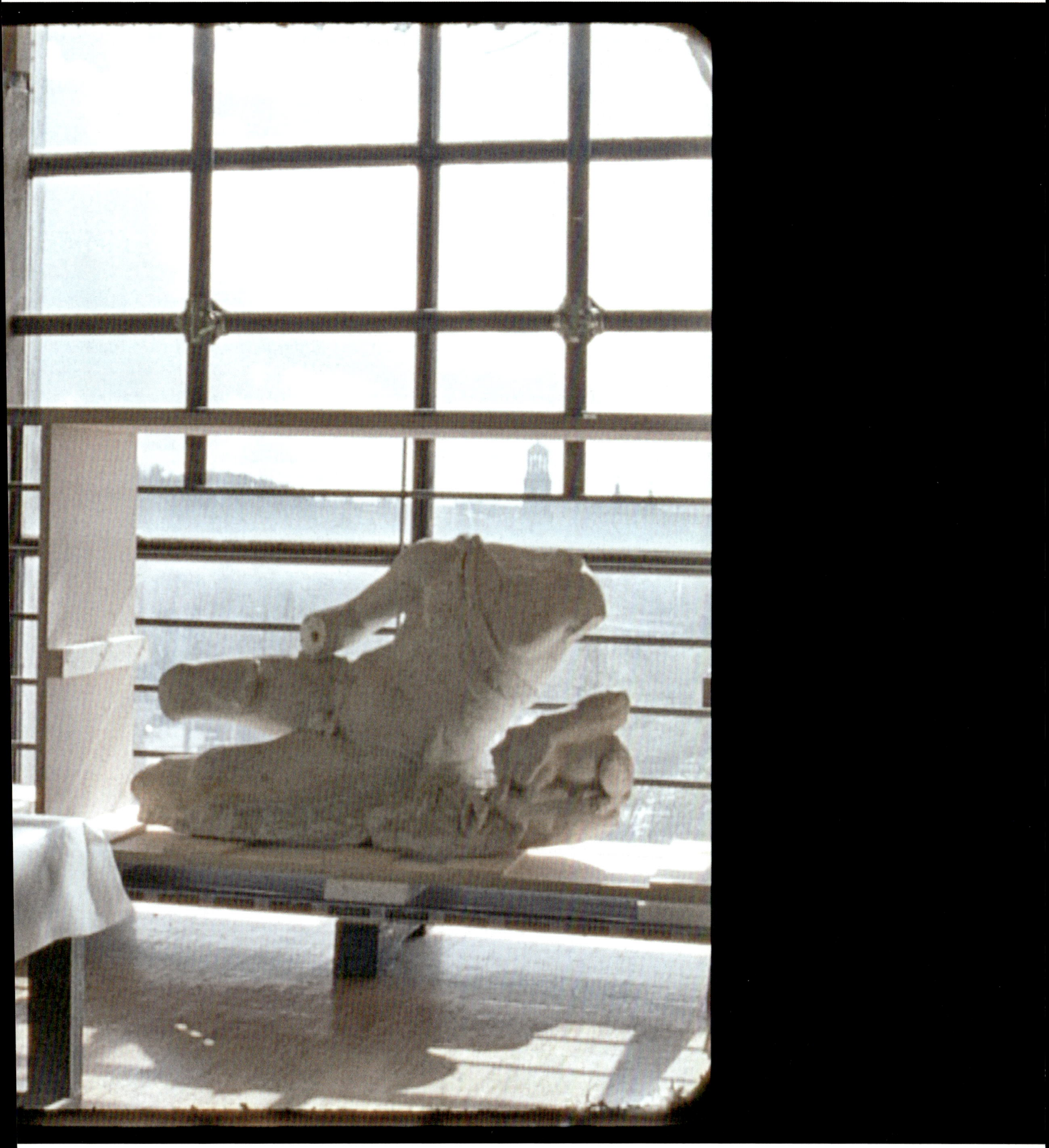

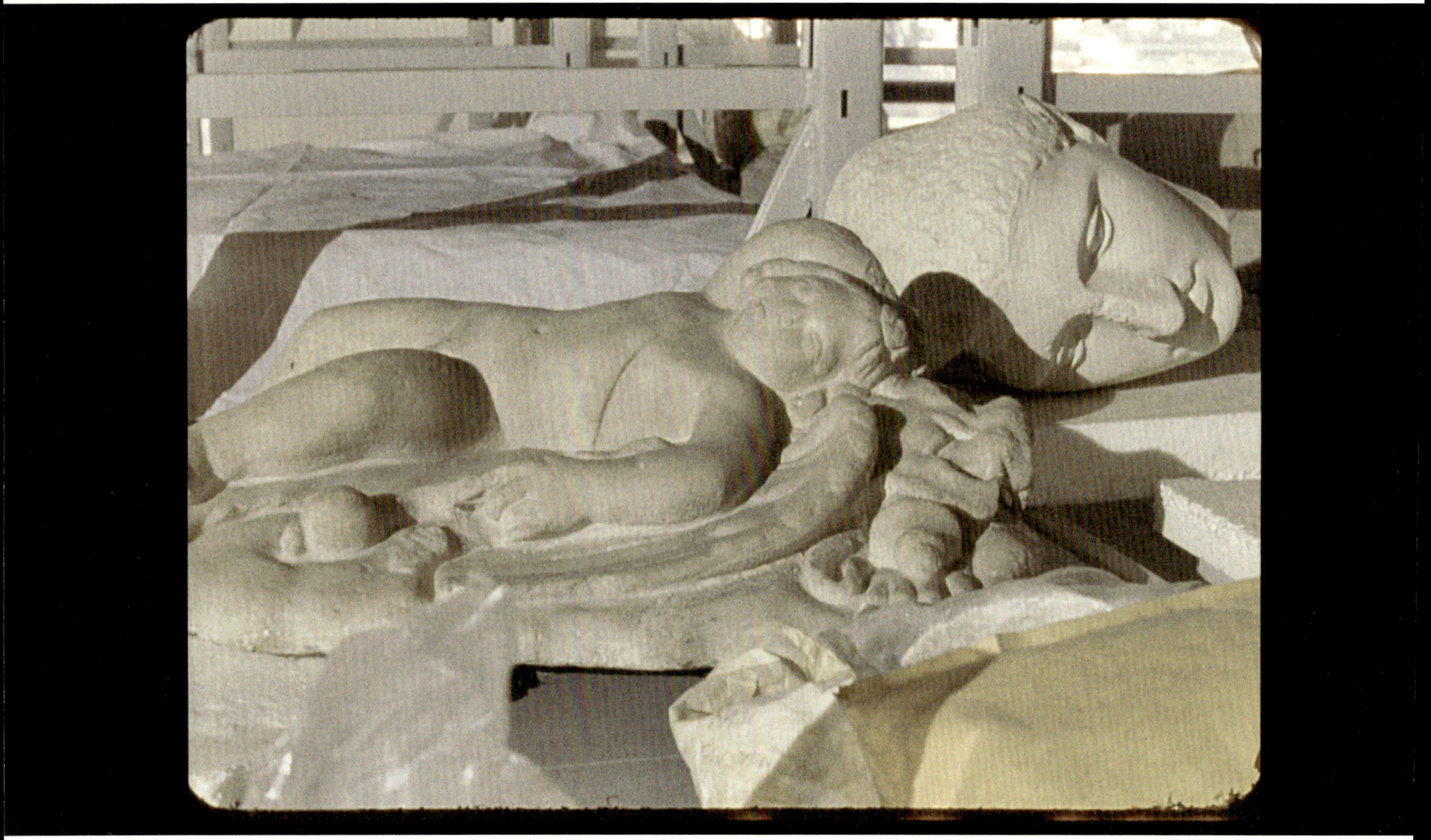

Above, right, and pages 160–63: *The Hidden Conference: A Fractured Play* (2011)

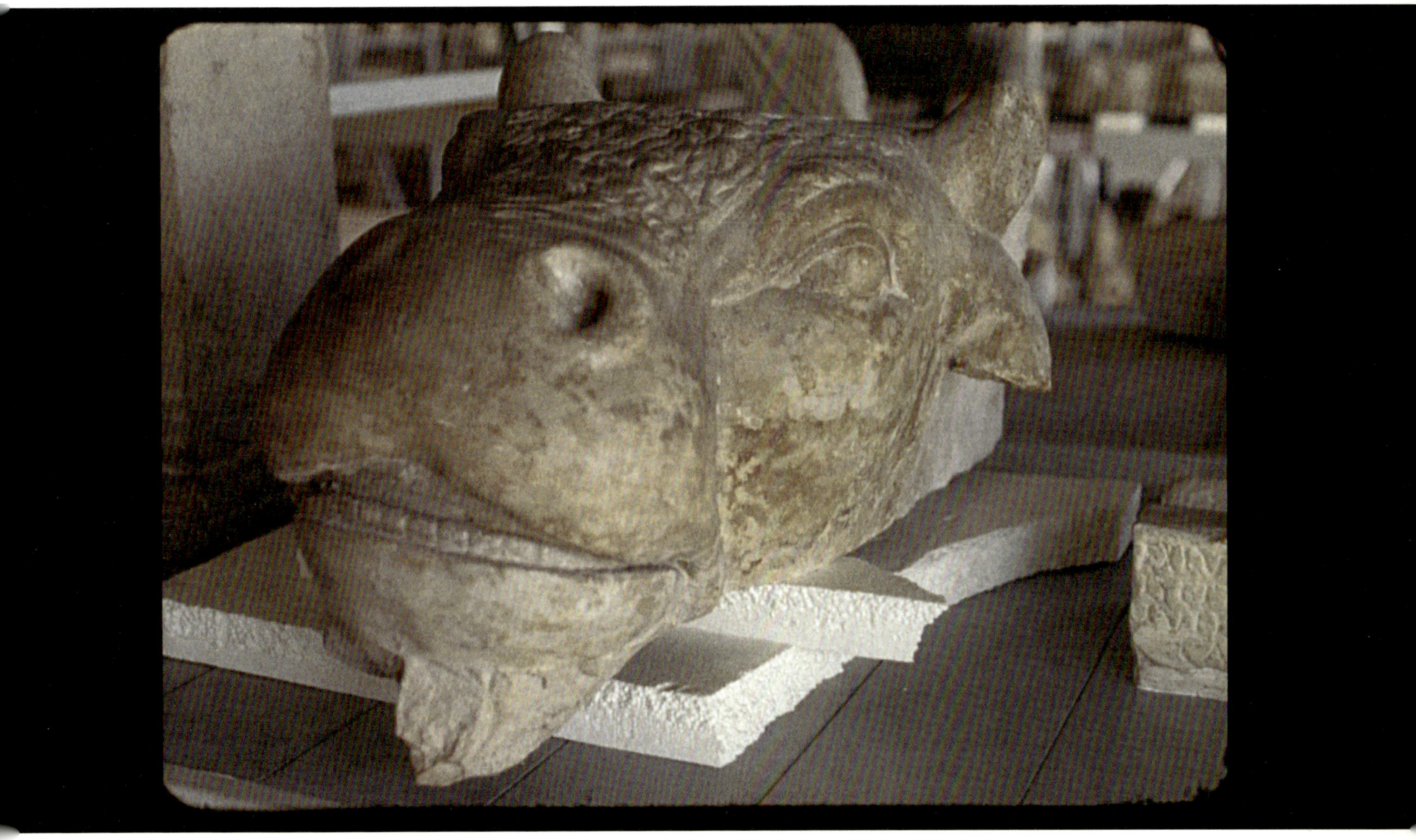

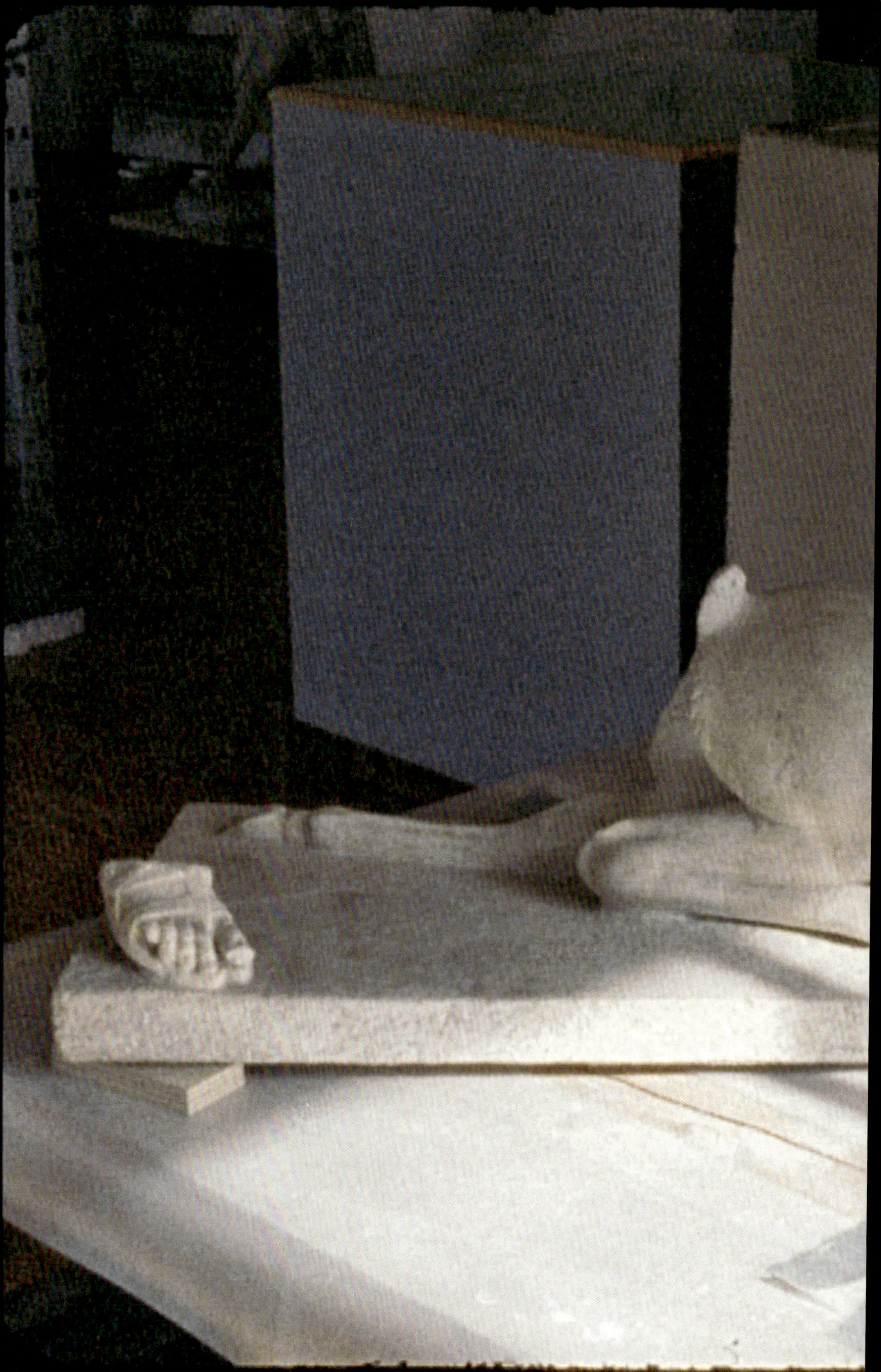

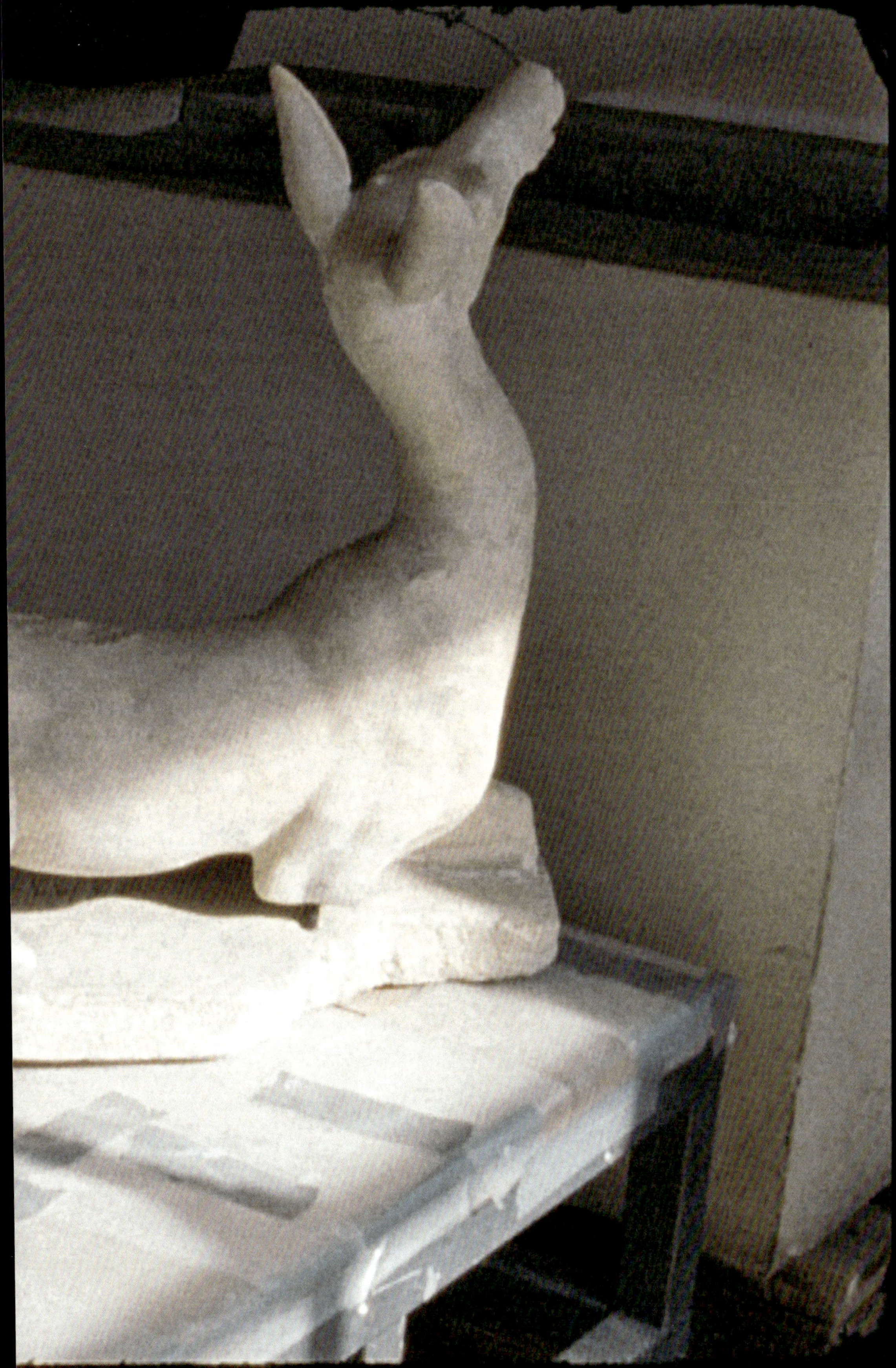

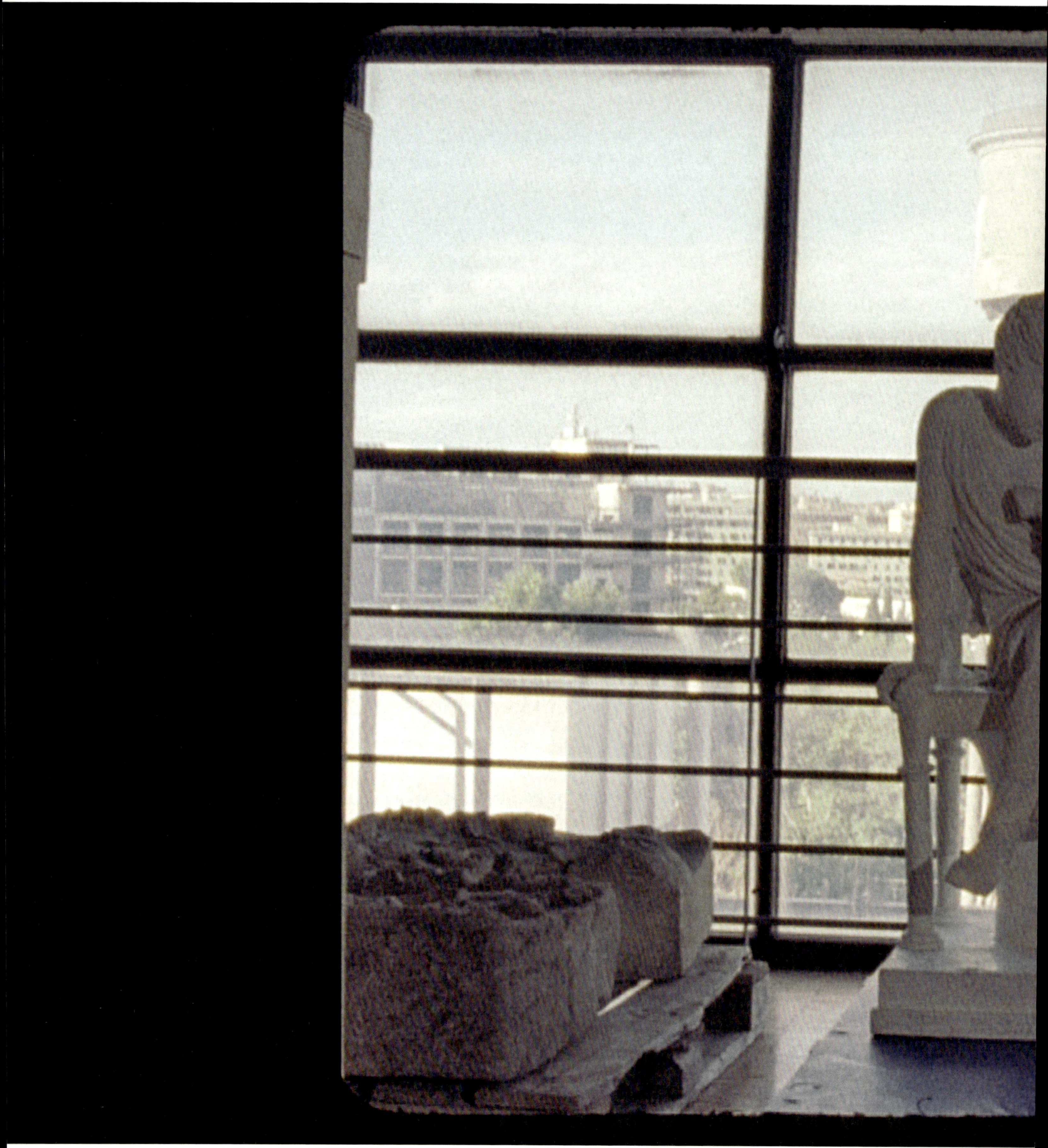

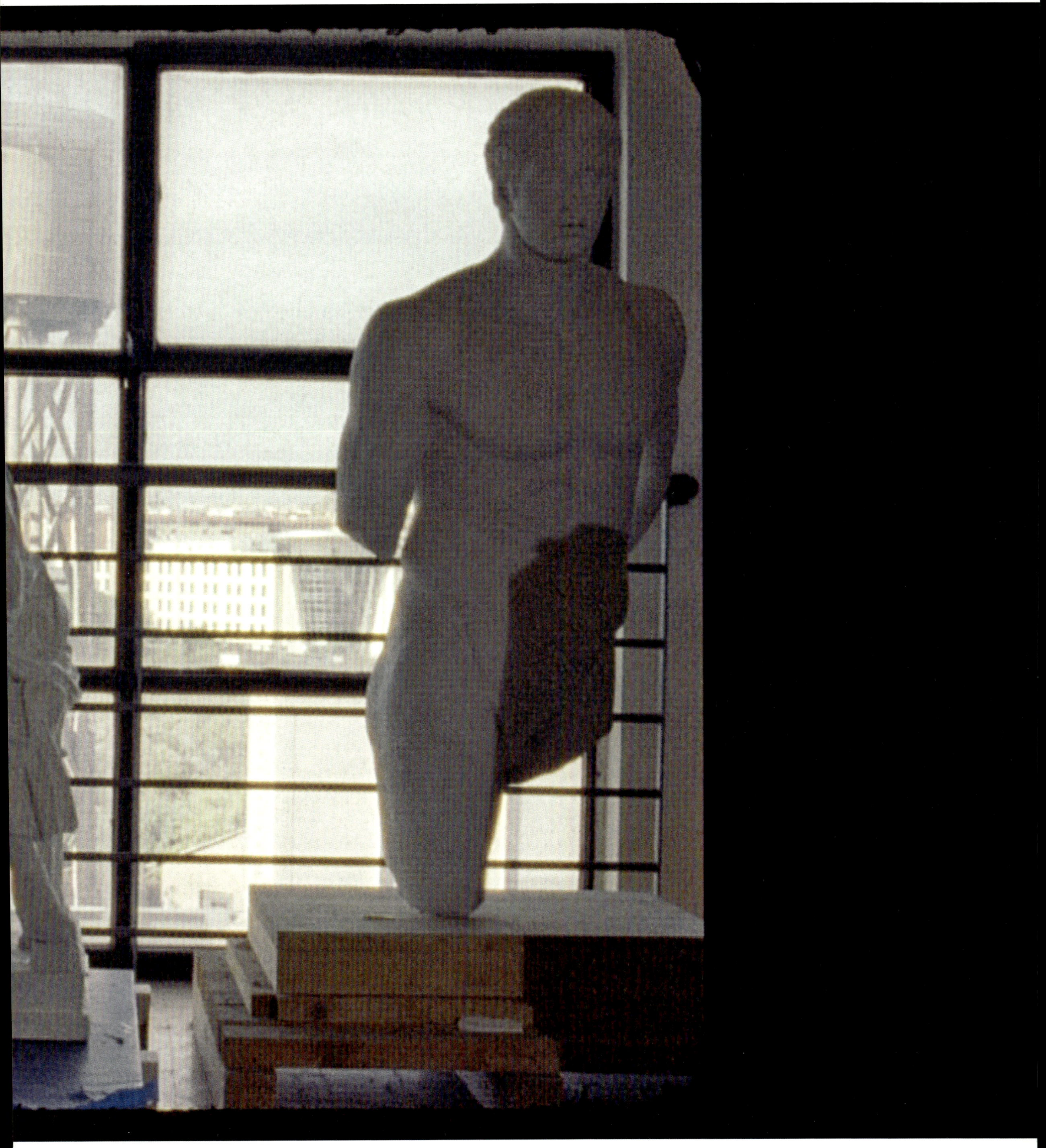

SUSPENDED STORIES: ROSA BARBA'S STRATEGIC NARRATIVITY

LYNNE COOKE

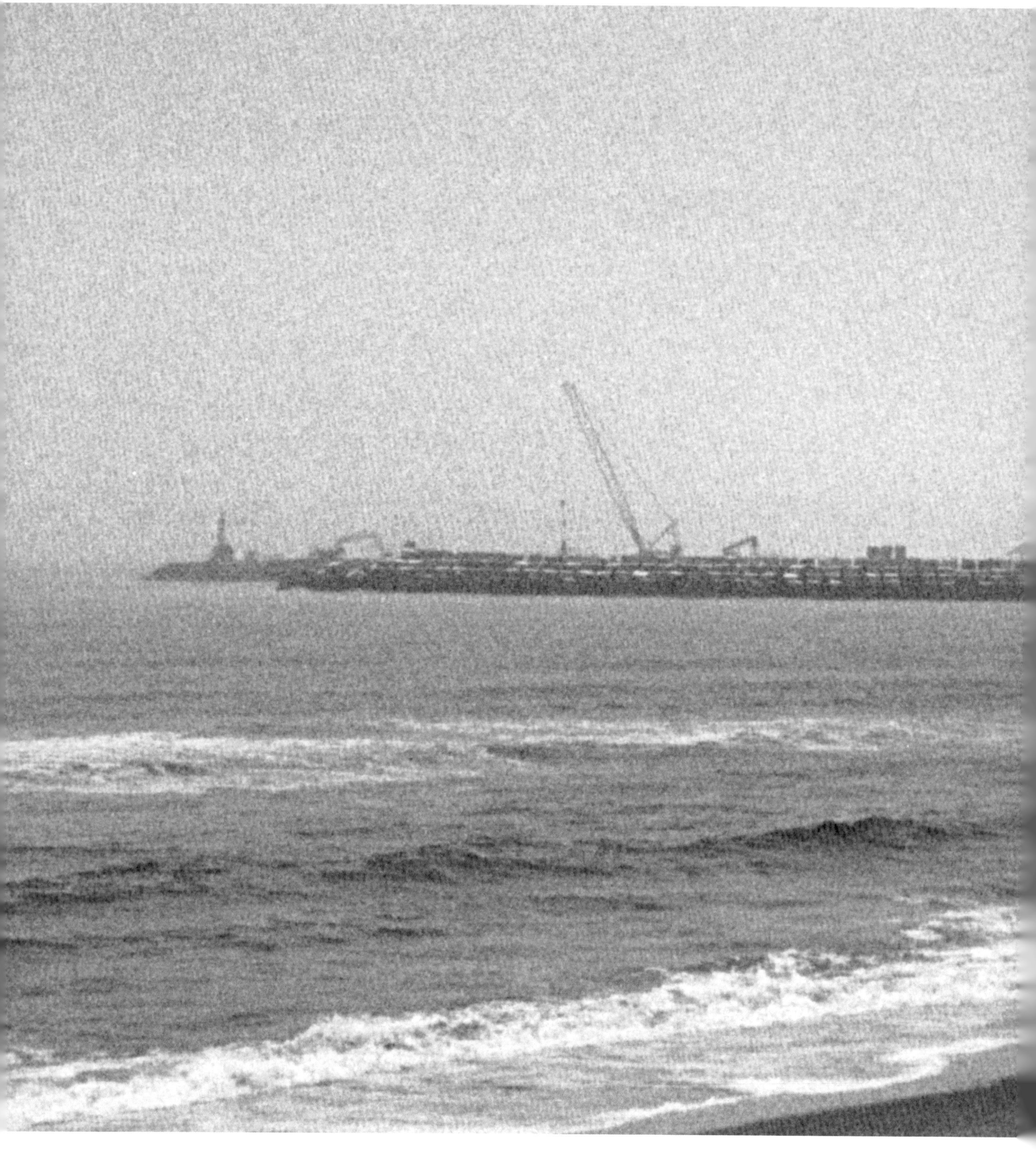

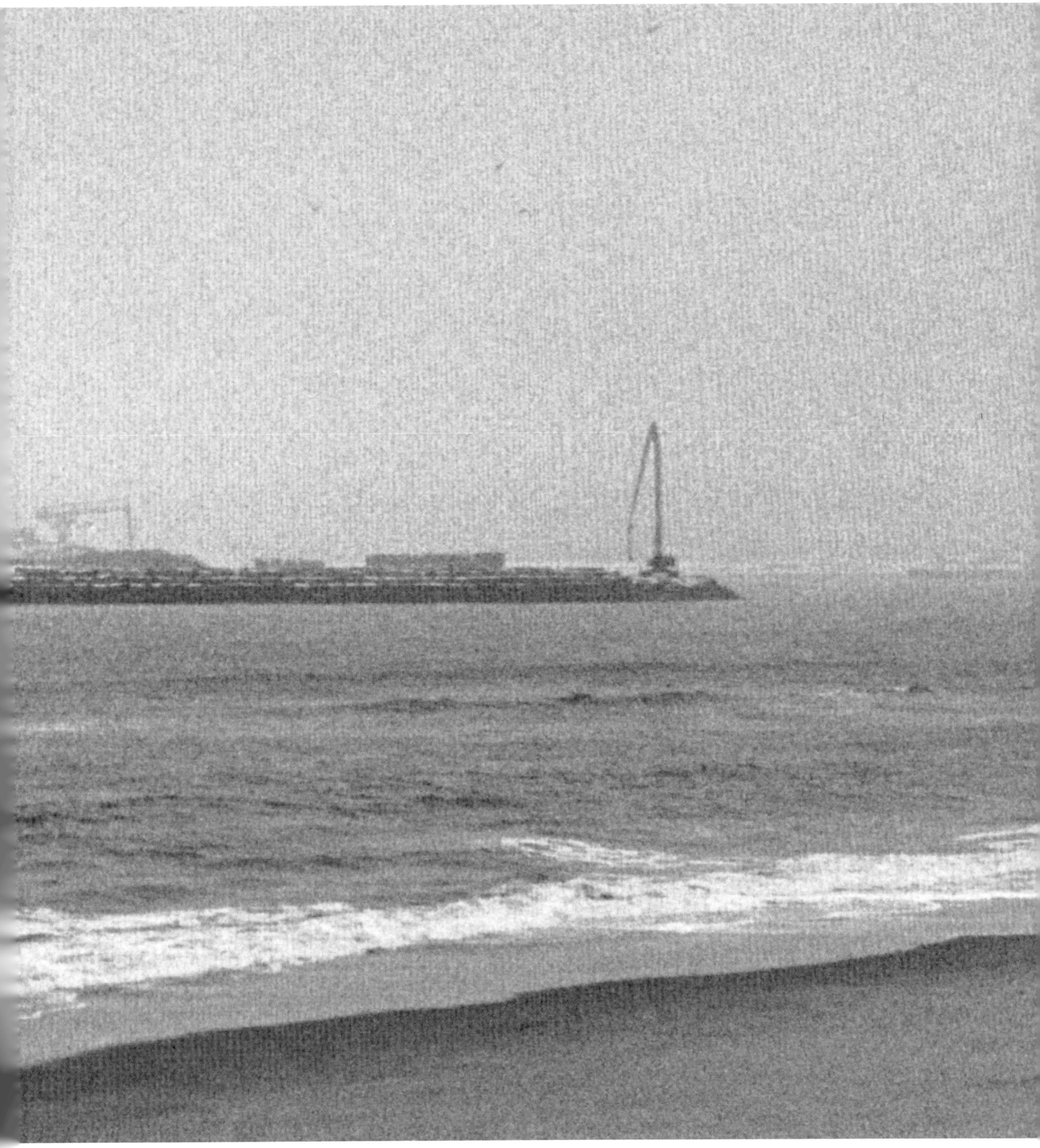

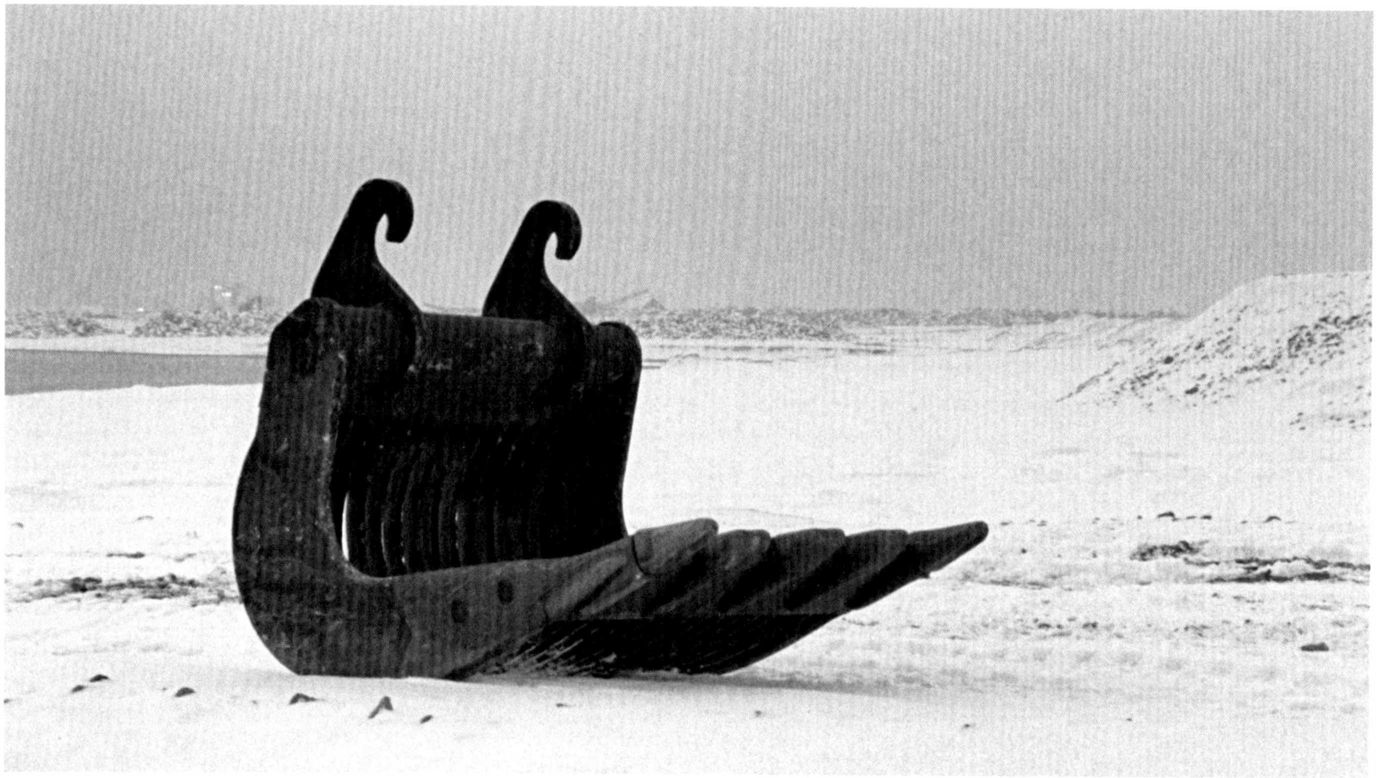

Above, preceding pages, and following pages: *Somnium* (2011)

"How can visual works of art . . . tell stories? . . . Narrative [must] become a tool not a meaning; a mediator not a solution; a participant not an outsider."
Louise Bourgeois

"A philosophy is characterized more by the formulation of its problems than by its solution of them."
Suzanne Langer

Rosa Barba's *Somnium* (2011), a 35-millimeter, 19:20-minute film projection, draws together many of the key concerns that have emerged in the artist's oeuvre over the past decade. Its point of departure is a short story by the German astronomer Johannes Kepler.[1] Although framed as a dream, this tale of a lunar voyage was devised to validate the radically seditious thesis of a heliocentric universe.[2] For over thirty years Kepler worked on this contentious theory, writing in Latin rather than the more accessible vernacular in the hope of warding off attacks from those who still believed that the earth was located at the center of the universe. Published posthumously in 1634 and only rarely reprinted over the next three centuries, his text was finally rescued from obscurity when translated into several European languages. Soon gaining an underground reputation among devotees of science fiction, today it is widely recognized as a pioneer in that genre. While writers such as J. G. Ballard have drawn profitably from it, filmmakers have not yet succeeded in giving it cinematic form. Research into *Somnium*'s checkered history has informed Barba's eponymous project. Borrowing Kepler's title in tribute, she has drawn upon both his tale and, equally importantly, his remarkable achievement in establishing a new ontology of vision.

One of the singular features of Kepler's novella is its curious structure. The story, such as it is, breaks off abruptly when the narrator suddenly wakes up from his lunar voyage and finds himself in his bed, his head muffled under his pillow. The author's recourse to the device of a dream is a blatant ruse that does little to mask the incendiary argument, the substance of which may be found in the extensive footnotes and commentaries that threaten to overwhelm the brief tale. Filled with scientific data and hypotheses, these appendices sometimes ground, and sometimes contest, the empirical observations and classical references proffered in the main body of the text. At the heart of Kepler's thesis is the conviction that rational scientific hypotheses can lead to theoretical truths neither accessible to nor necessarily verifiable by pragmatic observational study. His prescient recognition of the limitations of direct observation and empirical enquiry led him to posit an ontology of vision based in scientific theory. A debate couched in similar terms is woven into Barba's work. Her film opens with the voice-over of an authoritative male speaker who dispassionately relays the information that, though the planet Somnium is currently devoid of all living forms, nature is in the process of reclaiming areas that until recently had been given over to human enterprises. A classic science-fiction beginning, this opening gambit promises the security of a grand narrative yet quickly destabilizes expectation by introducing a variety of narrative modes that undermine notions of authorial omnipotence and coherence. Suturing documentary material to fictional narrative, and interleaving dissenting eyewitness accounts with the reports of officialdom, she counterpoints the evidentiary with the theoretical. A second voice is then heard. Colloquial in tone as well as address, it rarely rises above a fearful whisper as it relays its suspicions that something is deeply wrong with the information being distributed publicly about the sweeping changes transforming the environment. Unlike Kepler's knowing narrator, Barba's unassuming if skeptical witness seems unaware of the polemical import of his observations. Ultimately the artist's film avoids reconciling contrary perspectives, ending provocatively with a quotation from the Renaissance mystic Giordano Bruno, who argued that "the observer is always at the center of things."

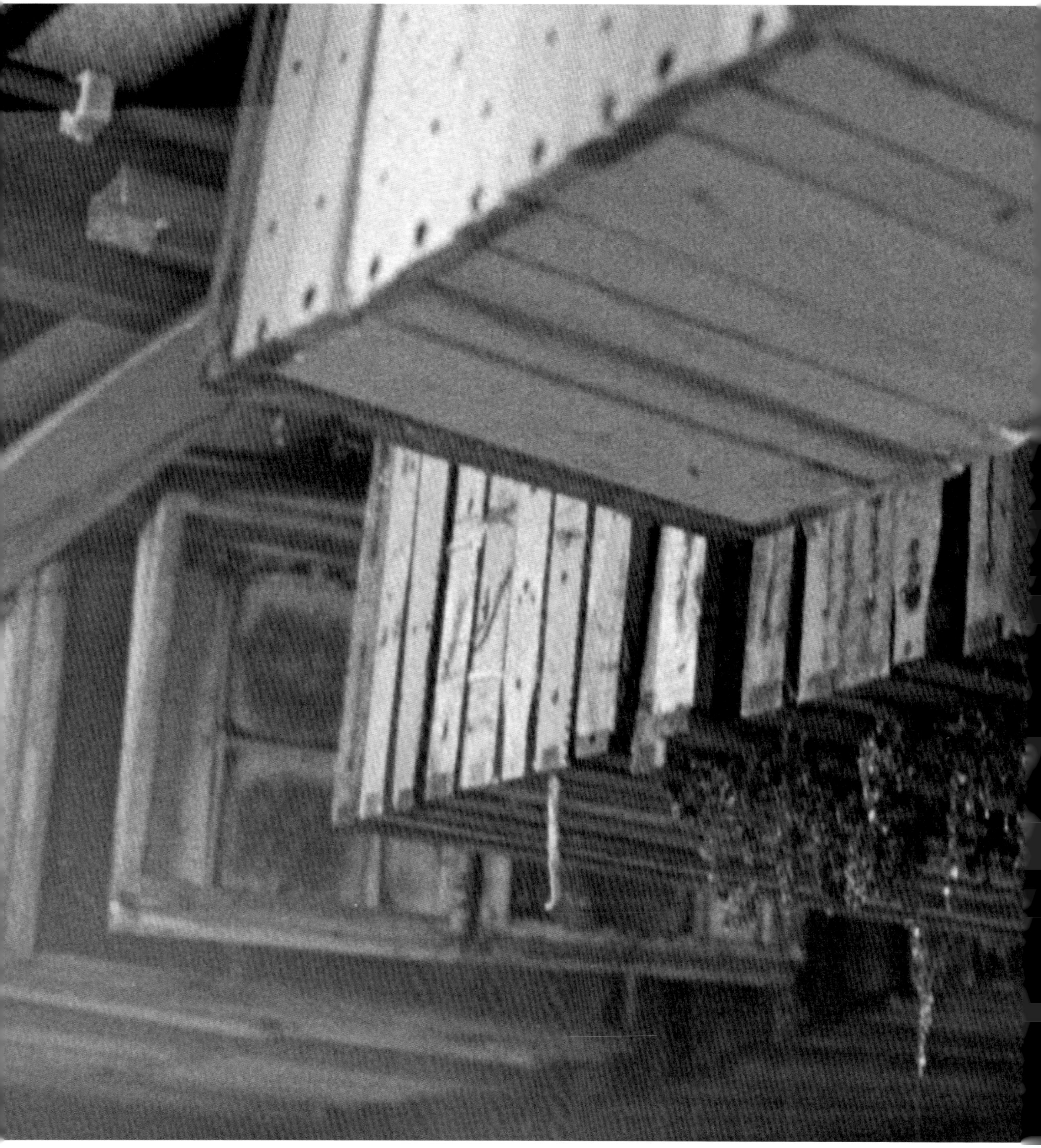

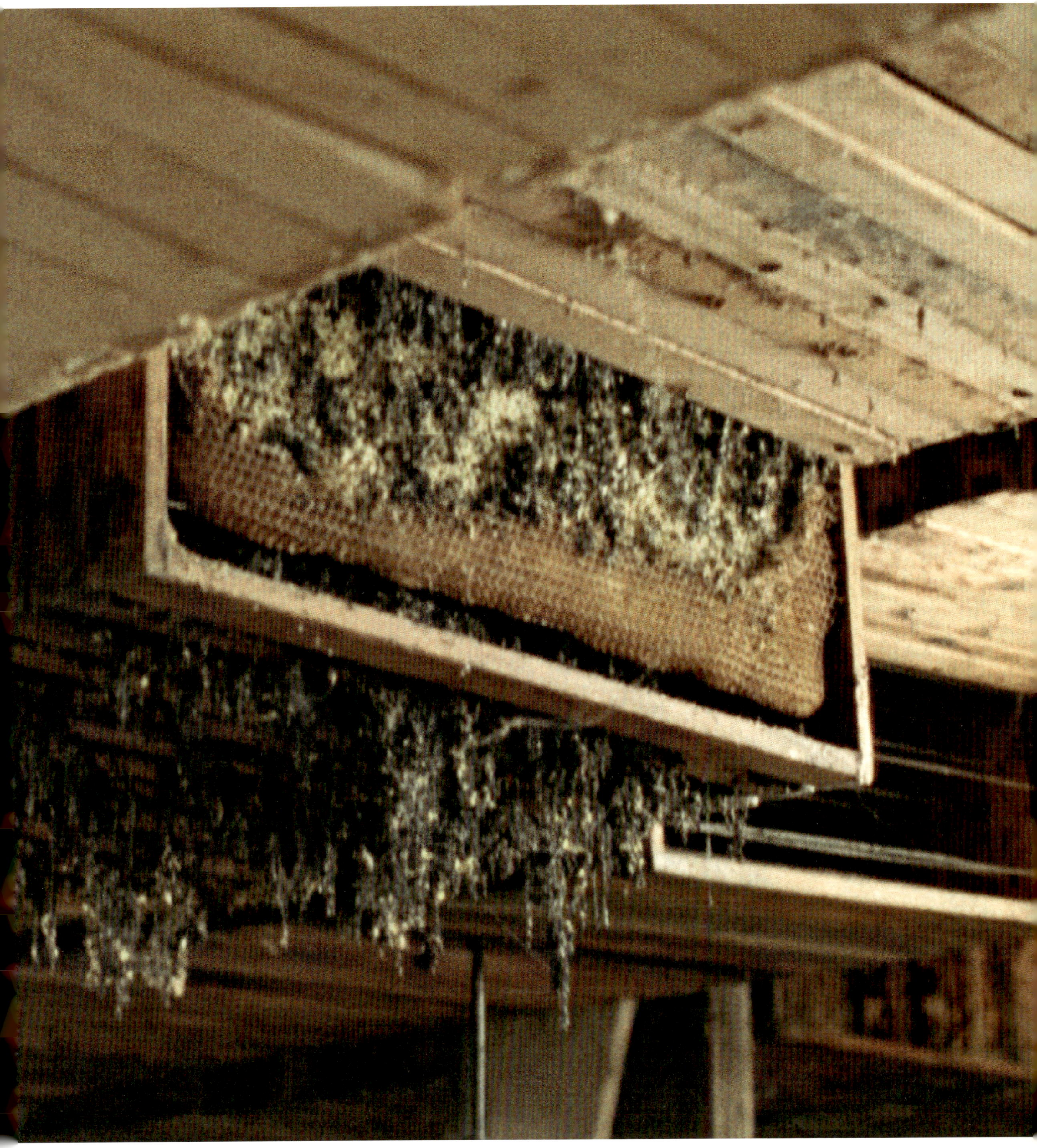

Subtle shifts within and among narrative voices in *Somnium* complement Barba's handling of the compelling visual imagery. Black-and-white photographs are reproduced of what can be assumed, due to cross-cutting between still and moving imagery, to be documents of the site in an earlier era. At other moments slow pans interrupt still shots that frame such details as a waste pipe cantilevered over an incline. Several images of this kind directly recall motifs that Robert Smithson highlighted in his landmark text "A Tour of the Monuments of Passaic, New Jersey," published in *Artforum* in December 1967. There Smithson reprised a trope of landscape art, transposing a canonical journey through a picturesque bucolic location to the dystopian industrial wastelands of a New Jersey backwater. Beguiled by such ruins, which, for him, could be best read as monuments to mankind's failed visions for a utopian technological future, Smithson returned repeatedly to this subject, above all in the great trio of works—sculpture, film, and essay—yoked under the collective title *Spiral Jetty*. *Somnium* clearly alludes to Smithson's seminal film, and not least to its hybrid wedding of first-person narrative to quotations and citations from science fiction, travel writing, literature, and science manuals in order to conflate disparate temporalities: past, present, and future; cyclical, linear, and entropic time-scales. The subtext of mnemonic images and references generated by Smithson's works is as central to any reading of *Somnium* as the film's debt to Kepler's literary gem. Barba's project newly animates these precedents. Far from being mired in a historical past, these works embody ahistorical voices, she contends; they are crucial components of a critical discourse that seeks to define the kind of vision required by a politically engaged contemporary cinema.

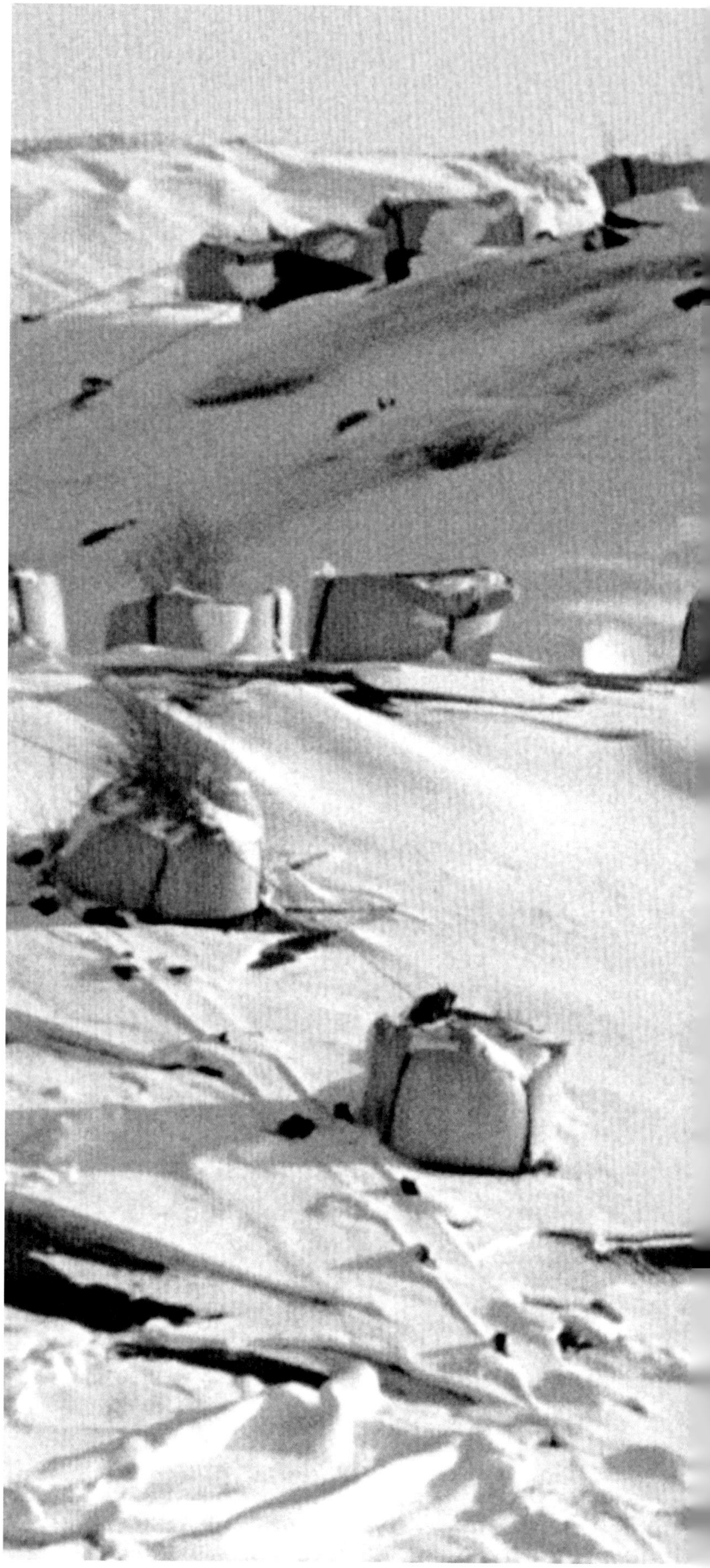

Right and following pages: *Somnium* (2011)

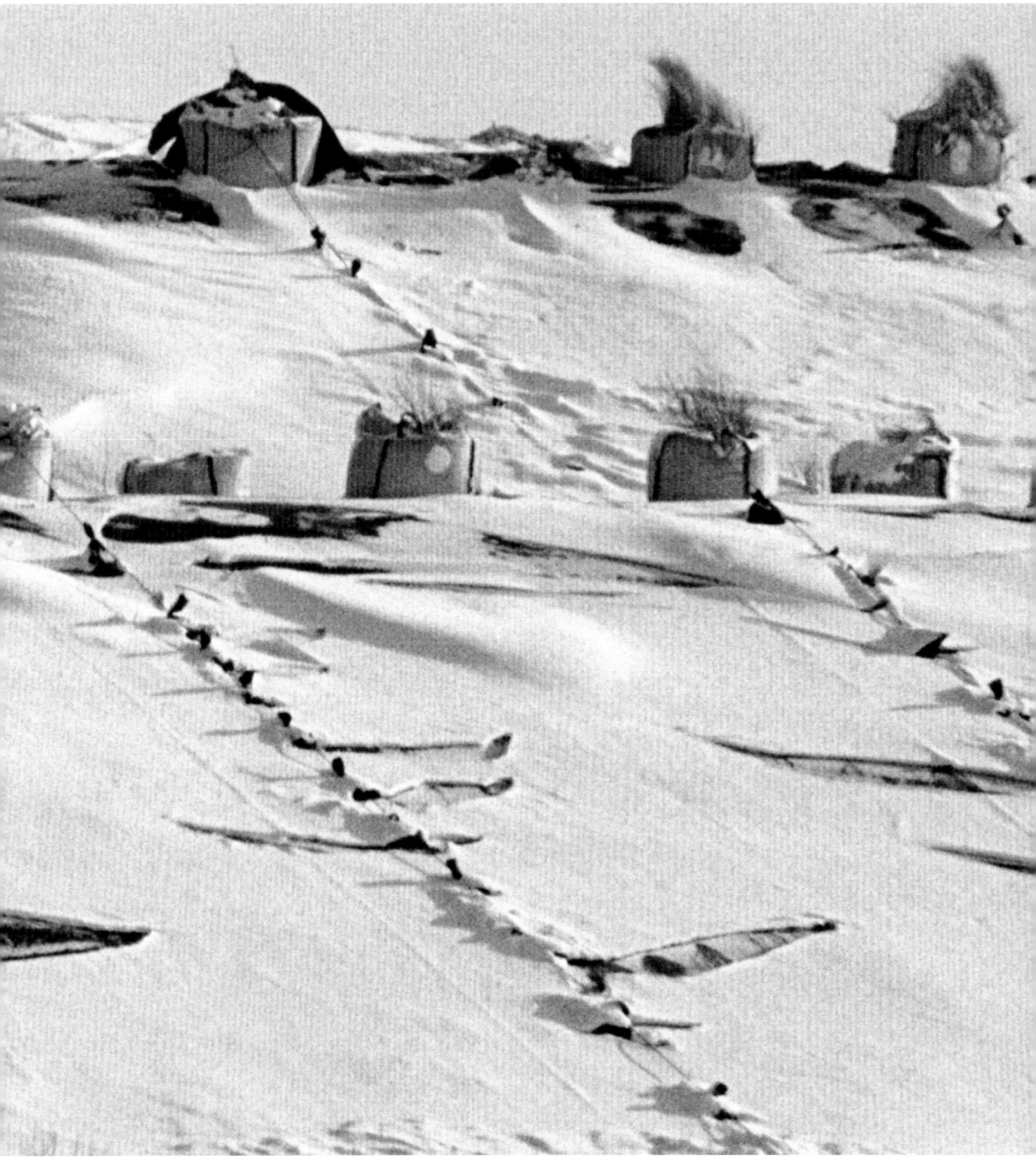

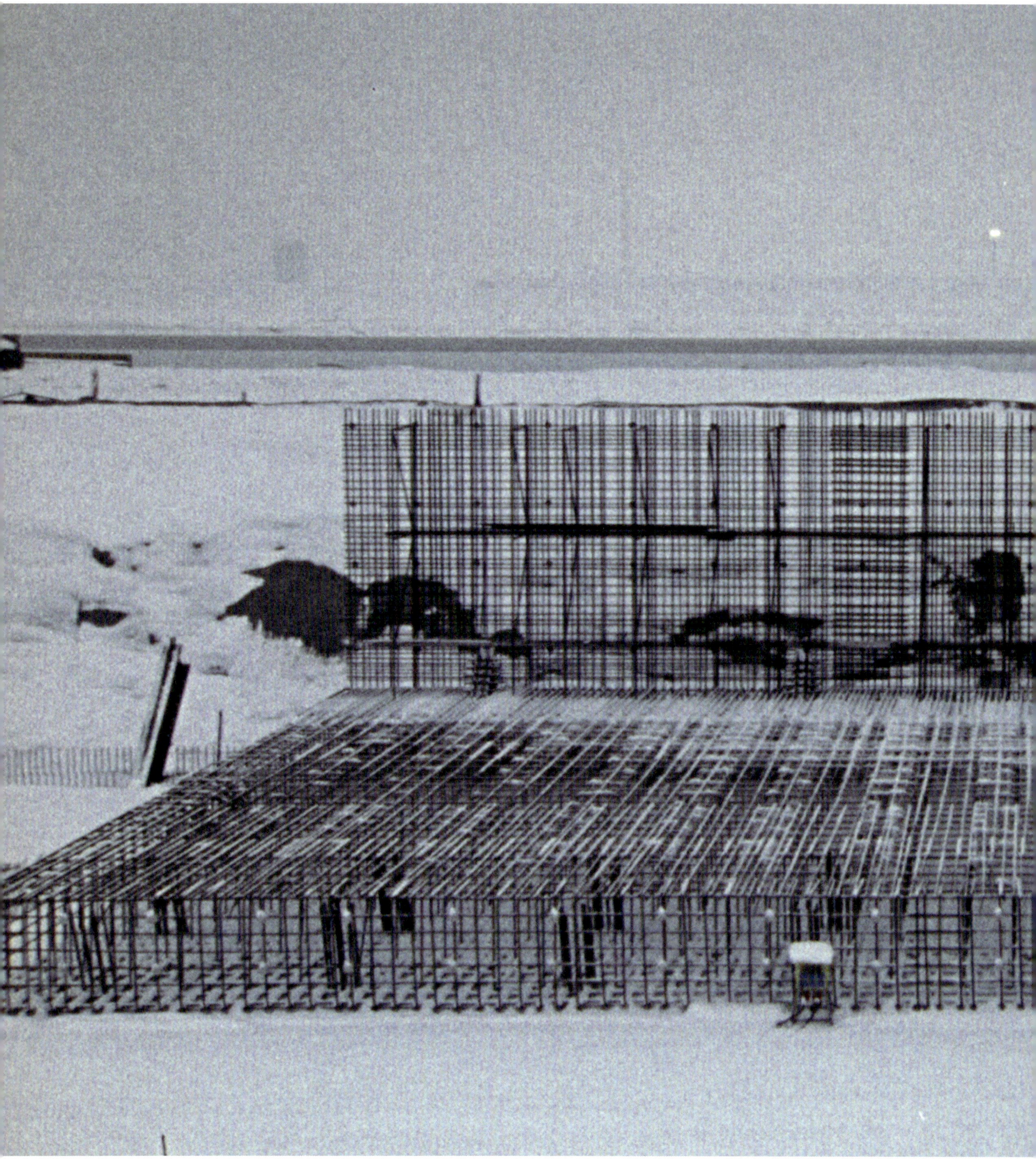

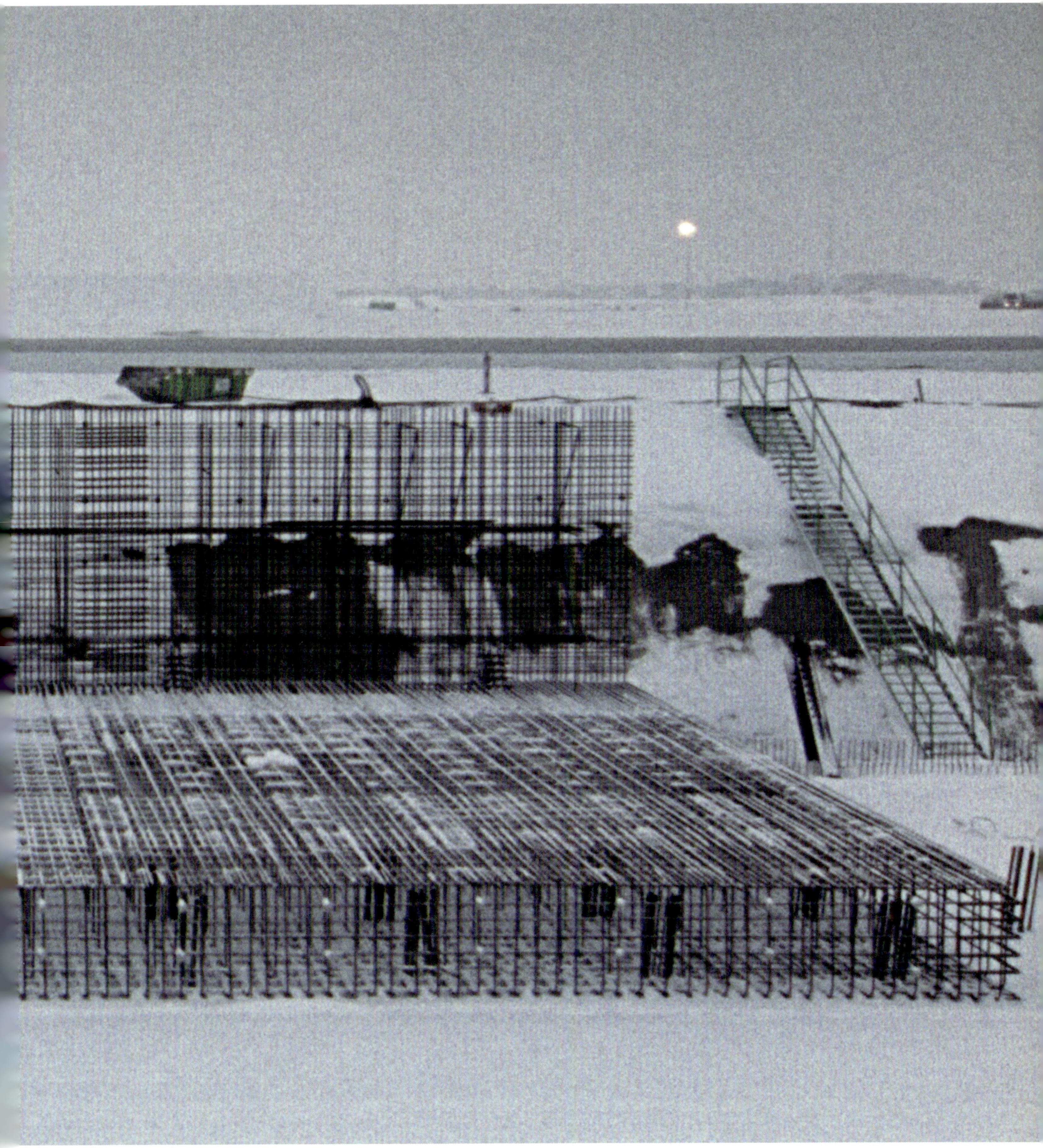

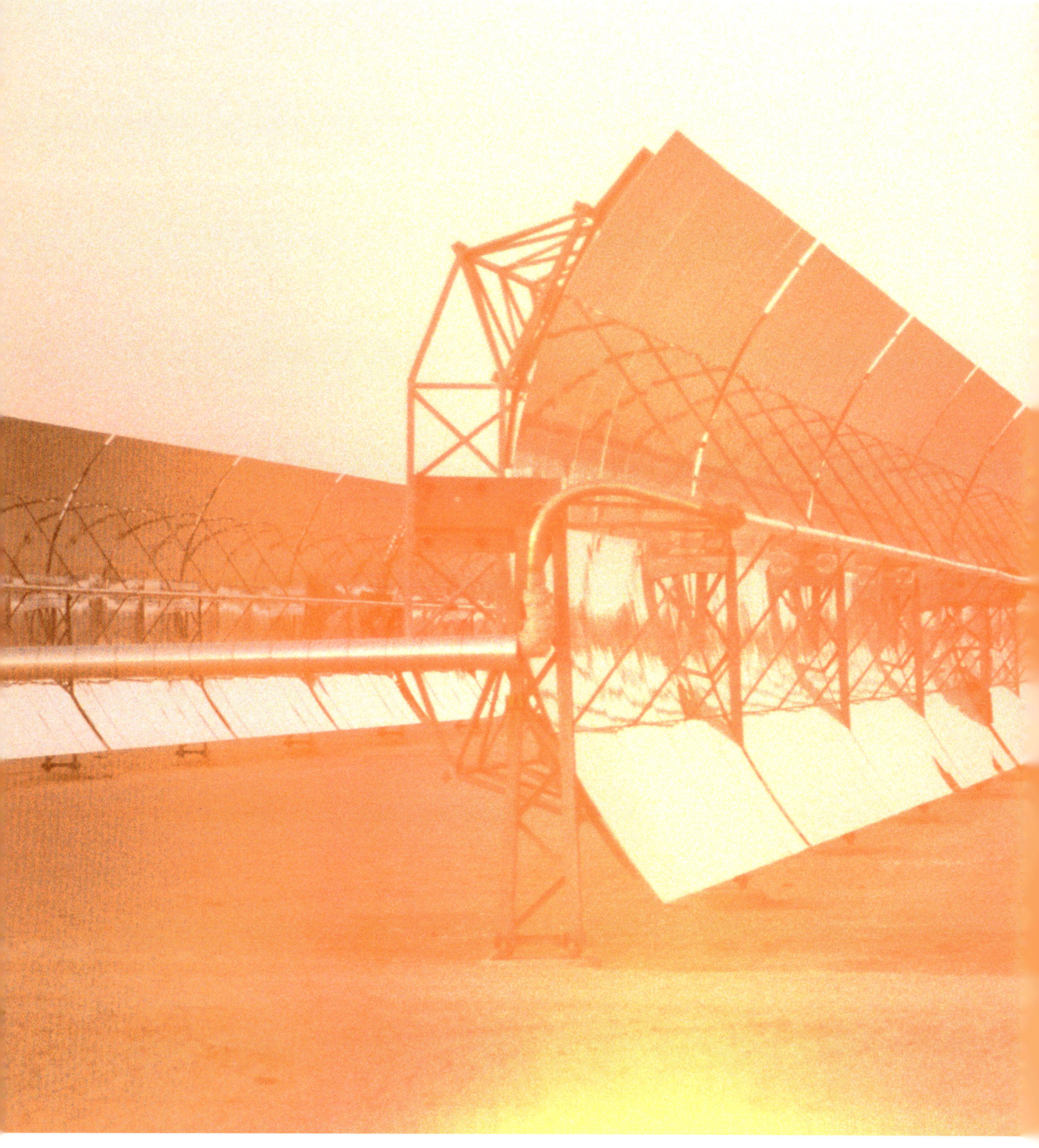

A more melancholy tone inflects *The Long Road* (2010), which, like *They Shine* (2007) and *The Waiting Grounds* (2007), was shot in the American Southwest. Seen initially from the air in a long tracking shot, the abandoned automobile test-site that is the work's visual focus resembles a prehistoric earthwork or a 1970s variant on the genre. Whether kin to the ancient Nazca lines only rediscovered as a result of air travel or to the industrial-scale incursions Smithson and his peers made into remote desert terrain in the postwar years, this elliptical incision in the earth's surface is similarly subject to decay and the predations of time. The soundtrack mingles techno-electronic sounds, from which haunting micro-tonal phrases emerge intermittently, with the throaty voice of Robert Creeley reading from his poem *The Long Road*. The memory of his father's death, coupled with a recognition, prompted by the sight of old school photographs, of the many decades that have elapsed since his passing, reminds the poet of his own mortality. The implication that the end of his long road may be approaching is picked up in the final shot in the film. Now positioned at ground level, the camera circles the test track; after rounding a curve, it enters a straight stretch, down which it speeds into the late-afternoon sun. Barba imbricates these shifting vantage points of eye and voice through her editing and pacing of the camera movements and her positioning and framing of the text within the audio track. As in *Somnium,* a mnemonic function based on direct and indirect reference to the works of other artists (a poet and nameless sculptors, in this case) is integral to the way content is elaborated.

They Shine (2007), untitled still

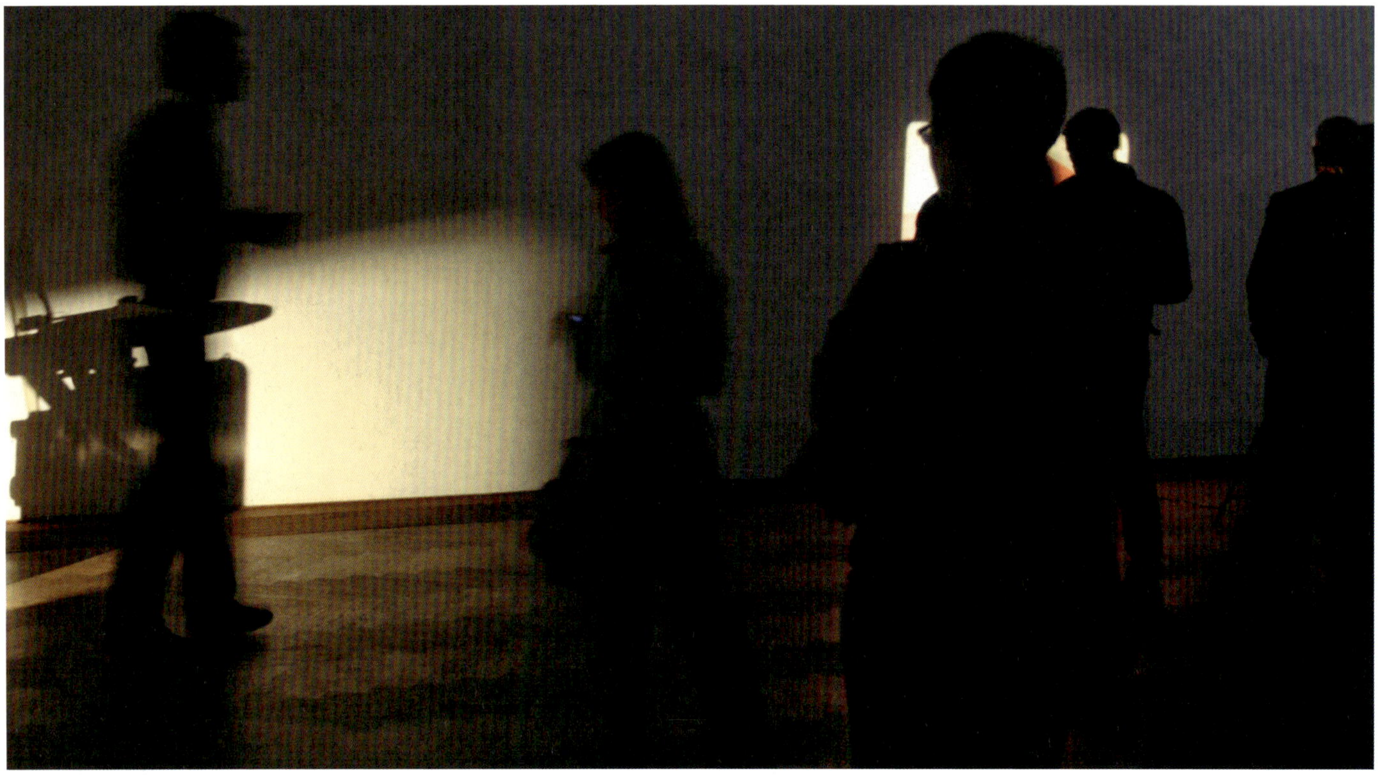

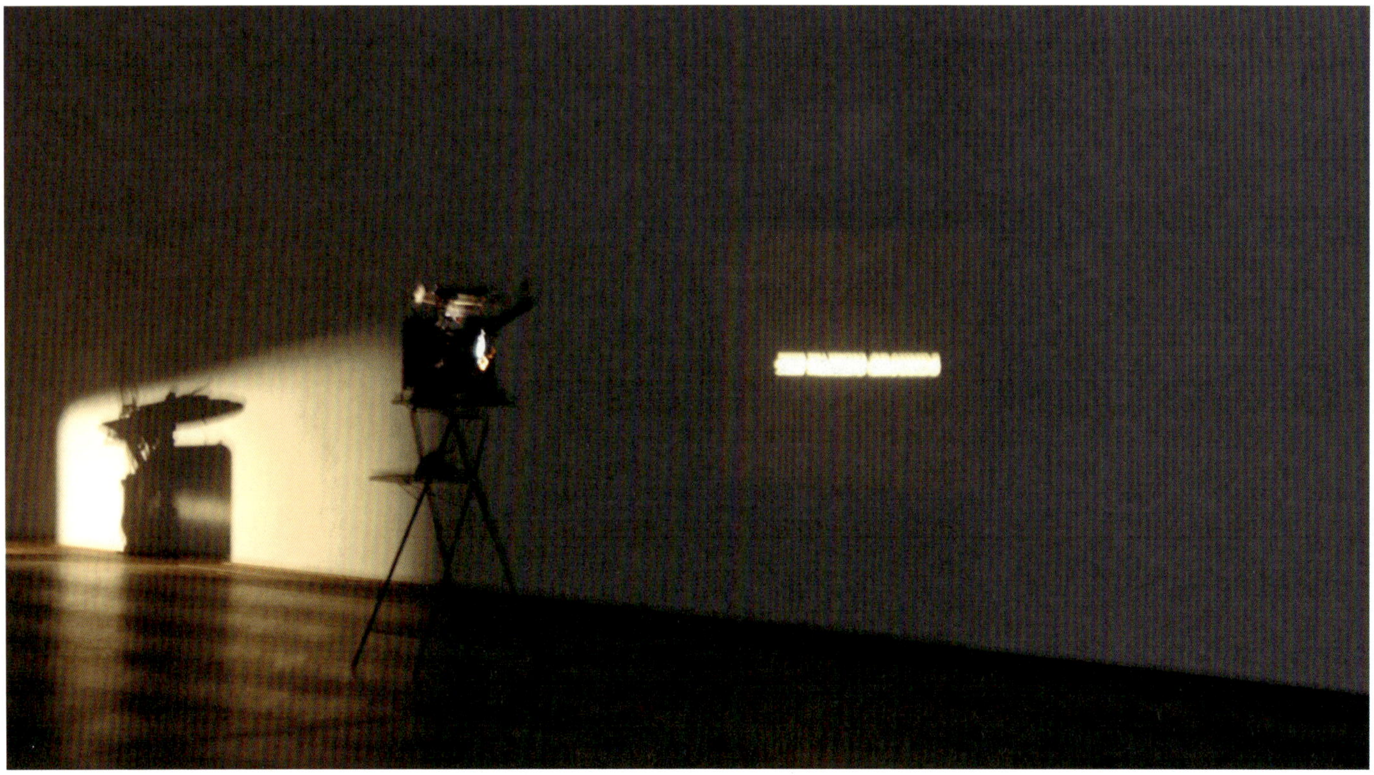

Waiting Grounds (2007) and *Western Round Table* (2007),
installation view, Kunsthalle Basel, 2008

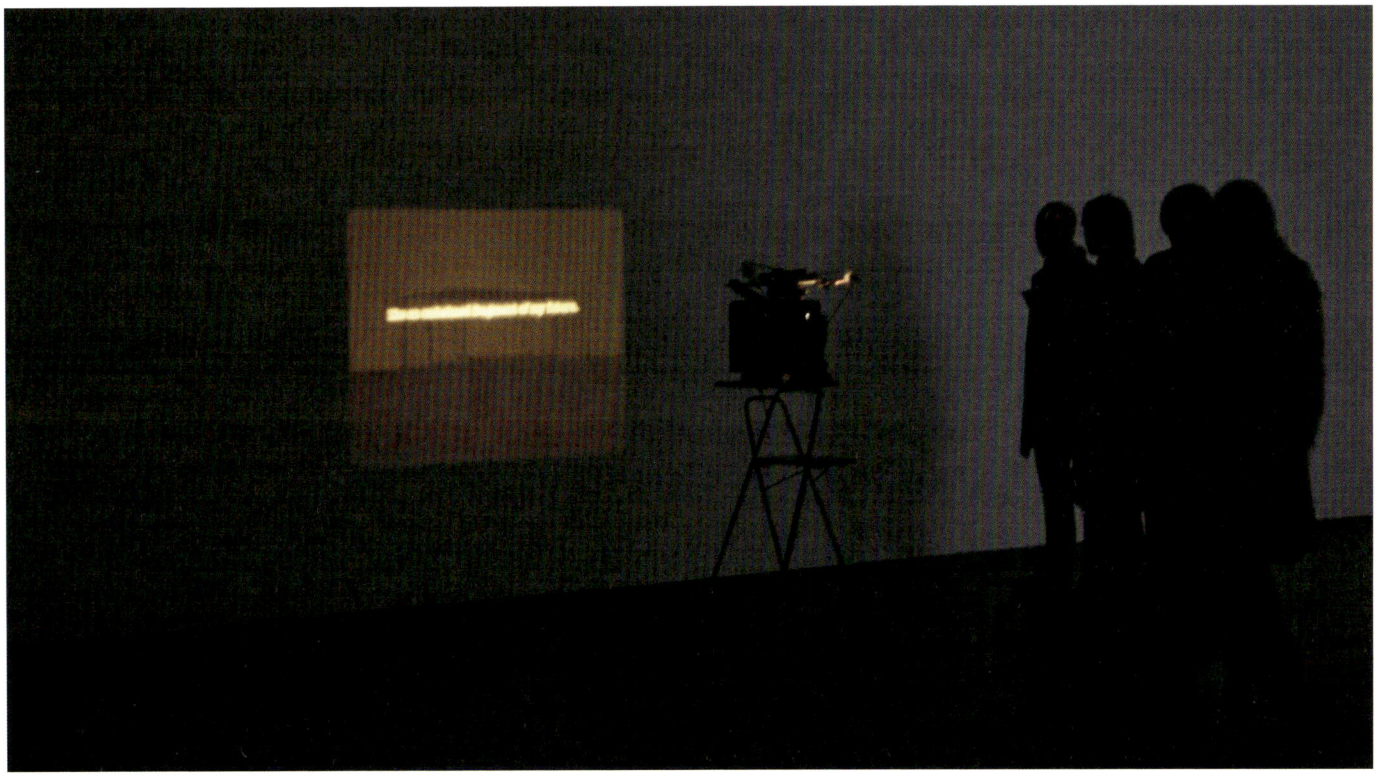

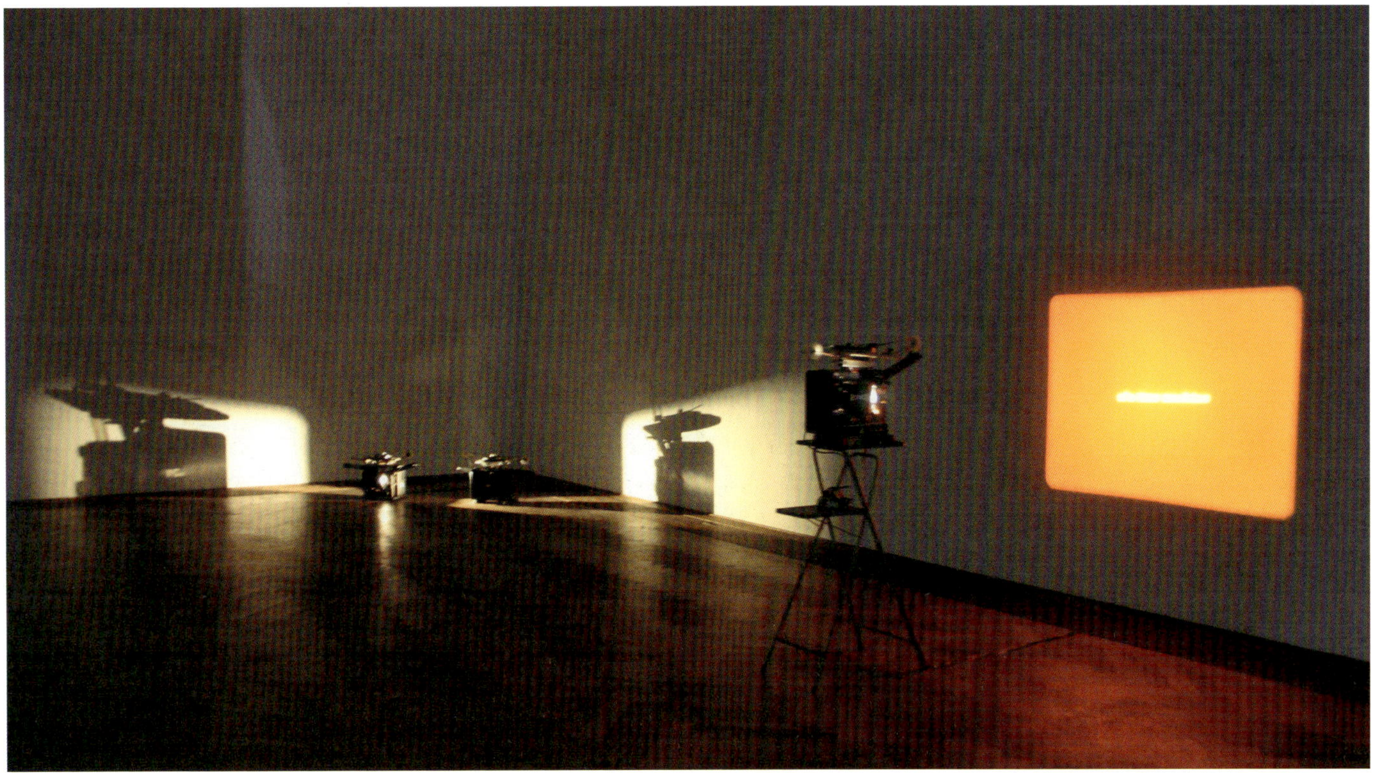

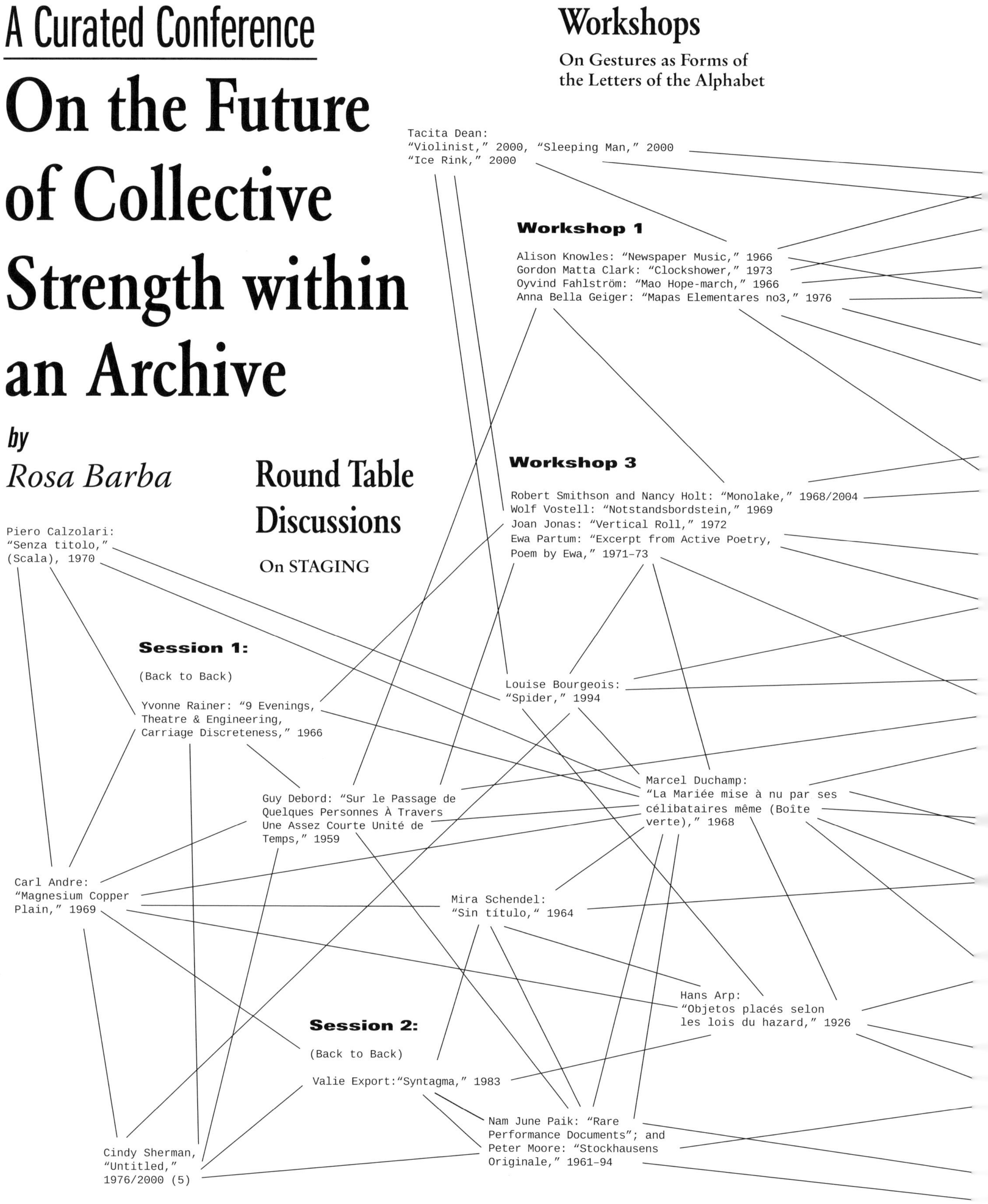

Above: *A Curated Conference* (2010)
Following pages: *A Curated Conference* (2010), model

Parallel Session

Dialogue as a Choir

Examining thematic and historical aspects in the present day, focusing on the significance of artists and films, from early pioneers to contemporary practitioners.

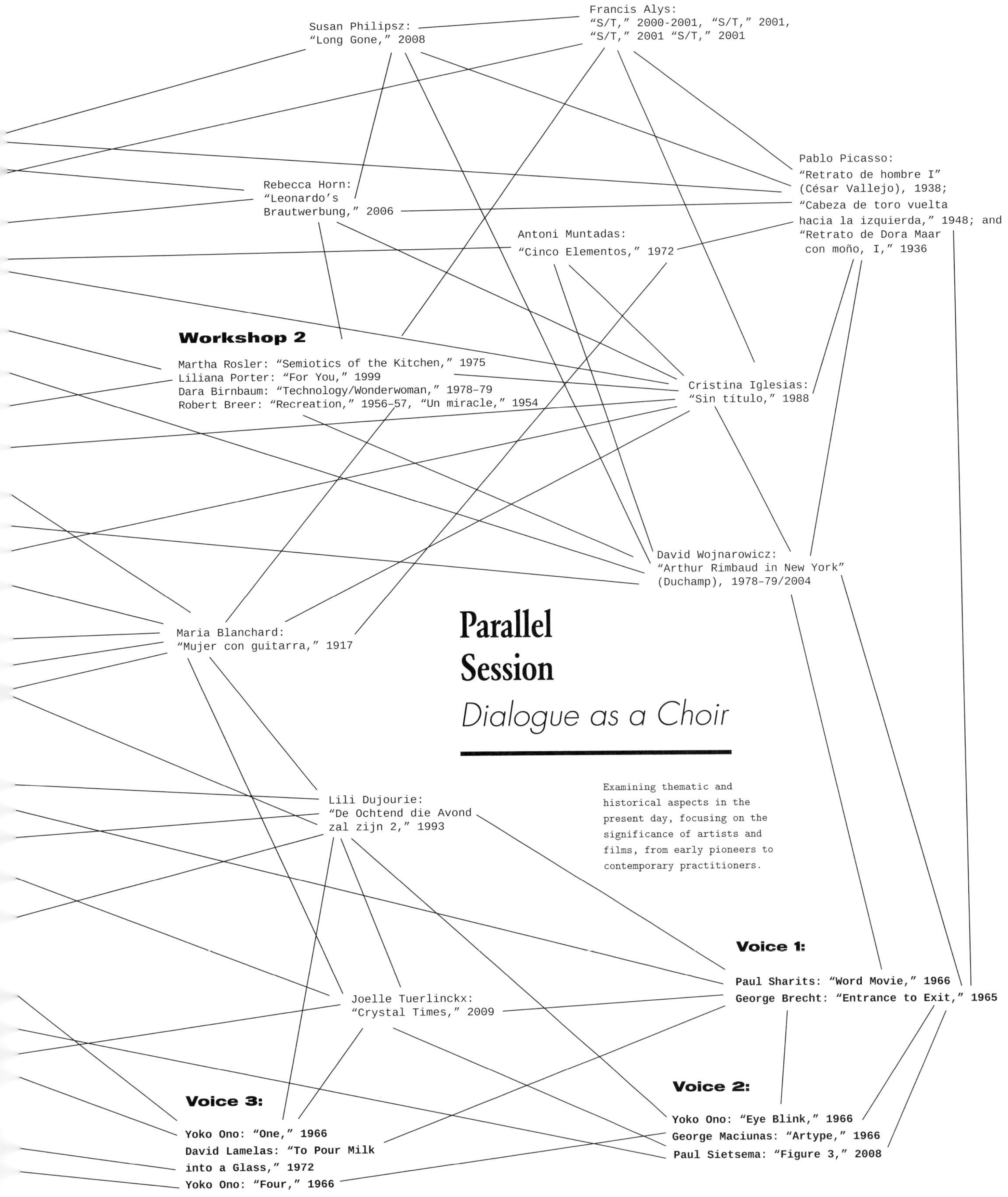

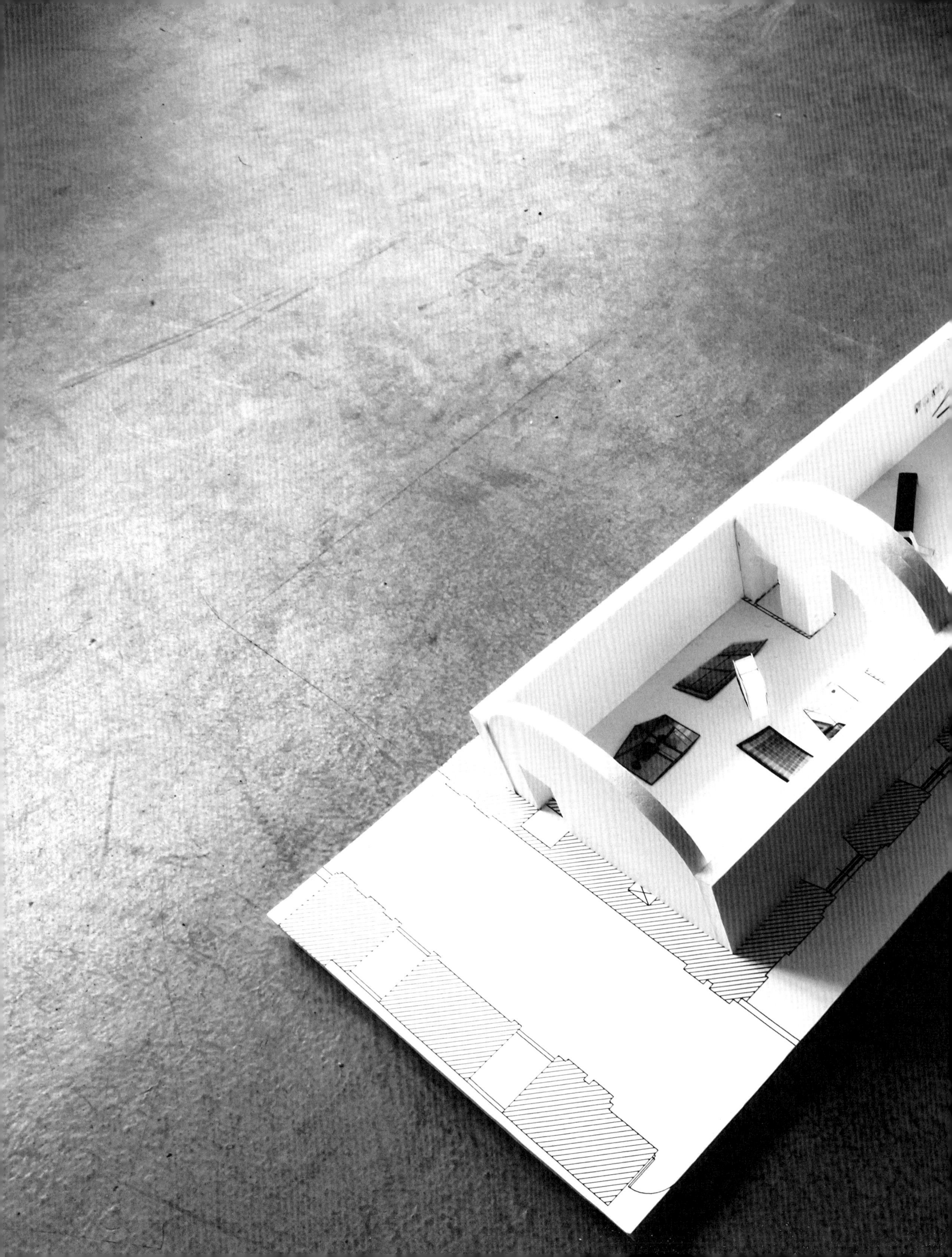

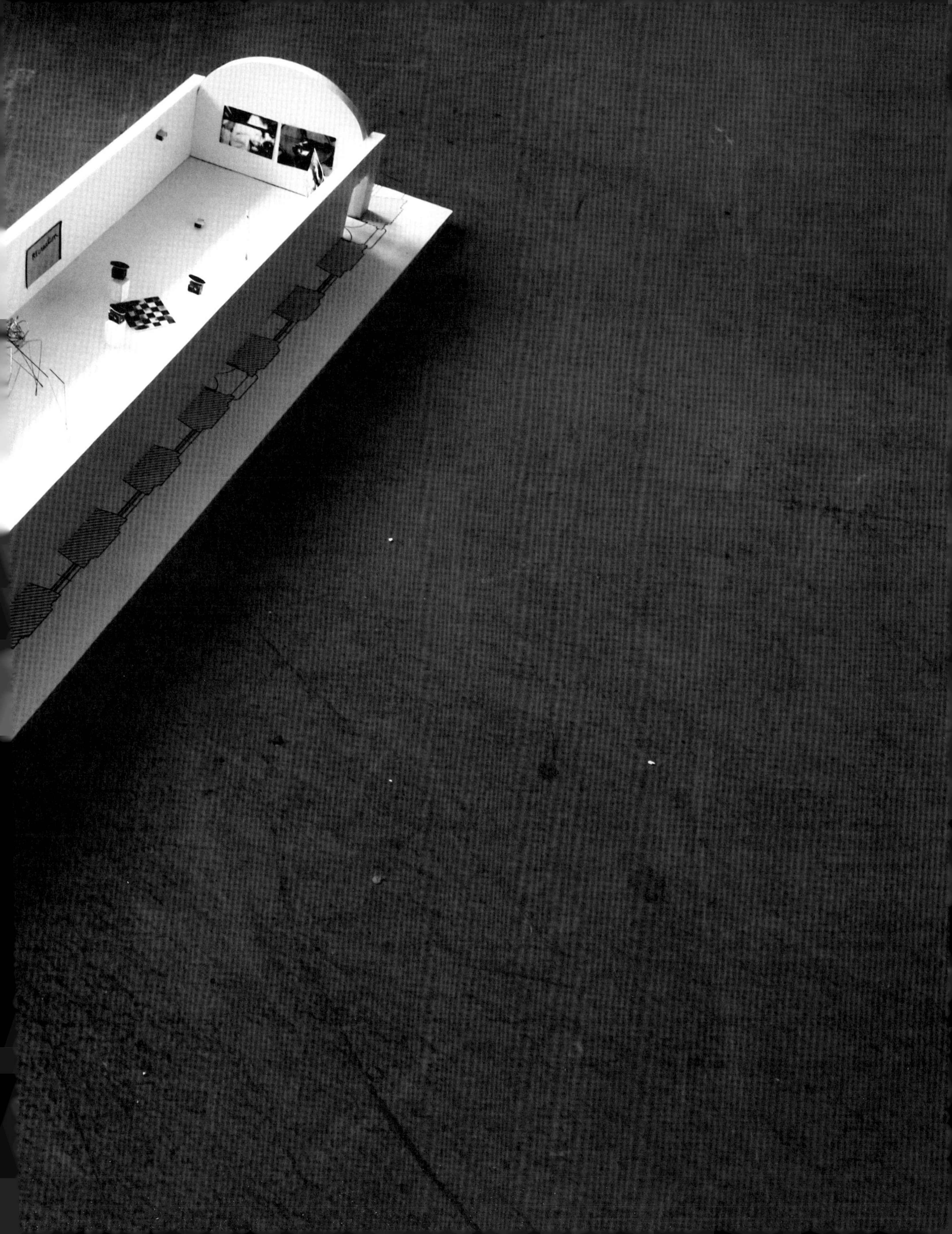

Barba's engagement with the place and role of works of art within the broader cultural imaginary was further clarified in her response to a recent commission from the Museo Nacional Centro de Arte Reina Sofía in Madrid. Invited to curate an exhibition from the museum's holdings, she responded with a proposal that she called "a curated conference." Her project comprised a presentation of some forty-three works, including film and video, photography, sculpture, painting, and drawings, which she installed in two adjacent galleries. "It is the aim of this conference to draw together a representation of artists from the twentieth and twenty-first centuries, and bring their informed opinions to bear on the significant questions of art," she wrote in the accompanying brochure.[3] Titled *On the Future of Collective Strength within an Archive* (2010), her display eschewed standard conventions of museological presentation, notably the segregation of art forms by medium and a linear hang arranged chronologically, in favor of an installation that juxtaposed and overlaid pieces made over the span of almost a century in close proximity. Rather than suppressing difference in service to an ideological imperative, the basis on which most collection displays are presented in contemporary art institutions today, she welcomed the anarchic outcome produced by a situation in which "each artist speaks with their own voice in their own language, temperament and volume." Recognizing that although some were recent additions, many of these artworks had long been in the collection, she invited the artists (through their works) to explore "the collective consciousness" within the archive. What would emerge, she anticipated, would be neither a consensual nor a coherent vision (the goal of museum professionals), but a "Babel of voices": the archive would be shown to be composed of "dateless individual expressions" that can be "choreographed like a musical score." She contends that "by negating the past and ignoring the future the artist can be free to make a radical statement which lasts over time . . . [and generates] an energy which connects artists of all ages."

Round-table discussions, workshops, a parallel session, and keynote speeches by Pablo Picasso, Mira Schendel, Louise Bourgeois, Martha Rosler, and others were also planned as part of the program. Several speakers brought up concerns adumbrated in Barba's own practice. Thus Picasso, for example, claimed, "All I have ever made was made for the present and with the hope that it will always remain in the present." George Maciunas underlined Barba's sense of collective identity when he termed this "community of individuals grouping together a vast quantity of behaviors and attitudes . . . a 'non-group' with no strict structures." Bourgeois, for her part, addressed the ways that visual works of art tell stories: she argued that through the interplay of formal qualities, "narrative becomes a tool not a meaning, a mediator not a solution." Although Barba omitted her own works, and hence her own voice, from the actual discussion, she made her position vividly clear by choosing as her principal speakers artists whose aesthetic and work instantiate the key terms in her own practice.

The archive was literally the source of Barba's exhibition-as-conference given that the checklist of works on view was drawn exclusively from the museum's storage areas. The term "archive" is also used more abstractly in order to refer to the system that, in Hal Foster's words, "structures the particular expressions of a particular period."[4] This discursive notion of the archive was also brought into play in Barba's project in that she critically engaged the ideology governing the presentation of the institution's collection elsewhere in its facilities, offering a subversive alternative to its norms of representational totality and historical accountability. Given her belief that artworks are "ahistorical," or "timeless," they may also be self-organizing, and can come together through their creators' initiatives, rather than depending on museum professionals who commandeer them to their orthodoxies.

Barba's innovative project can also be read through the model of the museum that Theodor Adorno addressed in an essay published in 1953 on what he called the "Valéry Proust Museum."[5] According to Adorno, Valéry embodied the position that the museum is "where we put the art of the past to death." "Museum and mausoleum are connected by more than phonetic association," he contended, for "museums are like the family sepulchers of works of art. They testify to the neutralization of culture." In opposition to the embalming, or reification, of the artwork that Valéry believed took place in the museum, Proust articulated a vision based on the idea of the artwork's reanimation. The museum is consequently for him a site of agonistic competition. Echoes of Proust's ideas may be heard in Barba's curatorial conference. However, whereas Proust accorded agency to the spectator, who was charged with reanimating the work, Barba tellingly leaves control in the hands of artists: their works embody their voices.

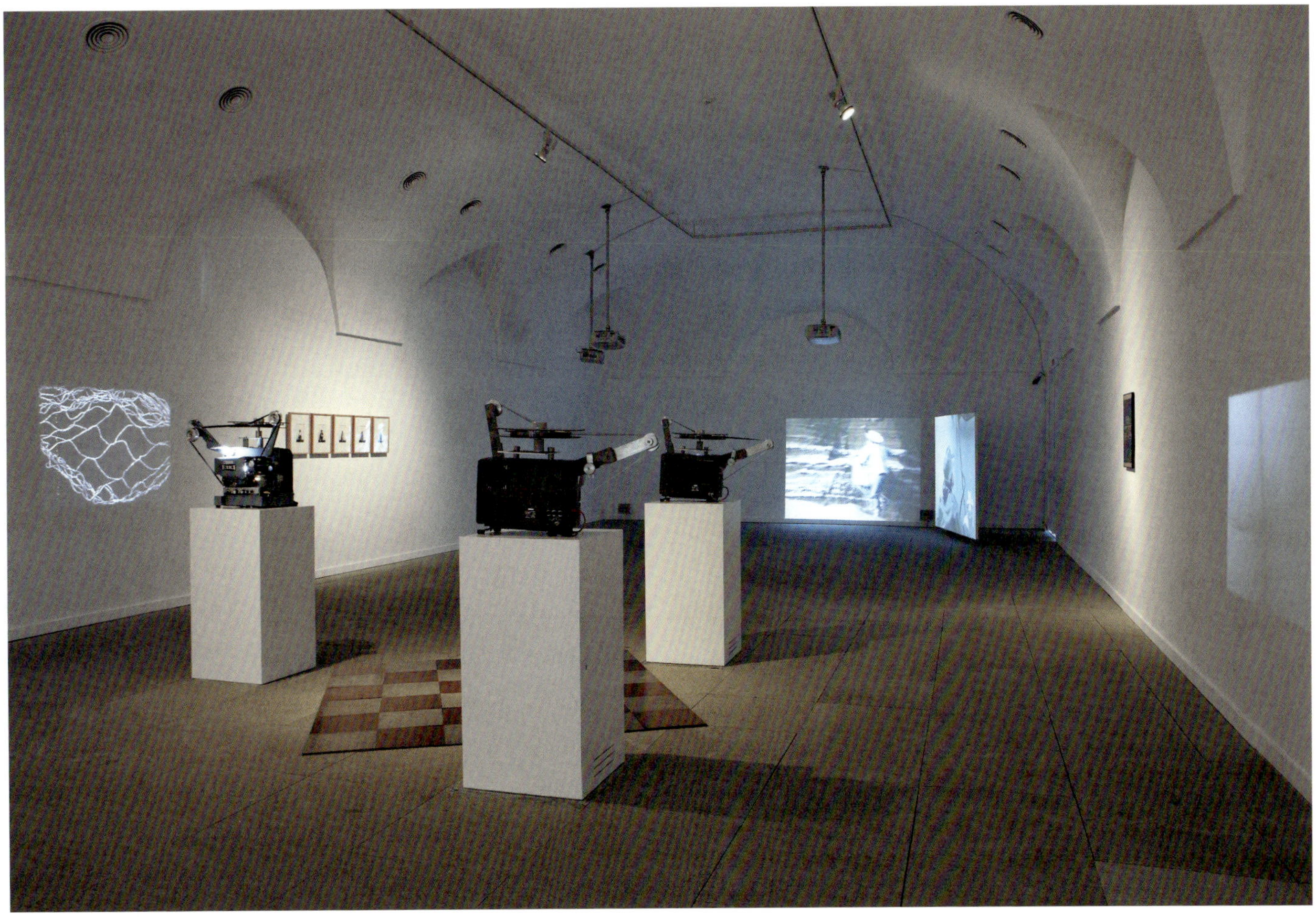

Above and following pages: *A Curated Conference* (2010), installation view, Museo Nacional Centro de Arte Reina Sofía, Madrid, 2010

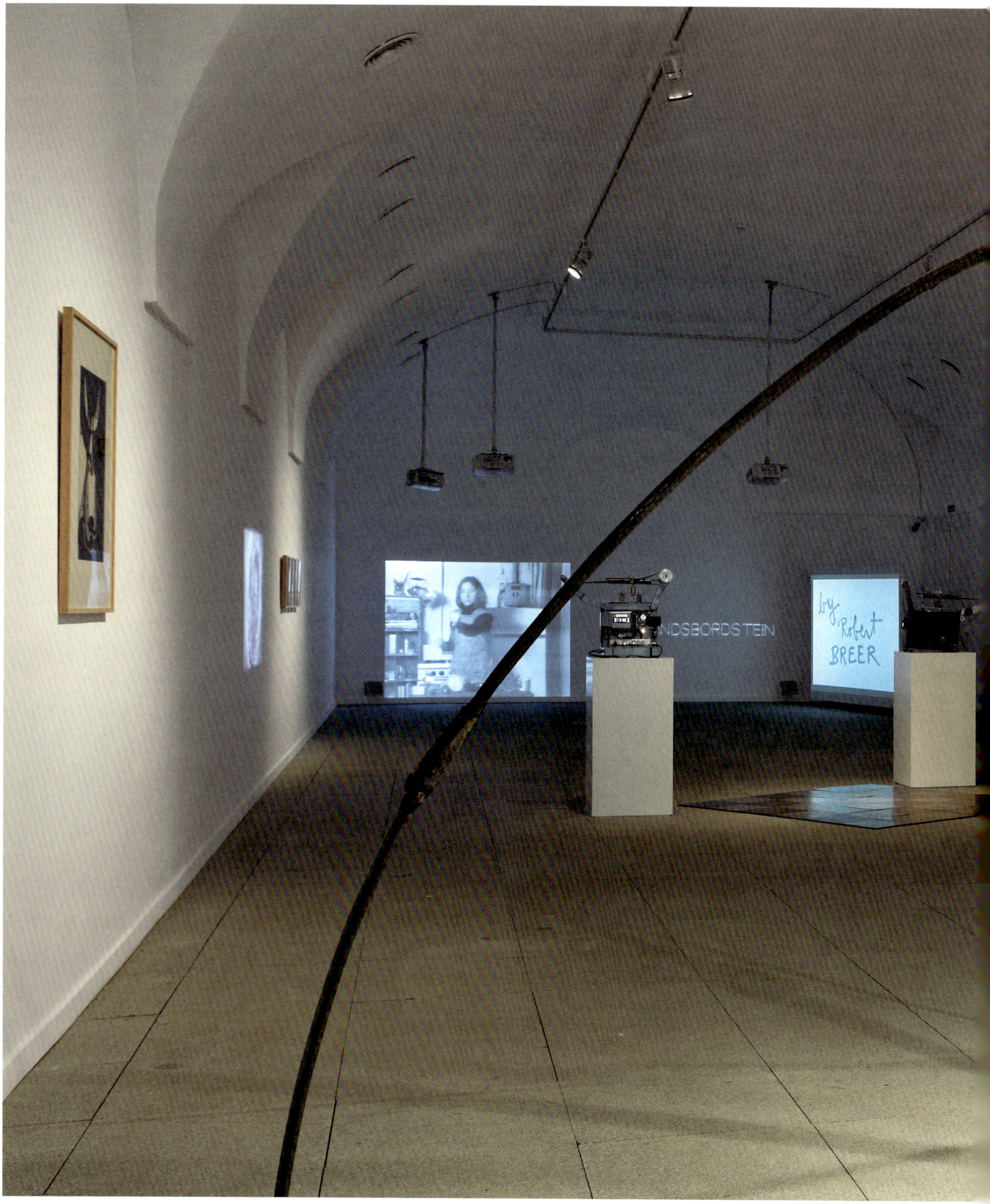
by Robert
BREER

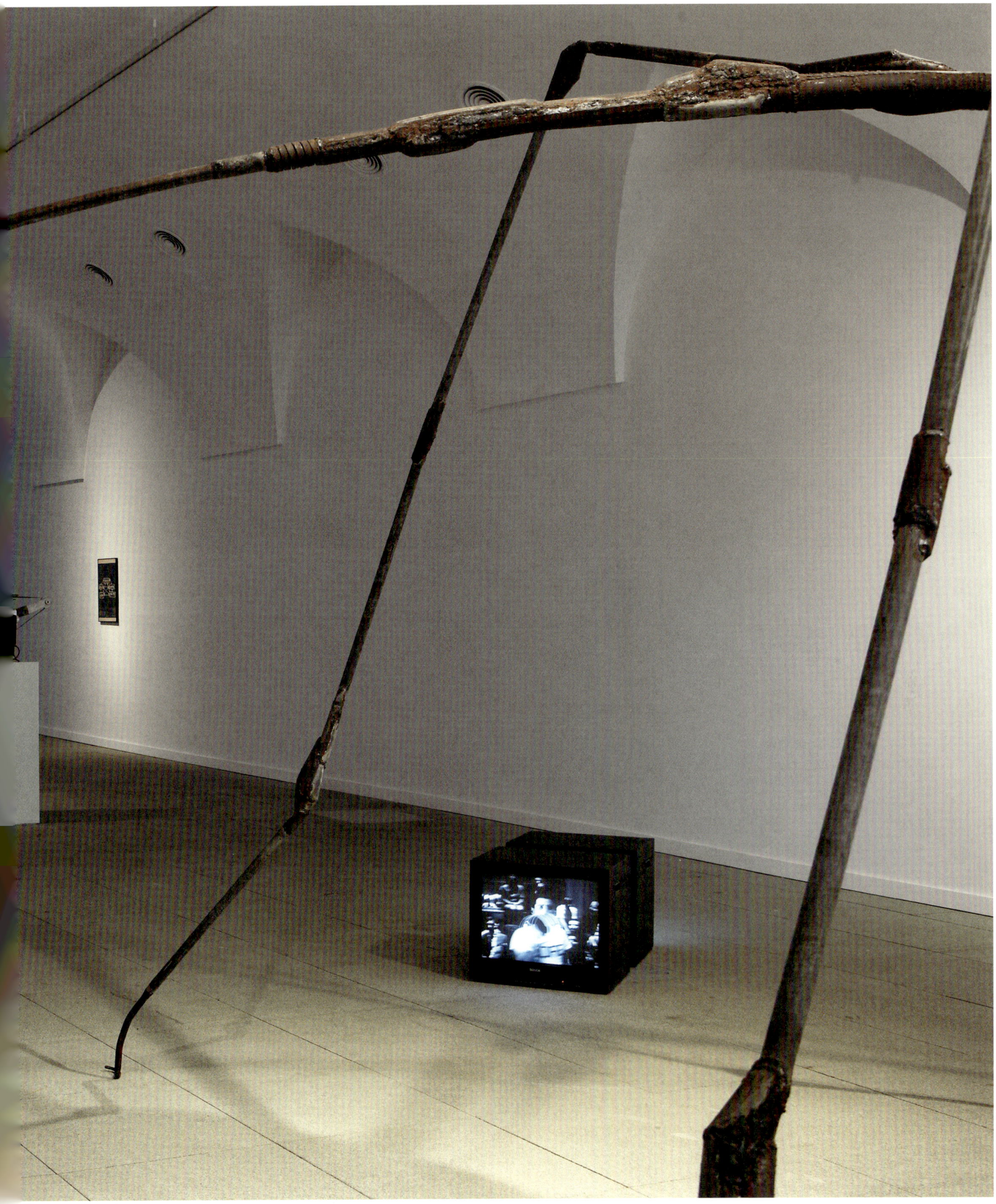

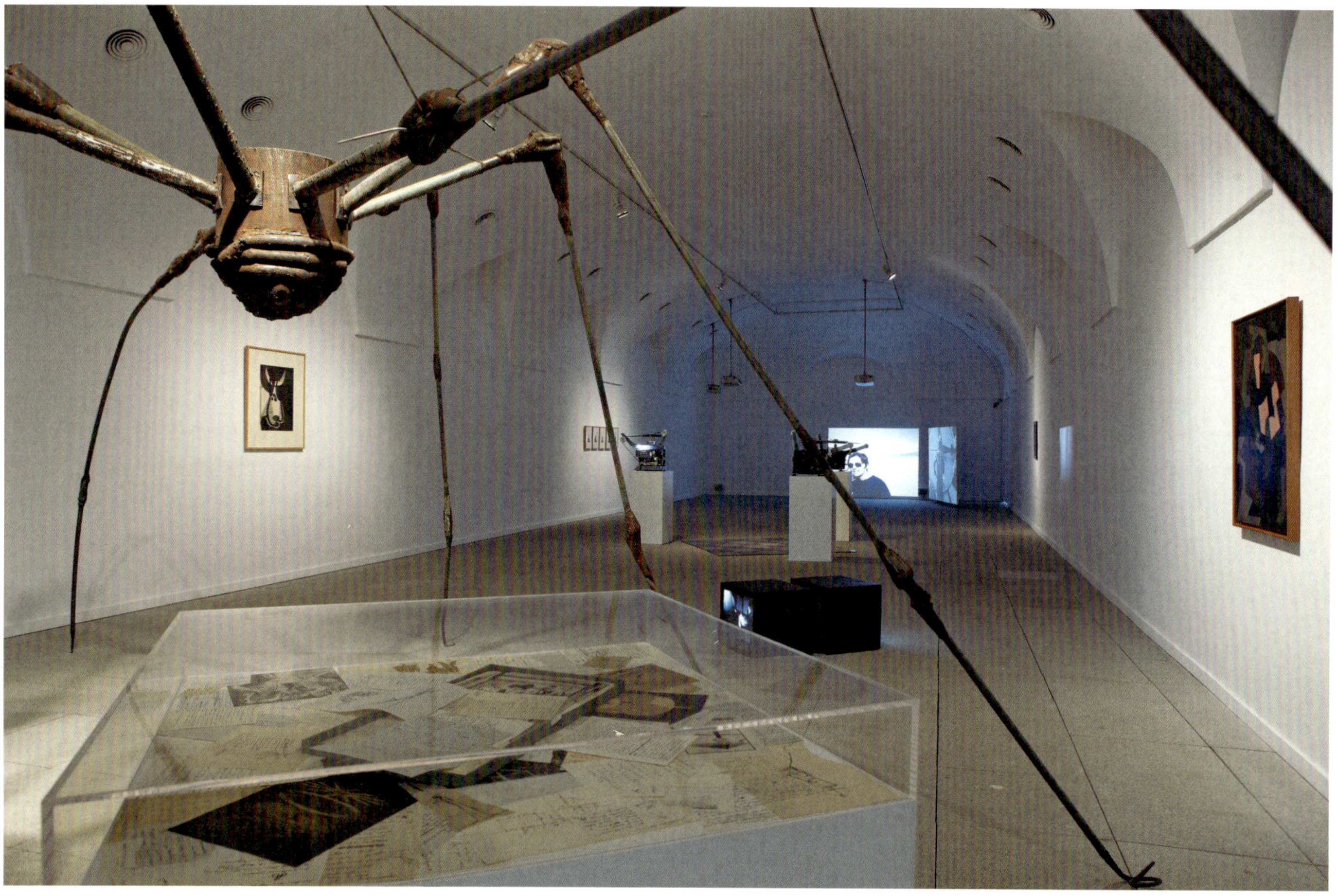

Above and right: *A Curated Conference* (2010), installation view, Museo Nacional Centro de Arte Reina Sofia, Madrid, 2010

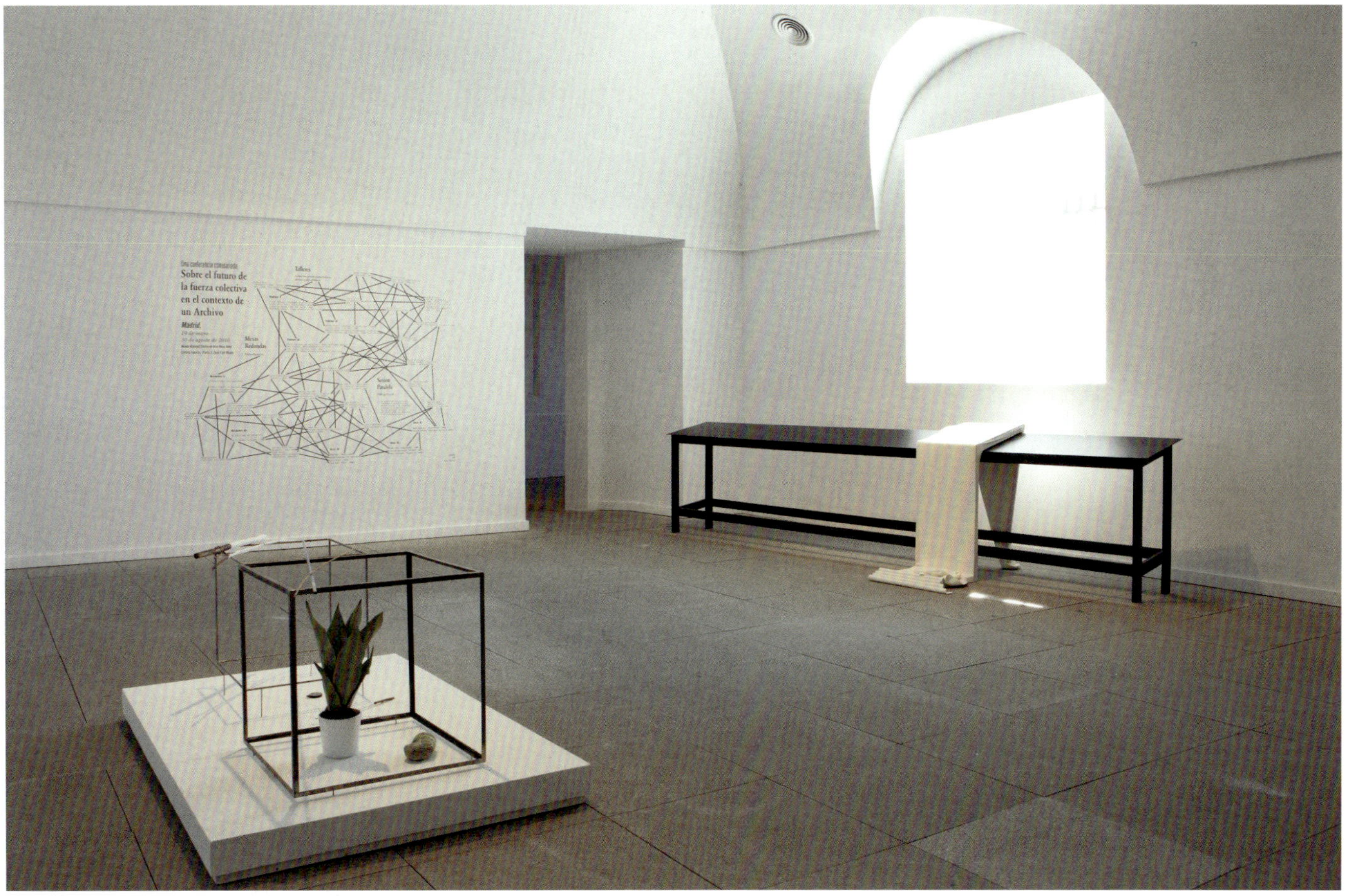
Sobre el futuro de
la fuerza colectiva
en el contexto de
un Archivo
Madrid.
Talleres
Mesas Redondas
Sesion Paralela

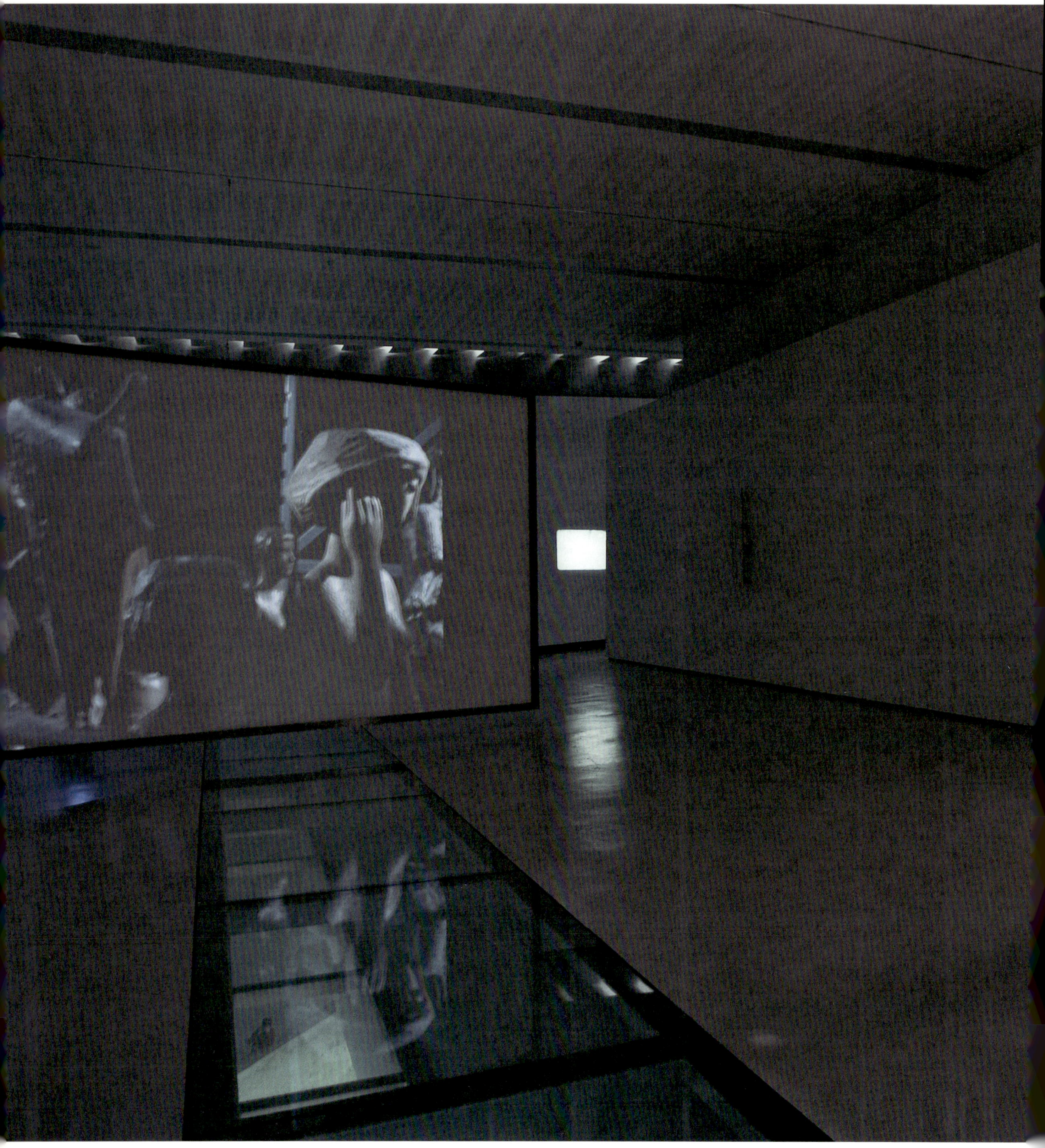

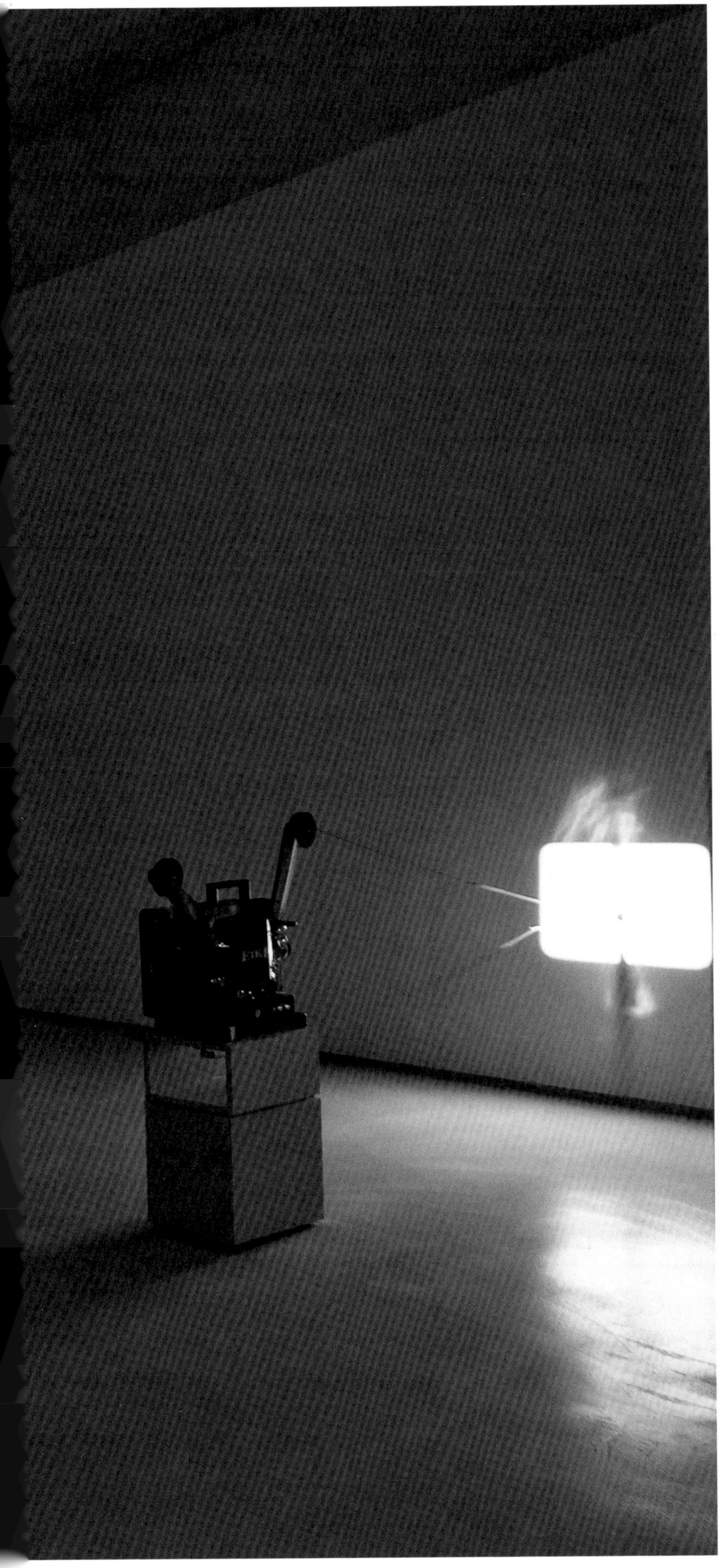

The Hidden Conference: About the Discontinuous History of Things We See and Don't See (2011), a 35-millimeter film shot shortly after Barba launched her project at the Museo Reina Sofía in Madrid, explores this debate further.[6] Set in an unidentified location (the storage area of the Neue Nationalgalerie in Berlin) and at "an unspecified point in time (in the future or in the past)," it brings to light a situation that although existing for years, the written prologue informs us, has now taken on a certain "degree of urgency." Nonetheless, the reason for the meeting is no longer known. As the camera choreographs a miscellaneous group of art objects shrouded in noirish lighting, fragmentary narratives emerge but never cohere. Once again narrative serves as "a mediator not [as] a solution." Speech is subsumed into corporeal performance, for the minimal soundtrack by Barba's long-time collaborator Jan St. Werner animates the works—by Ernst Barlach, Renee Sintenis, Gerhard Marcks, and others now sunk into anonymity—creating a sense of play through gesture, stance, posture, and regard. Far from challenging the paradigm of the archive as a failed futuristic vision, this clandestine conference confirms its rhetoric. Pathos surrounds the museum's erstwhile ambitions to representational totality, making moot the possibility of the redemptive salvaging of these misplaced shards of a fractured history.

Left: *The Hidden Conference: About the Discontinuous History of Things We See and Don't See* (2010) and *Invisible Act* (2010), installation view, MAXXI—Museo Nazionale delle Arti del XXI Secolo, Rome, 2010
Following pages: *The Hidden Conference: About the Discontinuous History of Things We See and Don't See* (2010)

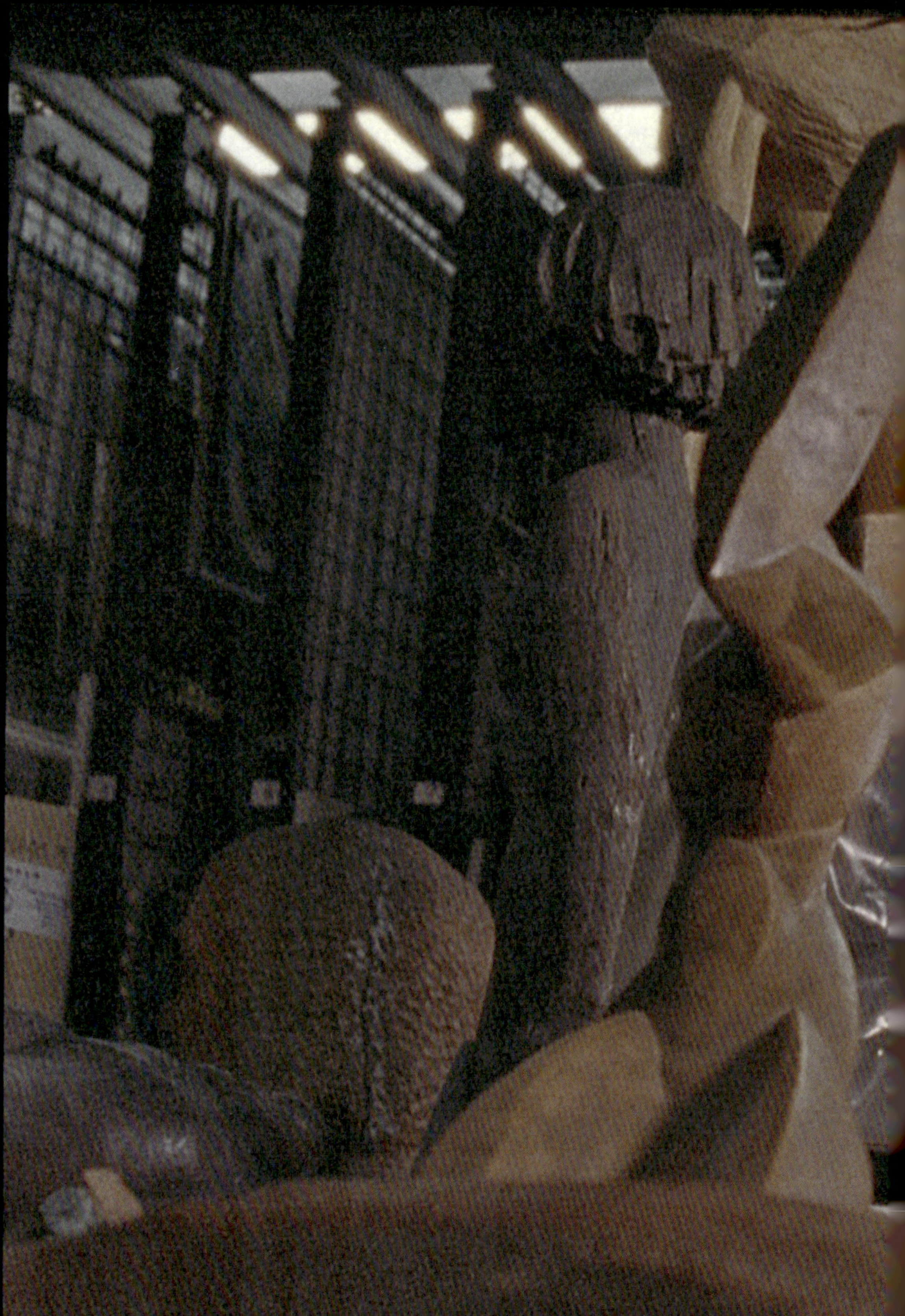

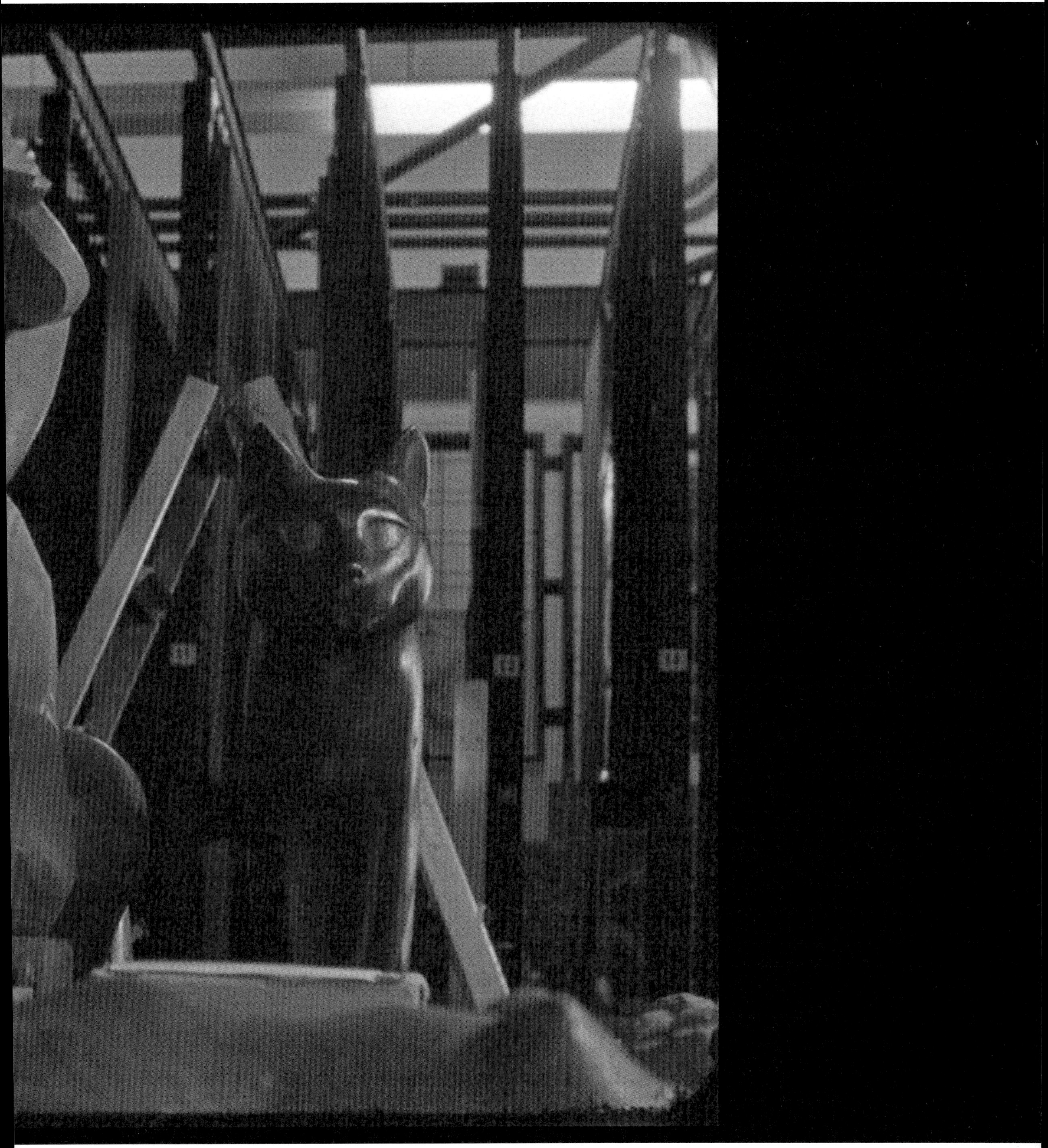

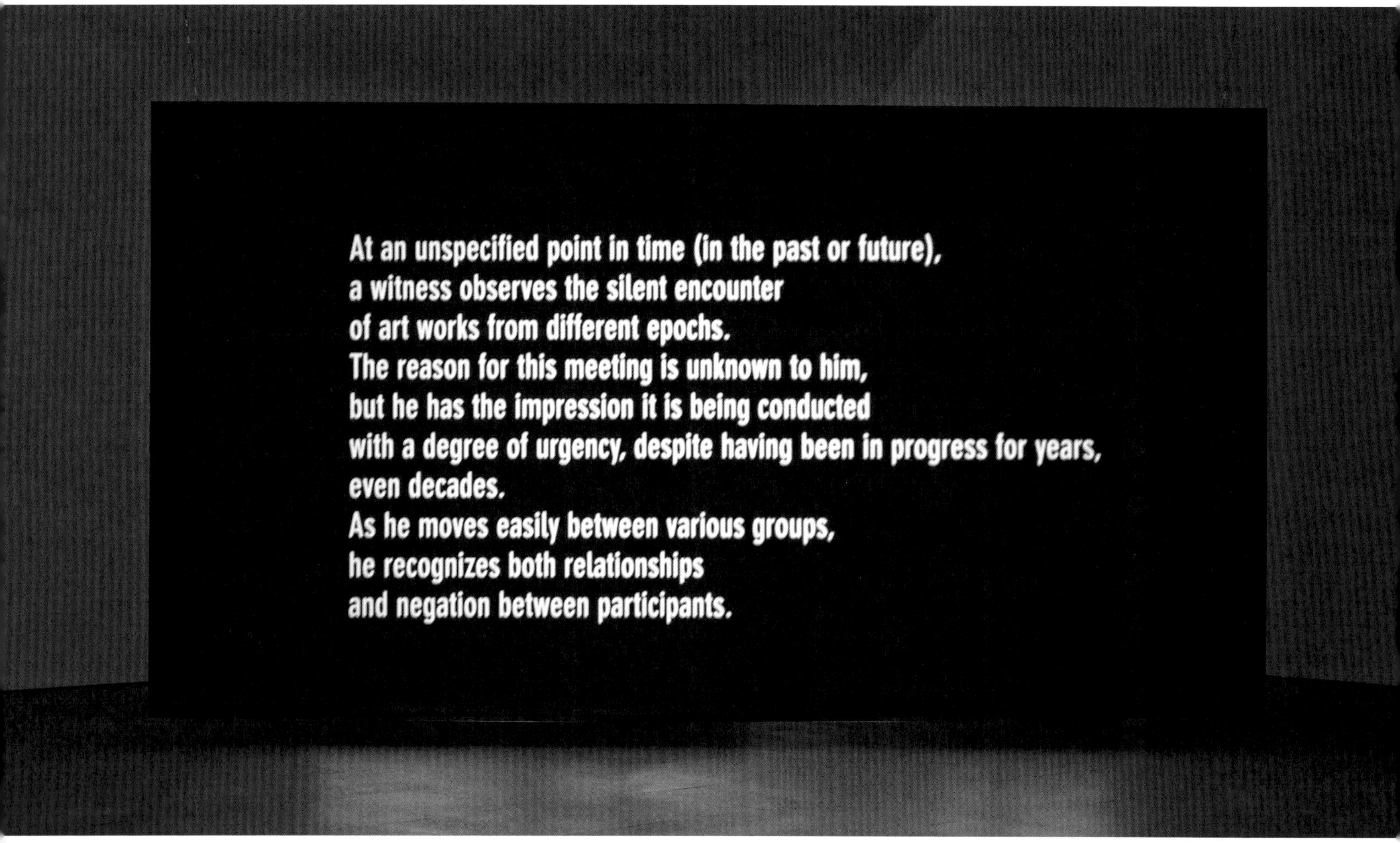

Above, right, and following pages: *The Hidden Conference: About the Discontinuous History of Things We See and Don't See* (2010), installation view, carlier | gebauer, Berlin, 2011

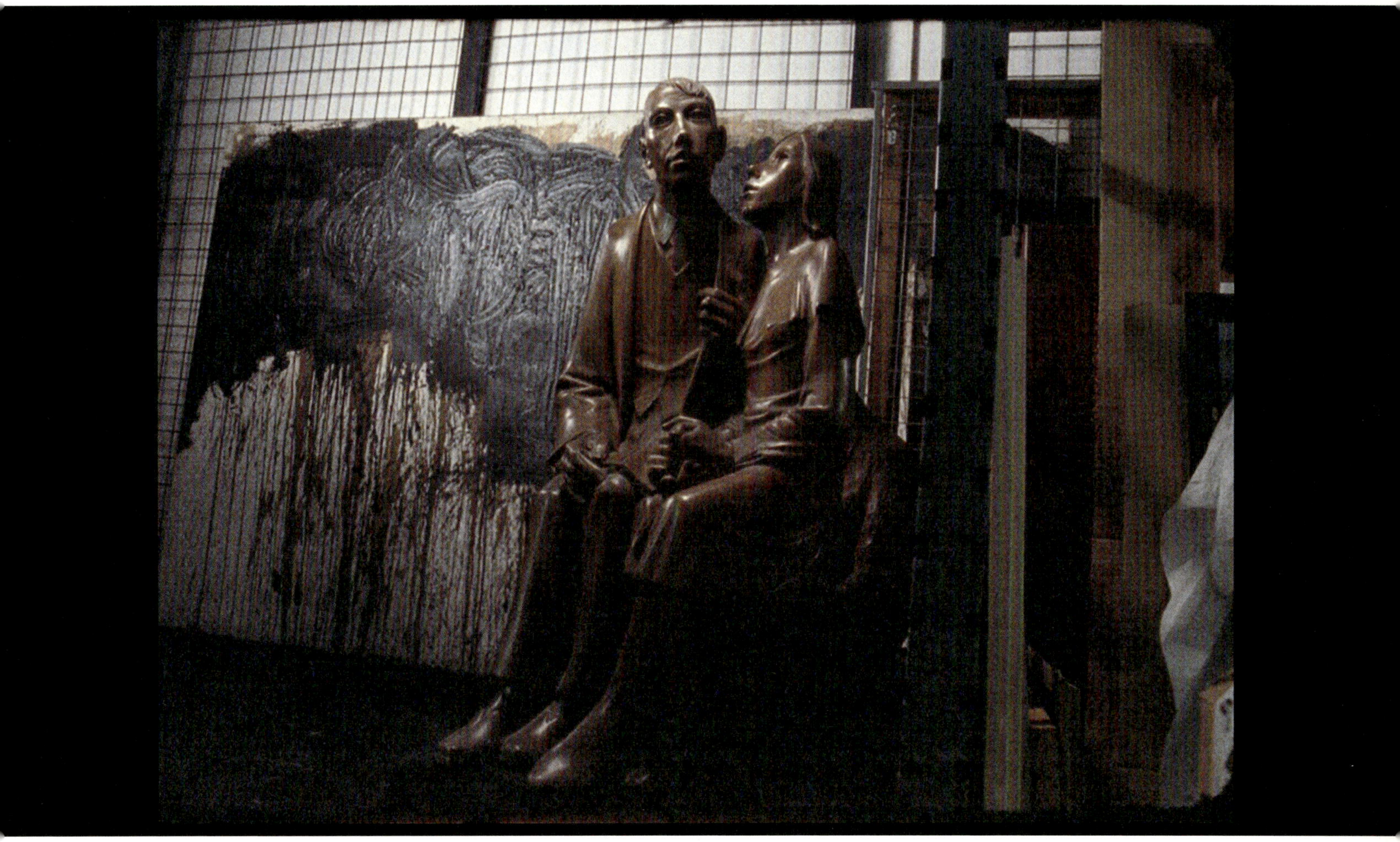

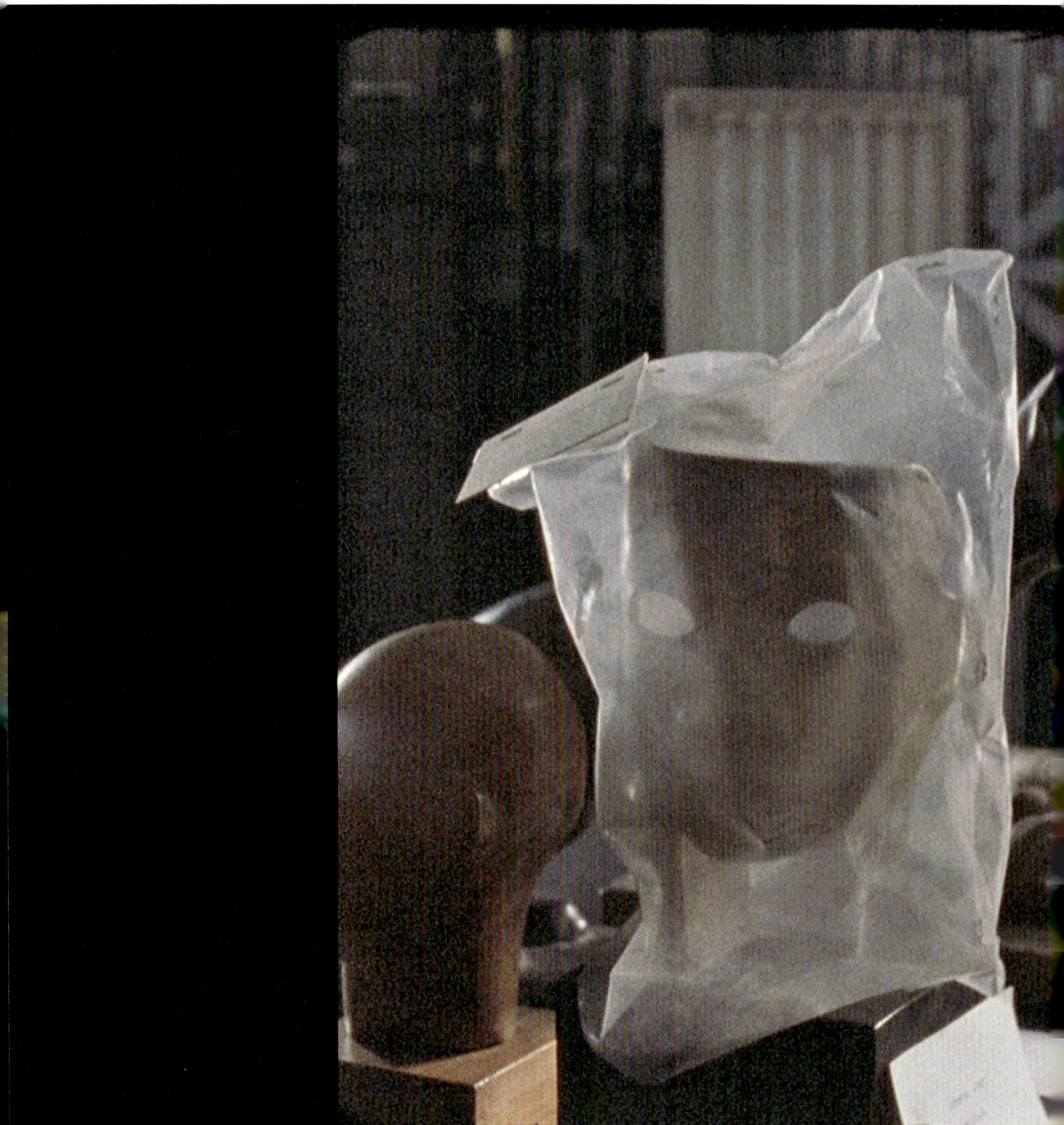

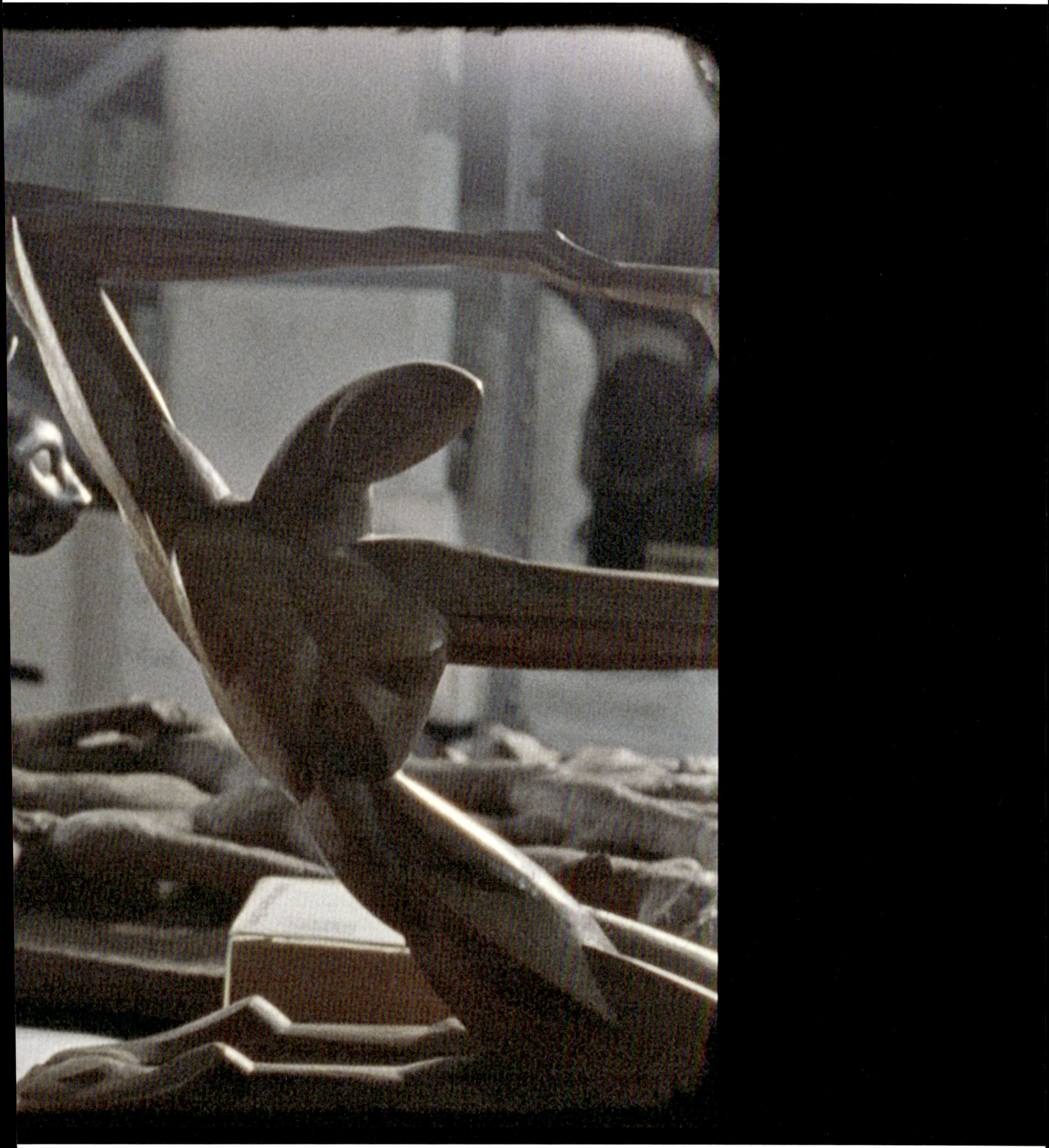

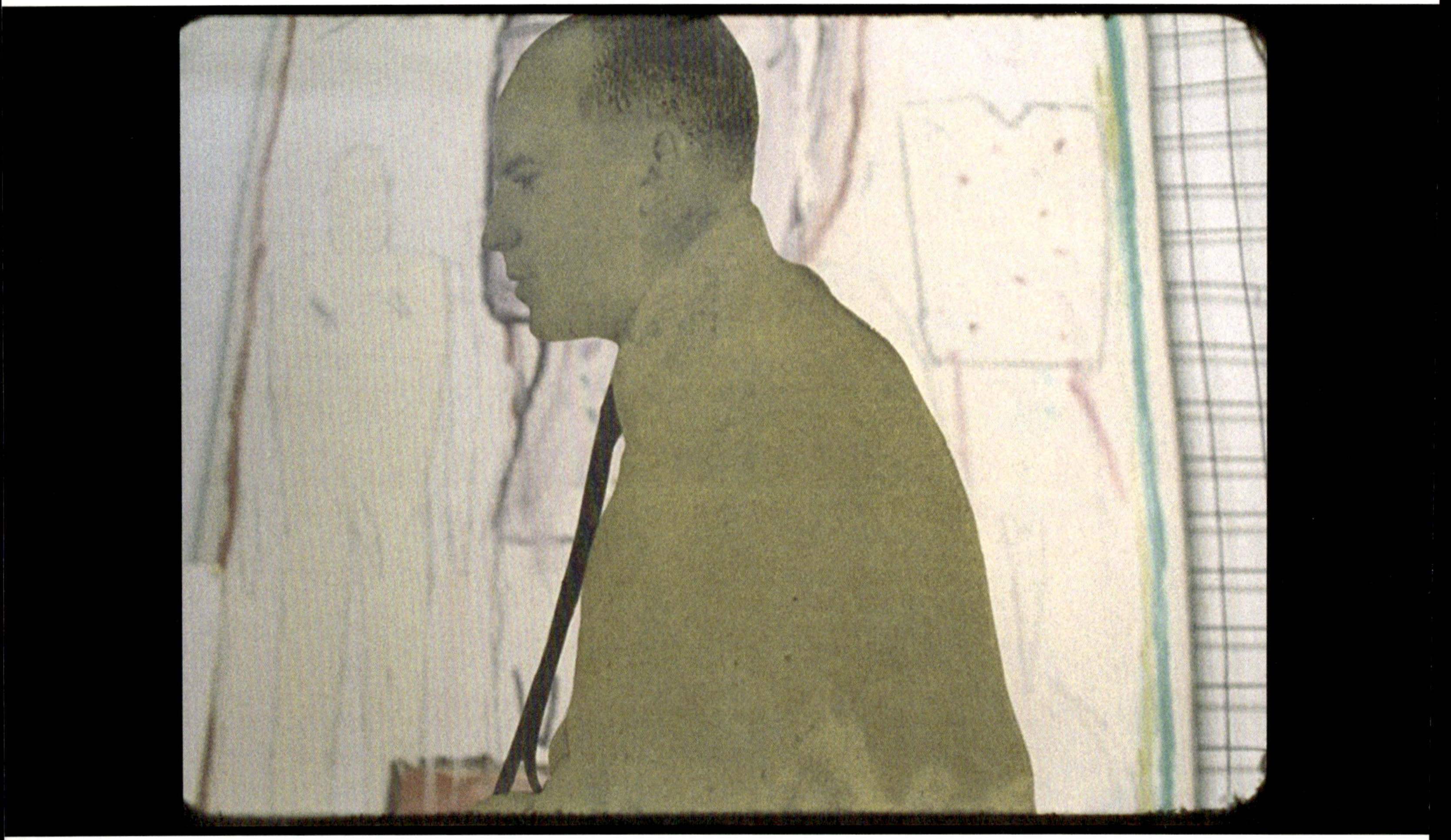

The Hidden Conference: About the Discontinuous History of Things We See and Don't See (2010)

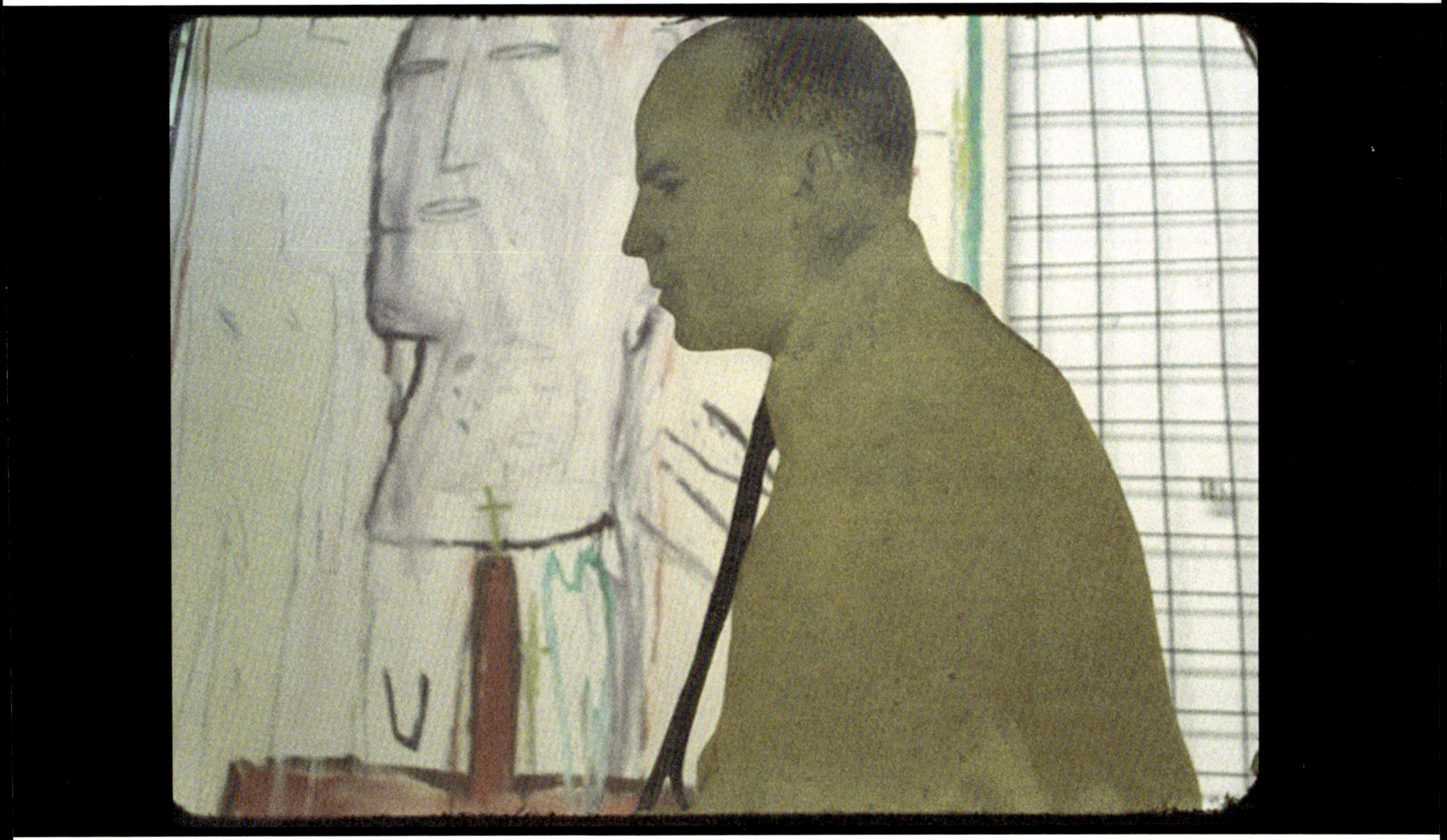

Several years ago, Barba had addressed the archive from a completely different perspective in *Western Round Table* (2007). Her source for the work was a symposium convened in San Francisco in 1949 under the heading "The Western Round Table on Modern Art." Aiming to "bring a representation of the best informed opinion of the time to bear on questions of art today," its distinguished lineup of (all male) discussants featured critics, artists, art historians, composers, museum professionals, and the like, including Marcel Duchamp, Frank Lloyd Wright, Darius Milhaud, Robert Goldwater, Mark Tobey, Alfred Frankenstein, Andrew C. Richie, and Gregory Bateson.[7] This time, Barba's riposte took the form of a sculptural projection. Two 16-millimeter projectors placed together on the ground spool clear celluloid. Each creates a spotlight of white light on an adjacent wall into which the looming architectonic shadow of its antagonist, the other projector, enters. The soundtrack is comprised of extracts from two Fellini films cut so that the projectors appear to be conversing with each other, albeit in terms far removed from the august tone of the proceedings of the West Coast conference. Never quite obliterated by the mechanical sound produced by the anachronistic projectors, the musical refrains are initially teasing, entertaining, and even captivating. Soon, however, the soundtrack becomes an earworm, unforgettable and ineradicable. An epigraph to the transcript of the proceedings by Suzanne Langer contains the claim that in characterizing a philosophy, the solutions offered to questions are less revealing than the formulation of the problems: "Its answers established an edifice of facts," she contends, "but its questions make the frame in which its picture of facts is plotted."[8] When filtered through Langer's observation, Barba's idiosyncratic embodiment of the proceedings of this celebrated event into a pair of somber architectonic silhouettes—dematerialized behemoths speaking imperviously over each other—may not be as negative as it initially appears.

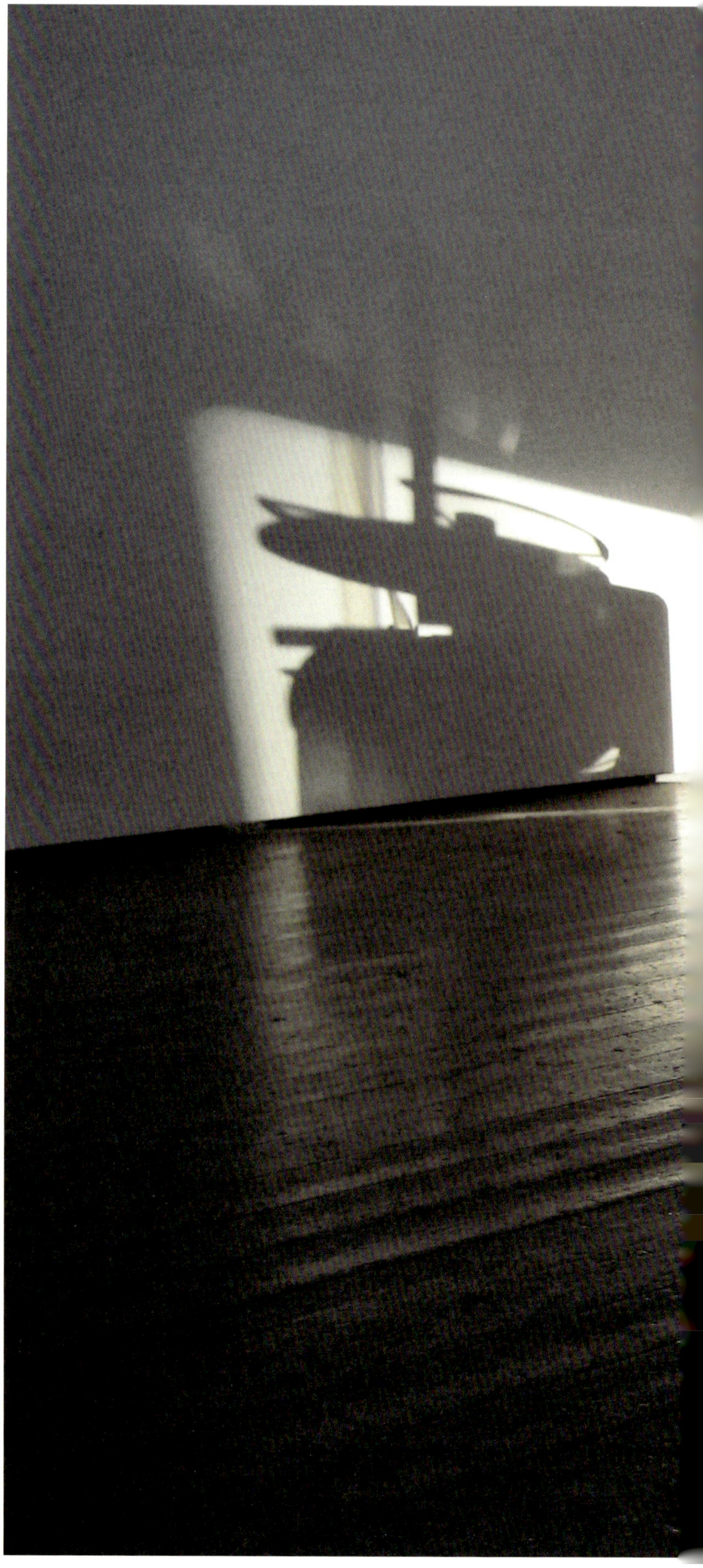

Western Round Table (2009), installation view, The Lux, London, 2009
Collection of the Museo Nacional Centro de Arte Reina Sofía, Madrid

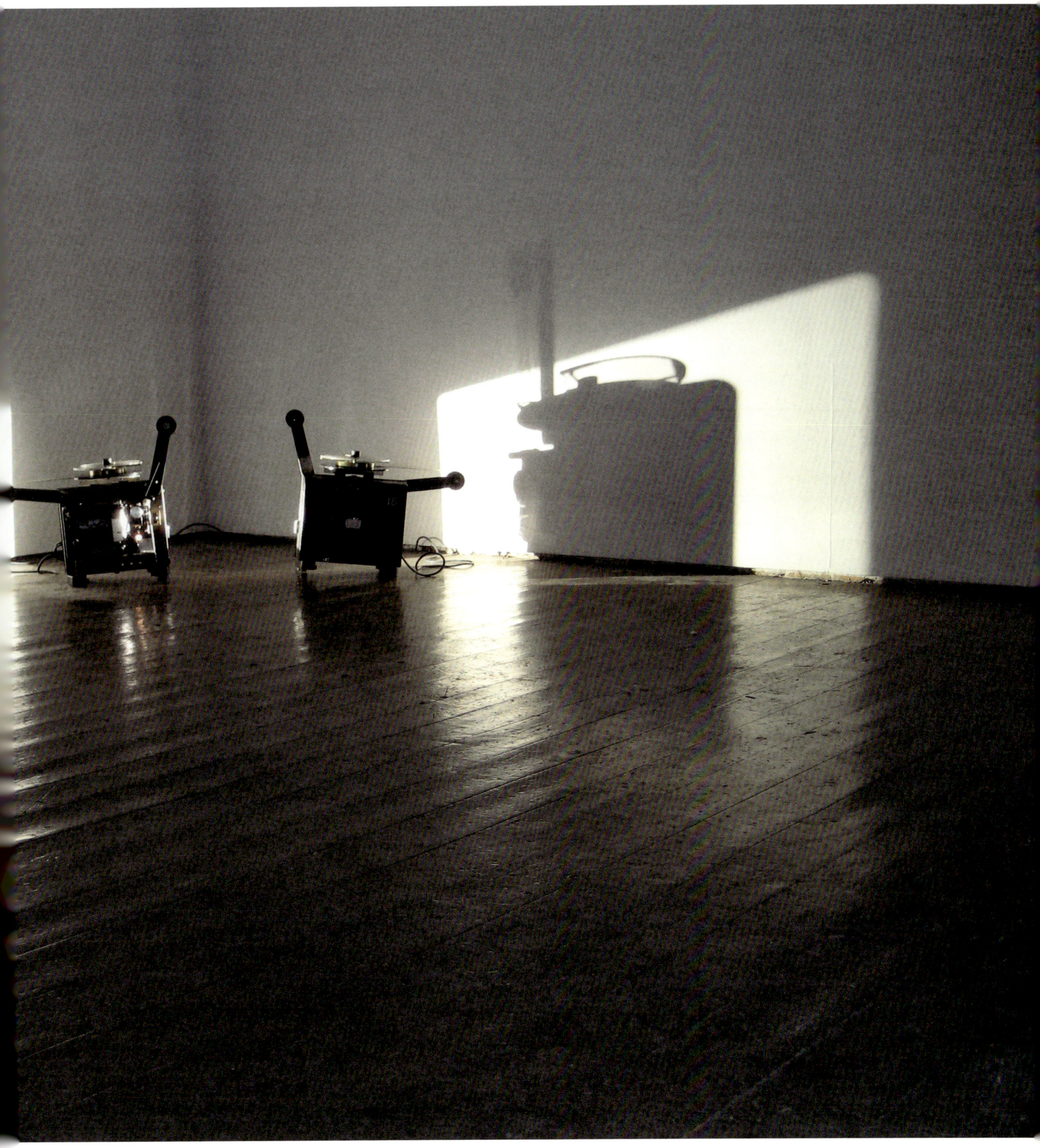

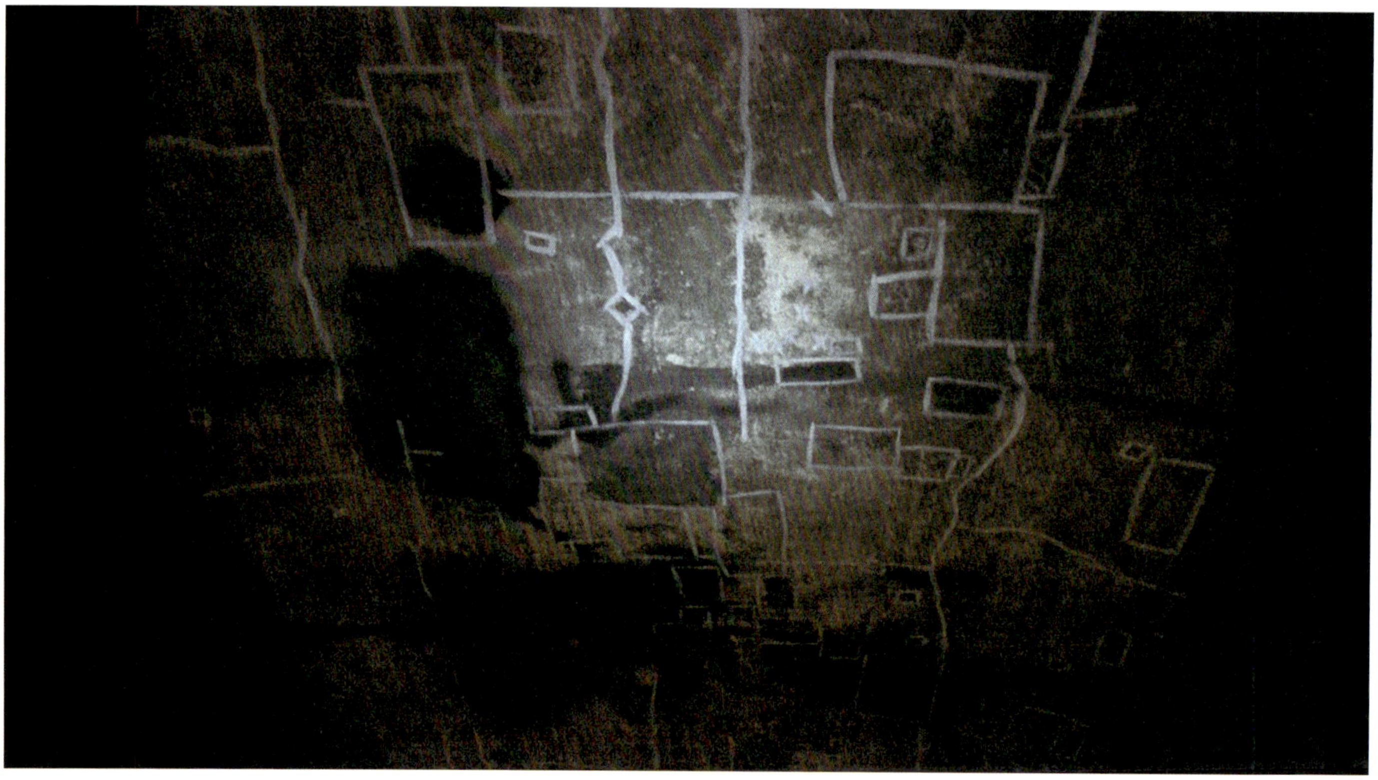

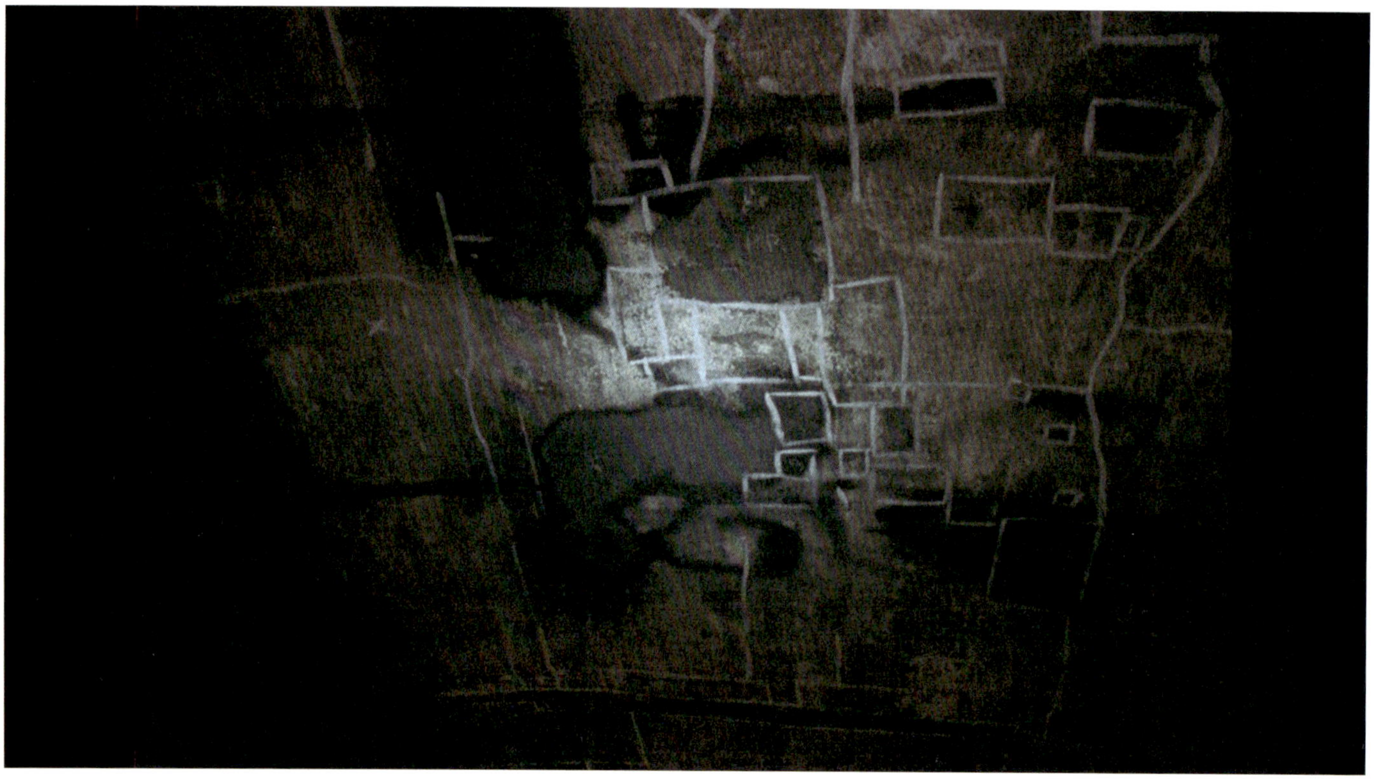

A Private Tableaux (2010)

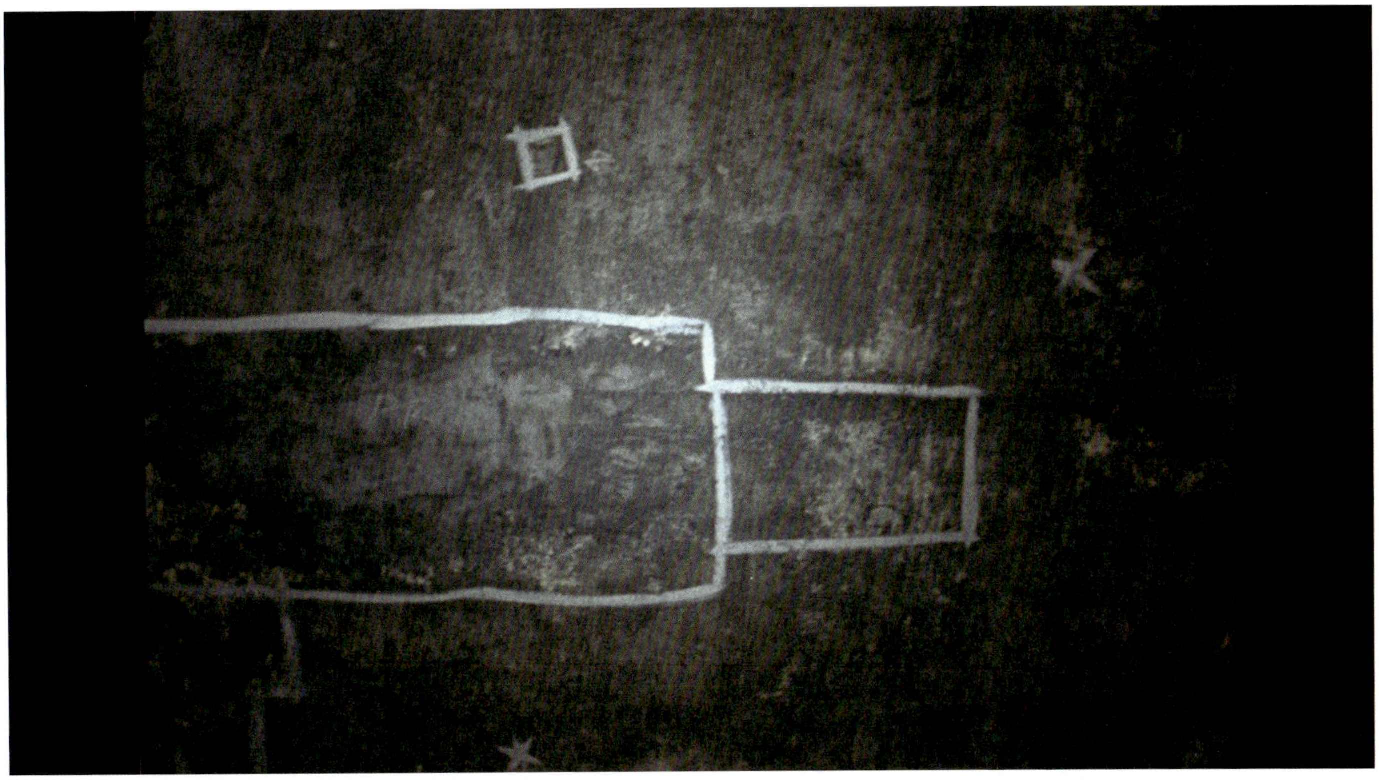

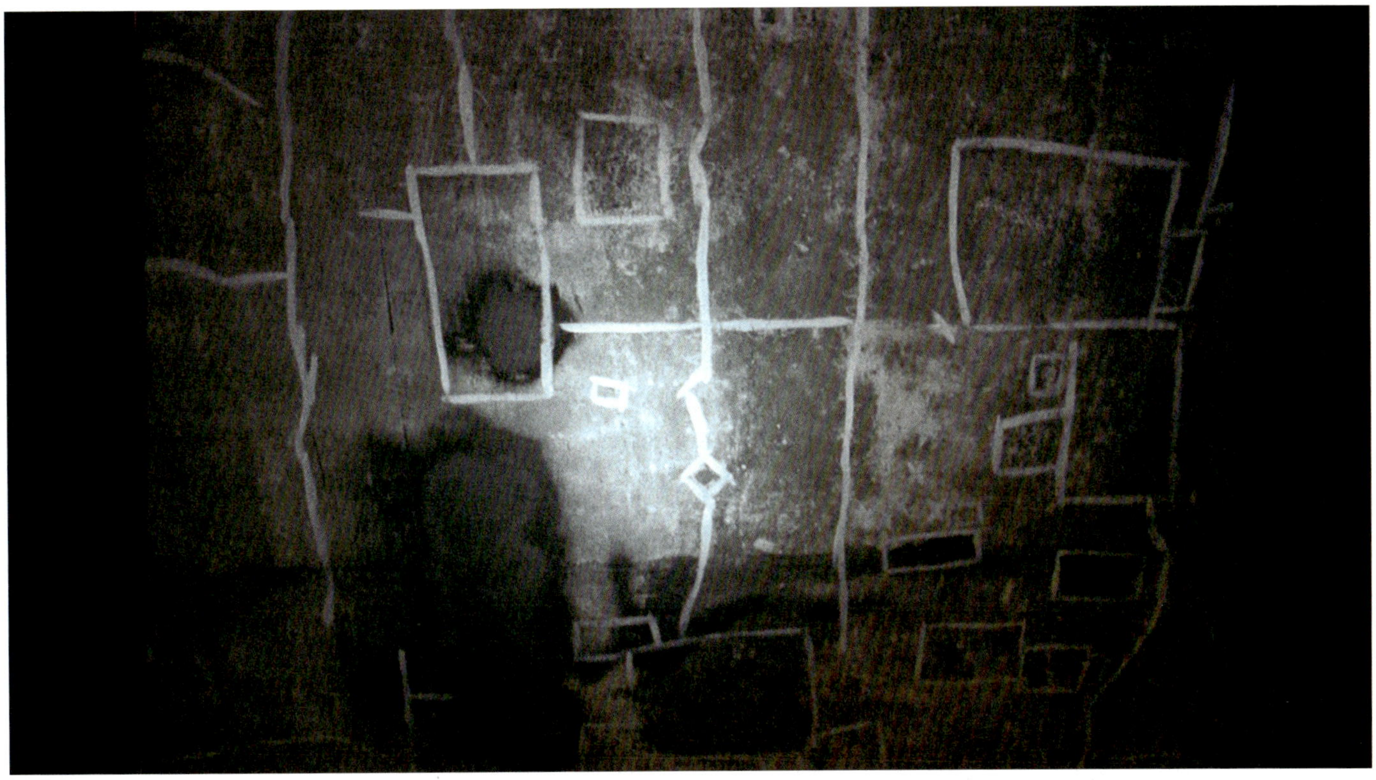

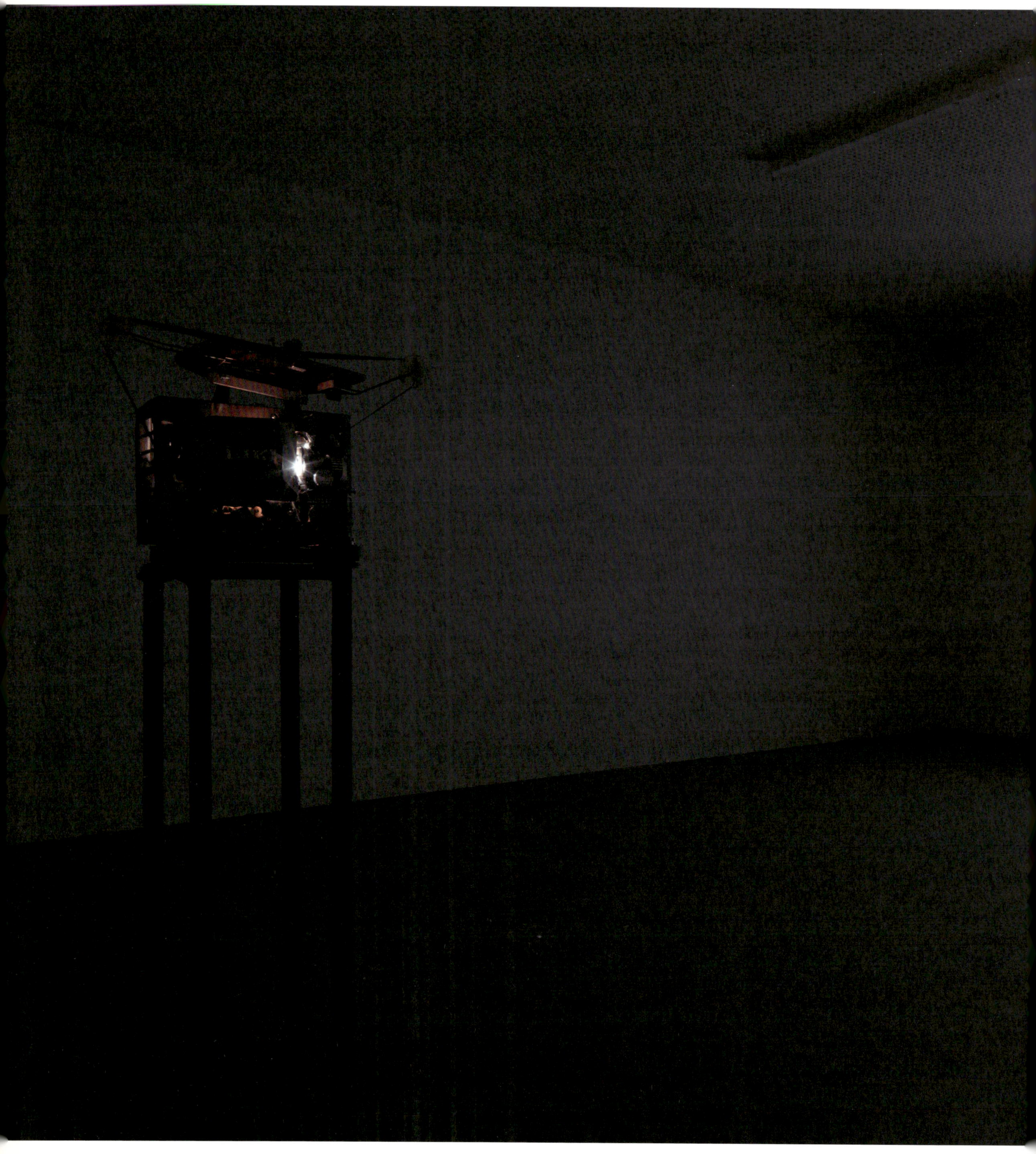

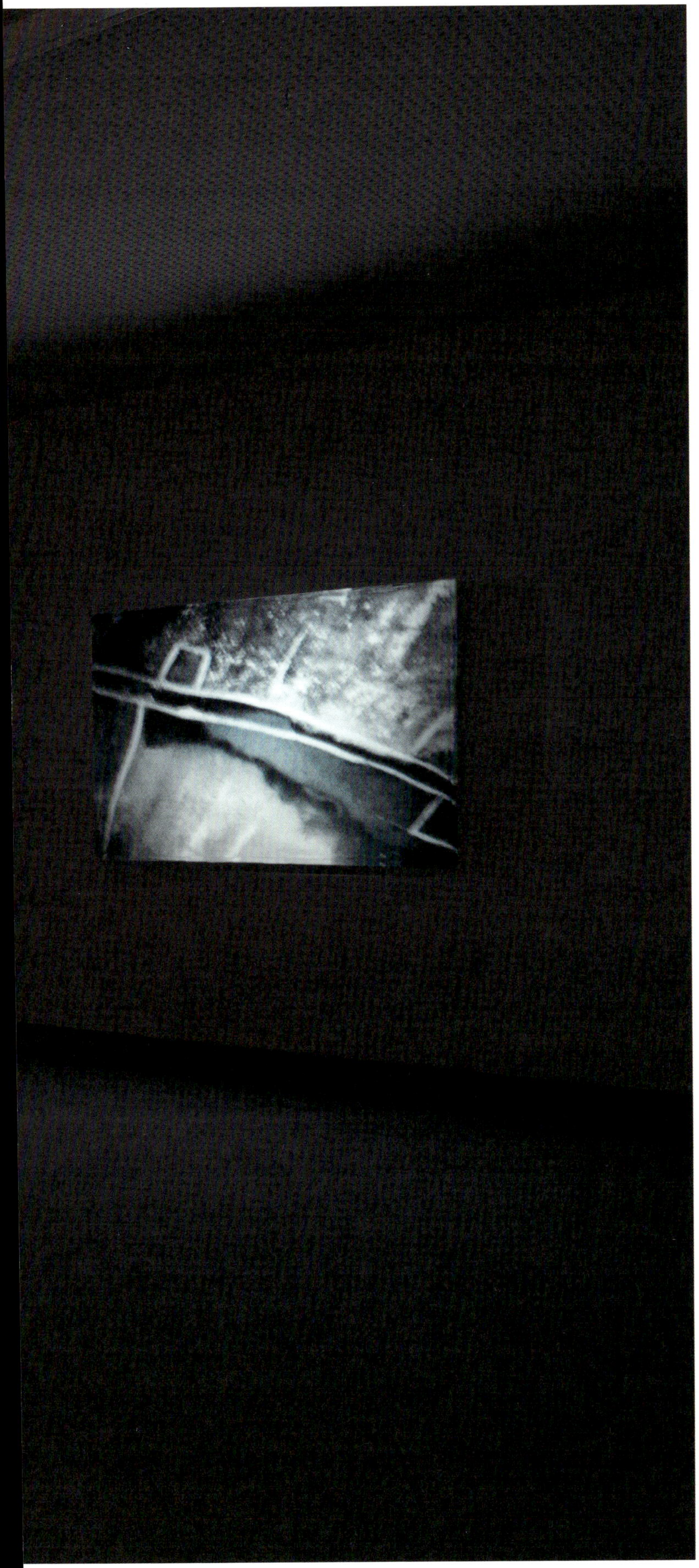

As *They Shine* attests, contemporary scientific imaginings are difficult to distinguish from what was once more properly the realm of science fiction.[9] Something quite different emerges, however, from *A Private Tableaux* (2010). Images resembling some kind of modern cave paintings are identified as the tracings left in passageways under the Mersey River in Liverpool over more than a century by engineers studying pressure points created by vehicles traveling in tunnels overhead. Barba, somewhat uncharacteristically, eschews an archaeological approach to this terse cartography in favor of a semiotic inquiry that reads the abstract signs as figurative symbols. Apparently ignorant of their origins, the commentator (whose report supplies the text in this film) likens them to a form of "automatic writing" made by the engineers' "subliminal selves" "for their own pleasure." He/she then attempts to characterize the markings that comprise these "private tableaux": in addition to "a flight machine" and "a carriage and horses," there is a portrait of a young man "drawn from memory." Comparing this face, with considerable latitude, to a drawing by Cocteau, the writer concludes that it "gave its creator much trouble and little satisfaction." Forgoing the dispassionate objective address proper to scientific interpretation, this fanciful semiotic parsing betrays a whimsicality rare in Barba's work. Yet it is precisely the risible character of these wild surmisings that throws attention back onto the terms in which the enquiry was formulated. Once again, Barba's primary concern is the structure that frames and governs the narrative impulse. Narrative as a form of cultural critique may serve as a means of both mediating history and making sense of contemporary experience. For Italo Calvino storytelling became a vehicle for galvanizing an audience that had grown passive, first under Fascist rule and then by rapid sociocultural developments in the postwar years. He came to believe that, far from requiring a polemical illustration of ideological positions, a committed literature required the deployment of style and craft in service to a form of realism that had nothing to do with naturalism. Fiction demanded attention, "first of all, [to] image and word, attitude, pace, style, contempt, defiance."[10] Realism, not naturalism, is also Barba's preferred mode; so, too, storytelling for her is a matter of style and attitude as much as one of craft. The sources of her narratives are culled from a wide range of literature. Sometimes, as in her use of Creeley's poem in *The Long Road,* she borrows directly; more often, as in *Somnium* and *Let Me See It* (2010), which is based on a story by Borges, she recasts or paraphrases the original text. Literature is nonetheless as fundamental to her conception of cinema as are its visual counterparts.

A Private Tableaux (2010), installation view, carlier | gebauer, Berlin, 2011

Whereas cinema is variously conceived as a kind of writing or inscription in many of Barba's film-works, sculpture is deployed to literally give material form to language.[11] *I Made a Circuit and then a Second Circuit* (2010) is one of a group of works that might be termed proto-cinematic devices, for each is composed from a sheet of felt suspended in space so that it functions as both screen and projector. When light is projected onto the dark lattice from which a text has been cut, a luminous script appears on the wall beyond. From the residues of one of these felt drapes Barba created *They Come and Go* (2009). The shards of language piled into a heap on a sheet of cloth laid on the floor and lit with the beam of a projector take on the form of an archive whose narrative potential is infinite.

Her acuity to text extends to its modes of delivery; the voices on her audio tracks are as particular as they are memorable. In *They Shine,* for example, the suave, matter-of-fact timbre of the narrator recalls the tones of the male leads in a certain type of Hollywood film. By cultivating that association Barba sought to underline the fact that the inhabitants of the uncanny milieu live between two phantasmic realities: the site on which the eerie array of reflectors was built is not far from Tinsel Town. Throughout her oeuvre, the monologues of (male) experts are always measured and cool, verging on laconic. However, when counterpointed with the indistinct, insecure voices of amateurs issuing uncertainly from the margins and interstices—as found in *Somnium*—these disciplinary tones sound slick, and their explanatory powers suspect.[12]

Storytelling depends as much on the reader/listener as on the authorial voice. In Roland Barthes' well-known formulation, reading (like viewing) creates a space of encounter where the reader and the multiplicity of writings that comprise any text "blend and clash." Barba's richly layered exploration of this encounter is perhaps nowhere more artfully manifest than in *It's Gonna Happen* (2005). An imaginary conversation that could plausibly have been part of the political machinations that have become known as Watergate provides the raw material for what may be a scene in a forthcoming feature film. The screenwriter's directions for this scene appear as phrases projected against a black ground, while on the soundtrack a reenactment of the conversation is played out in the form of a brief phone call. Viewers simultaneously read the texts and listen to the terse conversation in which two men plot a kidnapping, conjuring the scene in their imagination. As they struggle to take in both the written and spoken words unfolding in tandem but not in sync, they find themselves occupying two antipodal spaces: they are at once inside this illusory realm and outside its fictive boundaries. Independent from yet intermingling with the audio track, the sound of the projectors is a spur to the realization that an unmediated experience of cinema is no longer possible; the technologies of film and our attitudes toward it are inevitably filtered through its histories, conventions, and genres. By requiring her audience to negotiate between two contradictory positions, Barba enjoins them to reflect on film as a medium, and on its traditions and genres. The politics of Watergate are here both a pretext and a foil to her abiding subject: the politics of viewing. Time and again, the forms of introspection that mark many of the medium's exemplary modernist projects assume a narrative guise in Barba's practice. Self-reflexive texts, suspended stories, and speculative imaginings become discursive vehicles, the means through which she constructs a mode of viewing—an ontology of vision—appropriate to today's cinema.[13]

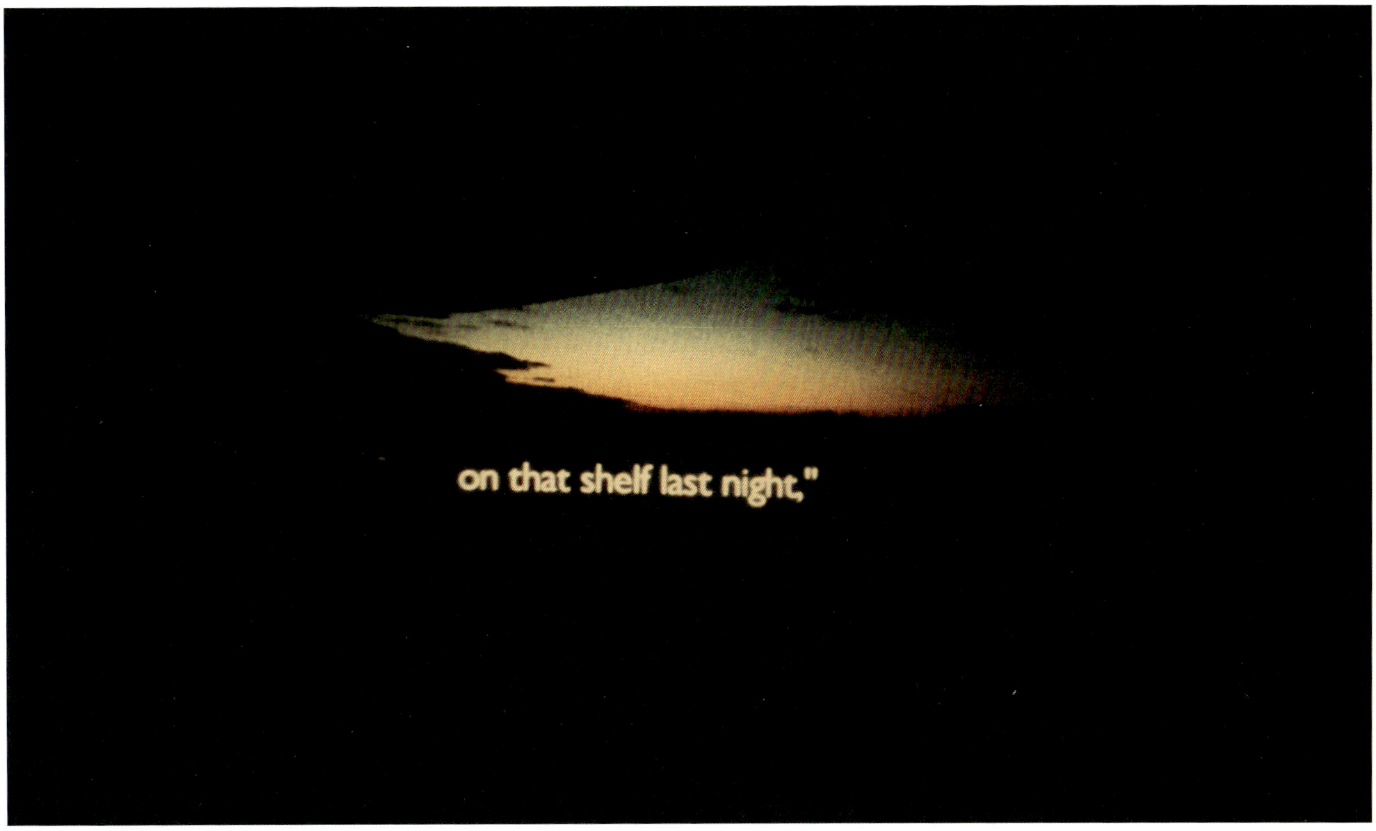

Above: *Let Me See It* (2011), installation view, Fondazione Galleria Civica–Centro di Ricerca sulla Contemporaneità di Trento, Trent, 2011
Following pages: *I Made a Circuit and then a Second Circuit* (2010), installation view, Kunstverein Braunschweig, 2011

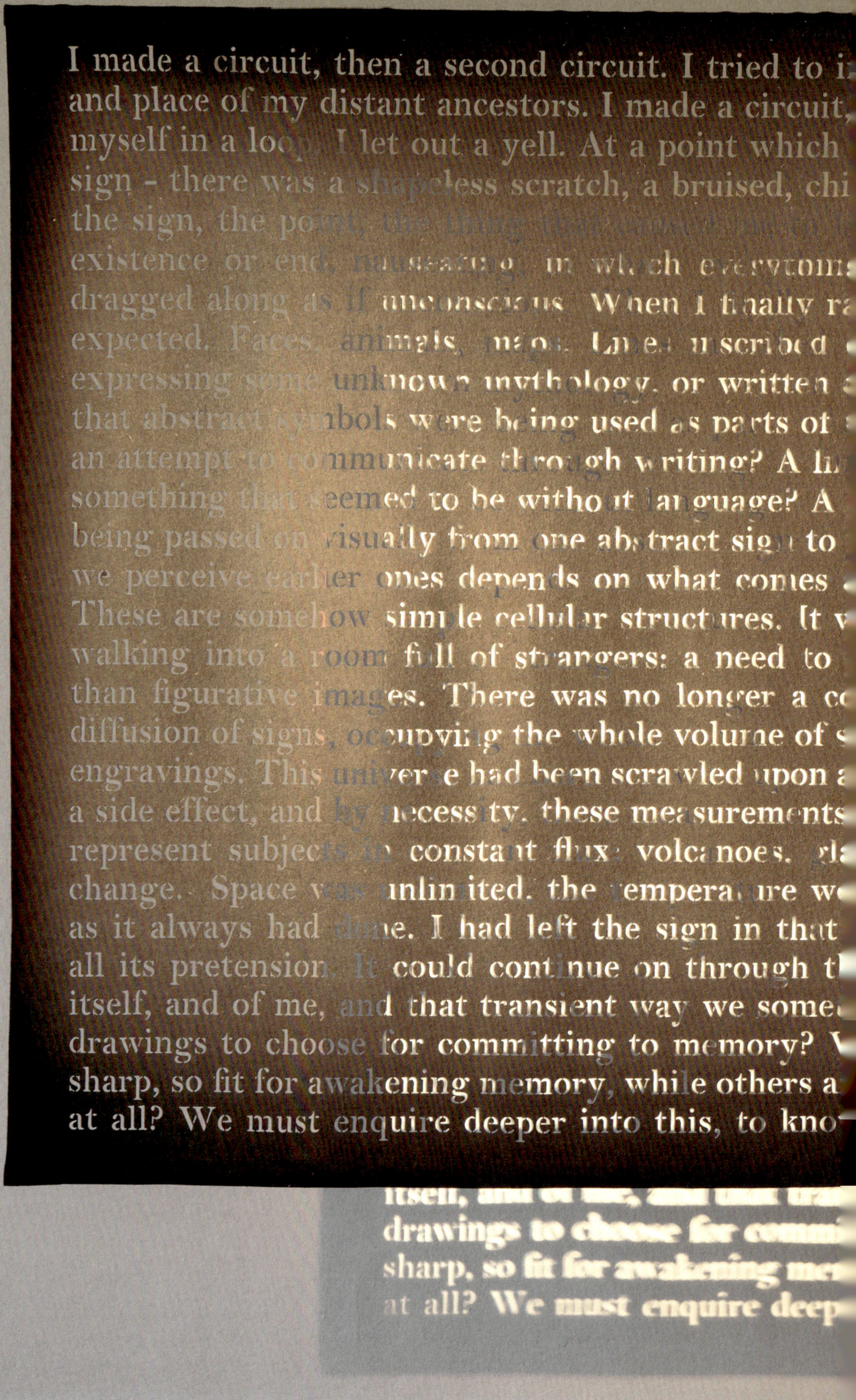

I made a circuit, then a second circuit. I tried to
and place of my distant ancestors. I made a circuit,
myself in a loop. I let out a yell. At a point which
sign - there was a shapeless scratch, a bruised,
the sign, the point,
existence or end, nauseating, in which
dragged along as if unconscious. When I finally
expected. Faces, animals, maps. Lines inscribed
expressing some unknown mythology, or written
that abstract symbols were being used as parts of
an attempt to communicate through writing? A
something that seemed to be without language? A
being passed on visually from one abstract sign to
we perceive earlier ones depends on what comes
These are somehow simple cellular structures.
walking into a room full of strangers: a need to
than figurative images. There was no longer a
diffusion of signs, occupying the whole volume of
engravings. This universe had been scrawled upon
a side effect, and by necessity, these measurements
represent subjects in constant flux: volcanoes,
change. Space was unlimited, the temperature
as it always had done. I had left the sign in that
all its pretension. It could continue on through
itself, and of me, and that transient way we
drawings to choose for committing to memory?
sharp, so fit for awakening memory, while others
at all? We must enquire deeper into this, to

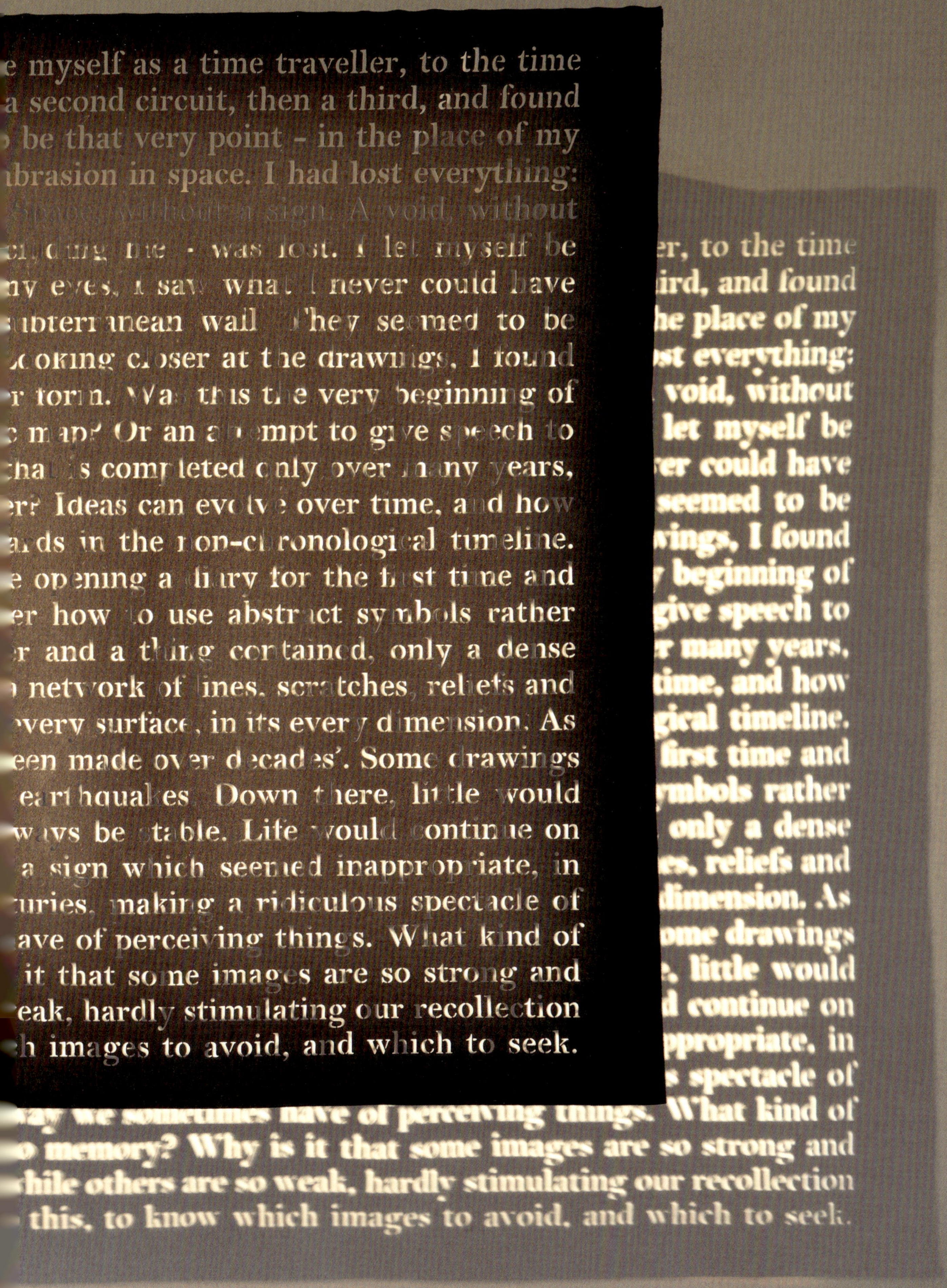
e myself as a time traveller, to the time
a second circuit, then a third, and found
be that very point - in the place of my
brasion in space. I had lost everything:
h images to avoid, and which to seek.
way we sometimes have of perceiving things. What kind of
memory? Why is it that some images are so strong and
while others are so weak, hardly stimulating our recollection
this, to know which images to avoid, and which to seek.

Hello there?

Hi

Everyone's gone

ok let's start

he said, he did not resign

what do you mean? Is he cheating us?

We are dealing with an enemy not like anything we've ever dealt with before

hmm ok

we have to follow this case

it has to be done carefully

clean, you know?

listen

meooow (a cat crossing the window)

i'm gonna have to stretch what i say a lot

possibly that's perfectly ok

this cat is driving me crazy

second, i think

well

it's a very tricky business

i mean

it has to be done

it has to be controlled without getting caught

ok

we are going to show them

we have to fight

the voice of the media has to be tuned to the same wavelength

for this story some people need to

you know

to go

i know

to start the whole thing going

we will call him on a phone

a phone that

well

we slip him a phone

someone will give him a phone

hmm

he will have no landline

no number from which he can be

It's Gonna Happen (2005), soundtrack script

reached

and then we will be able to hold him in a room

with his wife and his sister's husband

who will happen to be in the house at that time

that the abduction occurs

the soldier will come into the house and order them not to use the phone

and to come immediately

and then they take them to the airport

put them in a plane

they fly for six hours or so

with the shutters down

hmmmm

i have to put a call into the members of conference

asking if they demand that the press might be given the opportunity to speak

that they might be given a press conference opportunity

that the people can hear directly from him

how he has been treated

the essential message is clear

he did not resign

he was taken by force from his residence

in the middle of the night

forced onto the plane

and taken away without being told where he was going

after that the mission starts

yeah, that's a bit too good

almost scary, man

It's gonna happen

listen to the code tonight

i call

A reenacted phone call between two presidents of the possible dialogue that might have initiated the Watergate affair.

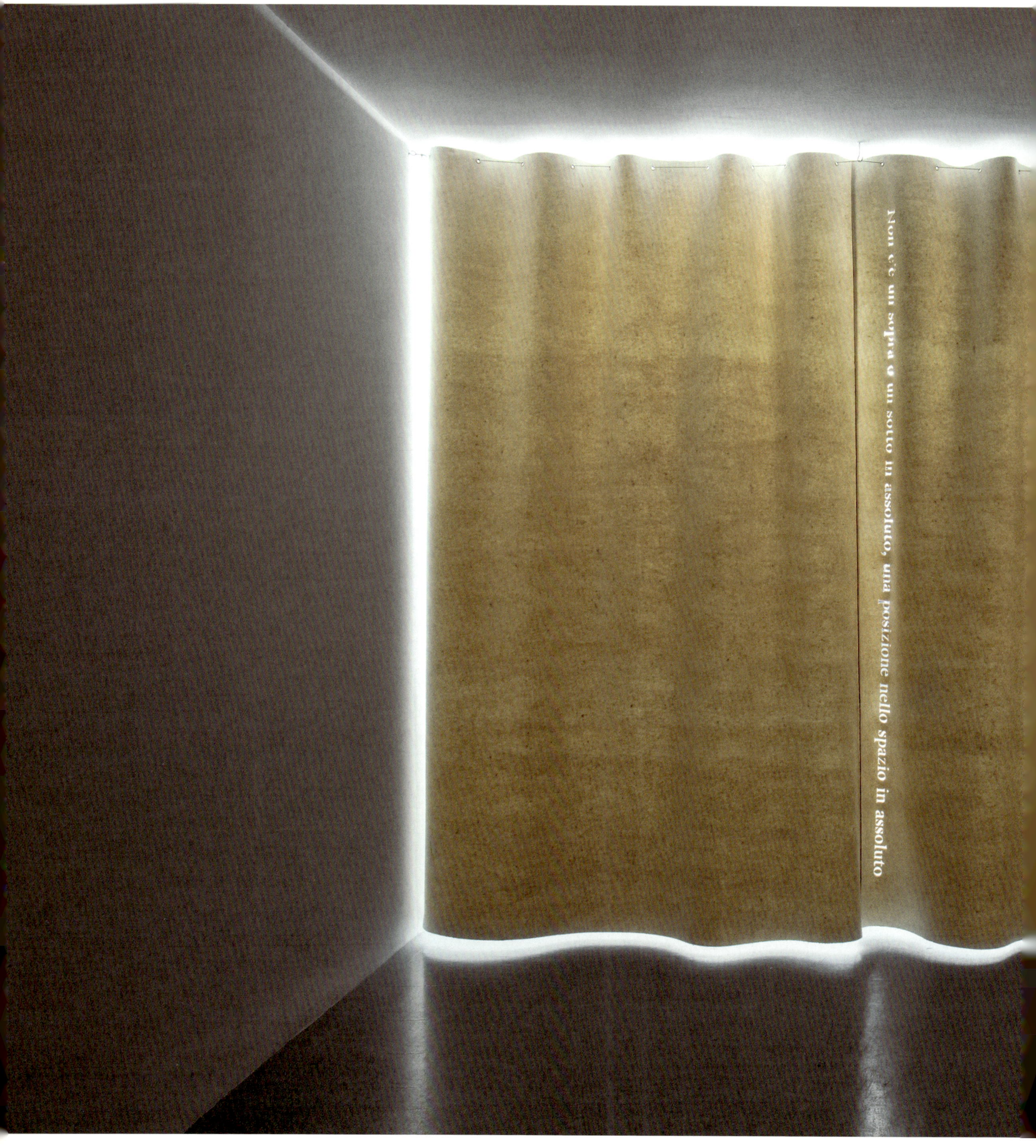
Non c'è un sopra e un sotto in assoluto, una posizione nello spazio in assoluto

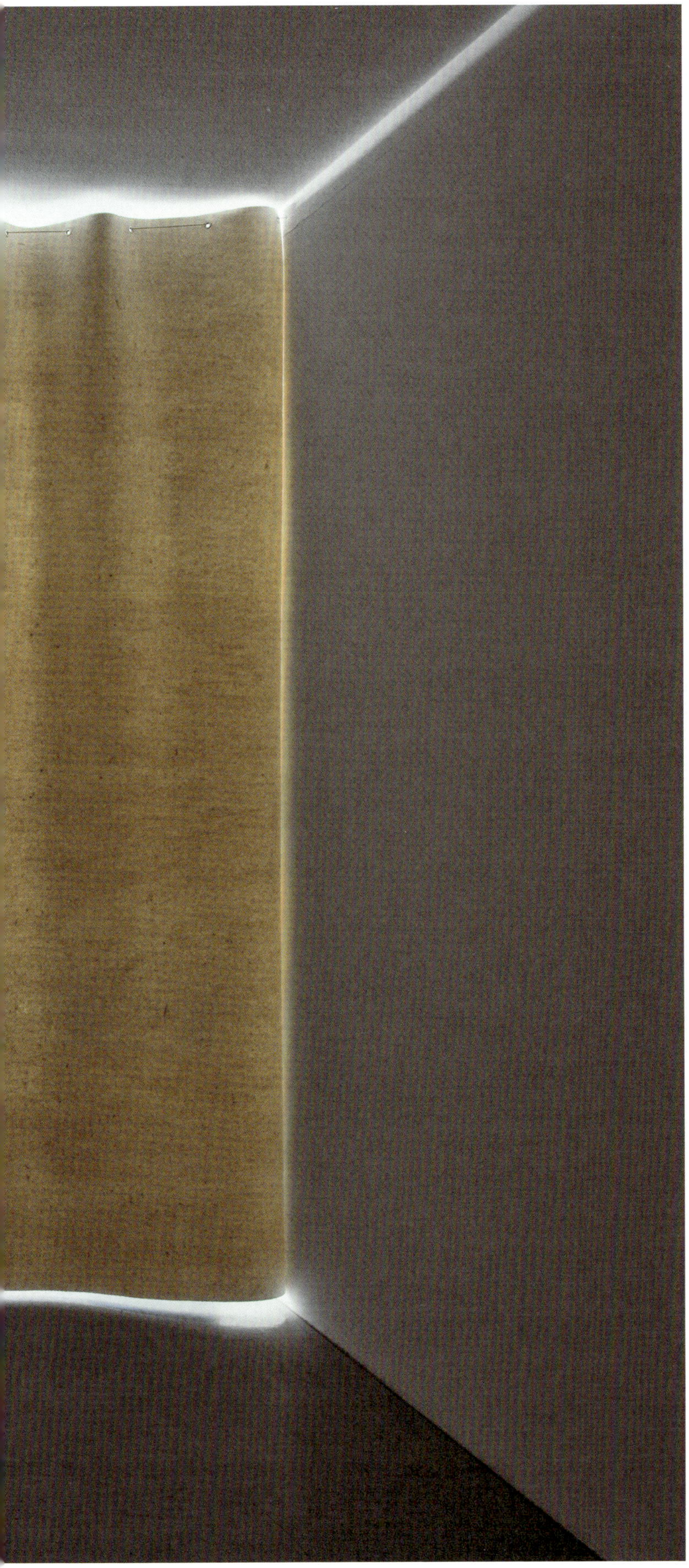

Notes

1. Gale E. Christianson, "Kepler's *Somnium:* Science Fiction and the Renaissance Scientist," *Science Fiction Studies* (March 1976), pp. 79–90. See also Raz Chen-Morris, "Shadows of Instruction: Optics and Classical Authorities in Kepler's *Somnium,*" *Journal of the History of Ideas* (2005), pp. 223–41.

2. The risk of publishing such highly controversial views in early-seventeenth-century Europe was considerable, as evidenced by the fact that an earlier version of the manuscript had led to the imprisonment of the writer's mother as a suspected witch.

3. Rosa Barba, *A Curated Conference: On the Future of Collective Strength within the Archive* (Madrid: Museo Nacional Centro de Arte Reina Sofia, 2010). All subsequent quotes are taken from this brochure.

4. See Hal Foster, "Archives of Modern Art," *October,* no. 99 (Winter 2002), pp. 81–95; see also idem, "An Archival Impulse," *October,* no. 110 (Fall 2004), pp. 3–22.

5. I am indebted to Foster's account of Adorno's essay. See Foster 2002 (see note 4), pp. 84–85. All subsequent quotes in this discussion are taken from Foster's text.

6. This is, in fact, the first of what is planned to be a four-chapter series; the second chapter, entitled *The Hidden Conference: A Fractured Play* (2011), had its debut in Trent in 2011.

7. For the transcripts of the conference, see "The Western Round Table on Modern Art (1949)," ed. Douglas MacAgy. Consulted online at: http://www.ubu.com/historical/wrtma/index.html (last accessed July 16, 2011).

8. Ibid.

9. The focus of *They Shine* (2007) is a vast array of futuristic structures, at once "glamorous" and "deadly," that purportedly ameliorates a hostile environment, transforming it into a habitable locale. It is subject to uneasy speculation and skepticism from bewildered locals. As in *Somnium,* a wryly ambivalent response to scientific imaginings in the face of nature seemingly running amok is the subject of Rivka Galchen's writings. (See, for example, Rivka Galchen, "Disaster Aversion: The Quest to Control Hurricanes," *Harper's Magazine* [October 2009], pp. 55–63. Consulted online at: http:www.harpers.orgarchive/2009/10.)

10. Italo Calvino, "Preface," *The Path to the Nest of Spiders* (Hopewell, NJ: The Ecco Press, 1976), pp. vii–viii.

11. *Printed Cinema* is the title she has given to an ongoing series of publications, each edition of which accompanies the production of a particular work or body of works and reflects on the process of its making.

12. The only exceptions to this roster of male voices are the two female speakers in *Parachutable* (2005). Though they do not interact, their voices interrupt and overlay each other, reinforcing the effects of contrast and resistance through which image and sounds are related.

13. "The real protagonists are stories suspended in air," states one of the two female voices in *Parachutable* (2005).

White Curtain (2011), installation view, Fondazione Galleria Civica–Centro di Ricerca sulla Contemporaneità di Trento, Trent, 2011

EPILOGUE

Rosa Barba's "Filmic Institution"

I. Space: *Est-ce que c'est une analogie à deux dimensions ou une métaphore?*

At first you do not take it in, but then you realize that you are entering a totally reorganized and transformed space, and that you are inside a large projector. You discover you are living out a story that is being told, in a place that changes as you move through it. You realize that you are in a film and inside the machine-museum that is projecting it. When you finally come across a 70-millimeter projector in the little theater, the last room of the Centre international d'art et du paysage de l'île de Vassivière—Rosa Barba's *White Museum* (2010), which seems prima facie to have been leaned against the wall—you realize that the whole museum functions like a centrifuge in which the narrative being recounted is fragmented into different works. You *are* the film, the film on which the exhibition is printed; your person, your emotions, and your musings are the exposed film that the institution constructs around you.

Rosa Barba creates mythologies and formulates hypotheses. She uses images to investigate and reconstruct. In her projects, she asks herself about the essence and function of film, musing about its structure as a medium and as an instrument used to create worlds—perhaps the principal creator of the modern imagination. Her work starts from a social, historical, naturalistic, scientific, and philosophical matrix and its intention is to provide a personal interpretation of real historical circumstances and facts. Her fascination for film concerns not only the medium's abstract aspect, but also its mechanical one. In Barba's installations, the technical instruments she employs—the projectors, the film, the speakers—perform a role in the film itself, transforming the space, modifying perception, and becoming a substantial part of the exhibition choreography. Together with the visitor, they engage in a continual sensorial loop. The mental process that the artist triggers through film, or her attitude towards film and, in a broader sense, the cinema, is about dissecting the medium and taking it apart, dividing it up into its different individual components so as to develop an awareness of it and to make the viewer part of it. What is more, Barba has an indisputable sensitivity for unusual places.

Barba's exhibition *Est-ce que c'est une analogie à deux dimensions ou une métaphore?* (Is It a Two-Dimensional Analogy or a Metaphor?), which was mounted at the Centre international d'art et du paysage de l'île de Vassivière, was entirely inspired by what most characterizes the island. The presence of water and the sense of luminosity are the fundamental elements of this strip of land that emerges from the middle of an artificial lake in the Limousin region of France. Playing with the very idea of the dichotomy of the artificial and the natural, Barba imagined that the fulcrum of the project could be the actual physical structure of the art center, which was designed by the Italian architect Aldo Rossi. The lake that surrounds the island thus becomes the narrating subject, and Barba uses it metaphorically as a projection screen. The light comes from a projector installed in the building beside the art center, the lighthouse, following an unexpected route through the Centre until it eventually strikes the lake. In illuminating the lake, the light seems to want to challenge the secret nature of this mirror of water. At the same time, an equally sophisticated mechanism in Barba's installation produces a sound, rippling the water's surface, so the viewer gets the sensation he can feel a sort of breath coming from the five villages that were drowned in the 1950s when the dam that created the lake was built. The result of this visionary operation is particularly effective, because thanks to the exhibition, it is immersed here in twin depths—that of the lake and that of the narrative that it triggers, transmits, and evokes. The work's continual cross-referencing between reality, fiction, perception, and absence is powerfully evident.

But Barba's work involves the museum's whole architectural structure. The building's nave houses *The Long Road* (2010), a new 35-millimeter film made on the site of a half-abandoned racing circuit in the Californian desert. The viewer has the feeling of traveling at a high speed around the loop that the artist creates while operating the camera. The traces of the tires of all the cars that have been round the circuit mark the asphalt and produce a double sensation, one that is simultaneously of a time long past and yet conveys the sense of an imminent threat. Suspended at the intersection of the present and the past, and perhaps also of the future, this place emerges from the sand like an immense drawing, the stigmata of a now abandoned and forgotten modernist culture ready to be transformed into something that is different and unexpected, not yet wholly expressed, and actually probably inexpressible.

Continuing out of the Centre's large nave to the first floor and into the study room, a 16-millimeter projector is placed on the ground and surrounded, or rather imprisoned, by film. This is Barba's *Enigmatic Whistler* (2009), which tells of nothing but itself. In the same room, another 16-millimeter projector is hung from the ceiling and supported

by its own celluloid film for the work entitled *Stating the Real Sublime* (2009). In these two works, the material prevails over the respective functions of the component parts, thereby animating the machine with a kind of anarchic life. The artist creates a new possibility, and once again, space tells a real story and creates its own fiction.
In the same room, Barba projects letters of light on the wall through cutout fabric in her works *The Indifferent Back of a View Rather Than Its Face* (2009) and *The Personal Experience behind Its Description* (2009). Here her work goes beyond cinematographic two-dimensionality. The letters filtered by the script are strewn on the ground, and the viewer finds himself on a three-dimensional, alienating narrative journey.
In Vassivière, the documentary aspect corresponds perfectly with that of the fiction, thereby creating potential hybrids of history and landscape.
The affinities between Vassivière and Barba's work are physiological. Aldo Rossi's watercolors, the lighthouse, the lake—everything coincides with a certain contemporary setting and with Barba's own poetics. The exhibition thus also challenges the subject of landscape, which, instead of being a constraint, paradoxically accommodates and contextualizes the feeling of the artist.
The art center in Vassivière is imagined as the stage for a mise-en-scène that is half inside, half outside. The spaces and times engage in a dialogue with one another, and the place assumes a mythical value, with everything foreshadowing the creativity that lies within the immense potential that has yet to be codified. Barba does not use the art center as a neutral space; rather, she succeeds in literally constructing a "museum" platform upon which to set up an exhibition that is an unexpected one with regard to the usual institutional and curatorial canons. It is as if the island were already Rosa Barba: all that remained for us to do was to present or offer it to her.

II. Time: *Stage Archive*

The joint exhibition at the Mart – Museo di Arte Moderna e Contemporanea di Trento e Rovereto and the Fondazione Galleria Civica–Centro di Ricerca sulla Contemporaneità di Trento was envisaged as being complementary to the preceding one in Vassivière, and so it developed around the theme of time—in a manner similar to how Barba tackled the theme of space in Vassivière—and the instrument dedicated to storing and inventing it: the archive. The exhibition thus recounts how much time shapes the identity and institutional activities of contemporary museums. Whereas the show in Vassivière focused on a spatial dimension through the narrative mechanisms of landscape and film, the one in Rovereto and Trento relates more to a temporal dimension, and to how time can be at once an objective dimension and an imaginary experience. The starting point of the project was a bit of research the artist did on documents from the Futurist period in the Mart's archives. The idea of the exhibition that resulted from this consists of presenting/representing—in the form of "sculpture–theatricality–abstraction"—screenplays and film treatments by the artist Fortunato Depero that were never realized as final films as well as documents from the period of the Futurist avant garde that make reference to other unfinished projects. The originals are preserved in the historical archives of the Mart. Barba thus reinterprets the archive, rescuing it from the realm of mere conservation and inserting it into one of fluid temporality. The exhibition is an active motor fueling the imagination and a source of new narratives, and it becomes an unusual hybrid: a stage archive on which the past and the future are represented in the present time of the museum.
In both Trento and Rovereto, the individual works maintain a dialectic relationship between them but are interconnected in a choreography provided by the setting that brings everything together to create a whole. The filmic and sound installation thus assumes the outlines of a "mechanical ballet" of Futurist inspiration. The individual protagonists are presented simultaneously on a single stage, which is represented by the exhibition. The show thus involves a two-fold "Futurist journey" comprised of texts, film, sculptural objects, and sounds. The result is a mechanical performance with a touch of anarchy, but also touches of harmony and science, like those characterizing a concert.
The exhibition becomes the hypothesis of a nonexistent Futurist archive that is being formed in real time within the museum and that is made up of a series of individual expressions, which can be made use of either separately or as a whole. It is a memorial dedicated to the Futurist avant garde that takes shape within the museum, proceeding like a fantastical entity engendered by the very archives in which it is preserved—an entity that is derived from a past characterized by the visionary force of Futurist aesthetics and research.
At the Mart, Barba intervenes in the museum's central space, setting up a nexus between the archive area in the basement and the exhibition rooms on the higher levels. The archives—the foundation of any institution—are usually relegated to the shadows, but here they assume the role of protagonist. The idea

of archaeological stratification is communicated through the vertical development of the exhibition, which highlights the transformation of the historical documents, rich with meaning in their unrealized potential. Two- and three-dimensional objects translate the original projects entrusted to historical documents into a film that does not exist.
The circular sculpture *Stage Archive* (2011) re-evokes the shape of the Fondazione Galleria Civica's large chandelier, which was designed by the architect Adalberto Libera for the central hall of the Palazzo della Regione Trentino–Alto Adige / South Tyrol in Trento. Inside the sculpture, a spool of film rolls just as it would if it were mounted on a film projector or being examined on a film editor's desk, but since it has not been printed with imagery, its activity produces nothing more than the sound of its own movement. In belonging to a specific mechanism, it seems to be seeking an image to project and a story to tell. In this work, the artist thus synthesizes the essence of the Futurist documents that inspired the exhibition. It is the representation of a utopia—the unspoken, potential energy—that characterizes these and reverberates through the museum via the exhibition.
The original use of the physical space transforms it into a mental and narrative space: the exhibition culminates in a large wall work (*Theory in Order to Shed Light,* 2011), a backdrop on felt whose textual content is projected as luminous forms on the museum's walls, as well as a number of small interventions at the front of the access staircase (*No Titles,* 2011) that, being integrated with the informative signage appearing on the museum's various floors, suggest the possibility of a further level upon which to interpret the museum, a more fluid, powerful, and purely mental spatiality and temporality that invite the visitor to read the institution "through time and space," merging past, present, and future, which is precisely what happens in the archives, where the documents of the past are active, topical objects in which different eras of time can overlap more freely.
The first two 35-millimeter films Barba produced as part of her series *The Hidden Conference: About the Discontinuous History of Things We See and Don't See* (2010) are projected in the main area of the Fondazione Galleria Civica in Trento.
The *Hidden Conference* series (2010–) has grown out of Barba's thoughts concerning the conservation of works of art in the storage rooms of some museums of ancient and modern sculpture. The artist creates an imaginary dialogue between the works, in their condition of silent and secret daily cohabitation within the institutional spaces in which they are kept.
In these films, which transform the stored items into a scenic backdrop shaped by light, as if the viewer had suddenly found himself on a theater or film set, the artist investigates the invisible links between the works of art and the network of linkages that generate the same idea of a "protected" space outside of time, like that of an archive. The artist narrates how, when invited by the Museo Nacional Centro de Arte Reina Sofía in Madrid to compile a selection of documents and works, she was fascinated by the archive itself, the idea of works that, far from the eyes of the public, continue to live on, contributing nonetheless to the construction of the identity of the museum and thus of our visual language, which develops in contact with it. She began to explore the invisible connections between the works preserved—the network of analogies that produce a collective idea of consistent space that, as a totality, acquired great value.
The precise order in which the works are conserved creates a new and elaborate system that the artist wants to recount in these films, thereby making us participants in the creation of meaning through these new and different compositions.
Barba asks herself: "What is the intrinsic quality of unseen art?" She investigates the long period of stasis a work endures after the difficult process of its acquisition and transfer from one owner to another, and all of the communication, negotiation, and complex transactions of the art market. Lastly, she wonders how the insertion of a new element into the collective memory of the entire archive (and, thus, into that of the museum) takes place. In her words, "There is a strange similarity between that moment and the random or labyrinthine process involved when we try to recall a name or word in our memory."
In relation to this pure institutional potential, which is suggested by the secretive dimension of the archive, Barba is presenting other works at the Fondazione that develop an analogous discourse. For instance, *Private Tableaux* (2010), a 16-millimeter film, draws on studies of basement architecture carried out over the years by numerous professionals.
By means of various drawings done by scientists for study purposes, the involuntary representation of a parallel history emerges, one in which a rich diffusion of signs occupies the entire volume of a space and a time that are prohibited. The grainy images of the 16-millimeter film *Let Me See It* (2009), which is more of an audio-play than a movie, depict a seascape at night, an aerial view of an archipelago in which only the lights of the houses on the ground illuminate the scenery. Two

men, one of whom is blind, talk about the objects around them, focusing in particular on a dodecahedron, an element that becomes crucial to the attempt on the part of one of the two men to recall his memories.
Invisible Act (2010) is a sculptural installation comprising a 16-millimeter projection in which a material object evokes an imaginative object, with one set inside the other within a dialogue consisting of contrasts and combinations. The work takes the document into account not just as a given object, but also as a moment of creation and reflection, as a fantastic transposition, and as a continuing possibility for transforming the image into matter and vice versa. *Optic Ocean* (2011) and *Time Machine* (2007) constitute the draft of a screenplay that is somewhere halfway between the real and the fantastical, and that stands out on the walls of the exhibition space, which has been transformed into a work document. *One Way Out* (2009) is comprised of a 16-millimeter projector whose film gets drawn upwards towards a little ravine in the exhibition space of which we become suddenly aware: it is the exit, the fantastical opening within the real institution that the entire exhibition seems to be seeking and evokes within the actual building of the museum.

III. From the Island to the Archive: Acknowledgments

As the curators of the exhibitions in Vassivière, Rovereto, and Trento, we would like to thank all of the people who contributed to their realization. Our gratitude goes first and foremost to Rosa Barba, who allowed us to discover a dimension of the museum institution of which we had previously been ignorant. Thanks to her, we have suddenly found the institution of the museum more fluid and colorful, and we have discovered its infinite potentialities; we have entered the secret passages of the "filmic institution" that Barba has introduced to us and to our visitors.
Special thanks go to Gabriella Belli, not only for having made it possible to carry out the project at Rovereto, but also for having shared the intuition that it could only arise from the historical archives of the Mart, from the museum's recollection and memory.
We would also like to thank the authors of the articles that comprise this catalogue: Lynne Cooke, Elisabeth Lebovici, Raimundas Malasauskas, Francesco Manacorda, Nataša Petrešin-Bachelez, and Ian White. This book constitutes, in fact, a sort of third exhibition, for it is the first extended monograph devoted to Rosa Barba's work since 2004.

Chiara Parisi, Director, Centre international d'art et du paysage de l'île de Vassivière

Andrea Viliani, Director, Fondazione Galleria Civica–Centro di Ricerca sulla Contemporaneità di Trento

Inside the Historical Archives of the Mart: A Work in Progress

In 2010, Rosa Barba began to take an interest in museum archives and produced two of the films belonging to her In Progress series, one of which is *The Hidden Conference: About the Discontinuous History of Things We See and Don't See,* thereby setting up a dialogue between the works preserved in the depositories of the two museums. In these films, the artist ponders the state of the works of art in their continuums as well as the multifaceted transitions between "public" and "private." Following this line of enquiry, Barba understandably approached the Mart – Museo di Arte Contemporanea di Trento e Rovereto and its historical archives. From the very outset, the Mart decided to elevate the importance of its inherited archives and bibliographical heritage, making them the cornerstone of a cultural identity parallel to that of the works of art. From the day it was instituted in 1987, the Mart has considered its possession of archival documentation relating to twentieth-century artists, architects, and art critics indispensable.
The term "archive" is very broad, both etymologically and philosophically. An archive can be defined as a complex of documents produced by a public or private subject in the course of its activity, but the term can also encompass the buildings that house such complexes and even the databases by which their contents are accessed. In addition to the rich documentation produced by official bodies (state, municipal, or ecclesiastical, for example) during the twentieth century, considerable attention has been paid to family and personal archives, ensembles of documentary materials collected by a family or an individual in the course of living their lives and carrying out their professional activities. Archives come into being unintentionally and spontaneously, but all recent historiography underlines how, as they grow, it often happens that a certain awareness develops which pushes subjects toward more selective and controlled forms of collection that are geared toward the creation of a specific profile. Therefore, the mechanisms of representation that are specific to all of the operations involved in passing on memory apply to this type of archive.
All types of archive are emblematically a piece of history in the making, and thus quintessentially not a finished outcome—like a book or work of art—but the sediment of a cultural history. Moreover, archives are a source of study that allows us to trace the phases of a work in development, and they are a fine instrument for setting up a dialogue between the history of art and all other historical, sociological, and even economic disciplines. Given this multifaceted richness, on several occasions shows, conferences, and publications by the Mart have led to the recovery and acquisition of collections and vice versa—the same exhibiting activity that has been carried on since the 1990s and has been inspired by the documentary collections the museum has been acquiring over time.
Rosa Barba's work is organized along the same lines, interweaving the documents preserved in the archives in the Mart's basement with the exhibition spaces of the museum's upper floors, and thereby making them communicate spatially and conceptually and displaying a possible temporal evolution of a creative project, the true potential of any archive. In particular, Barba did a lot of research on the archives relating to the Futurists due to both the presence of the Mart's substantial nucleus of Futurist documents—which gave rise to the Centro Internazionale di Studi sul Futurismo (CISF; International Center of Futurist Studies)—and the coincidence of the expressive means that she and the Futurists employed—i.e., film and text.
Futurism displayed a schizophrenic attitude toward the past. On the one hand it dismissed the past, but on the other hand it disseminated its own aesthetic and ideas (even quite strategically) by means of poetry, manifestos, magazines, and series of publications, all of which were aimed at creating a record or memory of the movement's ideas in order to exert a controlled influence on public opinion. Part of this archive is the collection of documents from the municipality of Rovereto relating to Fortunato Depero, which includes the archive's holdings relating to theater and cinema scripts that were never actually used. Depero began his involvement with cinematographic activity late in his career and came to it rather indirectly through his passion for the theater. It was, in fact, only in the mid-1920s that the Roveretan painter began to try his hand at film writing, producing a number of screenplays for film. Before then, film, which was considered a field of almost entirely unexplored experimentation in artistic languages, does not seem to have particularly attracted Depero's attention; instead, his curiosity led him to enthusiastic experimentation in theater. We may recall, for example, the bizarre audacity of the spectacle *I balli plastici* (Plastic Dance) that he worked out with Gilbert Clavel and staged at the Costanzi Theater in 1918, or the funambulatory *Teatro Magico* (Magic Theater), with its dancers springy with rubber.
If we think of the attraction that the

possibility of trying out all the creative opportunities of the artistic idiom always exercised on Depero above and beyond any disciplinary boundaries, this belated use of film is curious to say the least. Back in 1916, Marinetti and his cosignatories Corra, Settimelli, Ginna, Balla, and Chiti published a manifesto on Futurist cinematography in which they proclaimed film as a "new art, immensely vaster and more agile than all existing ones," including, we must therefore suppose, theater. In the manifesto, the many fields of application of film were singled out with great clarity and were understood precisely as "the means of expression most suited to the multiple sensibility of a Futurist artist." Poems, speeches, poetry, musical research, simultaneity, the interpermeation of times and places, states of mind, dramas of disproportion and potential dramas, linear plastic-chromatic equivalences—all this is set out as the exclusive appanage of polyexpressive cinematographic inquiry, an all-embracing exploration by definition, inasmuch as all the other arts come together in it. As the manifesto declares, "Painting + sculpture + sculptural dynamism and words set free + noisemakers + architecture + synthetic theater = Futurist cinematography." However, the transition from theory to practice revealed a certain difficulty in transforming the complexity of these definitions into a repertory of representative imagery. *Vita Futurista* (Futurist Life), the film that officially inaugurated the Futurist film season the very same year, is a significant example of this. In directing short films, Marinetti put forward once more the same mise-en-scène comprised of comic surprises and mocking tricks—i.e., absolute nonsense—that was typical of many of the offerings of Futurist theater at the time. Giovanni Lista has commented that it was a "cinema of juxtaposed *little forms* of mechanical gesturality, the grotesque, and whoops of laughter. The model can be traced back to the vaudeville stage, which is to say that the films were very similar to the theater, with its surprises, syntheses, and scenic improvisations." Also, the few indications that Depero has left us concerning the montage and sequence of his scripts make it clear how strongly the artist intended that film be at the service of the written word. This concept emerges with clarity in analyzing the narrative rhythm and spatio-temporal sequence of the texts in his various scripts, which depart so marginally from his vast literary production as to disappear into it. It is within this context, one so very rich in possible interpretations and developments, that Rosa Barba's project for the Mart fits, for it makes the utopian Futurist impetus topical and utilizes the museum's archive as an expressive platform. With her site-specific interventions for the empty central space of the museum, the artist translates the polysemanticism of (interlocutory and at times contradictory) thought preceding the realization of a work of art or an intervention that are, as the artist herself defines them, a "work in progress."

Gabriella Belli, Director, Mart – Museo di Arte Moderna e Contemporanea di Trento e Rovereto

FRENCH TRANSLATION

UNE IDÉE EN TROIS DIMENSIONS

IAN WHITE

«La cendre commençait à tomber sur nous, quoiqu'en petite quantité. Je tourne la tête, et j'aperçois derrière nous une épaisse fumée qui nous suivait, en se répandant sur la terre comme un torrent. ‹ Pendant que nous voyons encore, quittons le grand chemin ›, dis-je à ma mère, ‹ de peur d'être écrasés dans les ténèbres par la foule qui se presse sur nos pas. › A peine nous étions-nous arrêtés, que les ténèbres s'épaissirent encore : on n'eût pas dit seulement une nuit sombre et chargée de nuages, mais l'obscurité d'une chambre où toutes les lumières seraient éteintes. »

(Pline le Jeune, lettre à Tacite (Livre VI, XX) sur les danger auxquels il fut exposé à Misène[1])

Les catastrophes sont terribles. Mais une catastrophe en puissance ne l'est pas moins. Une catastrophe en puissance peut être même encore plus dangereuse. Elle peut ne pas exister. On ne peut pas l'ignorer. Peut-être n'existe-t-elle qu'à l'état de concept, un territoire imaginaire aux frontières floues et aux lois irrationnelles, un lieu vaste et ardent, arraché à la vie pour faire office de salle d'attente (dont il est impossible de s'échapper), où la peur, voir la menace, l'inéluctabilité, la vérité, la rumeur, la preuve, l'analyse, l'invisibilité, la fiction deviendraient autant de leviers par lesquels exercer le pouvoir. Etat d'absolue incertitude, comme une obscurité absolue, la catastrophe en puissance est très utile pour ceux qui possèdent le pouvoir, ou bien ceux qui désirent s'en emparer, du fait de l'importance prépondérante qu'elle permet au contrôle de l'information (quel éclairage on nous en donne) ainsi qu'au temps et à l'espace qu'elle autorise pour le faire. Elle peut également être le lieu des possibles – terribles peut-être, mais aussi chargés d'utopie – un terreau propice aux absolus des idéalismes et des idéalistes, quelle que soit leur position sociale.
Ainsi, nous pourrions paraphraser la série de documentaires politiques *The Power of Nightmares* du réalisateur britannique Adam Curtis, conçue pour la BBC en 2004. Dans cette série, il émet l'hypothèse selon laquelle le politicien moderne a trouvé un moyen de récupérer le pouvoir en se posant, non plus en idéologue ou en organisateur de la société civile, mais en protecteur. Un protecteur qui met le public – ses sujets – à l'abri de la menace bien spécifique (et considérée comme immense) du terrorisme international. En d'autres mots, il décrit le terrible usage que font les puissants de la conviction du public qu'une catastrophe est imminente. C'est un jeu de l'esprit. Le générique de chaque épisode, dans lequel Curtis expose brièvement ce postulat de départ, montre une série d'images (tous ses films combinent images d'archives et interviews qui servent de support à sa thèse) qui évoque un moment de l'histoire récente. Ces images mettent en place une fiction parlant de chaos à venir et préparent le spectateur à ce qui va lui être raconté : l'éclairage d'un stade est coupé, un studio de télévision (d'une chaîne d'information ?) est démantelé, des phares de voiture n'éclairent qu'une petite portion de route, de majestueux lustres en cristal sont éteints, l'ombre s'étend … En résumé, les ténèbres descendent, comme une métaphore de l'exploitation potentielle de cet état d'incertitude que l'on peut aussi attribuer à la catastrophe en puissance ; de même que les ténèbres descendent dans l'auditorium comme la condition première à l'expérience narrative ultime que représente le cinéma commercial. Le film catastrophe est peut-être l'un de ses genres ultimes, mais la catastrophe en puissance est à la fois la situation et la condition même de l'industrie du cinéma.
C'est dans ce cadre que je souhaite orienter mon approche du travail de Rosa Barba. Non parce qu'il présente des arguments sur l'utilisation politique de la peur du terrorisme international, mais à cause de son subtil questionnement et de son appropriation du cinéma commercial, en tant que sujet, au travers de ce que nous pourrions appeler diverses « mises en scène » – du « local », du non-acteur, du geste, du genre, de l'information, de l'expertise et de l'autorité – en marge d'un certain réalisme social par le prisme duquel elles seraient observées et données comme des composantes de l'œuvre, prêtes à être cadrées, redessinées, représentées. L'effet alors produit remet en cause et redistribue les rôles entre la vérité et la fiction, le mythe et la réalité, la métaphore et la matière jusqu'à un degré de trouble tel, qu'il donne corps à une pratique conceptuelle qui opère également une redistribution du rôle du spectateur et de sa propre mise en scène par un renversement radical et grisant : passant de simple récepteur d'une image (donc assujetti au contrôle) à celui qui est aux commandes de l'image, dans la salle des machines, qui regarde vers l'extérieur.

Souvent, les œuvres de Rosa Barba montrent des communautés pré ou post-apocalyptiques, apparemment abandonnées, et principalement occupées par une menace ou un désastre. Dans ces espaces, les personnes dépeintes, tout comme les dangers qui les menacent peuvent être tout aussi bien considérées comme réels que comme fictionnels : à tel point que le fait de savoir s'il s'agit de l'un ou de l'autre devient un facteur d'ambiguïté qui est, en fait, le moteur conceptuel premier des œuvres. Il ne s'agit ni plus ni moins que d'une variation sur cet « acte de foi » que le public réuni dans une salle de cinéma se doit d'accomplir ; ici cependant, au lieu d'une immersion dans une narration en tous points crédible, on tend plutôt vers la mise en place d'un méta-récit. Les films *Panzano* (2000), réalisé en collaboration avec Ulrike Molsen, et *Outwardly From Earth's Center* (2007) fonctionnent, de différentes manières, explicitement sur ce procédé (tout comme l'œuvre en ligne *Vertiginous Mapping* (2008)). Il en va de même pour *The Empirical Effect* (2010), et c'est sur cette œuvre que je voudrais m'arrêter en la considérant comme un point de cristallisation dont on peut retrouver la trace et en approfondir la compréhension dans les œuvres les plus anciennes, et que l'on pourra étendre à de brèves méditations sur les sculptures de l'artiste réalisées avec des projecteurs 16 mm, sur la place du visiteur en relation à ces objets et à leur réunion dans des expositions ou chaque œuvre devient un élément d'une constellation prééminente.
The Empirical Effect est tourné sur les pentes du Vésuve, volcan encore actif près de Naples, au centre de l'Italie, et dont l'éruption en l'an 79 de notre ère nous a légué Pompéi, parfaitement préservée, l'objet d'étude archéologique définitif et source de la plus ancienne description d'une éruption volcanique, écrite par Pline le Jeune, dont

un extrait ouvre le présent texte. Sa dernière éruption majeure a eu lieu en 1944 et la prochaine est présumée imminente – si l'on considère que la durée de la période de silence et d'inactivité du volcan est inversement proportionnelle à l'augmentation du nombre d'analyses et de spéculations, de leur manipulation et de leur contestation, et à la magnitude estimée de l'éruption à venir. Silence et inactivité étant tous deux les symboles et la fonction même de la menace. On pourrait imaginer que personne ne vit à cet endroit et pourtant les pentes du volcan n'ont jamais été aussi peuplées. Tous ceci n'en est pas moins une situation que le film ne fait que traiter de façon allusive, volontairement, comme pour changer les faits en anecdotes.

Le film s'ouvre avec une voix d'une intensité toute cinématographique : sur des images qui évoquent une lave sombre et bouillonnante, de la fumée, des charbons ardents, on entend une ténébreuse voix masculine décrivant l'activité du Vésuve à travers un mélange de faits et de mythes (renforcés par notre propre attente du récit d'un désastre) et s'achevant par des consignes d'évacuation. Notre attente est à son comble. Le décor est dressé. Sinistre. Mais l'œuvre ne s'engage pas dans cette direction. Le film de genre ainsi ébauché est abandonné. La caméra nous montre désormais un réseau d'instruments scientifiques de mesure, électroniques, peut-être des sismographes. Un bâtiment désert, ni résidentiel, ni civil, mais conçu pour le genre de recherches qui nécessite une architecture bien spécifique. Pas de présence humaine. Des images d'archives d'une scène de rue, probablement du début du XXème siècle. Des promeneurs regardant une montagne : le Vésuve. Des outils de mesure anciens, immobiles, dans des vitrines, inutilisés. Puis, soudain, une vue aérienne des pentes du Vésuve depuis un hélicoptère – dont on entend le bruit – révèle les villas et les villages, comme le générique d'un Dynasty méditerranéen. Retour dans ce bâtiment que nous appellerons un centre de recherches. Comme par magie, un groupe de personnes, pour la plupart âgées, apparaît sur une carte de la région recouvrant le sol ; ils se tiennent là comme des objets, éloignés les uns des autres (ils ont l'air, étrangement, hors de toute interaction sociale mais aussi calmes, à l'aise, en scène), alors que parmi eux bêlent un certain nombre de moutons. Présents et impliqués mais agents, ils commencent à examiner les cartes, ils semblent jouer les enquêteurs, leurs mouvements attentifs et leur rythme évoquent une chorégraphie. Une femme porte des lunettes de soleil avec une large monture en plastique blanc comme un accessoire de science-fiction ; ou bien comme sorties de cette image célèbre de *La société du spectacle* de Guy Debord où les spectateurs d'une salle de cinéma portent tous les mêmes lunettes 3D pour regarder un film. Ils s'interpellent par gestes en se parlant, mais sans que l'on puisse entendre ce qu'ils se disent. Des machines sont amenées sur un chariot, leur fonctionnement semble totalement étranger au groupe et le groupe à elles. L'examen qu'ils en font semble empreint de reproches qui s'étendent à la technologie même. Ils se mettent au travail. On entend un Archiviste qui explique que la communion entre la population et son environnement est autant une bénédiction qu'une malédiction qu'ils courent le risque de vivre désastre et dévastation et qu'ils le font délibérément, à cause de l'état particulier de renaissance qui en résulte…

Et la vidéo suit ainsi son cours, une alternance rythmée et irrégulière d'anachronismes, de différents registres, mêlant les genres et les scènes ; si bien qu'on ne remarque pas les incohérences entre les images utilisées parce que nous sommes dans, et parmi elles. Ou plutôt, ce que nous voyons et entendons est cohérent parce que nous sommes dans, et parmi elles. Rien n'est montré qui n'est pas mis en scène d'une manière ou d'une autre ; l'enquête scientifique n'est que décor et jeu d'acteurs ; le mystère, comme le mouvement des corps, est chorégraphié : les têtes tournées vers le ciel, un doigt pointé ; la caméra explore l'architecture avec une symétrie régulière, pas avec le tremblement de la main ou l'instabilité de l'œil ; le groupe de personnes âgées est semblable à un chœur antique qui se contenterait de chanter et de danser, plutôt que de commenter. L'absurdité vaut le raisonnement. Différent processus d'investigation existent en parallèle (cinématographique, documentaire, scientifique, amateur, mystique, théâtral) ; de cette manière, il n'y a pas de vérité. On ne nous apprend rien, pas de fait, pas d'histoire, pas de point de vue. Cet ensemble de scènes n'est pas le portrait d'une expérience commune, mais son interprétation sous la forme d'une représentation symbolique des idées, une traduction dans les champs de la performance et de la représentation ; et en ce sens il est plus proche de quelque chose de tangible qu'il ne s'en éloigne. Le confort du grand récit promis dans l'ouverture du film est mis en déséquilibre par une variété de modalités par lesquelles la situation initiale peut être pensée et expérimentée, plutôt que simplement racontée, comme si l'on était à l'intérieur et de la même matière que le média.

Vers la fin du film, une rangée de quatre vieux messieurs alignés sur un canapé, agitent leurs bras au-dessus de leur tête en rythme les uns avec les autres. Le son simulé d'une sirène occupe toute la bande-son. Pour la première fois, à la place d'individus isolés et du chœur de personnes âgées, de plus grands groupes de gens de tous âges sont montrés en train de « fuir » dans les rues (en réalité ils fuient comme si il y avait une urgence, en interprétant l'instruction « fuyez comme s'il y avait une urgence »). Certains portent un objet – une représentation en plâtre de la Vierge, une photographie, un sac en plastique. Ils jouent l'évacuation. Il peut s'agir d'un exercice d'évacuation réel. Ici, dans le film, il s'agit bel et bien d'une évacuation et non un document la représentant. Le registre de ce que l'on voit est le même que celui de toutes les situations mises en scène qui précèdent. Tout ce que les autorités locales peuvent demander à une communauté de faire pour tester les plans mis en place actuellement en cas d'éruption, pour démontrer combien de temps est nécessaire pour évacuer entièrement la région, combien et quel type de moyen de transport serait le plus efficace, quel délai d'alerte est suffisant pour permettre à chacun de se mettre en sécurité ; toutes les choses de ce type que recensent les comptes-rendus en ligne de ces exercices sont une preuve qui équivaut à n'importe quoi d'autre présenté dans l'œuvre. Une inversion radicale se produit alors. La réalité de l'œuvre vient englober une autre « réalité » : quelque chose qui était feint au moment où il a été filmé acquiert une sorte de vraisemblance à l'écran. La communauté n'est pas décrite, elle est construite : un communisme de représentations et une manifestation d'une toute autre forme d'empirisme que celle consistant à observer le monde extérieur. Une communauté (de spectateurs) est constituée par notre acte de visionnage et l'accord collectif qu'il suggère à propos de ce que nous pouvons ou ne pouvons pas dire, pas à propos du récit d'une situation périlleuse réelle, mais à propos de l'œuvre elle-même : ses vérités et ses mensonges, la nature de ses sources, ses strates de mise en scène. Un hyperréalisme, créé par et à partir

des situations et des conditions du cinéma industriel en tant que catastrophe en puissance qui deviendrait son propre sujet.
Nombreux sont les dispositifs utilisés dans *The Empirical Effect* que l'on peut retrouver dans les travaux précédents de Rosa Barba. En particulier *Outwardly From Earth's Center*, avec lequel le film partage de nombreux points communs, et *Panzano* avec ses situations dramatiques auto-référencées qui sont, au niveau filmique, plus proches de la juxtaposition.
Le développement d'un modèle spécifique dans ces trois films peut être circonscrit autant qu'il fait sens. Il est tout d'abord mis en place dans *Panzano*. Comme les deux autres, ce film est également un portrait (d'une relation triangulaire entre deux hommes et une femme) et la construction d'une réalité, l'interprétation d'une série de relations personnelles développées dans une représentation qui est le fruit d'un travail d'observation, de collaboration et de traduction - une situation réelle rendue étrange à travers divers artifices cinématographiques ou théâtraux (bande-son décalée, éclairage, cadrage, scénario, etc.). Non seulement chacune des trois personnes que le film met en scène joue un rôle scénarisé, mais elles sont aussi montrées dans ce que l'on présume être leur propre habitation : une maison isolée dans la campagne, pauvre et délabrée. Pour autant, elles y apparaissent par la magie de la surimposition, un fauteuil vide qui se change soudain en fauteuil occupé, etc. Ici, ce qui est implicite (la catastrophe en puissance) est leur peur (ou la menace) de leur disparition respective. Elles existent à la fois dans le réel et dans la fiction cinématographique (comme tous les acteurs, mais ici le paradoxe est particulièrement prononcé), ces deux éléments étant – comme ces trois personnes – dépendants l'un de l'autre, l'un toujours conditionné par l'autre. Entre eux, se jouent d'absurdes situations dramatiques qui tiennent du mélodrame. A un moment, l'homme le plus âgé dit au plus jeune, pendant une partie de baby-foot, que la femme n'a pas dormi dans son lit la nuit dernière : incompréhension, impuissance, jalousie ? Peur. Mais je voudrais attirer l'attention sur le point culminant du film. Une lumière mystique, brillante et aveuglante, baigne la maison. Est-ce que le plus vieux des deux hommes est en train de se faire enlever par des extraterrestres ? Il avance vers la lumière. Il y aperçoit un jeune homme et, soudain, un cri nous apprend qu'il a disparu. Qu'il ne reviendra jamais. Ce qui veut dire, bien sûr, qu'il n'est plus ni dans la maison ni dans le film. Seulement il revient, apparaissant dans les ténèbres alors que le jeune homme en deuil repose sa tête sur l'épaule de la femme au moment où elle dit : « Ferme les yeux et il reviendra ». Engendré par les ténèbres, il revient, au moins dans le film sinon dans la maison, comme une – ou la – présence cinématographique. Une image que nous connaissons, dont nous doutons et dont nous sommes reconnaissants, une image – comme le fantôme et la matière du médium – dont ils sont tous deux, comme nous, les témoins.
Outwardly From Earth's Center se rapproche de *The Empirical Effect* en ce sens qu'il s'agit aussi de l'examen d'un lieu (de liens, et non plus d'une relation) en danger : une île, presque déserte, qui dérive continuellement vers le Pôle Nord de plusieurs mètres par an. Le film présente une série d'habitants et d'experts qui sont identifiés par leur activité plutôt que par leur nom, un peu à la manière d'un livre d'histoires : Le Gardien de Phare, Les Archéologues, l'Architecte, l'Archiviste, etc. Leurs différentes théories (ou mythologies) et leurs solutions au problème de l'île sont le sujet et le résultat de la mise en scène de Rosa Barba : ils sont dans le registre du sublime, l'information est présentée dans un espace théâtralisé, projetée sur des écrans comme dans un décor pour la dramaturgie et le mystère de tableaux et de diagrammes à demi expliqués, ou considérée au titre de folklore et pourtant incluse dans des documents officiels. Ces histoires sont entrecoupées de plans bergmaniens d'un personnage solitaire sur une plage, regardant la mer au loin, monochrome, quintessence du romantisme ; et d'une série d'images de formations rocheuses sur lesquelles on entend une voix qui semble répondre au test de Rorschach, nommant ce qu'il voit dans chaque image, comme pour nous demander si nous le voyons aussi, comme pour nous offrir un exemple de l'intention qui préside à l'acte de cadrer et des problèmes que cela génère. Comme dans *The Empirical Effect*, ce film s'attache à mettre en œuvre un autre jeu de preuves qui vient recouvrir, contredire, supplanter et mystifier la réalité de cette autre catastrophe en devenir. Et comme dans cette autre œuvre, elles deviennent équivalentes du fait de la fonction enveloppante de l'œuvre, consumer par son acte de création même. Cela dit, cette œuvre non plus n'est pas un document, un enregistrement d'une situation réelle, mais la projection d'une situation réelle au moyen d'un vocabulaire, qui est visuel, fantastique, sa propre preuve (équivalente aux autres relatives) et cinématographique.
Vers la fin du film, de larges pieux de bois sont alignés sur le sable comme des hiéroglyphes verticaux. D'énormes et larges cordes, recouvertes de glace, sont tirées autour d'eux. A partir d'une vue aérienne de l'île, des rayons de soleil frappent la terre à travers les nuages, un phénomène qui fait écho à ces cordages, nombreux maintenant et que l'on voit comme de noires lignes ordonnées qui rayonnent (comme la lumière solaire) depuis la côte vers un point d'ancrage hors champ. L'île est « sauvée ». Comme dans un fantastique problème insoluble, qui est lui-même un symbole et une exploration des possibilités de la cohésion sociale, finalement résolu ; dans le film et dans notre acceptation des fictions qu'il cristallise.
C'est ce modèle que *The Empirical Effect* développe plus avant, comme si le film pouvait être vu comme une percée significative. Après avoir imaginé que la population ait été « emmenée » à l'abri, le chœur de personnes âgées reste sur place. Il n'y a aucun triomphalisme, mais on devine une détente. Ils dansent sur une terrasse dominant la mer avec un doux abandon qui suggère que tous ces tests, ces preuves, ces collectes d'indices, comparaisons, re-présentations, compétitions, expériences n'ont pas été vains, mais étaient aussi fictionnels et réels que l'éruption qu'ils essayaient d'anticiper ; et qui a et n'a pas eu lieu. Elle a (seulement) eu lieu à l'intérieur et au travers d'un complexe réseau fictionnel que nous ne devrions même pas remarquer, qui est le film lui-même, comme une sorte de réalité singulière.
De mon point de vue, les deux fins dont nous venons de parler nous mènent à celle de *The Empirical Effect*. Elles offrent toutes l'éventualité de quelque chose de joyeux qui se serait passé, et non un désastre ; quelque chose qui ressemble à une libération. J'émettrais l'hypothèse qu'il s'agit à la fois de l'acte de faire un film en soi, mais aussi du fait d'avoir échappé aux pièges du contrôle ; qui sont les autres plaisirs du cinéma commercial auxquels nous pourrions accepter d'être soumis (comme choisir avec joie de vivre à côté d'un volcan en activité). Si la situation et la condition du cinéma commercial peuvent être, en définitive, lues comme le (méta)sujet de Rosa Barba, ce qui est en jeu est une sorte de retournement de cette situation et de ces conditions

qui deviendraient un espace qui pourrait être occupé et détruit dans le même temps, à l'aide de ces propres outils.

Deux réflexions, liées entre elles, découlent de ce constat. La première concerne les sculptures de Rosa Barba constituées de projecteurs 16 mm, où le projecteur lui-même dans diverses configurations, est éteint ou projette seulement son propre faisceau lumineux et est considéré en tant qu'objet. *Stating the Real Sublime* (2009) en est un bon exemple. Dans cette sculpture, un projecteur est suspendu au plafond par la même pellicule transparente qu'il projette, ce film vierge est entraîné par une série de poulies avant de s'enrouler autour de la machine qu'il suspend. Au premier regard on peut voir cet objet comme une innovation. Quelle est cette machine ? Sa pellicule ne porte pas d'images, elle ne fonctionne pas selon son standard, elle est presque fétichisée. C'est presque comme si elle portait ses entrailles à l'extérieur, ou le matériau qu'habituellement elle ingère en son sein pour le transformer en cette œuvre d'art immatérielle ultime qu'est la projection. Mais il n'y a pas d'image, juste une machine prise, maintenue, fonctionnant du fait de son propre mécanisme. Contenue en elle-même, bizarrement à l'envers sans pour autant l'être mécaniquement. Selon moi, cela doit bien représenter quelque chose. Son sujet n'est pas le formalisme. C'est une image d'elle-même qui me place à ses côtés (je suis littéralement à ses côtés) tout en me proposant l'expérience d'une similaire inversion de moi-même. Elle devient comme une chose vivante. Je l'occupe et je la démonte tout comme je m'occupe et me démonte moi-même. Je suis assujetti à la situation et aux conditions d'une idée de cinéma, une qui existe en ce moment, disons le cinéma commercial auquel je ne participe ni physiquement, ni architecturalement, ni perceptivement mais dont je fais partie du mode de fonctionnement dans la mesure où, conceptuellement, il s'agit autant de sa métaphore que de son contenu. Sa situation en apesanteur est à la fois une absence de corporalité et l'infinité.

Si l'on va plus loin, un processus englobant similaire commence à se produire quand certaines de ces œuvres sont montrées ensemble : une combinaison de sculptures-projecteurs et de films projetés. Structurellement, ils sont le reflet les uns des autres et arrivent à intégrer le spectateur dans cette salle des machines conceptuelle comme des moyens nécessaires à leur réinvention et à la révélation d'un ensemble de liens que l'on appellerait ailleurs « soumission ». Il n'y a pas de meilleur exemple que l'exposition de Rosa Barba *Est-ce que c'est une analogie à deux dimensions ou une métaphore ?* (2010), qui occupait la quasi-totalité des espaces du bâtiment postmoderne unique du Centre international d'art et du paysage de l'île de Vassivière. En fait, l'exposition s'empare du bâtiment et de la circulation du visiteur dans les salles et au-delà comme une œuvre en soi. On était ainsi projeté depuis la tour d'un simulacre de phare le long du faisceau d'un projecteur 70 mm jusque dans les salles d'exposition proprement dites, où l'on se retrouvait confronté à la lumière du projecteur (et l'ombre de notre propre mouvement) que l'on découvrait sur les vues aériennes d'une piste d'essais automobiles dans le désert californien, avant d'être poussé plus loin dans le bâtiment dans une salle avec des sculptures-projecteurs et des textes projetés découpés dans des pièces de feutre suspendues au plafond comme un décor. Après une porte – dans la même progression linéaire – on arrivait dans un auditorium vidé de ses meubles et transformé en cabine de projection, où un autre énorme projecteur est placé contre une petite fenêtre. A la nuit tombée, il projette un rectangle de lumière blanche, immobile, sur l'herbe, les arbres et les buissons en contrebas qui bougent comme les images d'un film que l'on peut voir d'une salle entièrement blanche, rien de moins qu'un musée, en dessous de l'auditorium. La nature est devenue image, et le spectateur est immobile, la terre tourne. Vous êtes à l'intérieur des mécanismes de contrôle auxquels vous étiez, à l'extérieur (autrement) assujetti. Ici, c'est le cinéma industriel avec les lumières allumées, une idée en trois dimensions.

Note

1. Traduit par William Melmoth et revu par F. C. T. Bosanquet ; http://ancienthistory.about.com/od/pompeii/a/PlinyPompeii.htm (dernière visite le 2 février 2011).

LOOKING FOR ROSA BARBA
ELISABETH LEBOVICI

I. Full Circle

Ce n'est pas parce que l'exposition récente de Rosa Barba en France s'est déroulée sur l'île du lac de Vassivière – paysage transformé en écran par l'utilisation que l'artiste a fait du bâtiment du Centre d'art, devenu un gigantesque projecteur de ciné-lumière – que son travail m'est apparu comme un archipel. Le motif de l'île et de ses alentours surgit souvent dans ses travaux, sous forme de sites, de cartes, de territoires arbitrairement délimités dans un désert, de cirques, de circuits, de routes en anneaux, de salles d'exposition, de pellicules enroulées dans leur boîte ou encore de boucles filmiques, projetées dans leur continuel retour, mais également rendues visibles dans la matérialité de leur parcours. Ainsi, le trajet baroque de l'une d'entre elles, depuis un projecteur suspendu à quelques mètres du sol dans la tour caverneuse d'Aldo Rossi à Vassivière : en permanence, elle s'aspire verticalement, pour s'enrouler et choir à la plus grande hauteur possible. Ces ilôts sont également sonores, bruités par des ritournelles électroniques ou les technologies des projections et des ventilations, comme par des conversations dont on ne saisit pas le sens. A la Biennale de Venise 2009, un chœur de textes était chorégraphié par la voie de cinq projecteurs, qui accompagnaient tels des inconscients sonores, des paroles écrites à l'écran, qui faisaient penser obliquement aux inserts d'un film muet fournissant autrefois les dialogues des images. Car ce qui nous tient tout autant en haleine chez Rosa Barba, ce ne sont pas seulement ces sites qu'elle délimite mais les dramatisations qui s'y trament, ces amorces de récit mêlant science et technosciences fiction et science-fictions, qui « s'écroulent dans le soleil de leur rayonnante guerre (ir)-réelle[1] ». Souvent, ainsi, une menace sourd sans qu'on puisse démêler si elle émane d'un passé resté secret ou d'un futur qu'elles anticipent, si elle provient des images auxquelles elle réfère ou des machines incluses dans le présent performatif de l'installation. L'île menaçant de dériver dans la mer et de se séparer du monde qui les lie à nous et le continent perdu ou les ruines d'un événement oublié (« *Forgotten* » : l'un des pays de Rosa Barba) se confondent dans une temporalité non linéaire, non chronologique, non canonique et peut-être, faisons en l'hypothèse, « non masculine[2] » ? Le texte qui va suivre constitue également un archipel, un réseau d'îles, qui dérive doucement. Certes suscité par les travaux de l'artiste et en référence à eux, il ne se propose pas comme un substitut à l'expérience des œuvres, mais comme un déplacement, qui, alors qu'on s'affaire à la recherche de Rosa Barba, semble s'être *oublié* ou distrait dans sa lancée à la recherche de la recherche.

II. La fissure

Les Bergers d'Arcadie, Nicolas Poussin, 1638, Paris, Musée du Louvre. Dans une nature plutôt sauvage et peu agreste, aux arbres coupés par les intempéries ou dont les feuilles brunies épousent la forme des abondants nuages gris/blancs (l'Arcadie est un ilôt canoniquement « éloigné de toutes côtes »), quatre personnages sont regroupés autour d'un caveau sans grâce. A droite, une femme debout, de profil, tient l'une de ses mains sur l'épaule d'un jeune berger qui, penché, appuyé sur son bâton, se retourne vers sa voisine, tout en désignant d'un doigt et d'un pouce ce que les deux autres bergers, à gauche, s'efforcent de déchiffrer. L'un debout, désinvolte et déséquilibré dans sa pose aux jambes croisées, s'appuie sur le tombeau pendant que l'autre barbu, un genou en terre, touche, pour lire, l'inscription perceptible sur la pierre. *Et In Arcadia Ego*. Ou plutôt : Et In Arcadia E/go, puisqu'une fissure dans le caveau cisaille le dernier mot. C'est l'Ego qui se cisaille, en effet, pendant qu'un des bergers voit son ombre portée dessiner le fantôme d'une faux mortifère.
Le tableau de Poussin a fait d'une inscription sur une pierre dans un jardin, le point de convergence de toutes les conversations, depuis celle du groupe qui se penche sur elles jusqu'à celles des historiens d'art qui ont, jusqu'à l'obsession, dialogué par textes interposés : Panofsky, Blunt, Klein, Gombrich, Marin … Tous ces hommes éminents se sont à leur tour employés à lire péniblement ou brillamment dans les signes, pour y trouver le sens juste et, par là, engager la foi de leurs travaux. De même, durant des séries de rencontres après la 2ème guerre mondiale, artistes, historiens et critiques d'art s'escrimèrent à deviner le destin de l'esthétique. Ainsi, grâce à Rosa Barba qui la cite en référence, est revenu dans le cours de l'actualité *The Western Round Table on Modern Art*. Celle-là eut lieu en 1949 à San Francisco, afin d'apporter « une représentation de l'opinion la plus informée de son temps, pour produire des questions sur l'art aujourd'hui[3] » – ne s'agissait-il pas également de répondre de ceux-là mêmes qui formulaient ces questions, de légitimer leur expertise ? De ce Western en forme de conversation, on trouve trace sur le fameux réseau Ubu – et, de fait, il brille, en effet, par la présence de Duchamp, Bateson, Wright, 'Schoenburg' (sic !), formulant l'unanimité masculine de ses participants : « a bunch of guys trying to think. Still more difficult, we were trying to think aloud and trying to communicate with each other – trying to get things clear that have never been gotten clear[4] ». De nouveaux bergers, en somme ! L'Arcadie a fait place à l'Ouest, ce mot qui désigne à la fois l'occident et le Grand-Ouest des Amériques, genre cinématographique compris. Une série panoramique est ainsi ici livrée à une bande de cow-boys blancs essayant d'avancer sur l'avenir déjà dépassé de leur civilisation et de leurs cultures ; oubliant que toute vision est incarnée par un corps. « All Western cultural narratives about objectivity are allegories of the ideologies governing the relations of what we call mind and body, distance and responsibility[5].» En 1949, également, Simone de Beauvoir publiait *Le Deuxième Sexe.* Que n'ont pas dit ces hommes sur cette inscription sans verbe « Et In Arcadia Ego » - : inachevée ? Achevée ? - Sa traduction, variant entre « Moi aussi, je fus en Arcadie » et « Même en Arcadie, je suis » a fait parler, alternativement, le mort et la mort. Du masculin au féminin. Tout diverge à partir de là, à partir de cette écriture, ces quatre mots qui les lie, détournant le paysage décrit. Le tombeau parle mais que dit-il ? Qu'il s'agisse *de la* mort qui prévient, ou *du* mort déjà sous le caveau, un drame s'est installé dans la région pastorale, qui devrait pourtant être immunisée en tant que pays de la félicité contre la déchéance et la décrépitude. Le personnage féminin pendant ce temps figure debout, sans qu'elle penche ou s'essaye à décrypter. Elle est une

image pensive, parallèle à la surface du tableau, finalement restant seule figure : n'est-ce pas par elle, ainsi, que s'opère un second regard, faisant état d'un processus de visualisation, que la peinture n'a pas à représenter ? La fissure, ainsi, en serait le signal.
La fissure, c'est le sésame que nous a donné Louise Bourgeois. C'est là, où la question de la séduction fait effraction dans le texte de l'art. Louise Bourgeois explique, en effet, la narrativité de son œuvre par ce qu'elle appelle « la fissure » : « Nous souffrions d'une fissure dans la cellule familiale, par laquelle mon père introduisait des maîtresses dans la maison[6]». Voir à la dérobée ou par en-dessous c'est aussi activement incarner un regard, dont Louise Bourgeois propose à son tour l'activation aux et par les spectatrices. L'esthétique s'introduit dans ce craquement familial par un certain nombre d'images qui plus que d'évoquer la psyché de la fabricatrice, produisent chez la spectatrice un certain état de faille subjective[7]. C'est aussi ce que fait Rosa Barba dans *Split Fields*, dont le grain filmique en noir et blanc transpose en apparition fantasmatique, le fantasme collectif, social, économique et politique de l'effondrement potentiel des villages aux abords du Vésuve. Au sein de la Tate Modern, *Shibboleth*, le projet dans le Turbine Hall conçu par l'artiste colombienne Doris Salcedo, consistait en une crevasse creusée et zigzaguant dans le sol de béton de l'institution. « Un espace négatif. Il évoque le trou de l'Histoire qui marque la différence sans fond qui sépare les blancs des non-blancs » indiquait l'artiste, dont le projet de ligne de démarcation a, dans sa réalisation, laissé une cicatrice indélébile dans le sol de l'institution.

III. Stories from the Landscape

Dans *Le Chant de l'Alouette,* roman de l'écrivaine américaine Willa Cather, figure le « Panther Canyon ». C'est un canyon d'Amérique. Elle le situe dans l'Arizona désertique et le dessine comme une fissure abrupte. « Perpendicular cliffs striped with even-running strata of rock » for the « first two hundred feet below the surface » (…) » « From there on to the bottom the sides were less abrupt, were shelving and lightly fringed with piñons and dwarf cedars. The effect was that of a gentler canyon within a wilder one. The dead city lay at the point where the perpendicular outer wall ceased and the V-shaped inner gorge began. There a stratum of rock, softer than those above, had been hollowed out by the action of time until it was like a deep groove running along the sides of the canyon. In this hollow (like a great fold in the rock) the Ancient People had built their houses of yellowish stone and mortar[8].» Méchant et gentil, habité et inhabité : tout une gamme d'émotions le charge. Ce texte, qui décrit le canyon comme une de ces failles façonnant l'histoire énigmatique de ce pays est, lit-on « one of the most thoroughly elaborated female landscape in literature[9] ».
A l'intérieur de la fissure, il y a donc tout un peuple natif et le chant de la terre révèle ainsi ses habitants, qui sont des bâtisseurs écologiques. Willa Cather, ou plutôt Thea Kronborg, cantatrice et personnage féminin de sa fiction, évoque les vestiges archéologiques des poteries faites par des femmes indiennes : pour elle(s), ils ont le potentiel de devenir l'objet de leur recherche esthétique. La transformation des objets de la recherche est un motif qu'on trouve souvent lorsqu'on s'intéresse à l'impact des femmes dans l'histoire canonique des beaux-arts et qu'on s'ouvre à des usages non disciplinaires, notamment l'artisanat, du travail de la terre et de la céramique. Entre le processus de création qu'opère ce qu'on appelle la nature et celui qu'on appelle fiction, se creuse un passage, qui est aussi un paysage. « It is when the first semblance of organic form is achieved that a work of art exhibits its general symbolic possibilities, like a statement imperfectly made or even merely indicated, but understandable in its general intent[10].» Voilà ce qu'écrit une philosophe un peu oubliée, Susanne Langer, qui mit le « feeling » en avant, un sentiment qui n'est pas seulement celui du plaisir ou du déplaisir mais qui s'identifie à l'espace vécu du monde c'est-à-dire aux faits de la vie de l'esprit.
L'évolution du terme de paysage s'associe à cette conception : d'abord dépiction esthétique – dessinée, peinte ou textuelle – connotant ultérieurement une vue, et donc un point de vue, puis une intervention esthétique au sein d'un lieu, le mot a dérivé dans le temps et l'espace, jusqu'à désigner « both a specific terrain and the general character of that terrain[11]», selon J.M. Coetzee. Le paysage est un agencement, une composition esthétique et une orientation. Rosa Barba : « So then, it was a story that emerged from a landscape…[12] ».

IV. L'écosystème des collaborations

Panzano (2000, 22') est une collaboration entre Rosa Barba, Ulrike Molsen et Valeria, Claudio et Dino : quelques rescapé/e/s de ce qui fut l'une des plus éminentes utopies des années 1970, l'anti-psychiatrie. C'est aussi un modèle un peu trop oublié d'une écologie de vie soucieuse des relations entre les êtres humains et d'autres organismes (ici, la caméra, la télé, le héros de radio-crochet) à leur environnement, qui inclut d'emblée des processus de création, des productions culturelles. L'ecosystème du film n'est pas le village de Toscane mais l'espace de l'écran, qui passe de l'optique à l'haptique avec ses surexpositions, ses compositions associant la physicalité de tous les acteurs, incluant également la technologie. « L'œil de la caméra » se combine avec la virtualité des histoires potentielles et des effets chimiques de superposition, comme avec les craquements qui s'opèrent entre l'extérieur et l'intérieur. Panzano, si l'on veut, c'est le paysage de la fissure, gueule béante.
Et si ce micro-climat de l'expérimentation se dilatait jusqu'aux terres non cultivables du désert ? Evoquant une autre région du monde, le Grand Ouest américain et un autre temps, le début du XXème siècle, Jonathan Goldberg[12] fait le récit d'une collaboration fictive, car elle n'aboutit pas, entre deux femmes qui fréquentèrent ce même immense territoire : l'écrivaine Willa Cather, (plus célèbre aujourd'hui pour avoir utilisé, dans ses lettres de 1890, le mot *queer* afin d'évoquer la déviance sexuelle), et Laura Gilpin, l'une des plus éminentes photographes des peubles Navajo et Pueblo entre 1920 et sa mort en 1979[13]. Le Western tombe ici hors du canon épique de la construction de l'Amérique blanche et mâle, c'est-à-dire de la volonté de déplacer les frontières et de les contrôler, qui articule aussi d'une conception du désert comme monument et monolithe : *Et in Arcadia Ego.* Dans son désert, Laura Gilpin photographie « l'Antiquité » américaine comme règne d'une unité entre les canyons – la sculpture de la nature – et les maisons des peuples indiens, avec les poteries qui caractérisent, selon elle

« L'Endurance Navaho », ainsi qu'elle titre l'un de ses plus célèbres livres. Chez Cather, le paysage, sa flore et sa faune, y compris les poteries archéologiques Sinagua qui s'y trouvent, figurent une texture symphonique où s'unissent des corpuscules en transformation, mêlant, transposant leurs influences et leurs styles, mais dont la matérialité évoque également la membrane sensible du diaphragme - c'est-à-dire du muscle qui construit la respiration du chant. La musique du canyon s'établit également dans une harmonie entre les chants des oiseaux, le bruit des cigales et des insectes, et le rythme de certaines cérémonies. Ainsi, dans l'écriture, le site devient un résonateur de la vitalité du corps. Du côté de la photographe, il s'agit de visualiser l'oubli, ce qui fut mais n'est plus, quitte à reconstituer le site de la vie pacifique qui y déroulait son fil en faisant poser des Indiens ou plutôt des Indiennes bien vivants, payé/es en tant que modèles. Une façon de faire, qui a embarrassé plus d'un thuriféraire : mais ce que Laura Gilpin inscrit dans son imagerie, c'est une projection, écrit Goldberg, qui s'opère dans sa façon réservée et non envahissante d'unifier ces femmes, le site qui les environne et les artefacts ; les poteries qui figurent dans les images sont les passeurs, des « monuments d'une grande beauté (...) nous donnant dans leur art une virilité et une beauté de conception, qui rend les nôtres faibles et quelque peu insignifiants. Et par-dessus tout, ils ont « endured – enduré et duré[14] ». Le lien entre l'écriture de Cather et les photographies de Gilpin, qui tiendrait en peu de mots à la résolution d'une banale explication sexuelle (l'homosexualité), apparaît bien plus subtile lorsqu'il s'agit d'énoncer le désert comme lieu d'un savoir intuitif, vital, qui ne désire pas d'explication. Comme dans les Bergers d'Arcadie, il revient au personnage féminin, non de déchiffrer mais au contraire de se détourner du pouvoir des signes. Non par indifférence mais parce qu'elle est déjà un signe dans le langage masculin.

Et In Arcadia E/go : L'arcadie n'est plus une utopie. L'E/go cisaillé par une barre qui formule au contraire une dystopie, comme l'écrivain Monique Wittig, lorsqu'elle l'écrit dans *Le Corps Lesbien*, pour relater une expérience dans un langage qui ne m/e constitue pas comme sujet. Monique Wittig : « J/e poses the ideological and historic question of feminine subjects[15] ». J/e est pour Wittig, la marque d'une division dualiste des sexes et l'imposition d'une logique de la différence comme vérité et valeur universelle, un système dans lequel et par lequel les hommes sont (faits) des hommes et les femmes sont (faites) des femmes.

V. De l'Ouest en d'Est, le désert

Pour Reyner Banham, le désert est l'espace où l'homme moderne doit se sentir « chez soi[16] ». Dans le cinéma d'Antonioni, il s'inscrit dans une histoire post-industrielle de désertion et de dérive, explorant aussi une vision ambivalente du monde technologique. *Le Désert Rouge* véhicule les thèmes de l'aliénation, de l'angoisse, de la désorientation spatiale et de situations existentielles genrées, perçues à travers des changements chromatiques. C'est une passagère féminine qui s'embarque à travers ce paysage « psychogéographique » où, comme l'écrit Zygmunt Bauman : « The present is always wanting,which makes it ugly, abhorrent and unendurable. The present is obsolete ... The moment it lands in the present, the coveted future is poisoned by the toxic effluvia of the wasted past[17] » - un texte qui pourrait également s'appliquer à *D'Est*, le film de Chantal Akerman. *Le Désert Rouge* s'aventure également dans une géographie explorant le paysage pictural abstrait de l'art américain moderne, d'ailleurs exporté en Europe et notamment en Italie, afin d'y présenter : « the logical culmination of a long-standing and inexor-able tendency towards abstraction in which what had been characteristically American now became representative of «Western culture» as a whole[18] ». *Le Désert Rouge* s'écarte, de même, des conventions filmiques figuratives. Les couples faisant l'amour dans le sable de *Zabriskie Point* (1969) s'inscrivent comme des points de capiton dans un espace terrien bombé, comme si l'appareil de projection en restituait la courbure à l'écran.

Les technologies de l'image permettent un processus d'objectivation particulièrement sophistiqué, détaillé, partiel et mobile des émotions attachées à ces technologies. Ainsi, le désert du Mojave dans *They Shine* de Rosa Barba, est recadré sur ses « Fabriques » de panneaux solaires tendus comme des boucliers contre toute incursion venue du ciel ou ces édicules dévastés et graffités, qui ont probablement aussi participé au projet scientifique de spéculer sur le potentiel industriel et matériel de l'Amérique contre la guerre atomique[19]. Les uns comme les autres, qu'ils brillent ou qu'ils se rouillent, misent sur les pouvoirs fictionnels de la nature c'est-à-dire aussi sur les capacités de celle-ci à camoufler des récits de capitalisation et de profits sous les ruines. Comme le désert dans la dernière installation d'Hito Steyerl, avec son cimetière d'avions délabrés. On pense également à l'explosion des biens de consommation dans *Zabriskie Point* de Michelangelo Antonioni comme aux photographies de Sophie Ristelhueber du désert-poubelle de la première guerre d'Irak (*Fait*, 1992). Et enfin, à la réclusion permanente du personnage féminin du film *Safe* de Todd Haynes, incarné par Julianne Moore, pour laquelle un abri dans le désert constitue l'ultime possibilité d'un Soi discipliné par la terreur de survivre au temps de l'apocalypse environnementale. Cette terreur environnementale est apparue, d'ailleurs, à partir de 1949 avec la guerre froide et la course aux armements atomiques, développant aux Etats-Unis un imaginaire de la ruine, devenu à la fois rituel privé et modèle de gouvernance, poussant dans sa logique, à jouer et rejouer la destruction physique de l'Etat-nation comme à concevoir des villes test, des simulacres de banlieues comme prototypes de survie dans le désert de l'Ouest.

VI. The Desert Is No Lady

The Desert Is No Lady est l'intitulé d'un livre qui va à l'encontre de son titre. Une fois assumée que l'analyse du paysage a longtemps été complètement masculinisée, que le « canon du canyon » et la géographie furent d'abord la propriété intellectuelle des hommes, centrée sur la présomption que les régions sont peuplées d'hommes, conquises par les hommes, que les hommes sont angoissés devant la nature, etc., les recherches ont fait état de ces fils invisibles qui découpent le terrain selon le genre, le sexe, la race, et ont créé d'autres espèces d'espaces. C'est un peu comme lorsqu'on part à la recherche de Rosa Barba, afin de mieux décrire ses œuvres. On ouvre le dossier d'un art non-urbain, d'une tradition paysagère, d'un imaginaire géographique et de productions culturelles en rapport avec un sujet ou une subjectivité féminine et d'abord, on n'a rien. Le désert ? Mais même le désert est peuplé de milliers d'indices sur ce que le paysage a « fait » aux femmes de cultures anglo, hispano, mexico, indienne dans le Sud Ouest de l'Amérique, depuis les tissus Navajo à Georgia O Keeffe, des paniers Hopi à Willa Cather et des poteries Pueblo à Andrea Geyer. Ces approches du paysage y trouvent une force et une libération créatives : « l'échelle vaste et indomptée de la région les libère des restrictions silencieuses liées à la féminité. Une énergie érotique venue de la terre… infuse l'écriture des femmes indiennes et cette rencontre sensuelle et sensée, sexualisée se retrouve dans l'œuvre de l'artiste qui va la chercher…[20] ».

Quelles perspectives, visuelles et sociales, organisent l'intrusion des femmes et des questions de genre dans le paysage ? Lorsqu'elle passe de la présentation directe de son corps en performance à une série de « dialogues entre le paysage et le corps féminin » (ce sont ses termes), hors de l'atelier et de son extension du White Cube, Ana Mendieta convoque, effectivement, un accouplement entre la terre et le corps, sous le terme de « earth/body sculptures ». La terre, le sable, les pierres, l'eau, la poudre à canon, le feu, les plantes, les fleurs, les arbres, le sang, la neige, les cheveux y participent pour formuler, avec chaque *Silueta,* silhouette découpée aux formes du corps, cette zone de contact. L'artiste engage, dès la première installation où une Silueta est, placée sur une tombe Zapotèque à Oaxaca (1973), un mouvement permanent : chaque pièce laisse un creux, celui du corps physique documenté par la photographie ou le film-souvenir, qui marque aussi le déplacement consécutif à l'exil. Comme l'a montré Lucy Lippard, Ana Mendieta établit des connections entre le paysage et l'histoire, entre le psychique et le social teintant la pratique des *earthworks* de connotations politiques et féministes spécifiques : d'ailleurs les Silueta seront exposées d'abord, au sein de la galerie A.I.R., collectif newyorkais de femmes artistes. *Untitled, Volcano Piece, Iowa,* 1980, y propose une silhouette inscrite dans un monticule oblong, transformée en vulve avec ses lèvres de terre sous l'effet du feu, qui explose après que de la poudre eut été répandue sur la forme. Mendieta a mis le feu, filmé l'incendie, la déflagration de fumée et les restes : sa silhouette brûlée crée un vide, qui est autant le vide de l'exil, que celui de l'invisibilité des non-hommes et des non-blancs dans le paysage des Etats-Unis. Elle propose également une représentation de la sexualité féminine par le feu, qui va à l'encontre de la légende prométhéenne, qui fait apparaître le feu comme phallus, du moins dans l'interprétation Freudienne[21]. « Mon art vient du déplacement et de la rage », dit Mendieta.

L'espace de l'exil, de la déterritorialisation, s'inscrit dans la matière même avec lesquelles l'artiste fabrique ses œuvres. De la même façon, Nancy Holt inclut dans les formes qu'elle donne à ses propositions, le passage du temps qui constitue à la fois sa matière et son contenu. En 1969, elle enterre des poèmes dans des sites choisis des déserts de l'Ouest. A la même époque, Gina Pane, en Italie enterre des pierres comme une sorte de cadran solaire. C'est sur un terrain acheté dans l'Utah que Nancy Holt réalise, entre 1973 et 76, ses Sun Tunnel. Elle a fait installer quatre énormes tuyaux de canalisation réalisés en ciment. Ces « buses » de plusieurs mètres de long et 2,50 de hauteur, se font face par paires autour d'un espace vide, dont le centre porte un cercle en ciment. Ils sont orientés en fonction des solstices d'hiver et d'été et les trous percés dans les surfaces de ciment formulent la topographie des constellations, dont les taches de lumière à l'intérieur reproduisent les figures. « Le jour est transformé en nuit et on assiste à une inversion du ciel[22] » , dit Nancy Holt, de sorte que le temps acquiert une présence physique et que la configuration spatiale de la Terre devient perceptible : il s'agit de remettre la terre sur son axe dans un lieu où l'humanité n'a pas cours, de diriger la vue pour suivre les différentes positions du soleil. Le paysage de Nancy Holt ne procède pourtant pas d'une effusion romantique avec le paysage mais d'un « calcul » :

« j'ai voulu ramener le vaste espace du désert à une échelle humaine. Je n'avais nul désir de construire un monument mégalithique. La vue panoramique est trop écrasante pour qu'on puisse se passer de repères visuels[23] ».

VII. Désert, Désir

Pour Roni Horn, le désert est glacé, fait de glace et de terre noire. Le désert est un miroir, qui ne renvoie qu'à soi-même et donc un désert désert, comme elle le dit dans l'une des 8 entrées consacrées à ce terme dans son livre *Roni Horn aka Roni Horn*[24]. Ces occurrences du mot désert précèdent le mot : désir et suivent le mot : dédicace.

VIII. Savage Dreams

En 1851, commence une bataille dans ce qui deviendra le parc National de Yosemite. Celle-ci s'opère contre les habitants indigènes. En 1951, à quelques centaines de kilomètres, une autre guerre commence, lorsque le gouvernement des Etats-Unis met en place des essais nucléaires dans un site du Nevada, nécessitant l'évacuation de la terre et des gens. C'est ce que raconte le livre de Rebecca Solnit[25]. « Savage Dreams is an exploration of these two paradigmatic landscapes – the nuclear test site, where more than 1,000 nuclear bombs have been set off, and Yosemite National Park, where the Indian Wars never really came to an end. Between 1951 and 1991 you have a nuclear bomb a month for wars that weren't supposed to have begun, along with Indian Wars that were supposed to have ended in the 19th century and yet never did. The Native people didn't vanish, and their right to be on the land was still contested, though the violence was more subtle. While Yosemite has this conventional image of paradise, it ended up being a kind of hell for social alienation. At a test site, of course, atomic bombs are hell, but the communities organized to resist them have made it a kind of paradise. So the ideas about paradise and hell got turned inside out for me because of this stalwart, broad community of Mormon downwinders, Hiroshima survivors, nuclear physicists, anarchists, environmentalists, Buddhist monks, and Catholic priests who were convening at that test site[26].» Cette interview est parue dans *Bomb*, le magazine.

IX. Reclamation / Restitution

Les interventions dans la morphologie des sites, les œuvres constituées d'éléments naturels, bruts ou manufacturés, d'essences vivantes ou inertes ont renouvelé un art du paysage réalisé dans le contexte plus large de l'effort écologique. Il n'est pas anodin qu'à côté des *earthworks,* et parfois en contradiction avec eux, il y ait eu cette attraction de certains artistes pour un art de réhabilitation des sites. Ceux-ou celles-ci ont utilisé le terme de « reclamation art » – confondant dans cette expression, comme le français « restitution », l'action de rétablir ce qui a subi des altérations et de rendre ce qui a été pris, la reconstruction et la remise de la nature à elle-même. Cela ne saurait avoir eu lieu sans l'émergence de l'écologie comme mouvement politique. Tournant le dos à une conception de la nature comme chaos et sauvagerie, mais aussi comme réservoir de ressources, les questions environnementales vont produire la notion d' « ecosystème », avec sa dynamique complexe d'énergie et de matière.

Dans la fabrication du paysage écologique, on trouve une autre collaboration qui n'eut jamais lieu, celle de deux femmes publiant conjointement des ouvrages devenus, depuis, des classiques : les travaux sur la planification urbaine de Jane Jacobs, dont le *Death and Life of Great American Cities* est publié en 1961 et, en 1962, le livre de Rachel Carson, *Silent Spring,* qui montre comment les dommages provoqués par les pesticides ont transformé la notion même d'environnement. Ces deux livres, en effet, permettent de s'écarter de la dichotomie entre espace urbain et naturel. Dans les deux cas, les limites disciplinaires et spatiales entre la ville et la nature craquent : les deux ouvrages utilisent un vocabulaire similaire pour ouvrir un nouveau champ, qui entretient des connexions entre les deux domaines. Ce paysage s'oppose à celui d'une modernité associée à l'efficacité et à l'hygiène, fabriqué par le réformisme social et le rationalisme, qui ont en ce sens renforcé les barrières entre ville et nature. Or, Carson met en avant un discours populaire de santé écologique critiquant le modèle disciplinaire de l'expert, et de son côté, Jane Jacobs observe la violence en puissance dans la ville moderne ; un thème sur lequel les premiers ouvrages féministes, ainsi *The Feminine Mystique* (1966) de Betty Friedan, vont renchérir, lorsqu'ils évoquent le problème « sans nom », c'est-à-dire l'isolement des femmes dans l'Amérique suburbaine des années d'après guerre. Tel est ainsi la force d'un paysage féministe, qui arrive à situer ses questions à l'intérieur d'un nouveau cadre conceptuel. Donna Haraway n'a-t-elle pas suggestivement montré à quel point les questions de genre recoupent des notions de géographie, deux savoirs qui ont besoin d'être « situés » ? « Feminism embodiement, then, is not about fixed location in a reified body, female or otherwise, but about nodes in fields[27]. » Chez Rosa Barba, dans *Outwardly from Earth's Center,* au temps et à l'espace incertains, l'île de Gotska Sandön n'existe que dans sa dérive potentielle. Les experts parlent, le Gardien du Phare, l'Architecte, l'Archiviste, le Politicien, tous au masculin et les habitants, hommes, femmes ou autres, ne parlent pas mais fabriquent ensemble une sculpture, une architecture de cordes et de piliers de bois, une grille, un processus et un déplacement : un paysage, pas un état, pas un territoire, pas une administration.

X. Désastres

« At one time, New York was a city on an island, a city with a location in the physical world. In this century, even the island itself has been replaced by the Borough of Manhattan. Paris was once situated in a vast and fertile plain. Now it is in France but France is an invention of Paris.[28] », s'écrie Jimmy Durham.

En 2007, Sanja Ivekovic transforme la place principale de la Documenta de Kassel en champ de coquelicots. Mierle Laderman Ukeles déjà pour l'exposition *Care*, de 1969, proposait de faire livrer au musée, quotidiennement, des déchets provenant pour une part de bennes-poubelles, pour une autre résultant de la pollution de l'air et des rivières, afin d'œuvrer littéralement à leur réhabilitation au sein des salles d'exposition, en installant des machines à purification, à dépollution, servant au recyclage, et à la préservation. Entre 78-83, la même artiste avait proposé de transposer 6 des « polders » newyorkais en zones « chaudes » de réhabilitation, suivant une esthétique qui soit libérée des clichés enchaînant les représentations des femmes à la nature imposés par les hommes.

« There is no such thing as a natural disaster[29] » explique Rebecca Solinit. Qu'il s'agisse de tremblement de terre ou d'éruption volcanique et c'est l'architecture, le bâti humain qui trinque d'abord, qui tuent les gens, qui produit le désastre collectif, social, qu'entraînent également l'ouragan, la tempête, l'inondation, le tsunami. C'est ce que montre, également, *The Empirical Effect* (2009) où Rosa Barba traite d'un même genre de désastre « non-original », comme dirait Haraway, puisqu'il n'est que le nuage en suspension d'un drame n'ayant pas eu lieu depuis 1944. L'éventualité d'un réveil explosif du Vésuve est devenu une menace permanente pour les habitants de Naples et les environs ainsi que les nombreuses activités illicites qui y fonctionnent, mais aussi et à la fois, un spectacle touristique se nourrissant du danger, qui renouvèle le thème de l'horreur exquise du sublime par la monstration des appareils de mesure, des sondes et sismographes et par la performance collective constituée des tests d'évacuation des résidents. Cette composition, à nouveau, « psychogéographique » participe du film de Rosa Barba, qui est la fiction d'une fiction, la répétition générale de la fuite organisée des habitants du Vésuve n'ayant pas eu lieu, elle lui revint, dit-elle, de l'organiser. Quelques-uns des témoins de l'explosion de 1944 font partie du cortège de personnages, qui court dans un village vide, dans un court-circuit temporel où ils performent la répétition anticipée de la catastrophe. Réfugiés dans un abri, un ilôt de ciment « safe », les protagonistes incarnent par leurs gestes des possibilités de langages, de communication de vivre ensemble qui résistent aux simplificatrices distinctions entre arguments rationnels et irrationnels.

Mais la course des personnages sédimente une histoire particulière du cinéma à Naples, traditionnellement filmée sur le motif, à la fois depuis une perspective aérienne et du point de vue de son activité de rue. Dans l'ouvrage consacrée à la réalisatrice napolitaine Elvira Notari[30], l'historienne culturelle Giuliana Bruno montre comment celle-ci conçoit des fictions cinématographiques, par exemple *Duie Paravise* (Deux Ciels, 1928), où la technologie permet de confronter la perspective aérienne et l'espace vécu de la marche au niveau de la rue, ouvrant à d'autres paradigmes visuels que celui de l'œil et de l'optique.

XI. Vertiginous Mapping

A partir de la *Carte du Pays de Tendre* et sa topographie dessinée que publia Madeleine de Scudéry en 1654 pour donner figure à un itinéraire d'émotions, un voyage amoureux, un paysage intérieur fournissant « une carte géographique de l'espace relationnel » et un « texte cartographique ouvert dont les nombreux itinéraires potentiels produisent un effet cumulatif[31]», Giuliana Bruno réinvente l'espace du cinéma et le mouvement des arts « spatiovisuels », comme elle dit. L'invention du film, site culturel cinétique, a inauguré une ère de circulation de plus en plus complexe, à mesure qu'on essaye, comme le fait Rosa Barba, d'impliquer à l'intérieur de la carte la dérive qui a lieu dans le procédé et les outils mêmes de la cartographie : d'où la production d'une cartographie vertigineuse. Vertigineuse, parce qu'elle implique dans sa texture, aussi bien les images que les technologiques, les écrans que les projecteurs, l'architecture et la machine. Rosa Barba fait du cinéma lui même, une ruine du futur, une science-fiction laissée par le cyberespace du XXIème siècle. Avec les développements des réseaux du Web, notre culture spatiale, signale encore Giuliana Bruno, ne réinvente-t-elle pas sans cesse la pulsion de faire contact et d'être connecté, de poser l'espace virtuel comme habitable et habité ?

XII. « Facts Run on Lightbeams These Days[32].»

Notes

1. En anglais "collapse into the sun of their radiant (ir)reality-war".
Donna Haraway, "Situated Knowledges: The Science Question in Feminism and the Privilege of Partial Perspective", *Feminist Studies* 14, N° 3 (Automne, 1988), p. 577.
2. Sur la réfutation du modèle canonique d'un "récit de l'antériorité", voir Mieke Bal, *Louise Bourgeois' Spider: The Architecture of Art-Writing* (Chicago et Londres : University of Chicago Press, 2001).
3. "The Western Round Table on Modern Art (1949)", ed. Douglas MacAgy. Consulté en ligne à : http://www.ubu.com/historical/wrtma/index.html (dernière visite le 8 mars 2011).
4. Ibid.
5. Donna Haraway, 1988 (Cf. note 1), p. 583.
6. Louise Bourgeois, dans un entretien avec Bernard Marcadé dans le film de Camille Guichard : *Louise Bourgeois* (New York, février 1993).
7. Mieke Bal 2001 (Cf. note 2).
8. Willa Cather, *The Song of the Lark* (Boston: Houghton, 1915), p. 297.
9. Ellen Moers, citée dans Ann Moseley, "The Creative Ecology of Walnut Canyon", in *Cather Studies*, vol. 5. Consulté en ligne à : http://cather.unl.edu/cs005_moseley.html (dernière visite le 8 mars 2011).
10. Susanne K. Langer, *Feeling and Form: A Theory of Art* (New York : Scribner's, 1953), p. 122.
11. J. M. Coetzee, cité dans Katie Brewer Ball et Julia Steinmetz, "Call for Papers: Feminist Landscapes" in *Women & Performance: a journal of feminist theory.* Cet appel à contributions a été publié sur différents sites internet avec une date limite de contributions fixée au 1er janvier 2010.
12. Rosa Barba, *Printed Cinema #3: Accidental Suspension.*
13. Jonathan Goldberg, "Photographic Relations: Laura Gilpin, Willa Cather", in *American Literature* 70, N° 1 (mars 1998), pp. 63-95. Consulté en ligne à : http://www.jstor.org/stable/2902456 (dernière visite le 8 mars 2011).
14. Jonathan Goldberg, *Willa Cather and Others* (Durham, NC : Duke University Press, 2001), pp. 158-59.
15. Monique Wittig, "Author's Note", in *The Lesbian Body,* traduc. David Le Vay (Boston: Beacon, 1986), pp.10-11.
16. Reyner Banham, *Scenes in the American Deserta* (Cambridge, MA : MIT Press, 1989).
17. Zygmunt Baumann, *Modernity and ambivalence,* (Cambridge, UK : Polity, 1991), p. 11.
18. Serge Guilbaut, *How New York stole the Idea of Modern Art: Abstract Expressionism, Freedom and the Cold War,* traduc. Arthur Goldhammer (Chicago: University of Chicago Press, 1983), p. 177.
19. Cf. Joseph Masco, "Fantastic City: Engeneering Ruins in Cold War America", *Cabinet* 20, (hiver 2005-2006), pp. 85-88.
20. Vera Norwood et Janice Monk, eds., The Desert is No Lady: *Southwestern Landscapes in Women's Writing and Art* (New Haven: Yale University Press, 1987), p. 87.
21. Sigmund Freud, "The Acquisition and Control of Fire", in *The Standard Edition of the Complete Psychological Works of Sigmund Freud, Vol. XXII (1932–36): New Introductory Lectures on Psycho-Analysis and Other Works,* pp. 183-94.
22. Nancy Holt, "Sun Tunnels", *Artforum* (avril 1977), pp. 34-35.
23. Ibid.
24. Briony Fer et Roni Horn, *Roni Horn aka Roni Horn* (Londres: Steidl, 2009).
25. Rebecca Solnit, *Savage Dreams* (Berkeley: University of California Press, 2000).
26. Astra Taylor, "Rebecca Solnit", *Bomb* 109 (automne 2009), http://bombsite.com/issues/109/articles/3327
27. Donna Haraway, *"Simians, Cyborgs and Women: The reinvention of Nature"* (New York : Routledge, 1990), p. 195.
28. Jimmy Durham, "Artists' Pages", *Art Journal* 51, N° 2, *Art and Ecology* (Eté 1992), p. 14.
29. Rebecca Solnit, entretien. Consulté en ligne à http://believermag.com/issues/200909/?read=interview_solnit (dernière visite le 8 mars 2011).
30. Giuliana Bruno, *Streetwalking on a Ruined Map, Cultural Theory and the City Films of Elvira Notari* (Princeton, Princeton University Press, 1993).
31. Giuliana Bruno, *Atlas of Emotion, Journeys in Art, Architecture and Films* (New York : Verso, 2002). Cet ouvrage est à consulter intégralement.
32. Donna Haraway, "Situated Knowledges: The Science Question in Feminism and the Privilege of Partial Perspective", in *Simians, op.cit.*, p. 248, note 2 (Cf. note 27)

LES FILMS «INFILMÉS» DE ROSA BARBA

FRANCESCO MANACORDA & RAIMUNDAS MALASAUSKAS

Dans sa célèbre suite pour piano de 1874 *Les Tableaux d'une exposition*, Modeste Moussorgski transpose en musique un récit de sa visite de l'exposition de son ami, l'artiste et architecte Viktor Hartmann. Chacun des dix mouvements fait écho à une œuvre d'art spécifique, pour la plupart impossibles à identifier aujourd'hui. Le titre des œuvres est bien utilisé pour chaque mouvement, mais la majorité d'entre elles sont perdues ou leur identification incertaine. Avec cette discontinuité, la musique fonctionne comme la spectaculaire archive fantôme d'une expérience passée et dont les sources ne seraient plus disponibles pour l'auditeur dans leur forme originelle. Son pouvoir d'évocation fait émerger tout un potentiel d'images du plus profond d'une mémoire qui n'a jamais été conservée visuellement ; tout comme il ne reste d'un film, dont les images ont été effacées par l'usure du temps, que la trace sonore « secondaire » qui les accompagnaient.

L'œuvre de Rosa Barba *Hidden Conference* – et en général toutes ses œuvres récentes qui traitent de la question de l'archive – fonctionne comme le reflet inversé des *Tableaux d'une exposition*. Plusieurs collections de biens culturels mis en réserve (peintures, sculptures, œuvres sur papier) sont utilisées par l'artiste comme un réservoir de personnages qui pourraient être activés dans un film dont le scénario serait le fruit de leur proximité fortuite dans ce lieu de stockage. Dans le regard de l'artiste, le potentiel des réserves de musée ou des archives réside dans le rôle latent que les objets qui y sont entreposés peuvent jouer dans une intrigue. Des liens entre œuvres et documents sont tissés pour créer une histoire et le lieu de conservation lui-même se transforme en décor de théâtre où un rôle est assigné à chaque œuvre, en fonction de son identité, au sein d'une chorégraphie élaborée.

Les éléments de la collection deviennent les protagonistes de nombreuses histoires, secrètes et fragmentées, qui racontent comment ces objets se sont trouvés rassemblés. A la manière des lettres de l'alphabet, les documents peuvent être utilisés pour dire de simples mots, des phrases entières, de multiples textes. Ce jeu combinatoire n'est pas très éloigné de l'activité du musée : il donne à voir ce qui ressemble aux efforts des archéologues pour reconstruire un passé enfoui dont on ne connaîtrait que quelques fragments. A partir de ceux-ci, c'est toute une histoire – ou plutôt, dans le cas des archéologues, l'histoire – qui doit être reconstruite, assemblée, évoquée. La différence entre l'archéologie et les récits de Rosa Barba tient à ce que l'unité du matériel archéologique peut être garantie par le lieu géographique de leur découverte et la cohérence de leur datation. Inversement, tous les possibles en gestation dans les archives sont par définition à la recherche d'une histoire, pas nécessairement de l'Histoire, et Rosa Barba semble bien disposée à les laisser confluer vers son story-board de celluloïd pour former autant de permutations intermittentes. S'agit-il alors de futurs possibles qui n'auraient pas eu lieu ? D'univers alternatifs explorés par le jeu des probabilités mathématiques ? Ou bien encore de pièces de théâtre qui résulteraient d'une séance de spiritisme où l'on aurait essayé de ranimer les fictions potentielles cachées dans les œuvres qui sont confinées dans ces espaces, construits pour stocker notre mémoire collective.

Pour son exposition à Rovereto, Rosa Barba a imaginé une installation devant la porte qui mène aux archives. La mise en scène inclut un lampe et un rideau de théâtre suspendu près du seuil séparant l'exposition et les réserves. La lampe, ronde, monumentale, est posée sur le sol et une longues bandes de film en celluloïd se déplace lentement à sa surface, comme un serpent. Cette lampe fonctionne comme un objet filmique de science-fiction qui filtrerait le passé pour le convertir en futur éventuel. Si, avec un projecteur de film traditionnel, la lumière traverse la pellicule pour permettre à des images fantomatiques et immatérielles de danser sur un écran blanc ; avec cette version modifiée, la pellicule permet à la lumière de s'échapper vers la porte des archives, comme si elle voulait attirer vers sa surface, à la manière d'un aimant, tous les personnages potentiels confinés dans les « loges » derrière le rideau de théâtre. Plutôt qu'un projecteur, la lampe est alors une caméra, un instrument spirite capable de faire revenir à la vie des objets inanimés. Le film dans la lampe sert à invoquer toutes les histoires non encore racontées qui surgissent des archives, et c'est pour cette raison qu'il est encore non exposé. Les documents, œuvres d'art, photographies et manuscrits sont attirés vers la pellicule comme si le celluloïd avait été traité chimiquement pour attirer à sa surface tout contenu culturel.

Parmi les documents de Depero conservés, on trouve un certain nombre de scénarii pour un film futuriste jamais réalisé. Dans ces documents, un artiste atteint la gloire grâce à l'invention d'un théâtre entièrement automatisé. Dans ses notes, il décrit : « des animaux mécaniques, des sauvages automatiques qui dansent, des papillons multicolores qui volent, des masques dansants à moustaches, un théâtre d'ombres construit de toutes pièces, une pluie de cigarettes … ». Ces éléments sont comme autant de mondes plongés dans la mémoire de quelqu'un d'autre et rappellent les histoires qui émergent de l'interview de Raimundas Malasauskas avec Jean Péchalat[1] : des fragments de récits d'un village aujourd'hui englouti. Tout comme les craquements nocturnes de la surface gelée du lac de Vassivière qu'évoque Jean Péchalat, les archives hurlent pour qui veut bien les entendre. Ce qui est sous l'eau peut facilement être ressuscité en un ballet mécanique.

Par définition, l'archivage tend à une sorte de complétude fictionnelle ; il essaie d'imposer l'homogénéité à une série d'individualités parfaitement hétérogènes. La rigueur scientifique passe à côté du fait que les collections et les fonds d'archives sont souvent réunis de manière fortuite. Même s'il s'agit peut-être là d'un usage défaillant de l'appareillage scientifique, ce potentiel non linéaire pour engendrer des fictions collectives est précisément l'élément que la pensée scientifique laisse de côté ; alors qu'il peut lier entre elles des visions d'autres mondes possibles. Il y a quelques temps, j'ai rencontré Arlette Farge – l'historienne française spécialiste des archives – pour l'interviewer sur la notion de document, et l'aspect le plus intéressant de sa pratique que je retiens de cette conversation reste sa méthode pour véritablement comprendre un document d'archive :

> A un moment, je me suis rendue compte que si je voulais vraiment travailler sur le XVIIIème siècle, je ne pouvais pas simplement résumer et prendre des notes. Je me suis dis que si je faisais une série de fiches, à la manière des historiens, je n'y arriverais jamais. Les sources que je ne connaissais pas bien, et quc j'cssayais de déchiffrer, me semblaient tellement riches que je me suis forcée – même si ça ne me dérangeait pas du tout – à copier les choses, à m'aventurer dans la syntaxe et le vocabulaire, et j'étais convaincu – ce que vous allez trouver parfaitement naïf – que même le mouvement de mon corps pendant que j'écrivais ne pouvait que me donner des idées ! Mon immersion a été un processus très long, mais cela me plaisait, je copiais pendant des heures et des heures, et j'ai senti que ce mouvement précis me donnait une sorte d'inspiration – plutôt que de résumer, suivre les discussions, la ponctuation et les hésitations pas à pas. J'imaginais les voix et j'entendais les sons. Mon immersion n'avait rien d'imaginaire, elle consistait plutôt à « être avec ».

Dans ce récit, les documents sont comme des scenarii et l'action de les recopier devient une performance d'acteur pour parfaitement entrer dans la peau du personnage à interpréter. Rosa Barba va plus loin avec cette intuition en imaginant des pièces d'archive anthropomorphes, comme à la recherche d'un scénario commun. Comme dans la célèbre pièce de Pirandello *Six personnages en quête d'auteur*, la réserve, considérée comme une scène, donne l'occasion à ces individus sans intrigue d'avoir leur mot à dire sur les raisons de leur présence ou sur l'absurdité d'une telle condition. Les archives et les réserves sont pleines de ces acteurs en puissance, tous capables de jouer différentes tragédies. On les conserve comme des cadavres prêts à être ranimés : ils sont invisibles dans l'obscurité. La définition de Robert Smithson comparant les musées à des cimetières, pourrait être complétée en émettant l'hypothèse que les réserves, que le visiteur de musée ne voit pas, sont les lieux où l'on garde les morts-vivants. Leur potentiel ne réside pas tant dans la possibilité qu'ils puissent retourner dans l'espace d'exposition mais plutôt dans le processus quasi spirite qui fait d'eux les personnages d'une histoire non encore contée qui se déroulerait dans un futur indistinct.

Note

1. Cf. le texte de Raimundas Malasauskas dans ce volume, pp. 237–40

Chère Rosa,

Merci de me demander à nouveau de te tenir au courant de la mission. Je dois avouer qu'il ne s'est pas passé grand chose ces derniers temps, mais il y a plusieurs choses qui pourront cependant t'intéresser. Hier nous avons marché sur le pont qui mène de la terre ferme à l'île au milieu du lac. Presque au moment où ton email est arrivé, nous posions le pied sur l'île.
Après être monté et descendu de la tour, avoir vu des centaines de mètres de pellicule et écouté les basses fréquences qui émanaient de l'eau, nous sommes partis nous promener autour de l'île avec Alexandra. Je ne me souviens pas si nous avons terminé la balade, mais une chose qui m'a particulièrement frappé est le fait que l'île est une création humaine récente. J'avais pourtant l'impression que nous marchions dans un endroit qui existait depuis des lustres. J'étais abasourdi. Toute ma perception du lieu venait de basculer : je comprenais que nous nous étions au sommet d'une petite colline qui avait été entourée par les eaux et était devenue une île il y a seulement quelques années.
C'est à ce moment qu'Alexandra m'a appris qu'il y avait un homme qui vivait sur l'île depuis le temps ou l'île n'en était pas une du tout. Cet homme, selon elle, connaît l'histoire de l'île mieux que personne, parce qu'il est plus vieux que l'île elle-même. Est-ce que tu peux imaginer ça ? Je ne pense pas qu'il existe une seule autre personne au monde qui est plus vieille que l'île qu'elle habite.
Nous sommes allés le voir sans perdre un instant. Je me suis dit qu'il devait sûrement savoir des choses qui pourraient potentiellement m'aider dans l'accomplissement de ma mission de recherche de nouvelles possibilités pour ton film. Cet homme devait connaître quelque chose qui pourrait indirectement être transposé dans les formes et les trajectoires propres à ton travail, par le truchement poétique d'instables chaînes de signifiants et de promesses réitérées. Monsieur Péchalat, l'homme qui vit sur l'île, nous a accueilli chaleureusement dans sa maison. Plusieurs chats, roux, si je me souviens bien, étaient blottis un peu partout. Il était sincère et aimable, et très enthousiaste à l'idée de répondre à mes questions. Des questions simples, sans ordre particulier : sa vie sur l'île, la vie de l'île, et les souvenirs partagés entre l'homme et son île, tout ce qui pourrait m'aider à récolter quelques faits que nous pourrions adapter plus tard dans le scénario. J'étais très curieux de la période où l'île est devenue une île, des rêves qu'il avait en dormant sur une île, et de n'importe quelle scène ou image dont il pourrait se souvenir en détail.
On dit que l'eau aussi a une mémoire, et je me demandais s'il avait eu l'occasion d'en être le témoin. J'étais curieux de ces scènes qui émergent parfois de notre mémoire si parfaitement détaillées, comme ces brefs moments qui se sont passés de nombreuses années en arrière et qui ne vous avaient pas traversé l'esprit depuis un demi-siècle et qui, d'un coup, nous reviennent comme si cela avait eu lieu deux minutes auparavant. Ou peut-être dans deux minutes : le futur doit bien se répandre dans le passé comme l'eau se mélange à l'eau, n'est-ce pas ? Et ce n'est pas seulement à cause de ce glissement du futur dans le passé que tu ne dois pas m'en vouloir de ne pas tenir mes délais. Tout d'abord, je suis chrono-dyslexique ; ensuite ma fille à quelque chose qui ne va pas pour la première fois de sa vie. Elle ne veut pas me dire ce que c'est, mais ça me distrait encore plus que d'habitude. Hier, elle m'a raccroché au nez alors que j'essayais de lui raconter une histoire pour la consoler avec la première image qui m'était venue à l'esprit. J'avais pensé que le sujet de cette image était raccord avec toute notre conversation. C'était la photo en couleurs d'un crocodile dans les pages de l'Encyclopédie Soviétique qu'il m'était arrivé de feuilleter quand j'étais enfant. « Il peut encore mordre », j'ai dit en riant à ma fille dans l'espoir de lui remonter le moral. C'est à ce moment qu'elle a raccroché.
La chrono-dyslexie est plus facile à comprendre : c'est une maladie chronique qui s'apparenterait à la capacité de voyager dans le temps,

mais de façon involontaire. La dernière fois tu m'as demandé « quand » j'étais à l'heure, et je n'ai pas pu te répondre avec précision, tu t'en souviens ? C'est ce qui m'arrive : la drôle de sensation d'être dans un état sans début ni fin, et pourtant chaque fois que quelque chose se termine j'ai la sensation que ça ne recommencera jamais plus. Ça me rend prématurément mélancolique.
Le voyage dans le temps repose sur de nombreux paradoxes. L'un d'eux est la conviction que le passé (comme le futur) reste immobile et ne change pas (comme une sorte de bulle monadique gelée ou un fossile). Selon cette hypothèse, si quelqu'un de l'année 2012 retourne à Berlin pendant l'été 1989, il trouvera le Mur encore intact. Mais, des allemands en colère seront déjà rassemblés pour l'abattre. Les événements qui se déroulent sont une répétition familière de ce qui est connu de tous. Mais imagine ce qui se passerait si en remontant le temps tu découvrais que toutes les choses du passé ont tout autant changé que ta propre vie, mais ni dans la direction à laquelle tu t'attendais ni dans l'ordre des événements qui ont conduit au passé que tu crois connaître. Dans ces conditions, on ne passe plus d'une époque à l'autre comme on change de morceau sur son lecteur mp3. A la place, il ne nous reste plus qu'à utiliser nos propres artifices et peut-être laisser plus de temps au temps.

« Alors, depuis quand vivez-vous là, Monsieur ? » j'ai demandé à Monsieur Péchalat. « Votre histoire sera peut-être enregistrée non seulement par le vent qui souffle dans les arbres de l'île, mais sur la surface du film de Rosa Barba. »
« Je suis là depuis 1936 – Ça fait un bail ! – rester au même endroit tout ce temps. »
« Vous êtes né ici ? »
« Non, je suis né à Eymoutiers. »
« Pourquoi êtes-vous venu vivre ici ? »
« C'est le travail. Je suis venu avec mes parents qui avaient pris une ferme dans l'île ; l'île n'était pas une île, il n'y avait pas d'eau tout autour. On a continué à travailler chez Mme Pascal. Je suis resté chez elle, quand le barrage s'est fait, elle m'a gardé. Parce qu'il y a beaucoup de gens qui sont partis, les gens qui sont des villages sous le lac sont partis et moi, j'étais sur une montagne et je ne suis pas parti, je suis resté à Vassivière. J'ai continué à travailler pour elle jusqu'à sa mort et même après. Et après le Syndicat est venu et il a pris l'île. Ça a changé la vie, c'était pas du tout pareil, ça a changé beaucoup de choses. C'est très difficile… Je ne sais pas comment vous expliquer ça. La vie a été bouleversée, ce n'étais plus le même travail. On a gardé la propriété, on avait les bêtes, on avait bien des choses. Autrement, bien sûr, ça fait de la peine, quand on voit monter l'eau doucement. Quand le barrage a été fini, on voyait monter l'eau doucement et on a eu beaucoup d'envahisseurs à ce moment-là, parce que ça a fait monter la vermine : les rats, les serpents… Ça les rapprochait. Les serpents se promenaient dans la cour. Il fallait voir ça, c'est quelque chose de formidable. On disait la vermine mais les lièvres, les lapins – tout le gibier – sont remontés ici avec les serpents et les rats ; ils sont venus et on a vraiment été envahis. »
« En quelle année le lac a-t-il été rempli ? »
« Ils ont commencé les travaux en 1946 et le lac a été mis en eau en 1949, la veille de Noël, mais les travaux n'étaient pas finis. Le barrage n'était fait qu'à moitié, mais l'eau ne les gênait pas pour travailler. Le matériel venait par voix aérienne. C'était comme les téléphériques que vous voyez à la montagne, ça amenait des wagonnets qui déchargeaient le ciment sur le barrage.»
« Pendant trois ans, ils ont préparé le lieu avant que l'eau n'arrive. Que s'est-il passé de 1946 à 1949 ? »
« Ils travaillaient à la main. Il n'y avait pas beaucoup de matériel mécanique, juste un petit peu ; on faisait beaucoup à la main. Il y avaient 3500 ouvriers à l'époque. »

(Rosa, ne sois pas surprise s'il nous faut trois ans pour produire le scénario. J'aimerais que nous soyons 3 500 travailleurs capables de transformer les quelques possibles en fondations pour le présent. Mais à la place nous avons seulement Francesco, jusqu'au cou dans les archives, et moi, parachuté dans cette forêt. Peut-être que nos efforts vont converger, mais pas nécessairement dans la même version de l'histoire. Est-ce que tu penses que nous sommes reliés par la croyance dans le potentiel caché du monde qui nous entoure ? Je n'en suis pas certain. Je suis même assez sceptique à l'encontre de tous ces artistes qui affirment qu'ils produisent des potentialités. Je pense qu'ils sont paresseux et qu'ils intellectualisent trop. C'était comme si j'affirmais que je produis de la paresse. Je ne le dirais jamais, bien sûr. Mais s'il nous faut trois ans pour produire un scénario ; dis-toi bien que c'est un signe de ma fidélité à accomplir cette quête plutôt qu'un échec, Dieu nous en préserve.)

« Est-ce que le barrage a été envisagé avant la Seconde Guerre mondiale ? »
« Non, ils ont commencé immédiatement après. Il y avait l'Indochine. La guerre était à peine finie quand ils ont commencé parce qu'il n'y avait pas assez de lumière, pas assez de chauffage central. Maintenant il y a des bois partout, mais avant c'était des landes de bruyères, les bêtes qu'on élevait, il y avait très peu de forêts. Les bêtes étaient élevées en petits groupes, pas en grands troupeaux comme maintenant. Il y avait aussi beaucoup de plantations, du seigle, de l'avoine, des pommes de terre… il y en avaient vraiment beaucoup à l'époque. »
« Entre 1946 et 1949, quand le gouvernement a proposé aux gens d'aller ailleurs, pourquoi avez-vous décidé de rester ? »
« J'étais sur une montagne ; ceux qui étaient au-dessous, ils ont bien été obligés de partir de force. Moi je ne les gênais pas, c'était seulement ceux qui étaient dans l'eau. »
« Vous n'avez pas été inquiet de vous retrouver dans une situation un peu isolée. Comme échoué sur l'île ? »
« Je n'y ai même pas pensé. Ça a changé la vie ; une page a été tournée comme on dit. D'une certaine façon, on est allé de l'avant. Ce qui m'a le plus touché, c'est la vidange en 1995. Revoir les terres toutes vides... C'est là que cela m'a fait un coup de revoir le pays que j'ai vécu. J'ai eu la chance de le voir en hélicoptère, pour pouvoir expliquer où il y avait un pont, un moulin, une église... »

(Je voudrais suggérer que nous ajoutions le Centre international d'art et du paysage à la liste des lieux qui ont été engloutis par les eaux. Notre scénario devrait culminer par un désastre et introduire une histoire alternative à l'aide d'un montage en parallèle. Nous n'aurons pas à être trop littéral, mais nous devons exercer notre droit à créer une alternative. Le bâtiment d'Aldo Rossi et de Xavier Fabre s'inscrit dans le paysage d'une manière qui n'est pas si différente de celle d'une église, ou d'un moulin englouti. Je vois très bien des poissons en train de nager autour d'un autel et s'arrêter dans la salle qui abritait jadis des projecteurs 35 millimètres suspendus dans les airs. Peut-être que tu peux demander à ton assistant si l'on peut attacher une caméra sur la tête d'un poisson ?)

« Avant que l'eau n'arrive, ils avaient tout détruit ? »
« Ils ont tout cassé. Les arbres ont été tous coupés, les maisons dynamitées. On ne voit plus que des petits tas de pierres Ils ont dynamité pour ne pas gêner les bateaux. A Vaugelade, il y avait le moulin qui était intact et, ailleurs, l'église ; mais je ne me souviens plus où. L'eau a certainement tout détruit maintenant.»
« Etes-vous allé dans cette église avant la guerre ? »
« Non, jamais. Je ne sais pas où c'est. Certains disaient qu'il y avait un cimetière au fond de l'eau, mais ce n'est pas vrai. Vassivière, c'était juste un hameau. Le vrai Vassivière, c'est ici. »

(Je crois que nous devons ramener du fond de l'eau plus que des associations d'idées. On doit travailler sur l'intensité de la parallaxe. Peut-être que nous pourrions nous focaliser sur les changements, les moments de transition, la solitude. Le souvenir de quelque chose de lointain, comme cet homme qui plonge dans l'eau en 1949, qui convergerait avec quelque chose de plus récent, comme le souvenir de Noël dernier ou une chanson de George Michael. Ou peut-être quelque chose d'encore plus proche, comme une chanson que tu aurais entendu ce matin. Tu t'en souviens ? S'agirait-il alors de futurs possibles qui n'auraient pas eu lieu ? D'univers alternatifs explorés par le jeu des probabilités mathématiques ? Ou bien encore de pièces de théâtre qui résulteraient d'une séance de spiritisme où l'on aurait essayé de ranimer les fictions potentielles présentes au cœur de toute cette eau emprisonnée dans le lac ?

« En trois jours, l'eau s'est étendue partout. Comment était-ce pour vous ? Parce que le paysage a changé immédiatement, n'est-ce pas ? »
« Bien sûr ! On le voyait disparaître. Les souches qui étaient coupées, l'eau était passée dessus, on ne les voyait plus. On était content sans l'être vraiment ; on ne savait pas ce que c'était. On n'avait jamais vu de barrage. Les gens n'étaient pas contre ce barrage, parce qu'ils sortaient de la guerre. Ils avaient tellement souffert que ça s'est passé sans problèmes. Mais après il a fallu la police pour protéger les sites d'autres barrages. Les gens ne voulaient pas céder leur terrain. Je me souviens d'un projet de barrage en Creuse, bien après la guerre, que les gens ont empêché. Aujourd'hui, il n'y a que les maisons qui tombent en ruine, et il y a des gens qui y reviennent mais le terrain appartient toujours à EDF.»
« Aviez-vous des amis que vous n'avez jamais revu ? »
« Il y en a que j'ai perdu complètement ; ils sont partis dans le fin fond de la Creuse, dans les villes. Surtout les femmes ; elles sont parties après la guerre. Elles ne sont pas restées dans les campagnes. Elles en avaient marre de l'agriculture en vieillissant, et même si elles n'étaient pas vieilles, elles sont parties dans les villes : Paris, Lyon. Je les ai perdues de vue. A part certaines qui reviennent me voir, qui me connaissent, mais moi je ne les connais plus. Elles sont vieilles. Ce sont surtout les femmes qui sont parties en ville, parce que le travail ici est pénible. C'est très pénible d'être cultivateur, voilà pourquoi elles sont parties. »

(Imagine que tu es la dernière créature vivante sur la terre : ton amour du vide est lié à son destin, tes histoires ne seront plus jamais racontées (même par quelqu'un d'autre), et ta voix compte pour rien. « Vous êtes la dernière personne sur terre », ça évoque une étiquette de mise en garde. Mais soudain tes yeux repèrent un moustique gorgé de sang sur le mur blanc de la pièce dans laquelle tu viens d'entrer. A qui appartient ce sang ? D'où vient-il ? Quelles informations contient-il ? Est-il porteur d'un message des générations qui vivaient avant la fin de l'humanité ? Ou bien un rétrovirus à réactiver ? Prolongera-t-il la fin du monde ou peut-il en inverser le cours ? Peut-il, par accident, te rendre immortelle : toi, qui était la dernière créature sur terre il n'y a pas une minute ? On pourrait développer cette scène dans l'un des espaces du Centre d'art.)

« Donc au tout début, il n'y avait pas de pont ? Comment faisiez-vous ? »
« Le pont montait en même temps que l'eau. Tous les travaux d'EDF avaient commencé en même temps. Tout se faisait au même moment, comme il y avaient 3500 ouvriers. La passerelle, le barrage, les routes, tout se faisait en même temps...»
« Quand avez-vous eu la télévision ? »
« Bien plus tard, longtemps après le barrage. Je ne pouvais pas me la payer, c'était trop cher. »
« Est-ce que vous alliez au cinéma ? »
« Pour aller au cinéma, il fallait aller à Eymoutiers, c'était trop loin : 15 kilomètres à pied. Après, il y en a un qui a ouvert à Beaumont, mais il n'était pas grand. Maintenant, c'est facile. On prend la voiture et on va loin ; on peut aller au cinéma à Limoges, même si, en définitive, on y va pas. A Eymoutiers, il y en a qui y vont parce qu'il y a un film toutes les semaines, je crois. Avant il n'y avait pas les voitures comme maintenant ; c'était tout à fait rare, les voitures.»
« Quel était votre film préféré ? »
« Les films, je ne me souviens pas de tous. »

(Ces films oubliés me rappellent une fête qui avait lieu au bout d'une autoroute inachevée en Allemagne. Elle était organisée par les fans de techno au début de l'époque des raves, et elle avait attiré un large éventail de créatures cyber glam du milieu des années 90 ; si étranges que toute la scène aurait très bien pu être un décor de film. En fait, quand la police est arrivée pour faire arrêter la fête, les raveurs on dit qu'ils tournaient un film. Les policiers n'ont même pas cherché à savoir s'il s'agissait d'un film qui se passait dans le futur ou bien quelque chose d'autre. La crédibilité cinématographique a sauvé la fête. Le film des raveurs n'a bien sûr jamais été filmé, mais cette fête reste très présente dans ma mémoire du fait qu'elle n'ait jamais été filmée. Juste au bord de cette *autobahn* inachevée, il y avait une frontière ballardienne. « Nous sommes tous des films », tu te souviens de Terrence McKenna ?)

« Tout à l'heure, vous avez parlé de ce moment où les animaux, la vermine, sont arrivés sur l'île ? Que s'est-t-il passé exactement ? »
« C'est l'eau qui a fait se rapprocher les bêtes, les serpents, les rats. Les rats ont été les plus embêtants : ils nous mangeaient les pommes de terres dans les champs, le grain. Il a fallu qu'on les empoisonne parce qu'il y en avait vraiment trop. Mais les rats n'étaient pas méchants comme les serpents. Les rats mordent, mais ils ne tuent pas ; alors que le serpent tuait les bêtes, piquait les gens. »
« Mais les serpents ne sont-ils pas bons pour tuer les rats ? »
« Oui, ils les bouffaient mais pas tous : il y en avait trop. Et puis, les serpents, j'en avais peur. Il y avaient des aspics, des vipères, des couleuvres… On dit que la couleuvre n'est pas méchante, mais elles ont du venin quand même. J'ai vu une femme tomber raide morte ; beaucoup ont été piqués… J'ai vu cette femme tomber : elle portait des javels de blés qu'il fallait lier à la main et, en passant sa main, le serpent l'a piquée et elle est morte. Quand le médecin est arrivé, elle était morte. Quand on est piqué on en garde le souvenir. Autrefois, il y avait des guérisseurs, mais je parle d'il y a très longtemps. Quand un serpent vous mordait, je ne sais pas ce qu'ils faisaient, on ne me l'a jamais dit ; ils faisaient quelque chose de secret. Quoi, je n'en sais rien, mais ils guérissaient les gens. C'est plus vieux que moi ce temps-là, je ne l'ai pas connu. Mais si on ne voyait pas cette personne, on mourait. »

(Je pense que nous devrions demander à Francesco d'élaborer quelque chose sur l'imagerie des serpents à partir de serpentins de pellicule sur le sol. Il devrait expliquer à tout le monde comment ils ondoient et ramassent la poussière de métaphores. Nous pourrions aussi profiter de cette opportunité pour faire allusion au fantôme de l'*Opisthostoma Vermiculum*. C'est le nom d'une étrange créature que des scientifiques ont découvert il y a peu. Cependant, quand la créature a été mise au jour par sa découverte, elle s'est éteinte. C'est un exemple assez courant de relation entre la science et un phénomène inconnu : l'appareil déployé pour l'identification du phénomène tue son objet d'étude. Ce n'est donc pas étonnant que même le nom de la créature ait disparu de Google.)

« Pourquoi les gens choisissaient un guérisseur et pas un docteur ? »
« Parce que les médecins ne pouvaient rien faire ; il n'y avait pas encore d'injections à cette époque. »
« Il y a bien une petite île qui s'appelle l'île aux serpents ? »
« On lui a donné ce nom comme ça, pour faire beau. Il y a eu des serpents sur les sept îles ; plus l'île était grande et plus il y en avait. »
« Est-ce que le lac gèle parfois ? »
« Oui ! Je l'ai traversé sur la glace quand elle faisait 40 centimètres d'épaisseur par moins 27° C, en 1954. Ça faisait un joli plancher. Quand le barrage se remplissait, il n'y avait pas de bruit ; mais quand il descendait – quand ça cassait – ça faisait un bruit la nuit, comme des coups de tonnerre. On entendait les cassures… c'était formidable. Cette année, la glace était aussi fine qu'une feuille de papier.»

(La description de ce son devrait être traduite à l'aide d'un dispositif émanant directement de l'eau, peut-être un autre type de son ou une fréquence qui fracasserait notre indifférence, nos attentes et nos rêves. Est-ce que je t'ai raconté que j'avais rêvé plusieurs fois d'écrans d'iPhone cassés ces derniers temps ? Encore et encore, j'ai rêvé de ces écrans brisés de l'immersion : surfaces brisées d'une perspective infinie, sans profondeur, glace brisée du toucher, métaphores brisées. Par contre les sonneries étaient intactes ; elles me réveillaient à chaque fois.

« Vous vous souvenez quand le Centre d'art a été construit ? »
« Oui ! Il y eu des discutions autour de ça, mais de là à dire l'année où ça a commencé … Je ne me rappelle pas. Pourtant j'y ai travaillé, pour la construction, pour les sculptures, pour amener du matériel. »
« Quand le Centre d'art est arrivé, avez-vous pensé que quelque chose de plus intéressant allait se passer sur l'île ? »
« Je ne peux pas le dire. Ce sont des choses qui me dépassent, c'est plus fort que moi. C'est un peu spécial, le Centre d'art. Ils y font des choses incroyables. C'est une autre vie qui me dépasse. »
« Vous allez y voir les expositions ? »
« En principe, chaque fois. »
« Vous ne vous êtes jamais ennuyé, en vivant ici sur l'île ? »
« En ce moment, j'ai bien le cafard, mais il faut bien le prendre. Je n'ai plus de voiture pour sortir. J'ai fait un tonneau. J'ai eu l'accident à Pierrefitte, après le village. En plein jour, je me suis endormi et je suis rentré dans le talus et la voiture s'est retournée. Moi, pas un brin de mal et la voiture cassée. Moi, j'aurai peut-être guéri tout seul, mais il n'y a plus de voiture. Ils m'ont retiré le permis, parce que j'ai eu l'accident et que je suis trop vieux ; mais je vais bien essayer d'en trouver une autre. Je n'ai fait arriver de mal à personne, mais ils ne veulent plus m'assurer. »
« Il faut reprendre l'hélicoptère !… Quand vous étiez dans l'hélicoptère, avez-vous ressenti quelque chose ? »
« Rien du tout. J'étais heureux ; c'est bien de voir le pays que j'ai connu, parce que le lac, il fait 1000 hectares… Ça fait une sacré distance ; ça a duré plus d'une heure. J'étais content. C'est un joli voyage pour moi. Tous les endroits, tous les ponts, les routes, tout… C'était comme être sur la lune : la terre avait séché, il y avaient des craquelures comme dans le désert, assez grandes pour y passer la main. C'était nu, il n'y avait plus de verdure. Il n'y avait plus rien, que des souches qui avaient été coupées et des maisons écrasées. Bien sûr, ça rend triste d'un côté, mais pour celui qui l'a connu, qui y a vécu et qui voit tous les recoins… Je sais que je ne le reverrai jamais comme ça. »
« Est-ce qu'il y a beaucoup de gens qui viennent vous voir, comme nous aujourd'hui, pour vous parler de l'histoire de l'île ? »
« Oui, j'en ai eu beaucoup, j'en ai beaucoup moins. Ça les intéresse moins ou plus du tout, peut-être. Autrefois, il en venait beaucoup. Parfois, cela durait toute la journée.»

(Rosa, je te le dis, ton film sur l'île devrait durer toute la journée … Une projection d'une journée pleine de choses qui se sont déjà produites et de choses qui ne sont pas encore arrivées, dans le même rayon de lumière, tu t'en souviens … ?

DE LA PERFORMANCE DES TRACES QUE NOUS LAISSONS DANS L'HISTOIRE

NATAŠA PETREŠIN-BACHELEZ

Les expositions de Rosa Barba ont été qualifiées, dans des textes récents, « d'installations chorégraphiées[1]». Si l'on peut en effet affirmer que Rosa Barba transpose les notions d'installation cinétique et de performeur directement sur le projecteur de cinéma et dans sa caméra (en particulier dans les films *They Shine*, 2007, où l'on suit la rotation des panneaux solaires installés dans le désert de Mojave, et *The Long Road*, 2010, où une caméra aérienne dessine les circonvolutions d'une piste d'essais automobiles désaffectée), l'idée de chorégraphie doit être entendue dans son acception la plus large, en laissant de côté ses racines grecques d'*écriture de la danse* pour n'en retenir que l'art de la mise en scène, même s'il s'agit toujours de définir et d'organiser des mouvements dans l'espace. Cette entrée en matière nous permet de faire émerger une analogie intéressante avec la relation de travail que Rosa Barba instaure avec des personnes ou des groupes de personnes dans au moins trois de ses films : *Panzano* (2000), *Outwardly from Earth's Center* (2007) and *The Empirical Effect* (2010), dans lesquels cette relation devient particulièrement tangible et vient s'incarner dans des scènes de groupe où alternent dialogues, moments parlés et gestuelle.

Pour *Panzano*, le premier film que Rosa Barba a réalisé en collaboration avec Ulrike Molsen, les deux artistes ont travaillé pendant plusieurs mois avec deux hommes et une femme vivant dans une communauté psychothérapeutique expérimentale située dans un village toscan. Les trois protagonistes que l'on observe à l'image, et qui sont – comme l'écrit Ian White[2] – « orchestrés » dans des rôles flous et interchangeables (incarnant parfois un couple et leur enfant ou suggérant à d'autres moments que ce nous voyons pourrait être simplement la vie quotidienne et les conversations d'une famille atypique), sont en réalité en train de rejouer leur expérience de vie dans le village. Cependant, en regardant la manière dont se nouent et se dénouent leurs relations, le spectateur commence alors à s'interroger sur le processus de tournage lui-même et notamment à quel moment les deux réalisatrices ont-elles su faire doucement émerger la trame de leur récit tout en laissant leurs interlocuteurs se comporter et s'exprimer comme ils le souhaitaient.

L'étrange île suédoise de Gotska Sandön est le sujet du film *Outwardly from Earth's Center* où une situation réelle – celle de cette île qui dérive lentement vers le pôle nord – est habitée par une fiction dans laquelle les habitants s'emploient à mettre en œuvre un procédé d'arrimage de l'île pour prévenir son inéluctable destin géologique. Le sujet du film est tout d'abord évoqué à travers plusieurs monologues, filmés à la manière d'entretiens télévisés, qui nous permettent de faire connaissance avec le Gardien de Phare, l'Architecte, les Archéologues, le Politicien et l'Archiviste, dans leurs contextes respectifs et présentant chacun les outils dont ils disposent pour agir. La scène avec l'Architecte offre une nouvelle analogie très claire avec le format de la conférence-performance, où l'Architecte lui-même apparaît sur une scène, dans un décor d'écrans blancs sur lesquels des images sont projetées, mais où ce qu'il dit et montre est en décalage avec le récit que nous entendons. Une séquence plus performative du film commence ensuite, une partie dans laquelle la musique électronique et le paysage sonore composés par Jan St. Werner et Folke Rabe offrent une toile de fond inquiétante au mouvement physique, lent et appliqué des habitants qui déplacent des branches sur la plage, tirent des cordages depuis la forêt jusqu'aux bateaux qui s'éloignent ensuite plus loin dans la mer. C'est cette même scène, filmée depuis le ciel, qui vient clore le film. La caméra filme les cordes en train d'être tirées, oscillant et tremblant, luttant contre leur propre poids, elle semble presque flotter avec elles alors qu'elles sont hissées à bord et tendues, elle donne à voir des images spectaculaires tant sur le plan de la composition esthétique que de la qualité performative. Dans le texte de Ian White, cité ci-dessus, la scène en question lui évoque « les amis et performeurs dans *Wind* de Joan Jonas[3] », sa performance filmée de 1968 où un groupe de performeurs marche dans un paysage battu par le vent.

Etrangement, un autre film de Rosa Barba, où l'on retrouve des tentatives d'apprivoisement de la nature, met en scène des performances collectives similaires. Ici, ce sont les souvenirs des protagonistes qui dialoguent avec un scénario où il est question d'un violent réveil du Vésuve. Pour *The Empirical Effect*, Rosa a réuni et a travaillé avec deux groupes différents parmi lesquels figuraient beaucoup d'habitants de la « zone rouge », la zone située en contrebas du volcan et où le risque est constant, ainsi que quelques témoins de la dernière éruption catastrophique du volcan en 1944. L'ancien observatoire (Osservatorio Vesuviano) à Naples, non loin du cratère du volcan, est utilisé comme plateforme scénographique pendant la première moitié du filme et fonctionne ainsi comme un point de référence de la performance qui s'y déroule comme dans un théâtre de la mémoire. Un petit groupe de personnes âgées se déplace dans l'observatoire au milieu des sismographes. Ils semblent communiquer entre eux autour de la maquette du Vésuve sans que l'on puisse cependant comprendre le moindre mot. Des moutons marchent parmi eux avant de s'immobiliser et d'occuper leur place avec les acteurs sur une grande carte de l'Italie. Avec l'utilisation de cette dernière, l'artiste attribue une dimension métaphorique à la figure du volcan : nous sommes en présence d'un élément de la relation instable que la société italienne actuelle entretient avec la politique. L'un des hommes du groupe amène de vieilles machines que les autres déballent et démontent, ils feuillettent des livres et regardent des photographies en noir et blanc qui évoquent un fonds d'archives que l'on n'arrive pas à identifier et que l'on retrouve dans la vidéo sous la forme des films des frères Lumière sur Naples. Dans les propositions fictionnelles de Rosa Barba, la volonté de montrer et d'énumérer ce matériel d'archive de manière à renforcer la crédibilité de la narration et à stimuler notre curiosité quant à son authenticité est déjà mise en œuvre dans *Outwardly from Earth's Center* avec le personnage de l'Archiviste. Le film continue avec une séquence fortement performative où l'on retrouve le groupe, dans un pièce qui ressemble à une salle de classe, en train de regarder un diaporama ou un film, mais l'on ne voit qu'eux et leurs corps en guise d'écrans de projection puisque des images indiscernables – mais très probablement à nouveau du matériel d'archive – se reflètent sur leurs visages, leurs lunettes et leurs corps assis. Nous sommes les témoins d'une performance silencieuse où leur propre mémoire est renvoyée sur leur propre corps. L'artiste décrit elle-même l'ambiance dans la communauté qu'elle décrit dans le film comme « une société [qui] vit dans un haut degré de tension, mais qui pourtant semble paralysée et somnambule ». L'attention portée à ce groupe laisse place à une foule sortant de leur maison et descendant les rues en regardant le ciel comme si l'éruption avait commencé.[4] Alors que l'on peut s'attendre à voir le chaos et la lave en fusion dans la scène suivante, Rosa Barba décide de calmer le tempo avec une dernière séquence où l'on voit le premier groupe de protagonistes, sur une grande terrasse de l'observatoire, en train de danser et de chanter de vieilles chansons. Ils s'immobilisent finalement en tournant le dos à la caméra. On peut également assimiler la dernière scène à une performance : filmée de loin, avec un montage qui répète les plans avec le même point de vue, mais où une personne se retourne légèrement au milieu du groupe immobile.

Ces « performances collectives[5] » ont été spécifiquement enregistrées et mises en œuvre pour le film. Elles suivent un ensemble précis de négociations et d'improvisation. Dans la terminologie associée à la danse contemporaine et à la performance, les notions de chorégraphie et d'improvisation ne s'opposent plus puisque l'improvisation peut être incluse dans des pièces chorégraphiques, tout comme elle peut elle-même être chorégraphiée. L'organisation du groupe de ces « acteurs », comme Rosa préfère les appeler, dans un ensemble performatif cohérent est, de la même façon, le résultat d'un processus où l'artiste leur raconte sa manière de concevoir le récit et le film et où ils sont ensuite invités à (re)jouer en fonction de leur personnalité propre, de ce qu'il représente pour l'artiste et de leur sentiment sur la manière dont le récit devrait être représenté dans le film : « J'invite les gens à se réunir et à jouer leur souvenirs (sur la base de faits et de documents) dans une sorte de performance collective ; c'est l'apogée de la partie fictionnelle des films. Je leur parle de mes idées à propos du film, mais je leur dis surtout pourquoi ça m'intéresse de travailler avec eux sur ce film. Nous en parlons beaucoup pendant le tournage lui-même, très peu au début quand je les rencontre. C'est un peu comme une réaction chimique entre eux et moi. Dès que la caméra tourne, l'espace devient une scène et ils commencent à jouer pour moi.[6] » Les personnages qui apparaissent dans les différents décors des films évoqués plus haut ne sont jamais joués par des acteurs professionnels, mais par des personnes qui ont un lien profond avec le lieu ou la situation décrite dans le film. Les personnes choisies « portent en eux l'histoire du lieu, et je les invite à raconter cette histoire dans un cadre performatif que j'instaure. Ce cadre est simplement une esquisse de départ qu'il vont compléter ou détruire pendant le tournage. Je leur donne des instructions, mais ils sont libres d'en faire ce qu'ils veulent[7] ».

Particulièrement utilisée dans le film *The Empirical Effect*, la méthode consistant à inviter des personnes à jouer leur propre souvenir tout en imaginant une fiction narrative se rapproche des développements récents du champ chorégraphique qui s'intéresse à la production de sensations kinesthésiques et à la relation affective avec le spectateur à travers l'utilisation de l'imagination et du langage dans le processus chorégraphique. Mette Ingvartsen, Alice Chauchat ou Eszter Salamon font tous trois partie de la jeune génération de chorégraphes qui mettent l'accent sur l'usage du langage de manière à stimuler l'imagination et la sensation sur un mouvement particulier chez le performeur lui-même. Je citerais deux exemples où l'on peut voir une correspondance avec le « processus chorégraphique » dans les films de Rosa Barba. Dans le travail de création du spectacle de Salamon *NVSBL* (2006) où quatre danseuses avancent lentement sur la scène au point de rendre leurs mouvements imperceptibles,

> « action et sensation se fondent pour le performeur en un processus unique, de même que pour le spectateur, mais dans un ordre différent : pour le performeur, les actions partent de la sensation alors que pour le spectateur la perception demande un tel effort qu'elle est vécue comme un processus actif… Le problème auquel le performeur est confronté était d'imaginer et de feindre le mouvement, l'endroit précis du corps où il est initié, sa qualité propre, la forme qu'il pourrait prendre dans un autre contexte. Le système qui pouvait produire une vision quasi-physiologique de l'intérieur du corps et qui, de fait, nécessitait de rendre vivantes ces sensations avec des images et des fictions à propos du mouvement, c'est le Body Mind Centering (BMC)… Au-delà du BMC, les performeurs ont appliqué une autre technique d'expression, de manière à composer leurs expressions faciales et à enrichir la qualité des mouvements du corps dans son ensemble. Ils invoquaient des images et des expressions, la mémoire qu'ils pouvaient avoir de la dynamique de certaines humeurs et émotions, ou bien ils replaçaient les mouvements qu'ils étaient en train de faire dans un autre environnement, avec une qualité qu'ils ne pouvaient pas avoir sur l'instant, mais seulement virtuellement sur scène ; par exemple, analyser les sensations lorsque l'on effectue ce mouvement en courant, se rappeler de la sensation de la course, tout en ne courant pas[8].»

La chorégraphe danoise Mette Ingvartsen a écrit un court manifeste à propos de la *Site-specific performance*, qui fait à nouveau écho a l'esprit du lieu et à sa mémoire telle que Rosa Barba l'utilise dans ses films :

> « 1. Une *Site-specific performance* met l'accent sur l'utilisation d'un environnement existant comme le point de départ de sa création et, de ce fait, l'utilisation de cet environnement comme une toile de fond, un décor de scène, voir comme un performeur.
> 2. Une *Site-specific performance* permet au processus artistique de naître d'une situation sociale et / ou politique, sans pour autant se réduire à la reproduction de cette situation.
> 3. Une *Site-specific performance* réactive son lieu d'accueil et en offre un nouveau « panorama ».
> 4. Une *Site-specific performance* est conditionnée et influencée par un espace particulier et devrait conditionner et influencer ce lieu en retour.
> 5. Une *Site-specific performance* renonce à l'autonomie de l'art et à la neutralité de l'espace théâtral.
> 6. Une *Site-specific performance* crée une fiction à l'intérieur de la réalité d'un lieu, suggérant au spectateur de remettre en cause ses perceptions « naturelles ».
> 7. Une *Site-specific performance* se fond dans l'environnement où elle se déroule et devient indiscernable de la réalité même du lieu.

8. Une *Site-specific performance* produit du doute sur ce qui appartient à la situation performée par opposition à ce qui appartient à la situation existant au préalable.
9. Une *Site-specific performance* ne peut pas être rejouée dans le sens où elle fait partie intégrante de l'endroit où elle a été créée. Cependant, les stratégies utilisées peuvent être réutilisées ou adaptées à d'autres contextes et produire de nouvelles spécificités en fonction du lieu.
10. Une *Site-specific performance* concerne et traite de formats, de conventions et d'attentes envers les expressions performées, de la même manière qu'elle questionne les logiques de reproduction, de circulation et de co-modification des œuvres de performance[9] ».

Dans ses deux films les plus récents, cette forme très particulière de « site-specific performance » s'éloigne des gens pour s'étendre à la caméra de cinéma (*A Private Tableaux*, 2010) et sur les objets d'art des réserves de musées (*The Hidden Conference: About the Discontinuous History of Things We See and Don't See*, 2011). Dans *A Private Tableaux,* le mouvement de la caméra est « scénarisé » par les lignes, les marques, les dessins et les éraflures laissés au fil des années par les ingénieurs et les scientifiques lors de recherches sur la stabilité des constructions souterraines. La caméra fait ressortir des détails de dessins muraux accompagnés par des sons électroniques, puis par des sons semblant émaner d'un chantier de construction, et elle répond de manière kinesthésique au balancement de la lumière qui lui permet de capter des formes que l'on devine dans l'obscurité.
The Hidden Conference, bien que muet, n'en demeure pas moins un film performatif qui évoque les dialogues et les discussions que les œuvres d'art dans les réserves des musées pourraient entretenir entre eux. Il s'agit d'un travail en cours qui confirme la volonté de Rosa Barba de poursuivre son investigation des archives et des lieux de stockage de la culture. Au début, la caméra tisse lentement un récit entre différentes petites sculptures sur les étagères, dans une atmosphère de gros plans et de clair-obscur, comme s'il s'agissait de présenter au spectateur les personnages principaux. Dans la seconde partie du film, la réserve devient elle-même un décor où les entrées et les sorties de scène sont jouées par les parois métalliques sur lesquelles les tableaux sont conservés. Le paysage sonore, comme toujours avec les films et les installations de Rosa Barba, demeure un acteur essentiel dans le processus de mise en fiction.

A travers ces exemples, on comprend la manière dont Rosa Barba cherche à rendre visible, comme elle le dit elle-même, la façon dont notre paysage intérieur interagit avec les paysages naturels qu'elle dépeint dans ses films, mais aussi comment elle s'intéresse aux phénomènes et aux traces que nous laissons dans l'histoire.

Notes

1. « Dans ce cette exposition, l'installation soigneusement chorégraphiée de Barba divise l'attention du visiteur entre l'image projetée et le projecteur lui-même et pose la question de savoir qui de l'un ou de l'autre est la narration et qui est le narrateur. » Extrait du communiqué de presse de l'exposition de Rosa Barba à la Tate Modern (2010-2011).
http://www.tate.org.uk/modern/exhibitions/rosabarba/default.shtm
2. Ian White dans un texte sur Rosa Barba, in *Camera Austria*, n°101, 2088.
3. Cf. note n°2.
4. Ces scènes ont été filmées pendant les exercices annuels d'évacuation massive d'urgence, obligatoires pour tous les habitant de la zone rouge.
5. Barba a elle-même utilisé ce terme lors de sa conférence pendant le séminaire Something You Should Know à l'EHESS en mai 2010 à Paris. La formulation exacte de Barba a été le déclencheur du présent essai et je voudrais la remercier chaleureusement pour tous nos échanges sur cette notion.
6. Rosa Barba dans un entretien avec l'auteur, Novembre 2010.
7. Ibid.
8.Bojana Cveji: « Researching: A Public Interview with Eszter Salamon », in *6M1L*, everybodys publications, 2009, pp.84-85 Le Body Mind Centering est une approche globale de transformation à travers la rééducation des mouvements, largement utilisée depuis peu en chorégraphie contemporaine. Développé par Bonnie Bainbridge Cohen, c'est une étude expérimentale qui procède par l'incorporation et l'application de principes anatomiques, physiologiques et psychologiques liés aux différents stades de développement en utilisant le mouvement, le toucher, la voix et l'esprit.
9. http://www.everybodystoolbox.net/?q=node/160

HISTOIRES EN SUSPENSION : NARRATIVITÉ STRATÉGIQUE CHEZ ROSA BARBA

LYNNE COOKE

« Comment les œuvres d'art peuvent-elles [...] raconter des histoires ? [...] La narration doit [obligatoirement] devenir un outil et non un moyen ; un médiateur et non une solution, un participant et non un outsider. »
Louise Bourgeois

« Une philosophie se caractérise plus par la formulation de ses problématiques que par la tentative d'y apporter une solution. »
Suzanne Langer

Somnium (2011) de Rosa Barba, une projection 35 millimètres de 19 minutes et 20 secondes, réunit nombre de préoccupations importantes qui sont apparues dans l'œuvre de l'artiste depuis une dizaine d'années. Le film trouve son origine dans une nouvelle de l'astronome allemand Johannes Kepler[1]. Bien que traitée comme un rêve, cette histoire d'un voyage dans la lune a été conçue pour valider la thèse radicalement subversive de l'héliocentrisme de l'univers[2]. Kepler a travaillé sur cette théorie controversée pendant plus de trente ans, écrivant en latin plutôt que dans une langue vernaculaire plus accessible dans l'espoir d'éviter les attaques de la part de ceux qui croyaient encore que la Terre était située au centre de l'univers. Publiée de manière posthume en 1634 et très rarement republiée pendant les trois siècles suivants, son texte sera finalement sauvé de l'oubli lorsque il est traduit dans plusieurs langues européennes. Il gagne rapidement en notoriété parmi les amateurs de science-fiction, au point qu'il est aujourd'hui unanimement reconnu comme l'un des pionniers du genre. Alors que des auteurs comme J. G. Ballard s'en sont largement inspirés, les cinéastes ne sont pas encore parvenus à lui donner une forme cinématographique. Des recherches sur l'histoire mouvementée de *Somnium* ont nourri le projet éponyme de Barba. Empruntant le titre de Kepler comme un hommage, elle s'est inspirée à la fois de son histoire et, de manière tout aussi importante, de sa remarquable capacité à définir une nouvelle ontologie de la vision.
L'un des éléments singuliers de la nouvelle de Kepler tient à sa structure étonnante. L'histoire, en tant que telle, s'interrompt brutalement lorsque le narrateur se réveille de son voyage lunaire et se retrouve dans son lit, sa tête enfouie sous son oreiller. Le recours de l'auteur au dispositif du rêve est une ruse évidente qui ne parvient pas à dissimuler son raisonnement contestataire dont l'on retrouve la vraie nature dans les notes de bas de pages et les commentaires extensifs qui menacent presque d'ensevelir la courte nouvelle. Remplis de données scientifiques et d'hypothèses, ces appendices viennent parfois confirmer, et parfois remettre en question, les observations empiriques et les références classiques contenues dans le corps principal du texte. Au cœur de la thèse de Kepler se trouve la conviction qu'une hypothèse scientifique rationnelle peut amener à une vérité théorique qui n'est ni accessible ni nécessairement vérifiable, au moyen de l'étude des observations pragmatiques. Son intuition des limitations posées par l'observation directe et la recherche empirique le conduit à formuler le postulat d'une ontologie de la vision basée sur la théorie scientifique. Un débat formulé en des termes similaires se retrouve au cœur de l'œuvre de Barba. Son film s'ouvre sur la voix off autoritaire d'un narrateur qui relaie de manière parfaitement dépassionnée l'information selon laquelle, et bien que la planète Somnium soit actuellement dénuée de toute forme de vie, la nature est en train de réinvestir des zones qui, jusqu'à une date récente, avaient été dévolues aux activités humaines. Classique ouverture de science-fiction, cette manœuvre introductive semble promettre la sécurité d'un grand récit mais déçoit rapidement nos attentes en introduisant un ensemble de modes narratifs qui viennent saper les notions d'omnipotence de l'auteur et de cohérence. Combinant matériel documentaire et fiction narrative, intercalant des témoignages oculaires discordant avec les rapports des autorités, elle oppose ce qui est de l'ordre de la preuve avec ce qui relève de la théorie. Une seconde voix se fait alors entendre. Le ton et le discours sont plus familiers, rarement plus haut qu'un murmure apeuré, la voix relaie la suspicion selon laquelle il y aurait quelque chose de profondément faux dans la manière dont le public est informé des changements radicaux qui transforment l'environnement. Contrairement au narrateur informé de Kepler, l'humble témoin sceptique de Barba ne semble pas avoir conscience de la polémique sous-tendue par ses observations. Enfin, le film de l'artiste évite soigneusement de réconcilier les approches contraires et se termine à dessein par une citation de Giordano Bruno, mystique de la Renaissance, qui affirme que « l'observateur est toujours au centre des choses ».
De subtils changements à l'intérieur et entre les voix narrant *Somnium* viennent compléter la manière fascinante dont Barba utilise l'imagerie visuelle. Des photographies en noir et blanc reproduisent ce que l'on est amené à considérer, du fait du montage parallèle entre images fixes et images en mouvement, comme des documents montrant le site dans un passé lointain. A d'autres moments, de lents panoramiques viennent interrompre des plans fixes qui cadre des détails comme cette canalisation d'égouts en porte-à-faux au dessus d'un talus. Plusieurs images de ce type rappellent directement des motifs que Robert Smithson mettaient en évidence dans son texte marquant « A Tour of the Monuments of Passaic, New Jersey », publié dans *Artforum* en 1967. Dans ce texte, Smithson reprend un cliché de l'art du paysage en transposant un canonique voyage dans un endroit pittoresque et bucolique pour les terrains vagues industriels et dystopiques d'un coin reculé du New Jersey. Attiré par ces ruines, qui pouvaient être vues selon lui comme autant de monuments à l'échec d'une vision utopique du futur technologique de l'humanité, Smithson reviendra sans cesse vers ce sujet, en particulier dans sa grande trilogie d'œuvres – sculpture, film et essai – placée sous la dénomination commune *Spiral Jetty*. *Somnium* fait clairement allusion au film originel de Smithson, tout particulièrement à ce mariage de narration à la première personne et de citations et d'emprunts à la science-fiction, aux récits de voyages, à la littérature et aux manuels de science de manière à combiner des temporalités disparates : passé, présent et futur ; chronologies cycliques, linéaires et entropiques. Le sens caché des images mnémoniques et des références induites par les

travaux de Smithson sont tout aussi essentielles à une interprétation de *Somnium* que ce que le film doit au joyau littéraire de Kepler. Le projet de Barba anime ces précédents d'une nouvelle vie. Loin de rester cantonner dans le passé de l'histoire, elle affirme que le discours de ces œuvres transcende leur portée historique ; qu'ils sont des composants vitaux d'un discours critique cherchant à définir la vision nécessaire à un cinéma contemporain politiquement engagé. Une couleur plus mélancolique vient teinter *The Long Road* (2010), qui, comme *They Shine* (2007) et *The Waiting Grounds* (2007), a été tourné dans le sud-ouest américain. D'abord vue du ciel dans un long travelling, la piste d'essais automobile abandonnée qui est le sujet de l'œuvre ressemble a un *earthwork* préhistorique ou à une variante seventies du genre. Qu'elle soit parente des antiques lignes de Nazca redécouvertes grâce au développement des voyages en avion ou des incursions à grande échelle que Smithson et ses pairs ont réalisé après-guerre dans le désert, cette incision elliptique sur le sol est toute aussi soumise à la destruction et aux ravages du temps. La bande-son mélange des sons techno-électroniques, d'où émergent par intermittence des phrases microtonales obsédantes, avec la voix rauque de Robert Creeley lisant des extraits de son poème *The Long Road*. Le souvenir de la mort de son père, combiné avec la prise de conscience des nombreuses décennies passées depuis sa disparition, déclenchée par la vue d'anciennes photos de classe, rappelle le poète à sa propre mortalité. L'évocation que le terme de sa longue route pourrait n'être plus très loin est reprise dans le dernier plan du film. Désormais sur la terre ferme, la caméra suit les contours de la piste d'essais ; après avoir négocié une courbe, elle s'engage dans une ligne droite où elle accélère dans le soleil couchant. De par son montage et le rythme de ses mouvements de caméra, de par le positionnement du texte au sein de la bande-son, Barba imbrique ces positions stratégiques et mouvantes du regard et de la voix. Comme dans *Somnium*, une fonction mnémonique basée sur des références directes ou indirectes aux œuvres d'autres artistes (un poète et des sculpteurs anonymes dans ce cas précis) fait partie intégrante de la manière dont le contenu est constitué.

L'engagement de Barba avec le lieu et le rôle de l'œuvre d'art au sein de l'imaginaire culturel au sens large s'est précisé avec sa réponse à une commande récente du Museo Nacional Centro de Arte Reina Sofía à Madrid. Invitée à assurer le commissariat d'une exposition à partir des collections du musée, elle à répondu avec une proposition qu'elle appelle « a curated conference ». Son projet comprenait la présentation de quarante-trois œuvres, dont des films et des vidéos, des photographies, des sculptures, des peintures et des dessins, installés dans deux galeries adjacentes. Elle écrit dans la brochure qui accompagnait l'exposition que « le but de cette conférence est de réunir une représentation d'artistes du XXème et du XXIème siècle et d'apporter leur opinion éclairée sur les questions importantes de l'art[3] ». Intitulée *On the Future of Collective Strength within an Archive* (2010), sa présentation évite les conventions standards de la muséologie, en particulier la séparation des objets par médium et un accrochage chronologique linéaire, au profit d'une installation qui juxtapose et fait dialoguer des œuvres réalisées sur une durée de près d'un siècle à proximité les unes des autres. Plutôt que de supprimer les différences au service d'un impératif idéologique, ce qui forme la base de la façon dont les collections sont présentées dans la plupart des institutions d'art contemporain actuelles, elle encourage le résultat anarchique produit par une situation où « chaque artiste parle avec sa propre voix dans son propre langage, sa propre humeur et son propre volume ». Reconnaissant que même si certaines étaient des acquisitions récentes, nombre de ces œuvres d'art étaient présentes dans la collection depuis longtemps, elle invite les artistes (à travers leurs œuvres) à explorer « la conscience collective » au cœur de l'archive. Elle anticipe que ce qui doit en émerger, ne sera pas une vision cohérente ou consensuelle (le but des professionnels des musées), mais une « Babel de voix » : l'archive étant composée « d'expressions individuelles non datées » qui peuvent être « chorégraphiées comme une partition musicale ». Elle affirme que « en niant le passé et en ignorant le futur, l'artiste est libre de créer une proposition qui perdure dans le temps … [et qui génère] une énergie capable de connecter les artistes de tous âges ».

Des tables rondes, des workshops, une session parallèle, et des présentations par, entre autres, Pablo Picasso, Mira Schendel, Louise Bourgeois, Martha Rosler font également partie du programme. Plusieurs des intervenants soulèvent des interrogations présentes dans la propre pratique de Barba. Ainsi, Picasso affirme par exemple : « tout ce que j'ai fait l'a été pour le présent et avec l'espoir que cela resterait toujours dans le présent ». George Maciunas souligne l'idée d'identité collective présente chez Barba lorsqu'il définit cette « communauté d'individus constituant ensemble une vaste quantité de comportements et d'attitudes… un "non-groupe" sans structure particulière ». Bourgeois, de son côté, se consacre à la manière dont les œuvres d'art racontent des histoires : elle affirme que grâce au jeu des qualités formelles, « la narration devient un outil et non un moyen ; un médiateur et non une solution ». Même si Barba n'avait pas inclus ses propres œuvres, et donc sa propre voix, dans la discussion, elle avait clairement affiché ses positions en choisissant comme ses principaux intervenants des artistes dont l'esthétique et le travail incarnent les éléments clés de sa propre pratique.

C'est la notion d'archive qui était la source réelle de l'exposition-comme-conférence de Barba étant donné que la liste des œuvres exposées était issue exclusivement des réserves du musée. Le mot "archive" est également utilisé de manière plus abstraite pour faire référence au système qui, selon Hal Foster, « structure les expressions particulières d'une période particulière[4] ». Cette notion discursive de l'archive est également mise en œuvre dans le projet de Barba dans le sens où elle formule une critique de l'idéologie qui gouverne la façon dont les collections sont présentées ailleurs au sein de l'institution, offrant ainsi une alternative subversive à ses normes de représentativité totale et de responsabilité historique. Etant donné sa conviction que les œuvres d'art sont "anhistoriques", ou "intemporelles", elles pourraient tout aussi bien s'auto-organiser et se réunir sur l'initiative de leurs créateurs, plutôt que de dépendre de professionnels des musées qui les réquisitionnent au nom de leurs orthodoxies.

Le projet innovant de Barba peut aussi être lu à travers le modèle du musée développé par Theodor Adorno dans un essai publié en 1953 sur ce qu'il appelle le "musée Valéry-Proust[5]". Selon Adorno, Valéry incarne la position selon laquelle le musée est « l'endroit où l'on met à mort l'art du passé ». Il affirme que « Musée et Mausolée sont liés par bien plus qu'une association phonétique », au sens où « les musées sont comme les caveaux de famille des œuvres d'art. Ils témoignent de la neutralisation de la culture ». Par opposition à l'embaumement ou la réification des œuvres d'art tel que Valéry pense qu'ils se produisent

dans les musées, Proust élabore une vision basée sur l'idée de la réanimation de l'œuvre d'art. De ce fait, le musée est pour lui le lieu d'une compétition agressive. On retrouve des échos de l'idée de Proust dans la conférence curatoriale de Barba. Cependant, là où Proust assignait au spectateur le rôle de réanimer l'œuvre, Barba laisse le contrôle entre les mains des artistes : leurs œuvres incarnent leurs voix.
The Hidden Conference: About the Discontinuous History of Things We See and Don't See (2011), un court-métrage 35 millimètres tourné peu de temps après le lancement du projet de Barba au Museo Reina Sofia à Madrid, explore ce débat plus en détails[6]. Situé dans un lieu non identifié (les réserves de la Neue Nationalgalerie de Berlin) et à « un moment non spécifié dans le temps (dans le futur ou dans le passé) », il met en lumière une situation qui bien qu'existante depuis des années, comme nous en informe un prologue écrit, a atteint un certain « degré d'urgence ». Pour autant, les raisons de cette rencontre ne nous sont pas données. Alors que la caméra chorégraphie un groupe disparate d'objets d'art baignés dans un clair-obscur, des fragments de récit émergent sans jamais faire sens. Une fois de plus le récit fait office de « médiateur et non [pas de] solution ». Le discours fait partie intégrante de la performance corporelle, alors que la bande-son minimale composée par le collaborateur de longue date de Barba, Jan St. Werner, anime les œuvres – de Ernst Barlach, Renee Sintenis, Gerhard Marcks, et d'autres maintenant plongés dans l'anonymat – créant un jeu de geste, d'attitude, de posture et de regard. Loin de remettre en cause le paradigme de l'archive comme l'échec d'une vision futuriste, cette conférence clandestine confirme sa rhétorique. Le pathos se répand sur les vieilles ambitions de représentativité totale, mettant en débat la possibilité d'un sauvetage, d'une rédemption, de ces fragments perdus d'une histoire en miettes.
Plusieurs années auparavant, Barba s'était intéressée aux archives depuis un point de vue totalement différent dans *Western Round Table* (2007). Sa source pour l'œuvre était un symposium tenu à San Francisco en 1949 sous le titre « The Western Round Table on Modern Art ». Ayant pour but de « réunir une représentation des opinons les mieux informées du moment pour réfléchir sur les questions de l'art d'aujourd'hui », son panel de prestigieux intervenants (uniquement des hommes) incluait des critiques, des artistes, des historiens de l'art, des compositeurs, des professionnels des musées et ainsi de suite, dont Marcel Duchamp, Frank Lloyd Wright, Darius Milhaud, Robert Goldwater, Mark Tobey, Alfred Frankenstein, Andrew C. Richie, et Gregory Bateson[7]. Cette fois-ci, la réplique de Barba prit la forme d'une projection sculpturale. Deux projecteurs 16 millimètres placés tous deux sur le sol déroulent de la pellicule transparente. Chacun crée une projection de lumière blanche sur un mur adjacent dans laquelle se dessinent les ombres architectoniques de son antagoniste, l'autre projecteur. La bande-son est constituée d'extraits de deux films de Fellini coupés de manière à ce que les projecteurs donnent l'illusion de converser l'un avec l'autre, en des termes cependant bien éloignés de l'auguste ton des débats de la conférence de la Côte Ouest. Jamais vraiment recouverts par le bruit du mécanisme des projecteurs anachroniques, les passages musicaux sont au départ attirants, entraînants, voir même captivants. Mais très vite, cependant, la bande-son devient obsédante, impossible à oublier et impossible à éradiquer de son esprit. Une épigraphe dans le compte-rendu du symposium par Suzanne Langer contient l'affirmation que lorsque l'on essaie de caractériser une philosophie, les solutions apportées aux questions nous en apprennent moins que la formulation des problèmes : « les réponses établissent un édifice de faits », prétend-elle, « mais les questions font le cadre dans lequel cette image de faits est tracée[8] ». Passée au travers du filtre de l'observation de Langer, l'incarnation idiosyncrasique de Barba des actes de cet événement reconnu dans une paire de sombres silhouettes architectoniques – deux monstres immatériels parlant de manière impénétrable l'un en direction de l'autre – ne semble pas aussi négative qu'il y paraît.
Comme l'atteste *They Shine*, l'imaginaire scientifique contemporain est difficilement discernable de ce qui était autrefois du seul ressort de la science-fiction[9]. Quelque chose de très différent ressort, cependant, de *A Private Tableaux* (2010). Des images qui ressemblent à des peintures rupestres modernes sont identifiées comme les traces laissées dans des passages situés sous la rivière Mersey à Liverpool pendant plus d'un siècle par les ingénieurs qui étudient les points de pression créés par les véhicules circulant dans les tunnels au-dessus. Barba, de manière peut être inaccoutumée, évite l'approche archéologique de cette cartographie laconique à la faveur d'une enquête sémiotique qui considère ces signes abstraits comme des symboles figuratifs. Ignorant apparemment leur origine, le commentateur (dont le rapport constitue le texte du film) les compare à une forme « d'écriture automatique » créée par le « moi subliminal » des ingénieurs » « pour leur propre plaisir ». Il / elle essaye alors de caractériser les marques qui composent ces « private tableaux » : en addition d'une « machine volante » et d'un « carrosse avec chevaux », on trouve le portrait d'un jeune homme « dessiné de mémoire ». Comparant ce visage, avec une latitude certaine, à un dessin de Cocteau, l'auteur conclut qu'il « avait donné à son créateur beaucoup de peine et peu de satisfaction ». En renonçant au ton objectif et dépassionné propre à l'interprétation scientifique, cette analyse sémiotique imaginée trahit une fantaisie rare dans le travail de Barba. Pourtant, c'est précisément le personnage risible de ces étranges conjectures qui renvoie l'attention sur les termes dans lesquels se formule l'enquête. Une fois de plus, Barba porte son intérêt sur la structure qui encadre et que dirige l'impulsion narrative.
Le récit comme forme de critique culturelle peut à la fois servir de véhicule à une médiation de l'histoire et donner du sens à l'expérience contemporaine. Pour Italo Calvino, raconter des histoires est devenu un vecteur pour galvaniser un public devenu passif, d'abord sous le joug d'un régime fasciste puis par le développement socioculturel des années d'après-guerre. Il en vint à croire que, loin de requérir l'illustration polémique d'une position idéologique, une littérature engagée demande le développement d'un style et d'une technique au service d'une forme de réalisme qui n'a rien à voir avec le naturalisme. La fiction demande de l'attention, « tout d'abord, [aux] images et aux mots, aux attitudes, au rythme, au style, au mépris, à la provocation[10] ». Le réalisme, plutôt que le naturalisme, est également le mode préféré de Barba ; pour elle également, raconter des histoires est une question de style et d'attitude tout autant qu'une question de technique. Les sources de ses récits proviennent d'un large éventail de littératures. Parfois, comme avec son utilisation du poème de Creeley dans *The Long Road*, elle fait des emprunts directs ; plus souvent, comme dans *Somnium* et *Let Me See It* (2010), qui est basé sur une histoire de Borges, elle redistribue ou elle paraphrase le texte original. La littérature est néanmoins tout aussi fondamentale à sa conception du cinéma que le sont ses équivalents visuels.
Alors que le cinéma est diversement conçu comme une écriture

ou une inscription dans de nombreuses œuvres filmées de Barba, la sculpture se déploie pour littéralement donner une forme au langage[11]. *I Made a Circuit and then a Second Circuit* (2010) fait partie d'un groupe d'œuvres que l'on pourrait qualifier de disposition proto-cinématographique, dans le sens où chacun d'eux est composé d'une pièce de feutre suspendue dans l'espace de manière à fonctionner à la fois comme un écran et comme un projecteur. Quand la lumière est projetée sur le support sombre dans lequel un texte à été découpé, une inscription lumineuse apparaît au-delà sur le mur. A partir des restes de l'un de ces rideaux de feutre, Barba a créé *They Come and Go* (2009). Les fragments de langage disposés en tas sur un morceau de tissu tendu sur le sol et éclairés par le faisceau d'un projecteur prennent la forme d'une archive au potentiel narratif infini.

Sa sensibilité au texte s'étend à la façon dont il est livré ; les voix de ses pistes audio sont tout aussi particulières que mémorables. In *They Shine*, par exemple, le ton neutre et suave du narrateur évoque les intonations des acteurs principaux d'un certain type de film hollywoodien. En cultivant cette évocation Barba cherche à souligner le fait que les habitants de cet étrange milieu vivent entre deux réalités fantasmatiques : le site sur lequel l'inquiétant alignement de réflecteurs a été construit est tout proche de la Mecque du cinéma et des paillettes. A travers toute son œuvre, les monologues des experts (masculins) sont toujours calmes et mesurés, voir pratiquement laconiques. Cependant, lorsque les voix indistinctes et mal assurées d'amateurs en provenance des marges et des interstices viennent en contrepoint – comme on le retrouve dans *Somnium* – ces tons autoritaires ont l'air trop onctueux, et leur pouvoir d'explication suspect[12].

Le fait de raconter des histoires dépend tout autant du lecteur / auditeur que de la voix de l'auteur. Dans la formulation bien connue de Roland Barthes, lire (comme regarder) crée un espace de rencontre où le lecteur et la multiplicité des écritures que comporte n'importe quel texte « se fondent et s'affrontent ». L'exploration en profondeur et en nuances de cette rencontre par Barba n'est nulle part plus artistiquement manifeste que dans *It's Gonna Happen* (2005). Une conversation imaginaire qui pourrait de manière plausible faire partie des machinations politiques que l'on connaît sous le nom de Watergate fournit le matériau brut de ce qui pourrait être une séquence d'un long-métrage à venir. Les indications du metteur en scène pour jouer cette séquence apparaissent sous la forme de phrases projetées sur un fond noir, alors que sur la bande-son défile une reconstitution de la conversation sous la forme d'un bref appel téléphonique. Les spectateurs lisent le texte tout en écoutant la conversation laconique dans laquelle deux hommes préparent un enlèvement, en faisant surgir la scène dans leur imagination. Alors qu'ils luttent pour suivre à la fois les mots écrits et parlés qui se déroulent en tandem mais ne sont pas synchronisés les uns avec les autres, ils se retrouvent à occuper deux espaces diamétralement opposés : ils sont en même temps dans le domaine de l'illusion et au-delà des frontières de la fiction. Indépendant et se mélangeant pourtant avec la bande-son, le bruit des projecteurs donne une impulsion à la prise de conscience qu'une expérience candide du cinéma n'est plus possible aujourd'hui ; les technologies du cinéma et notre attitude à leur égard passent inévitablement par le prisme de son histoire, de ses conventions, et de ses genres. En demandant à son public de négocier entre deux positions contradictoires, Barba les oblige à réfléchir aux films en tant que médium, mais aussi sur ses traditions et ses différents genres. Les manœuvres politiques du Watergate sont ici à la fois un prétexte et une mise en échec de son éternel sujet : la politique du regard. Encore et toujours, les formes d'introspection qui sont la marque de nombreux projets modernistes exemplaires prennent une parure narrative dans la pratique de Barba. Des textes auto-réflexifs, des histoires en suspension, des pensées spéculatives deviennent des vecteurs de discours, les moyens avec lesquels elle construit une façon de voir – une ontologie de la vision – appropriée au cinéma d'aujourd'hui[13].

Notes

1. Gale E. Christianson, "Kepler's Somnium: Science Fiction and the Renaissance Scientist," *Science Fiction Studies* (Mars 1976), pp. 79–90. Voir aussi Raz Chen-Morris, "Shadows of Instruction: Optics and Classical Authorities in Kepler's Somnium," *Journal of the History of Ideas* (2005), pp. 223–41.
2. Le risque pris en publiant des vues aussi largement controversées au début du XVIIème siècle était considérable, pour preuve le fait que l'une des premières versions du manuscrit a conduit à l'emprisonnement de la mère de l'auteur, soupçonnée d'être une sorcière.
3. Rosa Barba, *A Curated Conference: On the Future of Collective Strength within the Archive* (Madrid : Museo Nacional Centro de Arte Reina Sofia, 2010). Toutes les citations qui suivent sont tirées de cette même brochure.
4. Hal Foster, "Archives of Modern Art," *October*, no. 99 (hiver 2002), pp. 81–95 ; voir aussi idem, "An Archival Impulse," *October*, no. 110 (automne 2004), pp. 3–22.
5. Je dois beaucoup au compte-rendu que Foster fait de l'essai d'Adorno. Voir Foster 2002 (voir note 4), pp. 84–85. Toutes les citations qui suivent sont tirées du texte de Foster.
6. Il s'agit, en réalité, du premier volet d'une série qui en comptera quatre ; le second chapitre intitulé : *The Hidden Conference: A Fractured Play* (2011) à été mis en place à Trento en 2011.
7. Pour les actes du colloque, voir "The Western Round Table on Modern Art (1949)," ed. Douglas MacAgy. Consulté en ligne à : http: / / www.ubu.com / historical / wrtma / index.html (dernier accès 16 juillet 2011).
8. Ibid.
9. Le sujet de *They Shine* (2007) est un vaste alignement de structures futuristes, à la fois « glamour » et « mortel », supposé améliorer un environnement hostile pour le transformer en localité habitable. Il fait l'objet de spéculations inquiètes et de scepticisme de la part de locaux abasourdis. Comme dans *Somnium*, les réactions ambivalentes et ironiques vis-à-vis des plans des scientifiques pour faire face à une nature qui semble se déchaîner est le sujet des écrits de Rivka Galchen. (Voir, par exemple, Rivka Galchen, "Disaster Aversion: The Quest to Control Hurricanes," *Harper's Magazine* [octobre 2009], pp. 55–63. Consulté en ligne à : http:www.harpers.orgarchive / 2009 / 10.)
10. Italo Calvino, "Préface," *The Path to the Nest of Spiders* (Hopewell, NJ: The Ecco Press, 1976), pp. vii–viii.
11. *Printed Cinema* est le titre qu'elle donne à une série de publications, toujours en cours, dont chaque édition accompagne la production d'une œuvre particulière ou d'un ensemble d'œuvres et se penche sur leur processus de production.
12. La seule exception à ce casting de voix masculines sont les deux narratrices de *Parachutable* (2005). Même si elles ne dialoguent pas, leurs voix s'interrompent et se chevauchent, renforçant les effets de contraste et de résistance qui lient le son aux images.
13. « Les vrais protagonistes sont les histoires suspendues dans les airs », déclare l'une des deux voix féminines de *Parachutable* (2005).

EPILOGUE

L'institution « filmique » de Rosa Barba

1- Espace : ***Est-ce que c'est une analogie à deux dimensions ou une métaphore ?***

Au début, vous ne vous en rendez pas compte, puis vous réalisez que vous entrez dans un espace totalement réorganisé et transformé. Vous êtes à l'intérieur d'un vaste projecteur de cinéma. Vous vous retrouvez au sein d'une histoire en train d'être racontée, dans un lieu qui change en même temps que vous le traversez. Vous réalisez que vous êtes dans un film et dans la machine-musée qui le projette. Quand, finalement, dans la dernière salle du Centre international d'art et du paysage de l'île de Vassivière, vous découvrez un projecteur 70 mm (*White Museum*, 2010) vous comprenez que vous êtes au cœur d'une machinerie complexe où le phare représente une des bobines. Vous êtes le film, la pellicule sur laquelle l'exposition est développée. Votre personne, vos émotions et vos pensées sont le film exposé que l'institution construit autour de vous.

Rosa Barba crée des mythologies et formule des hypothèses. Elle utilise les images pour enquêter et pour reconstruire. Dans ses projets, elle questionne l'essence et la fonction du cinéma, médite sur sa structure en tant que médium et en tant qu'instrument pour créer des mondes. Son travail commence toujours par une matrice sociale, historique, naturaliste, scientifique et philosophique, il naît de la volonté de donner une lecture singulière des faits réels et des circonstances historiques. Sa fascination pour le cinéma concerne autant son aspect abstrait que son versant mécanique. Dans les installations de Rosa Barba, les instruments techniques - les projecteurs, la pellicule, les haut-parleurs - jouent un rôle dans le film lui-même. Ils transforment l'espace, modifient nos perceptions et deviennent un élément essentiel de la chorégraphie de l'exposition. Ils agissent, pour le visiteur, comme un constant référentiel sensoriel. Le processus mental que l'artiste déclenche vis-à-vis du cinéma, son attitude à l'égard du film au sens large, est une posture qui consiste à le disséquer et à le mettre en pièces, à le réduire à la somme de ses composants individuels.

L'exposition de Rosa Barba *Est-ce que c'est une analogie à deux dimensions ou une métaphore ?* au Centre international d'art et du paysage de l'île de Vassivière s'inspire de ce qui caractérise le plus l'île. L'eau et la lumière comme éléments fondamentaux de cette terre qui surgit au milieu d'un lac artificiel dans la région française du Limousin. Ainsi, en jouant sur les idées d'artificiel et de naturel, Rosa Barba imagine que le cœur de son projet pourrait être la structure même du Centre d'art, conçu par l'architecte italien Aldo Rossi. Le lac qui entoure l'île devient alors narrateur et il est utilisé par Rosa Barba, métaphoriquement, comme un écran de projection.
La lumière arrive d'un projecteur installé dans le bâtiment principal dont le faisceau - qui le traverse entièrement - achève son long et improbable parcours en allant toucher le lac. En l'illuminant ainsi, la lumière semble défier la nature secrète de ce miroir d'eau. Un dispositif tout aussi sophistiqué produit un son qui vient effleurer la surface de l'eau si bien que le visiteur à l'impression de percevoir une respiration en provenance des huit hameaux engloutis dans les années 1950, lors de la construction du barrage qui donna naissance au lac. Le résultat de cette opération visionnaire est particulièrement efficace, au travers de l'exposition, le visiteur est immergé dans une double profondeur : celle du lac et celle de la narration qu'il enclenche. Les croisements permanents entre réalité, fiction, perception et absence deviennent évidents. Mais c'est toute l'architecture a être impliquée. La salle principale du Centre d'art, la nef, abrite *The Long Road* (2010), un nouveau film en 35 mm, réalisé dans le désert californien sur le site d'un circuit automobile, presque désaffecté. Le visiteur a l'impression de parcourir à grande vitesse la boucle créée par les mouvements de caméra de l'artiste. Les traces des pneus de toutes les voitures qui ont roulé sur ce circuit griffent l'asphalte et produisent un sentiment ambivalent : celui d'un passé désormais révolu et dans le même temps l'impression d'une menace imminente. Suspendu à l'intersection entre le présent et le passé, et peut-être le futur, cet endroit sort du sable comme un immense dessin. Stigmates d'une culture de la modernité oubliée, aujourd'hui abandonnée, prêts à être transformés en quelque chose de différent et d'inattendu, quelque chose qui n'est pas encore totalement exprimé est sans doute inexprimable.
Après la vaste nef, en poursuivant au premier étage dans la salle des études, un projecteur 16 mm est placé sur le sol, entouré, ou plutôt emprisonné, par sa propre pellicule. Il s'agit d'*Enigmatic Whistler* (2009) qui ne raconte rien d'autre que lui-même. Dans la même salle, *Stating the Real Sublime* (2009) un autre projecteur 16 mm, accroché au plafond, est suspendu à nouveau par sa pellicule. Dans ces deux œuvres, les instruments du cinéma prennent le pas sur les fonctions qui leur sont propres et offrent à ces machines l'occasion d'une vie anarchique.
Avec *The Indifferent Back of a View Rather Than Its Face* (2009) et *The Personal Experience Behind Its Description* (2009) - toujours dans la même pièce, Rosa Barba projette sur le mur au travers d'un tissu de feutre découpé des lettres de lumière. Ici, elle va au-delà des deux dimensions du cinéma. Les lettres du scénario découpées jonchent le sol, en désordre, et le visiteur se retrouve dans un étrange parcours narratif en trois dimensions.

A Vassivière, l'aspect documentaire et l'aspect fictionnel coïncident parfaitement et créent de potentiels hybrides, entre l'histoire et le paysage. Le travail de Rosa Barba entretient des affinités physiologiques avec Vassivière. Les aquarelles d'Aldo Rossi, le phare, le lac, tout concourt à un scénario contemporain avec la poétique propre de Rosa Barba. L'exposition vient défier le paysage et paradoxalement accueille et contextualise la perception de l'artiste.
Le Centre d'art est conçu comme le théâtre d'une mise en scène en équilibre, entre l'intérieur et l'extérieur. Les différents espaces et les différentes temporalités entrent en dialogue. Le lieu assume une valeur mythique et tout préfigure un acte de création à partir de cet immense potentiel encore non codifié. Rosa Barba n'utilise pas le Centre d'art comme un espace neutre : elle réussit littéralement à constituer une plateforme « muséale » pour mettre en place une exposition innovante et inattendue qui bouscule les canons de l'institution et du commissariat d'exposition. C'est comme si l'île appartenait déjà à Rosa Barba ; il ne nous restait qu'à la lui offrir.

2- Temps : *Stage Archive*

L'exposition commune au Mart – Musco di Arte Moderna e Contemporanea di Trento e Rovereto et à la Fondazione Galleria Civica–Centro di Ricerca sulla Contemporaneità di Trento naît en complémentarité avec la précédente et se développe - de la même manière que Rosa Barba avait abordé la question de l'espace à Vassivière - autour de la question du temps et de l'instrument dévolu à son enregistrement et à son invention : l'archive. Rosa Barba explore la manière dont l'archive façonne l'identité et l'activité institutionnelle des musées contemporains. Si à Vassivière, l'artiste se concentre sur l'espace au travers des mécanismes de la narration cinématographique, à Rovereto et à Trento, elle se réfère au temps, comme à une dimension objective et une expérience de l'imagination.
A l'origine, ce projet se structure autour d'une œuvre de recherche que l'artiste a réalisée autour des documents originaux de la période du Futurisme conservés dans les archives historiques du Mart. L'idée de l'exposition est de présenter / représenter - sous la forme « sculpture-théâtralité-abstraction » - des scénarios et des dispositifs filmiques, jamais réalisés. L'archive est réinterprétée par l'artiste qui la fait s'échapper du territoire de la conservation, pour l'emmener sur celui d'une temporalité mouvante. Moteur actif de l'imaginaire et source de nouveaux récits, elle devient un nouvel hybride : une archive-scène sur laquelle le passé et le futur sont représentés dans le présent du musée.

Dans les deux lieux, à Trento et à Rovereto, chaque œuvre entretient une relation dialectique avec les autres, la chorégraphie, constituant un cadre, vient les réunir pour composer un ensemble. L'installation, qui combine son et image filmique, prend la forme d'un « ballet mécanique » d'inspiration futuriste.
Chaque protagoniste est présenté en même temps sur une même scène, qui est représentée dans l'exposition. Elle implique donc un double « voyage futuriste » qui inclut textes, films, objets sculpturaux et sons. Le résultat est une performance mécanique qui laisserait une place pour l'anarchie mais qui aurait l'harmonie d'une chorale.
L'exposition formule alors l'hypothèse d'une archive futuriste qui n'existe pas, mais qui serait en train de se constituer en temps réel, et qui serait composée d'une série d'expressions individuelles utilisables séparément ou comme un tout cohérent. Un mémorial dédié à l'avant-garde futuriste qui prend corps dans le musée et devient une entité autonome qui naissant au sein même des archives où il est conservé.

Au Mart, l'artiste intervient dans l'espace central du musée, mettant en relation la zone des archives, au sous-sol, et les espaces d'exposition, aux étages supérieurs. L'idée de la stratification archéologique s'incarne dans le développement vertical de l'exposition. Cœur de toute institution, les archives, conventionnellement reléguées dans l'ombre, assument ici le rôle de protagoniste. Rosa Barba met en scène la transformation des documents historiques, denses de signification dans leur état d'inachèvement et à travers des objets bi et tri dimensionnels qui traduisent les projets futuristes dans un récit hypothétique.

Une sculpture circulaire (*Stage Archive*, 2011) reprend la forme du grand lustre. A l'intérieur de la sculpture, comme dans un projecteur ou sur une table de montage, passe une pellicule vierge qui ne produit que le son de son mouvement. Tout cela est la représentation de l'inexprimé, de l'énergie potentielle qui contiennent et qui caractérisent les documents futuristes et qui rejaillissent dans le musée au travers de l'exposition.
L'exposition s'achève avec une grande œuvre murale (*Theory in Order to Shed Light*, 2011). Un scénario sur feutre qui reproduit des éléments textuels et graphiques de documents futuristes ainsi que quelques interventions discrètes de signalétique sur l'escalier d'accès (*No Titles*, 2011). Ils viennent s'intégrer dans les panneaux informatifs disposés aux différents étages et suggèrent une spatialité et une temporalité, plus fluide et potentielle qui invitent les visiteurs à une lecture de l'institution « à travers le temps » mélangeant passé, présent et futur comme cela arrive normalement avec les archives, où les documents du passé qui sont, pour les chercheurs, des objets actifs, projectifs, actuels dont les temps peuvent se superposer plus librement.

Dans l'espace principal de la Galleria Civica di Trento, sont projetés les deux premiers films en 35 mm réalisés par l'artiste et intégrés à la série : *The Hidden Conference: About the Discontinuous History of Things We See and Don't See* (2010).
Le premier chapitre de cette série a été tourné dans les archives de la Neue Nationalgalerie de Berlin, le second dans les archives des Musées du Capitole à Rome. La série *Hidden Conference* provient de la réflexion menée par Rosa Barba depuis 2010 sur la conservation des œuvres d'art dans les réserves de certains musées de sculpture ancienne et moderne. L'artiste crée un dialogue imaginaire entre ces objets, dans leur état de constant silence et de secrète cohabitation avec les institutions qui les conservent.
Dans ces films où les objets entreposés sont transformés en toile de fond, découpés par la lumière, comme si nous nous trouvions soudain projetés dans un décor de cinéma ou de théâtre, l'artiste interroge les liens invisibles entre les objets d'art et le réseau de liens qui convergent vers l'idée d'un espace « protégé », hors du temps, au même titre que les archives. L'artiste raconte comment, invitée par le Museo Nacional Centro de Arte Reina Sofia à Madrid pour rassembler une sélection de documents et d'œuvres, elle s'est retrouvée fascinée par l'archive elle-même, par l'idée que des œuvres continuent de vivre loin du regard du public tout en contribuant, pourtant, à la construction de l'identité du musée et, de fait, à la construction de notre langage visuel qui se développe à son contact. Elle a commencé à explorer les relations invisibles entre les œuvres conservées, le réseau d'analogies qui produit l'idée collective d'un espace donné lequel, dans son ensemble, acquiert une grande valeur.
L'ordre méticuleux dans lequel les œuvres sont conservées crée un système inédit et complexe que l'artiste entend faire partager dans ces films, faisant de nous des participants au sein de ces nouvelles et singulières compositions.

L'artiste s'interroge : « Quelle est la qualité intrinsèque de l'art qu'on ne voit pas ? » Elle enquête sur le long sommeil d'une œuvre après le difficile processus d'acquisition et le passage d'un propriétaire à un autre, la communication, les négociations et les transactions complexes du marché de l'art.
Elle se demande comment s'ajoute les nouveaux éléments dans la mémoire collective des archives dans leur ensemble (et donc dans celle du musée). L'artiste écrit qu'il « existe

une étrange similarité entre ce moment et le processus aléatoire et labyrinthique lorsque nous essayons de trouver un nom ou un mot dans notre mémoire ».

En relation avec cette pure potentialité institutionnelle, suggérée par la dimension secrète de l'archive, Rosa Barba présente d'autres œuvres à la Fondazione qui développent un discours similaire : *A Private Tableaux* (2010), un film en 16 mm, traite des études sur l'architecture souterraine menées depuis des années par de nombreux professionnels. Aux travers des nombreux dessins réalisés par des scientifiques dans le cadre de leurs recherches, émerge la représentation involontaire d'une histoire parallèle, où une large diffusion de signes occupe tout le volume d'un espace-temps interdit. Dans le film en 16 mm, *Let Me See It* (2009), les images, présentant un grain très marqué, dépeignent un paysage nocturne, une vue aérienne d'un archipel dans laquelle seules les lueurs de maisons sur la terre ferme éclairent la scène. Deux hommes, dont l'un est aveugle, parlent des objets qui les entourent, en s'attardant sur la figure du dodécahèdre, élément qui devient crucial pour le voyage de l'homme à la recherche de ses souvenirs.
Invisible Act (2010) est une installation sculpturale qui comprend une image, projetée en 16 mm, dans laquelle un objet matériel évoque un objet imaginaire, disposés l'un dans l'autre et à l'intérieur d'un dialogue fait de contrastes et de combinaisons.
L'œuvre tient compte du document non pas simplement comme un objet donné, mais aussi comme un moment de création et de réflexion, comme une transposition, comme une possibilité permanente de transformer l'image en matière et inversement. *Optic Ocean* (2011) et *Time Machine* (2007) sont la compilation d'un scénario, entre réel et fantastique, qui s'étendent sur les murs de l'espace d'exposition en le transformant en document de travail. *One Way Out* (2009) est composé d'un projecteur 16 mm dont la pellicule est aspirée vers un petit renfoncement de l'espace d'exposition que l'on remarque soudain. C'est en fait la sortie, une ouverture fictive que toute l'exposition semble attendre, évoquée dans le bâtiment réel du musée.

3 - De l'île aux archives. Remerciements

En tant que commissaires des expositions à Vassivière, Rovereto et Trento, nous voulons remercier tout ceux qui ont contribué à les rendre possibles. En tout premier lieu à Rosa Barba qui nous a fait découvrir une dimension de nos institutions que l'on ignorait complètement malgré notre pratique quotidienne. Rosa Barba nous a révélé des lieux plus connectés, plus aventureux ; nous a montré ainsi qu'aux visiteurs leur infini potentiel, les passages secrets de ces « institutions filmiques ».

Un remerciement va à Gabriella Belli, non seulement pour avoir fait en sorte que le projet de Rovereto voit le jour mais aussi pour avoir partagé l'intuition qu'il ne pouvait naître que des archives historiques du Mart, du cerveau et de la mémoire du musée : de son cœur.

Nous voulons particulièrement remercier les auteurs des textes de ce catalogue qui constitue, en fait, une quatrième exposition, la première monographie exhaustive consacrée à l'artiste : Lynne Cooke, Elisabeth Lebovici, Nataša Petrešin-Bachelez, Ian White, Francesco Manacorda et Raimundas Malasauskas.

Chiara Parisi, Directeur du Centre international d'art et du paysage de l'île de Vassivière

Andrea Viliani, Directeur de la Fondazione Galleria Civica–Centro di Ricerca sulla Contemporaneità di Trento

Dans les Archives Historiques du Mart : *A Work in Progress*

En 2010, Rosa Barba commence à s'intéresser aux archives des musées et elle réalise deux des films de sa série *In Progress*, dont *The Hidden Conference: About the Discontinuous History of Things We See and Don't See*, instaurant ainsi un dialogue entre les œuvres conservées dans les réserves des deux musées. Dans ces films, l'artiste engage une réflexion sur la temporalité et la nature même des œuvres d'art ainsi que sur les multiples facettes de la transition entre « public » et « privé ».
Il est donc tout à fait compréhensible qu'en poursuivant ses recherches, Rosa Barba soit entrée en contact avec le Mart et ses archives historiques. Dès l'origine, le Mart a pris la décision de mettre l'accent sur son patrimoine bibliographique et sur les archives dont il est l'héritier, de faire de ces documents la pierre angulaire d'une identité culturelle qui suivrait une voie parallèle à celle des œuvres d'art. Depuis le jour de sa fondation en 1987, le Mart a toujours jugé indispensable de posséder un fonds d'archives en lien avec les artistes du XXème siècle, les architectes ou les critiques. La notion d' « archive » est très vaste, aussi bien sur le plan étymologique que du point de vue philosophique. Une archive peut se définir comme un ensemble de documents produits par une entité publique ou privée durant sa période d'activité, mais il peut également englober le bâtiment qui abrite cet ensemble, voir même la base de données qui permet l'accès à son contenu. En plus de la riche documentation produite par les institutions officielles (l'État, les villes ou l'Église par exemple) au cours du XXème siècle, une attention considérable a été portée aux archives familiales et personnelles, ensembles de sources documentaires réunies par une famille ou un individu au cours de leur vie ou de leur activité professionnelle. Une archive naît souvent de manière fortuite et spontanée, mais toute l'historiographie récente souligne comment, au fur et à mesure de son enrichissement, une certaine prise de conscience émerge et pousse le sujet vers une forme de collecte plus sélective et plus raisonnée qui tend à créer un profil spécifique. De ce fait, les mécanismes de représentation mis en jeu dans toute opération de transmission de la mémoire s'appliquent à ce type d'archive.

Emblématiquement, tous les types d'archive sont un morceau de l'histoire en train de se faire et, de fait, ils ne représentent pas la quintessence d'un aboutissement – comme un livre ou une œuvre d'art – mais plutôt un sédiment d'une histoire de la culture. De plus, les archives sont un objet d'étude qui nous permet de retracer les différentes phases de développement d'une œuvre, et elles sont un parfait instrument pour instaurer un dialogue entre l'histoire de l'art et toutes les autres disciplines historiques, sociologiques, voir même économiques. Du fait de cette grande richesse, des expositions, des conférences ou des publications initiées par le Mart ont, à plusieurs occasions, conduit à la redécouverte et à l'acquisition de collections et inversement – la même programmation d'expositions mise en place depuis les années 1990 a été largement inspirée par les fonds documentaires acquis par le musée au fil du temps.
Le travail de Rosa Barba est organisé selon les mêmes lignes de force, entrelaçant les documents préservés dans les archives, elles-mêmes conservées dans le sous-sol du Mart, avec les espaces d'exposition du musée situés aux étages supérieurs, les faisant ainsi communiquer spatialement et conceptuellement tout en mettant au jour l'évolution possible d'un projet créatif dans le temps, le vrai potentiel de toute archive.
Rosa Barba mena tout particulièrement une recherche extensive sur les archives liées aux Futuristes en raison à la fois de la présence au Mart d'un noyau substantiel de documents futuristes – qui permirent la création du Centro Internazionale di Studi sul Futurismo (CISF ; Centre International d'Études Futuristes) – et la proximité des moyens d'expression qu'elle et les Futuristes ont en commun (le film et le texte par exemple).
Le Futurisme fait montre d'une attitude schizophrène envers le passé. D'un côté, il rejette le passé, mais d'un autre côté, il propage sa propre esthétique et ses idées (de manière assez stratégique) au moyen de la poésie, de manifestes, de magazines et d'une série de publications toutes destinées à créer un registre ou une mémoire des idées du mouvement de manière à exercer une influence maîtrisée sur l'opinion publique.
Une partie de ces archives provient d'un fonds de documents de la municipalité de Rovereto lié à la figure de Fortunato Depero, incluant un ensemble associé à des scripts de théâtre et de cinéma qui ne furent jamais mis en œuvre. Depero ne commença à s'impliquer dans des activités cinématographiques que tardivement au cours de sa carrière et il y vint, de manière assez indirecte, au travers de sa passion pour le théâtre. En réalité, c'est seulement au milieu des années 1920 que le peintre de Rovereto s'essaya à l'écriture cinématographique en produisant nombre de scenarii de films. Avant cela, le film, qui était considéré comme un territoire largement inexploré de l'expérimentation des langages artistiques, ne semble pas avoir particulièrement attiré l'attention de Depero ; en revanche, sa curiosité le conduisit à mener des expérimentations enthousiastes dans le champ théâtral. On peut évoquer, par exemple, l'étrange audace du spectacle *I balli plastici* (Les danses plastiques) qu'il conçut avec Gilbert Clavel et mis en scène au théâtre Costanzi en 1918, ou le funambule *Teatro Magico* (Théâtre Magique), et ses danseurs élastiques en caoutchouc.
Si l'on songe à l'attraction qu'avait toujours exercé sur Depero l'opportunité d'expérimenter toute les possibilités d'expression artistique bien au-delà de toute barrière disciplinaire, cet usage tardif du film est pour le moins curieux. Déjà en 1916, Marinetti et ses cosignataires Corra, Settimelli, Ginna, Balla, and Chiti avaient publié un manifeste sur le cinéma futuriste dans lequel il proclamait que le film était « le nouvel art, tellement plus vaste et plus souple que tous ceux qui existent », y compris, on peut donc le supposer, le théâtre. Dans le manifeste, les nombreux champs d'application du film étaient isolés avec une grande précision et étaient clairement compris comme « les moyens d'expression les plus adéquats pour un artiste Futuriste ». Les poèmes, les discours, la poésie, la recherche musicale, la simultanéité, la porosité de l'espace-temps, les états d'esprit, la dramaturgie de la disproportion et les drames en puissance, les équivalences plastiques et chromatiques linéaires – tout ceci est conçu comme l'apanage exclusif d'une recherche cinématographique polyexpressive, une exploration globale par définition, de telle sorte que tous les arts s'y retrouvaient combinés. Comme le déclare le manifeste, « La peinture + la sculpture + le dynamisme sculptural et les mots libérés + les faiseurs de bruits + l'architecture + le théâtre synthétique = le cinématographe Futuriste ».
Cependant, la transition de la théorie à la pratique révéla une certaine difficulté à transposer la complexité de ces définitions dans un répertoire d'images représentatives. *Vita Futurista* (La vie futuriste), le film, qui inaugura officiellement la saison du film futuriste cette même année, est un bon exemple de ce phénomène. En réalisant des courts-métrages, Marinetti mettait une nouvelle fois en avant la même mise en scène faite de moments et tours comiques inattendus sur le ton de l'ironie – par exemple un non-sens absolu – qui étaient typiques de ce que pouvait proposer le théâtre futuriste au même moment. Giovanni Lista note qu'il s'agissait d'un « cinéma de *petites formes* juxtaposées de gesticulations mécaniques, de grotesque et d'éclats de rire. Le modèle doit en être recherché sur la scène du vaudeville, ce qui revient à dire que les films étaient très proches du théâtre, avec ses surprises, ses synthèses et ses improvisations sur scène ». De plus, les quelques indications que Depero nous a laissées concernant le montage et le séquençage de ces scenarii montrent clairement la façon très affirmée de l'artiste de mettre le film au service de l'écrit. Ce concept émerge très clairement si l'on analyse le rythme narratif et les séquences spatio-temporelles des textes de ces différents scenarii, qui ne s'écartent que très marginalement du reste de sa vaste production littéraire au point de s'y perdre. C'est dans ce contexte, si riche d'interprétations et de développements possibles, que s'insère le projet de Rosa Barba pour le Mart, dans le sens où il actualise l'impulsion futuriste et utilise les archives du musée comme une plateforme d'expression. Avec son intervention *in situ* dans l'espace central vide du musée, l'artiste traduit la polysémie de la pensée (interlocutoire et parfois contradictoire) qui précède la réalisation d'une œuvre d'art et d'une intervention qui sont, comme l'artiste les décrit elle-même, un « work in progress ».

Gabriella Belli, Directeur, Mart – Museo di Arte Moderna e Contemporanea di Trento e Rovereto

ITALIAN TRANSLATION

UN'IDEA A TRE DIMENSIONI

IAN WHITE

> "Cadeva già della cenere, non però ancora fitta; mi volto e vedo sovrastarmi alle spalle una densa caligine che quale torrente spargendosi per terra ci incalzava. Deviamo, io dissi, finché ci si vede, per non essere travolti, una volta raggiunti, dalla folla che ci viene dietro.
> Appena fatta questa considerazione si fa notte, non di quelle nuvolose e senza luna, ma come quando ci si trova in un luogo chiuso, spente le luci".

(Seconda lettera di Plinio il Giovane a Tacito sui pericoli di Miseno[1])

Le catastrofi sono terribili. Ma è terribile anche una catastrofe che attende di accadere. Una catastrofe che attende di accadere può essere più pericolosa. Può non esistere. Non può venire ignorata. Forse è interamente concettuale, un territorio immaginato con confini ambigui e leggi irrazionali (speciali), un grande spazio vorace ricavato nella vita per fare da sala d'attesa (una sala d'attesa da cui non si può uscire) in cui paura e minaccia, inevitabilità, verità, chiacchiera, segno, analisi, invisibilità, finzione diventano le leve con cui viene esercitato il potere. Uno stato di assoluta ignoranza, come l'oscurità assoluta, la catastrofe in attesa serve a chi detiene il potere e a chi lo vuole conquistare per mezzo della particolare, amplificata importanza che essa conferisce al controllo dell'informazione (a come la si accende) e al tempo e allo spazio che hanno per fare questo. E rappresenta anche una serie di possibilità (forse terribili, ma anche potenzialmente utopistiche), un terreno soffice, facile, che fa appello agli assoluti degli idealismi e degli idealisti, indipendentemente dal rango.

Così si potrebbe parafrasare la serie televisiva del 2004 del regista britannico di documentari politici Adam Curtis, trasmessa dalla BBC, *The Power of Nightmares*, in cui l'autore suggerisce che i politici di oggi abbiano trovato il modo di riacquistare potere rimodellando se stessi, non più come ideologi o gestori della cosa pubblica ma come protettori, che proteggono il pubblico, i loro sottoposti, in particolare dalla minaccia (rappresentata come immensa) del terrorismo internazionale. In altre parole, Curtis descrive il terribile valore d'uso, per chi ha potere, della convinzione comune che ci sia una catastrofe che attende di accadere. È un trucco mentale. La sequenza di apertura di ogni episodio, sulla quale Curtis pronuncia questo breve slogan, mostra una serie di immagini (tutti i film di Curtis uniscono materiale d'archivio e interviste come mezzo per veicolare gli argomenti) che in parte richiamano un periodo della storia recente, creando una narrazione di destino imminente e preparando lo spettatore per la storia che si sta per raccontare: le luci dello stadio si abbassano, uno studio televisivo (di telegiornale?) vuoto viene smantellato, i fanali di una macchina che corre illuminano solo una piccola porzione della strada, maestosi lampadari vengono spenti, le ombre si allungano... in poche parole, l'oscurità scende come una metafora dello stato di ignoranza da sfruttare che potremmo anche attribuire a quella della catastrofe imminente, e il buio cala nell'auditorium come la condizione stessa di quella esperienza narrativa definitiva, il cinema industriale. Il "disaster movie" potrebbe essere uno dei suoi generi fondamentali, ma la catastrofe in attesa rappresenta sia la situazione che una delle condizioni del cinema industriale.

È in questo quadro che voglio collocare una discussione sul lavoro di Rosa Barba. Non perché proponga il tema dell'uso politico della paura del terrorismo internazionale, ma per via della sua sottile analisi, e cooptazione, del cinema industriale in quanto soggetto, per mezzo di diversi tipi di quelle che si potrebbero interpretare come "messe in scena" – del "locale", il non-attore, il gesto, il genere, l'informazione, l'autorevolezza e l'autorità, il banale – rimosse dal realismo sociale all'interno del quale sono state osservate e che le qualifica come elementi dell'opera, da inquadrare, riprogettare, rappresentare. L'effetto è quello di contestare e ri-pensare verità e finzione, mito e realtà, metafora e materiale fino a un livello di disorientamento che alla fine si estende a una pratica concettuale che anch'essa ripensa la messa in scena personale dello spettatore come atto di rovesciamento radicale e inebriante: dall'essere il destinatario di un'immagine (soggetto a controllo) al ritrovarsi all'interno e in mezzo alla/e sua/e sala/e macchina/e guardando verso l'esterno.

Spesso l'opera di Rosa Barba rappresenta comunità pre- o post-apocalitticamente abbandonate, almeno in apparenza, impegnate dall'ipotesi di una minaccia di disastro in cui sia le persone rappresentate che i disastri che le minacciano potrebbero essere letti ugualmente come reali o inventati, fino al punto che essere l'una o l'altra cosa, diviene non irrilevante, ma un'ambiguità che è il mezzo stesso che fa funzionare le opere dal punto di vista concettuale. Si tratta di una variazione sull'"atto di fede" richiesto al pubblico di un teatro, ma che, invece di un'immersione in una narrazione credibile, tende verso l'instaurazione di una meta-narrazione. I film *Panzano* (2000) realizzato con Ulrike Molsen e *Outwardly From Earth's Center* (2007) funzionano esplicitamente, in modi diversi, intorno a questa struttura, come anche l'opera online *Vertiginous Mapping* (2008). Così anche *The Empirical Effect* (2010), ed è su quest'opera che voglio concentrarmi come su una specie di cristalizzazione strutturale che può essere compresa ulteriormente cercandone le tracce all'indietro nei primi lavori, ed estesa a brevi meditazioni sulle sculture dell'artista di proiettori di pellicole a 16mm, sulla posizione dello spettatore in relazione a essi e sulla loro raccolta in mostre nelle quali le singole opere divengono parti di una costellazione complessiva.
The Empirical Effect è realizzato sulle pendici del Monte Vesuvio, un vulcano ancora attivo vicino a Napoli, la cui eruzione del 79 d.C. ci ha lasciato Pompei perfettamente conservata, il soggetto archeologico fondamentale, e la prima descrizione di un'eruzione vulcanica scritta da Plinio il Giovane, da cui ho ripreso la citazione in apertura. L'ultima eruzione importante del Vesuvio ebbe luogo nel 1944, e si presume che la prossima sia imminente: la durata del silenzio e dell'inattività del vulcano è inversamente proporzionale al volume crescente delle analisi e della speculazione, alla sua manipolazione e contestazione e alla presumibile gravità della futura eruzione. Silenzio e inattività sono ambedue simboli e funzione della minaccia. Ci si aspetterebbe che nessuno viva qui, e invece le pendici sono più popolate ora di quanto siano mai state. Tutto ciò è tuttavia una

situazione di cui il film fa solo un resoconto ellittico, e questo è significativo, come a voler rendere fatto un aneddoto.

Il film si apre con una voce fuori campo su una scala che potremmo descrivere come cinematografica: si sente un uomo che grida, in parte informando e in parte mitizzando (per mezzo dell'aspettativa di una narrazione minacciosa) l'attività del Vesuvio, e termina con l'esortazione a fuggire, su un'immagine di ciò che sembra lava scura e ribollente, fumo e carboni ardenti. L'aspettativa è inscenata. Il pericolo. Ma non è così che continua l'opera. Il genere è stabilito per essere abbandonato. Ridotto a un reticolo di attrezzature scientifiche di controllo, forse sismografi elettronici. Un edificio vuoto, pensato per uno scopo non residenziale né civile, ma per il genere di ricerca che richiede un tipo specifico di architettura. Non ci sono persone. Riprese d'archivio di una scena in strada, probabilmente dell'inizio del XX secolo. I passanti guardano una montagna, il Vesuvio. Attrezzi di misurazione antiquati, immobili, in teche di vetro, non usati. D'un tratto, una ripresa aerea delle pendici del Vesuvio, da un elicottero di cui sentiamo il rumore, rivela ville e paesi, come nelle sequenze iniziali di una *Dinasty* mediterranea. Poi si torna all'edificio che chiameremo centro ricerche. Una mappa della zona ricopre il pavimento e come per magia compare un gruppo di persone perlopiù anziane, che non si toccano fra loro, restando lì come oggetti (stranamente desocializzati, ma anche calmi, a proprio agio, consapevolmente esposti), e fra loro un certo numero di pecore belanti. Le persone cominciano a esaminare le cartine, mettendo in scena un'indagine, muovendosi e camminando come in un accenno di coreografia, presenti e coinvolti, ma attanti. Una donna porta occhiali scuri con una grande montatura di plastica bianca dall'aria fantascientifica, che somigliano a quelli della famosa fotografia del pubblico che in un cinema indossa occhiali 3-D tutti uguali ne *La società dello spettacolo* di Guy Debord. Tutti gesticolano gli uni verso gli altri e parlano, ma noi non sentiamo cosa dicono. Poi vengono fatte entrare delle apparecchiature tecniche, estranee a loro e a cui loro sono estranei, fisicamente, funzionalmente: il loro esame e il modo in cui questa teconologia a loro appare, è un'idea da respingere con orrore. Vanno a lavorare. Si sente un archivista che descrive la comunione della popolazione con l'ambiente come una maledizione e una benedizione allo stesso tempo: rischiano il disastro e la rovina e sono là per scelta, per il tipo particolare di rinascita che ne deriva...

E così l'opera continua, un susseguirsi irregolare di anacronismi, registri diversi, generi e scene evocativi al punto che non notiamo l'incoerenza del materiale perché ci siamo dentro e in mezzo; o meglio, quello che vediamo e sentiamo è coerente *perché* ci siamo dentro e in mezzo. Non accade niente che non sia in qualche modo messo in scena; la ricerca scientifica è scena e recitazione; il mistero, come il movimento fisico, è coreografato, le teste rivolte verso il cielo, un'indicazione; la cinepresa esplora l'architettura con scorrevole simmetria, senza il tremare di una mano o l'instabilità di un occhio; il gruppo di persone anziane ricompare come un coro greco ma senza commentare, infine cantando e danzando. L'assurdo equivale all'argomento. Modi diversi di indagine (cinematografico, documentaristico, scientifico, dilettantistico, mistico, teatrale) coesistono, non esiste verità in *quel* senso. Non ci viene raccontato nulla, né fatto, né storia, né opinione. Questa serie di scene non è il ritratto dell'esperienza comune, ma la sua interpretazione in rappresentazioni simboliche delle idee, traduzioni in un campo di performance e rappresentazione; e in questo modo risulta più vicina a qualcosa di materiale, invece di allontanarsene ulteriormente. La sicurezza di una grandiosa narrazione promessa dall'apertura del film viene destabilizzata in una varietà di modalità attraverso cui questa situazione potrebbe essere pensata o sperimentata anziché raccontata, come all'interno di, e appartenente a, un mezzo.
Verso la fine del film quattro uomini anziani, seduti in fila su un divano, agitano le braccia sulla testa a tempo fra loro. Una finta sirena inghiotte il sonoro. Per la prima volta, invece di individui isolati o degli anziani del coro, si vedono "correre" per strada gruppi più numerosi di persone di tutte le età (cioè, corrono *come se* ci fosse un'emergenza, eseguendo l'ordine, "correte come se ci fosse un'emergenza"). Alcuni portano un oggetto (una statuetta in gesso della madonna, una fotografia, una borsa di plastica). Recitano l'evacuazione. Potrebbe essere una vera esercitazione di evacuazione. Qui nel film *è* l'evacuazione, non una sua documentazione. La registrazione di ciò che vediamo è l'equivalente di una qualsiasi delle situazioni messe in scena che abbiamo visto prima. Quello che un'amministrazione locale potrebbe aver chiesto di fare a una comunità per testare i piani ufficiali in caso di eruzione, per dimostrare quanto tempo ci vorrebbe per evacuare completamente la zona, che tipo di trasporti, e quanti, sarebbero piú efficaci, quanto preavviso servirebbe per la sicurezza di tutti o altre cose del genere, di cui rendono conto le documentazioni online di queste esercitazioni – tutto ciò è una prova equivalente a qualsiasi altra cosa presentata in quest'opera. In questo momento ha luogo un rovesciamento radicale. Il film in sé diventa una prova delle sue stesse invenzioni, indagini, rappresentazioni. Una realtà viene inglobata in quella dell'opera: qualcosa di recitato nelle condizioni reali quando viene filmato diventa una sorta di realtà. La comunità non viene rappresentata ma costruita, un comunismo di rappresentazioni e una manifestazione di un tipo di empirismo completamente diverso da quello che comporta l'osservazione del mondo esterno. Una comunità (di spettatori) viene creata per mezzo del nostro atto di guardare ora insieme all'accordo collettivo, attraverso questi termini, che suggerisce ciò che possiamo e non possiamo dire, non sulla documentazione di una reale situazione di pericolo, ma dell'opera stessa, le sue verità e le sue menzogne, le sue testimonianze e la natura di esse, i suoi strati di messa in scena. Un iper-realismo, mostrato a partire da e da parte della situazione e della condizione del cinema industriale come catastrofe-in-attesa che qui è reso soggetto esso stesso.

Molti degli espedienti usati in *The Empirical Effect* si trovano già nei lavori precedenti di Rosa Barba. In particolare in *Outwardly From Earth's Center*, che con il film ha molto in comune, e con i drammi filmicamente autoreferenziali del più associativo *Panzano*.
Lo sviluppo di un modello particolare in questi tre lavori può essere individuato con chiarezza, ed è importante. Per la prima volta viene creato in *Panzano*. Come gli altri due, questo film è anche al tempo stesso un ritratto (di un rapporto a tre fra due uomini e una donna) e la costruzione di una realtà, la messa in scena di una serie di rapporti personali sviluppati in una rappresentazione dopo l'osservazione, la collaborazione e la traduzione: rendere strana una situazione reale per mezzo di vari effetti cinematografico-teatrali (suono non sincronizzato, luci, inquadratura, sceneggiatura ecc.). Non solo

ciascuna delle tre persone descritte occupa un ruolo definito da un copione, ma esse sono anche mostrate in quello che assumiamo come il loro habitat: una casa isolata, rurale, misera, fatiscente. Eppure vi compaiono grazie alla magia della sovrimpressione, con una poltrona vuota che d'un tratto si trasforma in una poltrona occupata ecc., e il sottotesto (la catastrofe imminente) è la loro paura (o la minaccia) della scomparsa dell'altro. Ambedue esistono sia nella realtà che cinematograficamente (come per tutti gli attori, con la differenza che qui il paradosso è più pronunciato), e le due cose dipendono l'una dall'altra come le tre persone, con l'una sempre condizionata dall'altra. Fra loro si svolgono assurdamente drammi che emulano melodrammi. A un certo punto l'uomo più anziano dice al più giovane, mentre giocano a calcio balilla, che la notte prima la donna non ha dormito nel suo letto: incomprensione, impotenza, gelosia? Paura. Ma quello su cui voglio portare l'attenzione è la climax del film. Fortissime e accecanti, luci ultraterrene inondano la casa. Il più anziano viene rapito dagli alieni? L'uomo avanza verso la luce dove si intravede un uomo giovane, e poi d'un tratto si sente gridare che se n'è andato. Che non tornerà mai più. Il che significa, naturalmente, che non è più né in casa né nel film. Ma invece ritorna, evocato dall'oscurità quando l'uomo più giovane, piangendo, posa la testa sulla spalla della donna e lei dice: "Chiudi gli occhi e lui tornerà". E uscendo dall'oscurità lui torna davvero, almeno nel film se non davvero nella stanza, come una – o la – presenza cinematografica. Un'immagine che allo stesso tempo conosciamo, di cui dubitiamo e per cui siamo felici, vista coi propri occhi dagli altri due e da noi come lo spettro e la materia del mezzo.

Outwardly From Earth's Center è più vicino a *The Empirical Effect*, essendo anche l'analisi di un luogo (relazioni, ma non un rapporto) in pericolo: un'isola, apparentemente quasi deserta, che scivola senza sosta verso il Polo Nord di alcuni metri all'anno. Essa presenta una serie di "abitanti" ed "esperti" che conosciamo per il lavoro che svolgono più che per nome, come in un libro di favole: il Guardiano del Faro, gli Archeologi, l'Architetto, l'Archivista ecc. I diversi tipi di teorie (o mitologie) e di soluzioni che queste persone hanno verso il problema dell'isola sono soggetti alla, e prodotti della, messa in scena di Rosa Barba; sono situati all'interno del sublime, le informazioni sono presentate in uno spazio teatrale, proiettate su schermi come su un set per il dramma e il mistero di tabelle e diagrammi spiegati a metà, o riferite come folklore ma al tempo stesso riportate su documenti ufficiali. Queste storie sono inframmezzate con riprese alla Bergman di una persona sola su una spiaggia, con lo sguardo perso lontano nel mare, monocrome, di estremo romanticismo, e con una serie di riprese di formazioni rocciose su cui si sente una voce maschile che risponde come a un test Rorschach, nominando ciò che vede in ognuna di esse come se chiedesse se le vediamo anche noi, come a esemplificare un atto registico di inquadratura e i suoi problemi. Chiaramente, come in *The Empirical Effect* questo film tratta una serie di prove che si sovrappongono, si contraddicono, si soppiantano a vicenda e fantasticano su quest'altra catastrofe in corso. E come nell'altra opera esse finiscono con il diventare pari fra loro a causa della funzione di accerchiamento dell'opera, del suo stesso vorace atto di creazione. In altre parole, anche quest'opera non è un documento, una registrazione di una situazione reale, ma la proiezione di essa in un vocabolario che è visivo, fantastico, dimostrazione di se stesso (equivalente fra relativi) e cinematografico.

Verso la fine del film si vedono grandi pali di legno accatastati nella sabbia come geroglifici verticali. Intorno ad essi vengono trascinate corde enormi e spesse, incrostate di ghiaccio. In una ripresa aerea dell'isola, raggi di sole colpiscono la terra attraverso le nuvole, una formazione rispecchiata da queste corde, che ora sono molte e sembrano linee scure e tese, che si diramano (come raggi di sole) dalla costiera dell'isola verso un luogo in cui vengono tirate, che però è fuori dallo schermo. L'isola è stata "salvata". Cioè la soluzione impossibile a un problema fantastico che è esso stesso un simbolo o un'esplorazione delle possibilità della coesione sociale è resa possibile nel film, e col nostro consenso alle sue finzioni che esso fa sedimentare.

È questo il modello che *The Empirical Effect* sviluppa ulteriormente, come se il film potesse essere letto come un punto di svolta. Dopo che abbiamo immaginato che la popolazione sia "fuggita" verso la salvezza, il coro degli uomini anziani rimane. Non c'è trionfalismo, ma distensione. Gli uomini danzano su una terrazza che dà sul mare, con un dolce abbandono che suggerisce che tutto quel verificare, dimostrare, raccogliere prove, confrontare, rappresentare, competere, sperimentare non sia stato inutile ma fittizio e reale come l'eruzione che cercavano di prevenire, che è accaduta e non è accaduta; che è accaduta (solo) all'interno e per mezzo di una complessa rete di finzione che potremmo non aver neanche bisogno di notare, che è il film soltanto, come un genere speciale di realtà.

Il punto che voglio affermare è che entrambi questi finali precedenti portano a quello di *The Empirical Effect*. Essi offrono, in modo simile, il suggerimento che sia accaduto qualcosa di gioioso, non disastroso, qualcosa di simile alla liberazione, e io a mia volta suggerisco che questa sia al tempo stesso un'operazione di filmmaking e la nostra via di uscita dai simboli del controllo che sono gli altri piaceri del cinema industriale, ai quali potremmo consentirci di soggiacere (come scegliere felicemente di vivere vicino a un vulcano attivo). Se la situazione e la condizione del cinema industriale alla fin fine vengono lette come il (meta)soggetto di Rosa Barba, quello che viene realizzato è una sorta di ribaltamento di quella situazione e condizione tale che essa diventa contenuto di superficie e può essere occupata e smontata al tempo stesso, con i suoi propri mezzi.

Ci sono due pensieri, connessi fra loro, che partono da questa considerazione. Il primo riguarda le sculture di proiettori 16mm di Rosa Barba, in cui il proiettore stesso, disposto in vari modi, non proietta niente, o solo il raggio di luce, e viene proposto come oggetto. Un buon esempio è *Stating the Real Sublime* (2009): un proiettore è appeso al soffitto con la stessa celluloide che sta proiettando, con la pellicola vuota che gira su una serie di carrucole e intorno al corpo della macchina che tiene sospesa. A prima vista si potrebbe leggere come una novità. Che cos'è questa macchina? Il supporto / celluloide non contiene immagini, funziona in modo diverso dal normale, in modo quasi feticistico. È quasi come se fosse rovesciato con la parte interna all'esterno, come se il materiale che di solito ingoia e trasforma nell'opera d'arte più immateriale di tutte, l'immagine proiettata, fosse la sua culla. Ma non c'è immagine, solo una macchina colta, trattenuta, funzionante sui suoi stessi meccanismi. Autosufficiente e stranamente rovesciata, senza esserlo davvero dal punto di vista meccanico. Nella mia mente arriva a rappresentare qualcosa. Il suo

tema non è il formalismo. È un'immagine di sé che mi colloca di fianco ad essa (io sono di fianco ad essa) mentre mi associa a una simile, indicibile condizione di rovesciamento. Diventa come un essere vivente. Io occupo e smonto sia lei che me stesso. Sono soggetto alla situazione e condizione di un'idea di cinema, che adesso è lì, diciamo un cinema industriale, a cui non prendo parte fisicamente, architettonicamente o dal punto di vista percettivo, ma di cui sono una funzione fino al punto che, concettualmente, questa è sia la sua metafora che il suo contenuto. La sua assenza di peso è anche assenza di corpo, e immensità.
Ancora, è proprio questo avviluppamento che comincia ad aver luogo quando un certo numero di queste opere è mostrato insieme, combinazioni di sculture-proiettore e film proiettati. Strutturalmente, si immaginano a vicenda e inglobano lo spettatore in questa sala macchine concettuale come mezzo per ri-immaginare e rivelare un insieme di relazioni che altrove costituiscono la sottomissione. Non c'è esempio migliore che nella mostra di Rosa Barba del 2010 *Is It a Two-Dimensional Analogy or a Metaphor?* che occupava praticamente ogni spazio degli eccezionali edifici postmoderni del Centre international d'art et du paysage de l'île de Vassivière. In effetti essa rivendicava il movimento dell'edificio e degli spettatori attraverso e oltre esso come l'opera stessa. Si veniva spinti dalla torre di un falso faro lungo il raggio di luce di un proiettore 70mm nelle gallerie vere e proprie, e ci si trovava davanti lo schema di un proiettore (e del nostro movimento stesso) scoperto da una ripresa aerea di un percorso di collaudo automobilistico nel deserto californiano, poi spinti oltre attraverso l'edificio fino a una stanza con sculture-proiettori e film-come-testo ritagliati da fogli di feltro che pendevano dal soffitto come scenario. Attraverso una porta (tutto questo nella stessa direzione lineare) si arriva in uno spazio di tipo teatrale privo di mobili che adesso è una cabina di proiezione, dove un altro enorme proiettore è collocato su una piccola finestra. Quando fa buio proietta un rettangolo statico di luce su erba, alberi e cespugli sottostanti, che si muovono come i fotogrammi di un film visibile da una stanza bianchissima, un museo, nientemeno, sotto questo spazio. La natura è diventata immagine, e lo spettatore è fermo, la terra gira. Ti ritrovi dentro i meccanismi di controllo a cui fuori (altrimenti) eri soggetto. Ecco il cinema industriale a luci accese, un'idea a tre dimensioni.

Note

1. Riletto da William Melmoth et revu par F. C. T. Bosanquet; http://www.arangioruiz.org/vesuvio/ovidio/PLINIO79.htm (ultimo accesso: 2 febbraio 2011).

LOOKING FOR ROSA BARBA

ELISABETH LEBOVICI

I. Full Circle

Non è perché la recente esposizione di Rosa Barba in Francia si è svolta sull'isola del lago di Vassivière – paesaggio trasformato in schermo dall'uso che l'artista ha fatto dell'edificio del centro d'arte, divenuto un gigantesco proiettore di cine-luce – che il suo lavoro mi è apparso come un arcipelago. No, il motivo dell'isola con i suoi rimandi si ritrova spesso nei suoi lavori, sotto forma di siti, di mappe, di territori arbitrariamente delimitati in un deserto, di circhi, di circuiti, di strade anulari, di sale d'esposizione, di pellicole avvolte nei loro contenitori o ancora di bobine di film, proiettate nel loro continuo ritorno e, al contempo, rese visibili nella materialità del loro percorso. Come quel tragitto barocco che origina da un proiettore sospeso qualche metro da terra nella torre cavernosa di Aldo Rossi a Vassivière: il nastro di pellicola quasi aspirato in verticale, per poi avvolgersi e ricadere dalla maggiore altezza possibile. Isole che sono ugualmente sonore, come effetti prodotti da ritornelli elettronici o da tecnologie di proiezione e ventilazione, o perché no, da conversazioni di cui non si afferra il senso. Alla Biennale di Venezia del 2009, un coro di testi veniva coreografato dalla voce di cinque proiettori, che accompagnavano come inconsci sonori, alcune parole scritte sullo schermo, a evocare in filigrana le didascalie di un film muto che ai tempi fornivano i dialoghi alle immagini. Giacché, ciò che ci tiene in sospeso nell'opera di Rosa Barba, non sono semplicemente quei siti che lei si affanna a delimitare, ma le drammatizzazioni ad essi sottesi, abbozzi di racconto in cui si fondono scienza e tecnoscienze, fantasia e fantascienze, che «precipitano nel sole della loro radiosa guerra (ir)-reale»[1]. Spesso quasi una minaccia sorda senza che si possa discernere se essa provenga da un passato rimasto segreto o da un futuro in qualche modo anticipato, se scaturisca da immagini cui si riferisce, o da macchine incluse nel presente performativo dell'installazione. L'isola che minaccia di andare alla deriva nel mare e di separarsi dal mondo che a noi li lega, il continente perduto o le rovine di un evento dimenticato (*"Forgotten"*: uno dei paesi di Rosa Barba) si confondono in una temporalità non lineare, non cronologica, non canonica e forse, ipotizziamo, «non maschile»[2]. Il testo che segue rappresenta ugualmente un arcipelago, una rete di isole, che lentamente va alla deriva. Certo, trae origine dai lavori dell'artista e ad essi fa riferimento, ma non si propone come un sostituto dell'esperienza delle opere, piuttosto come uno spostamento, e intanto che siamo immersi nella ricerca di Rosa Barba, sembra essere *dimentico* o distratto nel suo slancio alla ricerca della ricerca.

II. La fenditura

I Pastori d'Arcadia, Nicolas Poussin, 1638, Parigi, Museo del Louvre. In una natura alquanto selvaggia e assai poco agreste, con gli alberi spezzati dalle intemperie e le foglie scurite che seguono la forma delle tante nuvole grigie / bianche (l'Arcadia è un'isola canonicamente «distante da qualunque costa»), quattro personaggi fanno cerchio attorno a una tomba spoglia. A destra, una donna in piedi, di profilo, tiene una mano sulla spalla di un giovane pastore che, proteso, si appoggia al bastone, voltandosi verso la sua vicina a indicare con un dito ciò che gli altri due pastori, a sinistra, cercano di decifrare. L'uno, in piedi, disinvolto e sbilanciato nella sua posa a gambe incrociate, si appoggia alla tomba, allorché l'altro, con un ginocchio a terra, tocca, per leggerla, l'incisione sulla pietra. *Et In Arcadia Ego.* O piuttosto: Et In Arcadia E / go, poiché una fenditura nella pietra recide l'ultima parola. È l'Ego che si spezza, in realtà, mentre uno dei pastori vede la propria ombra proiettare il fantasma di una falce portatrice di morte. Il quadro di Poussin ha fatto di un'iscrizione su una pietra, in una radura, il punto di convergenza di tutte le conversazioni, a cominciare da quella del gruppo che si protende su di esse fino a quelle degli storici dell'arte, i quali hanno dialogato fino all'ossessione per testi interposti: Panofsky, Blunt, Klein, Gombrich, Marin... Tutti questi eminenti personaggi si sono a loro volta applicati a leggere, chi a fatica e chi con successo, attraverso i segni, per trovarvi il significato giusto, sul quale poi dar prova di perizia nei propri lavori. Parimenti, dopo la seconda guerra mondiale, nel corso di una serie di incontri, artisti, storici e critici dell'arte cercarono di prefigurarsi le sorti dell'estetica. Così, grazie a Rosa Barba che ne fa esplicito riferimento, è tornata alla ribalta dell'attualità *The Western Round Table on Modern Art*. Questa tavola rotonda si era svolta nel 1949 a San Francisco, allo scopo di riunire «una folta rappresentanza dell'opinione pubblica più informata dell'epoca, per produrre domande sull'arte dell'oggi»[3], ma non si trattava in realtà di rispondere anche di quegli stessi soggetti che formulavano quelle domande, di legittimare la loro "expertise"? Di questo Western in forma di conversazione, si trova traccia nel famoso sito Ubu – e, in realtà, esso brilla per la presenza di Duchamp, Bateson, Wright, 'Schoenburg' (sic!), esprimendo l'unanimità maschile dei suoi partecipanti: «Un manipolo di uomini che cercava di pensare. E, cosa ancora più difficile, cercavamo di pensare ad alta voce e di comunicare l'uno con l'altro – cercando di fare luce su cose che non erano mai state chiare»[4]. Dei nuovi pastori, in definitiva!
L'Arcadia ha lasciato il posto all'Ovest, parola che al contempo indica l'occidente e il Grande-Ovest delle Americhe, ivi compreso il genere cinematografico. Una serie panoramica viene così consegnata a una banda di cow-boy bianchi che cerca di avanzare verso l'avvenire già obsoleto della loro civiltà e delle loro culture, dimenticando che qualunque visione è incarnata da un corpo. «Tutte le narrazioni della cultura occidentale sull'oggettività sono allegorie di ideologie che regolano le relazioni di ciò che chiamiamo mente e corpo, distanza e responsabilità»[5]. In quello stesso 1949, Simone de Beauvoir pubblicava *Il secondo sesso.*
È stato detto di tutto su quell'iscrizione senza verbo «Et In Arcadia Ego»: – Incompiuta? Compiuta? – la sua traduzione spaziando da «Anch'io fui in Arcadia» a «Io sono anche in Arcadia» ha fatto parlare alternativamente il morto e la morte. Dal maschile al femminile. Tutto diverge a partire da qui, a partire da questa scrittura, queste quattro parole che li uniscono, deviando dal paesaggio descritto.
La tomba parla, ma cosa dice? Che si tratti della morte che si preannuncia, o del morto che giace ormai nella tomba, un dramma si è insediato nella regione pastorale, che dovrebbe invero esserne immune, in quanto paese della felicità al riparo da ogni decadenza e decrepitezza. Il personaggio femminile per tutto quel tempo sta in piedi, senza chinarsi né tentare di decifrare alcunché. È un'immagine pensosa, parallela alla superficie del quadro, quella che in definitiva resta solo una figura: non è forse attraverso di lei, allora, che si opera un secondo sguardo, che dà conto di un processo di visualizzazione, che la pittura non può rappresentare? La fenditura, in tal senso, ne costituirebbe il segnale.
La fenditura è l'"apriti Sesamo" che ci ha lasciato Louise Bourgeois. È qui che la questione della seduzione produce un'effrazione nel testo dell'arte. Louise Bourgeois spiega, di fatto, la narratività della sua opera mediante ciò che lei definisce "la fenditura": «Noi soffrivamo di una fenditura nel nucleo familiare, attraverso la quale mio padre introduceva le sue amanti in casa»[6]. Vedere furtivamente o di sottecchi è lo stesso che incarnare attivamente uno sguardo, di cui a sua volta Louise Bourgeois propone l'attivazione alle e per le spettatrici.
L'estetica si introduce in questa incrinatura familiare attraverso un certo numero di immagini che più che evocare la psiche di colei che le ha fabbricate, producono nella spettatrice una sorta di stato di frattura soggettiva[7]. Lo stesso fa Rosa Barba in *Split Fields*, la cui grana filmica in bianco e nero traspone, in apparizione fantasmatica, il fantasma collettivo, sociale, economico e politico del potenziale crollo dei paesi ai piedi del Vesuvio. In seno alla Tate Modern, *Shibboleth*, il progetto nella Turbine Hall concepito dall'artista colombiana Doris Salcedo, consisteva nello scavare una crepa che procedeva a zig-zag nel pavimento di cemento dello spazio espositivo. «Uno spazio negativo. Esso evoca il buco della Storia che segna la differenza che separa i bianchi dai non-bianchi», spiegava l'artista, il cui progetto della linea di demarcazione ha lasciato, nella sua realizzazione, una cicatrice indelebile nel pavimento della Turbine Hall.

III. Stories from the Landscape

In *The Song of the Lark,* romanzo della scrittrice americana Willa Cather, figura il «Panther Canyon». Si tratta di un canyon americano, che l'autrice colloca nel deserto dell'Arizona e raffigura come una fenditura scabrosa. «Pareti a strapiombo brulle e ricoperte di sola roccia» per la «prima sessantina di metri sotto la superficie [...]». «Da lì fino a giù le pareti erano meno scoscese, degradanti e ornate di pini e di cedri nani. L'effetto era quello di un canyon più ospitale all'interno di uno più selvaggio. La città morta giaceva là dove finiva la parete ripida e cominciava il profondo taglio della gola. In quel punto, uno strato di roccia più tenero rispetto a quelle sovrastanti, era stato scavato dall'azione del tempo fino a diventare un enorme canale che correva lungo le pareti del canyon. In questa depressione (simile a una grande piega nella roccia) l'Antico Popolo aveva costruito le proprie case di pietra giallastra e malta»[8]. Temibile e benevolo, abitato e disabitato: tutta una gamma d'emozioni lo affolla. Questo testo, che

descrive il canyon come una di quelle fratture che modella la storia enigmatica di questo paese è «l'esempio più compiuto di paesaggio femminile in letteratura»[9].
All'interno della fenditura, c'è dunque tutto un popolo nativo e il canto della terra rivela così i suoi abitanti, che sono dei costruttori ecologici. Willa Cather, o piuttosto Thea Kronborg, cantante lirica e personaggio femminile del suo racconto, evoca le vestigia archeologiche delle terrecotte plasmate dalle donne indiane: per lei/loro, esse hanno la potenzialità per divenire l'oggetto della loro ricerca estetica. La trasformazione degli oggetti della ricerca è un motivo che si trova spesso quando ci si interessa all'impatto delle donne nella storia canonica delle belle arti e si considerano gli usi non disciplinari, in particolare l'artigianato, il lavoro della terra e della ceramica. Tra il processo di creazione che agisce in ciò che definiamo natura e in ciò che definiamo finzione, si scava un passaggio, che è anche un paesaggio. «Quando si porta a compimento la prima immagine di una forma organica, è allora che il lavoro artistico mostra le sue generiche e simboliche possibilità, esattamente come un'affermazione imperfetta o solo abbozzata, comprensibile però nel suo intento generale»[10].
Così scrive una filosofa un po' in disuso, Susanne Langer, che pone il "feeling" in primo piano, un sentimento che non è soltanto quello del piacere o del dispiacere ma che si identifica con lo spazio vissuto del mondo, vale a dire con i fatti della vita dello spirito.
L'evoluzione del termine paesaggio si associa a questo concetto: in primo luogo rappresentazione estetica – raffigurata, dipinta o testuale – a connotare ulteriormente una visione, e quindi un punto di vista, poi un intervento estetico in seno a un luogo, la parola è andata alla deriva nel tempo e nello spazio, fino a designare secondo J.M. Coetzee «sia uno specifico terreno che il carattere generale di quel terreno»[11].
Il paesaggio è una concatenazione, una composizione estetica e un orientamento. Così, Rosa Barba: «Era quindi una storia che emergeva da un paesaggio...»[12].

IV. L'ecosistema delle collaborazioni

Panzano (2000, 22') è una collaborazione tra Rosa Barba, Ulrike Molsen e Valeria, Claudio e Dino: alcuni superstiti di quella che fu una delle più rilevanti utopie degli anni settanta, vale a dire l'anti-psichiatria.
Un modello fin troppo dimenticato di un'ecologia di vita che ambiva a relazioni fra gli esseri umani o altri organismi (in questo caso, la macchina da presa, la televisione, il personaggio da concorso canoro radiofonico) e il loro ambiente, che include prima di tutto alcuni processi di creazione e produzioni culturali. L'ecosistema del film non è il borgo della Toscana ma lo spazio dello schermo, che passa dall'ottico all'aptico con le sue sovraesposizioni, le sue composizioni che associano la fisicità di tutti gli attori, comprese anche le tecnologie. "L'occhio della macchina da presa" si combina con la virtualità delle storie potenziali e degli effetti chimici di sovrapposizione, così come con le incrinature che agiscono tra l'esterno e l'interno. Panzano, se vogliamo, è il paesaggio della fenditura, quasi una bocca spalancata.
E se questo micro-clima della sperimentazione si dilatasse fino alle terre incolte del deserto? Evocando un'altra regione del mondo, il Grande Ovest americano, e un altro tempo, l'inizio del XX secolo, Jonathan Goldberg[13] fa il racconto di una collaborazione fittizia, giacché non si compì mai, tra due donne che frequentarono quello stesso immenso territorio: la scrittrice Willa Cather, (più famosa oggi per aver adoperato, nelle sue lettere del 1890, la parola *queer* al fine di menzionare la devianza sessuale), e Laura Gilpin, una delle più apprezzabili fotografe dei puebli Navajo e Pueblo tra il 1920 e il 1979, data della sua morte. Il Western ricade qui fuori dal canone epico della costruzione dell'America bianca declinata al maschile, ovvero della volontà di spostare le frontiere e di controllarle, facendosi portavoce anche del concetto di deserto come monumento e monolite: *Et in Arcadia Ego*. Nel suo deserto, Laura Gilpin fotografa "l'Antichità" americana quale regno di unità tra i canyon - sculture della natura - e le case delle popolazioni indiane, con le terrecotte che rappresentano, a suo avviso "La Resistenza Navaho", come recita il titolo di uno dei suoi libri più famosi. In Willa Cather, il paesaggio, con la sua flora e la sua fauna, comprese le terrecotte archeologiche Sinagua che vi si trovano, rappresentano una struttura sinfonica in cui si uniscono dei corpuscoli in trasformazione, a fondere e trasporre le loro influenze e i loro stili, ma la cui materialità evoca parimenti la membrana sensibile del diaframma – vale a dire del muscolo che permette la respirazione del canto. La musica del canyon si fonda anche sull'armonia tra il canto degli uccelli, il verso delle cicale e i ronzii degli insetti, e il ritmo di particolari cerimonie. Allo stesso modo, nella scrittura, il luogo diviene un risonatore della vitalità del corpo. Sul fronte della fotografa, si tratta invece di visualizzare l'oblio, ciò che fu ma non è più, a costo di ricostituire il sito della vita pacifica che vi si svolgeva facendo posare gli Indiani o piuttosto le Indiane vive e vegete, pagati/e per fare da modelli/e. Un sistema, questo, che ha imbarazzato più di un adulatore: ma ciò che Laura Gilpin inscrive nella propria iconografia, è una proiezione, scrive Goldberg, che si verifica nel suo modo riservato e affatto invadente di unificare queste donne, il luogo che le circonda e i loro manufatti; le terrecotte raffigurate nelle immagini sono i veicoli di «monumenti di grande bellezza [...] che ci offrono nella loro arte una virilità e una bellezza di concezione, che al confronto i nostri sono deboli e anche un po' insignificanti. E soprattutto, essi hanno «*endured* – resistito e durato»[14]. Il legame tra la scrittura di Cather e le fotografie di Gilpin, che si potrebbe far risalire banalmente a una spiegazione di natura sessuale (l'omosessualità), appare in realtà ben più sottile allorché si tratta di presentare il deserto come luogo di un sapere intuitivo, vitale, che rifugge da ogni spiegazione. Come nei Pastori d'Arcadia, sta al personaggio femminile non decifrare ma al contrario allontanarsi dal potere dei segni. Non per indifferenza ma perché essa è già un segno nel linguaggio maschile.
Et in Arcadia E/go: L'Arcadia non è più un'utopia. L'E/go diviso da una barra che viceversa enuncia una distopia, così come fa Monique Wittig, quando la introduce ne *Il corpo lesbico*, per riportare un'esperienza in un linguaggio che non m/i rappresenta come soggetto. Monique Wittig: «I/o pone la questione ideologica e storica dei soggetti femminili»[15]. I/o è per Wittig, il segno di una divisione dualista dei sessi e l'imposizione di una logica della differenza come verità e valore universale, un sistema nel quale e per il quale gli uomini sono (fatti) di uomini e le donne sono (fatte) di donne.

V. Di Ovest in Est, il deserto

Per Reyner Banham[16], il deserto è lo spazio in cui l'uomo moderno deve sentirsi "a casa propria". Nel cinema di Antonioni, si inscrive in una storia post-industriale di diserzione e deriva, esplorando anche una visione ambivalente del mondo tecnologico. *Deserto Rosso* veicola i temi dell'alienazione, dell'angoscia, del disorientamento spaziale e di situazioni esistenziali di genere, percepiti attraverso cambiamenti cromatici. È un passeggero femminile quello che viaggia attraverso questo paesaggio "psicogeografico" in cui, come dice Zygmunt Bauman: «Il presente è sempre deficitario, e pertanto minaccioso, ripugnante e insopportabile. Il presente è obsoleto... L'istante approda nel presente, il tanto atteso futuro è ammorbato dagli effluvi venefici del passato che è stato consumato»[17]; un testo che potrebbe ben adattarsi anche a *D'Est*, il film di Chantal Akerman. Allo stesso modo, *Deserto Rosso* si avventura in una geografia che esplora il paesaggio pittorico astratto dell'arte americana moderna, peraltro già esportato in Europa e in particolare in Italia, al fine di presentare «la logica conclusione di una tendenza inesorabile e di vecchia data nei confronti dell'astrazione» nella quale «ciò che era stata una caratteristica prevalentemente americana ora diventa rappresentativa della "Cultura occidentale" nel suo complesso»[18]. *Deserto Rosso* si allontana ugualmente dalle convenzioni filmiche figurative. Le coppie che fanno l'amore tra la sabbia di *Zabriskie Point* (1969) si inseriscono come "punti di trapuntatura" in uno spazio terrestre convesso, come se il proiettore restituisse la curvatura allo schermo.
Le tecnologie dell'immagine permettono un processo di oggettivazione particolarmente sofisticato, dettagliato, parziale e mobile delle emozioni legate a queste tecnologie. Così, il deserto del Mojave in *They Shine* di Rosa Barba, è rinquadrato sulle sue "fabbriche" di pannelli solari tesi come degli scudi contro chissà quale incursione venuta dal cielo o quelle piccole costruzioni devastate e coperte di graffiti, che probabilmente hanno partecipato al progetto scientifico di speculare sul potenziale industriale e materiale dell'America contro la guerra atomica[19]. Gli uni come gli altri, che brillino o che arrugginiscano, puntano sui poteri della finzione della natura, vale a dire sulle capacità di quest'ultima di nascondere i racconti di capitalizzazione e di profitti sotto le rovine. Come il deserto dell'ultima installazione di Hito Steyerl, con i suoi cimiteri di rottami d'aerei. Viene da pensare anche all'esplosione dei beni di consumo in *Zabriskie Point* di Michelangelo Antonioni così come alle fotografie di Sophie Ristelhueber del deserto-immondizia della prima guerra in Irak (*Fait*, 1992). E infine, alla reclusione permanente del personaggio femminile del film *Safe* di Todd Haynes, con il volto di Julianne Moore, per la quale un rifugio nel deserto costituisce l'ultima possibilità di un Sé sottomesso al terrore di sopravvivere al tempo dell'apocalisse ambientale. D'altronde, questo terrore ambientale è apparso fin dal 1949 con la guerra fredda e la corsa agli armamenti nucleari, sviluppando negli Stati Uniti un immaginario della rovina, divenuto allo stesso tempo un rituale privato e un modello di *governance*, spingendo nella sua logica a giocare continuamente alla distruzione fisica dello Stato-nazione così come a concepire delle città-test, dei simulacri di periferie come prototipi di sopravvivenza nel deserto dell'Ovest.

VI. The Desert Is No Lady

The Desert Is No Lady è un libro che va contro il suo titolo. Una volta partiti dall'assunto che l'analisi del paesaggio è stata per lungo tempo declinata al maschile, che il "cannone del canyon" e la geografia furono in primo luogo proprietà intellettuale degli uomini, basate sulla presunzione che le regioni sono popolate da uomini, conquistate da uomini, che gli uomini sono angosciati davanti alla natura, ecc., le ricerche hanno preso atto di questi fili invisibili che dividono il terreno secondo il genere, il sesso, la razza e hanno creato altre specie di spazi. È un po' come quando si parte alla ricerca di Rosa Barba, con l'intento di descrivere meglio le sue opere. Si apre il fascicolo di un'arte non urbana, di una tradizione paesaggistica, di un immaginario geografico e di produzioni culturali in rapporto con un soggetto o una soggettività femminile e per cominciare, non si ha niente. Il deserto? Ma anche il deserto è popolato da migliaia di indizi su ciò che il paesaggio ha "fatto" alle donne di culture anglosassoni, ispaniche, messicane, indiane nel Sud Ovest dell'America, a partire dai tessuti Navajo a Georgia O'Keeffe, dalle ceste Hopi a Willa Cather e dalle terrecotte Pueblo ad Andrea Geyer. Questi approcci del paesaggio vi trovano forza e liberazione creative: «la vasta e indomita scala della regione le libera dalle restrizioni silenziose legate alla femminilità. Un'energia erotica venuta dalla terra [...] permea la scrittura delle donne indiane e questo incontro sensuale e sensato, sessualizzato si ritrova nell'opera dell'artista che va a cercarla [...]»[20].
Quali prospettive, visive e sociali, organizzano l'intrusione delle donne e delle questioni di genere nel paesaggio? Quando passa dalla presentazione diretta del suo corpo in performance a una serie di "dialoghi tra il paesaggio e il corpo femminile" (i termini sono suoi), fuori dal laboratorio e dall'estensione di esso che è il White Cube, Ana Mendieta genera, di fatto, un accoppiamento fra la terra e il corpo, con il termine di *earth/body sculptures*. La terra, la sabbia, le pietre, l'acqua, la polvere da sparo, il fuoco, le piante, i fiori, gli alberi, il sangue, la neve, i capelli vi partecipano per esprimere, in ogni *Silueta* (sagome tagliate secondo le forme del corpo), questa zona di contatto. L'artista dà l'avvio, fin dalla prima installazione in cui una *Silueta* è collocata su di una tomba Zapoteca a Oaxaca (1973), a un movimento permanente: ogni pezzo lascia un vuoto, il vuoto del corpo fisico documentato dalla fotografia o dal film-ricordo, che segna anche la dislocazione conseguente all'esilio. Come ha ben mostrato Lucy Lippard, Ana Mendieta stabilisce delle connessioni tra il paesaggio e la storia, tra lo psichico e il sociale tingendo la pratica delle *earthworks* di specifiche connotazioni politiche e femministe: e non è casuale che le *Silueta* all'inizio verranno esposte proprio alla galleria A.I.R., collettivo newyorkese di donne artiste. *Untitled, Volcano Piece, Iowa,* 1980, propone una sagoma inscritta in un cumulo oblungo, trasformata in vulva con le sue labbra di terra sotto l'effetto del fuoco, che esplode dopo essere stata cosparsa di polvere da sparo. Mendieta ha appiccato il fuoco, filmato l'incendio, lo sprigionarsi del fumo e i resti: la sua sagoma bruciata crea un vuoto, che è allo stesso tempo vuoto dell'esilio e vuoto dell'invisibilità dei non-uomini e dei non-bianchi nel paesaggio degli Stati Uniti. Essa propone ugualmente una rappresentazione della sessualità femminile attraverso il fuoco, andando in senso contrario alla leggenda prometeica, incentrata sul fuoco come fallo, almeno secondo l'interpretazione che ne dà Freud[21].

«La mia arte viene dalla dislocazione e dalla rabbia», afferma Mendieta. Lo spazio dell'esilio, della deterritorializzazione, si inserisce nella materia stessa con la quale l'artista costruisce le sue opere. Allo stesso modo, Nancy Holt include nelle forme che dà alle sue proposizioni, il passaggio del tempo che costituisce sia la sua materia sia il suo contenuto. Nel 1969, l'artista sotterra dei poemi in alcuni siti scelti dei deserti dell'Ovest. Nello stesso periodo, Gina Pane, in Italia sotterra delle pietre come una sorta di quadrante solare. Ed è su un terreno acquistato nell'Utah che Nancy Holt realizza, tra 1973 e il 1976, i suoi *Sun Tunnels*. L'artista ha fatto installare quattro enormi tubi per condutture, realizzati in cemento. Questi «condotti» di circa 6 metri di lunghezza e 2,50 di altezza, sono posti uno di fronte all'altro a coppie intorno a uno spazio vuoto, con al centro una circonferenza di cemento. Sono orientati in funzione dei solstizi d'inverno e d'estate e i buchi disseminati sulle superfici di cemento rappresentano la topografia di alcune costellazioni, le cui figure sono riprodotte dalle chiazze di luce all'interno. «Il giorno è trasformato in notte e si assiste a un capovolgimento del cielo»[22], dice Nancy Holt, di modo che il tempo acquisti una presenza fisica e la configurazione spaziale della Terra diventi percettibile: si tratta di rimettere la terra sul proprio asse in un luogo in cui l'umanità non è più attuale, di dirigere lo sguardo per seguire le differenti posizioni del sole. Il paesaggio di Nancy Holt non deriva tuttavia da una effusione romantica con il paesaggio ma da un "calcolo": «ho voluto riportare il vasto spazio del deserto a una scala umana. Non era mio desiderio costruire un monumento megalitico. La visione panoramica è troppo opprimente perché si possa fare a meno di riferimenti visivi»[23].

VII. Deserto, Desiderio

Per Roni Horn, il deserto è ghiacciato, un misto di ghiaccio e terra nera. Il deserto è uno specchio, che rimanda solo a se stessi e quindi un deserto deserto, come lei stessa lo definisce in uno degli 8 lemmi consacrati a questo termine nel suo libro *Roni Horn aka Roni Horn*[24]. Queste occorrenze della parola deserto precedono la parola desiderio, e seguono la parola dedica.

VIII. Savage Dreams

Nel 1851 ha inizio una battaglia in quello che in seguito diventerà il parco Nazionale di Yosemite. Questa battaglia è perpetrata ai danni degli abitanti indigeni. Nel 1951, a qualche centinaio di chilometri di distanza, un'altra guerra comincia, allorché il governo degli Stati Uniti decide di dare l'avvio ai test nucleari in un sito del Nevada, ricorrendo per forza di cose all'evacuazione del territorio e delle persone. Questo è quanto racconta il libro di Rebecca Solnit[25]. «*Savage Dreams* è un'esplorazione di questi due paesaggi paradigmatici – il sito dei test nucleari, dove sono state esplose più di mille bombe nucleari, e il Yosemite National Park, dove le guerre contro gli Indiani non sono mai realmente finite. Fra il 1951 e il 1991 si conta una bomba atomica al mese per delle guerre che evidentemente non sono mai iniziate, insieme alle guerre contro gli Indiani che si presumeva fossero finite nel diciannovesimo secolo e che invece non si sono mai concluse. La popolazione indigena non sparisce, ma il suo diritto ad abitare nel territorio è continuamente messo in discussione, benché la violenza ora sia più sottile. Mentre Yosemite mantiene l'immagine convenzionale di paradiso, finisce per essere una sorta di inferno di alienazione sociale. Naturalmente, come sito dei test nucleari si tratta di un autentico inferno, ma se consideriamo le comunità che si sono organizzate per resistere, vediamo che queste hanno generato una sorta di paradiso. Così le idee sul paradiso e sull'inferno per me si sono come ribaltate a causa di questa coraggiosa e vasta comunità di Mormoni *downwinders* [persone esposte alle radiazioni dei test nucleari], sopravvissuti di Hiroshima, fisici nucleari, anarchici, ambientalisti, monaci Buddisti e preti Cattolici riuniti nel sito dei test atomici»[26]. Questa intervista è apparsa sulla rivista "Bomb".

IX. Rimostranza / Restituzione

Gli interventi sulla morfologia dei siti, le opere costituite da elementi naturali, grezzi o lavorati, di essenze vive o inerti hanno rinnovato un'arte del paesaggio realizzata nel contesto di un più ampio sforzo ecologico. Non è secondario che a fianco delle *earthworks*, e talvolta in contraddizione con esse, ci sia stata un'attrazione da parte di alcuni artisti per un'arte di restauro dei siti. Questi o queste hanno usato il termine di *reclamation art* - coniugando in questo termine, così come nell'italiano "restituzione" - l'azione di ristabilire ciò che ha subito delle alterazioni e di rendere ciò che è stato preso, ovvero la ricostruzione e al contempo la riconsegna della natura a se stessa. Questo non sarebbe potuto accadere senza l'emergenza ecologica organizzata in movimento politico. Contro una concezione della natura come caos e ferocia, ma anche come mera riserva delle risorse, i problemi ambientali daranno vita alla nozione di "ecosistema", con la sua complessa dinamica di energia e materia. Nella costruzione del paesaggio ecologico, troviamo un'altra consonanza che però non ha mai avuto luogo, quella di due donne che nello stesso periodo pubblicano due opere divenute, nel tempo, dei classici: i lavori sulla pianificazione urbana di Jane Jacobs, di cui *Death and Life of Great American Cities* viene pubblicato nel 1961 e, nel 1962, il libro di Rachel Carson, *Silent Spring*, che mostra come i danni provocati dai pesticidi abbiano trasformato la nozione stessa di ambiente. Questi due libri, di fatto, permettono di allontanarsi dalla dicotomia fra spazio urbano e spazio naturale. In entrambi i casi, i limiti disciplinari e spaziali tra città e natura si sgretolano: le due opere utilizzano un vocabolario simile volto ad aprire una nuova dimensione, capace di mantenere delle connessioni fra i due diversi ambiti. Questo paesaggio si oppone a quello di una modernità associata all'efficienza e all'igiene, costruito dal riformismo sociale e dal razionalismo, che in tal senso hanno rafforzato le barriere tra città e natura. Ora, Carson avanza una tesi popolare di salute ecologica criticando il modello disciplinare propugnato dagli esperti, mentre dal canto suo, Jane Jacobs osserva la violenza imperante nella città moderna; tema sul quale le prime opere femministe, quali

The Feminine Mystique (1966) di Betty Friedan, rincarano la dose, quando evocano il problema "senza nome", ovvero l'isolamento delle donne nell'America suburbana degli anni del dopoguerra. Tale è la forza del paesaggio femminista, che arriva a porre le sue questioni all'interno di un nuovo quadro concettuale. Donna Haraway non ha forse esemplificato in modo suggestivo fino a che punto le questioni di genere si intersechino con le nozioni di geografia, due saperi che hanno bisogno di essere "situati"? «L'incarnazione femminista, non attiene a una posizione fissa in un corpo reificato, femminile o altro, bensì alle ramificazioni nei diversi campi»[27]. Nell'opera di Rosa Barba, *Outwardly from Earth's Center,* dal tempo e spazio incerti, l'isola di Gotska Sandön esiste soltanto nella sua potenziale deriva. Gli esperti parlano, il guardiano del faro, l'architetto, l'archivista, il politico, tutti al maschile, mentre gli abitanti, uomini, donne o altri, non parlano ma costruiscono insieme una scultura, un'architettura di corde e di pilastri di legno, una grata, un processo e una dislocazione: un paesaggio, non uno stato, non un territorio né un'amministrazione.

X. Disastri

«Un tempo, New York era una città su un'isola, una città con una collocazione nel mondo fisico. In questo secolo, persino l'isola è stata rimpiazzata dal Distretto di Manhattan. Parigi una volta era situata in una vasta e fertile pianura. Ora è in Francia ma la Francia è un'invenzione di Parigi»[28], dichiara Jimmy Durham.
Nel 2007, Sanja Ivekovic trasforma la piazza principale di Documenta a Kassel in un campo di papaveri. Mierle Laderman Ukeles già per l'esposizione *Care*, del 1969, proponeva che fossero consegnati al museo, quotidianamente, i rifiuti provenienti in parte dai cassonetti dell'immondizia e in parte derivanti dall'inquinamento atmosferico e dei corsi d'acqua, allo scopo di contribuire letteralmente al loro recupero all'interno delle sale d'esposizione, installando delle macchine di depurazione, disinquinamento, per il riciclaggio e la conservazione. Tra il 1978 e il 1983, la stessa artista aveva proposto di trasferire 6 "polder" newyorkesi in alcune zone "calde" di recupero, propugnando un'estetica che fosse libera dai cliché imposti dagli uomini, per i quali le rappresentazioni della donna sono assoggettate alla natura.
«Non c'è niente che possa essere paragonato ai disastri naturali»[29], dichiara Rebecca Solinit. Che si tratti di terremoti o di eruzioni vulcaniche, è sempre l'architettura, la costruzione umana che ha la peggio, che uccide le persone, che produce il disastro collettivo, sociale, conseguenza dell'uragano, della tempesta, dell'inondazione, dello tsunami. Questo è ciò che mostra anche *The Empirical Effect* (2009–10), in cui Rosa Barba tratta di uno stesso genere di disastro *non-original*, come direbbe Haraway, perché è soltanto la nuvola sospesa di un dramma che non si è più ripresentato dal 1944. L'eventualità di un risveglio eruttivo del Vesuvio è diventata una minaccia permanente per gli abitanti di Napoli e dintorni, così come le numerose attività illecite che vi pullulano, ma è allo stesso tempo uno spettacolo turistico che si nutre del pericolo, rinnovando il tema dell'orrida raffinatezza del sublime attraverso la presentazione di apparecchi di misurazione, di sonde e sismografi e mediante la performance collettiva costituita dalle prove di evacuazione dei residenti. Questa composizione, ancora una volta, "psicogeografica" è presente nel film di Rosa Barba, come finzione di una finzione; non avendo mai avuto luogo la prova generale dell'evacuazione degli abitanti del Vesuvio, dice l'artista, le venne in mente di organizzarla. Alcuni testimoni dell'eruzione del 1944 fanno parte del corteo di persone che corre in un paese vuoto, in un cortocircuito temporale in cui si performa la prova anticipata della catastrofe. Rifugiati in una sorta di riparo, un'isola di cemento *safe*, i protagonisti incarnano attraverso i loro gesti differenti possibilità di linguaggi, di comunicazione del vivere insieme, resistendo alle distinzioni semplificatrici tra argomenti razionali e irrazionali.
Ma la corsa dei personaggi sedimenta una storia particolare del cinema a Napoli, tradizionalmente filmata dal vivo, sia da una prospettiva aerea sia dal punto di vista delle sue molteplici attività di strada. Nell'opera dedicata alla regista napoletana Elvira Notari[30], la storica della cultura Giuliana Bruno mostra come la Notari concepisca le sue narrazioni cinematografiche, ad esempio in *Due Paradisi*, 1928, dove la tecnologia permette di confrontare la prospettiva aerea e lo spazio vissuto in cui si cammina a livello della strada, aprendo in tal modo ad altri paradigmi visivi aldilà di quello dell'occhio e dell'ottico.

XI. Vertiginous Mapping

A partire dalla *Mappa del paese della tenerezza* e della sua topografia illustrata che pubblicò Madeleine de Scudéry nel 1654 per dare l'immagine a un itinerario di emozioni, a un viaggio amoroso, a un paesaggio interiore che fornisse «una carta geografica dello spazio relazionale» e un «testo cartografico aperto, le cui tante, potenziali opzioni di percorso producono un effetto cumulativo»[31], Giuliana Bruno reinventa lo spazio del cinema e il movimento delle arti "visive e dello spazio", per dirla con le sue parole. L'invenzione del film, sito culturale cinetico, ha inaugurato un'era di circolazione sempre più complessa, sempre che ci si sforzi, così come fa Rosa Barba, di coinvolgere all'interno della mappa la deriva presente nel processo e gli stessi strumenti della cartografia: da cui la produzione di una cartografia vertiginosa. Vertiginosa, perché essa implica nella sua struttura tanto le immagini quanto le tecnologie, gli schermi e i proiettori, l'architettura e la macchina. Rosa Barba fa dello stesso cinema una rovina del futuro, una fantascienza lasciata dal cyberspazio del XXI secolo. Con lo sviluppo del Web, la nostra cultura spaziale, osserva ancora Giuliana Bruno, non reinventa forse la pulsione di fare contatto e di essere connesso, di porre lo spazio virtuale come abitabile e abitato?

XII. "Facts Run on Lightbeams These Days"[32]

Note

1. In Inglese: "collapse into the sun of their radiant (ir)reality-war" da Donna Haraway, *Situated Knowledges: The Science Question in Feminism and the Privilege of Partial Perspective*, "Feminist Studies", vol. 14, n. 3, (Autunno 1988), p. 577.
2. Sulla confutazione del modello canonico di "narrazione dell'anteriorità", vedi Mieke Bal, *Louise Bourgeois' Spider: The Architecture of Art-Writing*, University of Chicago Press, 2001.
3. "The Western Round Table on Modern Art (1949)", edizione a cura di Douglas MacAgy. Consultato sul sito: http: / / www.ubu.com / historical / wrtma / index.html
4. Ibid.
5. Donna Haraway 1988, op. cit., p. 583.
6. Louise Bourgeois, in un'intervista di Bernard Marcadé nel film di Camille Guichard: *Louise Bourgeois*, (New York, Febbraio 1993).
7. Mieke Bal 2001, op. cit.
8. Willa Cather, *The Song of the Lark*, Houghton, 1915, p. 297.
9. Ellen Moers, citata da Ann Moseley, *The Creative Ecology of Walnut Canyon*, in "Cather Studies", vol. 5. Consultato sul sito: http: / / cather.unl.edu / cs005_moseley.html
10. Susanne K. Langer, *Feeling and Form: A Theory of Art*, Scribner's, 1953, p. 122.
11 J. M. Coetzee, citato da Katie Brewer Ball e Julia Steinmetz in *Call for Papers: Feminist Landscape*, in "Women & Performance: A Journal of Feminist Theory".
12. Rosa Barba, *Printed Cinema #3: Accidental Suspension*.
13. Jonathan Goldberg, "Photographic Relations: Laura Gilpin, Willa Cather ", *American Literature* 70, n. 1 (Marzo 1998), pp. 63-95. Consultato sul sito: http: / / www.jstor.org / stable / 2902456
14. Jonathan Goldberg, *Willa Cather and Others*, Duke University Press, 2001, pp. 158–159.
15. Monique Wittig, "Nota dell'autrice", ne *Il Corpo Lesbico*, Edizioni delle Donne, 1976.
16. Reyner Banham, *Deserti americani*, Einaudi, 2006.
17. Zygmunt Baumann, *Modernità e ambivalenza*, Bollati Boringhieri, 2010.
18. Serge Guilbaut, *How New York Stole the Idea of Modern Art: Abstract Expressionism, Freedom and the Cold War*, University of Chicago Press, 1983, p. 177.
19. Vedi Joseph Masco, *Fantastic City: Engineering Ruins in Cold War America*, "Cabinet 20", (Inverno 2005-2006), pp. 85-88.
20. Vera Norwood e Janice Monk, *The Desert Is No Lady: Southwestern Landscapes in Women's Writing and Art*, Yale University Press, 1987, p. 87
21. Sigmund Freud, "L'acquisizione del fuoco", 1932, ne *L'uomo Mosé, la religione monoteistica e altri scritti 1930-1938*, Bollati Boringhieri, 2003.
22. Nancy Holt, *Sun Tunnels*, "Artforum", (Aprile 1977), pp. 34-35.
23. Ibid.
24. Briony Fer e Roni Horn, *Roni Horn aka Roni Horn*, Steidl, 2009.
25. Rebecca Solnit, *Savage Dreams*, University of California Press, 2000.
26. Astra Taylor, *Rebecca Solnit*, "Bomb 109", (Autunno 2009). Consultato sul sito: http: / / bombsite.com / issues / 109 / articles / 3327
27. Donna Haraway, *Simians, Cyborgs and Women: The Reinvention of Nature*, Routledge, 1990, p. 195.
28. Jimmy Durham , *Artists' Pages*, in "Art Journal 51", n. 2: "Art and Ecology", (Estate 1992), p. 14.
29. Intervista a Rebecca Solnit. Consultata sul sito: http: / / believermag.com / issues / 200909 / ?read=interview_solnit
30. Giuliana Bruno, *Rovine con Vista. Alla Ricerca del Cinema Perduto di Elvira Notari*, La Tartaruga, 1995.
31. Giuliana Bruno, *Atlante delle Emozioni. In Viaggio tra Arte, Architettura e Cinema*, Bruno Mondadori, 2006. Opera da consultare integralmente.
32. Donna Haraway, "Situated Knowledges: The Science Question in Feminism and the Privilege of Partial Perspective", in *Simians*, op. cit., p. 248, nota n. 2.

I FILM "NON FILMATI" DI ROSA BARBA

FRANCESCO MANACORDA &
RAIMUNDAS MALASAUSKAS

Nella sua famosa suite per pianoforte del 1874 *Quadri da un'esposizione*, Modest Musorgskij traspose in musica la visita alla mostra del suo amico artista e architetto Viktor Hartmann. Ciascuno dei dieci movimenti della suite è legato a uno dei quadri, la maggioranza dei quali oggi non può essere identificata. Per ogni movimento sono usati i titoli dei quadri, ma la gran parte di essi sono andati perduti o sono di difficile individuazione. A causa di questa sconnessione, la musica funziona come uno spettacolare archivio fantasma di un'esperienza del passato la cui fonte non è più disponibile per l'ascoltatore nella sua forma originale. Il suo potere suggestivo consente di evocare immagini potenziali dal buio di una memoria che non è stata mai documentata visivamente, come in un film le cui immagini si sono deteriorate e cancellate lasciando la traccia uditiva di "secondo grado" che le accompagnava. Dal punto di vista dell'analisi testuale, gli ascoltatori vengono posti da questo pezzo in uno stato di amnesia forzata che la musica tenta di compensare.
L'opera di Rosa Barba *The Hidden Conference*, e in generale i suoi ultimi lavori sul concetto di archivio, funziona in modo speculare a *Quadri da un'esposizione*. L'artista usa raccolte diverse di dati culturali immagazzinati (quadri, sculture, opere su carta) come riserva di personaggi che potrebbero essere portati alla vita in un possibile film la cui sceneggiatura è creata per mezzo dell'uso della loro casuale vicinanza nel deposito. La potenzialità del deposito museale e dell'archivio risiede, per l'artista, nei ruoli potenziali che gli oggetti raccolti possono recitare in una trama. Le connessioni fra opere d'arte o fra documenti vengono usate per dar forma a una storia, e l'archivio stesso viene trasformato in un palcoscenico teatrale sul quale alle opere viene dato un ruolo che tiene conto della loro identità all'interno di una complessa coreografia.
Gli elementi delle collezioni non esposte diventano protagonisti delle molteplici storie non raccontate e non lineari che li hanno messi insieme. Come lettere dell'alfabeto, i documenti possono essere usati per comporre parole singole, frasi complete, scritti diversi. Il gioco combinatorio non è dissimile dal lavoro museale: il risultato è qualcosa di analogo allo sforzo dell'archeologo nel ricostruire un passato sepolto di cui ha ricevuto solo qualche frammento. Da questi frammenti dev'essere ricostruita, rimessa insieme, evocata una storia – o meglio, nel caso dell'archeologo, la Storia. La differenza fra il lavoro archeologico e le narrazioni di Rosa Barba risiede nell'unità del materiale che l'archeologo può garantire attraverso la collocazione geografica dei reperti e la corrispondenza della datazione. Viceversa, le molteplici possibilità di un archivio sono per definizione in cerca di una storia, non necessariamente della Storia, e Rosa Barba sembra incline a lasciare che esse si uniscano sul suo storyboard di celluloide formando permutazioni discontinue. Si tratta di possibili futuri che non hanno mai avuto luogo? Di universi multipli esplorati da giochi di teoria della probabilità? O ancora di pièces teatrali nate da una seduta spiritica che ha tentato di dare nuova vita alla narrazione

potenziale presente negli oggetti confinati nelle stanze costruite per immagazzinare la memoria collettiva?
Per la mostra a Rovereto, Rosa Barba ha progettato un'installazione di fronte alla porta che dà accesso all'archivio. La *mise en scène* comprende una lampada e un sipario teatrale posti sulla soglia che separa la mostra dal deposito. La monumentale luce circolare è installata sul pavimento, e su di essa delle lunghe pellicole di celluloide si muove lentamente come un serpente in cima a una superficie illuminata.
La lampada funziona come un congegno fantascientifico che filtra il passato convertendolo in un potenziale futuro. Se in un proiettore cinematografico tradizionale la luce passa attraverso la celluloide consentendo a immagini fantasmatiche e immateriali di danzare su uno schermo bianco, in questa versione modificata la celluloide fa filtrare la luce verso la porta dell'archivio, come attraendo magneticamente sulla sua superficie i personaggi del film potenziale confinati nei "camerini" dietro il sipario. In questo senso, piuttosto che un proiettore, la lampada è una cinepresa, uno strumento per sedute spiritiche in grado di rianimare oggetti inanimati. La pellicola dentro la lampada ha lo scopo di evocare le molte possibili storie non raccontate che emergono dall'archivio, e per questo è ancora non impressionata. Documenti, opere d'arte, fotografie e scritti sono attirati verso la pellicola, come se la celluloide fosse stata trattata chimicamente per poter attrarre contenuti culturali sulla sua superficie.
Fra i documenti lasciati da Depero vi sono alcune sceneggiature mai realizzate per un film futurista, in cui un artista raggiunge il successo con l'invenzione di un teatro completamente automatico. Depero descrive "animali meccanici, selvaggi automatici danzanti, farfalle variopinte che volano, maschere baffute che ballano, danze di ombre costruite, pioggia di sigarette...". Elementi del genere sono come mondi sommersi nella memoria di qualcun altro, e richiamano alla mente le storie che emergono dall'intervista di Raimundas Malasauskas a Pechalat[1]: frammenti narrativi di un paese ora conservato sott'acqua. Come nei suoni notturni del rompersi della superficie ghiacciata del lago di Vassivière evocati da Pechalat, l'archivio grida a chi vuole sentire. Ciò che è sommerso può facilmente essere resuscitato come balletto meccanico.
I due mondi distanti di Pechalat e del Futurismo si uniscono in *Underwater Forward Amnesia*, il nuovo film realizzato da Rosa Barba dopo tre anni di ricerche condotte in collaborazione con Malasauskas e con me fra Vassivière e Trento. La proiezione, che dura un giorno intero, richiama suoni e scenari di un mondo sommerso, come se fosse il rovescio di un archivio: un palcoscenico senza una storia, perché la storia è stata completamente cancellata dalla memoria. Frammenti di altre storie rubate da altri archivi separati possono abitare la scena come modelle che indossano un vestito dopo l'altro. Come nel teatro meccanico futurista, le storie si svolgono in quello che pare un inverso futuro di Atlantide, una civiltà sommersa, prima abbandonata e poi ripopolata dopo che un disastro ambientale ha reso impossibile agli uomini vivere sulla superficie terrestre. Il film riesce a dare la sensazione dell'atemporalità nonostante le sue 24 ore di durata, tutto ciò che è immerso nell'acqua acquista il lucore di un mondo visto attraverso la sfera di cristallo di un indovino morto tanto tempo fa. Il futuro avrà ancora bisogno dei racconti per dare ordine al mondo?
Ogni archivio, per definizione, tende alla costruzione di una completezza fittizia col tentativo di imporre generi diversi di omogeneità a una serie eterogenea di individualità. È un approccio scientifico che trascura la casualità con cui spesso sono raccolti archivi e collezioni, ed è proprio il potenziale non lineare di narrazioni collettive, l'elemento che sfugge al pensiero scientifico, ma, malgrado si tratti di un uso forse sbagliato dello strumento intellettuale, esso può legare insieme visioni di mondi alternativi del passato o del futuro. Qualche tempo fa ho incontrato Arlette Farge, la storica francese specializzata nel lavoro d'archivio, per intervistarla sul concetto di documento, e l'aspetto più interessante del suo lavoro che è emerso dalla conversazione è stato il suo metodo per comprendere appieno un dato documento:

> A un certo punto ho capito che se volevo davvero lavorare sul XVIII secolo non potevo solo prendere note e poi fare il riassunto. Mi dissi che se facevo una serie di schede come fanno gli storici, non sarei mai riuscita a cavare un ragno dal buco. Il materiale che non mi era familiare, e che tentavo di decodificare, mi sembrava così ricco che mi costrinsi (ma non mi pesava) a copiare le cose, ad avventurarmi nella sintassi e nel vocabolario, e mi convinsi (cosa che troverai assolutamente ingenua) che perfino il movimento del mio corpo mentre scrivevo poteva darmi delle idee! La mia immersione è stata un processo lungo, ma mi è piaciuto; copiavo per ore e ore, e sentivo che quel particolare movimento mi dava una specie di ispirazione - invece di riassumere frasi e seguire argomenti, segni di interpunzione ed esitazioni passo dopo passo. Immaginavo le voci e sentivo i suoni. La mia immersione non era qualcosa di immaginario, ma piuttosto un "essere con".

In questo racconto i documenti sono come sceneggiature, e l'atto di copiarli diventa una performance attoriale per calarsi completamente nel ruolo del personaggio da evocare. Se nel lavoro scientifico l'evocazione deve essere considerata come un emergere dal passato, nella finzione narrativa il continuum spazio-temporale può essere capovolto e si può considerare il personaggio evocato come se arrivasse dal futuro. Rosa Barba porta ancora oltre questa intuizione immaginando materiali d'archivio antropomorfizzati in cerca di un copione condiviso. Come nel famoso dramma di Pirandello *Sei personaggi in cerca d'autore*, il magazzino concepito come palcoscenico fornisce individualità senza una trama che hanno l'occasione di dire la loro sui motivi per cui si trovano lì o sull'assurdità della loro condizione. Archivi e depositi sono pieni di questi attori potenziali, tutti in grado di recitare in tragedie diverse e inventare il mondo utopico da cui sono appena giunti. Vengono conservati come cadaveri pronti a essere riportati in vita: sono nascosti nel buio. La definizione di Robert Smithson dei musei come cimiteri potrebbe essere ulteriormente modificata fino a postulare che i depositi, essendo invisibili ai visitatori dei musei, sono lo spazio in cui tenere i non-morti. Il loro potenziale non risiede nella possibilità di essere tirati fuori ed esibiti nello spazio espositivo, ma piuttosto nel processo simile a una seduta spiritica che li rende protagonisti di una storia non ancora raccontata che si svolge in un futuro non specificato.

Note

1. Cfr. il testo di Raimundas Malasauskas pubblicato qui di seguito in questo volume, pp.265–68

Cara Rosa,

Grazie per avermi chiesto ancora di tenerti informata sulla missione. A dire il vero, ultimamente non è successo granché, ci sono però tante cose che potranno senz'altro interessarti. Ieri abbiamo percorso il ponte che dalla terra ferma conduce all'isola in mezzo al lago. Più o meno nel momento in cui mi è arrivata la tua mail, stavamo mettendo piede sull'isola.
Dopo essere saliti e scesi dalla torre, aver visto centinaia di metri di pellicola e ascoltato le basse frequenze che provenivano dall'acqua, con Alexandra siamo andati a fare un giro intorno all'isola. Non ricordo se abbiamo concluso o meno la passeggiata, una cosa però mi ha particolarmente colpito, ed è il fatto che l'isola sia una creazione umana recente. E dire che avevo avuto l'impressione di camminare in un luogo che esisteva chissà da quanto tempo. Davvero, ero sbalordito. La mia percezione del luogo era completamente sovvertita: mi rendevo conto che ci trovavamo in cima a una collinetta che era stata circondata dalle acque e diventata un'isola non più di qualche anno prima.
È stato in quel momento che Alexandra mi ha parlato di un uomo che viveva lì fin dal tempo in cui l'isola non era affatto un'isola. Quell'uomo, a suo avviso, conosceva la storia di quel luogo meglio di chiunque altro, essendo ben più vecchio della stessa isola. Ti rendi conto? Non credo che ci sia nessun altro al mondo più vecchio dell'isola in cui abita.
Siamo andati a trovarlo senza perdere un minuto di più. Certamente lui doveva sapere tante cose che potenzialmente mi potevano aiutare nel compimento della mia missione, alla ricerca di nuove possibilità per il tuo film. Quell'uomo doveva conoscere qualcosa che indirettamente si poteva trasporre nelle forme e nei percorsi propri del tuo lavoro, tramite la poetica di instabili catene di significanti e di promesse reiterate.
Monsieur Péchalat, così si chiama l'uomo che vive sull'isola, ci ha accolto calorosamente nella sua casa. Tantissimi gatti, di colore fulvo, se non ricordo male, se ne stavano rannicchiati un po' dappertutto. Lui era sincero e gentile, e particolarmente entusiasta all'idea di rispondere alle mie domande. Domande semplici, senza un ordine preciso: la sua vita sull'isola, la vita dell'isola e i ricordi che l'uomo e la sua isola condividevano, tutto quello che poteva servirmi per raccogliere episodi che più tardi avremmo potuto adattare nella sceneggiatura. Ero assai curioso del periodo in cui l'isola era diventata un'isola, dei sogni che lui faceva dormendo da sempre su un'isola, e di chissà quale scena o immagine che avrebbe potuto ricordarsi nei particolari.
Si dice che anche l'acqua possieda una memoria, e io mi chiedevo se lui avesse avuto l'occasione di esserne testimone. Ero curioso delle scene che a volte emergono dalla nostra memoria così perfettamente dettagliate, come quei brevi momenti accaduti parecchi anni prima e che per cinquant'anni non ci sono mai tornati alla mente, ma che d'un tratto ci ricordiamo come se fossero accaduti due minuti prima. O magari due minuti dopo: il futuro deve pur espandersi nel passato come l'acqua si mescola all'acqua, no?
E non è soltanto per via di questo slittamento del futuro nel passato che tu non devi avercela con me perché non rispetto le scadenze. Tanto per cominciare, io sono un crono-dislessico; e poi mia figlia per la prima volta in vita sua ha qualcosa che non va. Non vuole parlarmene, e la cosa mi disorienta ancora più del solito. Ieri, mi ha riattaccato in faccia mentre per consolarla cercavo di raccontarle una storia ricorrendo alla prima immagine che mi era venuta alla mente. Pensavo che il soggetto di questa immagine fosse in sintonia con la nostra conversazione. Era la foto a colori di un coccodrillo sulle pagine dell'Enciclopedia Sovietica che mi era capitato di sfogliare quando ero bambino. «Può ancora mordere», le ho detto ridendo nella speranza di tirarla su di morale. È stato in quel momento che ha riagganciato.
La crono-dislessia è più facile da capire: si tratta di una malattia cronica che avrebbe a che fare con la capacità di viaggiare nel tempo, ma in modo del tutto involontario. L'ultima volta mi hai chiesto «quando» sarei stato puntuale, e io non sono riuscito a risponderti con precisione, ti ricordi? Mi succede proprio così: ho la strana sensazione di essere in uno stato senza inizio né fine, eppure quando qualcosa finisce sento che non ricomincerà mai più. Questo mi rende prematuramente malinconico.
Il viaggio nel tempo poggia su svariati paradossi. Uno di questi, è la convinzione che il passato (come il futuro) resti immobile e non cambi (come una sorta di bolla, di monade congelata o di fossile). Secondo quest'ipotesi, se qualcuno nell'anno 2012 tornasse a Berlino durante l'estate del 1989, troverebbe il Muro ancora intatto. Ma, dei tedeschi arrabbiati sarebbero già radunati là sotto per abbatterlo.
Gli avvenimenti che si svolgono sono una ripetizione familiare di ciò che tutti conoscono. Immagina però cosa succederebbe se tornando indietro nel tempo tu scoprissi che tutte le cose del passato sono cambiate quanto la tua stessa vita, ma non nella direzione che ti saresti aspettata né nell'ordine degli avvenimenti che hanno portato a quel passato che credi di conoscere. Da questo punto di vista, non si passa più da un'epoca all'altra come si cambia un brano sul proprio lettore mp3. In fin dei conti, non ci resta altro che utilizzare i nostri artifici e magari lasciare più tempo al tempo.

> «Allora, da quant'è che vive qui?» ho chiesto al signor Péchalat. «La sua storia sarà forse registrata non soltanto dal vento che soffia tra gli alberi dell'isola, ma anche nel film di Rosa Barba.»
> «Vivo qui dal 1936 – non è roba da poco! – restare nello stesso luogo per tutto questo tempo.»
> «È nato qui?»
> « No, sono nato a Eymoutiers.»
> «Come mai è venuto a stare qui?»
> «Il lavoro, è stato per il lavoro. Sono venuto con i miei genitori che avevano preso una fattoria nell'isola; all'epoca, l'isola non era un'isola, intorno non c'era l'acqua. Poi abbiamo continuato a lavorare dalla signora Pascal. Io sono rimasto con lei, quando è stata fatta la diga mi ha tenuto con sé. C'è invece tanta gente che è andata via, quelli che vivevano nei paesi al di sotto del lago se ne sono andati mentre io, che vivevo in cima a una montagna non sono partito, sono rimasto a Vassivière. Ho continuato a lavorare per lei fino alla sua morte e anche in seguito. Dopo di che è arrivato l'Ente e si è preso l'isola. Da allora, la vita è cambiata, non era più quella di prima, sono cambiate moltissime cose. È difficile da spiegare… non so come dirvi. La vita è stata sconvolta, non era più lo stesso lavoro. Certo, abbiamo mantenuto le nostre proprietà, avevamo le bestie, avevamo tante cose. Beh… sa, si stringe il cuore a vedere l'acqua che sale lentamente. Quando la diga è stata ultimata, vedevamo l'acqua salire piano

piano ed è allora che abbiamo avuto parecchie intrusioni, perché è arrivato di tutto qui: topi, serpenti... È stato per via dell'acqua. I serpenti andavano a spasso nel cortile. Dovevate vederli, una roba incredibile! Ma non solo loro, però, in realtà anche lepri, conigli – ogni tipo di selvaggina – sono risaliti fin su insieme ai topi e ai serpenti; sono arrivati e ci hanno letteralmente invaso.»
«In che anno è stato riempito il lago?»
«I lavori sono cominciati nel 1946 e il lago è stato varato nel 1949, la vigilia di Natale, i lavori però non erano finiti. La diga era solo a metà, ma l'acqua non impediva loro di lavorare. Il materiale veniva trasportato per via aerea. Un po' come le teleferiche che si vedono in montagna, arrivavano dei piccoli vagoni che scaricavano il cemento sulla diga. Per tre anni, hanno preparato il luogo prima che arrivasse l'acqua.»
«Cos'è successo tra il 1946 e il 1949?»
«Il lavoro veniva fatto quasi tutto a mano. Non c'erano molti strumenti meccanici, solo qualcuno; si lavorava molto a mano. All'epoca, avevano 3.500 operai.»

(Rosa, non meravigliarti se ci dovessero occorrere tre anni per scrivere la sceneggiatura. Mi piacerebbe che fossimo 3.500 lavoratori capaci di trasformare gli esigui possibili in fondazione per il presente. Ma in loco abbiamo soltanto Francesco, sommerso dagli archivi, e io, paracadutato in questa foresta. Forse i nostri sforzi convergeranno, ma non necessariamente nella stessa versione della storia. Credi che siamo legati perché confidiamo nel potenziale nascosto del mondo che ci circonda? Io non ne sono così sicuro. Sono anche piuttosto scettico sull'incontro di tutti questi artisti che affermano di produrre potenzialità. Penso che siano pigri e troppo intellettuali. Sarebbe lo stesso che io affermassi di produrre pigrizia. Cosa che non direi mai, ovviamente. Ma se dovessimo aver bisogno di tre anni per produrre una sceneggiatura, sappi che sarebbe non un segno di fallimento – che Dio ce ne scampi! – ma della mia fedeltà al compimento di questa ricerca.)

«La diga era stata progettata prima della Seconda Guerra mondiale?»
«No, hanno cominciato immediatamente dopo. C'era la questione dell'Indocina. La guerra si era appena conclusa; hanno iniziato perché non c'era abbastanza luce e i riscaldamenti centralizzati erano pochi. Ora ci sono alberi ovunque, ma prima c'erano solo lande di erica, animali d'allevamento, e pochissime foreste. Gli animali venivano allevati a piccoli gruppi, non in grosse mandrie come adesso. C'erano anche parecchie piantagioni, di segale, avena, patate... ce n'erano davvero tante all'epoca.»
«Tra il 1946 e il 1949, quando il governo ha proposto alla gente di andare altrove, perché lei ha scelto di restare?»
«Io stavo sulla montagna; quelli che erano sotto, sono dovuti partire per forza. Io non gli davo fastidio, semplicemente loro stavano in mezzo all'acqua.»
«Non ha mai avuto paura di ritrovarsi in una situazione un po' isolata. Come si fosse arenato sull'isola?»
«Non ci ho mai pensato. La vita è cambiata completamente; si è voltato pagina, come si suol dire. In un certo senso, eravamo andati avanti. La cosa che mi ha toccato di più, è stato lo svuotamento del 1995. Rivedere quelle terre tutte vuote... Allora, sì, è stata una stretta al cuore rivedere il paese in cui avevo vissuto. Ho avuto la fortuna di vederlo dall'elicottero, per segnalare dove un tempo c'era un ponte, un mulino, una chiesa...»

(Vorrei suggerire di aggiungere il Centro internazionale d'arte e del paesaggio alla lista dei luoghi inghiottiti dalle acque. La nostra sceneggiatura dovrebbe culminare con un disastro e introdurre una storia alternativa ricorrendo a un montaggio in parallelo. Non saremo troppo letterali, ma piuttosto eserciteremo il nostro diritto di creare un'alternativa. L'edificio di Aldo Rossi e di Xavier Fabre si inscrive nel paesaggio in un modo non troppo dissimile da quello di una chiesa o di un mulino inghiottito.)

«Hanno distrutto tutto, prima che arrivasse l'acqua?»
«Hanno spazzato via tutto. Gli alberi sono stati tagliati, le case fatte saltare con la dinamite. Sono rimasti solo dei piccoli cumuli di pietre. Hanno disintegrato tutto con la dinamite per non ostacolare le barche. A Vaugelade, c'era solo il mulino ad essere rimasto intatto e, altrove, la chiesa, ma non ricordo più dove. L'acqua ormai avrà distrutto tutto.»
«È mai andato in questa chiesa prima della guerra?»
« No, mai. Non so nemmeno dove sia. Alcuni dicevano che ci fosse un cimitero in fondo all'acqua, ma non è vero. Vassivière era appena una frazioncina. La vera Vassivière è qui.»

(Credo che dovremmo attingere dal fondo dell'acqua piuttosto che dalle associazioni di idee. Si deve lavorare sull'intensità della parallasse. Magari potremmo focalizzarci sui cambiamenti, sui momenti di transizione, sulla solitudine. Il ricordo di qualcosa di lontano, come quell'uomo che si inabissa nell'acqua nel 1949, che potrebbe poi convergere in qualcosa di più recente, come il ricordo dell'ultimo Natale o una canzone di George Michael. O perché no, in qualcosa di ancora più vicino, come una canzone che hai sentito stamattina. Ti ricordi? Si tratterebbe, allora, di futuri possibili mai accaduti? Di universi alternativi esplorati dal gioco delle probabilità matematiche? O meglio ancora di pièce teatrali risultanti da una seduta spiritica in cui si sarebbe cercato di riportare in vita le potenziali finzioni presenti nel profondo di tutta quest'acqua imprigionata nel lago?)

«Ha visto davvero il livello dell'acqua che saliva?»
«Sì, di continuo. La vedevamo arrivare, ma non saliva in fretta; saliva lentamente. Ci pensavamo certo, ma senza prestarci chissà quale attenzione. Comunque sia, saliva. Non tanto rapidamente perché quell'anno ha fatto parecchio caldo, per cui non c'era molta acqua, che poi all'epoca proveniva solo dalla Maulde. Ci sono molti fiumi che si riversano nel lago: c'è la Vienne che viene intercettata a Servières, lassù nel Corrèze, attraverso delle gallerie sotterranee che vanno a finire nella Maulde contribuendo al suo rifornimento, e poi ci sono altri fiumi e ruscelli – non me li ricordo tutti – che confluiscono là.»
«In tre giorni, l'acqua ha invaso tutto. Com'è stato per lei? Dato che il paesaggio deve essere cambiato di punto in bianco, giusto?»

«Proprio così! Lo vedevamo sparire. Sui tronchi tagliati, c'era passata sopra l'acqua, e non si vedevano più. Eravamo contenti senza esserlo per davvero; non sapevamo più cosa fosse. Non avevamo mai visto una diga. La gente non era contraria, perché veniva fuori dalla guerra. Aveva talmente sofferto che la faccenda della diga è passata senza tanti problemi. Dopo però, c'è voluta la polizia per proteggere i siti di altre dighe. La gente non voleva cedere i propri terreni. Mi ricordo del progetto di una diga nella Creuse, qualche tempo dopo la guerra, che la gente ha impedito di realizzare. Oggigiorno, ci sono soltanto le case che cadono in rovina, e ci sono persone che ci tornano ma il terreno appartiene sempre all'EDF.» (Électricité de France - NdT).

«Aveva degli amici che non ha più rivisto?»

«Ci sono quelli che ho perso completamente; sono partiti nella lontana Creuse, nelle città. Soprattutto le donne; se ne sono andate via dopo la guerra. Non sono rimaste nelle campagne. Invecchiando non sopportavano più l'idea di fare le contadine, e se anche non erano vecchie, sono partite lo stesso alla volta delle città: Parigi, Lione. Le ho perse di vista. A parte alcune che tornano a trovarmi, che mi conoscevano, ma io non le riconosco più. Sono invecchiate. Sono soprattutto le donne che se ne sono andate in città, perché il lavoro qui è faticoso. È molto faticoso fare l'agricoltore, ecco perché se ne sono andate.»

(Immagina di essere l'ultima creatura vivente sulla faccia della terra: il tuo amore per il vuoto è legato al suo destino, le tue storie non saranno mai più raccontate – nemmeno da qualcun altro – e la tua voce non conta più nulla. "Lei è l'ultima persona sulla terra", sa di avviso che ti mette in guardia. Ma d'un tratto i tuoi occhi individuano una zanzara gonfia di sangue sul muro bianco della stanza in cui sei appena entrato. A chi appartiene quel sangue? Da dove viene? Quali informazioni contiene? È portatore di un messaggio delle generazioni che vivevano prima della fine dell'umanità? Oppure un retrovirus da riattivare? Prolungherà la fine del mondo o piuttosto ne invertirà il corso? Può accidentalmente renderti immortale: tu, che eri l'ultima creatura sulla terra soltanto un minuto prima?)

«Quindi, all'inizio il ponte non c'era? Come faceva?»

«Il ponte cresceva allo stesso ritmo dell'acqua. Tutti i lavori dell'EDF erano cominciati contemporaneamente. Tutto veniva fatto nello stesso momento, dato che c'erano 3.500 operai. La passerella, la diga, le strade, tutto veniva fatto allo stesso tempo... »

«Quand'è che ha avuto la televisione?»

«Ben più tardi, parecchio tempo dopo la diga. Non potevo permettermela, era troppo cara.»

«Andava al cinema?»

«Per andare al cinema, bisognava andare a Eymoutiers, ed era troppo lontano: 15 chilometri a piedi. In seguito, ne hanno aperto uno a Beaumont, ma non è grande. Ora, è più semplice. Si prende la macchina e si va lontano; si può andare al cinema a Limoges, anche se, in fin dei conti, non ci si va mai. A Eymoutiers, ci vanno in tanti perché credo diano un film tutte le settimane. Prima non c'erano le macchine come adesso; erano rare, le macchine.»

«Quale era il suo film preferito?»

«Non me li ricordo proprio i film.»

(Questi film dimenticati mi ricordano una festa che si era tenuta in fondo a una autostrada incompiuta in Germania. Era stata organizzata dagli amanti della techno all'inizio dell'epoca dei rave party, e aveva richiamato una folta rappresentanza di creature cyber glam della metà degli anni '90; creature così bizzarre che tutta la scena avrebbe potuto essere benissimo il set di un film. E in effetti, quando è arrivata la polizia per impedire la festa, i partecipanti dissero che stavano girando un film. I poliziotti non hanno nemmeno cercato di sapere se si trattava di un film ambientato nel futuro oppure di qualcos'altro. La credibilità cinematografica ha salvato la festa. Il film del rave party naturalmente non è mai stato girato, ma questa festa resta presentissima nella mia memoria proprio perché non era mai stata filmata. Lungo quella *autobahn* incompiuta, si apriva una frontiera ballardiana. «Siamo tutti dei film», ti ricordi di Terrence McKenna?)

«Poco fa, ha parlato di quando sull'isola sono arrivati gli animali e tutti quei topi e serpenti. Cos'è successo esattamente?»

«È stata l'acqua a far avvicinare le bestie, i serpenti, i topi. I topi ci hanno dato parecchio fastidio: mangiavano le patate nei campi, il grano. Abbiamo dovuto avvelenarli perché erano veramente troppi. Non erano però cattivi come i serpenti. I topi mordono, ma non uccidono; mentre i serpenti uccidevano le bestie, morsicavano le persone.»

«Ma i serpenti non vanno bene contro i topi?»

«Sì certo, se li mangiavano, ma non tutti: ce n'erano troppi. E poi, dei serpenti, io ne avevo paura. C'erano aspidi, vipere, bisce... Dicono che la biscia non sia cattiva, ma comunque anche lei ha sempre un po' di veleno. Ho visto una donna cadere morta stecchita; in parecchi sono stati morsicati... Ho visto quella donna cadere: trasportava dei covoni di grano, che doveva legarsi intorno alla mano e, mentre lei passava la mano, il serpente l'ha morsicata ed è morta. Quando è arrivato il medico, era già morta. Se uno è stato morsicato se lo ricorda per sempre. Un tempo, c'erano i guaritori quando si veniva morsi da un serpente, ma sto parlando di tantissimo tempo fa. Non so esattamente cosa facessero, non me l'hanno mai detto; facevano qualcosa di segreto. Che cosa, non ne ho proprio idea, però guarivano la gente. Sto parlando di un tempo più vecchio di me, che io non ho mai conosciuto. Se però non si ricorreva a questa persona, si moriva.»

(Credo che dovremmo chiedere a Francesco di elaborare qualcosa sull'iconografia dei serpenti a partire dalle serpentine di pellicola sul pavimento. Dovrebbe spiegare a tutti come ondeggiano e raccolgono la polvere delle metafore. Potremmo anche approfittare di questa opportunità per fare allusione al fantasma dell' *Opisthostoma Vermiculum*. È il nome di una strana creatura che alcuni scienziati hanno scoperto recentemente. Purtroppo però, quando la creatura è stata resa nota in virtù della sua scoperta, è morta. Questo è un tipico esempio di relazione tra la scienza e un fenomeno sconosciuto:

l'apparecchio disposto per l'identificazione del fenomeno uccide il suo oggetto di studio. Non bisogna quindi meravigliarsi se perfino il nome della creatura sia scomparso da Google.)

«Perché la gente ricorreva a un guaritore anziché a un dottore?»
«Perché i medici non potevano farci niente; all'epoca non esistevano ancora le iniezioni.»
«C'è anche un'isoletta che si chiama l'isola dei serpenti?»
«Le hanno dato questo nome, così, tanto per fare. C'erano serpenti in tutte e sette le isole; più l'isola era grande e più ce n'erano.»
«Il lago gela ogni tanto?»
«Come no! L'ho attraversato quando il ghiaccio aveva 40 centimetri di spessore, con meno 27° C, nel 1954. Sembrava un bellissimo pavimento. Quando la diga si riempiva, non faceva rumore; ma quando scendeva – quando il ghiaccio si rompeva – faceva un rumore la notte, come un rombo di tuono. Si sentivano le crepe... era incredibile. Quest'anno, il ghiaccio era fine come un foglio di carta.»

(Si dovrebbe rendere questo suono attraverso un dispositivo proveniente direttamente dall'acqua, o magari con un altro genere di suono o una frequenza che spezzerebbe la nostra indifferenza, le nostre aspettative e i nostri sogni. Ti ho per caso raccontato che ultimamente ho sognato spesso display di iPhone in frantumi? E poi ancora, ho sognato display frantumati in immersione: superfici frantumate da una prospettiva infinita, senza profondità, vetri frantumati solo a toccarli, metafore frantumate. In compenso le suonerie erano intatte; sono queste a svegliarmi ogni volta.)

«Si ricorda di quando è stato costruito il Centro d'arte?»
«Sì! Ci sono state molte discussioni al riguardo, ma da qui a dire l'anno in cui è cominciato... Non me lo ricordo. Eppure ci ho anche lavorato, alla costruzione, alle sculture, per portare il materiale.»
«Quando è arrivato il Centro d'arte, ha pensato che sarebbe successo qualcosa di più interessante sull'isola?»
«Non saprei. Sono cose più grandi di me, che mi sopravanzano. È particolare, il Centro d'arte. Ci fanno cose incredibili. È un'altra vita più grande di me.»
«Va a vedere le mostre?»
«All'inizio, sì, tutte le volte.»
«Non le è venuto mai a noia di vivere su quest'isola?»
«In questo momento, sono un po' giù di morale, ma insomma sono cose che succedono. Non ho più la macchina e non posso più uscire. Ho fatto un incidente a Pierrefitte, subito dopo il paese, ho cappottato. In pieno giorno, mi sono addormentato e sono finito nella scarpata, e la macchina si è ribaltata. Io nemmeno un osso rotto ma la macchina distrutta. Magari sarò guarito da solo, comunque la macchina non c'è più. Mi hanno ritirato la patente, per via dell'incidente e perché sono troppo vecchio; ma cercherò di trovarne un'altra. Non ho fatto male a nessuno, loro però non mi vogliono più assicurare.»
«Le toccherà riprendere l'elicottero!... Quando era in elicottero, ha avuto qualche problema?»
«Assolutamente no. Ero felice; è bello vedere il paese che hai conosciuto, perché il lago, sa, sono 1000 ettari... è una grossa distanza; ci abbiamo messo più di un'ora. Ero contento. È stato un bel viaggio per me. Tutti quei luoghi, i ponti, le strade, tutto... Sembrava di stare sulla luna: la terra si era seccata, era piena di crepe come nel deserto, così grandi che ci poteva passare anche una mano. Era tutto spoglio, non c'era più vegetazione. Non c'era più niente, aldilà dei tronchi tagliati e delle case distrutte. Certo, per un verso è triste, ma solo per uno che l'ha conosciuto, ci ha vissuto e ritrova ogni minimo angolo... So che non lo rivedrò mai più così.»
«C'è molta gente che viene a trovarla, come noi oggi, per parlarle della storia dell'isola?»
«Sì, ne sono venuti parecchi, adesso però molti meno. Forse la cosa non li interessa più tanto o per niente. Un tempo, ne venivano molti. A volte, la cosa durava tutta la giornata.»

(Rosa, ascolta, il tuo film sull'isola deve durare tutta la giornata... Una proiezione di una giornata piena di cose che sono già successe e altre che non lo sono ancora, nello stesso raggio di luce, ti ricordi...?)

SUL METTERE IN SCENA LE TRACCE CHE LE PERSONE LASCIANO NELLA STORIA

NATAŠA PETREŠIN-BACHELEZ

Di recente le esposizioni di Rosa Barba sono state descritte come «installazioni coreografate»[1]. Se possiamo affermare che Barba traspone i concetti di installazione cinetica e di performer sui proiettori cinematografici e sulla sua macchina da presa (soprattutto nei film *They Shine*, 2007, dove seguiamo il movimento di rotazione dei pannelli solari nel deserto del Mojave, e *The Long Road*, 2010, dove la pista provvisoria è "disegnata" in cerchio con la macchina da presa a volo d'uccello), qui dovremmo usare il termine "coreografia" nel senso più ampio, lasciando da parte il suo significato etimologico greco di «scrivere la danza» e trasferendolo sull'attività di direzione registica, che così progetta e organizza il movimento nello spazio. Questo punto di partenza trova una emozionante analogia con i rapporti di lavoro che Rosa Barba intrattiene con singoli o gruppi di persone in almeno tre dei suoi film: *Panzano* (2000), *Outwardly from Earth's Center* (2007) e *The Empirical Effect* (2010), in cui proprio questo rapporto diventa concreto laddove vi sono momenti di apparizioni di gruppo che comprendono dialoghi, discorsi e movimento.

In *Panzano*, il primo film che Rosa Barba ha realizzato insieme a Ulrike Molsen, le due artiste hanno lavorato per alcuni mesi con due uomini e una donna che vivevano in una comunità psicoterapeutica sperimentale di un paese toscano. Le tre persone che osserviamo, e che vengono "orchestrate", come scrive Ian White nel suo testo[2], in ruoli piuttosto indefiniti e interscambiabili (a volte formando una coppia con un figlio, altre semplicemente suggerendo la possibilità che ciò che stiamo guardando potrebbe essere una famiglia atipica colta nelle abitudini e nelle conversazioni di tutti i giorni), hanno messo in scena la loro vera esperienza di vita quotidiana nel paese. Guardando come si formano e si svolgono i rapporti fra di loro, tuttavia, per lo spettatore comincia a svelarsi un'altra attività immaginativa: quella di porsi domande sul processo stesso delle riprese, in cui le due filmmaker hanno lasciato con delicatezza che la narrazione del film emergesse da sola man mano che le persone coinvolte agivano e cercavano di esprimere se stesse.

La strana isola svedese di Gotska Sandön è il soggetto del film *Outwardly from Earth's Center*, nel quale la situazione reale, quella dell'isola che scivola lentamente verso il Polo Nord, racchiude una narrazione di fantasia in cui gli abitanti si cimentano in un ancoraggio dell'isola per salvarla dal suo destino geologico. L'argomento è presentato dapprima per mezzo di una serie di monologhi simili a interviste, nel corso dei quali incontriamo il Guardiano del Faro, l'Architetto, gli Archeologi, il Politico e l'Archivista, ognuno nel suo contesto e ognuno presenta il materiale con cui lavora. La scena con l'Architetto offre un'altra chiara analogia con il genere della "lezione-performance", dove il personaggio stesso compare in una situazione di tipo teatrale davanti a schermi bianchi su cui vengono proiettate le immagini, e quello che dice e mostra non è sincronizzato con la narrazione che ascoltiamo. Poi comincia un'altra parte performativa del film, quella in cui la musica e il paesaggio sonoro elettronico composti da Jan St. Werner e Folke Rabe offrono un'atmosfera di mistero a un movimento molto lento, fisico e accurato degli abitanti, che posano i pali di legno per tutta la spiaggia, trascinano le corde dai boschi alle barche e poi dentro il mare, scena con cui finisce anche il film, con riprese dall'alto. Le riprese che stringono sui personaggi che trascinano le corde, barcollano e vacillano sotto il loro peso, quasi galleggiando insieme ad esse mentre le assicurano alle barche, sono spettacolari nella loro composizione estetica e qualità di esecuzione. A Ian White, nel testo citato sopra, questa particolare scena ricorda "amici e performer in *Wind* di Joan Jonas"[3], la performance filmata del 1968 dove un gruppo di performer si muove attraverso un paesaggio spazzato via dal vento.

In modo enigmatico, un altro film di Rosa Barba, dove la posta in gioco è il tentativo di domare la natura, comprende performance collettive analoghe in cui i ricordi dei personaggi interagiscono con lo scenario su un virulento risveglio del vulcano Vesuvio. Per realizzare il film *The Empirical Effect* l'artista ha messo insieme due gruppi diversi, dei quali facevano parte sia molti abitanti della "zona rossa", quella sotto il vulcano e quindi in costante pericolo, sia alcuni dei protagonisti dell'ultima catastrofica eruzione del 1944. Il vecchio Osservatorio Vesuviano di Napoli, che è situato vicino al cratere, è stato preso come piattaforma scenografica per la prima parte del film, offrendo così un'importante allusione a una performance che si colloca all'interno di un teatro di memoria. Un gruppo più piccolo di persone anziane si muove intorno alle attrezzature sismografiche dell'osservatorio, interagisce intorno al modello del Vesuvio senza che noi possiamo sentirne le parole, intorno ci sono delle pecore che stanno a guardare e occupano insieme agli attori il loro posto sulla grande mappa dell'Italia – e con la presenza di queste ultime si dispiega una metafora che l'artista ascrive al vulcano: stiamo osservando una parte del rapporto instabile fra società e politica nell'Italia di oggi. Uno dei membri del gruppo porta in scena delle vecchie macchine che gli altri tolgono dagli imballaggi e smontano, poi passano in rassegna libri e foto in bianco e nero che fanno accenno a del materiale d'archivio che non conosciamo ma che compare di nuovo sotto forma dei film dei fratelli Lumière su Napoli. L'importanza di mostrare ed elencare il materiale d'archivio per consolidare la plausibilità della narrazione e stimolare la nostra curiosità per l'autenticità delle sue proposte narrative è già evidenziata in *Outwardly from the Earth's Center* col ruolo dell'Archivista. Poi c'è un'altra sequenza fortemente performativa in cui il gruppo è seduto in una stanza che somiglia a un'aula scolastica a guardare delle diapositive o un film, ma noi vediamo solo loro e i loro corpi come schermi, perché sui loro volti, occhiali e corpi seduti sono riflesse delle riprese non riconoscibili, ma, probabilmente, di nuovo d'archivio. Assistiamo a una performance silenziosa in cui sul loro corpo è ri-proiettata la loro stessa memoria. L'artista stessa ha descritto l'atmosfera della comunità ritratta in questo film come "la società [che] vive a un alto livello di tensione, eppure paralizzata e sonnambulistica". Poi l'attenzione da questo particolare gruppo viene spostata su una massa di persone che corrono fuori di casa e per strada, guardando il cielo come se fosse cominciata l'eruzione[4]. Pur avendo creato in noi spettatori l'aspettativa di vedere l'eruzione di lava e il caos nelle scene seguenti, Barba decide di rallentare il ritmo di questa potente atmosfera con un'ultima sequenza col primo gruppo di attori, in cui li vediamo ballare e cantare vecchie canzoni su una grande terrazza dell'osservatorio. Alla fine si fermano e voltano le spalle alla cinepresa. L'immagine finale potrebbe essere considerata un'altra performance, ripresa da lontano, con un montaggio che ripete la stessa scena dallo stesso punto di vista, con una sola persona che si muove leggermente nell'altrimenti immobile gruppo di persone.

Queste particolari "performances collettive"[5] sono state riprese e pensate per questo film e seguono un preciso insieme di regole concordate e improvvisazioni. Nella terminologia contemporanea di danza e performance, coreografia e improvvisazione non sono più opposti, perché l'improvvisazione può essere compresa nei pezzi coreografati o essere addirittura coreografata essa stessa. Organizzare il gruppo di questi «attori», come preferisce chiamarli Rosa, in entità performative coerenti è, analogamente, il risultato di un processo in cui l'artista dice loro il suo modo di immaginare la narrazione e il film e loro sono invitati a (re)agire in base a chi sono, che cosa rappresentano per l'artista e come pensano che la narrazione andrebbe rappresentata nel film: "Invito le persone a riunirsi e a mettere il scena i loro ricordi (attraverso fatti, documenti) in una sorta di performance collettiva; è il punto più alto della parte inventata dei film. Racconto loro le mie idee, ma soprattutto spiego perché mi interessa lavorare con loro a questo film. Ne parliamo molto di più durante le riprese vere e proprie, mentre quando ci incontriamo all'inizio non ne parliamo molto. È una specie di reazione chimica fra me e loro. Appena la macchina da presa si accende, lo spazio diventa un palcoscenico e loro cominciano ad agire insieme a me"[6]. I personaggi che compaiono nei film di cui abbiamo parlato non sono mai impersonati da attori professionisti, ma da singoli profondamente legati al luogo o all'argomento rappresentato nel film. Queste persone selezionate con attenzione "portano con sé la storia del luogo scelto, e io li invito a raccontare questa storia in un quadro performativo che allestisco io. Questo quadro è solo un abbozzo con cui cominciare, poi loro lo ampliano o lo infrangono nel corso delle riprese. Io do loro le istruzioni, ma sono liberi di farci quello che vogliono"[7].

Utilizzato soprattutto nel film *The Empirical Effect*, il metodo di invitare le persone a mettere in scena i loro ricordi immaginando al tempo stesso una narrazione di fantasia si avvicina agli ultimi sviluppi della coreografia, che si occupa della produzione di sensazioni propriocettive e del rapporto affettivo con lo spettatore attraverso l'uso dell'immaginazione e del linguaggio nel processo coreografico. Mette Ingvartsen, Alice Chauchat ed Eszter Salamon sono tre esponenti della generazione più giovane di coreografi che mettono l'accento sull'uso del linguaggio per stimolare l'immaginazione e la sensazione su un dato movimento del performer stesso. Cito due esempi in cui possiamo trovare qualche corrispondenza con il "processo coreografico" dei film di Rosa Barba. Nel processo di lavorazione per lo spettacolo *NVSBL* di Eszter Salamon (2006), dove quattro danzatrici avanzano sul palcoscenico tanto lentamente da rendere impercettibili i loro movimenti,

> "azione e sensazione si fondono in un unico processo sia per i performer che per gli spettatori, eppure in una ripartizione diversa: per i performer, è la sensazione a dare inizio alle azioni, mentre per gli spettatori la percezione esige uno sforzo tale da venire vissuta come azione... Il problema che dovevano affrontare i performer era immaginare e fingere il movimento, il punto del corpo in cui inizia, la qualità corrispondente che possiede, l'immagine che potrebbe prendere in un contesto diverso. Il sistema che forniva un'intuizione di tipo semi-fisiologico all'interno del corpo e che perciò richiederebbe l'introduzione di immagini e storie sul movimento all'interno delle sensazioni era il *Body Mind Centering* (BMC)... Oltre al BMC i performer mettevano in atto un'altra tecnica di espressione: allo scopo di atteggiare il viso e arricchire la qualità dei movimenti dell'intero corpo, evocavano immagini di espressioni, il ricordo che avevano della dinamica di certi stati d'animo ed emozioni, o collocavano i movimenti che stavano compiendo in quel momento in un'altra ambientazione, con una qualità che non si poteva avere nella realtà ma solo virtualmente, sul palcoscenico; per esempio, come ci si sentirebbe a fare questo movimento mentre si corre, ricordare la sensazione del correre mentre in realtà non si sta correndo."[8]

La coreografa danese Mette Ingvartsen ha scritto un breve manifesto sulla *Performance Site-Specific*, che di nuovo riprende l'atmosfera dello spazio e il suo ricordo come vengono impiegati da Rosa Barba nei suoi film:

> "1. La performance site-specific sostiene l'uso di ambienti preesistenti come punto di partenza per la sua creazione, utilizzando così l'ambiente come sfondo, retroscena o addirittura performer.
> 2. La performance site-specific fa emergere l'idea artistica da una situazione reale, sociale e/o politica, pur non riducendo l'espressione alla riproduzione di tale situazione.
> 3. La performance site-specific riattiva la sua posizione e offre una nuova "vista" sullo specifico.
> 4. La performance site-specific è condizionata e influenzata da uno spazio particolare, e dovrebbe a sua volta condizionare e influenzare tale spazio.
> 5. La performance site-specific si discosta dall'autonomia dell'arte e dalla neutralità dello spazio teatrale.
> 6. La performance site-specific crea una narrazione all'interno della realtà del luogo, suggerendo allo spettatore di ripensare le sue percezioni "naturali".
> 7. La performance site-specific si scioglie nell'ambiente in cui viene eseguita, diventando indistinguibile dalla realtà del luogo.
> 8. La performance site-specific produce dubbio su ciò che fa parte della situazione che viene messa in scena, rispetto a ciò che faceva parte della situazione già in precedenza.
> 9. La performance site-specific non può essere portata in tournée perché è parte integrante del luogo dove nasce. Tuttavia, le strategie usate possono essere ristabilite o riadattate ad altri contesti e produrre nuove specificità.

10. La performance site-specific tratta e si dedica a formati, convenzioni e aspettative della messa in scena delle espressioni, e mette in dubbio le logiche di riproduzione, diffusione e mercificazione delle opere di performance. "[9]

Nei suoi due ultimi film, questa particolarissima "performance site-specific" filmata si estende dalle persone alla cinepresa (*A Private Tableaux*, 2010) e agli oggetti d'arte conservati nei depositi dei musei (*The Hidden Conference: About the Discontinuous History of Things We See and Don't See*, 2011). In *A Private Tableaux*, il movimento della cinepresa è "sceneggiato" da linee, segni, disegni, graffi lasciati negli anni da ingegneri e scienziati nel corso delle loro ricerche sulla stabilità dell'architettura sotterranea. La macchina da presa fa emergere dettagli di dipinti murali e i suoni elettronici che li accompagnano, e più oltre i suoni che sembrano arrivare da un cantiere, e risponde cinesteticamente alla luce oscillante che rende possibile cogliere nel buio quelle che paiono delle forme.
The Hidden Conference è un film muto ma performativo che evoca i dialoghi e le discussioni che potremmo immaginare abbiano luogo fra le opere d'arte nei depositi dei musei. È un work in progress, che conferma e annuncia al tempo stesso la costante indagine di Rosa Barba in magazzini e archivi culturali. All'inizio è la cinepresa a intessere lentamente la narrazione fra le piccole sculture sulle scansie, fornendo un'atmosfera fatta di primi piani e chiaro-scuro e dando la sensazione di presentare agli spettatori i protagonisti principali. Nella seconda parte del film, il deposito si trasforma in un palcoscenico dove le entrate e le uscite teatrali sono messe in scena dalle pareti di ferro dove sono conservati i dipinti. Il paesaggio sonoro, come sempre accade nei film e nelle installazioni di Rosa Barba, ha la stessa grande importanza nel sostenere il processo di narrativizzazione.

È in questi esempi che possiamo vedere l'interesse dell'artista nel portare alla visibilità, come dice lei stessa, i modi in cui i paesaggi interiori umani interagiscono con i paesaggi naturali che ritrae nei suoi film e in fenomeni e tracce che le persone lasciano nella storia.

Note

1. "In questa mostra, l'installazione accuratamente coreografata di Barba divide l'attenzione degli spettatori fra l'immagine proiettata e il proiettore stesso, ponendo domande su quale sia la narrazione e quale il narratore". Brano tratto dal comunicato stampa sull'esposizione di Rosa Barba alla Tate Modern (2010-2011). http://www.tate.org.uk/modern/exhibitions/rosabarba/default.shtm
2. Ian White nel testo su Rosa Barba, in "Camera Austria", n. 101, 2008.
3. Ibid.
4. Queste scene sono state riprese durante l'annuale esercitazione di evacuazione di massa a cui sono sottoposti tutti gli abitanti della zona rossa.
5. Barba ha usato questo termine al seminario *Something You Should Know*, all'EHESS di Parigi nel maggio del 2010. La sua formulazione precisa è stato il vero innesco per questo articolo, e vorrei ringraziarla di cuore per tutti i nostri scambi su questo concetto.
6. Rosa Barba in una conversazione privata, Novembre 2010.
7. Ibid.
8. Bojana Cveji, "Researching. A Public Interview with Eszter Salamon", in *6M1L*, everybodys publications, 2009, pp.84-85. Il *Body Mind Centering* è un approccio integrato all'esperienza trasformativa attraverso la rieducazione dei movimenti, ultimamente molto usato nella coreografia contemporanea. Sviluppato da Bonnie Bainbridge Cohen, è uno studio empirico basato sull'incarnazione e sull'applicazione di principi anatomici, fisiologici, psicofisici ed evolutivi, con l'uso di movimento, tatto, voce e mente.
9. http://www.everybodystoolbox.net/?q=node/160

STORIE SOSPESE: LA STRATEGIA NARRATIVA DI ROSA BARBA

LYNNE COOKE

"Come possono le opere d'arte visiva... raccontare storie? ... La narrazione [deve] diventare uno strumento e non un significato; un mediatore e non una soluzione; un partecipante e non un outsider".
Louise Bourgeois

"Una filosofia è caratterizzata più dalla formulazione che dalla soluzione dei problemi".
Suzanne Langer

L'opera di Rosa Barba *Somnium* (2011), un film in 35 millimetri della durata di 19 minuti e 20 secondi, mette insieme molti dei temi chiave emersi nell'ultimo decennio nell'opera dell'artista. Il punto di partenza è il racconto di un viaggio sulla Luna scritto dall'astronomo tedesco Giovanni Keplero[1] che, seppure strutturato sotto forma di sogno, era inteso a convalidare la tesi radicalmente sovversiva di un universo eliocentrico[2]. Keplero lavorò per oltre trent'anni a questa controversa teoria, scrivendo in latino anziché nella più accessibile lingua volgare, nella speranza di respingere gli attacchi di chi ancora credeva che la Terra fosse al centro dell'universo. Il suo testo, pubblicato postumo nel 1634 e ristampato solo di rado nei tre secoli successivi, fu infine salvato dall'oblio con la traduzione in varie lingue europee e oggi, dopo aver guadagnato una vasta fama underground fra gli appassionati di fantascienza, è ampiamente riconosciuto come un testo pionieristico del genere. Vi hanno attinto con successo scrittori come J. G. Ballard, benché nessun regista sia ancora riuscito a dargli forma cinematografica. È stata la ricerca sulla movimentata storia di *Somnium* a ispirare il progetto eponimo di Rosa Barba. Prendendo in prestito il titolo come omaggio, l'artista ha attinto sia dal racconto che, in misura altrettanto importante, dal suo notevole risultato nello stabilire una nuova ontologia della visione.

Uno degli aspetti più singolari del racconto di Keplero è la sua curiosa struttura. La storia in sé si interrompe bruscamente quando il narratore improvvisamente si sveglia dal suo viaggio lunare e si ritrova nel proprio letto con la testa sotto il cuscino. Il ricorso all'espediente del sogno è un esplicito stratagemma che fa ben poco per mascherare la sovversività dell'argomento, la cui sostanza si ritrova nelle ampie note e nei commentari che rischiano di soffocare la breve storia. Queste appendici, piene di dati scientifici e di ipotesi, di volta in volta sostengono o contestano le osservazioni empiriche e i riferimenti classici proposti nel corpo principale del testo. Il cuore della tesi di Keplero è la convinzione che le ipotesi razionali e scientifiche possano condurre a verità teoriche che non sono né accessibili né necessariamente verificabili dallo studio basato sull'osservazione pragmatica. La preveggenza con cui Keplero riconobbe i limiti dell'osservazione diretta e della ricerca empirica lo portò a postulare un'ontologia della visione basata sulla teoria scientifica. Nell'opera di Rosa Barba è intessuto un dibattito espresso in termini analoghi. Il film si apre con la voce fuori campo di un uomo dal tono autorevole che comunica in modo distaccato l'informazione che, benché il pianeta *Somnium* sia al momento privo di qualunque forma di vita, la natura sta riconquistando aree che fino a poco tempo prima erano state lasciate alle imprese dell'uomo. Questa mossa di apertura, un classico incipit da racconto di fantascienza, promette una narrazione coinvolgente ma subito destabilizza le aspettative introducendo svariate modalità narrative che minano alla base i concetti di coerenza e onnipotenza dell'autore. Saldando fra loro il materiale documentario e la narrazione di fantasia, e intercalando resoconti contrastanti di testimoni oculari a rapporti ufficiali, l'artista costruisce un contrappunto fra empirico e teorico. Poi si sente una seconda voce: colloquiale nel tono e nei modi, raramente si alza sopra un sussurro angosciato mentre riferisce il sospetto che ci sia qualcosa di profondamente sbagliato nelle informazioni diffuse pubblicamente sugli enormi rivolgimenti che stanno trasformando l'ambiente. A differenza del narratore consapevole di Keplero, il testimone di Rosa Barba, modesto ma scettico, sembra ignaro della portata polemica delle sue osservazioni. Alla fine, il film evita di riconciliare queste prospettive contrastanti, e si chiude provocatoriamente con una citazione del mistico rinascimentale Giordano Bruno, secondo cui "l'osservatore è sempre al centro delle cose".

In *Somnium,* sottili slittamenti all'interno delle voci narrative e fra di esse, integrano il modo in cui Barba gestisce le affascinanti immagini visive. Riproduzioni di foto in bianco e nero di quelli che, per il montaggio parallelo fra immagini ferme e in movimento, possono forse essere identificati come documenti che rappresentano il luogo come era in un'epoca precedente. In altri punti del film, lente panoramiche interrompono fotogrammi di dettagli, per esempio una tubatura di scarico che attraversa un pendio. Varie immagini di questo tipo richiamano i motivi sottolineati da Robert Smithson nel suo testo, ormai una pietra miliare, *A Tour of the Monuments of Passaic, New Jersey*, pubblicato su "Artforum" nel dicembre 1967, nel quale l'autore riprende una figura tipica della Landscape art, trasponendo il classico viaggio in luoghi bucolici e pittoreschi, nel paesaggio industriale abbandonato e distopico di una palude del New Jersey. Smithson rimane affascinato da queste rovine, che per lui si leggono come monumenti al fallimento delle visioni dell'umanità su un utopistico futuro tecnologico, e torna ripetutamente sull'argomento, soprattutto nel grande trittico di opere (scultura, film e saggio) raccolte sotto il titolo collettivo di *Spiral Jetty. Somnium* allude chiaramente a questo film seminale di Smithson, come anche alla sua narrazione ibrida tra prima persona e citazioni da racconti di fantascienza, testi di viaggio, letteratura e manuali scientifici, allo scopo di fondere insieme temporalità disparate tra passato, presente e futuro, e tra cronologie cicliche, lineari ed entropiche. Il subtesto di immagini e riferimenti mnemonici generati dalle opere di Smithson è fondamentale per la lettura di *Somnium*, ed è pari almeno al debito del film nei confronti della gemma letteraria di Keplero. Il progetto di Rosa Barba dà nuova vita a questi precedenti. L'artista sostiene che, lungi dall'affondare in un passato che ormai è storia, queste opere incarnano voci a-storiche, e sono componenti cruciali di un discorso critico che vuole definire il genere di visione richiesto da un cinema contemporaneo impegnato politicamente.

Un tono più malinconico pervade *The Long Road* (2010) che, come *They Shine* (2007) e *The Waiting Grounds* (2007), è stato girato nel sud-ovest degli Stati Uniti. La pista di collaudo automobilistico che rappresenta il centro visivo dell'opera, e che inizialmente vediamo in una lunga carrellata dall'alto, somiglia a un terrapieno preistorico o a una variazione sul genere risalente agli anni Settanta. Che ci sembri più simile alle antiche linee di Nazca riscoperte grazie ai voli aerei o alle incursioni su scala industriale in remoti territori desertici realizzate da Smithson e dai suoi compagni negli anni del dopoguerra, questa incisione ellittica sulla superficie terrestre è, come quelle, soggetta al decadimento e alle ingiurie del tempo. La colonna sonora mescola suoni tecno-elettronici, dai quali a intermittenza emergono frasi micro-tonali in cui la voce gutturale di Robert Creeley legge passi della sua poesia *The Long Road*. Il ricordo della morte del padre, insieme al pensiero improvviso, suscitato da alcune vecchie foto del tempo della scuola, dei tanti decenni trascorsi da questa morte, ricorda al poeta il fatto che anche lui è mortale. Il sospetto che la fine della sua lunga strada possa essere vicina, viene esplicitato nell'ultimo fotogramma del film. La cinepresa, posta al livello del suolo, gira intorno alla pista; dopo una curva, percorre un tratto diritto, prendendo velocità nel sole del tardo pomeriggio. Rosa Barba sovrappone questi mutevoli punti di vista di occhio e voce nel corso di tutto il montaggio, nei movimenti della macchina da presa e nella collocazione del testo nell'ambito della colonna sonora. Come in *Somnium,* la funzione mnemonica basata su riferimenti diretti e indiretti alle opere di altri artisti (un poeta e alcuni scultori senza nome, in questo caso) è parte integrante del modo in cui viene elaborato il contenuto.

L'interesse di Rosa Barba per il ruolo e la posizione delle opere d'arte all'interno dell'immaginario culturale è risultato ancora più chiaro con la risposta dell'artista al recente incarico del Museo Nacional Centro de Arte Reina Sofía di Madrid. Invitata a curare una mostra del patrimonio di opere del museo, l'artista ha replicato con una proposta che ha definito "una conferenza da curatore (*a curated conference*)". Il progetto prevede la presentazione di circa quarantatre lavori, fra cui film e video, fotografia, scultura, pittura e disegni, che l'artista ha installato in due sale adiacenti. "Lo scopo di questa *conferenza* è di riunire insieme una rappresentanza di artisti del XX e XXI secolo, con le loro opinioni di esperti sulle questioni più importanti dell'arte", ha scritto nella brochure di presentazione[3]. L'esposizione, intitolata *On the Future of Collective Strength within an Archive* (2010), evitava le convenzioni standard della presentazione museologica, in particolare la separazione delle opere per mezzo espressivo e la disposizione cronologica lineare, a favore di un'installazione che contrapponeva pezzi creati in un periodo di quasi un secolo, collocandoli a stretto contatto. Anziché nascondere le differenze in ossequio a un imperativo ideologico, la base su cui oggi vengono presentate gran parte delle collezioni nelle istituzioni artistiche contemporanee, Rosa Barba ha accolto positivamente l'anarchia prodotta da una situazione in cui "ogni artista parla con la propria voce nella propria lingua, con il proprio temperamento e al proprio volume". Sapendo che, nonostante alcune aggiunte recenti, molte delle opere facevano parte della collezione da molto tempo, Rosa Barba ha invitato gli artisti (attraverso i loro lavori) a esplorare "la coscienza collettiva" dell'archivio. Il risultato, anticipava l'artista, non sarebbe stata una visione consensuale o coerente (l'obiettivo dei professionisti dei musei), ma una "Babele di voci": l'archivio si sarebbe rivelato come composto da "espressioni individuali senza tempo" che possono essere "coreografate come una partitura musicale". Rosa Barba afferma che "negando il passato e ignorando il futuro, l'artista è libero di fare una dichiarazione radicale che dura nel tempo... [e genera] un'energia che mette in connessione artisti di ogni epoca".

Nel programma erano previste anche tavole rotonde, laboratori, una sessione parallela e la ripresa di interventi di Pablo Picasso, Mira Schendel, Louise Bourgeois, Martha Rosler e altri. Alcuni relatori hanno sollevato argomenti adombrati anche nelle opere di Rosa Barba. Così Picasso, per esempio, sosteneva: "Tutto ciò che ho fatto l'ho fatto solo per il presente, e con la speranza che resterà sempre nel presente". George Maciunas sottolineava il senso dell'identità collettiva dell'artista quando definiva questa "comunità di individui che raggruppano insieme una grande quantità di comportamenti e atteggiamenti... un 'non-gruppo' privo di strutture rigide". Louise Bourgeois, per parte sua, parlava dei modi in cui le opere di arte visiva raccontano delle storie, sostenendo che per mezzo dell'interazione delle qualità formali "la narrazione diviene uno strumento e non un significato, un mediatore e non una soluzione". Pur non partecipando alla discussione con proprie opere e quindi con la propria voce, Rosa Barba ha reso in modo estremamente chiaro la propria posizione scegliendo come principali relatori, artisti la cui estetica e il cui lavoro rappresentano concretamente le parole chiave della sua personale pratica artistica.

L'archivio è stato, letteralmente, la fonte della "mostra come conferenza" realizzata da Rosa Barba, dal momento che la lista di opere esposte era stata stilata pescando esclusivamente dai depositi museali. Il termine "archivio" viene usato anche, in modo più astratto, per riferirsi al sistema che, per dirla con Hal Foster, "struttura le espressioni particolari di un particolare periodo"[4]. Questo concetto discorsivo dell'archivio era stato messo in scena anche nel progetto di Rosa Barba, che affrontava criticamente l'ideologia che guida la presentazione della collezione del museo in altre sedi, offrendo un'alternativa che sovverte le norme di rappresentazione totalizzante e di responsabilità storica. Vista la sua convinzione che le opere d'arte siano "astoriche" o "senza tempo", esse possono anche essere auto-organizzatte, e possono unirsi per mezzo dell'iniziativa dei loro creatori anziché dipendere dai professionisti dei musei che le arruolano a forza nelle loro ortodossie.

Il progetto innovativo di Rosa Barba può essere letto anche attraverso il modello del museo a cui si riferiva Theodor Adorno in un saggio, pubblicato nel 1953, su ciò che l'autore chiamò il "Museo Valéry Proust"[5]. Secondo Adorno, Valéry incarnava la posizione secondo cui il museo è "dove mettiamo a morte l'arte del passato". "Museo e mausoleo sono connessi da più che un'associazione fonetica", sosteneva, perché "i musei sono le tombe di famiglia delle opere d'arte. Essi testimoniano la neutralizzazione della cultura". Di contro all'imbalsamazione, o reificazione, dell'opera d'arte che secondo Valéry aveva luogo nel museo, Proust articolava una visione basata sull'idea della rianimazione dell'opera d'arte. Per lui, di conseguenza, il museo è un luogo di competizione agonistica. Nella conferenza curatoriale di Rosa Barba si sente l'eco delle idee di Proust. Tuttavia, laddove Proust accordava allo spettatore la possibilità di agire, assegnandogli il compito di infondere nuova vita all'opera, Rosa Barba lascia efficacemente il controllo nelle mani degli artisti: le loro opere incarnano la loro voce.

The Hidden Conference: About the Discontinuous History of Things We See and Don't See (2011), un film in 35 millimetri realizzato poco dopo

il lancio del progetto di Rosa Barba al Museo Reina Sofia di Madrid, esplora ulteriormente questo argomento[6]. Il film, ambientato in un luogo non identificato (i depositi della Neue Nationalgalerie di Berlino) e in "un momento temporale non specificato (nel futuro o nel passato)", porta alla luce una situazione che, benché in atto da anni, come ci informa il prologo scritto, ha ora assunto un certo "livello di urgenza". Tuttavia il motivo della riunione non è più noto. Mentre la macchina da presa coreografa un gruppo eterogeneo di oggetti d'arte avvolti in una luce da film *noir*, emergono narrazioni frammentarie che non diventano mai coerenti. Ancora una volta la narrazione serve da "mediatore, non [da] soluzione". Il discorso viene incluso nella performance corporea, perché la colonna sonora minimale di Jan St. Werner, assiduo collaboratore di Rosa Barba, anima le opere (di Ernst Barlach, Renée Sintenis, Gerhard Marcks e di altri ormai caduti nell'oblio) creando un senso del ruolo attraverso il gesto, l'atteggiamento, la postura e lo sguardo. Lungi dal mettere in dubbio il paradigma dell'archivio come visione futuristica fallita, questa conferenza clandestina ne conferma la retorica. Il pathos circonda le passate ambizioni del museo nella totalità della rappresentazione, proponendo la possibilità della redenzione attraverso il salvataggio di questi frammenti sperduti di una storia in frantumi.
Molti anni fa Rosa Barba aveva affrontato l'archivio da un punto di vista completamente diverso in *Western Round Table* (2007). La sua fonte era stata un simposio riunito nel 1949 a San Francisco sotto il titolo "The Western Round Table on Modern Art". Lo scopo era di "portare una rappresentanza delle opinioni meglio informate del tempo ad affrontare le questioni dell'arte oggi", e il prestigioso gruppo (tutto al maschile) di relatori comprendeva critici, artisti, storici dell'arte, compositori, professionisti del museo e via dicendo, fra cui Marcel Duchamp, Frank Lloyd Wright, Darius Milhaud, Robert Goldwater, Mark Tobey, Alfred Frankenstein, Andrew C. Richie e Gregory Bateson[7]. Questa volta, la risposta di Rosa Barba ha preso la forma di una proiezione scultorea. Due proiettori 16 millimetri posizionati a terra vicini, fanno girare pellicola non impressionata. Ciascuno crea sul muro adiacente una macchia di luce bianca, nella quale entra lentamente l'ombra architettonica dell'antagonista, l'altro proiettore. La colonna sonora è composta di estratti da due film di Fellini, montati in modo tale che i due proiettori sembrino conversare fra loro, sebbene in termini ben lontani dai toni solenni del simposio. I refrain musicali, mai del tutto sovrastati dal suono meccanico prodotto dai vecchi proiettori, inizialmente sono intriganti, divertenti e perfino affascinanti, ma presto la musica diventa ossessiva, impossibile da dimenticare o estirpare. Un'epigrafe di Suzanne Langer alla trascrizione degli atti contiene l'affermazione che, nel caratterizzare una filosofia, le soluzioni offerte alle domande sono meno rivelatrici della formulazione dei problemi: "Le risposte hanno eretto un edificio di fatti" afferma la Langer, "ma sono le domande a costruire la struttura in cui i fatti sono fissati"[8]. Filtrata attraverso l'osservazione di Suzanne Langer, la peculiare incarnazione degli atti di questo famoso evento realizzata da Rosa Barba sotto forma di due oscure sagome architettoniche (sorta di Behemoth smaterializzati che si parlano addosso imperterriti) può essere meno negativa di come appare in un primo momento.
Come testimonia *They Shine*, le fantasie scientifiche contemporanee sono difficili da distinguere da quello che una volta era il regno della fantascienza vera e propria[9]. Qualcosa di molto diverso emerge però da *A Private Tableaux* (2010). Immagini che somigliano a un qualche tipo di pittura rupestre moderna sono identificate come le tracce lasciate nelle gallerie sotto il fiume Mersey a Liverpool nell'arco di oltre un secolo dagli ingegneri che studiavano i punti di pressione creati dai veicoli che percorrevano le gallerie sovrastanti. Rosa Barba, in un modo piuttosto insolito per lei, evita l'approccio archeologico a questa cartografia così limpida a favore di un'indagine semiologica che legge i segni astratti come simboli figurativi. Evidentemente ignaro delle loro origini, il commentatore (il cui resoconto costituisce il testo del film) li paragona a una forma di "scrittura automatica" creata "a livello subliminale" dagli ingegneri "per il loro piacere". Tenta di caratterizzare i segni che comprendono questi "tableaux privati": oltre a una "macchina per volare" e "un carro coi cavalli", c'è il ritratto di un giovane "disegnato a memoria". Confrontando questo volto, in modo piuttosto libero, con un disegno di Cocteau, lo scrittore conclude che "ha portato al suo creatore molti problemi e poca soddisfazione". Questa fantasiosa analisi semiotica, con la rinuncia all'approccio spassionato e oggettivo proprio dell'interpretazione scientifica, tradisce una stravaganza rara nelle opere di Rosa Barba. Eppure è proprio il carattere risibile di queste congetture in libertà che riporta l'attenzione sui termini in cui è stata formulata l'indagine. Ancora una volta, l'interesse primario dell'artista è sulla struttura che regola e governa lo slancio narrativo.
La narrazione come forma di critica culturale, può servire come mezzo per mediare la storia e al tempo stesso, dare un senso all'esperienza contemporanea. I libri di Italo Calvino, per esempio, divennero un veicolo per risvegliare una società che si era fatta sempre più passiva, prima sotto il regime fascista e poi a causa della rapidità dei cambiamenti socio-culturali del dopoguerra. Calvino era arrivato alla convinzione che, lungi dal richiedere di illustrare posizioni ideologiche in modo polemico, la letteratura impegnata dovesse dispiegare stile e abilità al servizio di una forma di realismo che non aveva niente a che fare col naturalismo. La narrativa richiedeva attenzione, "innanzitutto, [a] immagine e parola, scatto, piglio, stile, sprezzatura, sfida"[10]. Il realismo, e non il naturalismo, è anche il registro preferito da Rosa Barba; perciò anche per lei la narrazione di storie è una questione di stile e atteggiamento tanto quanto di abilità. Le fonti delle sue narrazioni sono scelte in un'ampia gamma di testi letterari. Talvolta, come nell'uso che fa della poesia di Creeley in *The Long Road*, prende a prestito direttamente; più spesso, come in *Somnium* e *Let Me See It* (2010), che si basa su un racconto di Borges, rielabora o parafrasa il testo originale. La letteratura è peraltro essenziale alla sua concezione del cinema quanto le sue controparti visive.
Mentre in molte delle sue opere filmiche il cinema è variamente concepito come un tipo di scrittura o iscrizione, la scultura è usata letteramente per dare forma materiale al linguaggio[11]. *I Made a Circuit and then a Second Circuit* (2010) fa parte di un gruppo di lavori che potremmo definire dispositivi proto-cinematografici, perché ciascuno di essi è composto da un telo di feltro sospeso nello spazio in modo tale che funga sia da schermo che da proiettore. Quando sulla griglia scura da cui è stato ritagliato un testo viene proiettata la luce, sulla parete retrostante appare una scritta luminosa. Da quello che restava di uno di questi oggetti, Rosa Barba ha creato *They Come and Go* (2009). I frammenti di linguaggio ammucchiati su un pezzo di stoffa steso a terra e illuminati con il fascio di luce di un proiettore, prendono la forma di un archivio dall'infinito potenziale narrativo.

Il suo acume per il testo si estende alle sue modalità di enunciazione: le voci sulle sue colonne sonore sono tanto peculiari quanto memorabili. In *They Shine,* per esempio, il timbro di voce gentile e pragmatico del narratore richiama i toni dei protagonisti maschili di un certo tipo di film hollywoodiani. Coltivando questa associazione, Rosa Barba vuole sottolineare il fatto che gli abitanti di quell'ambiente irreale vivono fra due realtà fantasmatiche: il luogo in cui è stata costruita la spettrale schiera di superfici riflettenti non è lontano da Hollywood. In tutta la sua opera, i monologhi degli esperti (maschi) sono sempre calmi e misurati, quasi laconici. Tuttavia, nel momento in cui vengono messi in contrappunto con le voci confuse e insicure di dilettanti che escono incerte dai margini e dagli interstizi (come accade in *Somnium*), questi toni ordinati suonano subdoli, e le loro spiegazioni sospette[12].
La narrazione di storie dipende tanto dal lettore / ascoltatore quanto dalla voce dell'autore. Nella nota formulazione di Roland Barthes, leggere (come vedere) crea uno spazio di incontro dove il lettore e la moltitudine di scritti che comprendono qualsiasi testo "si mescolano e si scontrano". L'analisi di questo incontro che Rosa Barba fa a tutti i livelli, forse da nessuna parte è altrettanto chiara e ben fatta che in *It's Gonna Happen* (2005), in cui una conversazione immaginaria che avrebbe potuto verosimilmente fare parte delle macchinazioni politiche divenute famose col nome di Watergate, fornisce la materia prima per quella che potrebbe essere una scena in un film di prossima realizzazione. Le indicazioni dello sceneggiatore compaiono come frasi proiettate su uno sfondo nero, mentre la colonna sonora riproduce la conversazione sotto forma di una breve telefonata. Gli spettatori al tempo stesso leggono i testi e ascoltano la stringata conversazione in cui due uomini tramano un rapimento, evocando la scena nella loro mente. Mentre si sforzano di seguire contemporaneamente le parole scritte e quelle pronunciate, che si svolgono in parallelo ma non in sincrono, gli spettatori si ritrovano a occupare due spazi agli antipodi: sono contemporaneamente all'interno del regno dell'illusione e all'esterno dei suoi confini fittizi. Il suono dei proiettori, che è indipendente dall'audio ma si mescola con esso, spinge a rendersi conto che ormai un'esperienza del cinema non mediata non è più possibile; le tecniche del film, e il nostro atteggiamento verso di esso, sono inevitabilmente filtrati attraverso le storie, le convenzioni e i generi. Chiedendo agli spettatori di negoziare fra due posizioni contraddittorie, Rosa Barba impone loro di riflettere sul film come mezzo espressivo, e sui suoi generi e tradizioni. La politica del Watergate qui è al tempo stesso un pretesto e uno smacco al suo tema di sempre: le politiche della visione. Ancora una volta, nella pratica artistica di Rosa Barba le forme di introspezione che segnano molti dei progetti modernisti esemplari sul mezzo espressivo, acquisiscono una maschera narrativa. Testi riflessivi, storie sospese e fantasticherie speculative diventano veicoli di digressione, attraverso cui l'artista costruisce una modalità del vedere (un'ontologia della visione) adeguata al cinema di oggi[13].

Note

1. Gale E. Christianson, *Kepler's Somnium: Science Fiction and the Renaissance Scientist*, in "Science Fiction Studies", (marzo 1976), pp. 79–90. Cfr. anche Raz Chen-Morris, *Shadows of Instruction: Optics and Classical Authorities in Kepler's Somnium,* "Journal of the History of Ideas", (2005), pp. 223–41.

2. Il rischio di pubblicare opinioni così controverse nell'Europa dell'inizio del XVII secolo era notevole, come testimonia il fatto che a causa di una versione precedente del manoscritto, la madre dello scrittore era stata arrestata con l'accusa di stregoneria.

3. Rosa Barba, *A Curated Conference: On the Future of Collective Strength within the Archive,* (Madrid, Museo Nacional Centro de Arte Reina Sofia, 2010). Tutte le citazioni che seguono sono tratte da questa brochure.

4. Vedi Hal Foster, *Archives of Modern Art*, "October", n. 99 (Inverno 2002), pp. 81–95. Vedi anche *An Archival Impulse*, "October", n. 110 (Autunno 2004), pp. 3–22.

5. Ringrazio Foster per il resoconto sul saggio di Adorno. Cfr. Foster 2002 (vedi nota 4), pp. 84–85. Tutte le citazioni che seguono sull'argomento, sono tratte dal testo di Foster.

6. Questo è in effetti il primo di quelli che saranno quattro capitoli di una serie; il secondo, intitolato *The Hidden Conference: A Fractured Play* (2011), è stato inaugurato a Trento nel 2011.

7. Per le trascrizioni della conferenza, vedi "The Western Round Table on Modern Art (1949)", edizione a cura di Douglas MacAgy. Consultato sul sito: http: / / www.ubu.com / historical / wrtma / index.html (ultimo accesso: 16 Luglio 2011).

8. Ibid.

9. Il centro di *They Shine* (2007) è un vasto spiegamento di strutture futuristiche, al tempo stesso "incantatrici" e "mortali", che pare migliorare un ambiente ostile transformandolo in un luogo abitabile. E' sottoposto alle congetture piene di ansia e allo scetticismo e sconcerto degli abitanti del posto. Come in *Somnium*, la risposta obliqua e ambivalente alle fantasie scientifiche di fronte a una natura che sembra impazzita, è anche l'argomento degli scritti di Rivka Galchen (cfr. per esempio Rivka Galchen, *Disaster Aversion: The Quest to Control Hurricanes*, "Harper's Magazine", (Ottobre 2009), pp. 55–63. Consultato sul sito: http:www.harpers.orgarchive / 2009 / 10).

10. Italo Calvino, "Prefazione", ne *Il sentiero dei nidi di ragno,* Einaudi, 1964.

11. *Printed Cinema* è il titolo dato dall'artista a una serie di pubblicazioni, tuttora in corso, ciascuna delle quail accompagna la produzione di una particolare opera o insieme di opere, e riflette sul processo della sua realizzazione.

12. Le uniche eccezioni a questa serie di voci maschili sono le due voci femminili in *Parachutable* (2005). Sebbene non interagiscano fra loro, queste voci si interrompono e si sovrappongono a vicenda, rafforzando gli effetti di contrasto e resistenza per mezzo dei quail vengono messi in relazione immagini e suoni.

13. "The real protagonists are stories suspended in air" ("I veri protagonisti sono le storie sospese nell'aria"), dice una delle due voci femminili in *Parachutable* (2005).

EPILOGO

L'istituzione "filmica" di Rosa Barba

1. Spazio: ***Est-ce que c'est une analogie à deux dimensions ou une métaphore?***

All'inizio non te ne rendi conto, poi ti accorgi di entrare in uno spazio totalmente ripensato e trasformato. E sei all'interno di un grande proiettore. Ti trovi ad abitare una storia che si sta raccontando, in un luogo che muta mentre lo attraversi. Sei in un film e all'interno della macchina-museo che lo proietta. Solo quando scopri un proiettore 70mm, *White Museum* (2010), nell'ultima sala del Centre international d'art et du paysage de l'île de Vassivière, realizzi che l'intero edificio del museo a mostra agisce come una centrifuga, dove si frammenta la narrazione in diverse opere. Tu sei il film, la pellicola su cui la mostra si imprime. La tua persona, le tue emozioni e le tue riflessioni sono il film impressionato, che l'istituzione costruisce intorno a te.

Rosa Barba crea mitologie e formula ipotesi. Usa l'immagine per indagare e ricostruire. Nei suoi progetti, s'interroga sull'essenza e la funzione del cinema, riflette sulla sua struttura come medium e come strumento creatore di mondi. Il suo lavoro parte da una matrice sociale, storica, naturalistica, scientifica e filosofica, nasce dalla volontà di fornire una propria lettura di dati, fatti reali e storici. La sua fascinazione per il cinema riguarda l'aspetto astratto, come quello meccanico.

Nelle installazioni di Barba, gli strumenti tecnici - proiettori, pellicola, casse audio - recitano un ruolo nel film stesso, trasformano lo spazio, modificano la percezione, diventano parte sostanziale della coreografia espositiva: agiscono in un rimando sensoriale continuo con il visitatore. Il processo mentale che l'artista innesca nei riguardi del cinema, il suo atteggiamento verso il film, è quello di sezionarlo e smembrarlo, dividerlo nelle singole e differenti componenti.

La mostra *Est-ce que c'est une analogie à deux dimensions ou une métaphore?* di Barba, presentata al Centre international d'art et du paysage de l'île de Vassivière, è stata ispirata proprio da ciò che più caratterizza l'isola. L'acqua e la luminosità, sono gli elementi fondamentali di questo lembo di terra che sorge nel mezzo di un lago artificiale nella regione francese del Limousin. E, giocando sull'idea di artificio e naturalità, Rosa Barba ha immaginato che il fulcro del progetto potesse essere la struttura stessa del Centro d'arte, disegnata dall'architetto italiano Aldo Rossi. Il lago che circonda l'isola diventa così soggetto narrante, e viene metaforicamente utilizzato da Barba come uno schermo.
La luce arriva da un proiettore installato nell'edificio principale, compiendo un lungo e imprevedibile percorso che lo attraversa interamente e va a colpire il lago. Illuminandolo, sembra voler sfidare la natura segreta di questo specchio d'acqua. Un altrettanto sofisticato meccanismo produce un suono, increspando la superficie e lo spettatore ha la sensazione di percepire un respiro proveniente dagli otto villaggi sommersi negli anni 50, quando nacque la diga che ha permesso la formazione del lago stesso. Il risultato di questa visionaria operazione è particolarmente efficace perché, attraverso la mostra, ci si immerge in una doppia profondità: quella del lago e quella della narrazione che la mostra stessa innesca. Il rimando continuo tra realtà, finzione, percezione e assenza è evidente.
Ma tutta la struttura architettonica del museo è coinvolta: la sala principale del Centro, la navata, ospita *The Long Road* (2010), un nuovo film in 35mm, realizzato sul sito di un circuito automobilistico semi-abbandonato nel deserto californiano. Lo spettatore ha la sensazione di percorrere a grande velocità il *loop* creato dall'artista-operatore. Le tracce dei pneumatici delle molte automobili che hanno percorso il circuito segnano l'asfalto e producono una doppia sensazione: quella di un passato ormai trascorso e, nello stesso tempo, quella di una minaccia imminente. Sospesi nel punto di intersezione tra presente e passato, forse futuro, questo luogo emerge dalla sabbia come un immenso disegno. Le stigmate di una cultura modernista ormai disertata, dimenticata, pronta a trasformarsi in qualcosa di diverso, inatteso, ancora non del tutto espresso e probabilmente inesprimibile. Proseguendo, al primo piano, dopo la grande navata, nella sala degli studi, un proiettore 16mm è posto al suolo e circondato, o piuttosto imprigionato, dalla pellicola.
Si tratta di *Enigmatic Whistler* (2009), che non racconta nulla, se non se stesso. Nella medesima sala, per *Stating the Real Sublime* (2009), un altro proiettore 16mm è sospeso al soffitto ed è sorretto dalle sue stesse pellicole di celluloide. In queste due opere, gli strumenti del cinema prevalgono sulle funzioni che gli sono proprie e offrono alla macchina un'occasione di vita anarchica.
Con *The Indifferent Back of a View Rather Than Its Face* (2009), e *The Personal Experience Behind Its Description* (2009), sempre nella stessa sala, Barba proietta sul muro, attraverso un tessuto ritagliato, lettere di luce. Qui si va oltre la bidimensionalità cinematografica, le lettere della sceneggiatura sono sparse a terra e lo spettatore si trova in un percorso narrativo tridimensionale e straniante.

A Vassivière, l'aspetto documentaristico coincide perfettamente con quello della *fiction*, creando potenziali ibridi storici e paesaggistici. Le affinità tra Vassivière e il lavoro di Barba, sono fisiologiche. Gli acquarelli di Aldo Rossi, il faro, il lago, tutto coincide con un certo scenario contemporaneo e con la stessa poetica dell'artista. La mostra è quindi anche una sfida al tema del paesaggio che, invece di essere una costrizione, paradossalmente accoglie e contestualizza il sentire dell'artista. Il Centro d'arte viene immaginato come un passaggio, una messa in scena che sta in bilico tra dentro e fuori. Gli spazi e i tempi dialogano fra loro, il luogo assume un valore mitico e tutto prelude a una creatività dal potenziale immenso e ancora non codificato. Il Centro d'arte non è stato usato da Barba come spazio neutro, ma l'artista ha saputo costruire letteralmente la piattaforma "museo" per far nascere una mostra inattesa rispetto ai canoni istituzionali e curatoriali: è come se l'isola fosse *già* di Rosa Barba: quello che rimaneva da fare è stato semplicemente offriglierla.

2. Tempo: ***Stage Archive***

La mostra congiunta al Mart – Museo di Arte Moderna e Contemporanea di Trento e Rovereto e alla Fondazione Galleria Civica–Centro di Ricerca sulla Contemporaneità di Trento, nasce come complemento della precedente e si sviluppa intorno al tema, speculare a quello dello spazio affrontato da Barba a Vassivière, del tempo, e allo strumento deputato a conservarlo e a invertarlo, l'archivio. La mostra racconta di quanto il tempo plasmi l'identità e l'attività istituzionale del museo contemporaneo. Se la mostra a Vassivière poneva al suo centro la dimensione spaziale, i meccanismi della narrazione cinematografica, quella a Rovereto e Trento si riferisce a una dimensione temporale e a come il tempo possa essere insieme dimensione oggettiva ed esperienza immaginaria.

Il punto di partenza del progetto è rappresentato da un lavoro di ricerca svolto dall'artista presso gli Archivi Storici del Mart su documenti originali del periodo futurista. L'idea della mostra consiste nella presentazione, nella rappresentazione, in forma di "scultura-teatralità-astrazione", di sceneggiature e trattamenti cinematografici mai realizzati. L'archivio è reinterpretato dall'artista che lo sottrae al territorio della pura conservazione e lo conduce in quello di una temporalità fluida. Motore attivo dell'immaginario, fonte di nuove narrazioni, diventa un inedito ibrido: un archivio-palcoscenico sul quale passato e futuro si rappresentano nel presente del museo.

In entrambe le sedi, Trento e Rovereto, le singole opere intrattengono una relazione dialettica tra loro, la coreografia fa da cornice accomunandole fino a comporre un insieme. L'installazione filmica e sonora accorpata assume i contorni di un "balletto meccanico" di ispirazione futurista: i singoli protagonisti vengono presentati simultaneamente su un unico palcoscenico, rappresentato dalla mostra. Si tratta dunque di un duplice "percorso futuristico" che comprende testi, film, oggetti scultorei e suoni. Il risultato è una performance meccanica che ha qualcosa di anarchico, ma anche di armonico come in una corale.
La mostra diviene l'ipotesi di un archivio futurista che va formandosi in tempo reale all'interno del museo e che si compone di una serie di espressioni individuali, fruibili separatamente o nel loro insieme.
Presso il Mart, l'artista interviene nello spazio centrale del museo, mettendo in relazione fra loro l'area degli Archivi al piano seminterrato e le sale espositive ai livelli superiori. L'idea di stratificazione archeologica è risolta con uno sviluppo verticale della mostra. Gli Archivi: fondamenta di ogni istituzione, convenzionalmente relegati nell'ombra, qui assumono un ruolo da protagonisti. Barba mette in scena la trasformazione dei documenti storici, densi di significato per la loro incompiutezza, attraverso oggetti bi- e tri-dimensionali, che traducono i progetti futuristi in un'ipotetica narrazione.
Una scultura circolare, *Stage Archive* (2011), rievoca la forma di un grande lampadario. All'interno della scultura scorrono, come in un proiettore cinematografico o sul tavolo di un montatore, tante diverse pellicole che, non essendo impressionate, producono solo il suono del loro stesso girare a vuoto. E' la rappresentazione dell'inespresso, dell'energia potenziale che caratterizza i documenti futuristi e che si riverbera, attraverso la mostra, sul museo.
Apice della mostra sono una grande opera a muro (*Theory in Order to Shed Light*, 2011), una sceneggiatura su feltro le cui parole si proiettano come forme di luce sui muri del museo e alcuni piccoli interventi segnaletici sul fronte dello scalone d'accesso (*No Titles*, 2011) che, integrandosi con i segnali informativi collocati ai vari piani, suggeriscono la possibilità di un livello ulteriore di lettura del museo, di una spazialità e temporalità più fluide e potenziali, che invitano il visitatore a una lettura dell'istituzione "attraverso il tempo, e lo spazio", confondendo passato, presente e futuro, come accade appunto negli archivi, dove i documenti del passato sono, per gli studiosi, oggetti attivi, proiettivi, attuali, in cui i tempi possono sovrapporsi più liberamente.

Nell'area principale della Fondazione Galleria Civica di Trento sono proiettati i primi due film in 35mm realizzati dall'artista nell'ambito della serie *The Hidden Conference: About the Discontinuous History of Things We See and Don't See* (2010).
La serie *Hidden Conference* nasce dalla riflessione condotta da Barba a partire dal 2010 sulla conservazione delle opere d'arte nei depositi di alcuni musei di scultura antica e moderna. L'artista crea un dialogo immaginario tra le opere, nella loro condizione di silenziosa e segreta convivenza quotidiana con i luoghi istituzionali in cui sono custodite.
In questi film, nei quali i depositi sono trasformati in un quinta scenica scolpita dalla luce, come se ci trovassimo improvvisamente su un set teatrale o cinematografico, l'artista indaga gli invisibili nessi tra le opere d'arte e la rete dei legami che generano l'idea stessa di uno spazio protetto e fuori dal tempo, come quello dell'archivio. L'artista racconta di come, invitata dal Museo Nacional Centro de Arte Reina Sofia di Madrid a compiere una selezione di documenti e opere, sia rimasta affascinata dall'archivio stesso, dall'idea delle opere che, lontane dagli sguardi del pubblico, continuavano a vivere, contribuendo comunque alla costruzione dell'identità del museo e, quindi, del nostro linguaggio visivo che si forma a contatto con esso.
Iniziò a esplorare le connessioni invisibili tra le opere custodite, la rete di analogie che producevano un' idea collettiva di spazio consistente che, nel suo insieme assumeva un grande valore. Esattamente l'ordine con il quale le opere vengono conservate, crea un nuovo ed elaborato sistema che l'artista, attraverso questi film, vuole raccontare, rendendendoci partecipi del senso di quelle nuove e differenti composizioni.
L'artista si domanda "Qual è la qualità intrinseca dell'arte non vista?" Indaga sul lungo sonno di un'opera dopo il faticoso processo di acquisizione e passaggio da un proprietario a un altro, la comunicazione, la negoziazione, e tutte le complesse transazioni del mercato dell'arte. Infine, si chiede come avvenga l'inserimento del nuovo elemento nella memoria collettiva dell'intero archivio e quindi del museo. "E' strana la similitudine tra questo momento e il processo casuale o labirintico di quando cerchiamo nella nostra memoria un nome o una parola" scrive Barba.
In relazione a questa pura potenzialità istituzionale suggerita dalla dimensione segreta dell'archivio, Barba presenta presso la Fondazione altre opere che sviluppano un analogo discorso: *A Private Tableaux* (2010), film in 16mm, trae spunto dagli studi condotti negli anni da numerosi professionisti sulle architetture sotterranee. Attraverso diversi disegni, realizzati dagli scienziati per ragioni di studio, emerge l'involontaria rappresentazione di una storia parallela, dove una densa diffusione di segni occupa l'intero volume di uno spazio e un tempo proibiti; nel film in 16mm *Let Me See It* (2009) le immagini sgranate mostrano un paesaggio notturno, una prospettiva aerea di un arcipelago, in cui solo i bagliori delle case sulla terraferma illuminano lo scenario. Due uomini, uno dei quali è cieco, parlano degli oggetti che li circondano, soffermandosi sulla figura

del dodecaedro, elemento cruciale per la regressione di uno dei due, alla ricerca dei suoi ricordi.

Invisible Act (2010) è un'installazione scultorea costituita da un'immagine proiettata in 16mm in cui un oggetto materiale evoca un oggetto immaginifico, composti l'uno nell'altro all'interno di un dialogo fatto di contrasti e combinazioni. L'opera tiene conto del documento non soltanto come dato oggettivo, ma anche come momento di creazione e riflessione, come trasposizione fantastica, come possibilità continua di trasformazione dell'immagine in materia e viceversa. *Optic Ocean* (2011) e *Time Machine* (2007) sono la stesura di sceneggiature, a metà fra reale e fantastico, che campeggiano sulle pareti dello spazio espositivo trasformato in documento di lavoro. *One Way Out* (2009), è costituita da un proiettore 16mm la cui pellicola viene risucchiata in alto, verso un piccolo anfratto del luogo espositivo che improvvisamente notiamo: si tratta della via d'uscita, di quel varco fittizio all'interno dell'istituzione reale di cui tutta la mostra sembra alla ricerca, evocandolo nell'edificio reale del museo.

3. Dall'isola all'archivio. Ringraziamenti

Desideriamo ringraziare, come curatori delle mostre a Vassivière, Rovereto e Trento, tutti coloro che hanno contribuito alla loro realizzazione. Il più grato dei ringraziamenti a Rosa Barba: ci ha permesso di scoprire una dimensione nell'istituzione che ignoravamo malgrado la nostra pratica quotidiana. L'abbiamo improvvisamente trovata più fluida e avventurosa, ne abbiamo scoperto le infinite potenzialità, abbiamo varcato i passaggi segreti di questa "istituzione filmica" in cui l'artista ci ha introdotto, insieme agli spettatori.

Un ringraziamento va a Gabriella Belli, non solo per aver reso possibile la realizzazione del progetto a Rovereto, ma per aver condiviso l'intuizione che esso non poteva che sorgere dagli Archivi Storici del Mart, dalla memoria e dal ricordo del museo, verso il suo destino futuro.

Desideriamo infine ringraziare gli autori dei testi a catalogo: Lynne Cooke, Elisabeth Lebovici, Nataša Petrešin-Bachelez, Ian White, Francesco Manacorda e Raimundas Malasauskas. Questo libro rappresenta, di fatto, una quarta mostra, la prima estesa monografia dedicata alle opere dell'artista a partire dal 2004.

Chiara Parisi, Direttore, Centre international d'art et du paysage de l'île de Vassivière

Andrea Viliani, Direttore, Fondazione Galleria Civica–Centro di Ricerca sulla Contemporaneità di Trento

Negli Archivi Storici del Mart: *A Work in Progress*

Nel 2010 Rosa Barba ha iniziato ad interessarsi agli archivi dei musei e ha prodotto due film dalla serie *in progress*, *The Hidden Conference: About the Discontinuous History of Things We See and Don't See,* mettendo in dialogo le opere conservate presso i depositi di due musei. In questi film l'artista riflette sulla condizione dell'opera d'arte nei suoi continui e sfaccettati passaggi tra "pubblico e privato". Seguendo questa linea di ricerca, Rosa Barba si è naturalmente avvicinata agli Archivi Storici del Mart.
Fin dai suoi esordi, il Mart ha deciso di incrementare il patrimonio archivistico e bibliografico ereditato, rendendolo il fulcro di una propria identità culturale, accanto alle opere d'arte. Dalla data della sua istituzione nel 1987, il Mart ha considerato irrinunciabile la presenza di fondi documentari di artisti, di architetti e di critici d'arte del Novecento.
Sia etimologicamente che filosoficamente, il termine "Archivio" è molto vasto: può essere definito come un complesso di documenti prodotti da un soggetto pubblico o privato nel corso della sua attività, ma si riferisce anche agli edifici che raccolgono tali complessi e persino alle banche dati informatiche. Oltre alla ricca documentazione prodotta dagli enti (ad esempio dallo Stato, dai Comuni, dalla Chiesa) nel corso del Novecento hanno suscitato notevole attenzione gli archivi familiari o personali, un insieme di materiali documentari raccolti da una famiglia o da un individuo, a corredo dello svolgimento dell'attività professionale e - in senso lato - della propria vita. Un archivio nasce in maniera non intenzionale, spontanea, ma tutta la storiografia recente sottolinea come nel corso della sua costituzione sia frequente che si sviluppi una certa consapevolezza che spinge i soggetti a forme di raccolta più selettive e controllate, mirate alla creazione di un ritratto specifico. Valgono dunque per questo tipo di archivi i meccanismi della rappresentazione, propri di tutte le operazioni di trasmissione della memoria.
Ogni tipo di archivio è in modo emblematico un pezzo di storia nel suo farsi, quindi per eccellenza non un risultato finale, come un libro o un'opera d'arte, ma il sedimento di una storia culturale. Gli archivi sono inoltre una fonte di studio che permette di risalire

alle fasi progettuali di un'opera e sono un fine strumento per mettere in dialogo la storia dell'arte con tutte le altre discipline storiche, sociologiche e persino economiche. Data questa poliedrica ricchezza, in più occasioni, mostre, convegni e pubblicazioni del Mart, hanno portato al recupero e all'acquisizione di fondi e viceversa: la stessa attività espositiva condotta lungo gli anni Novanta fino ad oggi, ha tratto spunto dalle raccolte documentarie che il Museo andava acquisendo. Su questa stessa linea si colloca il lavoro di Rosa Barba, che intreccia, facendoli comunicare spazialmente e concettualmente, i documenti conservati negli Archivi del seminterrato con i piani superiori, dedicati a spazio espositivo delle opere, mostrando un possibile svolgimento temporale di un progetto creativo, vero potenziale di ogni archivio. L'artista ha svolto in particolare un lavoro di ricerca sugli archivi futuristi, sia per il cospicuo nucleo di documenti qui conservati, che hanno dato origine al Centro Internazionale di Studi sul Futurismo (CISF), sia per una coincidenza di strumenti espressivi: il cinema e il testo.
Il Futurismo ha manifestato un atteggiamento schizofrenico nei confronti del passato in quanto da una parte, proclamava necessario il suo azzeramento, ma dall'altra, fin dagli esordi, ha propagandato, anche strategicamente, la propria estetica e le proprie idee tramite poesie, manifesti, riviste e collane di libri, tesi a costituirne una memoria e ad influenzare in maniera regolata l'opinione pubblica. Una parte di questo archivio è costituita dal Fondo Fortunato Depero, proveniente dal Comune di Rovereto, al cui interno è contenuto il Fondo relativo alle sceneggiature per teatro e cinema mai realizzate. Depero approda all'esperienza cinematografica piuttosto tardi e vi giunge non direttamente, ma guidato dalla sua passione per il teatro. E' solo dalla metà degli anni Venti infatti, che il pittore roveretano si cimenta con la scrittura cinematografica, realizzando alcune sceneggiature per film. Prima di questa data, il cinema, inteso nella sua valenza innovativa di campo pressoché inedito di sperimentazione dei linguaggi artistici, non sembra sollecitare particolarmente la sua attenzione e la sua curiosità, rivolta invece con instancabile entusiasmo alla sperimentazione teatrale. Proprio in quest'ultimo settore ricordiamo per esempio la fantasiosa temerarietà dello spettacolo elaborato con Gilbert Clavel *I Balli Plastici*, andato in scena al teatro Costanzi nel 1918, o la funambolesca creazione del *Teatro Magico* con i suoi ballerini molli di caucciù.
Se pensiamo all'attrazione che sempre esercitò su Depero la possibilità di sperimentare tutte le opportunità creative del linguaggio artistico, al di là e al di sopra di qualsivoglia confine disciplinare, questo uso tardivo del cinema è un fatto perlomeno curioso. Già nel 1916 i firmatari Corra, Settimelli, Ginna, Balla e Chiti, capeggiati da Marinetti, diedero alle stampe il manifesto *La cinematografia futurista*, nel quale avevano proclamato il cinema come "arte nuova, immensamente più vasta e più agile di tutte quelle esistenti", dunque, si suppone, anche del teatro. Nel manifesto, con estrema chiarezza, furono individuati i molteplici campi di applicazione del cinema, inteso appunto come "il mezzo di espressione più adatto alla plurisensibilità di un artista futurista": poemi, discorsi, poesie, ricerche musicali, simultaneità e compenetrazione di tempi e luoghi, stati d'animo, drammi di sproporzioni e drammi potenziali, equivalenze lineari plastico-cromatiche, tutto questo venne indicato come esclusivo appannaggio della ricerca poliespressiva cinematografica, ricerca onnicomprensiva per definizione in quanto in essa venivano ad assommarsi tutte le altre arti. "Pittura + scultura"- si legge infatti nel manifesto - "+ dinamismo plastico + parole in libertà + intonarumori + architettura + teatro sintetico = cinematografia futurista". Il passaggio dalla teoria alla pratica rivelò tuttavia una certa difficoltà nel trasformare la complessità di queste definizioni in un repertorio di immagini rappresentative. Significativo esempio è *Vita futurista*, il film che sempre nello stesso anno, inaugurò in via ufficiale la stagione cinematografica futurista. Nella regia del cortometraggio, Marinetti ripropose quella messa in scena costituita da sorprese comiche e trovate dissacranti, di assoluto *nonsense*, che negli stessi anni caratterizzava molte delle *pièces* del teatro futurista: "cinema delle *piccole forme* giustapposte - commenta Giovanni Lista - della gestualità meccanica, del grottesco, dello scoppio di riso. Il modello si rifaceva alla scena del varietà: film dunque molto simili al teatro con le sue sorprese, le sue sintesi e le sue improvvisazioni sceniche".
Anche le scarse indicazioni lasciateci da Depero circa il montaggio e la sequenza delle sue sceneggiature, fanno comprendere quanto l'artista intendesse il cinema come al servizio della parola scritta. E ciò si evince con chiarezza analizzando il ritmo narrativo e la sequenza spazio-temporale dei testi nelle diverse sceneggiature, che molto poco si discostano dalla sua vasta produzione letteraria, tanto da confondersi con essa.
In tale contesto, pertanto ricchissimo di possibili interpretazioni e svolgimenti, si inserisce il progetto proposto da Rosa Barba al Mart, che attualizza la spinta utopica futurista a distanza di tempo, utilizzando l'archivio come piattaforma espressiva. Con i suoi interventi *site-specific* per lo spazio centrale vuoto del museo, l'artista traduce la polisemanticità del pensiero, interlocutorio e a volte contraddittorio, che precede la realizzazione di un'opera d'arte e di un intervento che, come li definisce l'artista stessa, sono un *work in progress*.

Gabriella Belli, Direttore, Mart – Museo di Arte Moderna e Contemporanea di Trento e Rovereto

List of Works

Coro Spezzato: The Future Lasts One Day, 2009
Installation
Five 16-mm color films, five modified projectors on pedestals
5 min. each
Ed. 3 + 1AP
Pages 134-39

A Curated Conference, 2010
An exhibition with works of the collection of the Museo Nacional Centro de Arte Reina Sofía, Madrid
Pages 180-89

Double-Whistler, 2011
Sculpture
Two 16-mm film projectors, projected text
1:33 min.
Ed. 2 + 1AP
Pages 29-31

The Empirical Effect, 2010
16-mm film transferred to Blu-ray Disc, color
27 min.
Sound: Jan St. Werner, Andi Toma
Camera: Benito Strangio, Rosa Barba
Produced by the Hermès Foundation, Paris
Netherlands Film Fund, Amsterdam
Ed. 5 + 2AP
Pages 23-27 and 148-53

Enigmatic Whistler, 2009
Sculpture
16-mm loop, modified projector
2 min.
Ed. 3 + 1AP
Pages 16-17 and 54

Free Post Mersey Tunnel, 2010
Pipes, sound
Unique
Pages 36-38

The Hidden Conference: About the Discontinuous History of Things We See and Don't See, 2010
35-mm film, color, optical sound
10:30 min.
Sound: Jan St. Werner
Ed. 5 + 2AP
Pages 190-99

The Hidden Conference: A Fractured Play, 2011
35-mm film, color, optical sound
5 min.
Sound: Jan St. Werner
Ed. 5 + 2AP
Pages 154-63

I Made a Circuit and then a Second Circuit, 2010
Cutout text on felt
180 x 240 cm
Ed. 3 + 2AP
Pages 208-209

The Indifferent Back of a View Rather Than Its Face, 2009
Cutout text on felt
450 x 180 cm
Ed. 3 + 2AP
Pages 18-21

Invisible Act, 2010
Sculpture
16-mm film, silver ball, celluloid
Ed. 3 + 1AP
Pages 34-35 and 154

It's Gonna Happen, 2005
16-mm film, color, optical sound
3 min.
Ed. 5 + 2AP
Pages 210-11

Let Me See It, 2009
16-mm film, color, optical sound
4:10 min.
Ed. 5 + 2AP
Page 207

The Long Road, 2010
35-mm film, color, optical sound
6:14 min.
Ed. 5 + 2AP
Front and back endpapers and 46-55 and 71

No Titles, 2011
Intervention on museum wall
Text on vinyl
Dimensions variable
Pages 100 and 104-105

One Way Out, 2009
Sculpture
16-mm film, optical sound, projector, ventilator, tube
2 min.
Ed. 3 + 1AP
Pages 30 and 113

One Way Out, 2010
Sculpture for lighthouse
35-mm film, ventilator, speculum in lighthouse
Unique
Pages 42-43

Optic Ocean, 2011
Silk-screen print on canvas, spotlight
180 x 270 cm
Ed. 5 + 2AP
Page 111

Outwardly from Earth's Center, 2007
16-mm film transferred to video
22 min.
Music: Jan St. Werner, Folke Rabe
Camera: Makan Ebrahimi, Rosa Barba
Produced by the Baltic Art Center, Visby
Ed. 5 + 2AP
Pages 81-83 and 140-47

Panzano, 2000
(with Ulrike Molsen)
16-mm film, color, magnetic sound
22 min.
Ed. 5 + 2AP
Page 65

Parachutable, 2005
Installation
Two 16-mm films, color, optical sound
3 min. and 2 min.
Voices: Laetitia Sadier, Ain Bailey
Ed. 5 + 2AP
Page 59

The Personal Experience Behind Its Description, 2009
Cutout text on felt
450 x 180 cm
Ed. 3 + 2AP
Pages 20-21

Printed Cinema # 10: Vertiginous Mapping, 2008
Artist's book
Page 86

A Private Tableaux, 2010
16-mm film, color, optical sound
7 min.
Ed. 5 + 2AP
Pages 202-204

Somnium, 2011
35-mm film, color, optical sound
19:20 min.
Sound: Jan St. Werner
Camera: Benito Strangio
Voices: Matt Didemus, Ivan Seal
Produced by SKOR | Stichting Kunst en Openbare Ruimte, Amsterdam, and the Harbor of Rotterdam
Pages 166-75

Stage Archive, 2011
Sculpture
35-mm film, perspex, guiding rollers, neon lamps, engines, control
Diameter: 320 cm
Ed. 1 + 1AP
Pages 98-103 and 106

Stating the Real Sublime, 2009
Sculpture
16-mm film, modified projector
2:30 min.
Ed. 3 + 1AP
Pages 40-41 and 55

Theory in Order to Shed Light, 2011
Cutouts on felt
180 x 240 cm each
Ed. 3 + 1AP
Pages 106 and 108-109

They Come and Go, 2009
Felt text
Dimensions variable
Ed. 3 + 2AP
Pages 17 and 54

They Shine, 2007
35-mm film, color, optical sound
4 min.
Sound: Jan St. Werner
Voice: Matt Didemus
Ed. 5 + 2AP
Pages 56, 60-62, and 176

Time Machine, 2007
Silk-screen print on canvas, spotlight
150 x 250 cm
Ed. 5 + 2AP
Pages 112-17

Vertiginous Mapping, 2008
Web project commissioned by the Dia Art Foundation, New York
Pages 86-93

Vesuvio Recording, 2009
Ink drawing with seismograph
Ed. 5 + 2AP
Pages 84-85

Waiting Grounds, 2007
16-mm film, color
4 min.
Ed. 5 + 2AP
Pages 66-68, 73, 76-77, and 178-79

Western Round Table, 2007
Sculpture
Two 16-mm films, two projectors, two loops, optical sound
2 min.
Ed. 3 + 2AP
Pages 178-79 and 201

White Curtain, 2011
Cutouts on felt
270 x 450 cm
Page 212

White Museum, 2010
Sculpture
70-mm film loop
Pages 8-10, 14-15, 118-23, and 130-31

White Museum Soundtrack, 2010
Sculpture
Underwater sounds
20 min.
Ed. 3 + 1AP
Pages 12-13

Biography

Rosa Barba

born in 1972 in Sicily, Italy
lives in Berlin

Education / Residencies

2007–2008 IASPIS, International Artists Studio Program, Stockholm, Sweden
2007 Museumsquartier, Vienna, Austria
Villa Aurora, Pacific Palisades, Los Angeles, USA
2006 Production in Residence, Baltic Art Center, Visby, Sweden
2003–2004 Two-Year Residency Programme, Rijksakademie van Beeldende Kunsten, Amsterdam, the Netherlands
2001/2002 C³: Center for Culture & Communication Foundation, Budapest, Hungary
1995–2000 Academy of Media Arts, Cologne, Germany
1993–95 Studies of Theatre and Filmscience in Erlangen, Germany

Solo Exhibitions (Selection)

2012 MUSAC, Museo de Arte Contemporaneo de Castilla y León, Spain, curated by Juan de Nieves; Kunsthaus Zürich, Switzerland, curated by Mirjam Varadinis

2011 *Stage Archive*, Fondazione Galleria Civica-Centro di Ricerca sulla Contemporaneità di Trento, Trento, and Mart – Museo di Arte Moderna e Contemporanea di Trento e Rovereto, Rovereto, Italy, curated by Chiara Parisi and Andrea Viliani
carlier | gebauer, Berlin, Germany
Kunstverein Braunschweig, Braunschweig, Germany
Somnium, XL, New Orleans, International Film Festival, Rotterdam, the Netherlands
Rosa Barba / David Maljkovic, la Pedrera, Barcelona, Spain, curated by Cristina Cámara

2010 *Rosa Barba*, Tate Modern, London, United Kingdom, curated by Ben Borthwick
A Curated Conference, Museo Nacional Centro de Arte Reina Sofía, Madrid, Spain, curated by the artist
Is It a Two-Dimensional Analogy or a Metaphor?, Centre international d'art et du paysage de l'île de Vassivière, France, curated by Chiara Parisi and Andrea Viliani
Rosa Barba, Center of Contemporary Arts, Tel Aviv, Israel, curated by Sergio Edelsztein

2009 *Western Round Table*, carlier | gebauer, Berlin, Germany
Cinema Prospectif, Centre Georges Pompidou, Paris, France
Stating the Real Sublime, Galleria Giò Marconi, Milan, Italy

2008 *Outwardly*, carlier | gebauer, Berlin, Germany
Vertiginous Mapping, web project (http://awp.diaart.org/barba/), Dia Art Foundation, New York, USA
Villa Romana, Florence, Italy, curated by Angelika Stepken
Handed Over (with David Maljkovic), Bakery, Annet Gelink Gallery, Amsterdam, the Netherlands
École des Beaux-Arts, Montpellier, France
Outwardly, Bildmuseet Umea, Sweden, curated by Jan-Erik Lundström
Handed Over (with David Maljkovic), Project Art Center, Dublin, Ireland, curated by Tessa Giblin
Western Round Table, Galerie Patricia Dorfmann, Paris, France, curated by Romain Torri

2007 *They Shine*, Stedelijk Museum Bureau, Amsterdam, the Netherlands, curated by Jelle Bouwhuis
Present Future, Artissima, Turin, Italy, curated by Cecilia Alemani
HAP Grieshaber Prize, Deutscher Künstlerbund, Berlin, Germany
With a Hidden Noise, Kunstverein Medienturm, Graz, Austria, curated by Sandro Droschl
Western Round Table, Koje Medienturm, Museumsquartier, Vienna, Austria

2006 Baltic Art Center, Visby, Sweden, curated by Johan Pousette
Who Can Tell If I Am Inventing?, Badischer Kunstverein, Karlsruhe, Germany, curated by Angelika Stepken
It's Gonna Happen (with David Maljkovic), Croynielsen, Berlin, Germany
Museum am Ostwall, Schaufenster Dortmund, Germany, curated by Inke Arns

2005 Transmission Gallery, Glasgow, Scotland
Kasseler Kunstverein, Fridericianum ev., Kassel, Germany
A Tangible Accomplishment, Galerie Vera Gliem, Cologne, Germany

2004 *Buckle and Jitter*, Argos, Brussels, Belgium, curated by Paul Willemsen

2003 *Compilation1* (with Jeanne Faust and Jennifer Nelson), Kunsthalle Düsseldorf, Germany, curated by Ulrike Groos and Peter Gorschlüter
Kunststiftung Baden-Württemberg, Stuttgart, Germany

2002 Sala d'arte contemporaneo, Lima, Peru, curated by Jose-Carlos Mariategui
Pirate Spaces, c/o Peter Gorschlüter, Meyer Riegger, Karlsruhe, Germany

2001 *Navigator*, Ancient Gallery, Cinematexas, Austin, USA
Flightmachine, Kunstverein Medienturm, Graz, Austria, curated by Sandro Droschl
Counter-Motion, C³: Center for Culture & Communication Foundation, Budapest, Hungary

2000 artothek, Cologne, Germany
Moltkerei Werkstatt, Cologne, Germany

Group Exhibitions (Selection)

2011 *Surviving the Future*, Murmansk Art Museum, curated by Jan-Erik Lundström
Magical Consciousness, Arnolfini Art Centre, Bristol, United Kingdom, curated by Nav Haq and Runa Islam
Terminal Convention, Cork Airport, Cork, Ireland, curated by Peter Gorschlüter
H-Box, MUDAM—Musee d'Art Moderne Grand-Duc Jean, Luxembourg
H-Box, Artsonje Center, Seoul, Korea

2010 *SI*, Magasin, Grenoble, France, curated by Yves Aupetitallot
Camera, Light, Action, ABC, Berlin, Germany, curated by Marc Glöde
Premio Italia, MAXXI—Museo Nazionale delle Arti del XXI Secolo, Rome, Italy
Transatlantische Impulse, Akademie der Künste, Berlin, Germany, curated by Markus Richter
Quando si parte, Assab One, Milan, Italy, curated by Gaia Fugazzi
La scultura italiana del XXI secolo, Fondazione Pomodoro, Milan, Italy
The Moon Is an Arrant Thief, David Roberts Foundation, London, United Kingdom, curated by Thom O'Nions, Luiza Teixeira de Freitas, and Oliver Martínez-Kandt
Faux Amis, vidéothèque éphémère, Jeu de Paume, Paris, France, curated by Marta Ponsa
Behind the Curtain, Galleria Giò Marconi, Milan, Italy
Autokino, Temporäre Kunsthalle, Berlin, Germany, curated by Phil Collins
H-Box (touring), New Museum, New York, USA, curated by Benjamin Wire
H-Box (touring), Fondation d'entreprise Hermès, Paris, France
H-Box (touring), Fondazione Beyeler, Basel, Switzerland
H-Box (touring), Laboratorio de Arte Alameda, Mexico City, Mexico
21/21: 21 Artists for the 21st Century, Fondazione Sandretto, Turin, Italy, curated by Francesco Bonami
And Nothing Turned Itself Inside Out, Galeria Miroslav Kraljevic, Zagreb, Cro atia
Biennale Cuvée, Ok Center for Contemporary Art, Linz, Austria
Terra Infirma, ICSP, New York, USA, curated by Chiara Sartori
A Generation, Petah-Tikva Museum of Art, Israel, curated by Avi Feldman
Rethinking Location, Sprüth Magers Gallery, Berlin, Germany, curated by Johannes Fricke Waldthausen
From the Liberty Square to Independent Square, Fokus Łódź Biennale, Łódź, Poland
Nam June Paik Award, Museum Kunst-Palast, Düsseldorf, Germany
Touched, Liverpool Biennale, United Kingdom, curated by Lorenzo Fusi
Octobersaloon, Belgrade, Serbia, curated by Johan Pousette and Celia Prado

2009 *Making Worlds*, Palazzo delle Esposizioni, 53rd Venice Biennale, Italy, curated by Daniel Birnbaum
Ecstatic Resistance, X-initiative, New York, USA, curated by Emily Roysdon
And Then Nothing Turned Itself Inside Out, WUK Kunsthalle Exnergasse, Vienna, Austria, curated by Antonia Majaca and Ivana Bago
The Boundary Layer, The Prairie Art Gallery, Grande Prairie, Canada, curated by Catherine Dean
New Acquisitions, Museo Nacional Centro de Arte Reina Sofía, Madrid, Spain, curated by Rosario Pérez
Museo Riso, Palazzo Sambucco, Palermo, Italy
Art at the Centre of a Responsible Transformation of Society 2009, Collezione FRAC Piemonte, Vercelli, Italy
Fondazione Pistoletto, Biella, Italy
Film as a Subversive Art, Lux at Zoo, London, United Kingdom, curated by Mike Sperlinger
Eppur si muove (And yet it moves), Fondazione Sandretto Re Rebaudengo, Fondazione Eduardo Garrone, Palazzo Ducale, Genoa, Italy
Italics: Italian Art between Tradition and Revolution, 1968–2008, Museum of Contemporary Art Chicago, USA, curated by Francesco Bonami
A Despot in Flora's Garden, Preston Gallery, New York, USA, curated by Jasper Sharp
What a Wonderful World, Göteborg Biennial, Sweden, curated by Celia Prado and Johan Pousette
Life Forms, Bonniers Konsthall, Stockholm, Sweden, curated by Sara Arrhenius
Solaris, Galleria Giò Marconi, Milan, Italy, curated by Cecilia Alemani
Just in the Dark, Mercati di Traiano, Museo dei Fori Imperiali, Rome, Italy, curated by Andrea Viliani
Images Festival, Harbourfront Gallery, Toronto, Canada, curated by Pablo Ocampa
Drifting Histories, CCS Bard, Hessel Museum, New York, USA, curated by Anais Lellouche
Six Tuesdays after Film as a Critical Practice, The Lux 28, London, United Kingdom, curated by Ian White

2008 *Rooms Look Back and Inserts* (with Ursula Mayer and Margret Salmon), Kunsthalle Basel, Switzerland, curated by Simone Neuenschwander and Annette Amberg
50 Moons of Saturn, Torino Triennale, Turin, Italy, curated by Daniel Birnbaum
Video Report Italia 2006/2007, Galleria Comunale d'Arte Contemporanea, Monfalcone, Italy, curated by Andrea Bruciati
Degrees of Remove: Landscape and Affect, Sculpture Center, Long Island, and Anthology Film Archive, New York, USA, curated by Sarina Basta and Andrew Lampert
Italics: Italian Art between Tradition and Revolution, 1968–2008, Palazzo Grassi, Venice, Italy, and Museum of Contemporary Art Chicago, USA, curated by Francesco Bonami

Map-Navigating the Present, Bildmuseet Umea, Sweden, curated by Brita Talje and Jan-Erik Lundström
Visible Cinema, Center of Contemporary Arts, Glasgow, Scotland, curated by Isla Leaver-Yap
We Want to Thank the Curators, Seventeen Gallery, London, United Kingdom, curated by Vincent Honoré
Soft Cell: Dinamiche dello spazio in Italia, Galleria Comunale d'Arte Contemporanea, Monfalcone, Italy, curated by Andrea Bruciati
Abstract of Syn, ar/ge kunst, Bolzano, Italy

2007 52nd Venice Biennale, Italy, Slovenian Pavilion film program, curated by Francesco Manacorda
Heterotopias, 1st Thessaloniki Biennale of Contemporary Art, Greece, curated by Jan-Erik Lundström
12th Biennial of Moving Images, Geneva, Switzerland
Loop, Centro Cultural Valentina, Barcelona, Spain
Project Arts Centre, Dublin, Ireland, curated by Tessa Giblin
Turtle Saloon, Slade Woburn Studios, London, United Kingdom, curated by Michael Shamberg
Nederclips, Stedelijk Museum, 's-Hertogenbosch, the Netherlands, curated by Bart Rutten
Dissecting the Ear, Sign Gallery, Groningen, the Netherlands, curated by Bojan Faifric
Editions, Jahresgaben Ausstellung der Atelierstipendiaten, Kölnischer Kunstverein, Cologne, Germany

2006 *Last Lives in the Universe*, Smart Project Space, Amsterdam, the Netherlands, curated by Tessa Giblin and Chiara Sartori
Revisie, Centraal Museum, Utrecht, the Netherlands
No Picture, Swiss Institute, New York, USA, curated by Gianni Motti
Bathhouse, Gouda, the Netherlands, curated by Theo Thegelaers
Almost Cinema, Kunstcentrum Vooruit, Ghent, Belgium

2005 *Gravity in Art*, de Appel arts centre, Amsterdam, the Netherlands, curated by Theo Thegelaers
Image and Sound, Senef Film Festival, Seoul, Korea
Horror, Science Fiction and Porn, Art Gallery of York University, Toronto, Canada, curated by Philip Monk
Murmur, Tent—Centrum Beeldende Kunst, Rotterdam, the Netherlands, curated by Edwin Carels

2004 *A Molecular History of Everything*, Center for Contemporary Art, Melbourne, Australia, curated by Juliana Engberg
Doku/Fiction, Kunsthalle Düsseldorf, Germany, curated by Mouse on Mars and Peter Gorschlüter
Pole Position, Mannheimer Kunstverein, Mannheim, Germany
FEEL the Old FEEL the New, Z33, Hasselt, Belgium, curated by Edwin Carels and Pieter Van Bogaert
The Ex, Palais des Beaux Arts, Brussels, Belgium
Club Transmediale 04, Club Maria, Berlin, Germany
Duo Track, Nederlands Cultuurhuis, Brussels, Belgium, curated by Paul Willemsen
Travelling without Moving, W139, Amsterdam, the Netherlands, curated by Ann Demeester
Born to Be a Star, Künstlerhaus, Vienna, Austria, curated by Ursula Probst

2003 *Streams of Encounter*, Museum of Fine Arts, Taipei, Taiwan

2002 Ex Teresa Arte Actual, Mexico City, Mexico, curated by Guillermo Santamarina
Vision, Muescarnok/Kunsthalle, Budapest, curated by Miklos Peternak

2001 *Köln-Kunst 6*, Josef-Haubricht Kunsthalle, Cologne, Germany
See You Hear, Akademie der Künste, Berlin, Germany, curated by Siegfried Zielinski
Kunstraum Fuhrwerkswaage, Cologne, Germany

2000 *Media Model*, Muescarnok/Kunsthalle, Budapest, Hungary
Wie man sieht, Museum Ludwig, Cologne, Germany, curated by Siegfried Zielinski
Insensatezza, Fondazione Teseco, Pisa, Italy, curated by Luca Cerizza

1999 *Copy and Paste*, Kunstraum Innsbruck, Austria
Masterclass, Montevideo, Amsterdam, the Netherlands

Awards / Commissions

2010 Nam June Paik Award, Museum Kunst-Palast, Düsseldorf, Germany
Premio Italia Arte Contemporanea, MAXXI—Museo Nazionale delle Arti del XXI Secolo, Rome, Italy, nominee
International Film Festival, Rotterdam, the Netherlands, nominated for Tiger Short Award

2008 Web project for the Dia Art Foundation, New York, USA

2007 Prix du Centre pour l'image contemporaine, 12th Biennale of Moving Images, Geneva, Switzerland
Project Grant Atelier, Kölnischer Kunstverein, Cologne, Germany
International Film Festival, Rotterdam, the Netherlands, nominated for Tiger Short Award

2006 Artist Book Award for Printed Cinema, Ontario Association of Art Galleries, Toronto, Canada
Kunstpreis Berlin, Akademie der Bildenden Künste, Berlin, Germany, Sponsorship Award
HAP-Grieshaber Preis, Kunstfonds, Bonn, Germany

2005 Hartware Grant, NRW, Germany Installation Award, Images Festival, Toronto, Canada
Kunstiftung NRW, Germany

2004 Netherlands Film Fund Special Award, Split Film Festival, Croatia
Rijksakademie van Beeldende Kunsten Acquisitions Prize, Amsterdam, the Netherlands

2003 Grant of the Kunststiftung Baden-Württemberg, Germany
DAAD Grant, Germany
Uriot Award, Rijksakademie van Beeldende Kunsten, Amsterdam, the Netherlands

2002 Chargesheimer Foto-Film-Video Prize, Cologne, Germany

2001 Music Video Prize, International Short Film Festival, Oberhausen, Germany
Hermann Claasen Förderpreis, Cologne, Germany

Screenings and Festivals (selection)

2011 *What Makes Art Popular, What Makes Popular Art?,* Dundee Contemporary Arts, Dundee, United Kingdom
First Screening, Premiere at Loopfestival, La Pedrera, Barcelona, Spain

2010 *Rosa Barba in Conversation,* Starr Auditorium, Tate Modern, London, United Kingdom
Rosa Barba in Conversation, Cornerhouse, Manchester, United Kingdom
International Film Festival, Rotterdam, the Netherlands, nominated for Tiger Short Award
Kopietheater, Arsenale, Berlin, Germany, curated by Ian White
BAM, New York, USA
Courtisane Festival, Ghent, Belgium

2009 Pavilion Projects, Toronto, Canada
Pecci Museum, Florence, Italy
Museo Nacional Centro de Arte Reina Sofía, Madrid, Spain
Art Film, Art Basel, Switzerland
Rosa Barba, Cinema Prospectif, Centre Georges Pompidou, Paris, France
Impakt Festival, Utrecht, the Netherlands
Size Matters, International Film Festival, Rotterdam, the Netherlands

2008 Anthology Film Archive, New York, USA
Kölnischer Kunstverein, Cologne, Germany
Flare #3, Languedoc Roussillon Cinema, Montpellier, France
Sugar Is Sweet, Filmbank Tour with Fiona Tan and Nora Martirosan, various cinemas and film museums throughout the Netherlands
Iaspis, Open House, Stockholm, Sweden
Filmwinter, Stuttgart, Germany

2007 *No Picture,* Swiss Institute, New York, USA
12th Biennale of Moving Images, Geneva, Switzerland
International Film Festival, Hamburg, Germany
Virtuous Siblings, (Werner Herzog), Goethe-Institut, Los Angeles, USA
Contemporary Passages, Tent, Rotterdam, the Netherlands
International Film Festival, Rotterdam, the Netherlands, nominated for Tiger short Award
International Film Festival, Gothenburg, Sweden
International Short Film Festival, Oberhausen, Germany

2006 *Refracted Lens,* The Pioneer Theatre, New York, USA
Rosa Barba, Goethe-Institut, Los Angeles, USA

2005 Senef Film Festival, Seoul, Korea
Museum of Contemporary Arts, Lyon, France
International Short Film Festival, Oberhausen
Emaf, Osnabrück

2004 San Francisco Museum of Modern Art, USA
CCA, Tel Aviv, Israel
Palais des Beaux Arts, Madrid, Spain

2002 Video Art Festival, Lima, Peru
Avanto Film Festival, Helsinki, Finland
Rosa Barba, Cinema Gejzir, Budapest, Hungary
International Short Film Festival, Oberhausen

2001 Invideo, Milan, Italy
Netmage, Bologna, Italy

2000 International Film Festival, Rotterdam, the Netherlands
FCMM film festival, Montreal, Canada
Internationales Film Festival Odense, Denmark
Cinematexas, Austin, USA
Murphy's Short Film Festival, Cork, Ireland
Internationales Film Festival, Dresden, Germany

1999 Cinema Nova, Brussels, Belgium
Video Art Festival, Lima, Peru

1998 12th Video Festival, São Paolo, Brazil
Golem Video Festival, Turin, Italy
Raindance Festival, London, United Kingdom

Public Collections

Collezione FRAC Piemonte, Vercelli, Italy
Fonds Régional d'Art Contemporain (FRAC) de Franche-Comté, Besançon, France
Fundación Tantica, Buenos Aires, Argentina
Galleria civica d'arte moderna e contemporanea (GAM), Turin, Italy
Lemaître Collection, London, United Kingdom
Louisiana Museum of Modern Art, Denmark
Mart – Museo di Arte Moderna e Contemporanea di Trento e Rovereto, Art Collection UniCredit, Rovereto, Italy
Museo Nacional Centro de Arte Reina Sofía, Madrid, Spain
Nomas Foundation, Rome, Italy
Sammlung zeitgenössischer Kunst der Bundesrepublik Deutschland, Germany
Sculpture park of the Centre international d'art et du paysage de l'île de Vassivière, France
Vehbi Koc Foundation, Istanbul, Turkey

Selected Bibliography

Artist's Books

Barba, Rosa. *Printed Cinema #1: Broadcasting from Home*, distributed with the magazine *springerin*, vol. 3 (2004), Vienna, 2004.
——. *Printed Cinema #2: Parachutable Obstacles*, distributed by the Australian Centre for Contemporary Art, Melbourne, 2004.
——. *Printed Cinema #3: Accidental Suspension*, distributed by the Art Gallery of York University, Toronto, and Harbourfront Centre, Toronto, 2005.
——. *Printed Cinema #4: Who Can Tell if I Am Inventing?*, distributed by the 9th Istanbul Biennale, Istanbul, 2005.
——. *Printed Cinema #5: Outwardly from Earth's Center*, distributed with the magazine *Ein und Alle* of the Kunsthalle Fridericianium, Kassel, and by the Kasseler Kunstverein, Kassel, 2005.
——. *Printed Cinema #6: Wrong Edit*, distributed with the magazine *Juni-Kunstzeitschrift* and by the Badischer Kunstverein, Karlsruhe, 2006.
——. *Printed Cinema #7: Waiting Hall / Terminal*, distributed by Gouda Lichtjaren, Gouda, 2007.
——. *Printed Cinema #8: They Shine*, distributed by the Stedelijk Museum Bureau Amsterdam and the Center of Land Use Interpretation, Los Angeles, 2007.
——. *Printed Cinema #9: Save the Drifting of Gotska Sandn*, distributed by the Baltic Art Center, Visby; Bildmuseet, Umea; and Index—The Swedish Contemporary Art Foundation, Stockholm, 2008.
——. *Printed Cinema #10: Vertiginous Mapping*, distributed by the Dia:Beacon, New York, 2008.
——. *Printed Cinema #11: Idea in Abstract*, distributed by Tate Modern, Level 2 Gallery, London, 2011.
——. *Printed Cinema #12: Stage Archive*, distributed by the Fondazione Galleria Civica–Centro di Ricerca sulla Contemporaneità di Trento, Trent, and Mart – Museo di Arte Moderna e Contemporanea di Rovereto, Rovereto, 2011.

Monographs

Barba, Rosa. *Printed Cinema #1–10, 2004–2008*. With an essay by Marina Vishmidt. Brussels and Cologne, 2008.
——. Contribution to *Gagarin: The Artists in Their Own Words*, no. 11 (May 2010): 42–48.
——. *Vertiginous Mapping*. Web-based project with an introduction by Sara Tucker. www.awp.diaart.org.
Bell, Kirsty. "Suspended Animation." *Frieze* (May 2011): 118–121.
Rosa Barba: off sites / sets. Edited by Ulrike Groos, with contributions by Carlos Garza, Peter Gorschlüter, Iris Kadel, Olaf Karnik, Micah Magee, José-Carlos Mariátegui, Ralph McKay, Nils Röller, Laetitia Sander, Klaus Sander, and Siegfried Zielinsk. Exh. cat. Kunsthalle Düsseldorf. Cologne, 2003.

Articles and Reviews

Alemani, Cecilia. "Rosa Barba interview by Cecilia Alemani." *klat*, no. 2 (Spring 2010): 18–35.
——. "Rosa Barba and David Maljkovic." *Modern Painters* (December 2008–January 2009): 52–53.
——. "It's Gonna Happen." *Artforum*, "Picks" (March 2006).
Berberich, Nina, and Christina Grevenbrock. "Gib mir Fünf! Ausstellungstipps." www.art-magazin.de (March 17, 2011).
Berner, Irmgard. "Projektionen mit Süchtigkeitsfaktor." *Berliner Zeitung*, May 27, 2011.
Birnbaum, Daniel. "Best of 2008." *Artforum* (December 2008): 263.
Borthwick, Ben, and Melissa Gronlund. "Rosa Barba: Changing Cinema." www.afterall.org (November 12, 2010).
Bria, Ginevra. "Archivi di Luce by Rosa Barba." *Atribune* (June 2011).
Brivio, Giulia. "Rosa Barba alla Galleria Giò Marconi." www.teknemedia.net (October 2, 2009).
Budde, Nine. "Stopping by at a Friend's Place." www.thehighlights.org (October 27, 2009).
Buhr, Elke. "Plastisch ausgedrückt: Rosa Barba baut in Braunschweig Filme zu Skulpturen um." *Monopol* (March 2011): 106–7; www.monopol-magazin.de (March 14, 2011).
Buhr, Elke. "Die Kunst das richtige zu sehen." *Berliner Morgenpost*, May 24, 2011.
Castiglione, Manuela. "Meeting the Ambasciata d'Italia in Berlin: A Place for New Opportunities." www.illywords.com (April 8, 2011).
Cavallo, Francesca. "Living by Vesuvius. Considerations on Rosa Barba's film The Empirical Effect.", London Consortium (2011)
Ceresoli, Jacqueline. "Rosa Barba: Giò Marconi Milano." *Flash Art* (October–November 2009): 54.
Comer, Stuart. "The Best Motion Pictures and Moving Images 2009." *Frieze Magazine*, no. 128 (January–February 2010): 28–29.
Cooke, Lynne. "Best of 2010." *Artforum* (December 2010): 203.
Cotter, Holland. "Ecstatic Resistance." *New York Times*, December 17, 2009.
Dillon, Brion. "Terminal Convention." www.frieze.com (March 29, 2011).
"Dos lecturas sobre la coleccion." www.museoreinasofia.com (May 2010).
Douglas, Sarah. "Art in the Shadow of Violence." www.artinfo.com (October 12, 2010).
Egger, Christian. "Rosa Barba." *Spike*, no. 13 (Autumn 2007): 117.
Erdmann, Petra. "Zu den Bildwelten der Medienkünstlerin Rosa Barba." *springerin* 8, no. 2 (2002): 14–15.
"Film as a Subservient Art." www.metamute.org (December 8, 2009).
Gandini, Manuela. "Rosa Barba nel deserto delle atomiche." www3.lastampa.it (October 26, 2009).
Gayer, John. "Terminal Convention." *Art Papers* (May–June 2011).
Guadagnio, Letizia. "Cultura Italiana Nel Mondo: Rosa Barba da Agrigento a Kunstverein da Brunswick, al Mart di Rovereto, alla Tate di Londra." www.italiannetwork.it (March 22, 2011).
Heingartner, Douglas. "Rosa Barba at Argos Brussels." *Frieze Magazine*, no. 84 (June–August 2004).
Herchenröder, Christian. "Die entspannte Art der Kunstvermittlung." *Handelsblatt* (May 7, 2011).
Hose, Gregor. "Frauen mit und ohne Kamera." www.creativeface.net (May 13, 2009).
Jones, Barbara, and Arthur Roberts. "52nd Renshaw Street." www.allmycolours.wordpress.com (February 12, 2011).
Keith, Kelsey. "Digital Art Revolution: Filtering Online Noise." www.flavorwire.com (August 19, 2009).
Kitamura, Katie, and Mike Sperlinger. "The Best Motion Pictures and Moving Images of 2010." *Frieze Magazine*, no. 136 (January–February 2011): 24.
Kuiper, Petra. "Preis Nam June Paik für Rosa Barba und Ali Kazna." www.derwesten.de (October 1, 2010).
Lorch, Catrin. "Düsseldorf: Compilation I in der Kunsthalle." *Kunstbulletin* (March 2003).
Lequeux, Emanuelle. "Rosa Barba enchante l'île de

Vassivière." *Beaux Arts Magazine* (February 2010): 25.
Leung, Gil. "White Is an Image." www.lux.org.uk (October 14, 2010).
Mania, Astrid. "Vertäute Fiktionen: Rosa Barba in der Galerie carlier I gebauer Berlin." www.artnet.de (November 2008).
Michely, Viola. "Compilation I." *Kunstforum International*, no. 164 (May 2003): 299.
Milliard, Coline. "Rosa Barba Tate Modern—Level 2 Gallery." www.artinfo.com (October 7, 2010).
Morgan, Jessica. "Rosa Barba. Stage Archive." *Artforum*, museum previews (Summer 2011).
Muñoz-Alonso, Lorena. "Rosa Barba: A Curated Conference." www.frieze.com (June 14, 2010).
O'Connell, Brian. "Flights of Fancy Become Reality." *Irish Times*, March 12, 2011.
Palma, Domenico. "Rosa Barba. Stage Archive." www.undo.net (June 2011).
"Rosa Barba at Tate Modern." www.tate.org.uk (September 2010).
"Rosa Barba / Tate Modern Level 2." www.wonderlandmagazine.com (September 15, 2010).
Rech, Claudia. "Rosa Barba." *Zoe Magazine*, no. 24 (2009): 50–52.
Renz, Seraina. "51.Oktobarski Salon: The Night Pleases Us . . . " www.kunsttexte.de (November 21, 2010).
Repiso, L. "El Reina Sofía desvela la obra de Rosa Barba: La artista italiana ingresa en la colección permanente del MNCARS." www.publico.es (March 9, 2009).
Robecchi, Michele. "La Storia è una scultura." *Kunstbulletin* 1, no. 2 (January-February 2011).
Sartori, Chiara. "Interview with Rosa Barba." *Arte e Critica*, no. 52 (September-November 2007).
Sassone, Gabriele Francesco. "Esegesi della Luce." *Flash Art Italia* (September 2011).
Scharrer, Eva. "Rooms Look Back." *Artforum*, "Picks" (November 2008).
Simi, Giulia. "Staging Utopia. Stage Archive: Interview with Rosa Barba." *www.digicult.it* (June 2011).
Stöber, Michael. "Rosa Barba im Kunstverein Braunschweig." *Kunstforum International*, no. 209 (2011): 236.
Szremski, Ania. "Eclipsed Histories." www.fnewsmagazine .com (December 8, 2009).
Teasdale, Paul. "Rush Job?" www.frieze.com (February 25, 2011).
Tenconi, Roberta. "Introducing Rosa Barba." *MOUSSE Magazine*, no. 16 (December 2008–January 2009).
Uran, Pelin. "Interview with Rosa Barba." *Archive Journal* (2009).
Valentini, Veronica. "The Future Lasts One Day." *Flash Art International*, no. 266 (May-June 2009): 84–86.
Van der Vlist, Eline. "Rosa Barba at Stedelijk Museum Bureau, Amsterdam." *Modern Painters* 3 (June 2008).
Weil, Benjamin. "Rosa Barba-Le corps des images." *artpress*, no. 367 (May 2010): 43-47.
White, Ian. "Rosa Barba." *Camera Austria*, no. 101 (2008): 21–26.

Exhibition Catalogues

15 Jahre Villa Aurora—Transatlantische Impulse. Exh. cat. Akademie der Künste. Berlin, 2010.
21/21: 21 Artists for the 21st Century. Exh. cat. Fondazione Sandretto Re Rebaudengo. Turin, 2010.
50 Moons of Saturn: T2 Torino Triennale. Edited by Daniel Birnbaum. Exh. cat. Castello di Rivoli, Rivoli; Museo d'arte contemporanea, Turin; and Fondazione Sandretto Re Rebaudengo, Turin. Milan, 2008.
51st October Salon. Edited by Svetlana Petrovic. Exh. cat. Belgrade Cultural Centre. Belgrade, 2010.
52nd Venice Biennale: Film Program, Slovenian Pavilion. Exh. cat. Slovenian Pavilion, 52nd Venice Biennale. Venice, 2007.
A Fine Red Line: A Curatorial Miscellany. Edited by Gaia Tedone et al. Exh. cat. Baltic Centre for Contemporary Art. Gateshead, 2008.
A Generation. Exh. cat. Petach-Tikva Museum of Art. Petach Tikva, 2010.
*A Molecular History of Everything (*Well Not Everything)*. Exh. cat. Australian Centre of Contemporary Art. Melbourne, 2004.
Autokino. Edited by Angela Rosenberg. Exh. cat. Temporäre Kunsthalle. Berlin, 2010.
Biennale Cuvée 2010. Exh. cat. Ok Center for Contemporary Art. Linz, 2010.
Bindner, Stefan, and Thomas Feuerstein. *Sample Minds*. Cologne, 2004.
Borthwick, Ben. "Level 2 Gallery: Rosa Barba." www.tate.org.uk (September 2010).
Cámara, Cristina. "Level 2 Gallery: Rosa Barba." www.tate.org.uk (September 2010).
Copy and Paste. Exh. cat. Kunstraum Innsbruck. Innsbruck, 1999.
Doku/fiction: Mouse on Mars Reviewed & Remixed. Edited by Peter Gorschlüter et al. Exh. cat. Kunsthalle Düsseldorf. Düsseldorf, 2004.
Eppur si muove (And yet It Moves). Exh. cat. Fondazione Sandretto Re Rebaudengo, Turin, and Fondazione Eduardo Garrone, Genoa. Genoa, 2009.
Future Cinema: The Cinematic Imaginary after Film. Edited by Jeffrey Shaw and Peter Weibel. Exh. cat. ZKM—Zentrum für Kunst und Medientechnologie. Karlsruhe, 2002.
Gronlund, Melissa. "Level 2 Gallery: Rosa Barba." www.tate.org.uk (September 2010).
Höller, Christian. *Pop Unlimited*. Vienna, 2001.
Italics: Italian Art between Tradition and Revolution 1968-2008. Exh. cat. Palazzo Grassi, Venice, and Museum of Contemporary Art Chicago. Milan, 2008.
Köln-Kunst 6. Exh. cat. Josef-Haubrich-Kunsthalle. Cologne, 2001.
Life Forms. Edited by Sara Arrhenius and Magnus Bergh. Exh. cat. Bonniers Konsthall. Stockholm, 2009.
Making Worlds / Fare Mondi. Edited by Daniel Birnbaum. Exh. cat. Palazzo delle Esposizioni, Giardini, 53rd Venice Biennale. Venice, 2009.
Magical Consciousness. Exh. cat. Arnolfini. Bristol, 2011.
Masterclass. Exh. cat. Montevideo TBA. Amsterdam, 1999.
Olivares, Rosa, ed. *100 Video Artists*. Madrid, 2010.
Pole Position. Exh. cat. Mannheimer Kunstverein. Mannheim, 2004.
Rooms Look Back. Edited by Simone Neuenschwander et al. Exh. cat. Kunsthalle Basel. Basel, 2009.
Soft Cell: Dinamiche nello spazio in Italia. Edited by A. Bruciati et al. Exh. cat. Galleria Comunale d'Arte Contemporanea. Monfalcone, 2008.
Streams of Encounter. Edited by Andreas Walther et al. Exh. cat. Museum of Fine Arts Taipei. Taipei, 2003.
Touched: Liverpool Biennial 2010. Edited by Paul Domela. Exh. cat. The Tea Factory. Liverpool, 2010.
Zielinski, Siegfried, and Eckhard Fürlus, eds. *Variantology 5: Neapolitain Affairs*. Cologne, 2011.
What a Wonderful World: Göteborg Biennial 2009. Edited by Celia Prado. Exh. cat. Göteborg Biennial. Göteborg, 2009.
Wie man sieht . . . Exh. cat. Museum Ludwig Köln. Cologne, 2000.

Exhibitions / Expositions / Mostre

Centre international d'art et du paysage de l'île de Vassivière
Rosa Barba. Est-ce que c'est une analogie à deux dimensions ou une métaphore ?

Commissaires / Curated by
Chiara Parisi, Andrea Viliani

Assistants commissaires / Curatorial assistants
Alexandra Bordes, Frédéric Legros

Chargé du projet / Project manager
Jean-Christophe Radke

Régisseur / Registrar
Florian Guillaume
avec la collaboration de / in cooperation with
Leslie Benayoum, Béatrice Darmagnac, Cédric Lopes, Astrid Rossignol, Anna Rousse, Myrtille Saad, Lu Zhang

Chargés de l'éducation artistique et de la documentation / Arts education and documentation
Madeline Dupuy-Belmedjahed

Chargé de la librairie, de l'accueil des publics et du relais artothèque / Bookshop, reception, and art-lending library
Guillaume Baudin

Responsable de la comptabilité / Accountant
Muriel Meunier

L'exposition *Est-ce que c'est une analogie à deux dimensions ou une métaphore ?* de Rosa Barba est réalisée en partenariat avec Mademoiselle Bio et Pro Natura. / The exhibition *Is It a Two-Dimensional Analogy or a Metaphor?* by Rosa Barba is realized in partnership with Mademoiselle bio and Pro Natura.

Mart – Museo di Arte Moderna e Contemporanea di Trento e Rovereto
Rosa Barba. Stage Archive

A cura di / Curated by
Chiara Parisi, Andrea Viliani

Direzione scientifica / Scientific director
Gabriella Belli

Curatore tecnico / Technical curator
Veronica Caciolli

Direzione amministrativa / Administrative director
Diego Ferretti

Registrar
Clarenza Catullo
con la collaborazione di / in cooperation with
Ilaria Calgaro

Allestimento / Installation
Claudio Merz *(Responsabile / Supervisor)*
con la collaborazione di / in cooperation with
Arteam-Trento, Gianpiero Coatti, Giovanni Pivato
e di / and
Alberto Couceiro, Andreas Marckscheffel

Archivi storici / Historical archives
Paola Pettenella *(Conservatore capo / Chief curator)*
Duccio Dogheria, Carlo Prosser, Federico Zanoner

Archivio fotografico / Photographic archives
Attilio Begher *(Responsabile / Supervisor)*
Serena Aldi, Maurizio Baldo

Responsabile comunicazione e relazioni esterne / Communication and public relations
Flavia Fossa Margutti

Ufficio stampa e sito internet / Press office and website
Luca Melchionna, Clementina Rizzi

Comunicazione e promozione / Communication and promotion
Silvia Ferrari, Carlotta Gaspari, Maria Elena Putz, Lodovico Schiera, Vanessa Vacchini, Francesca Velardita

Si ringraziano / Many thanks to
Provincia autonoma di Trento

con / in partnership with

per le attività didattiche / for educational activities

Fondazione Galleria Civica–Centro di Ricerca sulla Contemporaneità di Trento
Rosa Barba. Stage Archive

A cura di / Curated by
Chiara Parisi, Andrea Viliani

Assistenza curatoriale / Curatorial assistants
Chiara del Senno, Giulia Corradi

Consulenza tecnica / Technical guidance
Alberto Couceiro, Jürgen Galli, Neli Wagner

Allestimento / Installation
Arteam, Trento; Giacca Srl Costruzioni Elettriche; Alpa Srl

Trasporti / Shipping
KDS Kunst und Druckservice Limited, OverdriveArt

Assicurazioni / Insurance
Augusta Assicurazioni Spa

Con il contributo di / With the contribution of
Fondazione Cassa di Risparmio di Trento e Rovereto; A22 Autostrada del Brennero Spa; Albergo Accademia, Trento; Goethe-Institut Mailand

Pubblicazione realizzata con il contributo della Regione autonoma Trentino-Alto Adige / This publication was made possible by a contribution from the Trentino-Alto Adige region.

CENTRE INTERNATIONAL D'ART & DU PAYSAGE
ÎLE DE VASSIVIÈRE

Centre international d'art et du paysage de l'île de Vassivière

Président / President
Stéphane Cambou

Directeur / Director
Chiara Parisi

Assistant exécutif de la direction / Executive assistant to the director
Frédéric Legros

Assistante / Assistant
Alexandra Bordes

Régisseur, Chargé de la production des expositions et du bois de sculptures / Production manager for exhibitions and sculpture wood
Jean-Christophe Radke

Régisseur adjoint / Assistant production manager
Florian Guillaume

Chargés de l'éducation artistique et de la documentation / Arts education and documentation
Madeline Dupuy-Belmedjahed, Jean-Denis Frater, Florian Guillaume

Chargé de la librairie, de l'accueil des publics et du relais artothèque / Bookshop, reception, and art-lending library
Guillaume Baudin

Responsable de la comptabilité / Accountant
Muriel Meunier

Responsable éditoriale de l'image / Image editing
Paola Manfrin

Le Centre international d'art et du paysage est financé par le Ministère de la culture et de la communication / Drac Limousin et le Conseil régional du Limousin et reçoit le soutien du Syndicat mixte « le Lac de Vassivière ». / The Centre international d'art et du paysage is sponsored by the Ministry of Culture and Communications/Drac Limousin and the Regional Board of Limousin and receives the support of the Syndicat mixte "le Lac de Vassivière."

Provincia autonoma di Trento
Comune di Trento
Comune di Rovereto

Museo di Arte Moderna e Contemporanea di Trento e Rovereto

Consiglio di amministrazione / Board of directors
Franco Bernabè (*Presidente / President*)
Isabella Bossi Fedrigotti (*Vicepresidente / Vice president*)
Lino Dainese, Massimo Egidi, Mariangela Franch, Michelangelo Lupo, Paolo Mattei

Direttore / Director
Gabriella Belli

Comitato scientifico / Scientific committee
Salvatore Settis (*Coordinatore / Coordinator*)
Umberto Allemandi, Guy Cogeval, Flavio Fergonzi

Collegio dei revisori dei conti / Board of auditors
Carlo Delladio, Luigi Matassoni, Giovanni Zani

Direttore amministrativo / Adminstrative director
Diego Ferretti

Archivi storici / Historical archives
Paola Pettenella (*Conservatore capo / Chief curator*)
Duccio Dogheria, Carlo Prosser, Federico Zanoner

Biblioteca / Library
Roberto Antolini (*Conservatore capo/ Chief curator*)
Mariarosa Mariech

Collezioni del XX secolo / 20th-century collections
Clarenza Catullo (*Conservatore capo e Registrar / Chief curator and Registar*)
Sabrina Azzolini, Veronica Caciolli, Ilaria Calgaro

Collezione VAF-Stiftung / VAF–Stiftung Collection
Daniela Ferrari (*Conservatore / Curator*)

Casa d'Arte Futurista Depero, Fondo Depero / Depero Fund
Nicoletta Boschiero (*Conservatore capo / Chief curator*)

Palazzo delle Albere, Collezioni del XIX secolo / 19th-century collections
Alessandra Tiddia (*Conservatore capo / Chief curator*)

Mostre temporanee / Temporary exhibitions
Beatrice Avanzi, Elisabetta Barisoni, Margherita de Pilati

Archivio fotografico / Photographic archives
Attilio Begher (*Responsabile / Supervisor*)
Serena Aldi, Maurizio Baldo

Segreteria della direzione / Secretarial staff
Babila Scarperi, Federica Tolimieri

Amministrazione / Administration
Marina Cindolo, Tiziana Cumer, Annamaria Folgarait, Roberta Galvagni, Daniela Gerola, Angela Gerosa, Arianna Gionta, Barbara Gober, Lina Mattè, Sabrina Moscher, Sabrina Polizzi, Mario Rigobello

Ufficio tecnico e informatico / Technicians and IT
Matteo D'Ignazio, Giusto Manica, Stefano Manica, Claudio Merz, Walter Pancin, Marina Peroni

Storage e allestimenti / Storage and installation
Giampiero Coatti, Mario Divina, Daniel Jorge Garcia, Giovanni Pivato

Comunicazione e relazioni esterne / Communication and public relations
Flavia Fossa Margutti (*Responsabile / Supervisor*)

Ufficio stampa e sito internet / Press office and website
Luca Melchionna, Clementina Rizzi

Comunicazione e promozione / Communication and promotion
Silvia Ferrari, Carlotta Gaspari, Maria Elena Putz, Lodovico Schiera, Vanessa Vacchini
Francesca Velardita

Servizi didattici / Education
Denise Bernabè (*Formazione e consulenza / Training and consultancy*)
Annalisa Casagranda (*Pubblico / Visitors*)
Carlo Tamanini (*Scuola / School*)
con la collaborazione di / in cooperation with
Ornella Dossi, Brunella Fait, Sabina Ferrario
e di / and
Karin Cavalieri, Stefania Fogolari, Amina Pedrinolla, Barbara Santi, Katjuscia Tevini

COMUNE DI TRENTO

Comune di Trento

Sindaco / Mayor
Alessandro Andreatta

Assessore cultura, turismo e giovani / Councillor for culture, tourism, and youth
Lucia Maestri

Dirigente servizio cultura, turismo e politiche giovanili / Manager of the culture, tourism, and youth office
Clara Campestrini

Capo ufficio servizio cultura, turismo e politiche giovanili / Head of the culture, tourism, and youth office
Donatella Turrina

Fondazione Galleria Civica–Centro di Ricerca sulla Contemporaneità di Trento

Presidente / Chairman
Danilo Eccher

Consiglio di amministrazione /Board of directors
Mauro Pappaglione, Mario Garavelli

Revisore dei conti / Accounting auditor
Filippo Degasperi

Comitato scientifico / Scientific committee
Gerald Matt, Hans Ulrich Obrist, Roberto Pinto

Direttore / Director
Andrea Viliani

Assistente di direzione / Director's assistant
Chiara del Senno

Assistente curatore / Assistant curator
Giulia Corradi

Servizi educativi / Educational services
Francesca Piersanti, Roberta Carturan, Angela Margoni

Reception
Rosa Cammarota

Ufficio stampa / Press office
adicorbetta, Milano / Milan

Soci fondatori / Founding members
Comune di Trento
Andrea Bert, Renzo Colombini, Daniele Dalfovo, Michele Dalfovo, Mario Garavelli, Mauro Giacca, Mauro Pappaglione, Paola Stelzer, Jurgen Todesco, Loris Todesco, Markus Walter Wachtler

Amici / Friends
Paola Ambrosi Rangoni, Fabio Bartolini, Marta Boglioli Ziglio, Gianfranco de Bertolini, Mauro De Iorio, Dario Ghidoni

The artist would like to thank the following people for their collaboration on this book and their support of her previous projects:

Chiara Parisi
Andrea Viliani
Gabriella Belli
Marie-Blanche Carlier
Gió Marconi
Ulrich Gebauer
Esther Quiroga
Lynne Cooke
Elisabeth Lebovici
Raimundas Malasauskas
Francesco Manacorda
Nataša Petrešin-Bachelez
Ian White
Cecilia Alemani
Daniel Birnbaum
Alexandra Bordes
Ben Borthwick
Jelle Bouwhuis
Veronica Caciolli
Cristina Cámara
Giulia Corradi
Alberto Couceiro
Sergio Edelsztein
Lorenzo Fusi
Peter Gorschlüter
Giovanni Giuliani
Markus Hartmann
Merten Houfek
Joachim Jäger
Karl Kliem
Gil Leung
Frieda Luczak
Christopher Mondt
Simone Neuenschwander
Bartolomeo Pietromarchi
Johan Pousette
Jimmy Robert
Tas Skorupa
Rupert Smyth
Angelika Stepken
Theo Thegelaers
Andi Toma
Sara Tucker
Cornelia Wagner
Hilke Wagner
Benjamin Weil
Ingrid Wiener
Oswald Wiener
Siegfried Zielinski
Jan St. Werner

Cover:

One Way Out, 2010
Courtesy of the artist, carlier | gebauer, Berlin, and Galleria Giò Marconi, Milan

Front and back endpapers:

The Long Road (2010)

This catalogue is published on the occasion of Rosa Barba's three solo exhibitions / Ce catalogue est publié à l'occasion des trois expositions personnelles de Rosa Barba / Questo catalogo è pubblicato in occasione delle tre mostre personali di Rosa Barba

Centre international d'art et du paysage de l'île de Vassivière
February 28 – June 27, 2010 / 28 février – 27 juin 2010 / 28 febbraio – 27 giugno 2010

Mart – Museo di Arte Moderna e Contemporanea di Trento e Rovereto
May 28 – August 28, 2011 / 28 mai – 28 août 2011 / 28 maggio – 28 agosto 2011

Fondazione Galleria Civica–Centro di Ricerca sulla Contemporaneità di Trento
May 28 – August 28, 2011 / 28 mai – 28 août 2011 / 28 maggio – 28 agosto 2011

Catalogue / **Catalogue** / **Catalogo**

Edited by / Commissaires / A cura di
Chiara Parisi, Andrea Viliani

Concept / Concept / Concetto
Rosa Barba

Copyediting / Suivi éditorial / Revisione dei testi
Krystina Stermole (English), Alexandra Bordes (Français), Giulia Corradi, Veronica Caciolli (Italiano)

Translations / Traductions / Traduzioni
Paul Aston (Italian–English); John Tittensor (French–English); Valeria Caredda, NTL (French–Italian); Irene Floriani, NTL (English–Italian); Jean-Denis Frater (English–French)

Graphic design / Maquette / Progetto grafico
Rupert Smyth

Typeface / Caractères / Caratteri
M-Thompson, Dante

Production / Production / Produzione
Christine Emter, Hatje Cantz

Reproductions / Photogravures / Riproduzioni
LVD Gesellschaft für Datenverarbeitung mbH, Berlin

Paper / Papier / Carta
LuxoArt Samt, 150 g/m²

Printed by / Imprimé par / Stampato da
Offsetdruckerei Karl Grammlich GmbH, Pliezhausen

Binding / Façonnage / Legatura
Buchwerk Darmstadt

Published by
Hatje Cantz Verlag
Zeppelinstrasse 32
73760 Ostfildern
Germany / Allemagne / Germania
Tel. +49 711 4405-200
Fax +49 711 4405-220
www.hatjecantz.com

You can find information on this exhibition and many others at www.kq-daily.de. / Si vous souhaitez obtenir de plus amples informations sur une exposition particulière, veuillez consulter notre site internet : www.kq-daily.de. / Per informazioni su questa mostra e altri si prega di visitare www.kq-daily.de.

Hatje Cantz books are available internationally at selected bookstores. For more information about our distribution partners, please visit our website at www.hatjecantz.com. / Les livres publiés par Hatje Cantz sont disponibles dans le monde entier dans les bonnes librairies. Pour tous les renseignements plus généraux, visitez notre site internet : www.hatjecantz.com. / Per i dettagli sulla distribuzione dei libri di Hatje Cantz si prega di visitare il nostro sito www.hatjecantz.com.

ISBN 978-3-7757-3019-8

Printed in Germany / Imprimé en Allemagne / Stampato in Germania

With support from the Kulturverwaltung des Berliner Senats

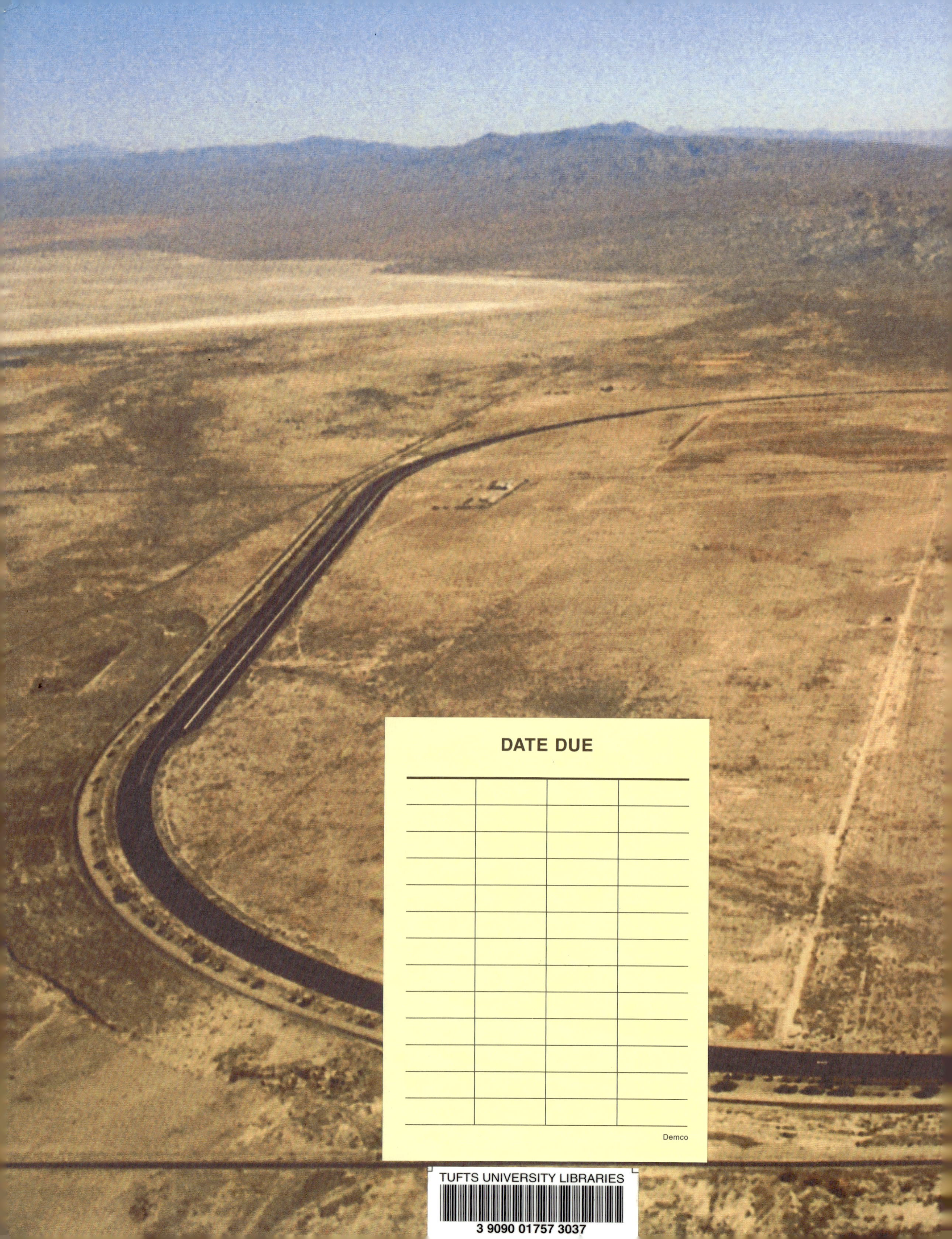